MAX YOUR MEMORY
the complete **visual** programme

Dr Pascale Michelon

LONDON, NEW YORK, MUNICH,
MELBOURNE, AND DELHI

Illustrator Keith Hagan at
www.greenwich-design.co.uk
Project editor Suhel Ahmed
Project art editor Charlotte Seymour
Designer Nicola Erdpresser
Editor Angela Baynham
Assistant to illustrator Sarah Holland
Senior production editor Jennifer Murray
Production editor Marc Staples
Production controller Alice Holloway
Creative technical support Sonia Charbonnier
Managing editors Penny Warren and Penny Smith
Managing art editor Marianne Markham
Art director Peter Luff
Catergory publisher Peggy Vance

First published in
Great Britain in 2012 by
Dorling Kindersley Limited,
80 Strand, London WC2R
0RL Penguin Group (UK)

Copyright © 2012 Dorling
Kindersley Limited
Text copyright © 2012
Dorling Kindersley Limited

1 2 3 4 5 6 7 8 9 10
001–182627–Jan/2012

A CIP catalogue record for this book is available
from the British Library.

ISBN 978-1-4053-9121-4

Printed and bound
in Singapore by
Tien Wah Press

Discover more at
www.dk.com

Contents

MAX YOUR MEMORY
the complete visual programme

How to use this book

A visual programme

If there is one magic word to open the door to a better memory, this word has to be "picture". It is a fact that pictures are easier to remember than words. As you will see, the method behind the majority of the memory-enhancing techniques presented in this book is to translate information into striking visual images and register these to enable better recall. This is one of the main reasons why *Max Your Memory* is a book that's visually led with fun and engaging illustrations and short chunks of easily digestible text.

Since learning becomes much easier when it is fun and relevant to us, most of the exercises throughout the book are not abstract but relate to familiar, everyday situations.

The chapters

The first step to boosting memory is to understand what memory is and how it works. Chapter 1 offers a clear, illustrated introduction to memory and brain potential. Chapters 2 and 3 focus on short-term and long-term memory respectively. The next two chapters offer key memory-enhancing techniques based on visualization and imagination (Chapter 4) and organization (Chapter 5). The book then explores memory for names (Chapter 6) and numbers (Chapter 7) and introduces key methods to improve memory capacity for both. The final chapter looks at some of the tweaks you can make to your lifestyle to maximize brain health: this includes information on nutrition, ways to manage stress, and tips to get adequate sleep and exercise.

"Super technique" pages offer proven methods for boosting memory power

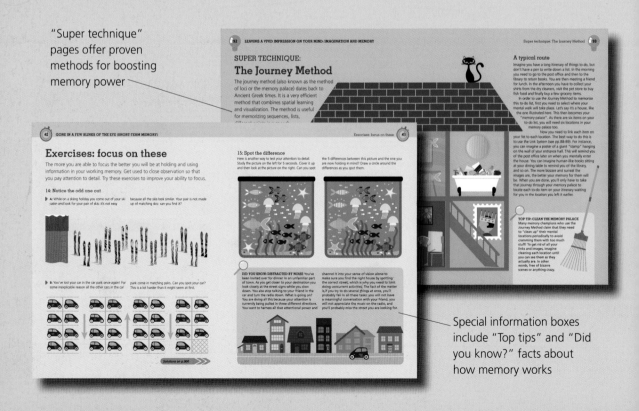

Special information boxes include "Top tips" and "Did you know?" facts about how memory works

Working through the book

The book is structured so that you can either choose a specific topic and focus on it alone, or work your way through from cover to cover. Chapters 2–7 start with check-in exercises to assess your current aptitude for a specific type of memory, e.g. long-term memory. Following a run-down of the key techniques and strategies, the check-out exercises at the end of the chapters encourage you to use these memory-boosting methods plus other tips to complete the exercises. You can then assess whether using these techniques has helped improve your memory.

Most of the exercises will ask you to memorize information and then cover it up, for which you will need a sheet of paper. In most instances, you will be asked to recall the information in the answer space provided. In cases where an answer space is not available, you will need an additional piece of paper to write down your answer. For exercises that test your long-term memory, you will be asked to complete an unrelated task to create a suitable time lag. These tasks will either be embedded in the question or framed in an illustrated tablet computer, which appears next to the main exercise.

Solutions

Finally, when applicable, you will find the solutions to the exercises at the back of the book. Look out for the solutions arrow on the relevant pages, which guides you to the specific page number.

Scoring boxes to assess your progress at the end of each check-in and check-out section

Detailed introductions precede exercises to provide essential information

Answer boxes to fill in as you work through the puzzles and exercises

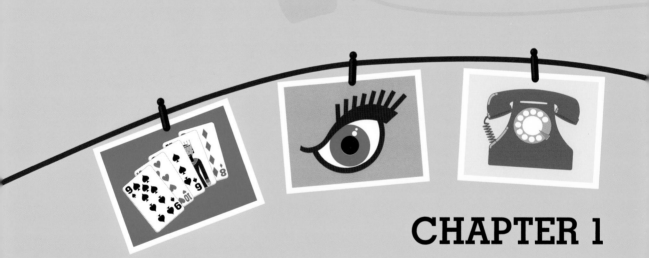

CHAPTER 1
YOU ARE WHAT YOU REMEMBER

What is memory?

Can you imagine living in the instant with no memories of the immediate or distant past? This is almost impossible to conceive: without any history or context, how would you know who the people talking to you are, what your favourite colour is, and what to make of things happening around you?

Organizing memories

Memory allows us to store and retrieve information about the world and how we react to it, which is vital to understanding who we are, our relationships with the people around us, and what the world means to us. In order to understand how memory works, imagine filing away into a photo album a set of photographs from your trip last summer. First, you need to identify what each photograph refers to. Then you need to put the photos in the right chronological order in the album. You are doing this so that when you want

to recount any part of the experience again, you can refer back to the album and retrieve the right photo without a problem. These three actions, namely, registering (also called encoding), storing, and retrieving, are the three fundamental steps involved in memorization.

A solid memory forms when it has been well registered because it can then be retrieved easily. As you will find out throughout this book, there are many things you can do to improve your memory. You will learn techniques to enrich information with meaning so that you make information more memorable when you register it. This will provide you with cues to retrieve it later on.

1: Using your mind's eye

Let's look at what happens in the mind when you register information you read in a text. Read this short passage and visualize the scene.

"It was a beautiful day, perfect for a picnic. The air smelled fresh. Flowers could be seen all around the park. Julie found an ideal spot under a large tree to unfold her blanket and set up her basket. Since the tree had not completely bloomed yet, the sun was shining through and warming her legs. As she pulled out her food, she noticed the light shimmering on the water ahead of her."

Now answer the questions on the right referring to the details you visualized:

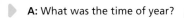

▷ **A:** What was the time of year?

▷ **B:** What colour were the flowers?

▷ **C:** What kind of tree did Julie settle under?

▷ **D:** What colour was Julie's blanket?

▷ **E:** What types of food did Julie take out of her basket?

▷ **F:** What kind of water feature caught Julie's attention?

What you have just done is delve into your own repository of memories to fill in the details. If you read the passage again, you will notice that none of your answers feature in the text. All we offered you were cues to trigger your imagination, which tapped into the vast archive of information you already possess. The visual details you recall when reading a text are powerful cues that can help you retrieve what you read later on.

TOP TIP: CREATE VISUAL MEANING So how does your mind process information? The information is first analysed and registered. For example, take the Spanish word "vaca" written above the picture of a cow. Your brain will identify the word and associate it with the visual image. So far so good: you know that you are reading the word "vaca" and that it means "cow" in Spanish. You have a good chance of remembering this, but your memory may be enhanced further if you also create visual meaning. How? Take a mental snapshot of the two pieces of information together. This way your brain will register the relationship between the object and the word. In doing so, you will increase the likelihood of remembering the word because visual information sticks in the mind more readily.

Does memory work automatically?

Try out these two exercises to learn more about how memory works. You'll find out whether it is always necessary to make a concerted effort to memorize in order to allow recall of information, or whether some things are memorized automatically.

2: Day at the beach

You are at the beach. Count how many toys you can put away directly (those on the table and chair) and how many you will have to clean up first (those on the sand).

Now cover up the picture. Although you weren't asked to memorize any of the toys, can you remember details about them? Answer these 5 questions:

A: Was the rubber duck wearing a hat?

B: What colour was the octopus?

C: What is the picture of on the bucket?

D: Were there any stars on the ball?

E: What colour was the truck's dumpster?

HOW IT WORKS: BRAIN ON AUTO-PILOT So do you always consciously commit stuff to memory? Or do you sometimes remember things without even trying? After completing the exercise above, you probably found that you registered some information unconsciously! The brain registers many facts and details without you being aware of them. It makes sense when you think about it: life would become exhausting if you were always telling yourself to remember everything. Although most of the information we register automatically never becomes conscious, the brain constantly refers to it to build or reinforce our ideas about the world around us.

3: It's a matter of size

Would these commonly known objects fit in a regular shoebox? Write "yes" or "no" in the answer box provided for each object. Then cover up the objects.

Although you didn't memorize what the various objects were or how they were grouped together, can you remember which objects were placed on which table?

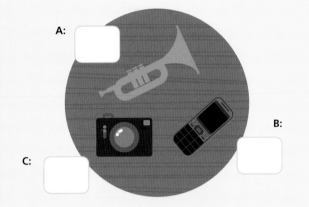

A:

B:

C:

D:

F:

E:

G:

H:

I:

▸ Round table

▸ Square table

▸ Triangular table

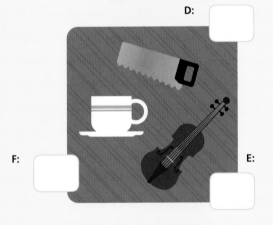

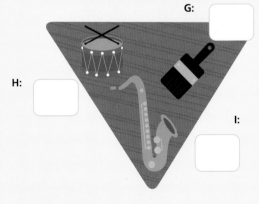

TOP TIP: CATCH THE MEANING If you were asked to memorize a passage of text, you would probably start by reading it over and over again, expecting the act of repetition to help encode the information in your mind. However, this isn't the most efficient way to absorb the meaning of the information you are trying to learn, which therefore increases your chances of forgetting it in the future. Ultimately, it is the ability to understand the meaning of the text that will lead to a stronger memory of it. The more you understand the meaning of what you read, the more connections you will make between the passage and what you know already, and the better your memory of it will be.

Solutions on p.180

Where in the brain do you keep your memories?

Are your memories stored at the back of your brain or at the front? Do we even know? Years of research have shown scientists that memories are not stored in any single place in the brain.

The main lobes

The brain weighs about 1.5kg (3lb 5oz) and can be divided into two hemispheres – right and left. Each of these can in turn be divided into four major lobes called the occipital lobe (situated at the back of the head, above the neck), the temporal lobe (situated beside the temples), the frontal lobe (situated just behind the forehead), and the parietal lobe (situated in the back of the head, at the top). It turns out that each lobe within the brain is responsible for different skills and functions.

What the lobes do

The occipital lobe is devoted entirely to analysing what we see. The parietal lobe is principally responsible for attention, processing sensations, such as touch, temperature, and pain, and spatial orientation. The frontal lobe is known for its role in higher abilities, which include decision-making, reasoning, impulse control, social behaviour, and memory. The temporal lobe deals mostly with the senses of hearing and smell, as well as language and memory. Located deep inside the temporal lobe is the limbic system, and the different parts of this support our appetites, emotions, and instincts. One part in particular, the hippocampus, is critical for learning, as it is involved with the formation of new memories.

As you can see, memory cannot be pinpointed to any specific part of the brain, but is dispersed throughout the different lobes and other sites. To summarize, a memory is the recollection and reconstruction of several pieces of information pulled together by mechanisms spread throughout the brain.

A:

B:

C:

D:

4: Label the brain

How much of what you have read so far can you remember? See if you can label this brain correctly by referring to the list on the right.

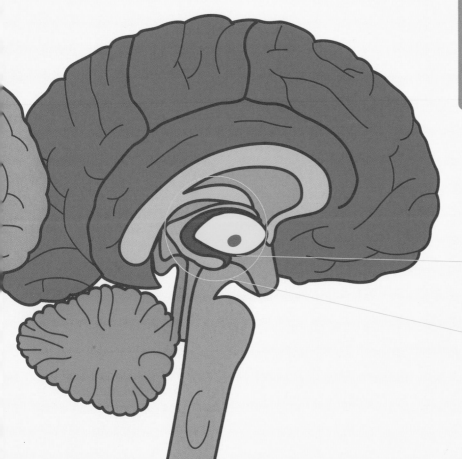

Sections of the brain:

Occipital lobe
Temporal lobe
Frontal lobe
Parietal lobe
Limbic system
Hippocampus

E:

F:

Solutions on p.180

HOW IT WORKS: NIMBLE NEURONS When you remember the face of a loved one, it is the result of the activity of brain cells (or neurons) in specific parts of your brain. Active neurons transmit information to each other using electrical impulses as well as chemical molecules, called neurotransmitters. This exchange occurs very rapidly through synapses (the tiny gaps between neurons). An average brain contains roughly 100 billion neurons. What's more, each neuron is connected to approximately 10,000 other neurons. This goes some way towards explaining our limitless capacity for creating and storing memories.

Why do we forget?

Our brain has the ability to hold on to lots of memories. However, it doesn't seem to keep hold of each one indefinitely. For example, you might never forget the name of your first love but always find it hard to remember where you left your keys. Why do we forget such things? As you know, memory works by first registering information and later retrieving it: things can go awry at either or both stages.

The science of forgetting

Let's look first at failure to register. Information that is registered poorly will be hard to retrieve. For example, it will be difficult to remember someone's name if you weren't paying enough attention when you were being introduced to that person.

Now let's look at retrieval failures. One possibility is that memories just fade away over time, especially if they are no longer accessed. Another possibility is that memories interfere with each other. For instance, you may not remember where you parked your car today because of interference from memories of where you parked your car yesterday. Finally, since most memories are attached to a context, a change of context may prevent you from retrieving a memory. For example, you might have trouble recalling the name of someone from your art class if you bump into them in the supermarket. This would happen because the contextual cues usually associated with this person, namely, the classroom setting, the teacher, and the other students, are absent in the supermarket.

5: Reading to the beat

Read the passage below. At the same time, tap your middle and index fingers on the table every 4 counts (count silently in your head). Once you've finished reading, cover it up, and answer the questions:

Joe was a forgetful person. He was always losing his keys and leaving his wallet at home. One day his mother asked him to run to the shops and buy a pint of milk, some bread and a packet of sausages. He came back an hour later after realizing that he forgot to take any money with him. His second trip was more successful even though he forgot the milk and instead bought a roast chicken. In the afternoon he managed to return six of his overdue books to the library.

A: What was the forgetful person's name?

B: Who asked him to go to the shops?

C: What was he supposed to buy?

D: What did he have to come back home for?

E: What kind of meat did he end up buying?

F: How many books did he return to the library?

Was it difficult to answer these questions? Finger drumming while reading the text divided your attention, which probably lowered your ability to register the information. This is an example of registering failure.

DID YOU KNOW: TIMES WHEN YOU WANT TO FORGET Have you seen the Hollywood movie *Eternal Sunshine of the Spotless Mind*? In the film a couple undergo a procedure to erase each other from their memories when their relationship turns sour. We'd all like to forget some memories, especially those that are traumatic. To date, there is no such procedure as the one depicted in the movie. However, one way memories can be suppressed is by actively trying to exclude them from our conscious thoughts. Although this may sound paradoxical, the process of conscious suppression has been shown to work in psychological experiments. Another way memories might be suppressed is by an unconscious mechanism called repression.

Exercises to show why we forget

How about doing a few more exercises to understand the nature of memory recall and forgetfulness? To experience interference first hand, try exercise 6. To feel the power of emotions on memory, as well as the benefit of cues when attempting to recall the past, try exercises 7 and 8.

6: Mixing up the lists

Below is a grocery list. Can you memorize it in 1 minute? When you are done, hide the words.

Here are the words that your niece wrote in a spelling test. Can you check that they are all spelled correctly? Mark a tick or a cross beside each spelling.

Brocoli   Juice
Steak   Yiogurt
Apple   Craker
Hamm

Carrots
Sausages
Pears
Turkey
Milk
Cheese
Biscuits

Do you still remember the grocery list you memorized? Try to write all the items down below.

How did you find that? Did you incorrectly write down some of the words from your niece's spelling test? This is a perfect example of interference in memory: both lists contained food items and those got mixed up in your mind, causing you to commit retrieval errors.

7: I wish I could forget

Look at each picture for 1 second then hide them all.
Then try to write down as many pictures as you can recall.

Did the two emotionally charged pictures feature in your answers? Unfortunately, negative or traumatic events tend to stick in our memory and are usually harder to forget. This is probably a way for us to catalogue negative experiences in our brain so that we can hopefully protect ourselves from something similar happening in the future.

8: Wonderful cues

Take no more than 30 seconds to memorize the names of the 8 Ancient Wonders of the World listed below. Cover up the names, count aloud to 15, and then using the country names as cues to help recall, write down the name of each "wonder" in the box next to the country to which it belongs.

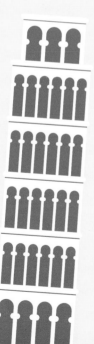

Peru	Machu Picchu
China	The Great Wall of China
Turkey	The Temple of Artemis
India	The Taj Mahal
Italy	The Leaning Tower of Pisa
Greece	The Statue of Zeus
Iraq	The Hanging Gardens of Babylon
Egypt	The Great Pyramid

China   _____

Egypt   _____

Iraq   _____

Turkey   _____

Peru   _____

India   _____

Italy   _____

Greece   _____

Can you improve your memory?

We are born with a finite memory capacity and nothing can be done about that. Would you say that this statement is true or false? Of course it's false! Your memory can be trained and improved at any age throughout your life.

Mnemonics

We can find great examples demonstrating the talents of a trained memory in societies (past and present) that rely on the use of oral tradition in the absence of written language. In these cases, human memory is the only way to store knowledge. A few individuals have to become memory experts. They train their memories so that they can orally pass knowledge on to future generations.

Unfortunately, there is no easy pill you can take to boost memory. Your memory will get better only if you use it regularly. Your memory will also improve if you use mnemonics. A mnemonic is the name given to any technique that helps your memory store information. Historically, mnemonics were used by the Ancient Greeks and they are still used today, especially by competitors at memory competitions around the world.

DID YOU KNOW: PRACTICE MAKES PERFECT Have you heard of Joshua Foer, the 2006 record holder in speed cards at the USA Memory Championships? In a "speed-card" contest, competitors race to memorize a pack of playing cards. Joshua Foer took only 1 minute and 40 seconds to memorize his pack successfully. A year earlier, Foer was a young journalist and a novice in the domain of memory training. He had decided to train to become a memory expert and it worked! How did he do that? He used mnemonics, especially those that involved creating complex visual images, which would readily stick in his mind.

9: Memorize fun facts

How about starting your memory-improving course by trying to memorize these fun facts? You never know, they may come in handy if you're taking part in a quiz, or if you just want to impress friends.

Take 2 minutes to memorize these facts. Then cover them up and write down as many as you can remember. The pictures below should help. Later today, recount at least 2 of these facts to someone you know.

▶ **A:** The opposite sides of a die always add up to 7.

▶ **B:** Frogs never close their eyes, even when they are sleeping.

▶ **C:** No piece of paper can be folded more than 7 times.

▶ **D:** A human eye has 6 muscles that control its movements.

▶ **E:** The pupil is actually a hole in the centre of the eye: it allows light to enter the retina.

▶ **F:** About 25 per cent of human beings sneeze when they look up at a bright sky.

▶ **G:** There are no clocks in Las Vegas gambling casinos.

▶ **H:** We use 100 per cent of our brain, not just 10 per cent.

Your plastic brain

No, your brain is not made of plastic! It is not a muscle either. But your brain has the ability to change depending on your daily experiences. This ability is called "plasticity" or "neuroplasticity" to be precise.

Plastic changes

Changes in the brain occur at the level of the synapses (the connections between neurons, see p.15). Exposed to challenging tasks, the synapses eventually become more efficient. The experience of the task also causes new synaptic connections to appear. The same can be said about neurons, with new ones also appearing and growing, even in an adult brain. This occurs especially in the hippocampus (this region is crucial for memory formation, see p.14). As you can probably guess, changes in the brain do not happen in a single day, but over a long period of time through the repeated use of a specific part of the brain.

Plastic changes occur a lot during childhood as the brain grows and matures. These changes can also take place following a brain injury. For instance, with access to proper rehabilitation, a person who has suffered a stroke can recover the use of an apparently non-functional limb thanks to neuronal re-organization in the brain. Finally, plastic changes occur during adulthood whenever new things are learned, memorized, and rehearsed. The good news is that the more you learn and memorize, the more connections are created and strengthened in your brain, which helps boost your ability to register and retrieve new information.

10: Wastebasket ball

Here is a simple exercise to demonstrate how repeated practice can lead to better performance. Your brain isn't likely to change dramatically during the course of this exercise, but it would if you were to challenge yourself by taking up a musical instrument, for example.

Use a wastebasket and a sheet of paper scrunched into a ball. Throw the "ball" repeatedly until you get 3 successful throws in a row. Increase the distance between you and the basket. Do the same exercise. With practice, you should find your aim improving over time.

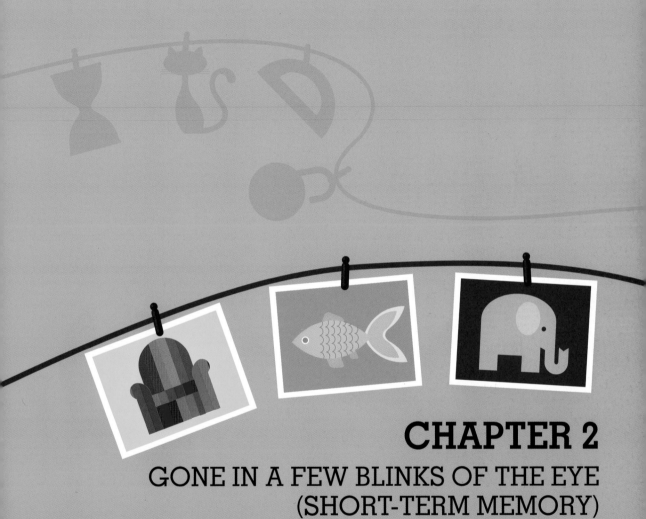

CHAPTER 2
GONE IN A FEW BLINKS OF THE EYE (SHORT-TERM MEMORY)

Check-in: how well do you remember the very recent past?

Memory for the very recent past (up to a minute ago) and memory for the past (everything beyond a minute) are different. The former is called short-term memory and the latter is known as long-term memory. Short-term memory allows you to hold in your mind what you have just heard, read, or seen. In the following exercises, your aim is to look at the material once, try to hold it in your memory, and then recall it as accurately as possible.

1: What is your limit?

Below are several series of numbers. To determine your memory span, starting with the shortest series, read the numbers once in your head and then cover up the series. Recall the numbers in the order you read them.

5 7 0 4 8 2 6 3 1 9

8 2 5 3 0 7 1 6 4

2 9 4 0 7 1 3 8

4 7 1 3 8 6 2

8 4 6 2 5 9

4 9 0 3 1

5 2 1 8

Your digit span = how many numbers you recalled correctly before you got your first series wrong.

Your score (your digit span):

_____
(from 4 to 10)

2: Sofa colours

In a phone conversation, the salesperson at the furniture store tells you the 6 colours the armchair you want to buy comes in. You need to remember the names of these colours until you can write them down on a piece of paper.

Read the names of these 6 colours once. Cover them up while repeating the 6 names to yourself for 10 seconds and then write them down in the space below.

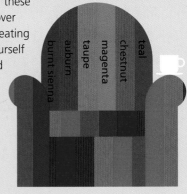

teal
chestnut
magenta
taupe
auburn
burnt sienna

Your score: _____
1–2 colours: 2 points
3–4 colours: 3 points
5–6 colours: 4 points

3: Cluster of shapes

Study this picture of overlapping shapes for 5 seconds. Then cover it up and reproduce what you remember in the space provided.

Your score: _____
2 errors+: 1 point
1–2 errors: 2 points
no errors: 3 points

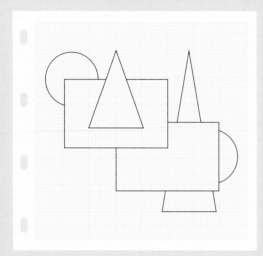 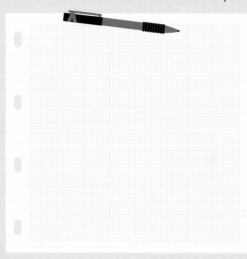

4: Cat invasion!

The 7 cats on the top wall have invaded your backyard. Look at them once, then cover them up and study the cats on the bottom wall. Very quickly, circle the cats that have never been in your backyard.

Your score: _____
1 cat spotted: 1 point
2 cats: 2 points
3 cats: 3 points

Solution on p.180

5: Write on your mental screen

You call for the bill after a meal with friends at a restaurant and have to divide it up among the group. It's a situation familiar to most of us, and often we reach for the calculator feature on our phones rather than relying on mental arithmetic. Practise dividing these numbers in your head and see how many you get right.

Restaurant

Divide 120 by 3 =

Divide 125 by 5 =

Divide 46 by 2 =

Divide 96 by 6 =

Divide 300 by 12 =

Divide 140 by 4 =

Your score: _____
1–2 correct: 2 points
3–4 correct: 3 points
5–6 correct: 4 points

Solutions on p.180

6: Gym locker

The receptionist at the gym gives you a new security code to access your locker. While rifling through your pockets for something to write it on, you have to hold the digits in your head for a few seconds. Read this series of digits once, then cover it up, and after 10 seconds write it in the space provided.

3 5 0 0 2 5 1 8

Your score: _____
1–3 digits: 2 points
4–5 digits: 3 points
6–8 digits: 4 points

7: March of the animals

Quickly study this procession of animals. Pay attention to which animals are shown as well as their order (from left to right). Then cover them up. Imagine that all the animals have turned around and are heading back to where they came from. Can you list them all starting with the last one in the procession (ie. the one on the right)?

Your score: _____
1–2 animals in the right place: 2 points
3–4 animals: 3 points
5–6 animals: 4 points

8: Four in a row

You're playing a popular game that involves arranging counters on a board. Unfortunately, during one game you accidentally knock the board over and so have to recreate the arrangement from memory.

Study the left board for 5 seconds. Then cover it up and reproduce the arrangement in the board on the right (you can write the initial of the correct colour in the appropriate circle, or colour it in).

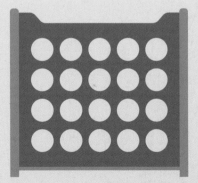

Your score: _____
1–2 counters: 2 points
3–4 counters: 3 points
5–6 counters: 4 points

HOW DID YOU DO?
Time to add up your points.
Your score: _____ **÷ 36 points**
= (_____ **x 100) =** _____ **%**
Are you surprised by your performance? Did you do better than you thought you would? In the next pages, you'll read about how your short-term memory helps you keep in mind a wide range of information, from a phone number while you are dialling it, to the shade of a colour while you are painting. As you will discover, focus is key to improving your short-term memory.

What is short-term memory?

Your short-term memory allows you to hold in your mind a piece of information while you are performing a task. The information will fade rapidly unless you actively try to retain it. This is crucial so that information relevant to the next task at hand can then be kept in mind.

Visual and verbal components

Depending on what you are holding in your mind, you use either your verbal or visual short-term memory. If you are trying to remember a phone number someone just told you, you repeat it to yourself until you can write it down, thereby using your verbal, or "phonological", short-term memory. If you want to copy down something you briefly saw on a screen, you keep a picture of it in your head, thereby using your visual short-term memory. How about doing the following exercises to test both components?

9: Where was it?

Take a look at this treasure map for no longer than 5 seconds and memorize the location of the hidden jewels. Then cover it up. Now mark on the empty grid below where the jewels were placed.

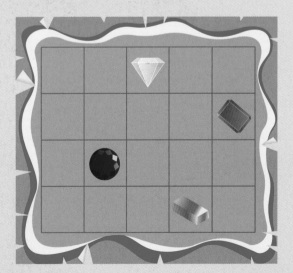

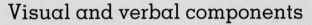

10: When order matters

Read each sequence of letters once, cover it up, and fill in the blanks.

T was in _____ position in the sequence.

P was in _____ position in the sequence.

L was in _____ position in the sequence.

D was in _____ position in the sequence.

DID YOU KNOW: STUCK ON SEVEN Short-term memory capacity is limited. In the 1950s, a psychologist called George Miller identified the magic number 7: it is the number of items that most people can hold in their short-term memory (plus or minus 2). Not very impressive when you realize that most phone numbers are generally 10 digits long! In the 1980s, an American college student who wasn't a memory expert memorized over 70 digits that were read to him one after the other. How was that possible? Aside from lots of practice, he used a technique called chunking (see p.154). This is something you can do, too.

Visual short-term memory

Visual short-term memory (VSTM) helps us keep in mind visual and spatial information for a very limited period of time so that it can be used to carry out ongoing cognitive tasks. The information might include the shapes and colours of things as well as the location of things around us.

Our mental sketchpad

Did you know that while we're moving our eyes (which happens quite often), we are unable to see? It is during this process that the VSTM plays an important role: it helps automatically fill in the tiny gaps between eye movements by momentarily storing what the world looks like.

On a more conscious level, VSTM can be thought of as a mental sketchpad on which you constantly draw and erase information.

You use it when you compare objects that are not near each other, such as when you are trying to choose between two types of wallpaper that happen to be located in different aisles of the DIY store. You use it when you're trying to reverse park your car by flitting your glance between the mirrors as you reverse into the tight space so as not to hit anything. You also rely on VSTM when you do spot-the-difference exercises. In all these cases, VSTM helps you retain visual information that is essential to complete the task at hand.

Using the mental sketchpad

Imagine a bowl of vanilla ice cream with a cherry on top. What you have just done is use your VSTM! All the images that appear in your mind's eye are formed on your mental sketchpad. You can then manipulate the image if that's what you need to do. (This process is discussed in detail on page 38.)

As you will find out throughout this book, the ability to visualize is important for boosting memory performance in general. This is a great motivation for stimulating your VSTM ability. You can begin right now by attempting the exercise on the next page.

11: Follow the path

Hold a path in your short-term memory. For each grid, briefly focus on the direction of the path and then cover it up. Hold the path in your mind's eye while counting to 5. Then reproduce the path in the empty grid.

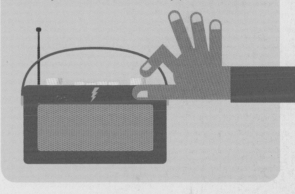

TOP TIP: MINIMIZE DISTRACTIONS Both verbal and visual short-term memories are very susceptible to distraction. Any interruption while you are holding information in this manner can make it disappear. Completing complex tasks in an environment free of distractions is essential for success. Turning the radio off, muting your email alerts, and avoiding using a screen saver that has a moving object are examples of simple things you can do to minimize distractions and help boost your short-term memory performance.

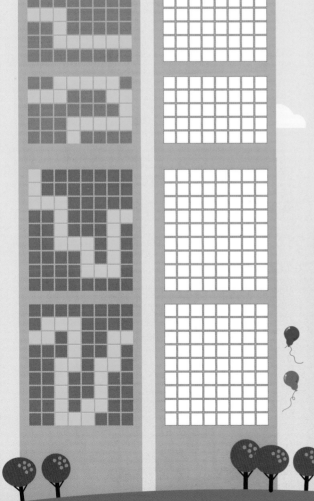

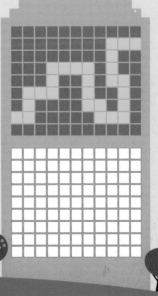

Working memory

Draw the letter J on your mental sketchpad. Now draw the letter D. Turn it 90° to the left and put it on top of the J. What does this shape resemble? An umbrella of course! You've just used your working memory. Our working memory is a crucial part of the memory system, not least because it helps us to work things out mentally.

Temporary workspace

Not only can we store information in our short-term memory, but we can also manipulate it. This is why short-term memory is sometimes also called the working memory. Working memory is our temporary workspace. We use it in everyday tasks ranging from driving (where you need to keep in mind the location of the cars around you as you navigate through the traffic), to preparing a budget (where you need to keep in mind one spending category while working on another), to writing a letter (where you need to keep in mind all you want to say while developing each point a sentence at a time).

Active thinking

Increasing or maintaining your working memory ability has enormous benefits in life. It could be compared to boosting the processing capacity of a computer. Working memory is where you do your active thinking and problem solving. So, a well-functioning working memory is key to successfully completing many complex activities that require you to reason, understand, and learn. Try the exercises opposite to use your mental workspace in different situations.

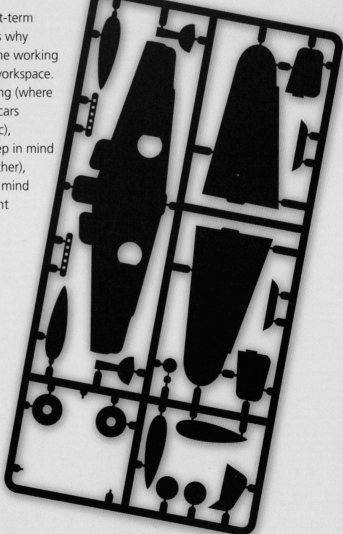

12: Mental rotation

When trying to find the right jigsaw puzzle piece, you often mentally rotate the ones you see on the table to "see" in your working mental space whether they would fit together. Let's practise mental rotation here. In each box below, study each part of the top figure for 5 seconds. Then cover it up and circle the figure in the bottom part that matches it. You will have to rotate the figures mentally to find the answer.

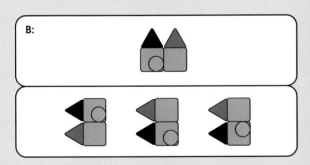

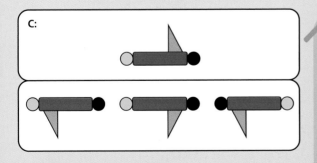

13: Backwards spelling

You are compiling a school quiz and one of the questions involves spelling several words backwards. Before asking the pupils to take part, you decide to try it yourself. Work on one word at a time. Read the word once, then cover it up and spell it backwards.

▶ A: **REARVIEW**

▶ B: **HORMONE**

▶ C: **ELEPHANT**

▶ D: **EXERCISE**

▶ E: **GYMNASTIC**

▶ F: **MEDITATION**

DID YOU KNOW: WORKING MEMORY VS IQ
Children at school need their working memory for various things, such as when doing maths, analysing information, or even when writing down homework instructions. Research shows that working memory scores at age 5, rather than IQ scores, are a better indicator of academic achievement when older (at age 11). This is good news, as working memory can be measured more easily and can also be improved.

Solutions on p.180 ⟫⟫

SUPER TECHNIQUE:

Be attentive to boost your working memory

Imagine holding a set of directions in your memory while driving. If a billboard advert catches your attention, it may invade your mental workspace and cause you to forget these directions. The same thing may happen if an unrelated thought suddenly comes to mind. Information in working memory fades away unless it is refreshed. Maintaining information in your short-term memory requires a lot of attention. The more you are able to focus on task-relevant information and ignore distractions, the better your memory performance will be. Irrelevant thoughts that enter your mental workspace and divide your focus may lead to information overload and ultimately errors.

Does multitasking really work?

Most of us lead busy lives these days, and one of the ways in which we try to get everything done is through multitasking. Multitasking requires you to hold information relevant to two or more tasks simultaneously in your working memory. This happens, for example, when you try to speak on the phone while also calculating how much you've spent on your last shopping spree: you have to be mindful of what your conversation is about while entering numbers in your calculator. First of all, attending to two actvities at the same time means

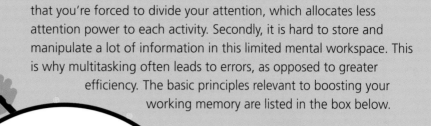

that you're forced to divide your attention, which allocates less attention power to each activity. Secondly, it is hard to store and manipulate a lot of information in this limited mental workspace. This is why multitasking often leads to errors, as opposed to greater efficiency. The basic principles relevant to boosting your working memory are listed in the box below.

Key memory-boosting principles

- Focus your attention on the task at hand.
- Reduce external distractions as much as possible.
- Avoid multitasking.
- Practise using your working memory – as with any brain function, working memory can become more efficient with practice.

HOW IT WORKS: WORKING MEMORY AND ADD These days increasing numbers of children seem to be diagnosed with Attention Deficit Disorder (ADD). There is also a tendency to seek medical help for this, but is resorting to medication the best solution? Maybe not. ADD usually goes hand in hand with working memory problems. Research has shown that training working memory leads to better attentional focus, better impulse control, and improved learning abilities. Working memory can be trained by performing regular computerized exercises that test your powers of concentratiion.

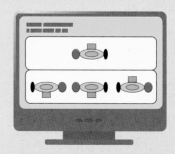

Exercises to test your concentration

The more you're able to focus, the better you will be at holding and using information in your working memory. Get used to close observation so that you pick up the smallest details. Try the following exercises.

14: Notice the odd one out

▶ **A:** While on a skiing holiday, you come out of your ski cabin and look for your pair of skis: it's not easy because all the skis look similar. Your pair is not made up of matching skis: can you find it?

▶ **B:** You've lost your car in the car park once again! For some inexplicable reason all the other parked cars come in matching pairs. Can you spot your car? This is a lot harder than it might seem at first.

Solutions on pp.180–1 ⟫

15: Spot the difference

Here is another way to test your attention to detail. Study the picture on the left for 5 seconds. Cover it up and then look at the picture on the right. Can you spot the 5 differences between this picture and the one you are now holding in your mind? Draw a circle around the differences as you spot them.

DID YOU KNOW: DISTRACTED BY NOISE You've been invited over for dinner in an unfamiliar part of town. As you get closer to your destination, you look closely at the street signs while slowing down. You also stop talking to your friend in the car and turn down the radio. What is going on? You are doing all this because your attention is currently being pulled in three different directions. You want to harness all that attentional power and channel it into your sense of vision alone to make sure you find the right house by spotting the correct street, which is why you need to limit doing concurrent activities. The fact of the matter is if you try to do several things at once, you'll probably fail in all these tasks: you will not have a meaningful conversation with your friend, you will not appreciate the music on the radio, and you'll probably miss the street you are looking for.

Check-out: exercise your short-term memory

Now that you know more about how your short-term memory and its various features work, as well as what you can do to try to boost it, let's assess how well you perform in the following exercises. Calculate your points for each exercise. Remember that attention is key here: eliminate potential distractions and make sure you maintain your focus throughout.

16: Letter strings

How many random letters can you hold in your mind? In other words, what's your letter span? Below are 7 series of letters. For each series, read the letters once in your head and then cover up the series. Recall the letters in the order you read them.

    F T H U
    U O S D B
    N C R P A L
    S I Q M Z T A
    O N X I G U V R
    E K D S P W A C J
    H U L D M Q V A P I

17: Mixed-up numbers

The numbers for the price tags for your garage sale are on the table in a messy pile. You look at them while crossing the room and then wonder which numbers you have. To answer this question, take 5 seconds to study the image of the numbers below. Then cover them up and list the numbers you remember by referring to the picture in your head.

Your score (your letter span):
_____ (from 4 to 10 points)

Your score: _____
more than 2 errors: 1 point

1-2 errors: 2 points
no errors: 4 points

18: Team colours

You're off to watch a 5-a-side soccer tournament involving 5 teams. Below is information on the strip colours of the teams. Focus on one team at a time.

Read the different colours of each strip while trying to picture it on your mental screen. Then cover up the information and fill in the missing colours of each strip.

▶ **Team A:** RAPID ROVERS Red jersey, black shorts, blue socks with yellow trim, white boots

▶ **Team B:** STRIKE FORCE Green jersey with black collar, orange shorts, white socks, black boots

▶ **Team C:** DASHING DYNAMOS Blue jersey, white shorts, green socks with yellow trim, red boots

▶ **Team D:** SILKY TOUCH Yellow jersey with black collar, grey shorts, red socks with blue trim, white boots

▶ **Team E:** GOALS GALORE Black jersey, red shorts with white stripes, blue socks with yellow trim, red boots

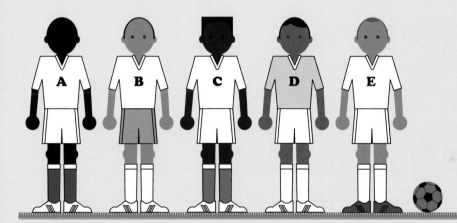

Your score: _____
1 strip: 1 point
2 strips: 2 points
3 strips: 3 points
4 strips: 4 points
5 strips: 5 points

19: Jumbo sandwich

Your friend asks you to buy him a sandwich at lunchtime. You need to remember his order until you can write it down on a piece of paper. Read the names of these 7 ingredients once, cover them up, close your eyes for approximately 10 seconds while repeating the 7 ingredients to yourself, and then write them down in the answer space.

Ingredients: Swiss cheese, chicken, tomatoes, bacon, green peppers, lettuce, light mayonnaise

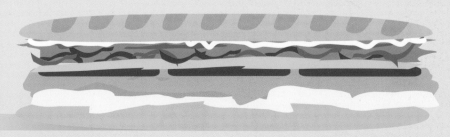

Your score: _____
1–3 ingredients: 1 point
4–6 ingredients: 2 points
all ingredients: 4 points

20: Number position

Read each sequence of numbers once, cover it up, and fill in the blanks.

▶ **A:**

8 4 3 2 6 7

3 was in _____ position in the sequence

▶ **B:**

9 2 8 1 7 3 6 5

1 was in _____ position in the sequence

▶ **C:**

6 1 4 0 8 5 3 7

5 was in _____ position in the sequence

▶ **D:**

3 5 0 2 7 4 1 7 6 8

6 was in _____ position in the sequence

21: Put the items back

You accidentally bumped into the shelving unit and 5 items fell on the floor. Can you put them back where they were? Take 5 seconds to look at where each item is in the unit on the left. Then cover it up and draw arrows to show where the items on the floor should go in the unit on the right.

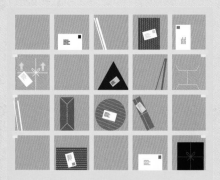

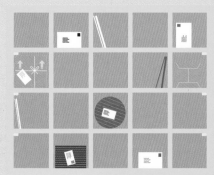

22: Mental drawing

Let's test how accurately you can draw on your mental sketchpad. Using the instructions, make a mental drawing of the picture. Then cover up the instructions and draw what you have visualized in the space below.

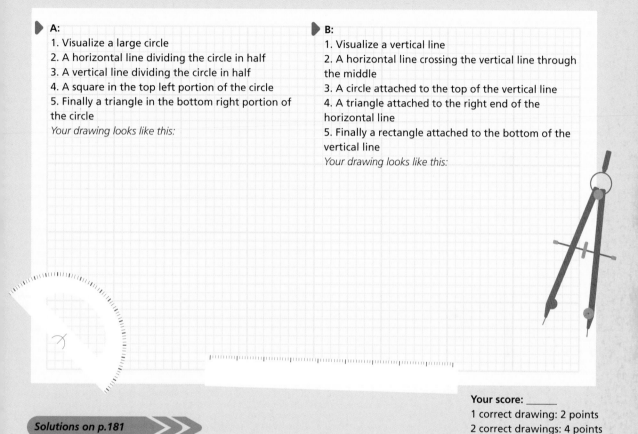

A:
1. Visualize a large circle
2. A horizontal line dividing the circle in half
3. A vertical line dividing the circle in half
4. A square in the top left portion of the circle
5. Finally a triangle in the bottom right portion of the circle
Your drawing looks like this:

B:
1. Visualize a vertical line
2. A horizontal line crossing the vertical line through the middle
3. A circle attached to the top of the vertical line
4. A triangle attached to the right end of the horizontal line
5. Finally a rectangle attached to the bottom of the vertical line
Your drawing looks like this:

Your score: _____
1 correct drawing: 2 points
2 correct drawings: 4 points

Solutions on p.181

23: Alien visit

These 7 aliens appeared in your street. Look at each of them once. Cover them up and then look at the aliens on the right. Ring the aliens that did NOT appear in your street.

Your score: _____   1 alien spotted: 1 point
2 aliens: 2 points
3 aliens: 3 points

24: An orderly hand

For each set of playing cards, look at each card once while placing it on your mental screen. Then cover up the set and mentally reorder the cards beginning with the lowest value. Write down the name of the cards (including the suit they belong to) in their new order.

25: A day at the zoo

You want to create a memorable day for your family so have decided to take them to the zoo. At the entrance you see a map showing you where all the enclosures are located. Quickly look at the map below and then cover it up. Try to remember where the different animal enclosures are and fill in the empty map with the names of the animals

Your score: _____   1 series: 6 points (value + suit)
2 series: 8 points (value + suit)
3 series: 10 points (value + suit)

Your score: _____   1–2 animals: 2 points
3–4 animals: 3 points
5 animals: 4 points

26: Alien words

On the right is a list of words that were transmitted during an alien broadcast. Read each word once, then cover it up and spell it backwards in the space below.

PRIGAL   ZATHERT

LUKAST

UFLITOR

SUVOLLEF

DEBOMET   *GRAXUM*

Your Score: _____ 1–2 words spelled correctly: 2 points
3–4 words: 4 points
5–6 words: 6 points
7 words: 8 points

27: Can you sing backwards?

▶ **A:** Do you know the lyrics of the nursery rhyme "Row row row your boat". Can you sing it backwards? Think about each line and then sing or say it backwards. Count how many lines you recite correctly in 1 minute.

▶ **B:** Now let's make it harder. Recite backwards each line of the nursery rhyme "Humpty Dumpty". Once again you have 1 minute to recite as many lines as you can.

A: Your score: _____ 1 line: 1 point
2 lines: 2 points
3–4 lines: 3 points

B: Your score: _____
1 line: 1 point
2 lines: 2 points
3+ lines: 3 points

28: Finding your way

You are visiting a friend in an unfamiliar town. You ask a stranger for directions and she tells you how to get to your destination. Read the set of directions once. Then cover it up and, starting at point A in the map below, use your memory to draw the route to your destination. Let's see how many instructions you can remember.

1: Head westwards and take the 1st right onto Easy Street
2: Keep walking northbound and take the 3rd left onto Bidas Walk
3: Walk to the end of Bidas Walk and turn right onto Judges Walk
4: Take the 1st left onto Chester Avenue and head to the end of the street

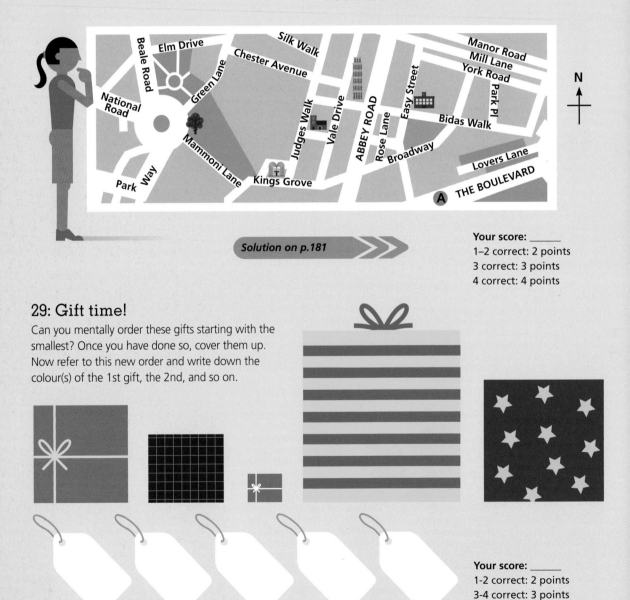

Solution on p.181

Your score: _____
1–2 correct: 2 points
3 correct: 3 points
4 correct: 4 points

29: Gift time!

Can you mentally order these gifts starting with the smallest? Once you have done so, cover them up. Now refer to this new order and write down the colour(s) of the 1st gift, the 2nd, and so on.

Your score: _____
1-2 correct: 2 points
3-4 correct: 3 points
5 correct: 4 points

30: The flag game

Study the top 2 flag garlands for 5 seconds. Then cover them up and colour in the blank spaces of the flags below, and write the name of the country each flag represents.

Your score: _____
1–3 correct: 2 points
4–5 correct: 3 points
6–7 correct: 4 points
8+ correct: 5 points

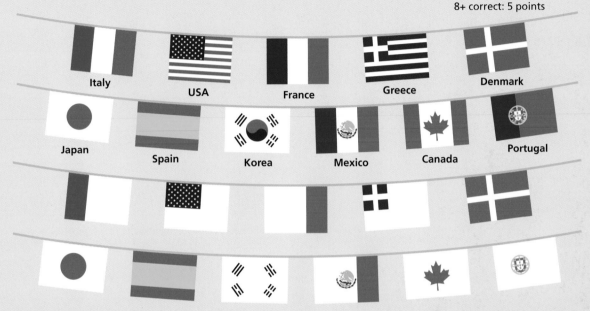

Italy   USA   France   Greece   Denmark

Japan   Spain   Korea   Mexico   Canada   Portugal

31: Identical layout

You have moved to a new house and want to arrange the furniture like it was in your previous home. For each room, look at the objects and their location once. Then cover it up and draw them in the empty plan below.

Your score: _____
1 room correct: 2 points
both rooms correct: 4 points

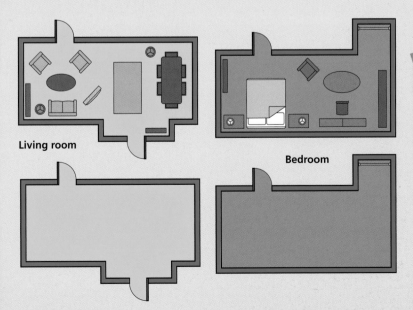

Living room

Bedroom

1 0

HOW DID YOU DO?
Time to add up your points.
Your score: _____ **÷ 83 points**
= (_____ **x 100) =** _____ **%**
Compare this score to the score you got for the check-in exercises. Have you made any progress? Of course, your brain workout doesn't stop here. To expand your short-term and working memory capacity, make sure you use it regularly and, above all, don't forget that it's all about maintaining focus!

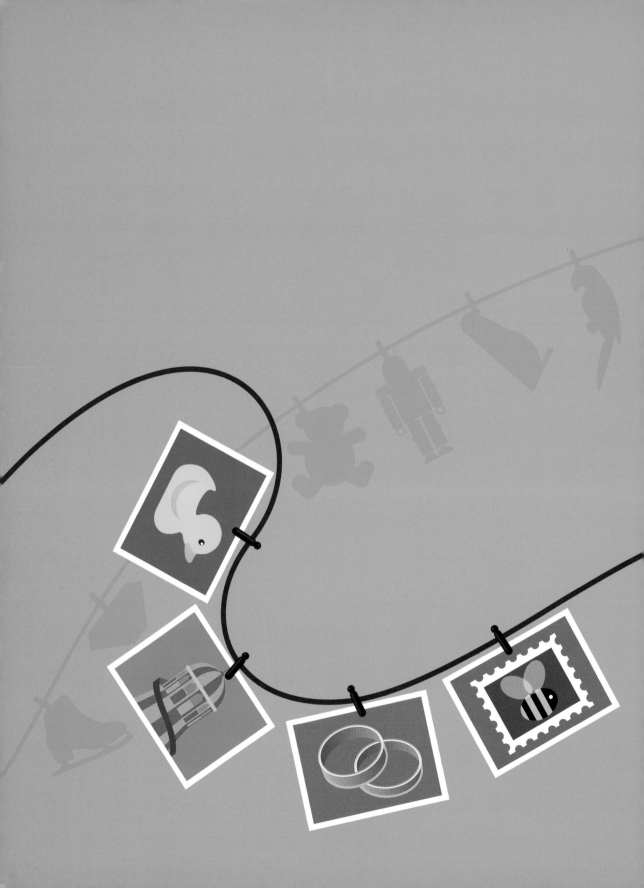

CHAPTER 3
IMPRINTING IT ON YOUR MIND
(LONG-TERM MEMORY)

Check-in: how well do you remember the past?

This chapter explores how long-term memory works and what you can do to improve it. Some exercises will ask you to retrieve memories from your own past while others will involve memorizing material and recalling it after a time-lag task.

1: Your life

Look back at your past and answer the following questions as accurately as possible. Leave the space blank if you cannot remember the answer.

▶ **A:** Where were you on Sunday a week ago?

▶ **B:** What was the name of your secondary school?

▶ **C:** What colour hair does your dentist have?

▶ **D:** What was your previous address?

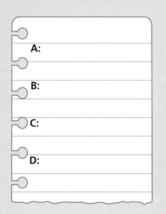

A:

B:

C:

D:

Your score: _____
1 point for each correct answer

2: Dining with the famous

A genie has granted you a wish to have dinner with 8 world-famous people (past and present). Write down on their plates what each person is famous for.

Your score: _____
1–4 correct: 2 points
5–8 correct: 4 points

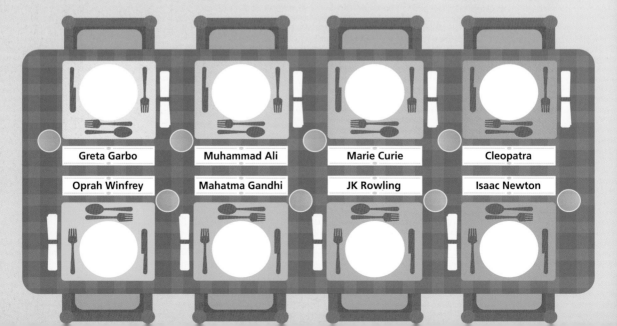

Greta Garbo

Muhammad Ali

Marie Curie

Cleopatra

Oprah Winfrey

Mahatma Gandhi

JK Rowling

Isaac Newton

3: Visual memories

How attentive are you? Try to answer the questions below using your visual memory of each object.

▶ **A:** How many wings do dragonflies have?

▶ **B:** Is the width of a credit card greater than 7.5cm?

▶ **C:** How many arrowheads does the universal recycling logo have?

▶ **D:** In Michelangelo's painting, *Creation of Adam*, with which hand is Adam reaching out to God?

▶ **E:** A standard ruler measures up to how many inches?

▶ **F:** Which colours make up the flag of the UK?

▶ **G:** What is the diameter of an adult human eye?

Solutions on p.181 ≫

4: Weekly shopping

Here is your food-shopping list. Will you be able to bring back all these items? Study the list for a few minutes. Then cover it up and name 12 countries in Asia. (This will provide the time lag.) Afterwards, try to recall as many items as possible.

Carrots, Biscuits, Milk, Leeks, Pears, Tape, Cheese, Sausages, Envelopes, Eggs, Tomatoes, Wine, Grapes, Cereals, Ham

Your score: _____
1-3 items: 2 points
4-7 items: 4 points
8-11 items: 6 points
12-15 items: 8 points

5: Wardrobe crisis

You are trying to help your friend reorganize her wardrobe after a dressing-up session. Below (left) is what the wardrobe originally looked like. Study it carefully for a few minutes and then cover it up.

Now take a minute to recite the 13 times table. Afterwards, return to the exercise – making sure the wardrobe on the left is still covered up – and draw arrows to show where the items were originally located.

Your score: _____
1–3 objects: 2 points
4–6 objects: 3 points
7–8 objects: 4 points
9–10 objects: 6 points

6: What were the questions?

The first exercise in this section asked you 4 questions about your life. Do you remember any of these questions? Write down as many as you can recall.

Your score: _____
1 question: 1 point
2 questions: 2 points
3–4 questions: 4 points

7: Dog sitting

You've offered to look after your friend's 3 dogs while she's away on holiday. When your friend brings the dogs to your house, she describes to you each one's personality. Take a few minutes to memorize the character traits of each dog and then cover up the words. Now to create time lag, spell out loud the first names of 8 family members. Afterwards, try to write the traits of the 3 dogs in the answer spaces below.

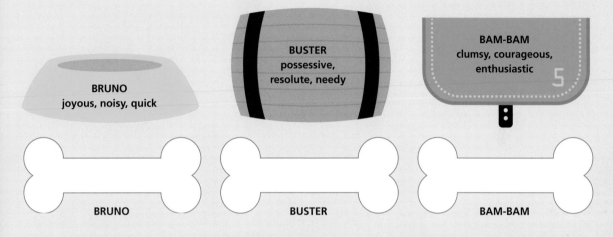

BRUNO
joyous, noisy, quick

BUSTER
possessive,
resolute, needy

BAM-BAM
clumsy, courageous,
enthusiastic
5

BRUNO

BUSTER

BAM-BAM

Your Score: _____
1–3 characteristics: 2 points
4–6 characteristics: 3 points
7–9 characteristics: 4 points

If you recalled all the characteristics and attributed them to the correct dogs, give yourself an extra 4 points:
Your score: _____

8: Shoes galore

Study these 16 types of footwear for a few minutes. Then cover up the picture and name 10 of your favourite cartoon characters to create a time lag. Afterwards, write down as many styles as you can recall.

Your score: _____
1–4 styles: 2 points
5–9 styles: 4 points
10–12 styles: 8 points
12+ styles: 10 points

1 0

HOW DID YOU DO?
Time to add up your points.
Your score: _____ ÷ **48 points**
= (_____ x 100) = _____ %
Did you fare better than you thought you would? You probably noticed that to complete these exercises, you could not rely on your short-term memory. In other words, you could not keep the information in your mental workspace because it was interrupted by another set of information during the time lag. So you had to sift through your long-term memory. Turn over to discover how your long-term memory works and discover ways to boost its aptitude.

What is long-term memory?

The image you have of your favourite schoolteacher, what you ate for breakfast this morning, and what you were doing 10 minutes ago are all in your long-term memory. Any memorized event that occurred outside the time limit of your short-term memory, which ranges from a few seconds to a minute, is in your long-term memory.

The two types

How many legs do flies have? What is the name of the secondary school you went to? You can probably recall that flies, like all insects, have six legs. You can probably name your old school quite easily, too. Although both these pieces of information are stored in your long-term memory, their nature is different: one is general knowledge, and you probably do not remember the context in which you learned it; the other is autobiographical and there are probably lots of emotions and other contextual memories attached to it.

The first type of information is called "semantic", and the second type is known as "episodic". A semantic memory is recalled as an isolated fact. In contrast, when an episodic memory is recalled, the person usually travels back in time and re-experiences the specific life episode along with the sensations attached to it.

The role of the hippocampus

All memories start as episodic memories. Over time, the context in which some were formed fades away and the memories become semantic.

The hippocampus (see p.14), which is a structure deep inside the temporal lobes of the brain, plays a crucial part in the formation of new episodic memories. Interestingly, some researchers believe that episodic memories are stored in the hippocampus, while others believe that it only stores episodic memories for a short time, after which the memories are consolidated to another part of the brain.

Are you ready to put your long-term memory to the test and try to recall some semantic and episodic memories? How about trying the two exercises on the opposite page?

9: Trip down memory lane

Write down 3 special moments from your childhood, 3 from your teenage years, and 3 from your adult life. Do you remember these moments like episodes of a favourite TV programme, with the different people involved, the locations in which they took place, and the emotions you were feeling at the time?

10: Where did I learn that?

Can you remember where you were and the source from which you learned the following pieces of information (e.g. a friend, television, newspaper, internet):

▶ **A:** The Statue of Liberty is in New York

▶ **B:** Mixing blue and yellow creates the colour green

▶ **C:** Blueberries are a good source of antioxidants

▶ **D:** Elephants are known to have good memories

All the questions above tested your semantic memory, so the chances are you had trouble trying to figure out where and from whom you learned each piece of information.

HOW IT WORKS: AMNESIA Long-term and short-term memories are independent and rely on different brain structures. For instance, people with total amnesia cannot register and/or retrieve long-term memories. They cannot learn new things, and cannot remember what happened five years or even five minutes ago. However, in some cases, the short-term memory is intact, enabling the person to hold information in their mind for a few seconds and manage tasks such as simple mental arithmetic.

Why do you never forget how to ride a bike?

Procedural, or "skill", memory is another type of long-term memory. This is the memory you use, for example, when you're riding a bike, playing a musical instrument or a video game. It is the memory for how to do practical things. We are all born with an instinctive ability to form procedural memories. It is how we learn to eat, walk, and talk.

Practice is key

Any procedural memory is developed through practice, and depends on different brain structures from the ones supporting memories, which can be communicated verbally. Once you develop a practical skill, you can apply it automatically. This means that when called upon, you retrieve it without the need for conscious attention. The memory for practical skills is also very long-lasting. How about trying the following exercises to develop two different practical skills?

11: Play that tune

The sequence of musical notes on the right corresponds to the tune for the opening line of "Happy birthday". Practise on the portion of the piano below with your right hand. Make sure you use the correct fingers, too. Try it out next time you come across a real piano!

D D   E D G   F

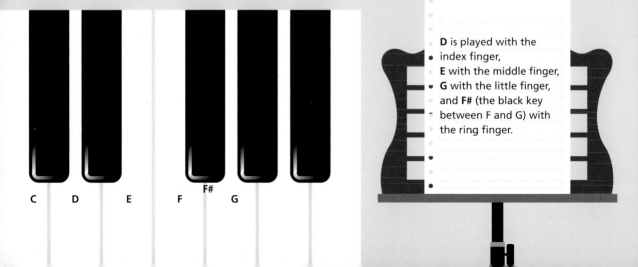

D is played with the index finger,
E with the middle finger,
G with the little finger,
and F# (the black key between F and G) with the ring finger.

C   D   E   F   F#   G

12: 3- and 4-strand braids

▶ **A:** Have you ever braided your own or somebody else's hair? This is a good example of a skill that stays with you forever once you have learnt it.

Here is how you make a 3-strand braid. Practise with hair or threads until you can do it without thinking.

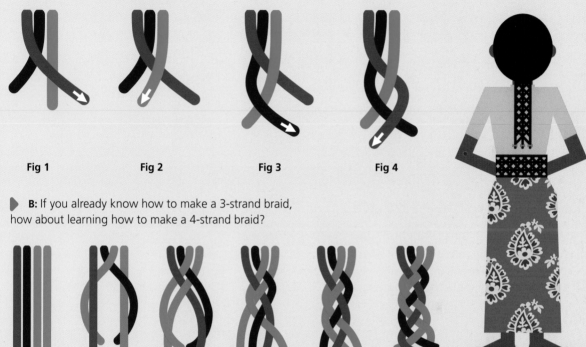

Fig 1   Fig 2   Fig 3   Fig 4

▶ **B:** If you already know how to make a 3-strand braid, how about learning how to make a 4-strand braid?

Fig 1   Fig 2   Fig 3   Fig 4   Fig 5   Fig 6

TOP TIP: HOW TO AVOID CHOKING UNDER PRESSURE Skills in procedural memory are practised so often that they become automatic. However, pressure can cause even a skilled performer to falter. You sometimes see this happen in a professional sport when a player starts making simple mistakes and ends up losing from a seemingly unassailable position. Choking under pressure is caused by concentrating too hard on trying to monitor an automatic skill. This is counterproductive because the brain structures underlying skill memory are not consciously accessible. A way to avoid choking is to practise under simulated pressure situations: the brain will then gradually adapt to the conditions and stop focusing on the skill. This will then alleviate excessive stress and allow your procedural memory to function naturally.

SUPER TECHNIQUE:

How to boost your memory of past events

"Curiosity is as much the parent of attention, as attention is of memory." These were the wise words of Richard Whately – educator, logician, and archbishop of Dublin in the 19th century – and form the basis of this technique.

The right frame of mind

If you didn't pay much attention to the details of the newspaper article you read this morning, the phone number of your doctor, or the name of the woman you met in yesterday's meeting, you probably won't be able to recollect any of these pieces of information. Is this such a surprise? You probably skimmed the article because it wasn't very interesting, you have your doctor's phone number on autodial so have no reason to ever refer to the number, and you'll probably never meet that woman again.

In short, we remember what we pay attention to, what we find interesting and surprising, what is important to us, and what has an emotional value (positive or negative). For example, a hobby that we are passionate about captures all of these things.

Memorability factor

Unfortunately, there are things we need to remember that do not possess these "hooks", such as the name of a medicine we have to take as well as the number of teaspoons, or the last place where we left our keys or reading glasses. The trick is to try to make day-to-day things such as these more memorable. This becomes possible when you apply the three key principles listed on the next page.

DID YOU KNOW: THE ACUTE MEMORIES OF SWAZI HERDSMEN
Can you recall what you bought for your dinner on the same day last month? Probably not. How about this then: herdsmen of the Swazi tribe of East Africa are able to remember in great detail each cow/bull bought a year ago, including who sold the animal, whether it was a bull, a cow, or a calf, its age and look, and what it was bartered for. Impressive, huh? Cattle have tremendous social and economic importance in the Swazi tribe. When the psychologist Barlett tested the same men on other kinds of detail, their memory wasn't better than the average person's. The conclusion we can draw from this is that we tend to remember stuff that matters most to us!

The key principles

Be attentive Although this seems obvious, paying attention to what you want to memorize is the first step towards successfully recalling it. For example, when you cannot remember where you last put your keys, your memory is not at fault. Most of the time this happens because you did not pay attention to where you placed them in the first place. The brain cannot retrieve information that it has not registered.

Be curious Memories that are rich in emotion and connected with many others are much easier to recall. Curiosity will help you create richer memories. By being curious, you will create connections between new and past events: you will feel more involved and this will trigger emotions. For instance, asking people questions about what they do and things they like will help you remember them and their names. Wondering how a medicine works may help you remember its name.

Be motivated Putting a concerted effort into memorizing plays a key role in how well you are able to retrieve a piece of information. Improving memory is like improving any skill. To master it requires continuous practice. It is not easy, but it can be done!

Create personal meaning

A married couple never forgets the memory of their wedding day, especially the moment they exchange the marriage vows and then, of course, the rings. This is because the occasion is full of personal meaning, which naturally commands attention, curiosity, and motivation – the key principles we've already discussed. To improve your memory for random pieces of information, you can attach personal meaning to them. Try exercise 13 below to see how applying this method can help with memorization.

13: It's mine!

Below are pictures of 12 objects that most people use around the house on a regular basis. How many of these objects do you think you will be able to memorize in 1 minute? Time yourself.

For each object, think about the one you have at home and where it is located. Spend 5 seconds developing a personal association with each object. When you are done, cover up the pictures. Then, to create a time lag, complete the maths problems on the right. Afterwards, return to the exercise and list as many objects as you can recall.

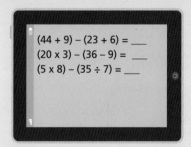

(44 + 9) – (23 + 6) = ___
(20 x 3) – (36 – 9) = ___
(5 x 8) – (35 ÷ 7) = ___

table

glass

fork

coat

sofa

mobile

bed

ironing board

bath

vacuum cleaner

mop

lamp

Solutions on p.181

14: Memorable day

Most of us are creatures of habit and our lives are bound by routine. This explains why what we did last Monday can be difficult to recall. To counter this, how about organizing a memorable day? You could take part in a unique activity that is enjoyable and meaningful to you.

Here are some ideas: go for a walk in an unfamiliar setting, buy something unusual for yourself or someone else, have coffee with a friend at a new venue, take a class in something novel, or visit a fun-packed place such as a fairground with friends or family.

15: Your favourite song

Listen to a song that used to be a favourite when you were a teenager. You might be surprised by how evocative this is and how long-forgotten emotions associated with the memories come flooding back. Write down the details and feelings that return to you.

DID YOU KNOW: FLASHBULB MEMORIES Do you remember how you spent New Year's Eve in 1999? Cast your mind back to the eve of the millennium, the place, and the people you were with. Your memory of this is probably quite vivid and rich in details. This is known as a flashbulb memory: a precise, concrete, and long-lasting memory of the context surrounding a special event. (The event can be a shocking one, too, such as the moment you find out that something tragic has happened.) There are two reasons why such memories stick in your mind. Not only was the moment they were registered very emotional, but they also tend to be retold or relived over and over again.

Does learning by rote work?

At school most of us memorized by rote material such as poems and maths formulas. Some of us still use this method to memorize information. Learning by rote is based on repetition. The idea is that the more you repeat something, the better the chance that it will stick in your mind.

Limitations of rote-learning

Going over a piece of information several times does increase the likelihood of remembering it. The major problem with this technique is that it doesn't require you to understand what you are learning. If the memorized information is not well understood, it will not become connected to existing knowledge (concepts) and, therefore, will be harder to retrieve later on. This explains why material memorized by rote is often forgotten if it is not rehearsed frequently. The perfect example is a student who crams information just before an exam, but doesn't remember much of it a few months later.

Self-testing

Meaningful learning, in which the new information is understood and connected to existing knowledge, usually leads to better and longer-lasting memories. Another effective learning method is known as "self-testing". When using this method, you test your memory several times at regular intervals for the facts you want to memorize, either on the same day or on different days. After you've tried to recall the information, you check the accuracy of your recall by looking back at the original facts. Self-testing is more effective than rote-learning, and a better way of training your brain to memorize. Try the following exercise.

16: Rote-learning vs self-testing

You want to remember the facts below for a game show in which you will appear as a contestant in a week's time. Use rote-learning to learn the first 3 facts: repeat each fact out loud 10 times.

Afterwards, use the self-testing method to learn the remaining 3 facts over the period of a day. Re-read the facts, and then test yourself again later in the day. Continue to do this until you can recall the 3 facts without making an error. Try to recall all 6 facts in 2 days' time (obviously making sure the facts are covered up).

• As of 2009, there were 528 million people living on the North American continent.
• In the UK, the life expectancy of men is 77.6 years and 81.7 years for women.
• The atmosphere on Venus is composed primarily of carbon dioxide.
• An oxymoron is the juxtaposition of two contradictory words (for example, a deafening silence).
• As of 2005, 34 per cent of the population aged 15 and over in Algeria was illiterate.
• The world track record for the 1-mile competition is held by a Moroccan athlete who ran it in 3 minutes 43 seconds in 1999.

DID YOU KNOW: ROTE-LEARNING OR PARROT FASHION? Different countries use a variety of colourful terms to refer to rote-learning. In Greece, rote-learning is known as *papagalia* "parrot-like learning", while in France it is called *par cœur* "by heart". It is not highly regarded in either country, where teachers tend to prefer comprehension instead. In parts of China, it is known as *tian yazi* "stuff the duck", while in Germany it is called *Der Nürnberger Trichter* "the Nuremberg Funnel", in both cases suggesting that knowledge is simply pushed into the pupil. However, China does consider rote-learning to be an integral part of its teaching culture.

Check-out: exercise your long-term memory

Now that you're familiar with the principles for effective memorizing, it's time to assess your long-term memory skills. Calculate your score for each exercise. Remember to be attentive and curious throughout. Some of the exercises will ask you to memorize information and then recall it after a delay or a time-lag task.

17: Panic at the toy store!

All the toys have been mixed up! Can you put them back where they belong? Study the diagram below showing which toys belong in which bucket. Then cover up the diagram. Before sorting the toys, take a minute to solve the maths problems below. Afterwards, sort the toys by writing the letter of the correct bin next to each one.

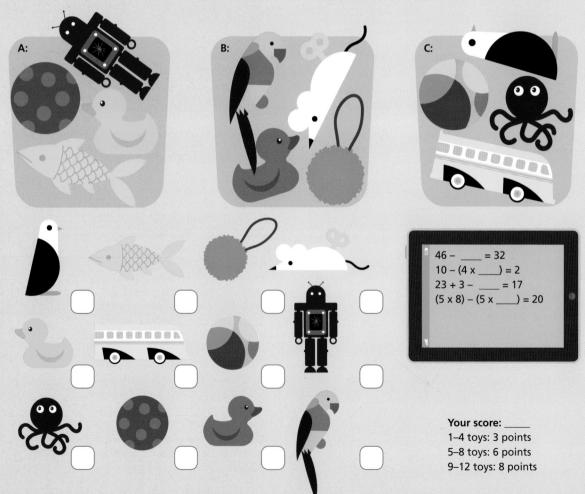

$46 - \_\_\_\_ = 32$
$10 - (4 \times \_\_\_\_) = 2$
$23 + 3 - \_\_\_\_ = 17$
$(5 \times 8) - (5 \times \_\_\_\_) = 20$

Your score: _____
1–4 toys: 3 points
5–8 toys: 6 points
9–12 toys: 8 points

18: Martian invasion

You're trying to read this old newspaper clipping. Some of the words have faded and are illegible. Can you figure out what the words that are missing should be? Cover the text when you are done. Then take a minute to recall the facts you learned in exercise 16 on page 67. Now write down as many of the missing words as you can recall, making sure the words you filled in in the first place are still covered up.

You may find that the easier it was to fill in the blank, the less attention you paid to the word and, probably, the more difficult it is to recall it.

Latest _____: a large Martian _____ is confirmed. The first spacecrafts were _____ this _____ over Spain and France. Further reports indicate that the fleet is heading towards Great _____. In London, the streets are filling up with _____ citizens gazing at the sky. _____ are full as people are trying to buy anything they can before the invasion. Cars and _____ are lining up on the main _____. Travelling may become _____ in a few hours.

Solutions on p.181

Your score: _____
1–3 words: 3 points
4–7 words: 6 points
8–10 words: 8 points

19: Origami puppy face

Have you ever tried origami, the Japanese craft of paper folding? Let's give it a go. Take 5 minutes to memorize the step-by-step instructions to create an origami puppy face. Use the illustrations to visualize each fold. Then close the book and get a square piece of paper. Now can you fold from memory?

Your score: _____
1–2 folds: 3 points
3–4 folds: 4 points
5 folds: 6 points

1. Fold along the diagonal to get a triangle, then fold the triangle in half to make a smaller triangle.

2. Hold the triangle with the point facing down and fold the 2 corners down. These are your dog's ears.

3. Turn the paper over and fold the tip of the triangle inwards.

4. Turn the paper over and draw 2 eyes, a nose, and a mouth.

20: Facing the enemies

Below are the different types of aliens that you will encounter in a video game. Your first job is to make sure you know which ones are your friends and which ones are the enemies. Study them carefully for several minutes. When you are done, cover up the chart. Then take a minute to solve the word puzzle on the right. Afterwards, on the second chart, mark a tick beside the friendly aliens and a cross beside the enemies.

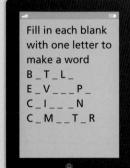

Fill in each blank with one letter to make a word

B _ T _ L _

E _ V _ _ _ P _

C _ I _ _ _ N

C _ M _ _ T _ R

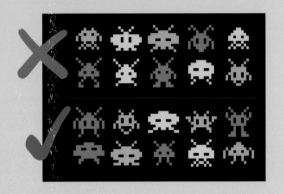

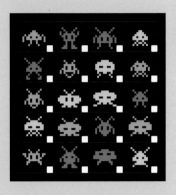

Your score: _____

1–5 aliens: 4 points

6–10 aliens: 8 points

10–15 aliens: 12 points

16–20 aliens: 15 points

21: Eyewitness

Have you ever wondered how accurate you would be if you were asked questions about a scene you had just witnessed? Let's give it a try. Study this scene for a few minutes. Then cover it up and solve the maths problems in the time-lag box. Afterwards, try to answer the questions below.

(10 x 7) – 45 = _____

(6 x 10) + (9 + 9) = _____

(7 x 4) – (15 x 0) = _____

(86 – 74) + (9 x 3) = _____

Solutions on pp.181–2

A: What instrument was the musician playing?

B: Was the woman pushing a pushchair or a pram?

C: Was the bus at a stop?

D: How many street lamps were in the picture?

E: Where was the bicycle in the picture?

F: Were both dogs on leashes?

G: What was the old man holding?

H: How many people were in the picture?

Your score: _____

1–3 correct: 3 points

4–5 correct: 5 points

6–8 correct: 7 points

22: Reading a map

You are getting ready for a long trip across Europe. Below is your itinerary. Study it for a few minutes and then cover it up. Then take a 2-minute break Afterwards, trace your route on the map next to the itinerary.

Your score: _____
1–3 cities: 3 points
4–6 cities: 6 points
7–8 cities: 8 points

Your itinerary:
Start in Paris (France),
then to Bern (Switzerland),
Florence (Italy), Rome
(Italy), Vienna (Austria),
Munich (Germany), Bonn
(Germany), Rotterdam
(Netherlands), and
back to Paris

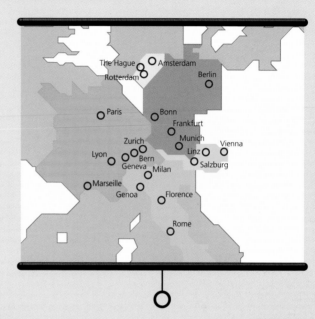

23: The "visiting girls" ceremony

Read the passage below, cover it up, and then take a minute's break before answering the questions below.

The Dai people of China practise an annual courtship ritual called "visiting girls". It starts out with young women sitting around a bonfire and turning their spinning wheels. They are approached by a group of men draped in red blankets who are playing musical instruments. Each man chooses a woman to serenade. If the woman of his choice finds him attractive, she'll take out a small stool from under her skirt and invite him to sit on it. Then the man will wrap her in his red blanket.

▶ **A:** In which country does the ceremony take place?

▶ **D:** What do the men wear?

▶ **B:** How often does the ceremony occur?

▶ **E:** What do the women keep under their skirts?

▶ **C:** What do the young men do?

▶ **F:** How do the women express their interest to the men?

Your score: _____
1–2 correct: 1 point
3–4: correct: 3 points
5–6: correct: 8 points

24: Moments from the past

Answer these questions accurately. Put a cross in the box if you don't know the answer:

Your score: _____
1–2 correct: 2 points
3–4 correct: 3 points
5–6 correct: 4 points

▶ **A:** What was your telephone number at your last address?

▶ **B:** What was your first job?

▶ **C:** What did you do on Saturday night two weeks ago?

▶ **D:** Can you name one of your primary school teachers.

▶ **E:** What was the title of the last book you read?

▶ **F:** What is the eye colour of your hairdresser/barber?

25: First glimpse of the ocean

Your friend is describing the first time he saw the ocean while on holiday. Try to visualize the scene as you read the postcard. When you are done, cover it up and recall the names of 10 people who were in your class in secondary school. Afterwards, draw what you can remember of the scene.

Your score: _____
1–3 correctly located objects: 3 points
4–6 objects: 5 points
7–10+ objects: 8 points

"I saw the ocean first. It was calm, with very gentle waves. There was a sailboat on the right in the distance. Closer up on the left there were two men about to board a small rowing boat. There were a number of seagulls: three above the two men and a group of four on the beach on the right. There was a single cloud in the sky, stretching over the sailboat. Next to the birds on the beach was a little girl playing with her dog. Her red bucket and her sandals were behind her."

26: Birthday wish

You accidentally spill water on your god-daughter's birthday wish list. The words become illegible so you try to remember what they were. Study this wish list for a few minutes. To create richer memories, try to think of each item in a personal context. Then cover up the list and try to find your way in the maze on the right. Afterwards, rewrite the list on the blank sheet below and see how many items you can remember.

- Jigsaw puzzle
- Dolls house
- Stickers
- Books
- Tea set
- Truck
- Doll
- Play-phone
- Dress
- Lollipops
- Guitar

Your score: _____
1–4 items: 3 points
5–8 items: 6 points
9–11 items: 8 points

27: Follow the recipe

You're tired of referring back to your cookbook to remember the ingredients you need for a recipe. How about trying to memorize them instead? Take 2 minutes to study the list of ingredients, then cover it up, and complete the time-lag task on the right. Now draw a circle around the ingredients you need.

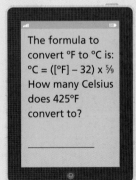

The formula to convert °F to °C is:
$°C = ([°F] − 32) \times 5/9$
How many Celsius does 425°F convert to?

_____

butter, onion, pasta, celery, mushrooms, flour, salt, milk, tuna, peas, cheese

Solutions on p.182

Your score: _____
1–4 ingredients: 3 points
5–8 ingredients: 6 points
9–11 ingredients: 8 points

28: Geography lesson

How much do you remember from your geography lessons at school?
Draw arrows to link each river with the sea or ocean it flows into.

River	Ocean/Sea
A: Mississippi	South China Sea
B: Jordan	English Channel
C: Seine	Dead Sea
D: Ganges	Atlantic Ocean
E: Danube	Persian Gulf
F: Euphrates	Black Sea
G: Amazon	Indian Ocean
H: Mekong	Gulf of Mexico

Your score: _____
1 point for each correct answer

Solutions on p.182

29: Who said what?

You are having dinner with new colleagues and each tells you something about themselves. Take a few minutes to memorize each quote and the face it belongs to. Then cover up the picture. After a 5-minute break, write the correct quote in each speech bubble.

Your score: _____
1–2 quotes: 3 points
3–4 quotes: 6 points
5–6 quotes: 8 points

I am on a diet

I'm learning to play golf

Gardening has always been my passion

I have 4 children: 3 boys and a girl

I do not like big cities

I go fishing whenever I can

30: All mixed up!

At a conference, you bump into a colleague and all the business cards you both have collected fall on the floor and get mixed up. Take a few minutes to memorize the names on the business cards in the holder. Then cover them up. Now, to create a time lag, recall the 8 Wonders of the World. Afterwards, identify your business cards from the pile.

Your score: _____
1–2 cards: 3 points
3–4 cards: 6 points
5–6 cards: 8 points

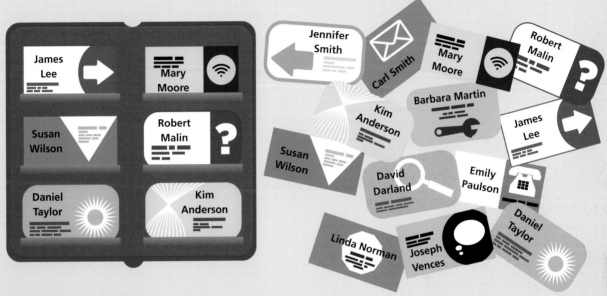

31: Stamp collector

You've spotted 10 stamps that you think may interest your friend who is an avid stamp collector. However, you're not sure whether he already has them. Take a few minutes to memorize the 10 stamps below (on the left). Then, to create a time lag, turn back to pages 72–73 and add up your score for the exercises on those 2 pages. Afterwards, return to this exercise (making sure the stamps you studied are covered up). Study your friend's collection and cross off the stamps that your friend already has.

1 0

HOW DID YOU DO?

Time to add up your points.
Your score: _____ ÷ 122 points = (___ x 100) = ___ %
Compare this score to the score you got for the check-in exercises. Are they different? How much were you able to focus your attention and create rich memories?

Do bear in mind that you cannot improve your memory over the course of a single day! What you can do is maintain the good work and make sure you keep applying the basic principles described in this chapter as often as possible when trying to memorize something.

Your score: _____
1–2 stamps: 3 points
3–4 stamps: 6 points
5–6 stamps: 8 points
7 stamps: 10 points

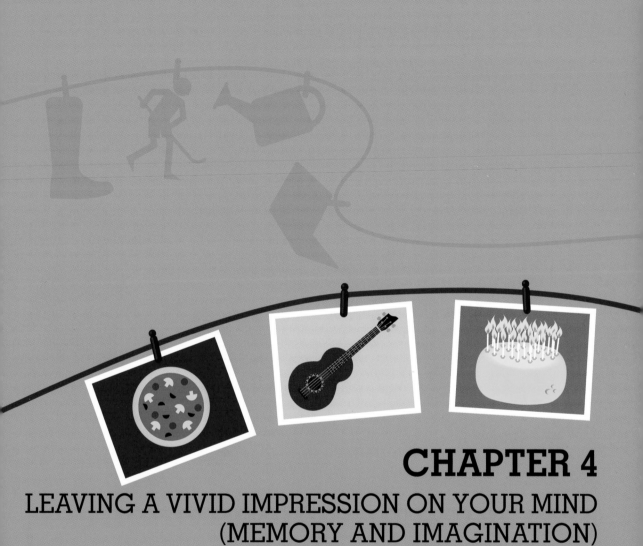

CHAPTER 4

LEAVING A VIVID IMPRESSION ON YOUR MIND (MEMORY AND IMAGINATION)

Check-in: what's your imagination like?

Recall a special moment in your life. Do images of the moment come to mind first? Of course they do. This is because we rely mainly on our sense of vision to build memories in the first place. This chapter looks at how honing the ability to create powerful mental images can lead to a better memory. Try the following exercises to assess your visualization skills.

1: Close your eyes to see

Visualize the following images and then rate the vividness of each image on a scale of 1 to 4:
1 = vague impression
2 = complete but lacking detail
3 = complete with a few details
4 = vivid impression

❯ **A:** Your mother's face. Your rating: ____

❯ **B:** A market stall. Your rating: ____

❯ **C:** The sun setting behind a mountain. Your rating: ____

❯ **D:** A cat warming up in the sun. Your rating: ____

❯ **E:** A forest in autumn. Your rating: ____

❯ **F:** A sailboat on a rough sea. Your rating: ____

What is your average rating (sum of all your ratings divided by 6)? Your Score: _____

2: What happens next?

Look at each scene and try to imagine what will happen next. You can either draw or describe the next scene in the space provided. Try to imagine something funny or surprising. You have 2 minutes.

Your score: ____
1 scene: 3 points
2 scenes: 6 points

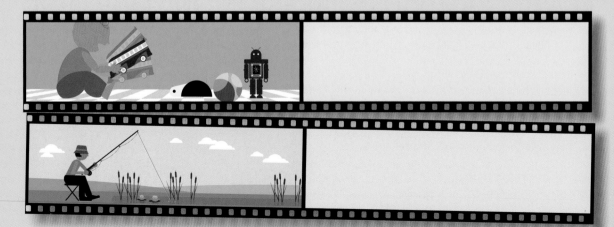

3: Back to front

Choose a room in your house (not the one you're currently in), and imagine all the furniture mirrored so that what's on the left is now on the right and vice versa. Draw an aerial plan of the mirrored room in the space below. Then go to that room and check how accurate your drawing is.

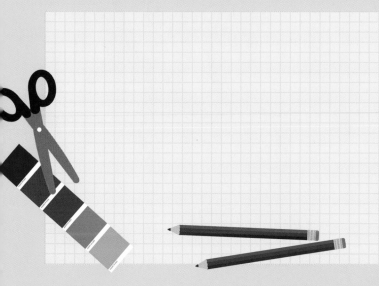

Your score: _____
2+ errors: 2 points
no errors: 4 points

4: Mental scale

Are the objects in the list smaller or larger than the size written beside them? In each case, always consider the length/height of the object, and NOT the width. Write "S" (smaller) or "L" (larger) beside each object.

▶ **A:** DVD case: 21cm (8¼ in)____

▶ **B:** Mobile phone: 7.5cm (3 in) ____

▶ **C:** Chequebook: 6cm (2⅓ in) ____

▶ **D:** Ballpoint pen: 9cm (3½ in)___

▶ **E:** Wine bottle: 36cm (14⅕ in) ____

▶ **F:** Cotton bud: 7cm (2¾ in)____

▶ **G:** Fork: 23cm (9 in)____

▶ **H:** Coffee mug: 13.5cm (5⅓ in)____

▶ **I:** Business card: 4cm (1½ in)____

Your score: _____
1–3 correct: 2 points
4–6 correct: 4 points
7–9 correct: 6 points

Solutions on p.182

1 2 3 4 5 6 7 8 9 10 11 12

1 2 3 4 5

5: Tactile memories

Can you recall what it feels like to walk on a warm sandy beach? If the answer is yes, you've just experienced a "kinaesthetic" image. In other words, you've just recalled the feeling you get when a part of your body touches something familiar.

How strong are your kinaesthetic images? Imagine the following actions and rate how difficult it is to recall the feeling on a scale of 1–4:
1 = very difficult, 2 = difficult, 3 = moderately easy, 4 = easy

A: Holding an ice cube. Your rating: _____

B: Stepping into a warm bath. Your rating: _____

C: A baby grasping your finger. Your rating: _____

D: Drinking cold water. Your rating: _____

E: Running barefoot on grass. Your rating: _____

F: Stroking a cat. Your rating: _____

What is your average rating (sum of all your ratings divided by 6)? Your score: _____

6: Imaginary turns

How good are you at mentally rotating objects? Let's give it a try. By mentally turning them left or right, decide whether the objects in each pair below are identical (I) or mirrored (M) images.

A:

B:

C:

D:

E:

F:

Your score: _____
1–2 pairs correct: 2 points
3–4 pairs correct: 4 points
5–6 pairs correct: 6 points

7: It's all in the detail

How precise are your mental images? Search your memory to answer the following questions.

▶ **A:** Do bears have short or long tails?

▶ **B:** What colour is the inside of a mango?

▶ **C:** Are flamingos pink all over?

▶ **D:** What's the colour of an uncooked shrimp?

▶ **E:** Do bats have large or small ears?

▶ **F:** What does the shape of Italy remind you of?

Your score: _____
1 point for each correct answer

Solutions on p.182 ▶▶▶

8: Zooming in

A butterfly appears bigger as you get closer to it, right? This can be experienced mentally, too. Imagine a butterfly on a flower 1 metre away from you and then begin zooming in on it. You can see the pattern on the wings. You may even be able to see its antennae and eyes. See, it works! Now imagine a caterpillar on a leaf 1 metre away from you. Zoom in on it and on a separate piece of paper list as many details as you can "see".

Your score: _____
1–3 details spotted: 2 points
4–6 details spotted: 3 points
7+ details spotted: 4 points

1 0

HOW DID YOU DO?
Time to add up your points.
**Your score = (_____ x 100) ÷ 40 =
_____ %**
Were you able to visualize images that were vividly detailed? Which aspect of visualization did you find the most challenging: colour, size, shape? During this chapter, you will find out why visualization is one of the keys to boosting memory. You will also learn two memory techniques that involve visualization.

How does visualization boost memory?

Pictures are more powerful than words to help retrieve a memory. This is because the brain registers pictures both at the conceptual and the visual level. For example, when you see a picture of a cheeseburger, you understand what it is (conceptual level) and you see what it looks like (visual level). In contrast, when you just hear the word "cheeseburger", you register it at the conceptual level and do not get any visual cues, so your brain has to work a little bit harder to access the memory.

The power of images

The superiority of images over words has been known for a long time. This is why most mnemonics boost your memory by asking you to convert what you want to learn into powerful mental images. The idea is that these images will stick in your mind because the brain registers them at both conceptual and visual levels, just as real pictures.

Mental images also help you to create connections between the different things you want to remember. For instance, if you want to memorize that your new neighbour has a white cat as well as a toddler child, try to picture both in a single image – you can imagine the cat licking the toddler's hand or the toddler riding the cat! Such images might seem silly, but they are powerful memory boosters.

Using the other senses

When you recall an object in your mind, you form a mental image of it, but you can also recall other sensory experiences of the object. For instance, if you're asked to think about chocolate, you probably begin by picturing your favourite chocolate bar, the packaging it's in, but then you can also imagine its smell, what it feels like on your fingers, and of course its taste when you put it into your mouth.

One way to create strong memories is to form images and enrich them with multi-sensory details. This will increase your chances of retrieving the memory. As with all the techniques featured in this book, the more you practise this multi-sensory technique, the better you will become at using it, and it will soon become a memory aid that you employ without even having to think about it.

9: Pictures and words

Take a few minutes to memorize the group of pictures and the list of words. When you are done, cover them up. Then, to make sure that none of these are still present in your short-term memory, recite the 8 times table backwards starting from 80. Afterwards, write down the pictures and words you can remember.

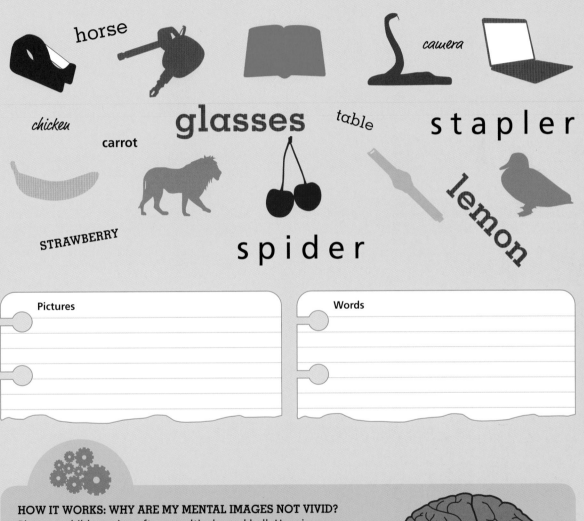

horse

camera

chicken

glasses

table

stapler

carrot

STRAWBERRY

s p i d e r

lemon

Pictures	Words

HOW IT WORKS: WHY ARE MY MENTAL IMAGES NOT VIVID?
Picture a child running after a multicoloured ball. How is your mental image? Is it richly detailed, full of colour, and as precise as a photograph? Or is it rather vague and dim? People report a lot of differences in the vividness of their mental images. Why is this? Research shows that the vividness of mental images is determined by the activity in the primary area of the brain which processes visual information (in the occipital lobe, at the back of your head). The more activity there is in this part of the brain, the more vivid your mental images.

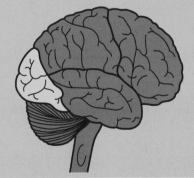

How do special moments stick in your mind?

We tend to remember moments, events, or things that are different from what we usually encounter. Our first experience of something is a perfect example, such as the first day of school, the first time we drive a car, or the first time we share a romantic kiss. Why is this?

The power of emotion

Such salient events attract our attention. This extra attention leads to a better memory of the event because more information becomes registered in the brain, and this additional information acts as a cue for retrieval later on.

In addition, salient events can sometimes rouse emotional states of surprise, pleasure, or shock. For example, most of us have no problem recounting our first day of school because we felt extremely curious, excited, and apprehensive on the day. Our heightened emotions triggered a state of arousal in which we were more alert and attentive. As a result, more information was registered during this event. In contrast, it's perhaps far more difficult to recount the memory of our third day at school because, as we became accustomed to our new surroundings, our emotions settled down.

Adding humour

There are many memory-boosting techniques that take advantage of the power of uniqueness on memory. This is the case, for example, in the Link System (see pp.88-89) in which the person creates surprising and original mental images using the material they are trying to memorize. These mental images tend to be funny too. This is because humour stimulates our attention substantially. For instance, it

is well known in the advertising world that humorous adverts are more memorable than serious ones. In fact, the next time you're watching television count the number of adverts you see that use humour to sell their product. You'll be surprised how often the scene, narrative, or strapline relies on humour to attract your attention. So the funnier you can make your mental images when using visual mnemonics, the better your memory of them will be.

10: Funny images

Spend 1 minute studying the 6 pictures that are on the front page of the magazine below. Then cover up the image and complete the maths problems in the time-lag task. Afterwards, write down as many objects as you can remember from the 6 drawings in the magazine.

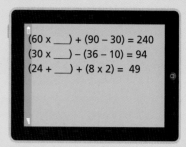

(60 x ___) + (90 – 30) = 240
(30 x ___) – (36 – 10) = 94
(24 + ___) + (8 x 2) = 49

Did you recall the objects that featured in the funnier/bizarre images more easily than the objects in the ordinary images? It is likely that the funnier scenes made a greater impact and stuck in your mind. This demonstrates the power of humour and uniqueness in memory formation.

Solutions on p.182

TOP TIP: CREATE A SURPRISE If you are organizing any type of event (whether it is a birthday party for a friend, an auction, or a fund-raising car boot sale) and would like it to be memorable, try to include a surprise. The surprise doesn't have to be something fantastic (no need to rent an elephant to wow the people, although that would really work!), but it has to be something that stands out and is unique to your event. Be as creative as you can.

Why can't you get that song out of your head?

Do you remember the songs you used to sing as a child? And can you easily recall the words to the songs you listened to as a teenager? Can you remember the melody as well as the lyrics? It is likely that you answered yes to these questions. How is it that songs seem to stick easily in our memories? There are three main reasons for this: repetition, the emotion we invested in the songs while listening to them, and the meaning of particular songs.

Making songs stick

We tend to hear songs we like over and over again. The more we like them, the more we listen to them, and if we like them a lot we tend to sing along, especially in the shower! Knowingly or unknowingly, we rehearse our favourite songs extensively, which increases the likelihood that they will stay with us forever.

Another reason why songs sometimes find a permanent home in our memories is because they are registered at several levels in our brain. First, both music and lyrics can trigger emotion, be it pleasure, joy, optimism, or sadness. Secondly, the lyrics of a song may hold special meaning for us. They might tell a poignant story, or encapsulate perfectly the moment we first fell in love. The combination of melody and lyrics makes a song both emotive and expository. This makes the memory of a song a very rich one and therefore easier to retrieve later on.

Other benefits

The relationship between music and memory is complex. Not only do songs we like stick in our heads, but music can also help alleviate anxiety and stress. Since a high level of stress is not good for memory (see pp.168–169), music can be considered to be an indirect memory booster. Its relaxing effect helps us to function better (though listening to music while studying may not be the smartest choice, see tip box opposite).

Interestingly, the context in which songs are heard often stays with us. This makes songs powerful tools to elicit autobiographical memories, especially when memory begins to decline with age.

Finally, because songs tend to stay in our memories for a while, they can be good tools to learn new facts. This can be achieved by replacing the lyrics of a well-known song with information you have to remember. Try the exercise "Singing to remember" on the next page to see how this works.

11: Singing to remember

You have 4 things to do today and decide to take advantage of the powerful effect of songs on memory to memorize your to-do list. You need a short and simple song. Let's pick a children's song that you probably know very well, such as "Frère Jacques".

Replace the lyrics of the song with the items on your to-do list. Sing the song several times with its new "lyrics". How fast can you learn the song (and thus memorize your list)? This also works very well when memorizing phone numbers, for example.

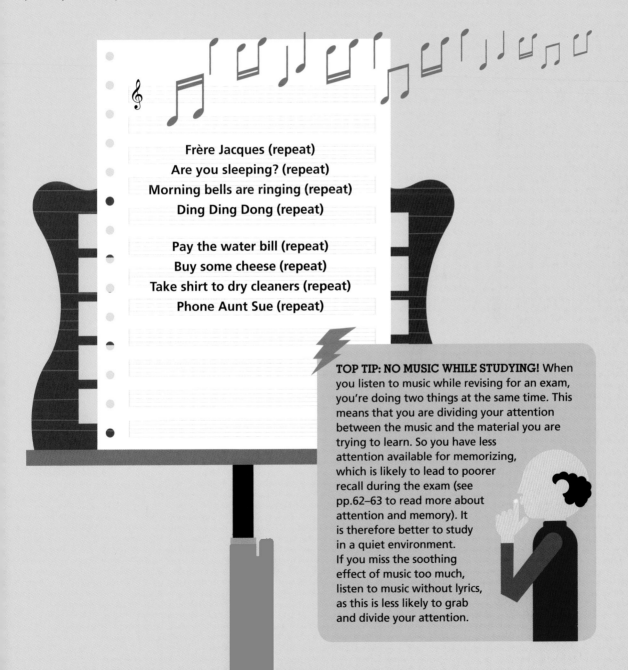

Frère Jacques (repeat)
Are you sleeping? (repeat)
Morning bells are ringing (repeat)
Ding Ding Dong (repeat)

Pay the water bill (repeat)
Buy some cheese (repeat)
Take shirt to dry cleaners (repeat)
Phone Aunt Sue (repeat)

TOP TIP: NO MUSIC WHILE STUDYING! When you listen to music while revising for an exam, you're doing two things at the same time. This means that you are dividing your attention between the music and the material you are trying to learn. So you have less attention available for memorizing, which is likely to lead to poorer recall during the exam (see pp.62–63 to read more about attention and memory). It is therefore better to study in a quiet environment. If you miss the soothing effect of music too much, listen to music without lyrics, as this is less likely to grab and divide your attention.

SUPER TECHNIQUE:
The Link System

A memory is rarely a single isolated fact. Most often it will be a collection of connected information. This is how learning happens in the brain: new facts are connected to old ones, and it is through this system of linkage that we store and retrieve information. This also explains why single facts, such as names, can be so difficult to remember.

We make natural connections

Sometimes connections form naturally when we encounter a new fact. For example, if your colleague tells you that he bought a new estate car, you will remember this because you can connect the information to something else you know about him, namely, that he has four kids so he needs a large car. Other times we come across isolated information and no connections come to mind. This might be the case when you meet Sally Kay for the first time. Your chances of remembering her name are slim without creating any connections. This is when the Link System (or association technique) comes in handy.

What is the Link System?

In the Link System, you use your imagination to create artificial links/ connections/associations between random objects. The more creatively you use your imagination, the stronger the links will be. And the stronger the links, the better your memory of those objects will be. There are two key methods to create strong links:

Exaggeration: links that are larger than life, strange, funny, or surprising are always more memorable.
Visualization: links that take the form of mental pictures rather than words are easier to recall.

How does it work?

Let's say you want to remember to buy cheese, candles, and paper napkins – the only items you still need for your friend's birthday party. A grocery list consisting of only three items seems pointless and, moreover, you are likely to lose it. Instead you could link cheese, candles, and napkin in the following funny image: picture your friend wearing a colourful paper napkin tucked into his shirt collar, blowing out 100 candles set on a giant Gouda cheese.

If you spend a few seconds thinking about this image, the chances are you will easily recall it when you are in the store.

DID YOU KNOW: NAME YOUR AUDIENCE When introduced to the 100 people who came to listen to his lecture on memory, Frank Felberbaum managed to memorize 90 of their names (both first and last). He attributed this incredible memory performance to the Link System he used. Frank Felberbaum is one of the world's leading memory experts, and he was also the winner of the Gold Medal at the World Memory Olympics, held in the United Kingdom in 1995.

Practise using the Link System

The following exercises will help you practise creating funny visual images to link random pieces of information and boost your memory of them. You will quickly see how easy and effective it is to use this technique.

12: Bizarre links

Create links for each set of random words listed below. Remember to create associations that are exaggerated and silly to help the objects stick in your mind. For example, if you had to link the words "pedicure" and "lemon pie", you could imagine squeezing lemons with your incredibly lovely feet to prepare the lemon pie. Yes, it's totally bizarre, but memorable! Now it's your turn. Use a separate sheet of paper if you require more space.

▶ **A:** apple – cow

▶ **B:** pencil – bridge

▶ **C:** phone – grass

▶ **D:** glasses – water

▶ **E:** bag – car – fork

▶ **F:** dog – flower – ruler

▶ **G:** umbrella – scissors – mouse

13: Crazy images

The funnier and crazier your visual images, the better. Let's practise visualizing events that are silly and surreal. Create a mental picture of each scene described below. Make sure your images are as detailed as possible. Spend at least 10 seconds on each.

▶ **A:** Marilyn Monroe standing on your sofa wearing a cowboy outfit

▶ **B:** A cockroach smoking a cigar while riding a large motorcycle

▶ **C:** A bearded man wearing only shorts, juggling baby elephants

▶ **D:** A kangaroo sitting in a bathtub filled with marmalade

▶ **E:** A woman with 4 arms playing the guitar and trumpet at the same time

▶ **F:** A talking lizard helping a group of blue children cross a busy street

▶ **G:** Bruce Lee in swimming trunks in your kitchen chopping carrots with his left hand

▶ **H:** You watering lollipops with a pink fluid on a bright summer's morning

14: Who's ordered what?

Imagine you are a waiter. Use the Link System to memorize the main courses ordered by each person at the table. To associate the food with a person, use exaggerated and surprising images. Picture each link/association in your mind for at least 10 seconds. Add as many details as possible to your images. When you are done, cover up the picture and say out loud 3 multiplication tables of your choice. Afterwards, write down the main courses that you remember next to the people who ordered them.

A cheese pizza

Fish and chips

Spaghetti with meatballs

Steak and baked potato

Shrimps with rice

Chicken with mushrooms

HOW IT WORKS: BIZARRE IMAGES IN THE BRAIN Which areas of your brain light up when you see (and probably also when you imagine) a bizarre, surprising image (a dog slowly morphing into a watering can, for example)? Neuroimaging studies show that two brain regions are active: a network of frontal and temporal brain areas, which are classically associated with the type of deep processing that leads to memory registration, and secondly regions of the brain usually associated with the state of arousal. This explains why such images are remembered so well.

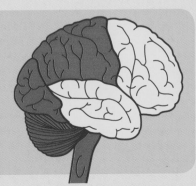

SUPER TECHNIQUE:

The Journey Method

The Journey Method (also known as the method of loci or the memory palace) dates back to Ancient Greek times. It is a very efficient method that combines spatial learning and visualization. The method is useful for memorizing sequences, lists, different points in a speech, material for a test, or even steps to operate a complex machine.

How does it work?

When using the Journey Method, you take a mental walk across a very familiar environment: it can be your house, the route you take to work, or even your own body. Your walk should always start in the same location (for instance, at the front door of your house) and follow the same route (first the dining room, then the kitchen, then the bathroom, the stairs, and so on).

The idea is to create a link between each item on your list and each visited location (or locus). You can merely "leave" an item in a location or more creatively connect the two. What matters is that you take the time to visualize the item in this location and enrich your mental image with as much detail as possible. Later on, when you need to recall the items on your list, you will walk along your mental path and "find" each piece of information where you left it.

A typical route

Imagine you have a long itinerary of things to do, but don't have a pen to write a list. In the morning you need to go to the post office and then to the library to return books. You are then meeting a friend for lunch. In the afternoon you have to collect your shirts from the dry cleaners, visit the pet store to buy fish food, and finally buy a few grocery items.

In order to use the Journey Method to memorize this to-do list, first you need to select where your mental walk will take place. Let's say it's a house, like the one illustrated here. This then becomes your "memory palace". As there are six items on your to-do list, you will need six locations in your memory palace too.

Now you need to link each item on your list to each location. The best way to do this is to use the Link System (see pp.88–89). For instance, you can imagine a poster of a giant "stamp" hanging on the wall of your entrance hall. This will remind you of the post office later on when you mentally enter the house. You can imagine human-like books sitting at your dining table to remind you of the library, and so on. The more bizzare and surreal the images are, the better your memory for them will be. When you are done, you'll only have to take that journey through your memory palace to locate each to-do item on your itinerary waiting for you in the location you left it earlier.

TOP TIP: CLEAN THE MEMORY PALACE
Many memory champions who use the Journey Method claim that they need to "clean up" their mental locations periodically to avoid cramming them with too much stuff! To get rid of all your links and images, imagine cleaning each location until you can see them as they actually are. In other words, free of any items or bizarre scenes.

Practise using the Journey Method

Complete the following exercises to become familiar with the Journey Method. Thereafter, keep using it as often as possible. Use it to memorize lists that you might refer to at home, school, or work. These could include shopping lists, the periodic table, or even the steps of CPR found in First Aid manuals.

15: Build a memory palace

Before using the method, you need to establish which memory palace you are going to use (see p.92 for examples). The key is to pick a location that you are familiar with and which you can navigate with ease.

Once you've chosen your memory palace, take a mental walk through it and pick at least 9 "rooms" (or landmarks) that you know very well.

Next, walk your mind through the same route several times until you know the journey by heart.

16: Holiday essentials

Use the Journey Method to memorize the holiday shopping list below. Spend 10 seconds placing the items at each location to create a journey filled with vividly detailed, surreal images. For more information on how to build suitable images, refer to the Link System described on page 88. When you are done, cover up the list and, to create a time lag, count backwards from 100. Stop after 2 minutes and then write down as many items on the shopping list as you can remember as you work your way through your memory palace.

Flip-flops
Sunglasses
Sun cream
Beach towel
Yellow cap
Puzzle book
Summer frock

24: Home redecorating

You are about to start some DIY work on your kitchen when you realize that you have to run to the store to get the 5 items listed below. Use the Link System to memorize your list. Then cover it up and take 2 minutes to think of as many words as you can that start with the letter V. Afterwards, recall your shopping list.

Masking tape
Packet of nails
Sand paper
Gloves
Screwdriver

Your score: _____
1–2 items: 2 points
3–4 items: 3 points
5 items: 4 points

25: The wedding speech

You are the best man at your friend's wedding. You have prepared a speech but prefer not to read it off a sheet of paper. Use the Journey Method to memorize the main parts of the speech. When you are done, solve the maths problem. Afterwards, recall out loud as much of the speech as possible (the exact wording does not matter).

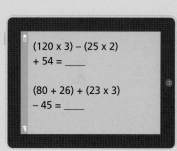

$(120 \times 3) - (25 \times 2)$
$+ 54 =$ ____

$(80 + 26) + (23 \times 3)$
$- 45 =$ ____

1. I have known Paul since Year 9 at school and back then he loved chasing girls. Fortunately he has changed a lot.
2. I was there when Paul and Eva met for the first time. It was not the most romantic situation: Paul was in the car with me when I accidentally hit the bumper of Eva's car at a set of traffic lights!
3. I remember how Paul would always tell me that he would never find a woman who was both smart and caring. Well he did.
4. I've known Paul and Eva for 5 years and can say that they are perfect for each other.
5. I have never seen them argue except for the time when Paul bought a ladder and they had to carry it all the way home because it did not fit in their car. I wish them to live happily ever after in their newly painted house (thanks to me!).

Your score: _____
1–2 parts: 2 points
3 parts: 4 points
4–5 parts: 6 points

Solutions on p.182 >>>

26: Does it fit in a shoebox?

Visualize each common object below (standard size) and decide whether or not it would fit in an adult shoebox. Mark a tick or a cross beside each item.

Your score: _____
1–4 items: 2 points
5–8 items: 4 points
9–10 items: 6 points

coat hanger

☐

colander

☐

hair dryer

☐

cereal box

☐

tambourine

☐

Child's doll

☐

table tennis bat

☐

bicycle pump

☐

laptop

☐

ice skates

☐

> *Solutions on p.182* ▶▶▶

27: Up in the sky

Try to memorize the 6 well-known constellations that are listed below using the Journey Method. Refer to the description of the constellations to create a concrete image of each one. When you are done, close the book and have a break. You can test your memory for them in 10 minutes' time.

▶ **A: The Great Bear:** its most famous feature is the Big Dipper

▶ **B: The Lesser Bear:** features a smaller dipper and the North Star is located at the end of the Little Dipper's handle

▶ **C: Cassiopeia: or the Queen,** is composed of 5 very bright stars that form a "W" shape

▶ **D: The Hunter: or Orion,** features 3 bright stars that form a belt-like pattern

▶ **E: The Swan:** one of the largest constellations, forms a cross-like shape

▶ **F: The Lion:** whose head and mane are marked by stars arranged like a reversed question mark

Your score: _____
1–2 constellations: 2 points
3–4 constellations: 4 points
5–6 constellations: 6 points

28: Learn the dance steps

Dancers often rehearse steps mentally when they are outside the dance studio. Let's try the same thing with the dance steps below. Read one step at a time and imagine performing it several times in your head. When you feel ready, stand up and give it a try! Record how many moves you remember to perform correctly.

1. Start, standing up, with both feet together

2. Step to the side with the right foot

3. Step across the right foot with the left foot

4. Step to the side with the right foot

5. Touch the left foot beside the right

6. Then, step back with the left foot

7. Step back with the right foot

8. Step back again with the left foot

9. Touch the right foot beside the left

Your score: _____
1–3 moves: 2 points
4–6 moves: 4 points
7–9 moves: 6 points

29: Surprise gifts

While shopping with your friend, you try to make a mental note of what she seems to like so you can come back later and buy her a surprise present. Use the Link System to memorize the items. When you are done, cover up the words and recite the 12 times table. Afterwards, write down the items you remember.

Scarf
Pearl necklace
Bracelet
Pocket mirror
Handbag
Pair of boots

Your score: _____
1–2 items: 2 points
3–4 items: 3 points
5–6 items: 5 points

30: Cube folding

Time for a quick visualization exercise! Let's test your ability to mentally fold and rotate an object. Carefully study the cube template below (left), and decide which of the 4 cubes it would become if you were to fold it.

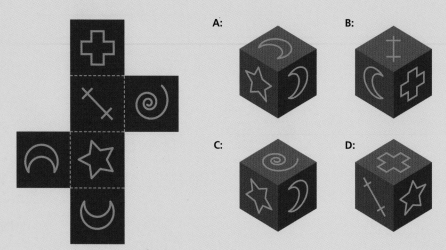

A:

B:

C:

D:

Your score: _____
Correct answer: 5 points

Solution on p.182

31: Red wines

You are applying for a job in a vineyard and need to memorize the different types of red wines and their characteristics. Try using the Journey Method to do this. Use the flavours to come up with a concrete image for each wine. When you are done, cover up the list and take a 10-minute break. Afterwards, recall each wine and its description on a separate sheet of paper.

Your score: _____
1–2 wines: 2 points
3–4 wines: 4 points
5–6 wines: 6 points

Shiraz: hearty and spicy Flavour: wild black fruit

Merlot: soft red Flavour: cherry and plum

Malbec: smooth with rich colour Flavour: plum, berry, and spice

Cabernet sauvignon: full-bodied and woody Flavour: currant and bell pepper

Pinot noir: delicate and fresh Flavour: cherry, strawberry, plum

Zinfandel: very versatile Flavour: berry, anise, and black pepper

32: Connect the four

Let's test the strength of your associations by assessing how long they last. Take 2 minutes to link/associate the 4 unrelated words below. Visualize your association. Then cover up the words and recite the 4 times table until you reach 64. When you are done, try to recall the 4 words. Then test your memory again after 30 minutes and once more after 1 hour.

Bucket   **Giraffe**   **Carrot**   **Bottle**

Your score: _____
1–2 words: 1 point
3–4 words: 2 points
30 minutes later:
1–2 words: 2 points
3–4 words: 4 points
1 hour later:
1–2 words: 4 points
3–4 words: 5 points

33: A full diary

You are a very busy person and have filled every day of the week with an activity. It is getting difficult to keep track of what you're doing on each day. Try using the Journey Method to memorize the sequence of activities.

When you are done, cover it up and add up the points you have scored in the check-out so far. Afterwards, list the activity you plan to do on each day of the week.

MON	Swimming
TUES	Tutoring school children
WEDS	Painting
THURS	Playing golf
FRI	Jogging
SAT	Fixing the taps
SUN	Voluntary work at the library

MON	
TUES	
WEDS	
THURS	
FRI	
SAT	
SUN	

Your score: _____
1–2 activities: 1 point
3–5 activities: 3 points
6–7 activities: 5 points

1 0

HOW DID YOU DO?
Add up the points you got for each exercise:
your score = (_____ x 100) ÷ 93 = _____ %
Are you getting used to the Link System and the Journey Method? Test yourself in a few days' time to see if you've held on to some of the information you memorized in these exercises: keep using the techniques until you master them to experience their full benefits.

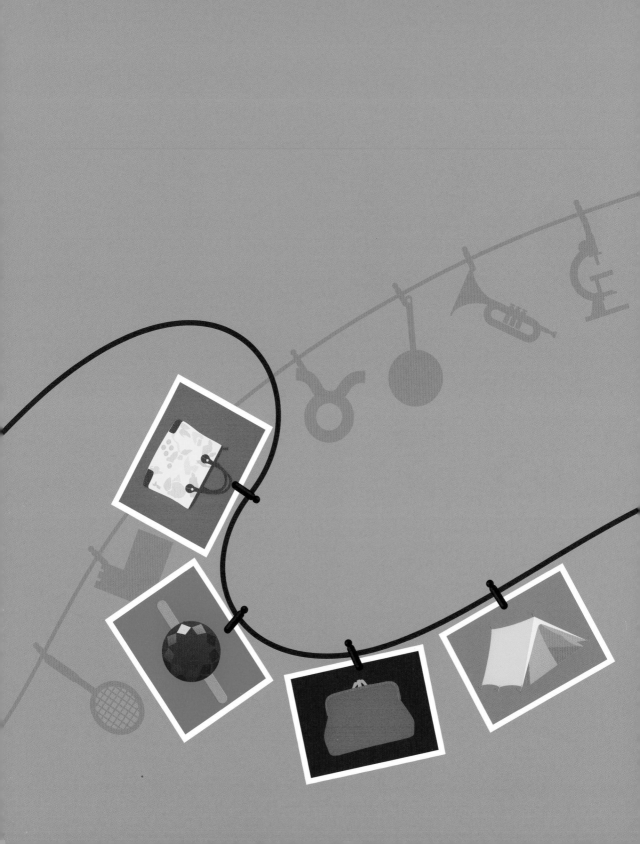

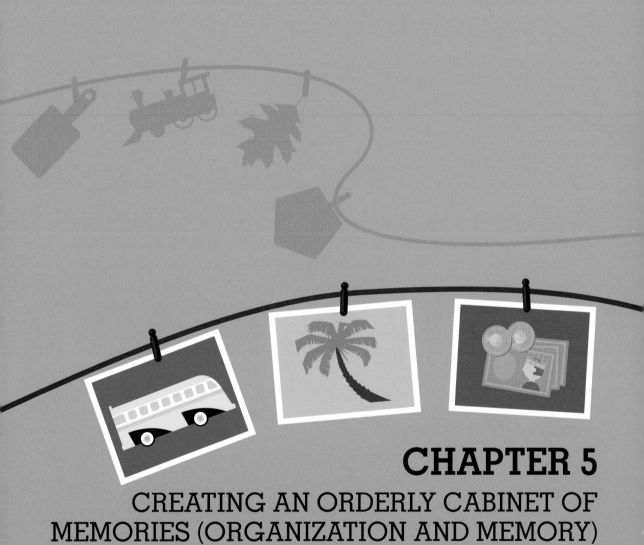

CHAPTER 5

CREATING AN ORDERLY CABINET OF MEMORIES (ORGANIZATION AND MEMORY)

Check-in: how organized is your mind?

You may be wondering what organization has to do with memory. First, the ability to organize information (text, words, pictures) in a meaningful way helps you to understand the information better. Secondly, it creates a system for you to be able to recall the items, which boosts your memory for that information. Before exploring the different ways information can be organized, let's test your natural ability to do this with the following exercises.

1: Accessories

Imagine you are working in a retail store and have been asked to display the accessories below. Can you group the accessories so that you have 3 different categories with 3 items on each shelf? You have 1 minute to do this.

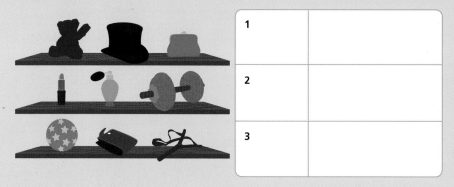

1	
2	
3	

Your score: _____
Found 1 group: 1 point
Found 2 groups: 2 points
Found 3 groups: 3 points

2: Ranking game

Below are pictures of a variety of random objects. Although they are unrelated, can you find 2 ways to rank or order the objects to help you memorize them?

1	
2	

Your score: _____
Found 1 way to order
the objects: 2 points
Found 2 ways to order
the objects: 4 points

3: What's on my kitchen table?

Look at the items on the table with the red tablecloth. Take 1 minute to figure out 3 meaningful groups/categories to put the items into. Then do the same with the items on the table with the blue tablecloth.

Your score: _____
Found 3 groups for table A: 3 points
Found 3 groups for tables A and B (6 groups in total): 6 points

Table A:

steak
corn
leek
cheese
ice cream
chicken
lamb   butter   bean
yoghurt   potato
turkey
sausage   milk   carrot
cream   pork
broccoli

Table B:

apricot
radish
lettuce   carrot
raspberry   artichoke
courgette   cherry
tangerine
orange
spinach
pumpkin   peas
strawberry
tomato

1	2	3

1	2	3

4: Going fishing

The fish below may look very similar but they actually belong to different species. Take 30 seconds to figure out how many species there are and identify the specific characteristic of each species you find.

Your score: _____
1 point for identifying each species and its specific characteristic

Solutions on p.183 ⟫⟫⟫

5: Who are they?

A: A baggage handler at the airport accidentally drops the suitcases belonging to 3 people. Unfortunately, the contents spill out and get mixed up. He has the idea of sorting them out according to the profession he can ascribe to each of them. Can you correctly sort out the contents and guess the profession of each person?

Profession 1
Profession 2
Profession 3

Your score: _____
1 profession: 1 point
2 professions: 2 points
3 professions: 4 points

B: Cover up the picture and list as many items as you can recall.

Your score: _____
1–5 items recalled: 2 points
6–9 items recalled: 4 points
10–12 items recalled: 5 points

6: Slide puzzle

Take no more than 10 seconds to mentally reorder the squares in the puzzle below so that you create a picture that depicts a famous event in history. Can you name the famous historical event?

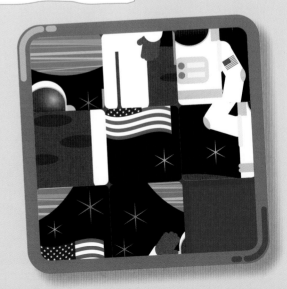

Your score: _____ 2 points for correct answer

7: Up for grabs

You are participating in a memory recall competition and would like to win first prize. Take 2 minutes to find a way to divide these objects into 2 meaningful groups to help you memorize them. Each group should have the same number of objects.

1	
2	

Your score: _____
Identified both groups:
4 points

8: Sorting shapes

Take 30 seconds to figure out the 3 ways to rank/order the shapes below.

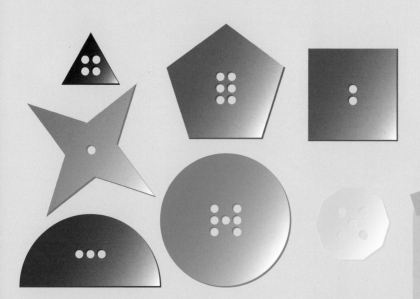

1
2
3

Your score: _____
1 ordering system: 1 point
2 ordering systems: 2 points
3 ordering systems: 3 points

Solutions on p.183

1 0

HOW DID YOU DO?
Time to add up your points. **Your score = (_____ x 100) ÷ 35 = _____ %** Does your score indicate that you have a natural talent for organizing information? How useful is this going to be in your quest for a better memory? Turn to the next page and begin to discover how (and why) organizing the material you want to remember can boost your memory.

Why keeping a tidy mind boosts your memory

If you are looking for a document on your desk, it is usually easier to find if your desk is organized. This is because an organized desk has been tidied up according to rules you have established and a logic that makes sense to you: mail may be stacked by date of arrival, to-do tasks could be in a separate pile, and official papers might be filed away in a specific drawer. So when you need to find something, you know where to look because the categories you used to arrange the contents of the desk act as cues to retrieve specific items.

Organizing information

Memory works in the same way. By organizing the material you want to memorize, you will create groups/categories that will serve as cues for later recall. In addition, the relationships between the items within each category will be strengthened simply because you have established a connection between them. And of course, you cannot organize material without really understanding it, which also helps boost your memory of it.

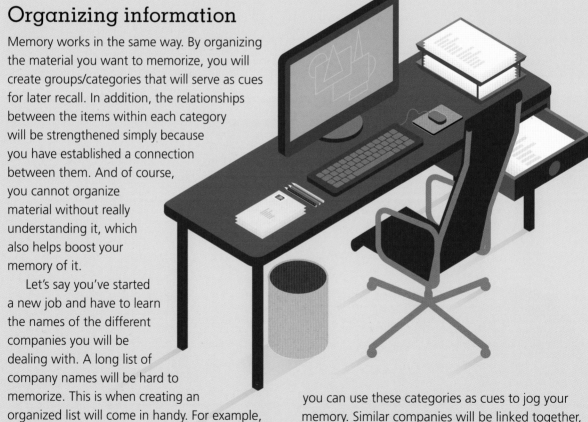

Let's say you've started a new job and have to learn the names of the different companies you will be dealing with. A long list of company names will be hard to memorize. This is when creating an organized list will come in handy. For example, grouping the companies according to the service they provide can help you form a memory of them. Later on, when you try to recall the company names, you can use these categories as cues to jog your memory. Similar companies will be linked together, too, which increases your chances of remembering them. How about using the same system to memorize the 24 pictures on the next page?

9: What belongs where?

Study the pictures below for 3 minutes and try to identify categories you can group them into (hint: you can form 4 groups). Then cover up the pictures, and to create a time lag, count to 90 in multiples of 3. Afterwards, try to recall as many of the pictures as possible.

▶ **A:** List below the categories you identified.

▶ **B:** How many pictures can you remember?

1
2
3
4

TOP TIP: YOUR PERSONAL SYSTEM IS THE BEST Many psychological studies have proven that material presented in an organized manner is better remembered than randomly presented material. In addition, creating your own system of organization works better than using one that is given to you. This takes advantage of another memory-boosting effect: we remember better what we come up with ourselves than what we passively receive. So do not hesitate to reorganize any material you need to learn according to a system that makes more sense to you.

Solutions on p.183 ▷▷▷

Ordering information

Grouping information into meaningful categories is one system of organization that can be used to boost memory. You can also organize information by ordering or ranking it. This can be done by alphabetical order, ascending size, brightness of colour, and so on. Use the exercises below to practise using grouping and ranking as a way to improve your memory.

10: Night at the casino

You are at the casino. You need a toilet break and leave your chips with a friend but want to make sure he doesn't gamble any of them in your absence. Take 2 minutes to memorize the chips below. To boost your recall, try ordering them by ascending value. Then cover up the chips and on a separate sheet of paper write down the names of 10 movies you've seen in the last year. Afterwards, try to recall all the chips.

11: The mobile zoo

The mobile zoo is visiting your local school. Memorize the different animals the zoo keepers will bring with them, pictured below, so that you can tell the other teachers. How about ranking the animals by size to enhance your recall? When you're done, cover up the animals. To create a time lag, return to exercise 10 and add up the values of all the chips. Afterwards, return to this exercise and try to remember all the animals.

12: Weekend shopping

Here is a list of the things you need to buy during the weekend. To make sure you do not forget any of the items, organize the list based on the 3 stores in which the items can be found. Once you are done, cover up the list and count backwards from 150. Stop at 115. Afterwards, try to recall all the items on your list.

watering can   plasters

nail polish   light switch

paint brush   rake

cotton balls   cough drops

compost   masking tape

flower seeds   Vitamin pills

Solutions on p.183 >>>

DID YOU KNOW: ACRONYMS AND ACROSTICS Acronyms (words that combine the initial letters of a series of words) are famous memory boosters. They organize material in a compressed form, which is easy to memorize. You can use these to remember lists. For instance, the to-do list "go to the **p**ost office, pay **E**lectricity bill, call **A**nna" could become PEA. When acronyms cannot be formed, acrostics can be used. These are memorable sentences or poems in which the letter at the beginning of each word or sentence spells a list of other words. For instance, in music, a well-known acrostic to remember the notes that fall on the lines in ascending order on the treble key is "**E**very **G**ood **B**oy **D**eserves **F**udge" (for E, G, B, D, F). You can create acrostics to remember many things, such as the planets in the solar system, the colours of the rainbow, and so on.

SUPER TECHNIQUE:

The Peg System

The Peg System is an efficient way of memorizing random lists of information, such as the 10 most populated countries in the world or the 12 signs of the zodiac. It works by learning a standard set of peg words on which you can hang the information you need to remember. The Link System (see pp.88–89) is used to hang or link information on the pegs.

Create your pegs

First you need to build your pegs. There are different types of pegs: the most common are the rhyming pegs and the alphabetical pegs.

Let's focus for now on the rhyming pegs. For this, you memorize a list of common words, which then become your pegs. You choose words that you can associate with numbers 1 to 10 through rhyme, for example 1 = gun, 2 = shoe, 3 = tree, 4 = door, and so on.

The resulting peg list will be easy to memorize. Remember that you do not have to use numbers. In the alphabetical peg system, letters are used instead to anchor the pegs. In fact, you can use any sequence that you already know by heart.

Once you have learned your peg list, you are ready to memorize any list of items. The peg list only has to be memorized once. Then it can be used over and over again by hanging items you

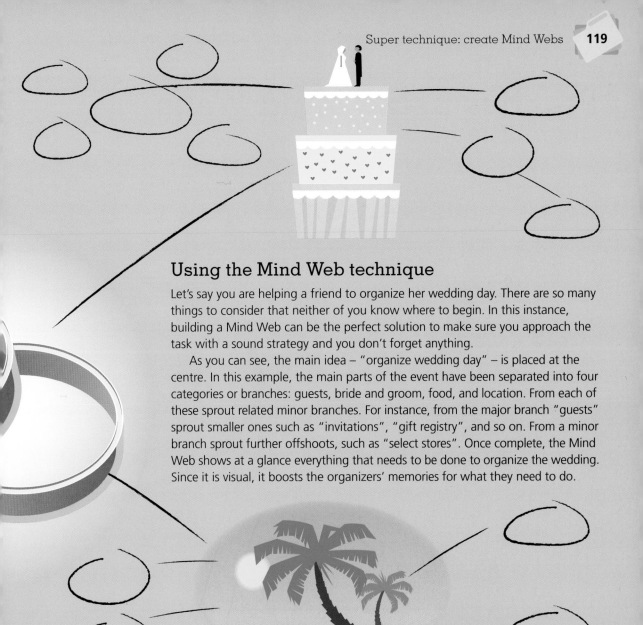

Using the Mind Web technique

Let's say you are helping a friend to organize her wedding day. There are so many things to consider that neither of you know where to begin. In this instance, building a Mind Web can be the perfect solution to make sure you approach the task with a sound strategy and you don't forget anything.

As you can see, the main idea – "organize wedding day" – is placed at the centre. In this example, the main parts of the event have been separated into four categories or branches: guests, bride and groom, food, and location. From each of these sprout related minor branches. For instance, from the major branch "guests" sprout smaller ones such as "invitations", "gift registry", and so on. From a minor branch sprout further offshoots, such as "select stores". Once complete, the Mind Web shows at a glance everything that needs to be done to organize the wedding. Since it is visual, it boosts the organizers' memories for what they need to do.

DID YOU KNOW: THE FIRST MIND WEB The use of Mind Webs can be traced back to the 3rd century when a Greek philosopher used one to illustrate a complex concept developed by Aristotle. However, it was not until the 1950s that the link between this kind of mental mapping and effective human learning was discovered (seminal work was carried out by Dr Allan Collins and Ross Quillian in the 1960s). Modern Mind Webs have been popularized by psychology author Tony Buzan, who has coined the term "mindmap" to describe this tool. Nowadays you can even find software that helps you build Mind Webs.

Practise using Mind Webs

Use the exercise below to create a Mind Web. The web is partly drawn to give you a head start. Begin with the main themes and then start branching out. There is no limit to the number of branches and sub-branches you can create. If the space provided on the page isn't enough then use a separate sheet of paper. Take all the time you need to complete the exercise.

17: Going travelling

You are thinking of going on a month-long trip to Bolivia and Brazil in South America. You start looking on the internet for more information and find a useful site: *www.travelindependent. info/america-south.htm*. Read the webpage and then draw a Mind Web to see whether you can visually organize the information that is most relevant to you. To get you started, we've already put down the central idea and 5 main branches. Complete the Mind Web. Test your memory 30 minutes after completion by writing down the information you can remember on a separate sheet of paper.

Clothes

Money

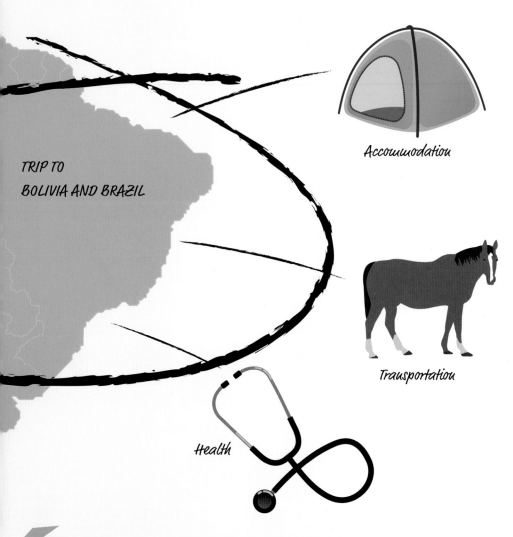

TRIP TO
BOLIVIA AND BRAZIL

Accommodation

Transportation

Health

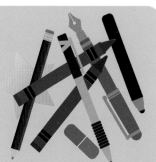

TOP TIP: BE CREATIVE When you are creating a Mind Web, do not hesitate to erase and redraw. Use different coloured pens and vary the thickness and length of lines. Include as many images as possible (small motifs representing ideas) and limit the amount of written information. It doesn't have to be a work of art, but something that triggers a memory. The more visual details you have in the Mind Web, the better. Include anything that seems relevant to your central idea. Above all, be creative! Creative maps will boost your power of recall the most because they are visually striking and also because you spend more time building them.

Check-out: exercise organizing information into solid memories

How good have you become at organizing information for a better memory? Do these exercises to discover the answer. Try to use the Peg System, a Mind Web, or a grouping system when recommended. Record your points for each exercise. You can complete the section over the course of a few days.

18: Bird watching

Below are 6 birds common to the UK. Take 1 minute to memorize their names. (Try putting them into 2 groups to boost your memory of them.) Then cover them up and move on to exercise 19. Afterwards, write down the correct name under each bird.

Your score: _____
1–2 birds: 2 points
3–4 birds: 4 points
5–6 birds: 6 points

Thrush
Robin
Chaffinch
Gold finch
Great tit
Blue tit

19: A trove of toys

Can you memorize all the toys pictured below? To boost your memory, group the toys into meaningful categories.

When you're done, cover up the toys and, on a separate piece of paper, list as many green-coloured fruits as you can think of in 2 minutes. Afterwards, try to recall the toys. (Do not forget to return to exercise 18.)

Your score: _____
1–4 toys: 3 points
5–8 toys: 6 points
9–12 toys: 9 points

20: The coldest places on Earth

Below is a list of the 10 coldest locations in the world. Try using your pegs to memorize them. When you are done, cover up the names and complete the maths problems. Then try to recall the locations in descending order starting from the coldest nation.

$(12 \times 6) - (4 + \underline{\quad}) = 56$
$(5 \times 8) + (7 - \underline{\quad}) = 42$
$(60 \div 4) + (26 - \underline{\quad}) = 29$

1. Antarctica   2. Russia   3. Greenland   4. Canada

5. Alaska (US)   6. Finland   7. Iceland   8. Mongolia

9. Kazakhstan   10. Estonia

1
2
3
4
5
6
7
8
9
10

How many locations did you remember in the correct order?

Your score: _____
1–3 locations: 2 points
4–6 locations: 4 points
7–10 locations: 6 points

Solutions on p.183

21: Ring fingers

Can you memorize all the rings on the woman's fingers? Work out the grouping system to help you here. Once you're done, cover up the rings and solve the time-lag problem. Afterwards, circle the rings you recognize in the display below.

Looking at the sequence of letters "OGIHD" is this statement true or false: "H is not preceded by G"?

_____

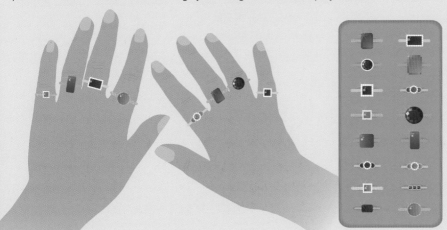

Your score: _____
1–3 rings: 2 points
4–6 rings: 4 points
7–8 rings: 6 points

22: Journalism school

You're keen to become a journalist. Do you know the 6 main questions you should answer when filing a report? The questions are:

Try using your pegs to memorize these questions. If your first peg is "gun", then you could visualize a scene in which someone in a mask is stealing your gun, prompting you to ask: "Who stole the gun?" When you are done, cover up the list and recite the 7 times table. Afterwards, try to recall the checklist questions.

Who is it about?

What happened (what's the story)?

When did it take place?

Why did it happen?

Where did it take place?

How did it happen?

Your score: _____
1–2 questions: 1 point
3–4 questions: 2 points
5–6 questions: 3 points

23: Beautiful bouquet

Imagine you are a florist. A customer calls to order a bouquet but your pen runs out of ink and you can't write down the order. Can you memorize the flowers he wants? How about organizing them by colour to improve your recall? When you are done, cover up the picture and write down on a separate sheet of paper as many types of tea as you can think of in 1 minute. Afterwards, write down below as many types of flowers as you can remember from the order.

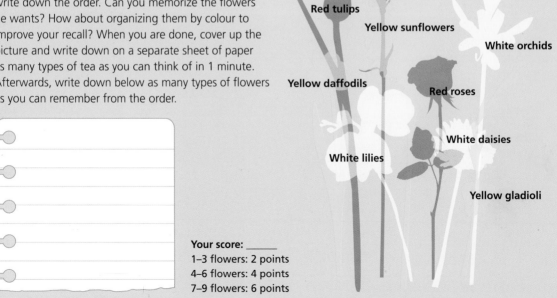

Red carnations

Red tulips

Yellow sunflowers

White orchids

Yellow daffodils

Red roses

White daisies

White lilies

Yellow gladioli

Your score: _____
1–3 flowers: 2 points
4–6 flowers: 4 points
7–9 flowers: 6 points

24: To the rescue

Your neighbour is an elderly lady for whom you often run errands. She called you this morning with a list of things for you to do. To make sure you remember all the tasks, use the Peg System (see pp.114–115) to memorize the to-do list. When you are done, cover up the list and take a 2-minute break. Afterwards, see how many tasks you can recall from the list.

take her prescription to the chemist

mow her lawn

order special socks online

check her bank statement

buy milk and flour for her

renew her newspaper subscription

show her how to send an email

Your score: _____
1–3 tasks: 2 points
4–5 tasks: 4 points
6–7 tasks: 6 points

25: Cloud gazer

Try to memorize as many cloud names as you can in the chart below. Use the shape of the clouds as well as their elevation as organization principles to help boost your recall. Then cover up the cloud names and complete the maths problems below. Afterwards, write down the correct name of each cloud in the blank chart.

cirrostratus

cirrus

cirrus-cumulus

cumulo-nimbus

altostratus

altocumulus

stratocumulus

stratus

nimbostratus

cumulus

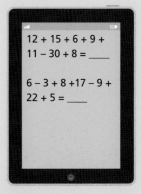

12 + 15 + 6 + 9 + 11 − 30 + 8 = ____

6 − 3 + 8 +17 − 9 + 22 + 5 = ____

Your score: _____
1–3 cloud names: 2 points
4–6 cloud names: 4 points
7–10 cloud names: 6 points

Solutions on p.184

26: The great outdoors

The last time you went on a camping trip you forgot several essential items. To make sure this doesn't happen this time round, you decide to memorize the most important items you'll need. Try using your pegs to do this. Then cover up the list and answer the question in the time lag box. Afterwards, write down as many items as you can remember.

List 4 favourite books from your childhood
1:
2:
3:
4:

Torch, soap, can-opener, bin bags, icebox, roadmap, socks, matches, sunscreen, pocketknife

Your score: _____
1–3 items: 2 points
4–6 items: 4 points
7–10 items: 6 points

27: Entertaining James

Your nephew James, who is 5 years old, is visiting you and your family next week. You need to keep him and your son busy and are looking for things to do with them. Using your nearest city as a model, plan for the week by drawing a Mind Web on a separate sheet of paper. Think of the things that are available in your area. Include any different kinds of entertainment you can think of (such as arts and crafts, outdoor activities, museums, playgrounds) and don't forget to add suitable places for lunches and snacks.

How comprehensive was your Mind Web?
Your score: _____
5 ideas/activities: 1 point
6–8 ideas/activities: 2 points
9–12 ideas/activities: 4 points
13+ ideas/activities: 6 points

28: Decathlon

Do you know the order of the events in a decathlon? As the name indicates, it includes 10 sporting disciplines that are spread over 2 days. Can you memorize what happens on each day? You may want to use the Peg System here. When you are done, complete the maths problems. Afterwards, try to remember the 10 events of a decathlon, in the correct order if possible.

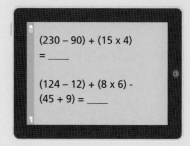

$(230 - 90) + (15 \times 4)$
= ____

$(124 - 12) + (8 \times 6) - (45 + 9)$ = ____

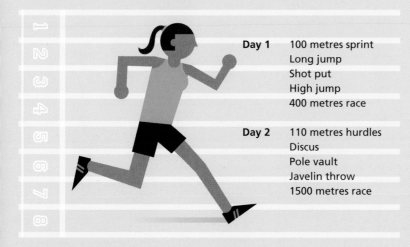

Day 1	100 metres sprint
	Long jump
	Shot put
	High jump
	400 metres race
Day 2	110 metres hurdles
	Discus
	Pole vault
	Javelin throw
	1500 metres race

Solutions on p.184

Your score: _____
1–4 events: 2 points
5–8 events: 4 points
9–10 events: 6 points
Add 2 points extra if you remembered the events in the correct order.

29: Fixing the house

You need to repair parts of your house before you can put it up for sale. The picture below shows the 8 most urgent things that need fixing. To aid memorization, try organizing the repairs from top to bottom. Then cover up the picture and take 2 minutes to think of as many boys' names as you can beginning with B. Afterwards, try to recall all the parts you need to repair.

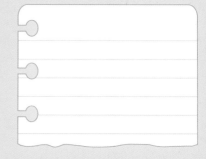

Your score: _____
1–3 parts: 2 points
4–6 parts: 4 points
7+ parts: 6 points

30: Time to limber up

It's difficult to do an exercise routine while referring to a fitness manual. Why not memorize the programme in advance? Here is a sequence of exercises that is great for building body strength. To memorize the exercises, try ordering them starting at the legs and then move upwards. When you are ready, cover up the exercises and count backwards starting from 65. Afterwards, see how many exercises you can remember.

Squat: squat slowly with your arms extended to maintain balance (target body part: thighs)

Shoulder press: start with arms half-extended to the side, raise both hands over your head (target body part: shoulders)

Calf raise: go up on your toes keeping your arms by your sides (target body part: calves)

Bicep curl: bend arms at 90° in front of you, curl upper arms towards shoulders (target body part: biceps)

Leg extension: hold your hips and raise one leg to the side and then alternate (target body part: buttocks)

Your score: _____
1–2 exersises: 3 points
3–5 exercises: 6 points

31: Caring for your car

Any car requires a variety of regular checks to ensure that it is safe to drive. Use the Peg System to memorize the essential maintenance checks. Once you're done, say the alphabet out loud missing out alternate letters. Afterwards, cover up the information in the top box and fill in the blank spaces below.

Your score: _____
1–2 words: 2 points
3–4 words: 4 points
5–6 words: 6 points

Maintaining a car
- Check fluids: brake fluid, transmission fluid, power steering fluid, oil, washer fluid, engine coolant
- Tyres: check pressure, balancing, rotation, wheel alignment, wear
- Inspect or replace: windshield wipers, air and fuel filters, oil, spark plugs, belts
- Check all lights

Maintaining a car
- Check fluids: brake fluid, _____, power steering fluid, oil, _____, engine coolant
- Tyres: check _____, balancing, rotation, wheel alignment, _____
- Inspect or replace: _____, air and fuel filters, _____, spark plugs, belts
- Check all lights

32: Vegetable garden

You have decided to plant the following fruits and vegetables in your new garden. Try using your pegs to memorize them. When you are done, cover up the garden and on a separate piece of paper list as many breeds of dogs as you can think of in 2 minutes. Afterwards, test your memory of the produce.

Your score: _____
1–3 foods: 2 points
4–6 foods: 4 points
7–10 foods: 6 points

33: Lost in the forest

Can you memorize the shapes of these different leaves and the names of the trees they belong to? To boost your recall, try putting the leaves into meaningful groups (such as those with pointy ends, those that are prickly, and so on). When you're ready, cover up the leaves and recite the 6 times table backwards from 60. Afterwards, draw the leaves and write down the names of the tree they belong to on a separate piece of paper.

Your score: _____
1–3 leaves: 2 points
4–6 leaves: 4 points
7–8 leaves: 6 points

1 0

HOW DID YOU DO?
Time to add up your points.
Your score = (_____ x 100) ÷ 98 = _____ %
You are working hard: congratulations! By now, you should have memorized your pegs and be ready to use them when required. Try drawing Mind Webs whenever you need to organize and memorize a lot of information. Of course, do not hesitate to review the techniques in the previous chapters so you can decide which best suits your needs.

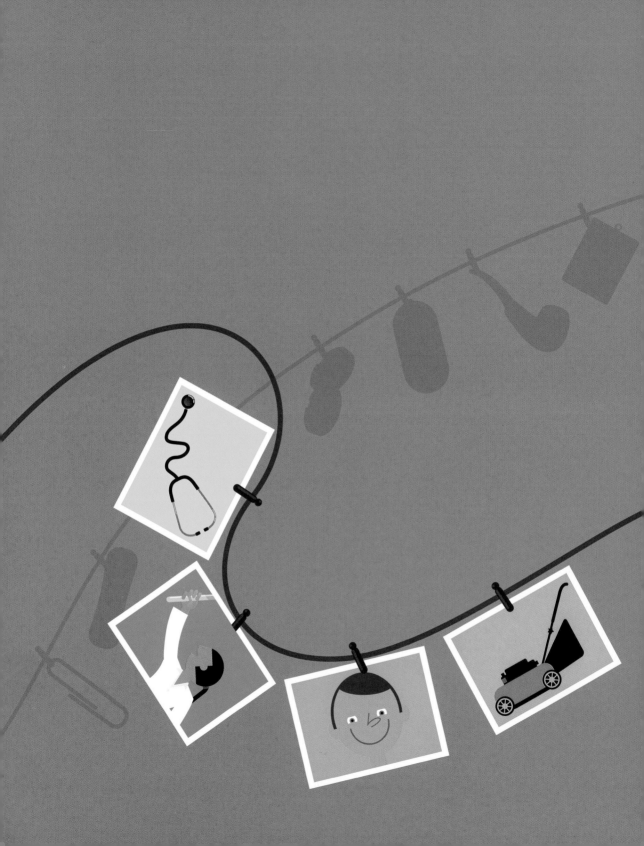

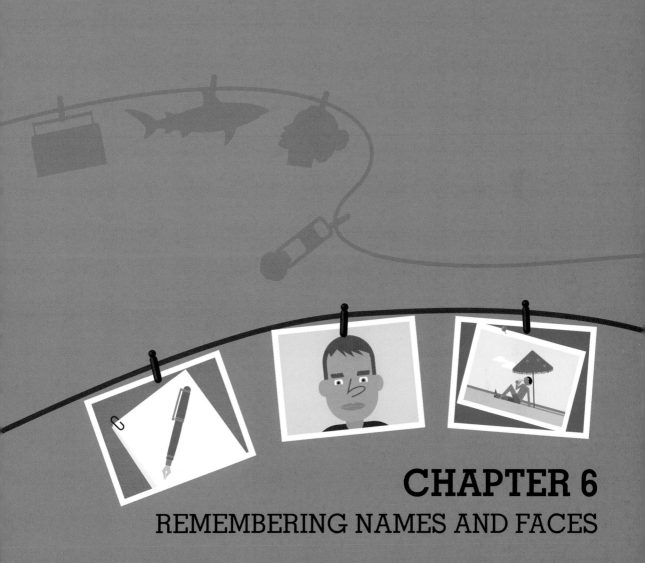

CHAPTER 6
REMEMBERING NAMES AND FACES

Check-in: how well do you remember names and faces?

Before learning how to boost your memory for names and faces, let's test your current ability. Once more, we've added an unrelated time-lag task for some of the exercises. Write down your score as you go along and add up your points at the end.

1: Meeting the board

Below are the names of the 8 members you want to speak with at the next board meeting. Take 1 minute to memorize their names. Then cover them up and count backwards from 30. Afterwards, see how many names you can remember.

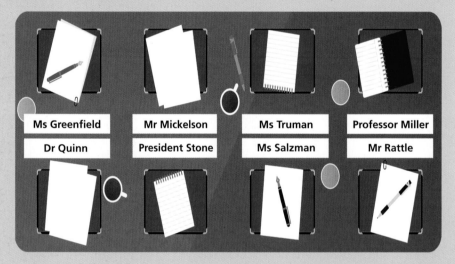

| Ms Greenfield | Mr Mickelson | Ms Truman | Professor Miller |
| Dr Quinn | President Stone | Ms Salzman | Mr Rattle |

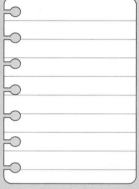

Your score: _____
1–3 names: 1 point
4–6 names: 2 points
7–8 names: 3 points

2: New bank workers

Study the faces of these 5 new bank employees. After 30 seconds, cover them up and recite the 7 times table backwards starting from 70. Afterwards, circle the 5 employees who match the ones below among the three rows of faces on the next page.

Your score: _____
1–2 faces: 1 point
3–4 faces: 2 points
5 faces: 3 points

3: Name the faces

Take 1 minute to memorize the names and faces on the right. Once you're done, cover them up and take a 2-minute break. Afterwards, write down the correct names under the faces below.

Ruth Raugh   **James Weisman**   **Nancy Kemna**   **Matthew Steele**

Your score:_____
1 point for each name recalled under the correct face

4: Observing faces

Take 2 minutes to look closely at the 4 faces below. Try to memorize as much as you can about them. Now cover up the faces and, to create a time lag, spell out 10 words that each consist of 6 letters. Afterwards, see how many of the questions on the right you can answer correctly.

▶ **A:** What is Mr A's hair colour?
▶ **B:** Is Ms B wearing glasses?
▶ **C:** Does Mr C have thin lips?
▶ **D:** Does Ms D have long hair?
▶ **E:** Does Mr A have thick eyebrows?
▶ **F:** Does Mr C have a flat or pointy nose?

Mr A   **Ms B**   **Mr C**   **Ms D**

Your score: _____
1–2 correct answers: 1 point
3–4 correct answers: 2 points
5–6 correct answers: 3 points

Solutions on p.184 ▷▷▷

5: Back to the bank

Without referring back to exercise 2 on page 132, can you still identify the 5 new bank employees from the array of faces below? (They are all now wearing a pair of glasses to make things a little more difficult.) Circle the correct faces.

6: Pairing up

You are introduced to 3 couples at a dinner party. Take 30 seconds to memorize the names and faces of each couple. Then cover them up and recite the alphabet backwards starting from the letter J. Afterwards, fill in the correct names under the picture of each couple.

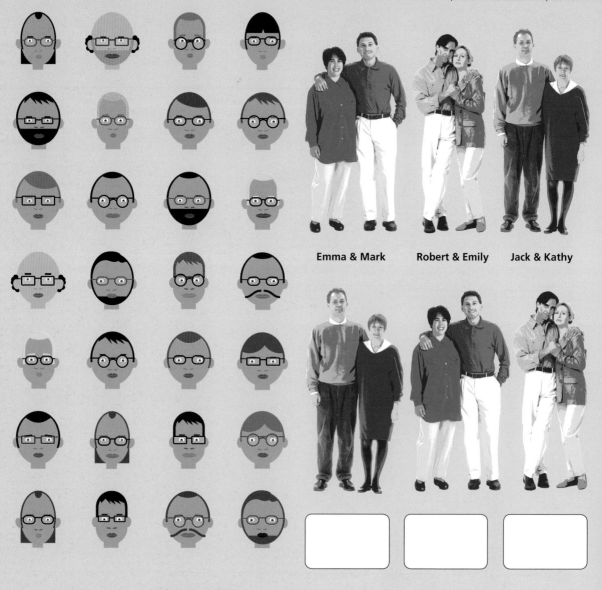

Emma & Mark   Robert & Emily   Jack & Kathy

Your score: _____
1–2 faces: 1 point
3–4 faces: 2 points
5 faces: 3 points

Your score: _____
1 point for each couple
identified correctly

7: Star-studded cast

You read a review of a Hollywood blockbuster starring 5 leading male actors. Take a few minutes to memorize the 5 names. Then cover them up and think of the names of 10 female actresses. Afterwards, see how many actors' names you can remember.

TOM HANKS   MATT DAMON

JOHNNY DEPP   BRAD PITT

LEONARDO DICAPRIO

Your score: _____
1–2 names: 1 point
3–4 names: 2 points
5 names: 3 points

8: On a day trip

Here are 5 children you have to look after during a trip to the aquarium. Take 1 minute to memorize their names and faces so that you can find them should they wander off. Then cover them up and solve the maths problems. Afterwards, recall their names and draw an arrow to the correct faces.

26 + 51 + 32 + 64 = _____
43 + 31 + 36 − 20 = _____
34 + 45 + 7 − 21 = _____
32 + 12 − 30 + 11 = _____

| Elsie | Daniel | Alice | Sanjeev | Ashley |

Solutions on p.184

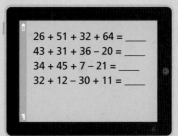

Your score: _____
1–3 faces only: 1 point
4–5 faces only: 2 points

1–3 faces + names: 3 points
4–5 faces + names: 4 points

1 0

HOW DID YOU DO?
Time to add up your points.
Your score: _____ ÷ **26 points**
(_____ **x 100**) = _____ **%**
Are you pleasantly surprised? Or do you feel your memory for names and faces needs to improve? Whatever the case, read on to understand why names are so hard to memorize. There are a few tricks that you can use to boost your memory for them, too. The next pages will help you master these.

SUPER TECHNIQUE:

The 3-Step Memory Booster

We all forget names at times, whatever our age. Names seem to have a habit of going in one ear and out the other. Remembering names is not impossible, though. Here are two simple and efficient methods to help you.

Two simple methods

The first method is repetition. Repeating someone's name when you first meet that person will increase your chances of remembering it later. The simplest way to do this is to use the name as you talk to the person. For example, "Rebecca, I was wondering whether…?", "What do you think about … Rebecca", and so on. The other method is the 3-Step Memory Booster. The goal of this technique is to associate the name to a concrete visual object, which will then become your cue to remember the name.

How does the 3-Step Memory Booster work?

This method makes use of association and visualization in the same way as the Link System (see pp.88–89). The first step is to give the name a concrete meaning. Some names, especially surnames, such as Miller or Greenfield, already have a meaning. However, although most names don't offer an immediate meaning, they can still remind you of something concrete. For instance, Watson may remind you of Dr Watson in Sherlock Holmes. If you listen to the sound of the name, you can also hear "what son?".

The second step is to observe the face of the person whose name you are trying to remember. Pay close attention to the individual features. Are the eyebrows thick and bushy? Is the nose big? Are there any moles? Select a facial feature that is striking to you. The third step is to link/associate the name and the face into a single image. To do this, imagine the object the name reminds you of attached to the striking facial feature you have selected. So "Mr Shelley" might have a multi-coloured shell stuck in his bushy eyebrows. Although silly, the image is memorable. This final step strengthens the link between face and name. However, the first two steps can be enough to boost your memory for the name.

Let's have a go!

You are introduced to Mrs Chisholm. To begin with, make sure you've got the name right. Ask her to repeat it, and maybe even spell it for you.

Step 1 What does the name remind you of? Maybe you know somebody else with the same name? Maybe the sound of the name makes you think of a "chisel" or a combination of "cheese" and "elm"? Let's say you pick "chisel".

Step 2 Study Mrs Chisholm's face. You need to focus on the individual features rather than the face as a whole. The way Mrs Chisholm ties her hair reveals a large forehead. She also has a mole on her chin. Pick either of these as your striking feature.

Step 3 Now combine the name and face in a memorable image using the Link System. Picture a chisel on her forehead, or perhaps an image of a white chisel on a black flag, which is sticking out of her mole. This is indeed ridiculous, but it is also why you will remember her name.

MRS. CHISHOLM
MYM 001

DID YOU KNOW: THE POWER OF THE 3-STEP MEMORY BOOSTER! Are you thinking that the 3-Step Memory Booster is far too complicated, time consuming, and frivolous? First, trust your brain: associations, links, and images come to mind very quickly. Secondly, note that the mere fact of adding meaning to names (step 1) can boost your memory for them. In one study, a group of people whose average age was 43 were trained for 6 hours over 3 weeks to give more meaning to new names they encountered by using step 1 of the 3-Step Memory Booster. As a result, their memory for names increased and the effect was still present 3 months later. So, yes, it is worth the effort, even if you do not feel like creating silly images every time you meet someone new.

Practise using the 3-Step Memory Booster

These exercises will help you practise the different steps involved in the 3-Step Memory Booster. You will be asked to give first and last names more meaning, observe faces closely, and, finally, associate names and faces to boost your powers of recall. Remember to be creative when it comes to links and associations.

9: New colleagues

Here are the names and faces of 4 new work colleagues. Use the 3-Step Memory Booster to memorize the names and the faces they belong to. For each name, write down what it reminds you of, then select a striking facial feature, and form an image that combines the two. When you are done, cover up the names and, to create a time lag, starting at 51 count down in 3s. Afterwards, write down the correct name beside each face.

Ms Muller

Mr Schwartz

Ms Siegel

Ms Nichols

10: Meaningless names?

Let's try to give the names below some concrete meaning. For each name below, write down whether you know someone with the same name (a friend, a celebrity, a work colleague), and then write down what the name reminds you of, in other words, what comes to mind when you read it or say it out loud.

A: Mrs Lucy Walford

B: Ms Carol Ratliss

C: Ms Sandy Walrack

D: Mr Edward Moskoni

E: Mr Harry Bockhurst

F: Mr Keith Rao

HOW IT WORKS: YOUR EYES SEE THE SUM OF ITS PARTS When you encounter a new face, you rarely focus on the individual features. Instead, your brain naturally identifies the relationships between the different features and then processes the configuration of the whole face. In fact, it's what helps you to recognize a face and differentiate it from others. There is a simple way to demonstrate this. Take a moment to study the two faces on the right. Can you see any differences between them?

Now turn the book upside down and take another look. Can you now see a difference?

Why was it harder to see the down-turned mouth and eyes of the right-hand face when it was upside down? It's because seeing it upside down disrupted your ability to process the configuration of the face.

Check-out: exercise your memory for names and faces

Now that you're familiar with the 3-Step Memory Booster, let's test your memory for names and faces again. When the exercise asks you to memorize a name, use only step 1 of the method and try to give more meaning to the name to boost recall. When a face is also shown, study it carefully and try to follow the other two steps of the method. You can complete this section over a few days.

11: The new batch

Imagine you're a teacher. Here are 4 new students who are joining your class this year. Take a few minutes to memorize their faces so that you can recognize them later today. Then cover up the faces and, to create a time lag, recite the 3 times table until you reach 60. Afterwards, circle the faces of your students in the group below.

Your score: _____
1 point for each face identified

12: Influential women

Listed below are a few of the most influential women of the 20th century. Take 2 minutes to memorize their names. Then cover them up and recite the 7 times table out loud until you reach 105. Afterwards, try to recall the women's names.

- **Susan Anthony** (American civil rights movement leader who fought for women's rights)
- **Dorothy Hodgkin** (awarded Nobel Prize in Chemistry for her work on the structure of both penicillin and insulin)
- **Mother Teresa** (humanitarian and advocate for the poor and helpless in India)
- **Indira Gandhi** (first female prime minister of India, who served for three consecutive terms)
- **Rosa Parks** (African-American civil rights activist)

Your score: _____
1–2 names: 2 points
3–4 names: 3 points
5 names: 4 points

13: Postcards aplenty

Over the summer you received many postcards. Can you memorize the names of the people who sent you these? After 2 minutes, cover them up and, starting at 52, count down by 4s. Afterwards, try to recall the names of the people who sent you a card.

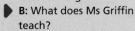

Jane

Melanie

Michael

Caroline

Michelle

Dominic

Dylan

Theo

Your score: _____
1–3 names: 2 points
4–5 names: 3 points
6–8 names: 4 points

14: Meet the teachers

Below are the names and photographs of 6 new teachers at your son's school, as well as the subjects they teach. Take all the time you need to memorize them using the 3-Step Memory Booster. Then cover up the names and faces, and take 2 minutes to remember 2 of your favourite teachers at school. Write down on a separate sheet of paper the reasons why you liked them. Afterwards, answer the questions below.

Ms Walker English	**Mrs Reed** Mathematics	**Ms Henderson** Geography
Ms Griffin Biology	**Miss Crawford** Physical education	**Mr Palmer** History

▶ **A:** Does Ms Henderson wear earrings?

▶ **B:** What does Ms Griffin teach?

▶ **C:** Who is the new mathematics teacher?

▶ **D:** Does Mr Palmer have facial hair?

▶ **E:** Does Ms Walker wear glasses?

▶ **F:** Who is the new physical education teacher?

Solutions on p.184

Your score: _____
1–2 correct answers: 2 points
3–4 correct answers: 3 points
5–6 correct answers: 4 points

15: Friends of a friend

Your friend introduces you to his friends. Take 1 minute to memorize their names and faces. Then cover them up and solve the time-lag problem. Afterwards, write down the names in the answer boxes with an arrow pointing to the correct faces in the picture.

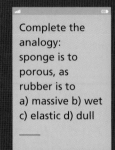

Complete the analogy: sponge is to porous, as rubber is to
a) massive b) wet c) elastic d) dull
_____

Rebecca   **Nathan**   **Tommy**   **Tanya**   **Jessica**

Your score: _____
1–2 names: 2 points
3–4 names: 3 points
5 names: 4 points

16: Who's the inventor?

Do you know the names of the people who invented many of the common objects we use today? We've listed a few below. Take 2 minutes to memorize their names and what they invented.

Then cover up the information, and take a 5-minute break. Afterwards, write down the name of the inventor under each invention illustrated below.

Alan Blumlein, UK:
the stereo (1933)

Edwin Beard Budding, UK:
the lawnmower (1830)

Douglas Engelbart, US:
the computer mouse (1963)

Whitcomb Judson, US:
the zip (1893)

Robert Adler, Austria/US:
the wireless remote control (1955)

Felix Hoffmann, Germany:
aspirin (1897)

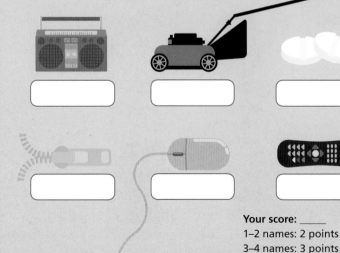

Your score: _____
1–2 names: 2 points
3–4 names: 3 points
5–6 names: 4 points

17: Business relations

4 people handed you their business cards at the last trade fair. Each card includes a photograph of the person. Take a few minutes to memorize the names using the 3-Step Memory Booster. Then cover up the business cards and complete the maths problems in the time-lag box. Afterwards, write down the correct names on the business cards below.

18: Too many docs!

Can you memorize the names of the doctors below and what they specialize in? Take as much time as you need, then cover them up and, on a separate sheet of paper, list the names of the memory techniques you have learnt so far in this book. When you're done, write down the correct doctor's name beside each specialism.

Katrina Sky

Gloria Jones

Rodney Appleton

Frederick Kraft

Dr Payne – Dentist
Dr Dunn – Ophthalmologist
Dr Snyder – Cardiologist
Dr Lawrence – Dermatologist
Dr Wheeler – Obstetrician
Dr Burton – Gastroenterologist

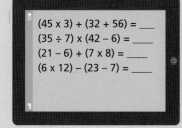

(45 x 3) + (32 + 56) = ___
(35 ÷ 7) x (42 – 6) = ___
(21 – 6) + (7 x 8) = ___
(6 x 12) – (23 – 7) = ___

Gastroenterologist

Cardiologist

Dentist

Ophthalmologist

Obstetrician

Dermatologist

Your score: _____
1–2 specialisms: 2 points
3–4 specialisms: 3 points
5–6 specialisms: 4 points

Your score: _____
1–2 names: 2 points
3–4 names: 4 points

Solutions on p.184–5

19: On first-name terms

Below are the name tags of the distinguished guests you would like to meet at the art exhibition coming to your local gallery. Memorize the names in 2 minutes, then cover them up and solve the time-lag problem. Afterwards, draw a circle around the names of the people you want to talk to in the list of names underneath.

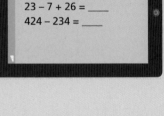

Place 6 Xs on the grid below without making 3-in-a-row in any direction.

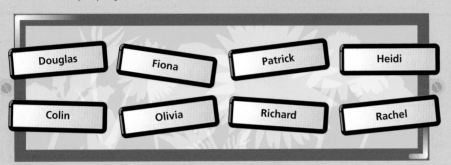

Douglas Fiona Patrick Heidi

Colin Olivia Richard Rachel

Rachel	Vanessa	Eleanor	Gabriel
Dustin	Patrick	Benjamin	Douglas
Pamela	Fiona	Olivia	Adam
Heidi	Colin	Philip	Ella
Oscar	Patricia	Bianca	Richard

Your score: _____
1–3 names: 2 points
4–6 names: 3 points
7–8 names: 4 points

20: Party time!

As you chat with the party hostess, 4 guests arrive and the hostess introduces them to you. Can you memorize their names and faces? Once you're done, cover up the names and faces and complete the maths problems. Afterwards, write down the correct name under each face.

$67 + 45 - 6 =$ _____
$34 + 4 - 8 =$ _____
$23 - 7 + 26 =$ _____
$424 - 234 =$ _____

Philip Wolaver **Sharon Druce** **Sara Winspear** **Mary Houseman**

Your score: _____
1–2 names: 2 points
3–4 names: 4 points

Solutions on p.185

21: Who's playing?

Imagine you've seen a poster advertising a concert in which 8 famous singers are performing. Can you memorize their names? Once you're done, cover up the poster, and on a separate sheet of paper, take 2 minutes to list as many words as you can think of beginning with the letter U. Afterwards, try to recall the singers' names.

Your score: _____
1–3 names: 2 points
4–6 names: 3 points
7–8 names: 4 points

Elton John
Prince
Celine Dion
Eric Clapton
Annie Lennox
George Michael
Whitney Houston
Alicia Keys

22: The philanthropic six

On the right are the names of the 6 volunteers who will help you organize a charity event. Try using the 3-Step Memory Booster to memorize their names. When you're done, cover up the names and faces, and take a 5-minute break. Afterwards, write down the names you remember under the correct faces below.

Mr Frazier   Ms Burke   Mr Vargas

Ms Pearson   Ms Chambers   Mr Osborne

Your score: _____
1–2 names: 2 points
3–4 names: 3 points
5–6 names: 4 points

1 0

HOW DID YOU DO?
Time to add up your points:
Your score = (_____ x 100) ÷ 48 points = _____ %
Compare this with your check-in score. Have you improved? Try using the 3-Step Memory Booster the next time you meet someone. You'll be surprised at how well you remember the person's name later on. The more you use the method, the easier it will become, and soon it will feel like second nature!

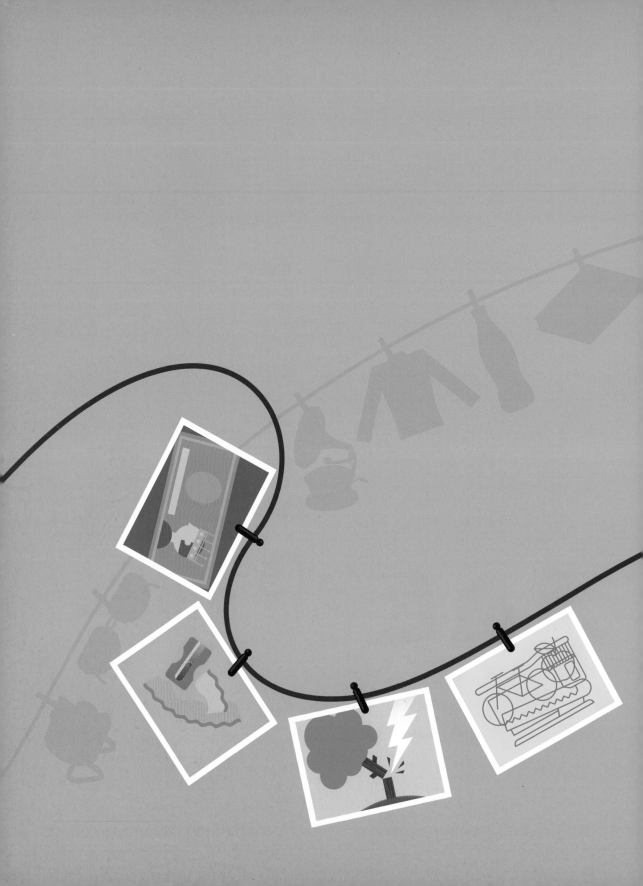

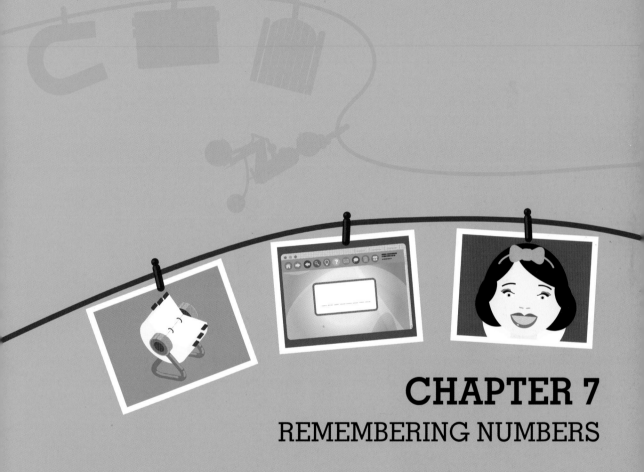

CHAPTER 7
REMEMBERING NUMBERS

Check-in: do you have a head for storing numbers?

For most people, it's a challenge to memorize numbers, be it a phone number or a pass code. Fortunately, a few simple techniques and a willingness to learn can help you become more proficient at memorizing numerical information. Before discussing these techniques, let's assess your current memory for numbers.

1: Window shopping

Can you memorize the prices of the following items of clothing? Study each price-tag for 10 seconds, then cover them up and, on a separate sheet of paper, list as many girls' names beginning with A as you can think of in 1 minute. This will create a time lag. Afterwards, recall the prices of the 3 items.

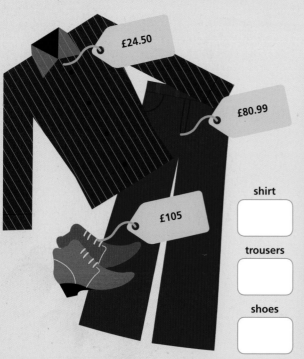

£24.50

£80.99

£105

shirt

trousers

shoes

Your score: ____
1 price: 1 point
2 prices: 2 points
3 prices: 3 points

2: Momentous years

Here are the dates of 3 historical events. Pick one you don't know already and memorize it. When you are done, move on to the next exercise. Afterwards, return to this exercise and recall the event and the year it happened.

- **1989:** The Berlin Wall falls, paving the way for German reunification
- **1982:** the first music album is released on CD
- **1994:** Nelson Mandela is elected president of South Africa, marking the end of the Apartheid.

Your score: ____
Event and year recalled:
3 points

3: Driving too much?

You are about to go on a 6-month trip abroad and reluctantly decide to leave your car with a friend. When your friend drives you to the airport, you think it might be prudent to memorize the reading on the odometer so that you can work out how much he drives the car in your absence. When you are done, cover it up and take a 2-minute break. Then recall your odometer reading. Afterwards, return to the previous exercise.

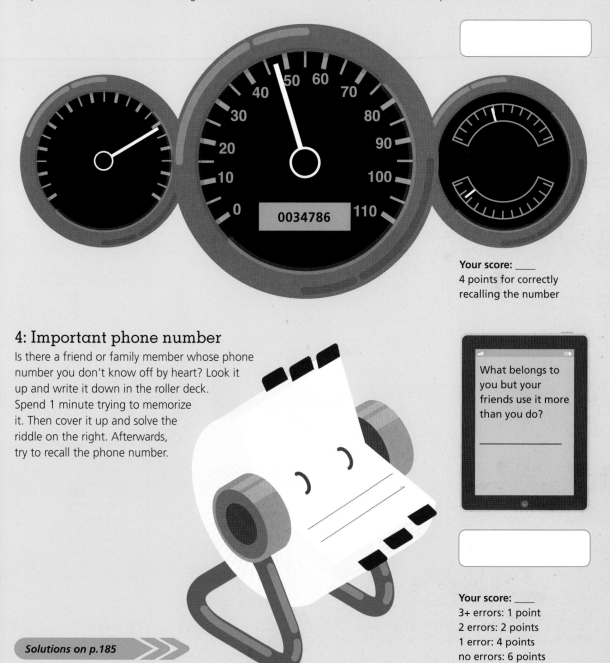

0034786

Your score: ____
4 points for correctly recalling the number

4: Important phone number

Is there a friend or family member whose phone number you don't know off by heart? Look it up and write it down in the roller deck. Spend 1 minute trying to memorize it. Then cover it up and solve the riddle on the right. Afterwards, try to recall the phone number.

What belongs to you but your friends use it more than you do?

_____

Your score: ____
3+ errors: 1 point
2 errors: 2 points
1 error: 4 points
no errors: 6 points

Solutions on p.185

5: Code to enter the site

You have registered for an online service, and have been provided with the following access code: **12254930**. Take 30 seconds to memorize it. Then cover it up and solve the riddle on the right. Afterwards, recall the code.

A basket contains 5 apples. How can you divide it among 5 children so that each has 1 apple and 1 apple stays in the basket?

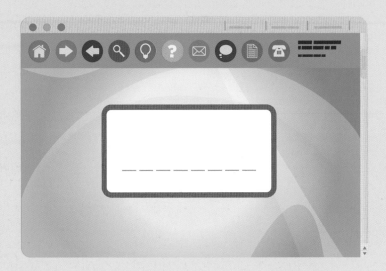

_ _ _ _ _ _ _ _

Your score: ____
3+ errors: 1 point
2 errors: 2 points
1 error: 4 points
no errors: 6 points

6: Age is just a number

Take 1 minute to memorize the birth years of the following people. Then cover up the dates and find your way in the maze. Afterwards, write down the correct birth year under each person.

1956

1967

1976

1989

Your score: ____
2 points for each year recalled correctly

7: Knitwear for Christmas

You're knitting sweaters for your 3 nephews this Christmas. Can you memorize their sizes? Take 2 minutes to study the measurements, then cover them up and solve the time-lag problem below. Afterwards, recall each set of sizes.

John
Chest: 66cm
Neckband: 30cm
Arm length: 51cm

Jason
Chest: 71cm
Neckband: 31cm
Arm length: 53cm

Jamie
Chest: 76cm
Neckband: 33cm
Arm length: 55cm

8: Tight security!

For security reasons, the entry codes to the main building at work and the car park change regularly. Can you memorize the 2 new codes? When you are done, cover them up and take a 2-minute break. Afterwards, try to recall the 2 entry codes.

Access code for the building:
431768

Access code for the car park:
086035

building

car park

Your score: _____
1 code: 3 points
2 codes: 6 points

1 0

How many left and right turns do you need to take to go from the circle to the triangle? (You're not allowed to rotate the book!)

Your score: _____
1 set of sizes: 1 point
2 sets of sizes: 3 points
3 sets of sizes: 6 points

HOW DID YOU DO?
Add up the points you got for each exercise.
Your score = (_____ x 100) ÷ 42 = _____ %
Did you have a hard time trying to memorize and recall all those digits? Or was it not as bad as you thought it would be once you applied yourself?
In the next pages, you will be introduced to a few techniques that can help you boost your memory for numbers.

Solutions on p.185

The beauty of chunking

The reason numbers are difficult to recall is because they are abstract concepts. They do not stick in your memory as readily as words or pictures, both of which you can usually attach a meaning to. However, chunking (or grouping) individual digits into larger units is an easy way to boost your memory for them.

Grouping long numbers

Can you memorize the following number inside 30 seconds: 3 4 1 9 9 8 7 4 7? Of course it would be much easier to write the number down than to attempt to cram it inside your head in the short space of time. OK, let's try grouping the number into three units instead: 341 998 747. You now have only three numbers to memorize instead of nine digits. If you repeat these three units out loud several times, your verbal short-term memory (see p.34) is likely to remember the number later on.

Finding meaningful groups

Memorizing numbers becomes even easier when you can attach meaning to them. How is that possible? Well, let's try to find some kind of meaning in what initially seems to have none. The number above can be chunked differently: 34 1998 747. Now, "34" may have been your age when you had your first child, "1998" may be the year you moved house, and "747" may remind you of the most popular aeroplane in Boeing's fleet. With these associations, the number would now be much easier to memorize and a lot harder to forget!

Of course, in many instances you won't be able to find such personal meanings in numbers. You will then have to be creative and imaginative. To get you started, here is a list of number-related information you may know well enough to use as meaningful chunks:

• Birth dates (of friends and family members, for example)
• Addresses (of places you go to often, for example)
• Historical dates (you learned at school, for example)
• Autobiographical dates (the date you were married, for example)
• The time you usually get up to go to work, have lunch, go to the gym
• The number on the jersey of your favourite sports player
• Famous numbers such as 007 (the fictional British secret service agent), Route 66 (the famous US highway), 3.14 (pi), and so on.

9: Trip to Beijing

You are organizing a trip to China, and frequently have to phone the travel agency in Beijing. The phone number is: **008610198253**. Use the chunking method to memorize this number. Try to recall the phone number in 10 minutes' time.

10: A slice of pi

It's perhaps one of the most widely recognized numbers in the world, but how much of it do you know? How about trying to memorize the first 10 digits of this infinite number: **3.141592653**. Once again, use the chunking method to help you. Then cover it up and solve the riddle below. Afterwards, recall the number.

What is black when you buy it, red when you use it, and grey when you throw it away?

_____

Solutions on p.185

TOP TIP: REMEMBER YOUR LICENCE PLATE NUMBER
Do you have a hard time recalling your licence plate number? Use chunking. Look at your plate number and try to find a chunk of digits or letters that make sense to you: do the digits form a number you know (a year, a memorable date, a special number)? How about the letters: do they remind you of a word? For example, the licence plate number "70 RSK" may remind you of the age of a close friend (70) and the letters "RSK" may remind you of the word "risk". Or, better still, you may combine both in a sentence such as "At the age of 70 it's riskier to go skiing!"

BOND 007

SUPER TECHNIQUE:

The Number-Association System

Here is another method to transform an abstract number into something more memorable: convert it into a picture. This way you can take advantage of the superiority of images in memory (see pp.82–83). There are at least three ways to do this using the Number-Association System.

What is the Number-Association System?

This is a mnemonic system in which numbers are converted into concrete objects, making them easier to visualize. You can do this by associating each number with:

- an object whose name **rhymes** with the number. For example, zero = snow, one = bun, two = shoe, and so on.
- an object whose **shape** looks like the written number. For example, zero = hole, 1 = candle, 2 = swan, and so on.
- an object whose **meaning** is associated with the number. It is up to you which method you choose to use.

Creating meaning

Let's focus on the third method (finding meaning). Here are objects to which each number could be matched:

0 = an empty glass or a black hole (represents nothingness)
1 = the sun (there is only one in our solar system)
2 = twins or eyes (we all have two eyes)
3 = a tricycle (it has three wheels) or a trident (it has three prongs)
4 = a lucky clover (it has four leaves)
5 = a hand (it has five fingers) or a foot (it has five toes)
6 = a fly (it has six legs)
7 = Snow White (because of the seven dwarfs)
8 = a spider (it has eight legs)
9 = a heavily pregnant woman (nine months of pregnancy)

Once you have a list of number-image associations, you need to learn it off by heart. Then you are ready to memorize any number. To do so, you need to convert each number into its corresponding object and imagine the objects interacting in a striking visual scenario.

How does it work?

Let's say you have been given a new Personal Identification Number (PIN) for your credit card –7542 – and you need to memorize it. First, convert each digit into an object: 7 = Snow White, 5 = hand, 4 = lucky clover, and 2 = twins. Now put together your scenario: Snow White is handing you a lucky clover before the twins can snatch it away. Add any details that make the scenario more striking and therefore more memorable (see pp.84–85): Snow White's hand is white and delicate, the leaf is a bright green colour, and so on. Chances are you will now recall your new PIN very easily.

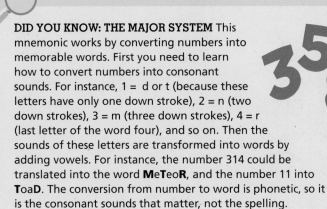

DID YOU KNOW: THE MAJOR SYSTEM This mnemonic works by converting numbers into memorable words. First you need to learn how to convert numbers into consonant sounds. For instance, 1 = d or t (because these letters have only one down stroke), 2 = n (two down strokes), 3 = m (three down strokes), 4 = r (last letter of the word four), and so on. Then the sounds of these letters are transformed into words by adding vowels. For instance, the number 314 could be translated into the word **MeTeoR**, and the number 11 into **ToaD**. The conversion from number to word is phonetic, so it is the consonant sounds that matter, not the spelling.

Practise using the Number-Association System

To use the Number-Association System, you need to build a list of number-image associations that works for you. Start by creating your list and then practise using your number-images to memorize birth dates and PINs.

11: From digits to images

▶ **A:** Transform digits 0 to 9 into visual objects. Create your own set of images using one of the 3 systems described on pp.154–155: rhyme, shape, or meaning. Doodle on a separate sheet of paper if it helps you come up with suitable ideas.

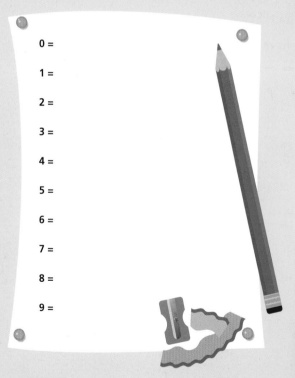

0 =

1 =

2 =

3 =

4 =

5 =

6 =

7 =

8 =

9 =

▶ **B:** Now memorize your list. Test your memory for your list over several intervals. Recall the list by saying it out loud, writing it down, drawing or visualizing the objects. If there's an object you can never remember, then change it. Perhaps it's not the best association for you.

12: Birth years

Use your number-images to memorize the birth years of 3 people you work with. If you happen to work from home, then use the years below:

1982   1978   1956

Once you have inserted your number-images into 3 vivid mental scenarios, cover up the years and solve the problem below. Afterwards, try to recall your scenarios and in doing so the 3 years.

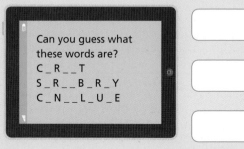

Can you guess what these words are?
C _ R _ _ T
S _ R _ _ B _ R _ Y
C _ N _ _ L _ U _ E

13: Safe delivery

Imagine you are a secret agent and have to deliver 2 briefcases containing sensitive documents. For added security, each lock has a different code: all the codes are shown below. Use the Number-Association System to memorize these codes. When you are done, cover up the numbers and solve the riddle in the time-lag box. Afterwards, try to recall the 4 codes.

Q: At night they come without being fetched, and by day they are lost without being stolen. What are they?

_____

▶ **A: Briefcase 1**

3 6 9 4   8 9 7 6

▶ **B: Briefcase 2**

2 1 5 3   4 7 3 2

▶ **A: Briefcase 1**   ▶ **B: Briefcase 2**

Solutions on p.185 ⟩⟩⟩

HOW IT WORKS: THE MENTAL DIVIDE When people (in a left–right reading culture) think of numbers, they automatically think in terms of a number line, with smaller numbers on the left and larger numbers on the right. How do we know this? In a computerized exercise, in which subjects had to press a key to the left of the keyboard when certain numbers appeared on the screen and a key to the right when other numbers appeared, the results showed that people reacted much faster when they had to press the left key for small numbers and the right key for larger numbers. This experiment reveals how the brain spatially maps numerical information in order of ascendancy, depending on the direction our eyes follow while we are reading.

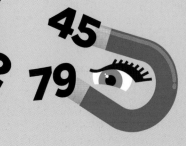

Check-out: exercise your memory for numbers

Now that you are familiar with the techniques, let's assess your memory for numbers once again. To score a higher percentage than you did for the check-in exercises, try using the chunking method and Number-Association System when suggested. Are you ready to chunk and use your number-images?

14: Airport pick-up

You are a chauffeur working for an international company. You are asked to pick up 4 clients from the airport who are arriving from different cities around the world. Memorize the 4 flight numbers so that you can check the arrivals board at the airport. Try using the Number-Association System. When you are done, cover up the numbers and solve the riddle in the time-lag box. Afterwards, try to recall the flight numbers.

> What can bring back the dead, make us cry, make us laugh, make us young? It's born in an instant and lasts a lifetime.
>
> _____

✈ Arrivals

From	Flight
T O K Y O	V S 6 2 3 4
M U M B A I	A I 1 5 2 3
M A D R I D	I B 9 3 1 6
C H I C A G O	A A 4 1 6 7

TOKYO

MUMBAI

MADRID

CHICAGO

Your score: ____
2 points for each flight number recalled

15: Speed demons

The speed of light and the speed of sound are two terms that have become part of our daily parlance, but do you know what the actual speeds are? Well now is your chance to memorize these numbers. You may want to chunk the numbers. Once you're done, cover up the numbers and take a 5-minute break. Afterwards, return to the exercise and try to recall the speeds.

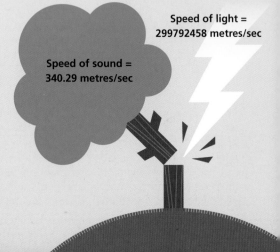

Speed of light = 299792458 metres/sec

Speed of sound = 340.29 metres/sec

Sound

Light

Your score: ____
1 speed: 2 points
2 speeds: 4 points

16: Banking details

A part of your job involves communicating with banks abroad. To do so, you need to memorize the codes that identify these banks. Let's say that the two banks you communicate with the most are identified by the codes written below. Memorize these using the chunking method. When you are done, cover up the codes and find your way through the maze. Afterwards, recall the codes.

 A:

2 0 6 9 8 7

A:

B:

3 1 4 6 5 7

B:

Your score: ____
1 code: 2 points
2 codes: 4 points

Solutions on p.185

17: Friendly neighbours

You are having a friendly chat with a couple of ladies at the local café, and during the conversation you discover that they live in a street close to yours. Use the Number-Association System to memorize their house numbers. When you are done, cover up the numbers and, on a separate sheet of paper, list as many different types of cake as you can think of in 2 minutes. Afterwards, try to recall the house numbers.

A:

B:

6 2 9

1 3 6

A:

B:

Your score: ____
1 house number: 2 points
2 house numbers: 4 points

18: Online library

Here is your new library access number. Instead of having to refer to your library card every time you request a book online, how about using the chunking method to memorize the number? When you are done, cover it up and try to answer the question in the time-lag box. You have 1 minute. Afterwards, try to recall the number.

Can you name an English word that has three consecutive double letters?

_____

Your score: _____
3+ errors: 2 points
1–2 errors: 4 points
no errors: 5 points

19: Eventful years

Below is a list of years in which a significant event occurred. Try using the Number-Association System to memorize each year and event. When you are done, cover up the dates and, on a separate sheet of paper, take 2 minutes to recall a significant event in your life. Afterwards, write down the year next to the picture relating to the event.

1886: The prototype recipe of Coca-Cola is created.

1940: John Lennon, founding member of The Beatles, is born.

1964: The Rolling Stones arrive in New York to begin their first tour in the US.

1969: Neil Armstrong becomes the first man to set foot on the Moon.

Your score: _____
2 points for each year recalled correctly

20: Sophie's new number

Your granddaughter calls to give you her new phone number. Will you be able to memorize it? See if chunking helps. When you are done, cover up the phone number and, on a separate sheet of paper, list as many names of childhood friends as you can remember in 2 minutes. Afterwards, try to recall the number.

0 8 5 3 7 4 5 4 9 7 7

Your score: _____
3+ errors: 2 points
1–2 errors: 4 points
no errors: 5 points

21: Tuning in

Do you sometimes find it difficult to remember the frequency of radio stations? The Number-Association System may be useful here: try it with these 3 radio stations. When you are done, cover up the frequencies and solve the analogies in the time-lag box. Afterwards, try to recall the numbers of each frequency.

A: Wolf is to pack as tree is to _____
B: Cat is to kitten as plant is to _____
C: Spin is to dizzy as fire is to _____

648 AM

105.7 FM

93.4 FM

Your score: _____
1 frequency: 2 points
2 frequencies: 4 points
3 frequencies: 6 points

Solutions on p.185

22: Uncle Fred's area code

Uncle Fred has moved to California, USA. Can you memorize his new ZIP code? Use the chunking method to give the number more meaning. When you are done, cover up the number and solve the riddle in the time-lag box. Afterwards, recall the ZIP code.

What always runs but never walks, often murmurs, never talks, has a bed but never sleeps, has a mouth but never eats? _____

Uncle Fred

California
90272 – 1016

Your score: _____
3+ errors: 2 points
1–2 errors: 4 points
no errors: 5 points

23: Card verification

During regular online security checks on credit cards, the system often asks for the last 4 digits of the card number instead of the whole series. So it's wise to memorize these digits. Let's practise with the 4-digit numbers below. You may want to use the Number-Association System to boost your memory of them. When you are ready, cover up the numbers and take a 5-minute break. Afterwards, try to recall the 4 numbers.

6532

9451

8648

4361

Your score: _____
1–2 card numbers: 2 points
3 card numbers: 4 points
4 card numbers: 6 points

24: Utility bill

Below is your account number for paying the water bill. Can you try to memorize it? See if the chunking method helps. When you are done, cover it up and figure out in the time-lag box what the 5 objects overlapping each other are. Afterwards, try to recall the number.

2 2 0 3 4 5 8 7 2 0

Your score: _____
3+ errors: 2 points
1–2 errors: 4 points
no errors: 5 points

Solutions on p.185 >>>

25: Eating cake

Try to memorize the number of calories in each cake pictured below using the Number-Association System. Then cover up the information and take a 2-minute break. Afterwards, fill in the calorie figure for each cake.

Jam doughnut (75g): 252 cal

Iced ring doughnut (70g): 268 cal

Fruit scone (40g): 126 cal

Sponge cake (53g): 243 cal

Cherry pie (90g): 390 cal

Iced ring doughnut [   ]   **Fruit scone** [   ]

Jam doughnut [   ]   **Sponge cake** [   ]

Cherry pie [   ]

Your score: _____
2 points for each calorie figure recalled correctly

1 0

HOW DID YOU DO?
Time to add up the points you got for each exercise. **Your score = (_____ x 100) ÷ 70 = _____ %**
Compare your score to the one you got for the check-in exercises. Were the chunking method and Number-Association System helpful? To develop a better memory for numbers, try to take advantage of them as much as you can in your everyday life.

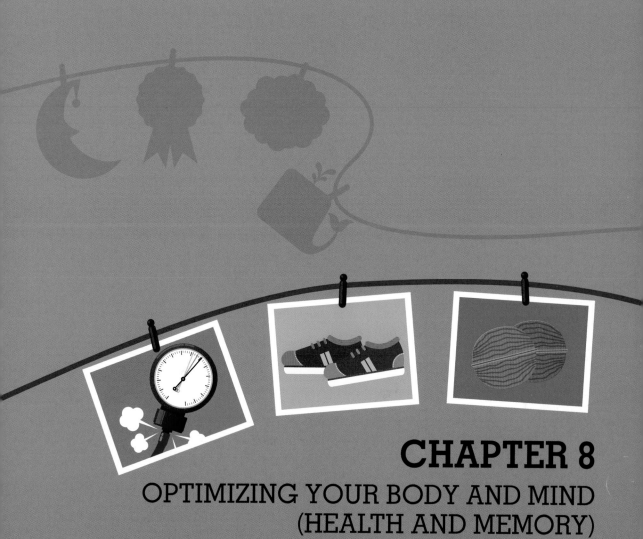

CHAPTER 8
OPTIMIZING YOUR BODY AND MIND
(HEALTH AND MEMORY)

It's not what it once was! Does age affect memory?

It's true that some brain functions, such as the working memory, slow down with age. We become more prone to distractions, too, which makes it harder to focus and register information in our long-term memory. Although still sound, our processing power might lose some of its zip. However, by taking more time and minimizing distractions, we can perform to the same level as we used to.

The aging brain

Is it possible to tell which brain is younger by comparing scans of a teenager's brain and the brain of an elderly person? Probably, yes. The older brain is likely to show the general wear and tear that comes from a lifetime of living. In particular, it may be smaller due to some atrophy. Closer observation may also show that the production of neurotransmitters (the chemicals transmitting information between nerve cells) has decreased. Having said that, some people's brains do not show such signs. In fact, individual differences can be quite extreme when it comes to how the brain deals with ageing.

Lifestyle choices

Our lifestyle impacts greatly on how our brains and memories age. This is because of "neuroplasticity" (see pp.22–23). Some things are good for brain health while other things are bad, and the extent to which your brain function remains sound throughout life depends partly on your lifestyle choices. The major things you can do to maintain a good memory is eat a balanced diet, manage stress, and exercise both mind and body on a regular basis.

1: It's on the tip of my tongue

Does the correct word sometimes elude you during a conversation? This phenomenon tends to become more frequent as we age. There is nothing pathological about it: in fact, relaxing and ignoring the issue is usually enough to bring the correct word back to mind only moments later. For now, let's assess how easily words come to you (also called your verbal fluency). Write down as many words as possible that may fall under each heading below. You have 1 minute for each. Use a separate sheet of paper if you need more space.

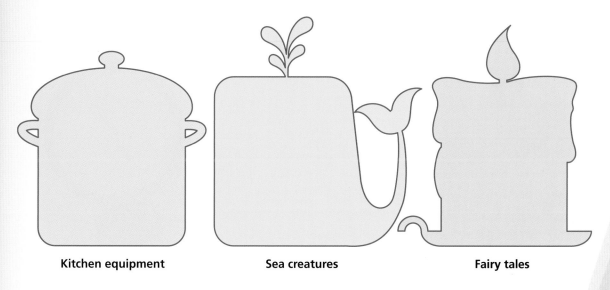

Kitchen equipment　　　　**Sea creatures**　　　　**Fairy tales**

DID YOU KNOW: A LIFESTYLE TO REMEMBER
Do you enjoy playing board games, card games, and crossword puzzles? Do you read newspapers, magazines, or books on a regular basis? Do you like listening to the radio, visiting museums, participating in discussions? Are you educated to a high level? Did you or do you have an intellectually demanding job? Answering yes to any of these questions means that you have a greater chance of maintaining your memory functions and having a resilient brain as you age. Indeed, it seems that the more people participate in activities that engage and stimulate their brain, the better their brain ages.

I'm losing my mind! How to manage stress

Sometimes you just have too much to do and not enough time. On top of that, you seem to be losing your mind: you become overwhelmed, frustrated, and begin forgetting things. Your memory is like a sieve! Does this sound familiar?

The importance of stress

Regardless of whether it is caused by tight deadlines, work overload, or an anxiety to succeed, pressure induces stress. Too much stress is likely to cause memory lapses, irrespective of age. An increase in stress is the body's way of reacting when it senses danger, be it physical or psychological. Stress helps us to take flight when we feel a physical threat, or keeps us on our toes when we engage in a high-pressure task, such as giving a presentation to a large audience. Stress triggers the release of stress hormones in the blood: adrenaline and cortisol. These hormones prepare the body for action as the heart starts pumping faster and the muscles tighten up.

Too much stress!

We've mentioned the positive effects of stress, when stress is occasional. However, chronic stress has negative effects on both your body and mind. It results in lowered immunity response and higher blood pressure. At the level of the brain, it can kill brain cells in regions supporting learning and memory, such as the hippocampus (see pp.14–15). Stress management should therefore be part of any good brain and memory maintenance and enhancement programme. Relaxation (through meditation or yoga), physical exercise, and socializing with friends are ways to lower stress. Complete the exercise on the next page to become familiar with meditation techniques.

2: Meditate for your brain health

Most meditation techniques fall into 3 major categories. One is the "open monitoring meditation", which is a type of practice in which you actively pay attention to what is happening inside you, but without reacting or judging. Another is "self-transcending meditation" in which you try to go beyond your own mental activity to reach a restful but alert state of consciousness. Finally, there is "controlled focus meditation" in which you focus attention on your breath, an idea, an image, or emotion. Are you ready to give meditation a try?

Let's start by rating your current stress level:
For each of the body parts depicted on the right, rate how relaxed it is on a scale of 1 to 4 under the "before" heading. (1 = very relaxed, 2 = quite relaxed, 3 = quite tense, and 4 = very tense)

Now follow these steps to enter a relaxed meditative state:
• Find a quiet spot where you can sit or lie down. Close your eyes.
• Take slow, deep breaths. Think about the rhythm of your breathing.
• Relax your body. Focus on each part of your body (start at the feet and work upwards) and relax each muscle until it feels heavy.
• Empty your mind. If negative thoughts or distractions come up, ignore them.
• After approximately 15 minutes, allow thoughts to return, but keep your eyes closed.
• Finally, open your eyes and stay seated for a few more minutes before getting up.
• Now rate your stress level again under the "after" heading.

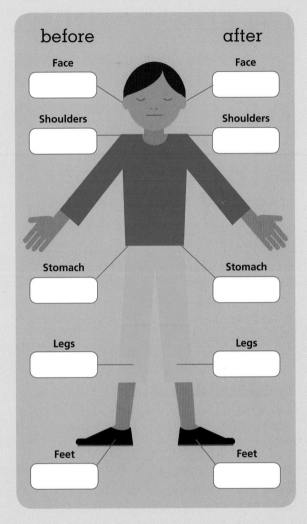

before   after

Face   Face

Shoulders   Shoulders

Stomach   Stomach

Legs   Legs

Feet   Feet

Did it work? Is your overall score lower now? As you probably noticed, it is not always easy to empty your mind. To counter this, you may want to choose a sound ("om"), a word, or a phrase that means something important to you, which you can repeat quietly to yourself during the exercise.

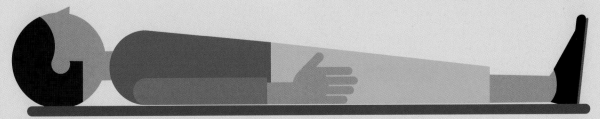

De-stress with yoga

Yoga is a physical, mental, and spiritual discipline that is more than 5,000 years old. The word *yoga* means "to join or yoke together", and the practice is all about finding harmony between the mind, body and spirit. Yoga involves exercise, breathing, and meditation. Its goal is to improve both physical and mental health. There are many different types of yoga. The most commonly practised is known as *Hatha* Yoga, which includes physical postures and movements as well as breathing techniques.

Yoga poses

Below are three poses to help you relax. Yoga is suitable for most adults of any age, but is not recommended for pregnant women, and children under 16. If you have not exercised in a while, it's advisable to go slowly. If you are not sure, you may want to check with your doctor first, especially if you suffer from back pain or a chronic injury to the wrists or knees.

3: Accomplished pose

This is a very popular seated position for meditation, which is easier than the famous Lotus pose. It opens the hips and lengthens the spine.

- Sit down on the floor with your legs extended. (It will probably be more comfortable if you use a yoga mat.)
- Bend the right knee and tuck the leg underneath you so that the heel presses against your bottom. Keep the knee on the floor.
- Bend the left knee and rest the outside of the left foot behind the right knee so that the left ankle is over the right ankle. The heel of the left foot should line up approximately with the navel.
- Rest your hands on your knees with the palms facing up and the index finger and thumb of each hand touching one another.
- Keep your spine straight and your head up, roll your shoulders back, and push your chest out.
- Relax your face and belly, and breathe. Hold the pose for as long as you feel comfortable.

4: Table pose

This pose is a starting point for other poses, such as the Cat Tilt pose (see below). It helps stretch and realign the spine.

• Start on all fours with your knees hip-width apart and your toes pointing behind you.
• Your hands are directly under your shoulders with your fingers spread wide.
• Keep your neck long and aligned with your spine and look several centimetres in front of you.
• Do not arch or round your back.
• Hold the pose for 5 to 10 breaths.

5: Cat Tilt pose

This pose stretches the shoulders and the middle to upper back.

• From the Table pose, exhale and tuck your tailbone under while rounding the spine.
• Let your head drop down.
• Press your palms on the ground to move your shoulders away from your ears.
• Raise your middle and upper back up towards the ceiling.
• Hold for 5 to 10 breaths.
• To release, inhale and relax back into the Table pose.

HOW IT WORKS: HOW DOES YOGA HELP RELIEVE STRESS? Research shows that yoga increases the level of gamma-aminobutyric acid (GABA), a chemical in the brain that regulates the activity of neurons. Depression and anxiety are typically associated with low GABA levels, while increased levels are associated with improved mood and decreased anxiety. A study showed that practising yoga for one hour three times a week for 12 weeks improved mood and decreased anxiety more than a comparable amount of walking. Another study showed that in experienced yoga practitioners, GABA levels increased by 27 per cent after a one-hour yoga session. In contrast, such an increase was not recorded after an hour of reading..

The importance of sleep

It's a simple matter of fact that sleep deprivation impairs memory and judgment. In contrast, a good night's sleep can improve your memory for what you learned yesterday, what you have to do today, and how to do things (procedural memory, see pp.60–61). This then begs the question as to what goes on inside your brain while you are sleeping?

The different stages of sleep

During a typical night, you go through four to six cycles of sleep. Each cycle is made up of four non-REM sleep stages followed by one REM sleep stage. Here is what a typical cycle looks like:

Stage 1 You are falling asleep. It is a light form of sleep from which you can be easily woken. Your brain begins producing theta waves (sleep waves), which are much slower than beta and alpha waves (waves while you are awake).

Stage 3 You are in deep sleep. Your breathing and heart rate are slow and regular. Your brain now also produces low-frequency delta waves. These are often referred to as slow sleep waves.

REM Stage You are still sleeping but your body temperature, and heart and breathing rates, increase. Your eyes move under closed lids and your limbs are temporarily paralysed. Alpha and beta waves are present in addition to theta waves. You are likely to be dreaming (although you can also dream during non-REM stages).

Stage 2 You are now asleep, but can still be easily woken. Your eyes stop moving. Your body temperature, your heart rate, and your blood pressure drop. Theta waves are still present.

Stage 4 You are now in a state of very deep sleep. It is difficult to wake you up. Delta waves are present.

Brain maintenance during sleep

Although research is ongoing as to how sleep affects memory, what we do know is that during sleep the brain seems to be refuelling, organizing information, while discarding what it regards as being irrelevant. Some connections between neurons (see pp.14–15) are eliminated while others are strengthened. Indeed, the processes by which memories become stable may be occurring while we sleep, culminating in the consolidation of memory.

Interestingly, different types of memory may be consolidated during different stages of sleep. For instance, REM sleep may play a role in consolidating "how-to" memories (how to play the violin, for example). In contrast, non-REM sleep stage 3 has been linked to the consolidation of spatial memories. Non-REM sleep stage 4 may play a role in enhancing verbal memories.

How do we know this? Well, boosting the slow sleep waves during non-REM stages (by passing a weak current via electrodes through the scalp) increases the recall of words learned before falling asleep. Also, brain scans of subjects have revealed the same pattern of brain activity occurring during REM sleep as during the learning of a motor task the day before.

6: Remembering dreams

So far there is no definitive answer as to why we dream. Nevertheless, dreams are usually fun to talk about (as long as you can remember what you dream about). A good way of remembering dreams is to keep a dream diary. Leave the diary close to your bed so that you can write down what you remember as soon as you wake up. See whether what happens to you, or what you experience during that week, has any bearing on the things you dream about.

TOP TIP: A GOOD NIGHT'S SLEEP Here are a few pointers to help you fall asleep and sleep soundly through the night:
• Avoid any caffeine, alcohol, or nicotine before bedtime.
• Do not eat a heavy meal before bedtime.
• Avoid strenuous physical activity (other than sex) within three hours of bedtime.
• Do not stay in bed for too long if you cannot fall asleep. Get up, do something relaxing, such as read a book (not a textbook), meditate, or listen to soothing music, and then try again when you start to feel a little drowsy.

Foods to sharpen your thinking

While it's necessary to feed our brain specific nutrients so that it functions to its highest potential, it's important to choose the right foods so that we absorb a good balance of nutrients. Let's see what's good for the brain and what's bad.

The GOOD

Omega-3 and omega-6

The membranes of brain cells as well as the protective substance that covers them are composed of polyunsaturated fatty acid molecules, such as omega-3 and -6. This explains why you probably have heard these names being associated with brain health and development. Our body doesn't manufacture omega-3 and -6, so we need to get them from our diet. A healthy diet contains a balance of the two fatty acids. Unfortunately, most North Americans and Europeans now get far too much of the omega-6s and not enough of the omega-3s.

• Omega-3 fatty acids are found in cold-water fish (salmon, sardines, mackerel, tuna, and trout) and in some seeds and nuts (flax seeds, chia seeds, and walnuts).
• Omega-6 fatty acids are found in seeds and nuts and the oils extracted from them (sunflower, corn, soy, and sesame oils).

Antioxidants

Antioxidants are molecules that prevent free radicals from damaging cells in our bodies, and this includes brain cells. Free radicals can be formed during oxidation, which is when oxygen interacts with other molecules inside the body. Free radicals can also enter the body via other sources, such as cigarette smoke, pollution, and pesticides. They trigger destructive chain reactions that antioxidants can stop. Fortunately, antioxidants (such as vitamins C and E and many other substances) can be found in a variety of foods, which include:

• Vegetables: spinach, artichoke, avocado, beans
• Dark-skinned fruits and berries: grapes, raisins, blueberries, blackberries, strawberries, raspberries, plums, acai berries, red grapes, cherries
• Nuts: almonds, pecans, walnuts
• Red wine, green tea, fruit juices
• Dark chocolate.

The BAD

Trans and saturated fats

These are not essential to our diet. In fact, consuming too much can increase the risk of cardiovascular disease (and thus Alzheimer's disease) by raising levels of "bad" LDL cholesterol and lowering levels of "good" HDL cholesterol. Trans fats are found in dairy products, meat, butter, and spreads. They are generally used in fast food, snacks, fried food, and baked products as well as many packaged foods. Anything fried has trans fats. Products containing saturated fats include dairy products, meat, eggs, chocolate, and nuts as well as some oils (coconut oil, palm oil, and palm kernel oil).

7: The best diet?

There is a diet that offers a healthy balance between omega-3 and omega-6 fatty acids. Studies have shown that people who follow this diet are less likely to develop heart disease and are at lower risk of cognitive decline. What is this diet? The clue's in the picture.

HOW IT WORKS: THE CAFFEINE HIT! Caffeine is a stimulant. It belongs to a chemical group called xanthine. When you drink coffee, your body falsely recognizes caffeine as adenosine, which is a naturally occurring xanthine in the brain that slows down the activity of brain cells (neurons). The caffeine is used by some neurons in place of adenosine. The result is that these neurons speed up instead of slowing down. This increased neuronal activity triggers the release of the adrenaline hormone, which affects your body in several ways: your heartbeat increases, your blood pressure rises, your breathing tubes open up, and sugar is released in the bloodstream for extra energy. Whether this results in increased brain performance is unclear. Studies show contradictory results. Scientists are equally uncertain as to whether caffeine offers any protective effect against age-related cognitive decline.

Answer on p.185

Exercise to jog the memory

It's no secret that physical exercise keeps the body healthy. But did you know that it also boosts your brain functions? Increasing evidence shows that exercise enhances the brain's performance and protects it from disease and natural decline.

How does it work?

Exercise triggers neuroplastic changes in the brain. Indeed, the volume of some brain regions, specifically regions associated with memory and learning (such as the hippocampus and the frontal lobes), can increase after a period of regular exercise. Studies on animals give us clues as to how exercise may cause this increase in volume. Exercise seems to enhance the production of growth hormones such as BDNF (brain-derived neurotrophic factor). This triggers both neurogenesis (the production of new brain cells) and angiogenesis (the development of new blood vessels). BDNF also helps neurons survive and plays a role in the biological processes associated with the consolidation of memory. In addition, exercise increases the levels of some neurotransmitters such as serotonin (see pp.14–15), thereby helping the transmission of information between neurons.

The best exercise

Aerobic exercise has been repeatedly shown to influence the brain's performance. Aerobic exercise is the kind of exercise that increases your heart rate over a sustained period of time, such as walking, jogging, swimming, cycling, or dancing.

Of course, you have to exercise regularly to reap the benefits. Guidelines recommend moderate exercise for 30 minutes, three times a week at least. Note that more intense exercise for shorter periods of time, or less strenuous exercise for longer periods of time, work just as well. Usually, you can experience positive and long-lasting effects on the brain about six months into the training. New evidence suggests that resistance and strength physical training (such as using free weights and exercise machines at the gym) for 60 minutes a week can also improve brain function.

The good news is that it is never too late to start exercising and benefiting from it. Age should not be a concern and neither should you worry if you've never exercised before. You just need to find the type of exercise that suits you and begin at an intensity that you find comfortable.

8: Exercise outside the gym

It is not always easy to find the time to go to the gym. Can you list at least 6 ways you can exercise physically during your day at home, at work, or your place of study?

1.
2.
3.
4.
5.
6.

Answers on p.185

9: Your aerobic routine

Here is a 10–minute (1 minute per move) aerobic routine to de-stress! You can do it anywhere. Increasing the duration and pace of the movement and adding arm movements will increase the intensity of the exercise. If you have not exercised in a while or if you are unsure, check with your doctor before doing this routine.

Warm up first: stretch arms and legs then march on the spot

Start jogging on the spot

Lift one knee, then the other, and repeat

Return to jogging on the spot

Jump up and down

Jog on the spot again

Step forward with your right leg, bring your foot back next to your left foot. Repeat with the left leg. Increase the pace

Return to jogging on the spot, gradually slowing down

March in place until your heart rate slows down

Stretch arms and legs

DID YOU KNOW: EXERCISE DEVELOPS BRAIN AGILITY In a study, 7- to 11-year-old overweight children who enrolled on a 14-week exercise programme showed improved brain functions and better performance in mathematical tasks after completing the programme. The exercise programme resulted in increased activity in the frontal regions of their brains. This study goes some way towards proving that children who play sports at school, take part in other "active" extra curricular activities, or merely enjoy a game of catch after school, appear to reap greater neurological benefit than previously thought.

The final word

So now you know some of the most effective ways to improve your memory and keep it in good shape throughout your life. You are also armed with the knowledge to optimize your brain health. If you continue to practise what you have learned in this book, you are definitely on the road to success.

Key things to remember

• Take advantage of your brain plasticity by using your memory on a daily basis. This will ensure that the brain areas supporting memory stay stimulated and potentially improve over time.

• When you are trying to memorize or learn anything, remember that attention, curiosity, and motivation are the natural triggers that can boost your ability to register the material.

• Memory-enhancing techniques have proven their efficiency on many occasions. As you've learned, the majority of these techniques ask you to order information and translate it into memorable images.

• To keep your brain and memory in good shape, it's important to pay attention to your general physical health: clean up your diet, do physical exercise regularly, get adequate amounts of sleep, and try to manage your level of stress.

Summary chart

Use the chart opposite to select the technique(s) that best fits the material you are trying to memorize. Practise using these on a regular basis and soon you will marvel at your growing memory power!

✔ Material to learn/remember	✔ Technique/strategy to use
Names and faces	*The 3-Step Memory Booster (pp.136–137)*
Numbers (phone number, PIN numbers, dates, and so on)	*The chunking method (pp.152–153)* *The Number-Association System (pp.154–155)* *The song method (pp.86–87)* *The major system (p.155)*
Any short list of items (1–5 items on a shopping or to-do list, simple recipe, and so on) **Random pieces of information** (historical events, names of clouds, birds' names, and so on)	*The Link System (pp.88–89)* *The song method (pp.86–87)* *The ordering method (pp.110–111 and pp.112–113)*
Any long list of items (5+ items on a shopping or to-do list, names of constellations, elements of Periodic table, an itinerary of activities, and so on)	*The Journey Method (pp.92–93)* *The Peg System (pp.114–115)*
Extensive amounts of information (a speech, material for a test, instructions to operate a complex machine, a long recipe, details of a project, and so on)	*Mind Webs (pp.118–119)* *The ordering method (pp.110–111 and pp.112–113)*

Solutions

Chapter 1

3: It's a matter of size

A: No (Trumpet)
B: Yes (Mobile phone)
C: Yes (Automatic digital camera)
D: No (Handsaw)
E: No (Violin)
F: Yes (Teacup)
G: Yes (Paint brush)
H: No (Drum)
I: No (Saxophone)

4: Label the brain

A: Parietal lobe
B: Occipital lobe
C: Temporal lobe
D: Frontal lobe
E: Hippocampus
F: Limbic system

12: Final destination

B: Meadow Close

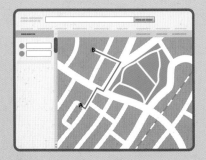

13: The memory quiz

1: B   **6:** A   **11:** B
2: A   **7:** B   **12:** C
3: A   **8:** B   **13:** A
4: C   **9:** A   **14:** A
5: C   **10:** B

Chapter 2

4: Cat invasion!

5: Write on your mental screen

Divide 120 by 3 = 40
Divide 125 by 5 = 25
Divide 46 by 2 = 23
Divide 96 by 6 = 16
Divide 300 by 12 = 25
Divide 140 by 4 = 35

14: Notice the odd one out

A:

B:

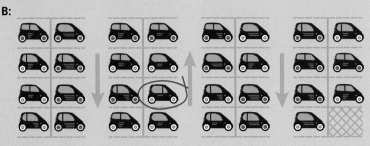

12: Mental rotation

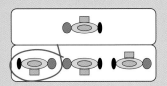

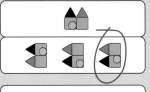

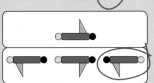

15: Spot the difference

22: Mental drawing

A:

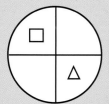

B:

23. Alien visit

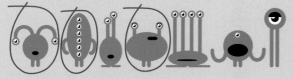

28: Finding your way

Chapter 3

2: Dining with the famous

Greta Garbo – Hollywood actress
Muhammad Ali – Heavyweight boxing champion
Marie Curie – Physicist & Chemist (Nobel prize winner)
Cleopatra – Ruler of Ancient Egypt
Oprah Winfrey – US chat show host and actress
Mahatma Gandhi – Political and spiritual leader of India
JK Rowling – Author of the Harry Potter novels
Isaac Newton – Physicist

3: Visual memories

A: 4 wings
B: Yes. It's approximately 8.5cm
C: 3 arrowheads
D: Left hand
E: 12 inches
F: Red, white, and blue
G: Approximately 2.5cm

13: It's mine!

Time-lag task:
$(44 + 9) − (23 + 6) = 24$
$(20 \times 3) − (36 − 9) = 33$
$(5 \times 8) − (35 ÷ 7) = 35$

17: Panic at the toy store!

Time-lag task:
$46 − 14 = 32$
$10 − (4 \times 2) = 2$
$23 + 3 − 9 = 17$
$(5 \times 8) − (5 \times 4) = 20$

18: Martian invasion

Latest headline: a large Martian **sighting** is confirmed. The first spacecrafts were **spotted** this **morning** over Spain and France. Further reports indicate that the fleet is heading towards Great **Britain**. In London, the streets are filling up with **worried** citizens gazing at the sky. **Supermarkets** are full as people are trying to buy anything they can before the invasion. Cars and **buses** are lining up on the main **roads**. Travelling may become **difficult** in a few hours.

20: Facing the enemies

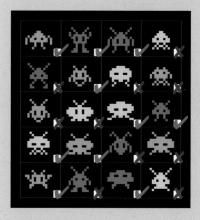

Time-lag task:
BATTLE
ENVELOPE
CHICKEN
COMPUTER

21: Eyewitness
A: Guitar
B: Pram
C: No
D: 10 lamps
E: Leaning against a lamppost
F: No
G: Walking stick
H: 10 people

Time-lag task:
$(10 \times 7) - 45 = 25$
$(6 \times 10) + (9 + 9) = 78$
$(7 \times 4) - (15 \times 0) = 28$
$(86 - 74) + (9 \times 3) = 39$

22: Reading a map

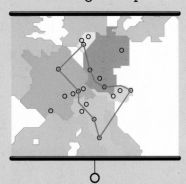

26: Birthday wish
Time-lag task:

27: Follow the recipe

Time-lag task:
218.3° Celsius

28: Geography lesson

River	Ocean
Mississippi	Gulf of Mexico
Jordan	Dead Sea
Seine	English Channel
Ganges	Indian Ocean
Danube	Black Sea
Euphrates	Persian Gulf
Amazon	Atlantic Ocean
Mekong	South China Sea

Chapter 4

4: Mental scale
A: DVD case: Smaller
B: Mobile phone: Larger
C: Chequebook: Larger
D: Ballpoint pen: Larger
E: Wine bottle: Smaller
F: Cotton bud: Larger
G: Fork: Smaller
H: Coffee mug: Smaller
I: Business card: Larger

6: Imaginary turns
A: Identical
B: Mirrored
C: Identical
D: Mirrored
E: Identical
F: Mirrored

7: It's all in the detail
A: Short tails
B: Yellow/orange
C: No, the tip of the beak and parts of the outer wing are black.
D: White/grey
E: Large ears
F: A boot

10: Funny images
Objects: lion, cage, ostrich, toothbrush, towel, bench, man, book, tree, frog, horse, green fence, scissors, hand, pink cat, biscuits, glass of milk, red and white straw, plate.
Time-lag task:
$(60 \times 3) + (90 - 30) = 240$
$(30 \times 4) - (36 - 10) = 94$
$(24 + 9) + (8 \times 2) = 49$

23: Memorize to music
Time-lag task:
The nail in a horseshoe
Footsteps

25: The wedding speech
Time-lag task
$(120 \times 3) - (25 \times 2) + 54 = 364$
$(80 + 26) + (23 \times 3) - 45 = 130$

26: Does it fit in a shoebox?
Coat hanger: No
Colander: No
Hair dryer: Yes
Cereal box: No
Tambourine: No
Child's doll: Yes
Table tennis bat: Yes
Bicycle pump: Yes
Laptop: No
Ice skates: No

30: Cube folding
Answer: C

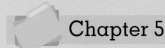 # Chapter 5

1: Accessories

For women: lipstick, perfume, purse
For men: dumbbell, top hat, wallet
For children: ball, slingshot, teddy bear

2: Ranking game

By size (small to large): diamond ring, calculator, telephone, vase, umbrella, laptop computer, car
By value: umbrella, vase, calculator, telephone, laptop computer, car, diamond ring

3: What's on my kitchen table?

Table A
1. 6 dairy products: cheese, milk, yoghurt, ice cream, butter, cream
2. 6 meats: sausage, steak, chicken, pork, turkey, lamb
3. 6 vegetables: corn, potato, bean, carrot, broccoli, leek

Table B
1. 5 orange-coloured fruit/vegetable: apricot, pumpkin, orange, tangerine, carrot
2. 5 red-coloured fruit/vegetable: strawberry, cherry, tomato, radish, raspberry
3. 5 green-coloured fruit/vegetable: courgette, spinach, peas, lettuce, artichoke

4: Going fishing

There are 4 species:
1. Tail type 1
2. Tail type 2
3. Blunt fins
4. Pronounced gills

5: Who are they?

Football player: football, football boots, pair of shorts
Artist: colouring pencils, sheet of paper, easel, paint set, ruler
Scientist: test tube, protective goggles, latex gloves, microscope

6: Slide puzzle

The picture depicts the first moon landing in 1969.

7: Up for grabs

1: Objects that make a sound when they're used: telephone, violin, baby's rattle, radio, bell, trumpet
2: Objects that do not make a sound when they're used: scissors, cup, pencil, book, sunglasses, bottle

8: Sorting shapes

First ordering system: colours of the rainbow
Second ordering system: number of sides in ascending order
Third ordering system: number of dots in ascending order

9: What belongs where?

The 4 categories are:
Vehicles (private modes of transport)
Vehicles (public modes of transport)
Facial features
Other body parts

12: Weekend shopping

DIY store: paint brush, masking tape, light switch
Chemist: cough drops, cotton balls, nail polish, plasters, vitamin pills
Garden centre: compost, flower seeds, rake, watering can

14: Let's go shopping

Time-lag task:
$(125 + 41) - (8 \times 2) = 150$
$(12 \times 6) + (71 + 28) = 171$
$(23 + 26) + (15 \times 4) = 109$
$(52 + 20) - (9 \times 8) = 0$

19: A trove of toys

Meaningful categories:
Sports equipment: football, badminton racket, cricket bat, shuttlecock
Toy vehicles: coach, train, jeep, tractor
Cuddly animal toys: teddy bear, panda, penguin, lion

20: The coldest places on Earth

Time-lag task:
$(12 \times 6) - (4 + 12) = 56$
$(5 \times 8) + (7 - 5) = 42$
$(60 \div 4) + (26 - 12) = 29$

21: Ring fingers

The rings can be grouped by the shape of their stone (circular, square, rectangular), or by colour (red: ruby, green: emerald, and blue: sapphire).

Time-lag task:
Answer: False

25: Cloud gazer

Organization principle: cloud levels
Low clouds: stratus, nimbostratus, cumulus,
Middle clouds: altostratus, stratocumulus, altocumulus
High clouds: cirrostratus, cirrus, cirrus-cumulus
Exception: Cumulonimbus

Time-lag task:
12 + 15 + 6 + 9 + 11 − 30 + 8 = 31
6 − 3 + 8 + 17 − 9 + 22 + 5 = 46

28: Decathlon

Time-lag task:
(230 − 90) + (15 x 4) = 200
(124 − 12) + (8 x 6) − (45 + 9) = 106

29: Fixing the house

 **Chapter 6**

2: New bank workers

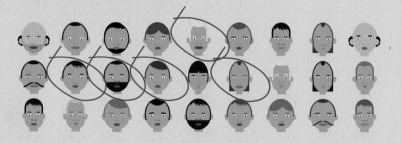

4: Observing faces

A: Light brown
B: Yes
C: No
D: No
E: Yes
F: A flat nose

5: Back to the bank

8: On a day trip

Time-lag task:
26 + 51 + 32 + 64 = 173
43 + 31 + 36 − 20 = 90
34 + 45 + 7 − 21 = 65
32 + 12 − 30 + 11 = 25

11: The new batch

14: Meet the teachers

A: Yes
B: Biology
C: Mrs Reed
D: No
E: No
F: Miss Crawford

15: Friends of a friend

Time-lag task:
Answer: C elastic

17: Business relations

Time-lag task:
(45 x 3) + (32 + 56) = 223
(35 ÷ 7) x (42 − 6) = 180
(21 − 6) + (7 x 8) = 71
(6 x 12) − (23 − 7) = 56

18: Too many docs!
Time-lag task:
1: Be attentive to boost memory (pp.40–41)
2: Basic principles to improve memory for the past (pp.62–63)
3: The Link System (pp.88–89)
4: The Journey Method (pp.92–93)
5: The Peg System (pp.114–115)
6: Mental Maps (pp.118–119)
7: The 3-step memory booster (pp.136–137)

19: On first-name terms
Time-lag task:

20: Party time!
Time-lag task:
67 + 45 − 6 = 106
34 + 4 − 8 = 30
23 − 7 + 26 = 42
424 − 234 = 190

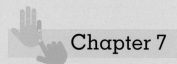

Chapter 7

4: Important phone number
Time-lag task:
Answer: Your name

5: Code to enter the site
Time-lag task:
Answer: Give the 4 children an apple each and then give the last child the basket with the apple in it.

6: Age is just a number
Time-lag task:

7: Knitwear for Christmas
Time-lag task:
3 x left turns
3 x right turns

10: A slice of pi
Time-lag task:
Answer: Charcoal

12: Birth years
Time-lag task:
Carrot
Strawberry
Cantaloupe

13: Safe delivery
Time-lag task
Answer: Stars

14: Airport pick up
Time-lag task
Answer: A memory

16: Banking details
Time-lag task:

18: Online library
Time-lag task:
Answer: Bookkeeper

21: Tuning in
Time-lag task:
A: Forest
B: Sapling
C: Hot

22: Uncle Fred's area code
Time-lag task:
Answer: A river

24: Utility bill
Time-lag task:

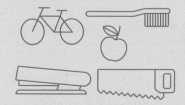

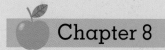

Chapter 8

7: The best diet
The Mediterranean diet. This diet does not include much meat. The emphasis is on whole grains, fresh fruits and vegetables, fish, olive oil, garlic, as well as a moderate amount of wine.

8: Exercise outside the gym
1: Always take the stairs instead of lifts
2: Park you car further than you normally would from your destination
3: Take a walk outside during your lunch break
4: Put on some music in the house and dance to it
5: Do some gardening
6: Housework (vacuuming the house offers a good physical workout)

Useful websites

GENERAL INFORMATION ON MEMORY

www.sharpbrains.com

www.dana.org

www.pbs.org/wnet/brain/

www.youramazingbrain.org/yourmemory/

www.improvememory.org

www.waystoimprovememory.com

www.memorise.org

www.memory-loss.org

www.gloo.com.au

MORE PUZZLES AND FURTHER INFORMATION

Short-term memory

www.fupa.com/play/Puzzles-free-games/short-term-memory

www.free-sudoku-puzzles.com/games/memory-game/short-term-memory-game.php

www.onlinegamescastle.com/game/short-term-memory

www.everydayhealth.com/longevity/mental-fitness/brain-exercises-for-memory.aspx

Long-term memory

www.lumosity.com

www.toimprovememory.com/longtermmemoryactivities.php

www.memoryjoggingpuzzles.com

Memory and imagination

www.enchantedmind.com/html/science/creative_memory.html

www.cul.co.uk/creative/puzzles.htm

www.supplementsformemorytips.com/Improve-Memory-When-You-Improve-Creativity.html

Memory and organization

www.web-us.com/memory/improving_memory.htm

www.npmanagement.org/Article_List/Articles/Organizational_Memory.htm

Remembering names and faces

www.memory-key.com/improving/strategies/everyday/remembering-names-faces

www.howtoimprovememory.org/names-faces/

www.mymemoryfix.com/remember_faces.html

Remembering numbers

www.braingle.com/mind/test_numbers.php

www.improvememory.org/how-to-improve-memory/memorization-techniques-remember-numbers

www.memorise.org/lesson3.htm
(For further information about the Major System)

Your body and mind

www.learningmeditation.com
(For more information on meditation)

NHS Direct
www.nhs.uk/conditions/stress
(Advice on symptoms of stress, treatment, and prevention)

The World Health Organization
www.who.int/occupational_health/topics/stressatwp/en/
(Advice on stress at the workplace)

The British Wheel of Yoga
www.bwy.org.uk
(Find a certified yoga teacher in the UK and overseas)

Further reading

Introduction to the brain

Searching for memory: The Brain, the Mind, and the Past by Daniel L. Schacter (Basic books), 1997

Learning and Memory: The Brain in Action by Marilee B. Sprenger (ASCD), 2003

The Rough Guide to the Brain by Barry Gibb (Rough Guides), 2007

The Human Brain: A Guided Tour by Susan Greenfield (Phoenix), 2001

Memory improving techniques and exercises

Don't Forget: Easy Exercises for a Better Memory by Danielle C. Lapp (DeCapo Press), 1995

Intelligent Memory: Exercise Your Mind and Make Yourself Smarter by Barry Gordon and Lisa Berger (Vermilion,) 2003

How to Develop a Brilliant Memory Week by Week: 52 Proven Ways to Enhance Your Memory Skills by Dominic O'Brien (Duncan Baird Publishers), 2005

Intelligent Memory by Barry Gordon and Lisa Berger (Vermilion), 2003

Exercises in Memory by Frank Channing Haddock (Kessinger Publishing), 2010

Maximize Your Memory: Techniques and Exercises for Remembering Just about Anything by Jonathan Hancock (Reader's Digest Association), 2000

Memory and creativity

Cognition: From Memory to Creativity by Robert W. Weisberg and Lauretta M. Reeves (John Wiley & Sons), 2012

The Mind Map Book: Unlock Your Creativity, Boost Your Memory, Change Your Life by Tony Buzan (BBC Active), 2009

Brainpower: Practical Ways to Boost Your Memory, Creativity and Thinking Capacity by Laureli Blyth (Barnes & Noble Books), 2002

Memory and health

Saving Your Brain: The Revolutionary Plan to Boost Brain Power, Improve Memory and Protect Yourself Against Aging and Alzheimer's by Jeffrey Ivan Victoroff (Bantum Doubleday Dell), 2004

How to Improve Memory and Brain Function as we Age by Parris Kidd (Keats Pub Inc.),1997

Yoga Mind, Body and Spirit: A Return to Wholeness by Donna Farhi (Newleaf), 2001

How to Activate Your Brain: A Practical Guide Book by Valentin Bragin M.D Ph.D (AuthorHouse), 2007

Super Body, Super Brain: The Workout That Does it All by Michael Gonzalez-Wallace (HarperOne), 2011

General

The Sharp Brains Guide to Brain Fitness: 18 Interviews with Scientists, Practical Advice, and Product Reviews, to Keep Your Brain Sharp by Alvaro Fernandez & Dr. Elkhonon Goldberg (Sharpbrains, Incorporated), 2009

My Stroke of Insight: A Brain Scientist's Personal Journey by Jill Bolte Taylor (Hodder), 2009

The Brain That Changes Itself: Stories of Personal Triumph from the Frontiers of Brain by Norman Doidge Science (Penguin), 2007

Spark: The Revolutionary New Science of Exercise and the Brain by John J. Ratey and Eric Hagerman (Quercus Publishing), 2008

The Memory Book: The Classic Guide to Improving Your Memory at Work, at School, and at Play by Harry Lorayne and Jerry Lucas (Ballantine Books), 1986

Index

About the Author

Dr Pascale Michelon

Pascale Michelon is a research scientist at Washington University in the Pychology department. Dr Michelon's passion for applying and sharing scientific knowledge led her into the field of brain fitness and memory improvement. She has worked with both young and older adults to understand how the brain processes information and memorizes facts. In 2006, she founded The Memory Practice to provide adults with challenging cognitive exercises to keep their brain fit. Dr Michelon has received several academic fellowships and awards. From 2004 to 2006, she received the Washington University Center for Aging award for her research into the effects of ageing on spatial reasoning. Dr Michelon is also an Expert Contributor for the website SharpBrains.com where individuals, companies, and institutions are provided with the best science-based information and guidance on brain health and fitness.

Acknowledgments

Author's acknowledgments

I would like to start by thanking my editor Suhel Ahmed for his thoughtful support, his rapid and enlightening feedback, and his enthusiasm for the project from start to finish. I would like to thank Keith Hagan for his fresh, colourful, and striking illustration, without which this book would clearly not be the same. Many thanks to Charlotte Seymour for overseeing every aspect of the book's design, and my gratitude also goes to Nicola Erdpresser who did a fantastic job of marrying the text and illustrations: it was always a pleasure to see the proofs during the book's production. Thanks also to Angela Baynham for her solid editorial work.

Finally, I would like to thank my family and particularly Pascal, for his continued support and his complete trust in my projects and dreams.

Publisher's acknowledgments

Dorling KIndersley would like to thank HIlary Bird for supplying the index and Alyson Silverwood for proofreading the book in such a short amount of time. Also, many thanks to them and their families for checking the puzzles and exercises.

We would like to extend our thanks to Giles Smith, the marketing manager at **www.travelindependent.info**, for providing us access to their online entry for South America on pp.120–121

Picture Credits

The publisher would like to thank the following for their kind permission to reproduce their photographs: (Key: a-above; b-below/bottom; c-centre; f-far; l-left; r-right; t-top)

16 John Foxx: (cr). **Getty Images:** Digital Vision (cra); Stockbyte (ca). **59 Getty Images:** McDaniel Woolf (ftr). **133 Getty Images:** Monica Lau (ca). **Imagestate:** (c, fcr, cl). **138 John Foxx:** (crb). **Imagestate:** (cr, cra, br). **141 John Foxx:** (bc, fbl, bl). **Getty Images:** C. Borland / PhotoLink (cb); Monica Lau (clb). **Inmagine:** (cl). **142 Imagestate:** (cl). **145 Getty Images:** Don Tremain (c). **150 Imagestate:** (br)

All other images © Dorling Kindersley
For further information see: www.dkimages.com

By the same Author

BUILDING CONSTRUCTION

Volumes One, Three and Four

JOINERY

By J. K. McKAY

BUILDING CONSTRUCTION

Volume Two

W. B. McKay
M.Sc.Tech., M.I.Struct.E.

Former registered architect and
chartered structural engineer and Head
of the Department of Building and
Structural Engineering in the
Manchester University Institute
of Science and Technology.

BUILDING CONSTRUCTION

VOLUME TWO

FOURTH EDITION (METRIC)

By J. K. McKay, B.A., B.Sc.Tech., A.R.I.B.A., C.Eng., M.I.Struct.E.

With drawings by the authors

Longman
Scientific &
Technical

Longman Scientific & Technical
Longman Group Limited,
Longman House, Burnt Mill, Harlow,
Essex CM20 2JE, England
and Associated Companies throughout the world.

First published 1944
Second Edition 1961
Third edition 1968
Fourth Edition (metric) 1970
Ninth impression published by Longman Scientific
& Technical 1987
Eleventh impression 1990
Twelfth impression 1991
Thirteenth impression 1993
Fourteenth impression 1995

ISBN 0-582-42217-5

Produced by Longman Singapore Publishers Pte Ltd
Printed in Singapore

PREFACE TO THE FOURTH EDITION

In this edition the various units have been converted to metric terms.

In the third edition, due to the replacement of the model Bye-Laws by the Building Regulations, the chapters dealing with fireplace construction and drainage, in addition to being extended, were rewritten and brought up to date. The corresponding drawings were modified or renewed entirely and a fresh one of a septic tank included.

The opportunity has been taken once more to revise parts of the text and figures.

J. K. McK.

1970

PREFACE TO THE FIRST EDITION

VOLUMES II and III are devoted to those parts of Building Construction which are regarded as suitable for a second-year course. Brickwork, drainage, masonry and mild steel roof trusses are dealt with in Vol. II (this volume), carpentry, joinery and roof coverings in Vol. III.

One of the aims of the author has been to treat the subject sufficiently comprehensively in order to meet, as far as possible, the individual requirements of both students and lecturers concerned with the examinations of the Royal Institute of British Architects and allied professional bodies, and for National Certificates and Diplomas in Building. A wide syllabus has therefore been adopted to meet a variety of needs. It is not intended that the whole syllabus should be covered by one class in one session, but rather that most classes should be able to select those parts of the syllabus that apply specially to them. The syllabus adopted has been divided into eight parts, and these appear as headings of the respective chapters of both volumes.

Materials have been treated at some length. Much of the description in smaller type is intended for the more advanced students and for reference purposes.

Because of the relatively large size of many of the drawings it has been possible to include associated details for convenient reference. Thus, for example, Fig. 51 incorporates complete details of the small steel roof truss. Again, the several openings showing the stone dressing in Fig. 42 are detailed in Fig. 43 on the opposite page. It is hoped that the arrangement of the details in the full-page drawings especially will be of assistance to students preparing homework sheets and testimonies of study. A Homework Programme appears on p. 137. This is suggestive only, to be departed from according to the requirements and capacity of the students. Its purpose is not the production of sheets identical in detail and composition.

The author wishes to express his appreciation to several colleagues for their valuable criticisms and suggestions during the preparation of this volume, and particularly to Mr V. C. Barnes, A.R.I.B.A., Mr D. A. G. Reid, B.Sc., A.M.I.C.E., and Mr A. V. Wilson, M.Sc.Tech., M.I.Struct.E. His thanks are also due the Controller, H.M. Stationery Office, for kindly allowing the inclusion of extracts from several British Standard Specifications, many more of which have been consulted. Acknowledgement has been made in the text to several firms who have readily supplied information on building materials and processes of manufacture.

JANUARY 1944   W. B. McK.

CONTENTS

LIST OF ILLUSTRATIONS

Note: UNLESS INDICATED OTHERWISE ALL DIMENSIONS ON THE FIGURES ARE GIVEN IN MILLIMETRES

CHAPTER ONE

BRICKWORK

Syllabus.—Extended description of the manufacture and characteristics of bricks, cements and limes; lime and cement mortars; concrete. Squint quoins and junctions in English and Flemish bonds; piers; cavity walls; circular work; reinforced brickwork; raking bonds; garden, cross, Dutch, brick-on-edge and facing bonds; recessed, elliptical, pointed and rere arches. Damp proofing of basements; dry areas. Stepped foundations. Concrete floor construction. Decorated brickwork. Fireplaces, flues, chimney breasts and stacks; building regulations. Setting out.

MATERIALS[1]

A BRIEF description of certain building materials is given in Vol. I. These will now be considered in greater detail.

BRICKS

Bricks are chiefly made from clay and shale, and are moulded either by hand or machinery. The principal elements of clay suitable for brick-making are alumina and silica. Alumina renders the clay plastic, and thus facilitates the moulding process; if incorrectly proportioned it will cause the bricks to crack, twist and shrink excessively when being burnt. The silica may be combined with the alumina or it may be free in the form of sand; if combined, it has a tendency to produce shrinking and warping, but if free it counteracts this tendency and assists in the production of hard, durable and uniformly shaped bricks; brittle bricks will result if the sand content is excessive.

Brick clays may also contain varying proportions of limestone, iron, magnesia, salts such as magnesium sulphate, sodium sulphate, potassium sulphate and calcium sulphate, in addition to organic matter and water.

Limestone or chalk has the effect of reducing shrinkage and acting as a flux during the burning process, causing melting and binding of the mass. It influences the colour of bricks. The limestone should be present only in a fine state of division (the size of the particles not exceeding " pin-heads "), otherwise the pieces of quicklime (see p. 20) will slake and expand if the bricks absorb moisture. Such expansion will crack or shatter the bricks. Fine grinding of the clay will prevent damage from this cause. An excess of chalk will produce mis-shaped bricks when being burnt.

Iron oxides and magnesia also influence the colour of bricks (see p. 12). Salts

---

[1] Consideration of much of this description of materials can be deferred until the Third Year of the Course. It is given here in somewhat extended detail for the purpose of reference.

may cause efflorescence (see p. 13). Organic matter, if in excessive quantity, may contain compounds which discolour plaster. Certain salts, particularly magnesium, may cause the bricks to decay.

Suitable clays for brick-making include "reds," "marls," "gaults," "loams," "Knotts" and "plastics."

Red Clays are found in many parts of the country and are extensively used for producing high-class bricks. As is implied, the colour of these bricks is red in various shades, depending upon the proportion of iron oxide present. Red bricks which are particularly noteworthy are those from Berkshire, Durham, Hampshire, Lancashire, Leicester, Yorkshire and the vicinity of Peterborough.

Marly or Limy or Calcareous Clays have a large chalk or limestone content and are commonly used. Sand is sometimes added to such clays to prevent the bricks fusing during the burning process. Marly clays are converted into *malm* by the addition of chalk in correct proportion. In producing malm, the clay and chalk are separately reduced to a slurry or slip in wash mills. The clay *wash mill* is a cylindrical tank in which harrows of vertical metal teeth, attached to horizontal arms, are rotated to churn up the contents. The mill is stopped at intervals to allow stones and larger grains of sand to settle to the bottom, leaving the liquid with the clay in suspension. The chalk is washed in a similar mill, but a spiked roller instead of the harrows is used to break up the lumps to a fine state of division. The washed clay and chalk are now mixed together in exact proportions and passed through a screen to a *wash-bank* or shallow settling tank where the surplus water is run off, leaving the malm. Marl and malm bricks are almost white in colour. The approximate analysis of marl includes 33 per cent. silica, 10 per cent. alumina, 30 per cent. chalk and 5 per cent. oxide of iron. Well-known white bricks are obtainable from Cambridgeshire, Lincolnshire and Suffolk.

Gault Clays are heavy, tough and of a bluish colour, but with sufficient chalk content to render the bricks a pale yellow or white colour when burnt. Bricks, called *gaults*, made from such clays are often perforated (see p. 19) or have a large frog to reduce the weight; they are very satisfactory for general building purposes.

Loamy or Mild Clays have a high silica content, and the addition of a flux, such as chalk, is often necessary. Shrinkage of these clays during burning is relatively small, and they produce bricks of excellent quality. Compared with marls, a loamy clay may consist of approximately 65 per cent. silica, 27 per cent. alumina, 0·5 per cent. chalk and 1 per cent. iron.

Knotts Clay is found in deep seams in the neighbourhood of Peterborough, and as it contains a relatively large proportion of finely distributed combustible matter, an economy in fuel for burning results. Fletton bricks (see p. 10) are produced from this clay in enormous quantities. The approximate composition is 50 per cent. silica, 15 per cent. alumina, 10 per cent. lime, 7 per cent. iron, 5 per cent. carbonaceous matter, together with water and traces of magnesia, potash and soda.

Plastic or strong Clays are composed chiefly of silica and alumina in combination, and chalk of a creamy consistency must be added to prevent distortion and excessive shrinkage in drying and burning. *London clay*, from which the well-known London stock bricks are made (see p. 11), is of this class.

Clay Shales, quarried in Durham, Lancashire and Yorkshire particularly, produce excellent bricks. Shale is a hard, laminated rock which is reduced to a plastic mass suitable for brick-making by weathering and the addition of water (see next column). It is found, often in the same quarry, with a varying content of oxides of iron, etc., and the careful blending of these shales produces bricks, used for faced work, of different shades. A typical shale may contain roughly 60 per cent. silica, 25 per cent. alumina, 0·6 per cent. chalk, 7 per cent. oxides of iron, 2 per cent. magnesia and traces of alkalis (potash and soda), organic matter and water.

Fireclay is quarried in Lancashire, Durham, Northumberland, Yorkshire, Staffordshire and other parts of the country. It contains a large proportion of silica (varying from 50 to 70 per cent.) and little, if any, lime and iron. Bricks made from such clay are highly resistant to high temperature and are therefore suitable for the lining of furnaces and fireplaces.

MANUFACTURE OF BRICKS

The various methods of production are determined very largely by the nature of the clay or shale, and may be divided into the (a) semi-dry or semi-plastic process, (b) stiff-plastic process and the (c) plastic process.

(a) *Semi-dry or Semi-plastic Process.*—The clay or shale is comparatively dry. It is ground to a fine powder by heavy rollers, passed through a screen, mixed to a uniform consistency, pressed and re-pressed in moulds by very powerful machinery (see p. 3) and burnt. Sometimes the screened material is damped by sprayed water. Because of the dryness of the material the bricks are taken direct from the moulding machine to the kiln, the usual intermediate drying stage being omitted. The process is relatively cheap. This process is adopted for the production of Flettons, owing to the suitability of the Knotts clay.

(b) *Stiff-plastic Process.*—This process, which is being adopted to an increasing extent, is similar to the above, except that the water content of the material is increased and therefore less powerful machinery is required to mould the bricks (see p. 3). A separate drying plant is not always necessary. The process is usually applied to hard, dry clays, such as marls, and certain shales; it may also be applied to wetter clays, provided they have been partially dried before being crushed.

(c) *Plastic Process.*—The clay suitable for this process contains a large proportion of moisture, and is used for making wire-cut and hand-made bricks (see pp. 3 and 4). The bricks must be carefully dried before being burnt.

The various processes of (1) preparation of the clay or shale, (2) moulding, (3) drying and (4) burning are briefly described in Vol. I.

1. Preparation.—The top soil, or *overburden* or *callow*, is first removed. Clay is dug by hand or by mechanical excavators (see Chap. I, Vol. IV), which consist of a jib having a bucket with steel claws attached. The bucket is pressed against the base of the quarry face, and as it ascends the claws remove the clay which passes into the bucket; the jib is swung round until the bucket is over a wagon which receives the clay discharged from it. Shale is usually loosened by blasting and then filled into wagons either by hand or by means of an excavating machine.

Weathering.—In the absence of crushing machinery, certain clays are subjected in winter to exposure to the weather. This is usual in small works where moulding and subsequent operations are only carried out during the spring and summer months and the clay is dug in the autumn. The excavated clay is spread over the ground for a slight depth (not more than 610 mm) to allow the action of the frost to break down the clay into minute particles. Stones, roots, etc., are removed, whilst at least once during the winter the clay is turned over to increase the exposure and improve its workability.

There are several methods of conveying the clay or shale from the quarry or pit. One form consists of an " endless wire rope " to which the bogies or wagons are attached; the moving rope drags the full wagons (which run on rails) up the incline to the mill as the empty wagons descend and return to the pit. Alternatively a motor tractor may be used to haul the wagons.

Cleaning.—Some clays require to be " cleaned." Stones, coarse vegetable matter, etc., may be removed either by hand picking, or the clay may be passed through a wash mill.

Blending.—Clay or shale used for making common bricks is usually taken as quarried direct to the crushing machinery. That for the more expensive bricks, especially multi-coloured facings (see p. 13), often requires the material from different strata to be mixed together as required. This important operation, known as blending, includes the removal of any undesirable material. The selection of the various clays or shales is made at the quarry-face and the blending is performed by one or more mechanical mixers, in conjunction with the grinding or crushing machine.

Reduction.—The machinery for reducing the clay or shale to a fine condition depends a good deal upon the character of the material. Thus, an *edge-running mill* is suitable for hard, dry clays which have been previously crushed by a *stone breaker*, whereas *crushing rolls* are effectively employed for plastic clays.

One form of stone breaker or disintegrator consists of a rapidly rotating shaft from which hammers are hung to break up the material to a coarse powder.

There are three types of *edge-runners* or *grinding mills*, i.e. (1) *dry* or *revolving pans*, (2) *wet pans* and (3) *pan mills*. A dry pan consists of two heavy metal rollers which rotate in a revolving pan having a perforated base; the latter may be 3 m in diameter and the size of the perforations varies from 1·6 to 13 mm; water is added to the clay or shale as required during the grinding operation, and the crushed material passes through the base to a pit or is conveyed by a belt to the moulding machine. A wet pan or *chaser mill* has two rotating rollers or runners which revolve in a fixed pan, the base of which is in the form of a grating having 6 to 19 mm slots through which the crushed material is forced; the material is softened by water which is sprayed over it. A pan mill or *tempering mill* consists of a pair of runners and a solid revolving pan which receives a measured charge of clay and a definite amount of water; grinding proceeds for about twenty minutes before the material is removed. A *pug mill* may be used in lieu of a pan mill, and consists of a vertical metal cylinder in which curved knives attached to a rotating shaft churn up the clay and force it downwards through the outlet at the base.

Crushing rolls are used for reducing clays of high plasticity. The rolls, driven at a speed which varies from 50 to 160 or more revolutions per minute, are in pairs, and are strong metal cylinders placed horizontally, side by side, with a space between; they are from 450 to 915 mm diameter and 660 to 915 mm long. The clay is fed between the rollers from a hopper fixed above them. The surface of the rolls may be smooth or they may be either toothed, spiked, corrugated, etc., when they are called *kibblers*. The rolls may consist only of a single pair, or there may be two pairs with one pair above the other. The space between a single pair should not be less than 13 mm if provided with a double pair of rolls, the upper pair are kibblers spaced up to 50 mm apart, and the lower pair of smooth rolls are closely spaced to a minimum of 0·8 mm. The kibblers grip and crush the clay sufficiently for fine reduction by the lower rolls, from which it passes in thin sheets.

Screening.—Clay or shale after being ground is generally passed through a screen to ensure that only fine, well graded material is passed forward for moulding. The coarse material retained on the sieve is returned for further grinding.

De-airing.—As is implied, de-airing means extracting air, and is a process which has been recently introduced into this country and applied to certain clays and shales prior to the moulding operation. During the grinding and pugging processes air is introduced between the fine particles. This entrapped air reduces the plasticity of the clay, preventing the mass from becoming thoroughly homogeneous, and causing defects such as blisters, laminations and cracks (see p. 14). The removal of the air therefore increases the workability of the clay and prevents the development of these defects. A de-airing machine simply consists of a chamber to which a vacuum pump is connected. The fine particles of clay or shale are forced into the chamber and the air is extracted as the material proceeds to the moulding machine.

De-airing has been particularly successful in connection with the manufacture of wire-cut bricks (see below), where the complete plant may consist of a pug mill or an *auger machine* with a *shredding plate*, a de-airing chamber, and a second auger which conveys the clay from the chamber and forces it through the *die* to the wire-cutting machine. An auger machine is a horizontal pug mill with a powerful metal screw or worm instead of the shaft with blades. The extruded clay as it leaves the die is in the form of a continuous band having smooth surfaces and sharp, well defined arrises.

Grog, which is burnt waste bricks or burnt clay ground to a powder, is sometimes added to the raw clay in the mill to reduce shrinkage of the bricks during the drying and burning processes.

2. Moulding.—The prepared clay or shale is machine-moulded by either the (*a*) wire-cut or (*b*) pressure processes, or it may be moulded by hand.

(*a*) *Wire-cut Process.*—The clay or shale, in the form of a continuous plastic band or column, is propelled from the pug mill or auger over oiled rollers to the *cutting table*. The exit, called the *die* or mouthpiece, is lubricated with water, steam or oil to reduce friction and ensure uniform movement of the column, and is approximately 247 mm by 188 mm; this size is variable, depending upon the shrinkage of the material, which may be 6·4 to 8·5 mm per 100 mm and which occurs during the drying and burning processes.

The usual type of cutting table consists of a frame containing several wires at a distance apart equal to the thickness of the bricks plus the shrinkage allowance, and is shown in the sketch A, Fig. 1. These wires are kept taut by means of screws. As the end of the column reaches the stop, the frame automatically moves forward and the wires cut the column transversely into brick slabs; these are pushed forward, placed on barrows and wheeled to the drying floor. In another type of cutting table the frame is fixed and the column, which has been cut to length, is pushed forward past the wires. The frame in another type rotates and the wires divide the column by a downward cut. In one of the latest machines two columns are extruded, and two cutting tables can produce 5 500 wire-cuts daily. As the column leaves the die a small roller under it impresses the trade mark of the firm on the clay at brick thickness centres.

(*b*) *Pressure Process.*—The prepared clay is automatically fed into rectangular metal die-boxes or moulds which are the size of a brick plus shrinkage allowance. Two of many machines used for this purpose are shown diagrammatically at B and C, Fig. 1. The horizontal rotary table of machine B contains a number of moulds which are brought in turn under the plunger; the latter charges the moulds with clay and consolidates it under great pressure; as the table rotates the pressed brick slabs are automatically pushed upwards clear of the moulds and removed. In the press C the clay in the mould or die-box is consolidated as the plunger descends. Some bricks are passed through two presses, the second press producing a better shape and further consolidation. After consolidation the slab is removed either by an upward movement of the base or by the dropping of the sides, which in one type of mould are hinged at the bottom and collapse outwards.

At one works, referred to on p. 10, the clay, after being ground and screened, passes on to a moving steel belt which traverses a huge kiln and feeds the moulding machine which presses four bricks at a time and is capable of moulding 2 600 bricks per hour. This machine travels on rails and is brought opposite the empty chambers of the kiln in turn and into which the moulded bricks are passed direct.

Wire-cut bricks for facings are often *re-pressed* to consolidate them and render their arrises sharp and square. Both types of presses, B and C, are suitable for this purpose, that at B having moulds with collapsible sides which become vertical as each box comes under the plunger. Spraying oil over the bricks facilitates their removal.

Hand-moulding Processes.—Although bricks can be made more cheaply and much more quickly when machine-made, hand-moulding is far from being an obsolete process. Hand-moulded facings have a rich texture, beautiful colouring and durability. Purpose-made bricks which depart from standard sizes, and clay blocks of special shapes to meet specific requirements, are hand-moulded. Except in certain districts, comparatively few common or *stock*[1] bricks are now moulded by hand.

The clay or shale is prepared by any of the methods described on pp. 2 and 3. In addition, *souring* or ageing the clay is sometimes resorted to. This merely consists of storing the plastic clay, for a period varying from one day to several weeks, in one or more cool chambers to ensure a uniform distribution of the water throughout the mass and the decomposition of any organic matter. This results in an increase in the plasticity and workability of the paste, and assists in preventing the development of cracks, blisters and other defects.

There are two methods of shaping bricks by hand, namely, (*a*) sand-moulding and (*b*) slop-moulding.

(*a*) *Sand-moulding.*—The wood-mould, shaped as shown at A, Fig. 2, has neither top nor bottom and is usually lined with brass or iron; its internal dimensions are those of the finished brick plus allowance for shrinkage (19 to 25 mm). This is called an *open-mould* or *stock-mould*, as distinct from a *box-mould* which has a fixed bottom and is used for special bricks.

The moulding operations are done on a wood bench or *moulding stool*, which is about 1·8 m long by 0·6 m wide by 0·9 m high. A "stock" of clay of the correct consistency, flattened on top, and a heap of sand are placed conveniently to hand on or near to the bench. The moulder sprinkles sand on a portion of the table and the inside faces of the mould (hence the name applied to the process) to prevent adhesion and facilitate the subsequent removal of the clay slab. Meanwhile an assistant (known as the "clot-moulder") cuts a portion of clay from the stock and kneads it into a rectangular "clot" which is about one-quarter larger than the mould. The moulder takes the clot, throws it into the mould and completely fills it by pressing the clay down with his fingers. The edge of a *strike* (a wood straight-edge which is dipped in water) is drawn across the top to remove the superfluous clay and level the surface of the slab. Finally, the moulder lifts the mould, and with a twist of the hand turns the slab on to a flat piece of wood called a *pallet board*. The slab is removed by a boy to the floor of the drying shed.

These bricks are often moulded on a piece of wood called a *stockboard*, which is nailed to the top of the bench. It has a raised centre or *kick*. The kick and stockboard are covered with brass as shown at B, Fig. 2. Four metal pegs are driven into the table, one at each corner of the stockboard, and the mould is placed upon them as shown. The thickness of the brick is regulated according to the extent to which the pegs are driven. The kick forms the characteristic frog in the bricks.

Approximately 1 000 bricks per day can be moulded by this method by a moulder and assistants.

Ornamental bricks and those of special shapes are sometimes moulded from

---

[1] "Stock" is a term which originally denoted hand-made bricks moulded on a stockboard (see Fig. 2). It is now loosely applied and generally indicates common wire-cuts.

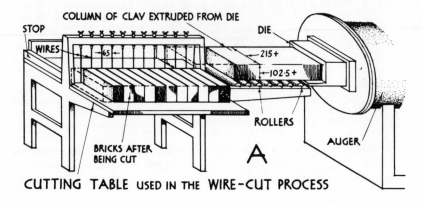

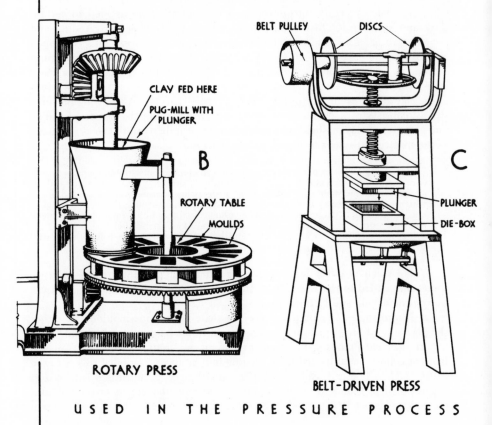

SKETCHES OF BRICK MOULDING MACHINERY

CUTTING TABLE USED IN THE WIRE-CUT PROCESS

ROTARY PRESS

BELT-DRIVEN PRESS

USED IN THE PRESSURE PROCESS

NOT TO SCALE

FIGURE I

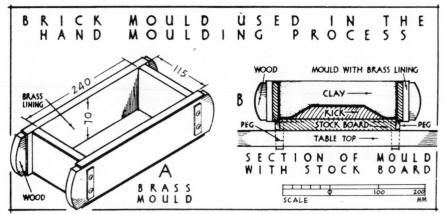

BRICK MOULD USED IN THE HAND MOULDING PROCESS

240 115

BRASS LINING 70

WOOD A BRASS MOULD

WOOD

B MOULD WITH BRASS LINING

CLAY →

KICK

PEG STOCK BOARD PEG

TABLE TOP →

SECTION OF MOULD WITH STOCK BOARD

SCALE 0 100 200 MM

FIGURE 2

wire-cut and pressed green bricks which are used instead of clots to fill the moulds.

(b) *Slop-moulding.*—This method is now rarely employed. The clay used in this method is more plastic than that used for sand-moulding. Sand is sprinkled on the prepared portion of the table or stockboard. The mould, entirely of wood, is dipped into a trough of water (provided on the bench) and filled with a clot as above described. As the bricks are not sufficiently stiff to permit of their immediate removal on a pallet, the full moulds are taken to the drying floor and there turned out.

3. Drying.—With exception of common bricks made by the semi-dry process (see p. 2) and certain pressed bricks moulded by the stiff-plastic process (p. 2), bricks must be dried before being placed in the kiln. This applies particularly to those made by the plastic process (p. 2), where the water content may exceed 25 per cent. Drying is effected by (a) artificial and (b) natural means.

(a) *Artificial Drying.*—The chief heating mediums are steam, direct heat from fires, and waste heat from kilns and boilers. The dryers include the (i) hot floor, (ii) shed, (iii) chamber and (iv) tunnel types.

(i) *Hot Floor System.*—This is commonly employed for drying plastic (wire-cut) bricks. The floor is usually that of the building in which the bricks are moulded and should be adjacent to the kilns. It consists of either steel plates or concrete slabs which cover conduits in which the steam pipes are laid. The steam is controlled by valves in order that the temperature may be regulated to suit the bricks. The steam may be generated from the boiler which provides the power for the crushers, grinding mills, etc.

When direct heat from coal or coke fires is the medium, a number of long flues are constructed immediately under the floor. The flues are about 450 mm square and are parallel to each other at about 2·5 m centres. Each flue is slightly inclined upwards from a fireplace at one end, and the upper ends are connected to a transverse flue which delivers into a chimney.

If waste heat from the kilns is used, the flues under the drying floor are arranged as last described, except that their lower ends are connected by a transverse flue which is connected to the kilns. The flow of gases from the kilns is controlled by a fan at one end of the upper transverse flue.

The bricks from the moulding machine or bench are preferably placed on end on the hot floor, with a space between each, when the heat gradually dries them from the bottom upwards. If the bricks are not stiff enough to permit of this, they are placed on bed on the floor. The time taken to dry bricks varies. Some bricks may be taken on barrows direct to the kiln after being left on the hot floor for one day only, whilst others may require five days before they are fit for removal to the kiln.

(ii) *Shed or Room Dryers.*—A shed is a 9 to 12 m wide single storey building containing *racks.* A rack is approximately 0·6 m wide and has ten of more shelves of narrow battens upon each of which a row of moulded bricks is "finger-spaced" on edge. The shed is heated by steam pipes, stoves or a hot floor. Drying is comparatively slow and somewhat irregular.

Sometimes the space above a continuous kiln (see p. 6) is partly utilized to store bricks which are dried by heat from the kiln.

(iii) *Chamber Dryers.*—A shed is divided into several chambers, each about 1·2 m wide, 2·4 m high and of variable length, with a door at each end. The bricks are placed, with a space between each, on loose narrow shelves or on cars. One type of car consists of a bogie (which runs on a track) having a metal frame or rack which supports loose pallet boards that are about 1·2 m long. Each board is loaded with a row of ten or more bricks as they are moulded and placed on edge with a space between. Another type consists of a bogie on the base of which is stacked *stool pallets.* The latter are narrow wood shelves, with 200 mm high end supports, for receiving the moulded bricks which are placed on edge. When rack-cars are used, each drying chamber has longitudinal bearers fixed to the side walls for their entire length and at about 300 mm intervals; these support the loaded pallet boards as they are removed from the cars. Stool pallets are stacked one above the other in each chamber. Loaded cars may be wheeled into the chambers in which they remain until the bricks are dry. The heat must be applied very gradually, otherwise the bricks will warp and crack.

In some dryers the bricks are gradually heated in a saturated atmosphere until they reach a temperature of about 32° C. The humidity is then reduced by the admission of dry air, and the temperature is increased as required. This greatly minimizes damage to the bricks.

(iv) *Tunnel Dryers.*—This type of dryer resembles the tunnel kiln shown in Fig. 4 and described on pp. 10 and 11. As the loaded cars traverse the tunnel, which is about 30 m long, hot air (steam or waste gases) enters at the unloading end, and the current is caused to flow towards the loading end by means of a fan. The rate of drying varies, but generally a car of dried bricks is removed and one of green bricks is added every hour. The tunnel dryer may be operated intermittently like a chamber dryer, it being filled with loaded cars of green bricks and the whole of them being removed after the drying operation has been completed.

(b) *Natural Drying.*—Whilst artificial means of drying is now generally adopted, bricks must be dried naturally if heat is not available. Natural drying is usual where clamp-burning (see p. 11) is resorted to and in yards where the output is small. A well ventilated shed may be used, in which the bricks are stacked on racks and dried by the circulation of un-heated air.

Alternatively they are hack-dried. A *hack* is simply a long double row of green bricks which are stacked to a maximum height of approximately 900 mm depending upon the softness of the bricks.

The hack-ground is level and well drained. There is a space of about 225 mm between each *line* or *blade* of bricks forming a hack; the bricks are placed on edge at 13 mm intervals to a height of from five to eight courses, the bricks in one course bridging the spaces between those in the course below. One course, which may be 60 m or more in length, is completed first to allow the bricks to stiffen before the next course is laid. The hacks are spaced at about 2·7 m apart and should run in a north-south direction so that both sides will be exposed to the sun. The bottom course is placed on planks or hollow rectangular tiles or 50 mm thick layers of sand, breeze, etc. As a temporary protection the top of each hack is covered with a series of portable light wood " caps " which are about 1·8 m long with sloping sides in the form of a roof. The sides are also protected by hurdles or screens called *loo-boards*; these are about 1·8 m long and 0·9 m high. This temporary protection is removed during favourable weather, but the hacks should be covered immediately when necessary, otherwise much damage to the bricks may be caused. The bricks are *scintled* when half dry, *i.e.*, they are set diagonally, with a 50 mm space between each and with alternate courses reversed.

As bricks containing moisture are readily damaged by frost, hack-drying can only be carried out during the six months of the year, from April to September inclusive. The process is extremely slow, the bricks taking from three to six weeks to dry, depending upon the weather and the nature of the clay.

4. Burning.—This is the final process in brick manufacture. Permanent kilns are chiefly used for burning bricks, although clamp-burning (see p. 11) is still adopted in certain parts of the country. Kilns may be classified into (*a*) intermittent, (*b*) continuous and (*c*) tunnel.

(*a*) *Intermittent, or Periodic or Single Kilns.*—These are permanent structures and may be divided into (i) down-draught, (ii) horizontal draught and (iii) up-draught kilns, according to the direction of the fire.

(i) *Down-draught Kiln.*—This is the most efficient form of intermittent kiln, and it is the only type adopted to any extent in this country. Even in works having large outputs, it is not unusual to find that the common bricks and certain facings are burnt in a continuous kiln (see next column), whilst best class sand facings and blue bricks are burnt in a down-draught kiln, as the heat which influences the colour can be controlled better in the latter.

The section of a down-draught kiln is shown at T, Fig. 3. That adopted for bricks is usually rectangular, although circular kilns for ware goods (see Chapter Two) are common. The capacity varies from 20 000 to 40 000 bricks. The rectangular chamber has four walls and an arched top which incorporates a heat-insulating ring composed of porous bricks (probably made of a fossil earth known as *kieselguhr*); this reduces the amount of heat transmitted through the structure and thus effects a saving in fuel. The kiln is lined with fire-bricks. Fireboxes are formed at intervals, and a special feature is the continuous screen wall, called a *flash-wall* or *bag-wall*, constructed parallel to and about 230 mm from the inside of each long wall. The heat from the fuel (which is usually small coal called *slack*) thus passes upwards to the arch, which deflects it down through the openly stacked green bricks (see p. 7), the gases escaping through perforations in the floor to a horizontal flue connected to a tall chimney. The screen walls are perforated at intervals near the bottom to allow sufficient heat to pass direct to the lower portion of the stack during the drying process. An opening or *wicket* is provided at one end through which the kiln is filled

and emptied. This is bricked up with a temporary wall after the green bricks have been set, and the outside of this wall is luted with clay.

Glazed bricks and certain red bricks (in addition to terra-cotta, etc.) must not be exposed to the direct flames from the fires, otherwise they would be damaged by the gases, dust, etc. Such bricks are heated in *muffle kilns*. This type of kiln consists of an outer rectangular chamber and an inner compartment. A simple form has a fireplace at one end of the chamber and a horizontal main flue, extending the full length, at the floor level. Cross walks at intervals are arched over this flue and these support the inner shell comprising firebrick bottom, sides, top and one end. There is a space between the inner shell and outer structure so that hot gases from the fire can completely traverse it before escaping through openings in the outer roof into an upper horizontal flue extending the full length. The bricks are stacked in the inner compartment and the open end is built-up and daubed with clay. Thus, these bricks are heated entirely by the heat transmitted through and radiated from the firebrick shell.

Sometimes six or more down-draught chambers are constructed to form what is known as a *semi-continuous kiln*. This type provides for the waste heat from one chamber being utilized to dry and heat the bricks in others. Thus, after chambers 1 and 2 have been loaded and the fire in No. 1 lighted, the heat not required passes through holes in the floor of No. 1 chamber, along a flue to an opening (controlled by a damper) in the division wall and over a flash wall into No. 2 chamber, where it circulates round the green bricks before entering the main flue to the chimney. The fire in chamber 2 is maintained, chamber 3 is loaded and the bricks in the latter are gradually heated by the waste gases from No. 2. Each chamber is progressively heated in this manner until the final one is reached. An economy in fuel thus results.

(ii) *Horizontal Draught or Newcastle kiln.*—Comparatively few of these are now in operation, it having been gradually replaced by the continuous type of kiln. It is a rectangular building with an arched top, and is approximately 4·5 m wide and not more than 9 m long. The fireplaces are arranged at one end, together with a perforated flash-wall, and a chimney is provided at the opposite end. The gases traverse horizontally and pass into the chimney at the floor level. A wicket in one or both long walls is formed to permit of loading and unloading.

(iii) *Up-draught or Scotch or Score Kiln.*—This is the most primitive form and is now almost obsolete. It is rectangular on plan, having three permanent brick walls and a temporary end wall; there is no roof, the top being open. The size is roughly 7·6 m by 4·9 m by 3 m high. Fire-openings are provided at intervals in the side walls at the ground level. Coal fires are gradually applied after the kiln has been loaded, and when the bricks are dry the top is closely covered with old bricks; these and the temporary end wall are daubed with clay paste. Hot fires are now maintained for two or three days, after which they are damped down and the bricks are allowed to cool. The heat is irregular and consequently there is a large proportion of over-burnt bricks at the bottom and under-fired at the top.

Intermittent kilns are not economical, as the walls have to be heated up at each setting of the kiln, and this results in a heavy fuel consumption.

(*b*) *Continuous Kilns.*—This type, evolved from the intermittent and semi-continuous kilns, is most suitable for large and regular outputs. It is so called because the operations are uninterrupted, each chamber in turn being loaded, dried, burnt, cooled and emptied, and the waste heat is utilized to dry and pre-heat the green bricks. The kiln is thus economical in fuel consumption.

The structure consists of walls of ordinary brickwork, lined with firebricks jointed with refractory cement, the top is generally arched and lined with purpose-made firebricks, and the floor is usually constructed of hard bricks bedded on sand or concrete. The kiln is divided into compartments or chambers. The divisions may be temporary (see C, Fig. 3) or permanent (see M). The number of compartments varies; twelve is considered to be a minimum, fourteen and sixteen are common, whilst the largest kiln in this country (see p. 10) has 224 chambers. The length of a chamber is usually from 3·7 to 4·9 m, the width varies from 2·7 to 3 m, and the height to the crown rarely exceeds 2·7 m. Best results are obtained if the total length of the chambers is not less than 60 m to permit of the efficient control of the various operations. Each chamber has an opening (known as a *wicket* or *door gap*) in the external wall for loading or " setting " and emptying or " drawing " the bricks; it has a flue, controlled by a damper, to convey the used gases to the main flue and thence to the chimney. In a more modern kiln, and especially those used for producing facing bricks, each chamber is connected to a hot-air flue (see p. 8). Small coal or slack is commonly used as fuel. This is fed through *feed-holes* situated in the top of the kiln, and these are preferably of fireclay blocks covered with movable metal airtight caps. The capacity of a chamber varies; the smallest will hold about 8 000 bricks, whilst a very large chamber will accommodate 40 000 or more bricks. It is customary for one chamber to be drawn and one to be filled daily. The rest of the kiln is divided into (1) drying, (2) pre-heating, (3) firing and (4) cooling zones (see U, Fig. 3).

(1) *Drying or Steaming or Water-smoking Zone.*—A brick, even after being treated in a dryer, has a comparatively large water content which often exceeds one-sixth of its dry weight. The process of eliminating this water is an important one, for, if not carried out gradually, the bricks will crack and their strength be considerably reduced by the formation of steam within the small voids or pores of the material. The bricks in the drying chambers of the kiln are gradually heated to a temperature of 120° C. by the admission of hot air from the pre-heating chambers. This hot air should be free from gases, such as sulphur dioxide, otherwise the bricks will be discoloured by a deposition on their exposed surfaces of a film called *scum* or *kiln-white* (see p. 14). The waste heat from the firing chambers should not be used for drying purposes in kilns in which facings are produced, as this contains gases which cause discoloration (see p. 8). Large volumes of steam are produced during the drying process, and for the production of good coloured bricks this steam must be rapidly removed through flues (see p. 14) to avoid condensation on the bricks. The length of the drying zone depends on the length of the chambers and the draught created by the chimney, but in a fourteen chamber kiln the zone usually comprises two chambers, and three will be required in a sixteen chamber kiln (see U, Fig. 3).

(2) *Pre-heating Zone.*—The bricks in this zone are gradually brought to a dark-red heat (600° C.), during which the chemically combined water is set free and removed, and then the burning is carefully controlled until the temperature is increased to approximately 950° C. During the latter stage the iron and other compounds are oxidized and the colour of the bricks is influenced; the burning must therefore not be hurried, otherwise the bricks will be dis-

coloured and hearting (see p. 13) will result. The length of the pre-heating zone is usually equivalent to four chambers (see U, Fig. 3).

(3) *Firing Zone.*—The bricks are vitrified during the final heating which takes place in this zone in which the maximum temperature may reach 1 100° C.[1] The number of chambers in full-firing zone is two and three in a fourteen and sixteen chamber kiln respectively (see U). Coal is added through the feed-holes every quarter of an hour, and fuelling of the kiln is confined to them, the chambers in the drying and pre-heating zones having been heated by waste heat from the cooling zone. The stoking is generally done by hand, although the employment of automatic feeders which discharge the required quantity of coal at regular intervals is increasing. The durability of the bricks depends upon the firing of the kiln at this stage; excessive temperature will cause the bricks to lose their shape, and under-burning will reduce their strength.

(4) *Cooling Zone.*—This usually consists of four chambers, as shown at U, although in the larger kilns the length of the zone is increased and the risk of damage, such as cracking, is correspondingly reduced. The temperature of the bricks in the unloading chamber, which adjoins the cooling zone, should be sufficiently low to enable them to be handled comfortably.

Setting.—There are several different arrangements of setting the green bricks in a kiln, much depending upon the stiffness of the bricks and the type of kiln. One form is to stack them on edge in a series of *bolts* or rows 225 mm thick, alternately as headers and stretchers and about 19 mm apart. Another arrangement, suitable for a continuous kiln, is shown in the section at A, Fig. 3. This shows three courses of bricks (headers) on edge, " finger-space " (about 19 mm) apart. A course of stretchers is placed upon these, followed by alternate double courses of headers and single courses of stretchers. Vertical flues, called *fire-columns*, are formed in the stack under the feed-holes. These extend from top to bottom, are about 125 mm square and serve as combustion spaces and for ashes.

The following is a description of some continuous kilns, including the Manchester, Zigzag, Hoffman and Habla kilns.

Manchester Kiln[2] (see A, B and C, Fig. 3).—That shown is a simple form of the Manchester kiln, and is suitable for the burning of common bricks.[3] It consists of two long compartments, separated by a longitudinal wall, and whilst it has no permanent division walls, it is divided into chambers by paper " partitions " (see p. 8), and it is therefore called a fourteen chamber kiln. Each chamber accommodates 8 000 bricks, and as one chamber of burnt bricks is emptied per day, the weekly output is approximately 50 000 bricks, which is considered to be the minimum for a continuous kiln. Whilst a smoke flue, controlled by a damper, can be provided for each chamber, the plan shows that one damper serves chambers 1 and 14, and similarly another damper is

[1] This varies; thus, for Fletton bricks the maximum temperature may not exceed 850° C.
[2] By courtesy of Messrs Dean, Hetherington & Co., Accrington. This is the smallest and simplest type of continuous kiln built by this firm.
[3] The Manchester kiln, incorporating a hot air flue, is used for the production of facing bricks.

common to both chambers 7 and 8; this is in order to simplify the kiln. The chamber flues are connected to two main flues which lead to a chimney 12 m high and 1·2 m internal diameter) conveniently near.

> To fire this kiln for the first time, six or seven chambers are set with green bricks and each section is separated by being papered off. Thin brown paper, obtained in rolls, is usually used for this purpose, and this is pasted over (liquid clay, called *slip*, being used as an adhesive) the last completed end face of stacked bricks. The wickets in these chambers, 2 to 7 inclusive, are bricked up with temporary walls, and a small fireplace is prepared in each. A temporary brick wall, shown at H on plan C, is built, and this is prepared with four fireplaces. Fires are lit in these fireplaces and the heat is steadily applied to the bricks in chamber 2. The damper controlling this section is open to allow the steam and gases to escape. When the temporary wall at H gets too hot to the hand, the paper partition separating chambers 2 and 3 will have burnt away. No. 2 damper is then closed and No. 3 damper is opened, thus allowing the heat to pass through chamber 2 to chamber 3, and hence into the main flue to the chimney. This is repeated until three or four chambers are red hot. Coal is then passed through the feed-holes and down the 125 mm square fire columns (see p. 7). Meanwhile further chambers will have been set with green bricks until all of the chambers, excepting No. 1, are filled. The open fires in the temporary wall at H and those in the wickets are maintained until a sufficient body of heat has been built up to light and support combustion of coal fed from the top. The open fires are then stopped in rotation, chamber 1 is set and papered over as described above, and the bricks in chamber 2 are removed. The kiln is now prepared for normal working, when one chamber is emptied and another is filled daily.

After the whole of the chambers have been fired, the following is a normal daily schedule for this kiln, assuming that the direction of the fire is clockwise as shown by the arrow, and that chamber 3 is being unloaded :—

Chamber	Bricks		Chamber	Bricks	
1	Drying	Temperature 25° C. (min.)	10	Heating	Temperature 700° C.
2	Being set	Cool	11	Heating	to
3	Being drawn	Cool or Cold	12	Heating	120° C.
4	Cooling		13	Heating	120° C.
5	Cooling	50° C.	14	Drying	(max.)
6	Cooling	to			
7	Cooling	1 000° C.	Wickets 2 and 3 are open, remainder are built up.		
8	Firing	1 000° C. (max.)	Damper 1 is open, rest are closed.		
9	Firing	700° C. (min.)	Paper partition pasted on bricks stacked in chamber 1 on face adjoining chamber 2.		

The cold air entering wickets 2 and 3, whilst cooling the bricks, gradually increases in temperature, especially when it traverses those in chamber 7 which had been subjected to the maximum temperature the previous day. This supplies the primary heat to burn the coal, which is fed in small quantities every fifteen minutes from the top of chambers 8 and 9. As the hot air proceeds on its travel, it pre-heats the bricks in chambers 10, 11, 12 and 13, and dries and steams those in chambers 14 and·1 before escaping down the branch flue No. 1.

This being a continuous process the operations are maintained in this sequence, but are advanced by one chamber daily. Thus, on the following day chamber 3 is filled and chamber 4 is emptied.

As the whole of the waste heat is utilized to dry the bricks in this kiln, and as that from the firing chambers may cause discoloration (see p. 14), it follows that the kiln is best suited for the manufacture of common bricks, for which purpose it is most economical. The provision of hot air flues (see below) is necessary for the production of good-coloured bricks.

> During the slack periods, when the output from half the kiln would be sufficient to meet the demand, it may be used intermittently as follows : Four small fireplaces are constructed in the external end wall of chamber 1, the two openings between chambers 1 and 14 and 7 and 8 are built up temporarily, and the chambers 1 to 7 inclusive are filled with green bricks. Fires in the end fireplaces are maintained until there is sufficient heat to fire coal fed through the feed holes. Top feeding of the chambers is continued until the bricks are throughly burnt, when the half kiln is emptied and re-set.

Zigsag Kiln (see J, K, L and M, Fig. 3).—This is one type of Zigsag kiln[1] which is divided by permanent walls into fourteen chambers. The fire is drawn in a zigsag direction owing to the position of the openings in the division walls being staggered, causing it to traverse each chamber diagonally.

Each chamber has a transverse *downcast flue* under the floor which is connected to the *main* or *smoke flue* and controlled by a damper from outside. There is, in addition, a *hot air flue* immediately over the main flue and extending the full length of the kiln. When required, each chamber is connected to this hot air flue by raising the damper controlled from the top of the kiln (see K and dampers 1, 14, 2, etc., at M). As mentioned on pp. 7 and 14, hot gases from the firing chambers must not be used to dry bricks if scumming is to be avoided, and only hot gases from the *cooling* chambers should be admitted for this purpose. Hence the necessity for this hot air flue. In addition to the downcast flue and hot flue dampers, each chamber has a third or main flue damper immediately over the crown of the smoke flue and controlled from the top of the kiln (see K and dampers 10, 5, 9, etc., at M). These, together with the downcast flue dampers, are opened wholly or partially as required in the drying chambers for the rapid removal of the steam.

The process is continuous, at least one chamber being loaded and one unloaded daily. The daily schedule of the operations varies according to the nature of the clay, quality of bricks, draught (velocity of the air created by the chimney or fan), length of fire circuit, etc.

The Zigsag is exceptionally efficient for the following reasons : (1) It can be effectively controlled; (2) it produces bricks of first quality, comparatively free from undesirable discoloration and other imperfections enumerated on pp. 13 and 14; and (3) the fuel consumption is relatively low.

Habla Kiln.—This has several features which resemble the Zigsag kiln. The plan is similar in that the *trace holes* (openings in the partitions) are staggered, causing the fire to take a zigzag course, but these partitions, instead of being permanent as in the Zigzag kiln, consist of dried bricks (without mortar) and are therefore temporary.

For the production of common bricks the kiln has not a permanent top, and it is therefore classified as of the " archless " type. After the loading chamber has been set, it is covered with either two courses of bricks laid close together with a layer of sand or ashes on top, or concrete slabs with metal trays containing kieselguhr, a highly porous earth which serves as a heat insulating material. The kiln is fired by pulverized

---

[1] From details supplied by Messrs John Jones & Sons, Buckley, Chester.

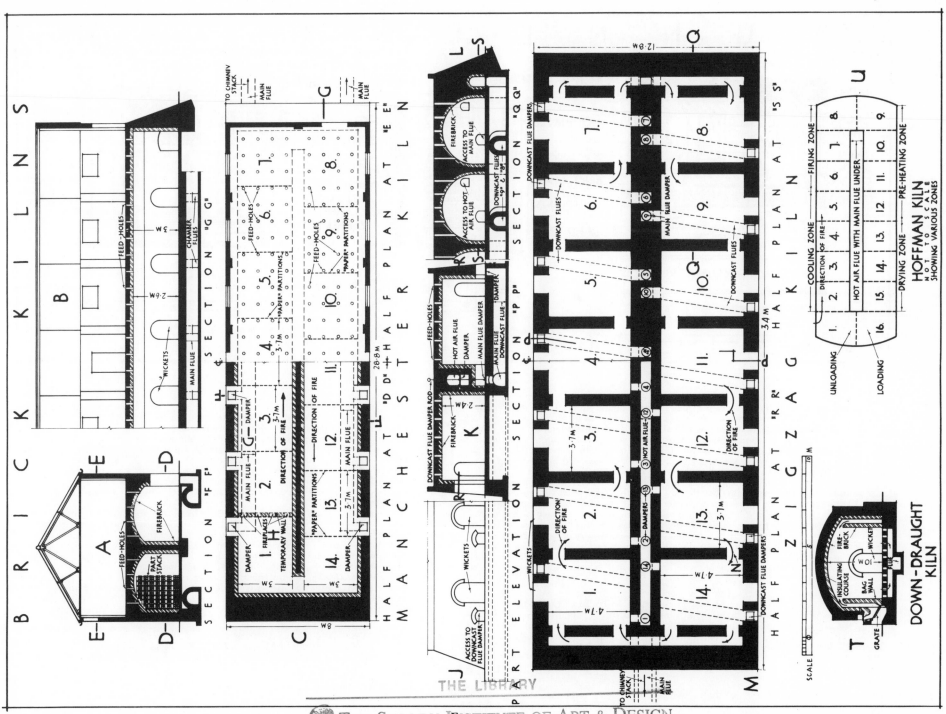

BRICK KILNS

SECTION "G"

SECTION "F"

MANCHESTER

HALF PLAN AT "E"

HALF PLAN AT "D"

PART ELEVATION

SECTION "P P"

SECTION "Q Q"

HALF PLAN AT "R R"

HALF PLAN AT "S S"

ZIGZAG KILN

HOFFMAN KILN
NOT TO SCALE
SHOWING VARIOUS ZONES

FIRING ZONE

COOLING ZONE

DIRECTION OF FIRE

HOT AIR FLUE WITH MAIN FLUE UNDER

DRYING ZONE

PRE-HEATING ZONE

UNLOADING

LOADING

DOWN-DRAUGHT KILN

SCALE

THE SURREY INSTITUTE OF ART & DESIGN
Farnham Campus, Falkner Road, Farnham, Surrey GU9 7DS

FIGURE 3

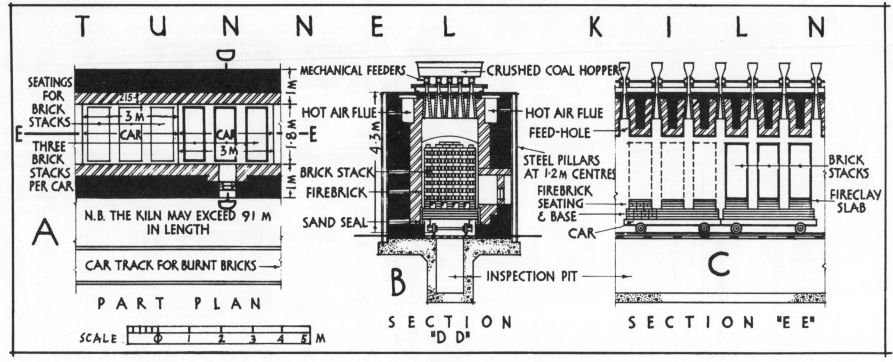

FIGURE 4

coal passed through feed-holes provided in the temporary top. It has main and hot air flues. An arched permanent top is best if facings are to be produced.

The Habla kiln, like the Zigzag kiln shown in Fig. 3, has a long length of travel, which facilitates the control of operations, and it is relatively cheap to construct.

Hoffman Kiln.—This is probably the best known kiln of the continuous type. The original kiln was circular on plan, the chambers (separated by paper partitions) being placed round a central tall chimney. This kiln has been improved, and a plan of the later type of Hoffman kiln is shown in the line diagram at U, Fig. 3. The number of chambers varies, but the largest of this type, used for the burning of Fletton bricks, has no less than 224 chambers.[1] In addition to the main flue which takes the products of combustion from each chamber, it has a central hot air flue to which are connected branch flues from the chambers, so that hot air from the cooling chambers may progressively be admitted to dry the bricks. Each chamber is further provided with a flue in the top to allow the steam to escape during the preliminary drying operation. One chamber is filled and another is emptied daily, as described on p. 8. Common bricks, together with a proportion of selected facings, are produced in this kiln.

---

[1] This kiln is at the works of Messrs The Marston Valley Brick Co. Ltd. Its length is 1 000 m. Each chamber has a capacity of 33 000 bricks. Fourteen chambers are subjected at the same time to the maximum temperature with fifteen chambers between each. Hence it is equivalent to fourteen 16-chamber kilns and the *weekly* output is approximately 3¼ million bricks.

(c) *Tunnel Kilns.*[1]—This kiln, shown in Fig. 4, is a brick structure which is traversed by cars or trucks upon which the bricks are stacked. The kiln may be from 90 to 137 m long, its internal width varies from 1·5 to 1·8 m, and its height to the crown of the arch is approximately 3 m. The kiln has three zones, *i.e.*, pre-heating, firing and cooling, thus for a 90 m kiln these are approximately 39 m, 30 m and 21 m long respectively. The firing zone and part of the cooling zone are lined with firebrick, and the walls of the former are constructed with a 230 mm thick layer of insulating material between the lining and the outer brickwork; this insulation protects the latter and conserves the heat. A metal door is provided at each end of the kiln.

The metal cars are 3 m long, and their bases are protected by three or four courses of firebricks. In a siding adjacent to the kiln each car is loaded in three stacks with a space between each; three seatings, each three courses high of firebricks covered with a fireclay slab, are provided on the base to receive the bricks. The approximate number of 215 mm bricks which a car will hold is 2 000. The kiln and tracks for loading and unloading the cars are under cover.

Rows of feed-holes are provided at intervals in the roof of the firing zone, the distance between each row being equal to that between the stacks of bricks. The fuel is crushed coal, and this is fed from hoppers which are placed over mechanical feeders fixed immediately over the feed-holes. Thus the coal dust is fired immediately

---

[1] By courtesy of Messrs Gibbons Bros. Ltd., Dudley.

it enters the kiln and the larger particles continue to burn as they pass down the spaces between the stacks to the base. The air for combustion, drawn in through the exit by means of a fan, is pre-heated as it passes through the cooling zone, and the temperature, which increases as the draught of air proceeds through the firing zone, is gradually reduced as it traverses over the bricks in the pre-heating zone. The combustion is so complete that little smoke escapes at the fan outlet, and a chimney stack is therefore not required. At the exit end of the cooling zone a vertical air flue is provided which is connected to a horizontal flue that is continued over the arch of the cooling zone, along each side of the firing zone (see B) and over the pre-heating zone arch to a fan which delivers the hot air to the brick drier. Scumming of the bricks is avoided by the provision of a number of waste gas flues at the front end of the pre-heating zone which are connected to a common flue controlled by an extraction fan to withdraw the gases. A sand seal is provided at each side of the kiln throughout its length; these consist of metal channels containing sand through which passes the lower edges of the metal plates fixed at the sides of the cars. The seals prevent loss of draught and protect the wheels and axles of the cars.

The cars are caused to travel on a track for the full length of the kiln by means of a powerful hydraulic ram. The movement is intermittent, the cars being pushed forward at regular intervals to the extent of one-third the length of the car or the equivalent of a stack and one space. This distance is maintained uniformly so as to ensure that the spaces (called *combustion chambers*) between the brick stacks are immediately under the feed-holes. As these spaces extend the full width and height of the stacks, a uniform temperature throughout is ensured and this results in the bricks being uniformly burnt. It takes from two to three minutes to move the load, and the interval between each movement varies from thirty to fifty minutes according to the output required. The rate of travel varies, but for a 90 m kiln, the time taken between a car entering and leaving the kiln is approximately three days and the weekly output is about 160 000 bricks. The working of the kiln is very flexible as it can be readily speeded up or slowed down as occasion demands by regulating the rate of travel and the amount of coal supplied by the mechanical feeders. As each car of finished bricks emerges from the kiln, another car of green bricks enters the charging end.

The advantage claimed for the tunnel kiln are: (1) The bricks are evenly burnt, and it is therefore particularly suited for the production of first-class facings; (2) the output is regular and only a small percentage of bricks are damaged in the process; (3) low maintenance costs; (4) flexibility of working; and (5) on account of the complete combustion which results, there is no smoke nuisance and the conditions of employment are improved, as the kiln is not entered to load and unload the bricks.

The disadvantage of this type of kiln are: (1) The relatively high initial cost, and (2) the additional cost of providing power for the ram, fans, etc.

Temperature Control in Kilns.—The temperature in kilns in which first-class facings are produced is sometimes controlled by the use of either *Segar cones* or a *pyrometer*.

Segar cones are small L-shaped pieces made from special clays, having a flat base with a vertical leg, and are tested to bend at certain temperatures. Thus, a " No. 022 cone " will bend (*i.e.*, the leg will gradually collapse until the top touches the base) when subjected to a temperature of 600° C., whilst a " No. 10 cone " will do likewise at 1 300° C. Generally three cones of the desired " temperature resistance " are placed in different parts of the kiln, and in positions in which they will be seen through spy-holes in the walls. Firing ceases when the required temperature in the kiln has been reached, indicated by the bending of the cones.

Electric pyrometers are usually used in gas-fired kilns. Such consists of an electrical conductor (containing a coil of platinum wound round a strip of mica) which is exposed to the heat. This is connected by leads to an electrical system which automatically records temperature movement on a chart, and the rate of firing in the kilns is regulated according to the readings.

Clamps.—A clamp simply consists of a large mass of green bricks stacked, with several intermediate layers of breeze (cinders) as described below, upon a

foundation of old bricks. It has neither walls nor roof. Clamp-burning preceded kiln-burning, and it is still adopted in certain parts of the country, particularly in Kent and Essex, where *London stocks* are made. Clamps are also occasionally used at works to provide temporary additional means of burning when the output of the permanent kilns is insufficient to meet heavy demands. The bricks are not uniformly burnt, and whilst a large proportion is satisfactory, those on the outside are underburnt, and those near the *live holes* (see below) and in the heart of the kiln are mis-shapen and cracked owing to the excessive heat.

A clamp is constructed in the following manner : The ground, which should be well drained, is paved with a layer of old bricks, placed on edge. The size of this paving is from 12 to 15 m square although this varies. The paving is slightly dished, rising slightly from the centre to the edges, to prevent the stacked bricks when being burnt from falling outwards. The clamp is built with a series of 3-brick thick walls (called *necks*), and the construction may be commenced either (*a*) at one end or (*b*) down the middle.

(a) *End Clamping.*—The end wall, known as the *upright*, extends the full width of the clamp. It is about 1·4 m thick at the base, and is formed with a vertical face internally and a battered face externally. The bottom course consists of old burnt bricks laid scintled (diagonally) on edge with 50 mm spaces between. The second course is also formed of burnt bricks laid on edge, but these are spaced as stretchers. Breeze and coal slack is placed in the spaces between the bricks, and the top is covered with a 150 or 175 mm layer of breeze. The first course of green bricks is laid as headers on top of this layer, the bricks being placed on edge and closely spaced. This is covered with a 100 mm layer of breeze, followed by the second course of raw bricks (stretchers) placed on edge, with a slight space between each. This course is given a 50 mm covering of breeze. The remainder of the wall is formed of alternate courses of headers and stretchers of raw bricks, placed on edge, slightly spaced and with a thin sprinkling of breeze between each course. The number of courses of green bricks is approximately thirty. A 75 to 150 mm layer of breeze is spread over the top course of raw bricks, and this is covered by a course of old bricks, closely set on edge, with the joints luted with clay.

The rest of the clamp is constructed with a series of parallel 3-brick thick walls or " necks," extending its full width, until the opposite end is reached, when an " upright " is built similar to the first with an external batter. These necks are formed exactly like the uprights, having alternate header and stretcher courses of green bricks on a double course of old bricks at the base, layers of breeze and a daubed hard brick finish. The breeze layers are continuous, and the bricks are so arranged that a stretcher course in one neck is opposite header courses in adjacent necks.

In the middle of each end neck a continuous horizontal flue (called a *live hole*) is formed between the double course of burnt bricks forming the base. It is formed by leaving a 215 mm wide space whilst constructing the base. Similar flues (which are 215 mm high) are constructed along the centre of every seventh or eighth neck. Dry brushwood is placed in these flues and this is covered by the 150 mm layer of breeze.

(b) *Middle Clamping.*—In this system the upright is constructed down the centre to the full extent of the clamp. It is built in a similar manner to the end uprights described above, except that it has a batter on each face, and a 215 mm by 215 mm horizontal flue is formed in the middle of the base for its entire length. The necks are formed on either side of the upright and with faces parallel to the batter. Three transverse horizontal flues (one in the centre and one at about 2·1 m from each end) are formed in the base whilst the necks are being built, and these are connected to the central live hole. These cross flues are filled with brushwood.

It is usual to construct a wall of old bricks on each face of the clamp and extending the full height. This is 215 mm thick at the base and 75 mm at the top. These walls are daubed over with clay, except where holes have been left for the admission of air. The clamp is fired by lighting the brushwood in the flues. Gradually the breeze begins to burn, and the fire passes upwards until the whole clamp is burning. London stocks and most of the bricks burnt by this primitive method are made of clay to which sifted breeze has been added; alternate layers of clay, breeze and washed chalk are stacked and allowed to weather (see p. 2); this is subsequently mixed and the breeze thoroughly incorporated. Such bricks therefore contain fuel, and the clamp continues to burn for two and a half to six weeks until this breeze has been consumed. Little attention is needed whilst the clamp is burning. If the fire is proceeding too quickly, the air holes are stopped to reduce the draught. Protection is sometimes afforded by boarded screens fixed on the windward sides.

Sizes of Bricks.—Brick dimensions are specified in B.S. 3921 : where the nominal sizes are given as follows :—

Length (mm)	Width (mm)	Depth[1] (mm)
215	102·5	65

The brick length of 215 mm plus the usual 10 mm vertical joint thus gives an effective unit length of 225 mm.

Samples of 24 bricks are used to ascertain if a consignment satisfies the dimensional standard. The method of sampling is given below. In testing the sizes place a sample of 24 bricks in contact on a level surface and then measure the overall dimension by means of a steel tape. According to the B.S. this should be within the following limits :—

Dimensions of a Sample of 24 Bricks		
Length (mm)	Width (mm)	Depth (mm)
5 160 ± 75	2 460 ± 43	1 560 {+ 60 / − 30}

Sampling.—Twenty-four bricks are taken from every consignment of 30 000 bricks or part thereof. These samples are stored in a dry place not in contact with the ground. They are taken at random (*a*) *preferably* when the bricks are in motion (such as loading or unloading), *or* (*b*) from a stack.

In method (*a*) the bricks are taken at random from each of a number of convenient positions. Sampling by method (*b*) entails the removal of part of the top of two courses of the stack so as to open a trench. The samples are then taken from the third or fourth courses below the top.

If a sample complies with the dimensional tests, the whole batch from which it is taken shall be deemed to comply. If the sample is below standard then the whole batch is deemed not to comply.

[1] In earlier B.S. another type of brick was mentioned as being nominally 50 mm deep. This is no longer specified in the latest B.S., although bricks of this depth are still available.

COLOUR OF BRICKS

There is a wide range of colours of bricks, such as white, grey, brown, red, purple, blue and black, with intermediate shades. Bricks of varying shades, called *multi-coloured*, have within recent years been in big demand for faced work. Some bricks are uniform in colour, whilst others are mottled or irregularly shaded. The colour is influenced by : (*a*) Chemical constitution of the clay, (*b*) temperature during burning, (*c*) atmospheric condition of kiln, (*d*) sand-moulding, and (*e*) staining.

(*a*) **Chemical Constitution of Clay or Shale.**—Iron oxides affect the colour considerably. Thus, clays which produce white bricks have little or no iron present, whilst blue bricks contain at least 7 per cent. oxide of iron. Careful blending of the clays and shales (see p. 2) is responsible for the production of many beautifully coloured bricks, and such colours are permanent.

(*b*) **Temperature during Burning.**—Light coloured bricks are often the result of the temperature of the gases in the kiln being too low, or the duration of the maximum temperature being too short, whilst, at the other end of the scale, Staffordshire blue bricks require a temperature which may reach 1 200° C.

(*c*) **Atmospheric Condition of Kiln.**—Certain white bricks can only be produced if they are protected in the kiln from smoke, whilst dark brown and purple coloured bricks are made by creating a smoky atmosphere in the kiln (see below).

(*d*) **Sand-moulding.**—Sand-moulded hand-made bricks (see p. 4) and pressed bricks which have sand sprinkled over their oiled surfaces whilst being moulded are richly coloured during the burning process. The nature of the sand used for this purpose depends upon that of the clay or shale, and a good deal of experimental work with different coloured sands is often necessary before the desired colour of the facing bricks is obtained.

(*e*) **Staining.**—Surface colours may be obtained by adding certain metallic oxides (such as manganese for browns, chromium for pinks, antimony for yellows, copper for greens, cobalt for blues, cobalt and manganese for blacks, etc.) which are crushed very finely and added to the sand sprinkled on the bricks prior to burning. Sometimes water is added to the oxides and brushed on the surfaces. Such colours, unlike those produced by blending (see above), are rarely permanent.

White bricks contain not more than a trace of iron and generally a large proportion of lime.

Cream bricks contain traces of iron and a small proportion of chalk.

Grey bricks are either commons which have been discoloured by scumming (see p. 14) or facing, such as *silver-greys*, which have been stained on the surface.

Buff bricks contain less than 2 per cent. of iron oxide.

Yellow bricks contain magnesia or sulphur (when clamp-burnt).

Red bricks contain at least 3 per cent. of iron oxide.

Brown and *purple* bricks may have a similar iron content to reds, but the difference in the colour is due to smoking and special firing.

Blue bricks contain 7 to 10 per cent. of iron oxide. A blue surface colour is also obtained by pouring coal-tar in the fireboxes of the down-draught kiln (or that of the firing chamber of a continuous kiln) just before the burning process has been completed. This produces a dense smoky atmosphere. The damper is partially closed. This is repeated three times at twenty-minute intervals, when the damper is closed and the chamber is left sealed for at least forty-eight hours. If salt is mixed with the tar the exposed surfaces of the stacked bricks will be glazed. Purple bricks may be produced in a similar manner.

Black bricks contain a similar amount of iron to the blue clay, in addition to certain manganese oxides. The iron, etc., content is responsible for the colour produced when the bricks are burnt. Black colour is also produced as described for blues, except that zinc and not tar is applied to the fires, and twenty-four hours' sealing of the chamber is usually sufficient.

Multi-coloured Bricks.—The diverse range of colours of these bricks is very largely due to (*b*) and (*c*)—see p. 12; the bricks are generally produced in a down-draught kiln (p. 6), as the temperature and smoking are best controlled in this type. The bricks are carefully stacked on *bed* to avoid damage, and so arranged that one end and one face of each is exposed. The kiln is fired as already described until the bricks have been subjected to the maximum temperature for a sufficient period, which varies according to the nature of the clay or shale. A *reducing atmosphere* is then produced in the kiln by restricting the admission of air to the kiln and heavily charging it with smoke. Thus the flue is partially closed by lowering the damper, and dense smoke is caused by charging the fireboxes with coal. Immediately the smoke has abated, more fuel is added to produce a dense smoky condition and, after these operations have been repeated over a period of approximately ten hours, the fireboxes and flue are closed for about four hours. The flue is then opened and the bricks are allowed to cool. Many variations in colour can be obtained in this manner, much depending upon the skill of the operator.

TEXTURE OF BRICKS

There is considerable variation in the texture (or surface finish) of bricks. Thus, machine-made commons and certain facings have smooth faces, whilst hand-made facings cannot be equalled for the richness of their texture; many machine-made bricks are characterized by roughened surfaces which have been purposely exaggerated. The pleasing texture of hand-made bricks is produced during the moulding operation, the hand-pressing of the clay or shale into the mould and the sand from the sides of the mould, which is stamped into the material, giving an irregular creasing or unevenness to the side and end surfaces. The fine colouring of a mass of brickwork constructed of such bricks, particularly after it has weathered for some time, is enhanced by the light and shade effect produced by the uneven surfaces. Such bricks are expensive, and therefore attempts have been made to imitate this texture and apply it to mechanically made bricks. Some of these attempts have been quite successful, even if the resulting texture is of less quality (chiefly because of the uniformity which results when the depressions or roughness are similar on every brick) than that of hand-made bricks.

The following are some of the means which are adopted to produce a mechanical texture :—

Wire-cut bricks are given a roughened appearance on three faces by a frame containing a horizontal and two vertical wires which is fixed about 25 mm in front of the mouthpiece of the auger (see p. 3). The horizontal wire is stretched across and just slightly below the top of the opening, and the distance between the two taut vertical wires is slightly less than the width of the die. These wires cut the band of clay as it is extruded from the machine, leaving roughened surfaces on the top and sides.

Rustication may also be obtained by plates containing fine projecting wires, one plate being fixed above and two at the sides of the clay column as it issues from the mouthpiece. The points of these wires slightly penetrate at varying depths the moving clay band and scratch the surfaces. Felt covered rollers partly smooth the excessive roughness as the column proceeds to the cutting table.

Hand or mechanical *stippling* is resorted to as an alternative. This consists of scrubbing or dabbing the top and sides of the clay band with brushes having metal bristles. Some of the irregularities are smoothed down by rollers.

A rustic effect can also be produced by *sand-blasting*. Specially selected sand is forced by compressed air through the nozzle of a pipe on to the top and sides of the extruded clay. This produces small depressions on the surface. Rustic pressed bricks can be treated in this manner.

Pressed bricks can be rusticated by using a mould or metal press-box having hinged sides. Relief (raised) patterns are engraved on the internal surfaces of these sides. Probably the most effective design is that resembling the bark of a tree. The collapsible sides are necessary to permit of the removal of the brick after the plunger has impressed the pattern on one or more faces as it consolidates the clay. The appearance of a wall is made more effective if bricks of several selected textures are built at random during its construction.

Rough sand-faced bricks, when wire-cut, are made by sprinkling sand (specially selected) through a sanding machine on to the clay band as it is being extruded. The sand is then passed in by top and side rollers.

Pressed sand-faced bricks are made by sanding the internal faces of the mould before being charged. Hand-made bricks are sand-faced during the normal process (see p. 4).

DEFECTS IN BRICKS

The following are the principal defects to which bricks are subjected :—

Black Core or Hearting.—This is fairly common in bricks made of red clays (p. 1) which have been heated too rapidly in the kiln, causing the surface to vitrify and the interior to remain black.

Bloating or Swelling.—This is attributed to the presence in the clay of an excess of carbonaceous matter and to bad burning.

Burring or Clinkering.—Clamp-burnt bricks, usually adjacent to the flues, which have been fused together by excessive heat are called *burrs* or *clinkers*. Such are only suitable for breaking up for coarse aggregate (see p. 28).

Chuffs or Shuffs.—These are badly cracked and mis-shapen bricks produced by rain falling on them when hot. They are useless.

Crazing is a defect common in glazed bricks (see p. 16) characterized by fine cracks. These are due to the glaze and the body (clay) not expanding and shrinking to the same extent.

Crozzling.—Excessive heating in the kiln may produce mis-shapen bricks known as *crozzles*. If not too badly shaped they may be used for brickwork below ground level, otherwise they are only suitable for aggregates.

Efflorescence.—Bricks made from clay containing a relatively large proportion of soluble salts, particularly calcium sulphate, are liable to become discoloured by the formation of a whitish deposit. Whilst this efflorescence or *salting* is particularly common to new brickwork, it may also form on the faces of old external walls which are subjected to excessive dampness. It is formed as follows : The salts are dissolved when water is absorbed, and as the bricks become dry the salt solution is brought to the surface by capillarity, evaporation takes place and the salts remain on the face. In mild cases the efflorescence gradually disappears as the brickwork is subjected to alternate wet and dry periods, the rain removing the deposit until the salts are gradually eliminated. If the bricks contain a high percentage of salts the efflorescence may persist over a long period, and where dampness is caused from defective rain-water pipes or the omission of a damp proof course, the unsightly appearance may continue until the defect or omission has been remedied. Crystallization of the salts may not occur on the outer surface of the bricks during evaporation but may take place just below the surface. This is called *crypto-florescence* and may result in the bursting off of the outer skin.

Portland cement mortar and certain lime mortars may cause efflorescence and affect the brickwork; soluble salts present in the soil, such as chlorides and nitrates, may also produce this condition when the ground water is absorbed.

Grizzling.—Common bricks, though of good shape, which are underburnt (indicated by a light colour and a dull sound when struck), and therefore weak, are called *grizzles*; only suitable for inferior internal partition walls when little strength is required.

Iron Spots.—These are surface dark spots, due to the presence of iron sulphide in the clay, which render the bricks unsuitable for facings.

Laminations are generally caused by the air in the voids between the particles of clay not being eliminated in the grinding, pugging, etc., processes, and producing the formation of thin laminæ on the faces of bricks which may scale off on exposure to the weather (see " de-airing," p. 3).

Lime Nodules.—Bricks containing pieces of limestone left uncrushed in the clay during its preparation are quite unsuited for external walls or internal walls which are to be plastered, as the lime will expand when water is absorbed, causing cracking or disintegration (see p. 1).

Scumming or Kiln-white.—This is an unsightly discoloration of bricks, particularly those containing lime and iron sulphide, which have been fired in a continuous kiln. Several causes contribute to this condition, but it is chiefly due to the hot gases from the firing chambers (which contain sulphur) coming in contact with the damp bricks in the early drying chambers, and producing a thin brownish-white or grey film (usually sulphate of lime) on the surface. Such bricks are only suitable for commons. Scum is prevented if provision is made for the escape of steam in the drying zone of the kiln (p. 7) and if clean hot air is only used to dry the bricks. Barium carbonate powder or barium hydroxide is sometimes mixed with the clay before moulding to prevent scum formation. The carbonate in a fine powder form may be added to the clay before it enters the auger or pug mill, or, as is usual, it may be mixed with water and the solution thoroughly incorporated with the clay.

Distortion may be produced by overburning. Badly worn auger mouth-pieces and press moulds will cause the bricks to be badly shaped. Cracking may be caused by drying and cooling the bricks too quickly in the kiln. Careless handling of green bricks during manufacture will cause damage. Chipped, cracked and broken bricks, especially if underburnt, are common results of improper handling in course of transit.

Terms which are gradually falling into disuse include *place bricks* (similar to grizzles, see above) and *shippers* (sound but imperfectly shaped bricks used as ships' ballast).

These have been referred to in Chap. I, Vol. I. Good bricks should be thoroughly burnt, as most well-burnt bricks are durable and capable of withstanding relatively heavy loads. As adequate firing in the kiln tends to eliminate any soluble salts in bricks, it follows that hard-fired bricks are relatively free from defects such as efflorescence and crypto-florescence (see adjacent column). Conversely, underburnt bricks (usually denoted by an abnormal light colour and a dull sound when struck together) are comparatively soft, easily broken, are neither durable nor pressure-resistant (see p. 15), and are liable to defects produced by salts.

Good bricks should be free from the defects enumerated above and, if used as facings, should conform to one or other of the colours and textures mentioned on pp. 12 and 13.

Permeability.—Bricks for external use must be capable of preventing rain-water from passing through them to the inside of walls of reasonable thickness. In this connection the practice of specifying the maximum amount of water a brick shall absorb (usually " one-seventh of its own weight of water after twenty-four hours' immersion ") is not now considered desirable, for it does not follow that a brick is impermeable if it has a relatively small absorption. Much depends upon the character of the pores.

Some pores are continuous from face to face, and therefore rain-water readily passes through them to the inside, whilst other pores or cavities are not interconnected but are entirely enclosed by material, and do not affect permeability. A close-pored brick will freely absorb water which will not readily evaporate. But a brick which is more open-pored will absorb less moisture, which will evaporate more easily because of the increased air circulation; it follows that such a brick (provided any connected pores are not too large as to allow the water to be blown through them) is more successful in preventing dampness on the inside.[1]

Further, it is difficult to lay certain dense and smooth-faced bricks owing to their lack of " suction," which prevents a ready adherence of the mortar. This lack of adhesion causes narrow fissures to appear between the bricks and the mortar joints. The result is that water penetrates through these cracks, and much dampness in solid brick walls is due to this course, even though the bricks may be impermeable (see p. 42). Hence, bricks should be porous to a certain extent, the pores being neither too fine nor too open, to permit strong adhesion of the mortar. Incidentally, even if the joints are well filled with mortar, especially if it is a rich mix (see p. 25), fine hair-like cracks may develop, when the mortar shrinks on drying, through which water will readily pass to the inside.

Permeability Test.—A simple apparatus used for measuring the rate of absorption of water consists of a flat pyramidally shaped brass cover which is fitted over the brick (or other) specimen, which is usually 100 mm square; a short length of vertical glass tubing, with its lower end fixed to the cover, is fitted to a fine bored glass tube (having a scale behind it) which is fixed horizontally at 200 mm above the top surface of the specimen; a rubber pipe from a glass cylinder containing water is connected to the vertical tube; the vertical faces of the specimen are waxed and thus made

---

[1] Briefly the distinction between absorption, permeability and porosity is as follows :—
Absorption is the property of allowing water to enter a material.
Permeability is the property of allowing water to pass through a material.
Porosity is the proportion of void space in a material.

impermeable. Water from the cylinder is admitted to occupy the space between the top of the specimen and the under side of the cover and to fill both vertical and horizontal tubes; the water is then shut off. As the water passes through the specimen, it flows along the horizontal tube; this rate of flow is obtained by observing the end (or meniscus) of the water and measuring from the scale the distance this travels in a given time. The 200 mm head of water gives a pressure in excess of that caused by a very strong force of wind against a wall down which rain is pouring (see also p. 108).

Strength.—It is only necessary to specify the strength of bricks when they are required for the construction of walls, piers etc., which have to support heavy concentrated loads. The reason for this is that the compressive strength of brickwork constructed of relatively inferior bricks will be quite adequate to resist the normal weight which it will be required to support. Thus, whilst the brickwork at the ground level of a two-storied house will not usually be subjected to a greater load than 134 kN/m², it would be a very poor brick which had a crushing strength of less than 6 435 kN/m². The average crushing strength of bricks serves as an approximate index only of the compressive strength of brickwork, as much depends upon workmanship, height in relation to thickness, etc. A rough approximation of the strength of brickwork built in cement mortar (1 : 3) and good hydraulic lime mortar (1 : 3) is respectively one-third and one-fifth that of the individual bricks.

The crushing strength of bricks is determined in a compression machine such as that shown at E, Fig. 9 (see p. 32). A brick is usually tested on bed and placed in the machine between two pieces of plywood, any frogs being filled flush with cement mortar. The compressive strength varies enormously between batches from the same kiln and even of individual bricks from the same burning. As an illustration of this, tests carried out in the Building Laboratory of the Manchester University Institute of Science and Technology on six bricks obtained from a kiln at the same time showed the crushing strength to vary between 10 MN/m² and 16·6 MN/m². This variation is partly due to the different position of the bricks in the kiln. It is because of this variation that at least six (preferably twelve) specimens of a brick should be tested and the mean figure taken.

This variation is also shown by the following figures in brackets which indicate the approximate crushing strengths of specimen wire-cut pressed and hand-made bricks (six of each type) from well known and reputable manufacturers : Wire-cut commons and facings (12·4 to 34·4 MN/m²), pressed commons and facings (17·2 to 41·3 MN/m²) and hand-made facings (13·8 to 34·4 MN/m²). Engineering bricks (see p. 17) have crushing strengths varying from 55 to 124 MN/m².

Frost Action.—External walls constructed of porous underburnt bricks are particularly vulnerable to damage by the action of frost. Such damage is due to the absorbed water expanding (to about one-eleventh of its volume) as it freezes and exerting pressure on the pore walls which the comparatively soft material is unable to resist. Disintegration thus results, and when this is repeated during severe winters, disfigurement due to pitting and cracking of the surface and damaged arrises may become very pronounced. Brickwork of poor quality bricks with overhand struck joints (see Chap. I, Vol. I), that below the ground level, and copings are particularly subject to damage by frost. It does not affect brickwork of sound, hard-burnt bricks.

Frost Resistance Test.—A simple, but effective, apparatus in which bricks and other building materials may be tested for frost resistance is shown in Fig. 39 and described on p. 110. This test can also be carried out in a watertight metal container which is partly filled with a freezing mixture consisting of 2 parts ice and 1 part common salt. The brick to be tested, after being immersed in water for twenty-four hours, is wrapped in a piece of cloth, totally immersed in the mixture, the lid is shut and the container is placed in a box so that it is encased by a 75 mm thickness of cork, sawdust or similar insulating material. After being frozen at −10° C. for eighteen hours the specimen is removed, thawed by running water, unwrapped and examined. The freezing and thawing cycle is repeated for at least ten times. Certain bricks, well known for their durable qualities, are not affected even if subjected to forty freezings, whilst others, only suitable for internal work, will show serious disintegration after ten freezings. This apparatus does not give such good results as that illustrated in Fig. 39, as the immersion of the specimens in the freezing mixture appears to improve their resistance to frost action on account of their impregnation with salt.

A good test, but one which does not give immediate results, consists of digging a hole and placing in it two bricks on end, one above the other, with the upper brick half exposed. These are left for a year. In a normal winter successive frosts will cause a poor brick to crack across at ground level, whilst the lower one may show signs of flaking. Sound bricks will not be affected.

Efflorescence Test.—A brick is partially immersed on end *in* a dish of distilled water, and the water absorbed is evaporated from its upper surfaces. Any salts liable to form efflorescence are brought to the surface by the water in its passage through the brick.

CLASSIFICATION OF BRICKS

Bricks may be classified according to (1) quality and (2) usage.

1. **Classification according to Quality.**—Bricks from a kiln are divided into three classes, namely : (*a*) *firsts*, which are best and are selected by hand; (*b*) *seconds*, which are selected bricks but are not equal to " firsts " on account of some imperfection in regard to colour or shape or both; (*c*) *thirds*, which are the remainder of the kiln, the best being only suitable for interior work.

2. **Classification according to Usage.**—A conveniently broad division of bricks is in accordance with their suitability for (*a*) interior purposes, (*b*) exterior purposes, (*c*) pressure-resisting purposes and (*d*) fire-resisting purposes.

(*a*) *Bricks for Interior Purposes.*—Common bricks are invariably specified for internal walls, as neither strength, durability nor appearance are important.

If the walls are to be plastered it is essential (especially if the bricks have a large suction capacity) that the walls shall be copiously watered before the first coat is applied, otherwise an excessive amount of water will be absorbed from the plaster and this may cause failure. It is also important that the bricks shall not contain nodules of lime (see pp. 1 and 14), as the water applied to walls prior to plastering will be absorbed, causing the lime to slake and the resultant expansion to crack or splinter the bricks.

It is essential that certain brick partition walls, particularly those on upper floors, shall be as light as possible, and perforated or hollow bricks or blocks (see U, V, W and Y, Fig. 5) are suitable for this purpose.

Sometimes facing bricks, and not commons, are required for internal walls, such as those for churches, corridors, class-rooms, etc. Light-coloured bricks, such as " silver-greys " (p. 12) and sand-lime bricks (p. 17) are used for such purposes on account of their satisfactory light-reflecting qualities. White, etc., glazed bricks (see next column) are also used for internal walls of dairies, factories, lavatories, etc.

(9) *Bricks for Exterior Purposes.*—The essential requirements of facing bricks are durability, colour, texture and freedom from defects. Colour and texture are not important if the walls are to be rough-casted or plastered, good quality commons being sufficient for this purpose. They should have sufficient suction capacity to ensure the thorough adhesion of the mortar (see p. 14). The crushing strength is not material unless heavy loads have to be supported, as any durable brick will safely support the load which has to be normally resisted. Bricks to be used below the horizontal damp proof course should be carefully selected, as these are subjected to the greatest frost action (p. 15), and absorption of certain salts from the soil may cause deterioration if the bricks are not durable.

(c) *Bricks for Pressure-resisting Purposes.*—These are required for the construction of piers, large-spanned arches, etc., where large stresses have to be resisted. Strength is therefore the chief requirement, and engineering bricks (p. 17) which are very strong and hard burnt are most suited for this purpose.

(d) *Bricks for Fire-resisting Purposes.*—Those best suited to resist high temperatures, as for lining furnaces, chimney stacks, boilers, etc., are fireclay, silica, ganister, bauxite and magnesite bricks (see below).

The following is a summary of several types of bricks which have not been already described :—

Firebricks.—These are capable of resisting very high temperatures and are used for lining fireplaces, tall chimneys, furnaces, gas retorts, etc. They are made from (a) fireclay, (b) silica rocks and (c) silica rocks together with *ganister.*

(a) *Fireclay Bricks.*—Fireclays or refractory clays are associated with coalfields, and are usually obtained by mining as distinct from quarrying. They are found in many parts of the country. The clay contains from 55 to 75 per cent. silica and 22 to 35 per cent. alumina.

The fireclay is crushed and finely ground. Grog (finely ground burnt fireclay) is often mixed with the material to reduce shrinkage. The mixture is then soured to increase its workability (p. 4), moulded (pressed), dried and hard burnt for about seven days. The maximum temperature for firing first-class bricks should not be less than 1 500° C. The bricks are of a cream or buff colour.

(b) *Silica Bricks.*—These contain 95 to 97 per cent. of silica and 1 to 2 per cent. lime. The rock is crushed by heavy rollers, then ground in a pan mill in which the lime is added in correct proportion and in liquid form; the lime acts as a binding material. Powerful presses are used to mould the bricks and the burning takes place in kilns of either the down-draught, chamber (similar to the zigzag) or tunnel type. Good siliac bricks should resist a minimum temperature of 1 300° C. They are very brittle. Well-known silica bricks are produced in South Wales (from the Dinas rock, quarried near Swansea) and they are particularly suited for the lining of metallurgical furnaces and coke ovens.

(c) *Ganister Bricks.*—Ganister is a dark-coloured sandstone containing up to 10 per cent. of clay. It is quarried in this country (Sheffield being an important centre), Wales and Scotland. Their manufacture is similar to that of silica bricks They are very refractory, as they are capable of withstanding a temperature of 1 800° C., and are therefore particularly suited for lining furnaces, etc.

Bauxite Bricks (made from an aluminous earth imported from France), **Magnesite Bricks and Chromite Bricks** (both also made from imported material) are other highly refractory products. They are used for lining special furnaces, such as steel and blast furnaces and cement kilns, and are generally gas-fired.

Rubbers or Cutters are soft red (chiefly), white or buff coloured bricks, consisting of washed loamy clay containing a large proportion of sand, and are usually hand-made in a box-mould (p. 4) and baked (not burnt) in a kiln. The colour is uniform throughout, and owing to their softness and fine-grained texture they are easily cut, rubbed and carved. They are used principally for gauged arches, decorated quoins and jambs.

Glazed Bricks.—Fireclays or shales are best for producing glazed bricks. As they are usually required to be built with joints not exceeding 3 mm thick, they must be true to shape, with fine straight arrises. They are therefore carefully pressed and sometimes re-pressed, with the arrises hand-trimmed with a strike. Glazed bricks are impervious and are of two kinds, namely : (1) salt-glazed and (2) enamelled.

1. *Salt-glazed Bricks* are usually produced in a down-draught kiln.[1] Salt is thrown on the the fires of the kiln after the bricks have reached a temperature of about 1 200° C. The heat vaporizes the salt and causes it to combine with the clay to form a vitreous or glassy surface which cannot scale off. Usually two, and not more than three, charges of salt are applied at about twenty-minute intervals when the bricks have reached the required temperature, a shovelful of salt being thrown on to each fire. The colour of the glazed surfaces is a brown of various shades. Such bricks are used for internal dadoes, lavatories, basements, areas, large brick sewers, inspection chambers, etc.

2. *Enamelled Bricks.*—These are now obtainable in a large variety of colours. There are two methods of producing these, namely : (a) dry-dripped and (b) wet-dripped.

(a) *Dry-dipped Process.*—These enamelled bricks are called *biscuit-ware.* They are moulded, dried, burnt to a temperature of approximately 1 200° C. (this is called *biscuit-burning*), cooled, prepared for glazing, coloured, glazed and re-burnt. The colouring, glazing and preparation (called *bodying*) are done on a bench in a shed. At least three vessels containing liquid or *slurry* of varying consistency are placed on the bench. The first vessel contains the *slip* or *engobe* or *body*, and is a mixture of china clay (which is slightly plastic and found in Cornwall, Devon and Dorset), crushed burnt flints, ball clay (more plastic than china clay), etc., and water. The second tub contains a similar mixture with the addition of metallic oxides (such as those stated on p. 12) to give the required colour. The liquid in the third vessel is called the *glaze*, and this is a mixture of china clay, felspar (a silicate of alumina with varying proportions of sodium, potassium, etc.), whiting and water. The proportions of the ingredients vary considerably. More than one tub containing colouring bodies are sometimes required to give the desired colour, the ingredients and proportions being determined as a result of experience and exhaustive tests. The bricks are first washed, one stretcher or one header face (or both) being hand-brushed with water. Each brick is then separately treated, the washed face(s) being hand-dipped into the slip, then into the colouring solution and finally into the glaze. After the edges have been trimmed with a wire brush to remove the surplus glaze, the bricks are very carefully stacked in the kiln and burnt to fuse the glaze. Thus, these bricks are subjected to two separate burnings. Coal and gas are the fuels used, gas kilns being most successful for this class of bricks.

(b) *Wet-dipped Process.*—The slip, colouring solution and glaze are applied direct to the bricks immediately after they have been moulded and dried. They are afterwards very carefully burnt. Whilst this is a cheaper method than (a), only one burning being required, the results are not so good and there is a large proportion damaged during the handling operations. Such bricks are only suitable for inferior work.

Glazed bricks, especially biscuit-ware, are used for first-class faced work as required for factories, dairies, certain shops, abattoirs, corridors, dadoes of classrooms, lavatories, areas, wells of large buildings, external facings, etc. The surfaces can readily be washed down, and white glazed bricks are particularly effective in areas of buildings and in places where the maximum reflected light is required.

Perforated Bricks.—Perforated bricks, such as is shown at U, Fig. 5, are made by the wire-cut process (p. 3), the small holes of varying diameter (9 to 20 mm) being formed as the clay column is extruded through the mouthpiece in which short horizontal bars are fixed. The advantages claimed for these bricks are : A saving

---

[1] Tunnel kilns are also used for this purpose.

in clay results, the drying and burning processes are facilitated, resulting in a reduction of fuel, thay are light to handle (the perforations reducing the weight by about one-fifth) and because of this comparative lightness the cost of carriage is reduced. Several forms of perforated bricks are used in *reinforced brickwork* (see p. 44). Additional mortar may be required for the bed joints, especially if the holes are large.

Air Bricks.—If of standard size, the green bricks are machine made in the usual manner (pressed or wire-cut), otherwise they are hand-made in a box-mould (p. 4). Each slab is then perforated thus : A templet of thin zinc, the size and shape of the bed and perforated as required, is placed on top of the slab (which usually has an oiled surface) laid on bed, fine sand is dusted over it, the templet is removed, leaving a light-coloured pattern of sandy squares on the surface. These serve as a guide for the moulder who takes a hollow steel tool, square in section and having sharp cutting edges, and presses it through the slab at each square of the pattern. The tool is withdrawn, and the clay within is removed by passing a solid metal rod down it. The section is similar to U, Fig. 32, Vol. I. Cheaper air bricks, having thin perforated panels, are stamped by a press.

Hollow, Cellular or Cavity Bricks (see V and W, Fig. 5).—The cellular type has 19 to 25 mm thick " walls " or " skins " with two or more " webs " or " diaphragms." They are light and are therefore suitable for partitions; their cavities also reduce heat transmission. They are machine pressed, the plunger, having solid metal cores, forming the cavities as they descend. These bricks are sometimes glazed and are often made of fireclay.

V Bricks (see A′ to E′, Fig. 5).—Developed by the Building Research Station these produce a wall which is equivalent to a 275 mm cavity wall (see p. 39) but which is only 215 mm wide. The brick (A′) incorporates a " cavity " bridged by four thin diaphragms which do not impair the weather resistance of the wall. The perforations amount to about 50 per cent. of the volume of the brick and so give good thermal insulation. The 215 mm cavity wall produced by these bricks can be built about 30 per cent. faster the the normal 275 mm cavity wall.

One V brick corresponds in volume to two standard bricks and weighs about 3·9 kg in comparison with the weight of one standard brick of 3·2 kg; it can be easily lifted by the bricklayer because the two outer large perforations form convenient handholes.

In laying V bricks mortar is spread along the two outer parts of the bed over the area of the small perforations; the bricks are thus laid on two *separate* strips of mortar, care being taken to prevent mortar from entering the centre handholes. This divided mortar joint is best made by using a special tray, alternatively a batten 75 mm wide and 16 mm thick is placed along the centre of the wall the mortar being spread either side of the batten. When the bricks are bedded on the strips some of the mortar is pressed into the small perforations to give a strong key and produce the normal 10 mm thick bed joint.

A special perforated brick (B′) is used with the V bricks at jambs and quoins as shown at C′ and D′. The concrete strip foundation (E′) need only be 430 mm wide (instead of about 510 mm for a 275 mm cavity wall). On this and up to d.p.c. level 215 mm standard bricks are used for the wall; at this level one course of split V bricks, the brick being split and diaphragms removed, is laid which allows the placing of the stepped d.p.c.

Hollow Blocks (see Y, Fig. 5).—These are used in the construction of partitions. Somewhat similar blocks are employed in the construction of fire-resisting floors.[1]

They are usually made of fireclays or shales by the wire-cut process (p. 3). The shape of the blocks depends upon the special provision made in the mouthpiece of the auger, and there are several patent devices for forming the hollows. One of the simplest consists of a strong thin metal frame which projects into the die from the front and two solid horizontal metal cores or bars which are secured to it. As the clay is pushed through the die, the cores produce two voids in the extruded column. At the same time any grooves in the sides are formed by projecting ribs of the sides of the die. The extruded column is passed to the cutting table, the frame being pivoted to cause the wires to cut it into the required lengths by a downward movement.

---

[1] Detailed in Vol. IV.

Some hollow blocks are solid-ended. One device fixed in the die to produce such blocks consists of a square shutter (the size of the cross-section of the void) which is fitted to the top and caused to descend and rise automatically at required intervals. When the shutter is down it occupies a central position in the die, and this produces the hollow portion of the column as it proceeds. When the shutter rises clear of the die, the section of the moving clay band is solid. Thus a column is produced which is hollow, having solid partitions at intervals, the thickness of the latter being equal to twice the finished thickness of an end. The column is then cut at the table, the wires being drawn centrally down through these solid portions. Drying and burning complete the process.

Pavings are very hard-wearing bricks used, as implied, for paving roads and paths. They are sometimes salt-glazed, each with one face roughened or chequered to increase the foothold. They are laid on edge on a concrete bed with a 13 mm bed joint of cement and sand (1 : 2) and the vertical joints, 2 mm thick, are grouted with cement and sand (1:1½). These bricks are now very rarely used.

Engineering Bricks.—These are exceptionally strong and durable, and are used for piers, bridges, sewers and similar engineering purposes. Those most noteworthy are Accringtons (pressed), Southwaters (pressed and wire-cuts), blue Staffordshires (wire-cuts and hand-made) and Hunzikers (made of crushed flint and lime).

Sand-Lime Bricks.—These are of the same size as ordinary clay bricks and are made of a mixture of sand, lime and water which is pressed into moulds and hardened. Their colour is grey or a dull white, although oxide pigments may be added to give other colours. The sand should be clean and well graded, and the normal proportion used varies from 92 to 95 per cent. of the dry mix. The 5 to 8 per cent. of lime which is mixed with the sand may be of any class, provided it can be thoroughly well slaked. It must be properly burnt (see p. 19) as overburnt lime does not readily slake and underburnt lime has a high calcium carbonate content which is valueless. The slaking or hydration must be complete before the mixture is pressed.

There are three stages in their production, namely : (*a*) mixing, (*b*) pressing and (*c*) hardening.

(*a*) *Mixing.*—The burnt lime (quicklime) is finely ground in a ball mill (p. 22) and passed through a sieve to eliminate coarse-grained particles. This is mixed with and in the correct proportion in an edge-runner (p. 2) and slightly more than the required amount of water added to slake the lime. The mixture is passed to a hopper or silo and left for a variable period (generally twenty-four hours) to ensure through hydration.

(*b*) *Pressing.*—The rotary table type of press (p. 3) is generally used, a measured quantity of the material being fed, pressed into a slab and removed. The pressure varies with the water content and must be sufficient to enable the bricks to be handled without damage.

(*c*) *Hardening or Autoclaving.*—A " kiln " in which the bricks are hardened is a 1·7 to 2·1 m diameter steel cylinder, varying from 9 to 21 m long, and is called an *autoclave.* The pressed bricks are stacked on cars (similar to those used in tunnel kilns, see p. 10), each truck taking up to 1 500 bricks. The loaded cars are run into the autoclave, the tight-fitting doors are closed, steam is admitted and the pressure gradually increased. The maximum steam pressure varies with the length of time at which it is steadily maintained, the greater the pressure the shorter the time of autoclaving; thus, if a steady pressure of 827 kN/m² is applied, the period varies from eight to twelve hours, whilst this time may be halved if the pressure is increased to 1 380 kN/m². After steaming for the required period the supply of steam is shut off and the bricks allowed to cool by opening a valve. The loaded cars are then removed.

Sand-lime bricks are of uniform colour, texture, size and shape, with square arrises. Their fine texture renders them suitable for carving, and figures carved *in situ* on the brickwork have successfully relieved the somewhat monotonous appearance of large uniformly coloured surfaces.

Although these bricks have not been subjected to prolonged tests, it is considered that those of best quality compare favourably with good quality common bricks as regards compression strength and durability. They are only moderately resistant to frost action and are therefore not suitable for brickwork below ground in water-logged sites. They have been used successfully as a cheap substitute for white glazed bricks in wells of buildings and similar positions where maximum light is required.

Cement and Concrete Bricks.—Portland cement is used to a relatively small extent in the making of bricks. Sand as a fine aggregate is added to the cement in varying proportions, suitable mixes being 1 part cement to 6 to 8 parts graded sand. The materials are well mixed in a machine, just sufficient water being added to ensure adhesion. The mixture is then pressed in moulds or in a rotary table machine, removed and dried slowly for at least a fortnight (preferably a month) before being used. The bricks are covered with damp cloths during the maturing period. Rapid-hardening cement (p. 24) in lieu of ordinary Portland cement expedites the setting period.

Concrete Blocks of various sizes and mixes are also made, the aggregates being sand, broken brick, broken stone, gravel coke breeze, etc. (see p. 28).

Cement and concrete bricks or blocks have not become popular in this country, chiefly on account of their dull, uninteresting appearance, although concrete slabs are often employed in the construction of internal partitions, (Chap. I, Vol. III).

Breeze Slabs of various sizes (usually 50 to 75 mm thick) and consisting of 1 part cement to 6 or 8 parts powdered breeze have been extensively used for partitions in positions where loads have not to be supported (p. 15). These are cast in wood moulds. Cavity walls (p. 39) are sometimes constructed of breeze slabs which are approximately 900 mm by 300 mm by 65 mm thick, placed on edge between reinforced concrete pillars.

Special Shaped Bricks.—A selection of special shaped bricks, most of which are standard, is shown in Fig. 5. They are kept in stock by the larger brick manufacturers, and are chiefly made by machinery (pressed or wire-cut). This results in a reduction in cost, as non-standard bricks can only be purposely made by hand in moulds which have to be constructed to the specified requirements. The increased availability of standard specials has also resulted in a saving of time of the bricklayer which was formerly occupied in cutting the bricks to shape.

Squint Bricks (see A, B, C and D, Fig. 5).—These are used in the construction of acute and obtuse squint quoins (see p. 36).

Bullnose Bricks.—A double bullnose brick is shown at Q, Fig. 2, Vol. I. It is difficult to cut neatly a mitre at the intersection between two bullnose arrises; special *returns* containing mitres are therefore useful. That at E, Fig. 5 shows an internal return; similar right and left handed returns on bed, edge and end are also available. An external return is shown at F. A *stop* is required to provide a satisfactory finish when a bullnose edge is continued by a square arris, as at the base of a pier or jamb; a double stop is shown at G; single stops are also made. That shown at H, sometimes called a *cownose*, is suitable for copings and jambs of 102·5 mm walls.

Dog-leg or Angle Bricks (see J).—These are also used at squint quoins, particularly of cavity walls (see E, Fig. 11).

Birdsmouth Bricks (see K, Fig. 5).—These may be used at alternate courses of internal squint quoins or for decorated serrated courses.

Circular Bricks (see stretcher L and header M).—These are used for circular work as in the construction of bay windows (see Figs. 15 and 29), apsed ends, staircase wells and tall chimneys. These are referred to on p. 44.

Coping Bricks.—A few standard shapes are shown at N, O and P. Bullnose bricks are used for the same purpose.

Pistol Bricks (see Q).—These are used for forming circular or coved angles between walls or between a wall and a floor.

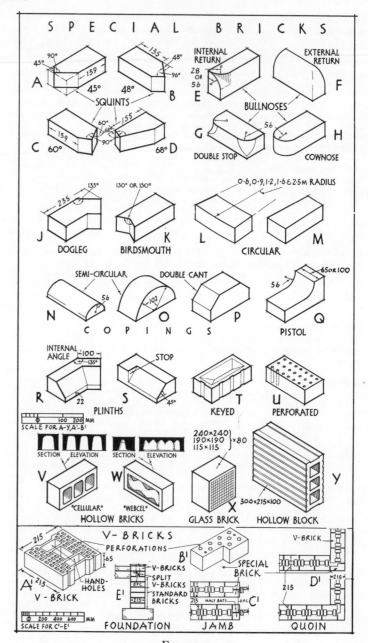

FIGURE 5

Plinth Bricks.—These are referred to in Chap. I, Vol. I. A dogleg internal angle plinth is shown at R, Fig 5 and a stop is shown at S. Right and left handed plinth internal returns, like the bullnose brick E, and external angles are also obtainable from stock.

Keyed or Nicked Bricks.—The type shown at T, manufactured by the London Brick Co. Ltd., has dovetailed grooves formed on one stretcher and one header face for the purpose of providing a mechanical bond with either plaster or roughcast which may be applied to the brickwork. They are obtainable as commons, as shown, or as cellulars (see V).

Perforated Bricks (see U and B').—These have small holes 10 to 16 mm in diameter) formed throughout their thickness, the object of which is to reduce their weight (pp. 15 and 16).

Hollow Bricks.—These are made of clay formed with one or more cavities which reduce their weight some 25 per cent. and increase insulation against heat and moisture (see p. 17). The cellular type V, made by the above firm, has three cells separated by tapered webs; these cells are open to one bed and extend to within about 6 mm from that opposite. The "Webcel," type W, manufactured by the Marston Valley Brick Co. Ltd., has a single void, shaped as shown. These bricks are laid with their solid beds uppermost and are particularly effective in the construction of partition walls.

Hollow Blocks.—One of several types of walling blocks is shown at Y. The thickness varies from 13 to 215 mm. Some have only two cells, whilst another type having a central web has ten cells. They are used for partitions; the fluted sides and beds provide a good key for the plaster, and the cells reduce the transmission of sound and heat, besides decreasing their weight (p. 17).

Glass Bricks (see X).—There are two types, *i.e.*, solid cast blocks of glass and hollow glass blocks, the latter being made in two halves before being joined and hermetically sealed. They are not capable of resisting heavy loads, but they can be built into panels to any practical height, and are being used to form semi-transparent walls and partitions to steel framed buildings, etc. (see Chap. I, Vol. III). The bricks are bedded and jointed with lime mortar like clay bricks, they are not usually bonded, the vertical joints being continuous. The mortar recommended consists of 1 part lime, 1 part Portland cement and 4 parts sand. Panels exceeding 1·8 m in width should be reinforced with hoop iron or expanded metal (see p. 44) at every third to fifth course; vertical rod reinforcement is necessary if the panels exceed 6 m in width. Provision must also be made for expansion at the sides and tops of panels. The bricks are made in various sizes and patterns, the largest size being 240 mm by 240 mm by 80 mm.

LIME

Manufacture.—Lime is produced by burning chalk or limestones in a kiln. There are two types of kiln, *i.e.*, (1) intermittent and (2) continuous.

1. *Intermittent Kiln.*—This is the simplest form of kiln and is one which is

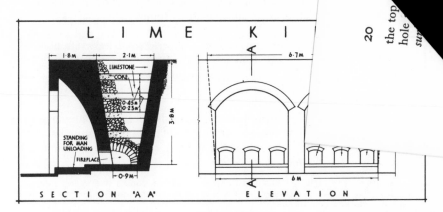

FIGURE 6

in use in many parts of the country. That shown in Fig. 6 is one of several kilns in which lime used extensively in the North of England is produced. The kiln is situated at the side of a cutting (often the face of the quarry); the four walls are tapered and are lined with firebrick; it is open at the top. A loosely built rough arch of pieces of the unburnt limestone is formed at the bottom, and this supports alternate 450 mm thick layers of limestone and 230 mm thick layers of fuel (25 to 40 mm coke nuts). Both the limestone and coke are charged into the kiln from side-tipping tubs which operate on a track on each side and at the top of the kiln. A coal fire is started in the fireplace below the arch and it gradually extends to the layers of fuel and limestone until the whole mass is brought to a bright red heat (900° C.). The period of burning is about four days. The burnt lime is then removed through the *eyes*, after which the kiln is again charged. The cover provided by the arched portion at the front of the kiln affords an adequate protection to the freshly burnt lime as it is withdrawn, and the top is generally protected by an open roof. The capacity of this kiln is about 20 320 kg of limestone and 8 128 kg of coke.

Lime produced in this manner is used for mortar.

Sometimes this form of kiln is charged wholly with pieces of limestone, and the fire is maintained at the bottom for a few days until the whole of the limestone or chalk has been thoroughly burnt. This is commonly known as a *flare kiln* and produces a white lime, free from discoloration and especially suitable for plastering.

2. *Continuous Kiln.*—The simplest form of continuous kiln is the *draw* or *tunnel kiln*. This is a brick structure, firebrick lined, in the form of an inverted truncated cone, about 4·9 m high, 2·4 m diameter at the top and 1·2 m diameter at the base, having a fireplace with grating at the bottom. It is charged with alternate layers of limestone and coal or coke. The process is continuous, the burnt lime being withdrawn at the base, and raw limestone and fuel added at

Some tunnel kilns have the lower half below ground, from the draw at the base of which is an inclined shaft or tunnel. Such are known as *k draw* or *tunnel kilns.*

Another form of continuous kiln consists of a steel cylindrical shaft, firebrick lined, some 15 m high and 2·5 m diameter, with several furnaces at the base, and so designed that only the hot gases come into contact with the limestone. Such kilns are economical in fuel consumption, and the lime which is withdrawn at suitable intervals is free from discoloration.

The Hoffman kiln, described on p. 10, is another form of continuous kiln used for burning lime and is suitable for the production of large supplies. The following is a brief description of such a kiln which has been in continuous use since the end of the nineteenth century[1].

It has twenty-eight firebrick lined chambers, each having a wicket and a damper controlled flue which is connected to the main horizontal flue leading to a central chimney stack. The kiln has no permanent partitions.

Two sections of the kiln, each of ten chambers, are drying, burning and cooling at the same time, and there is a gap of four chambers between each section to permit of stacking, unloading and the carrying out of repairs. A party of men is constantly removing the cool burnt lime from the front of each section, whilst another gang is stacking the limestone at the back of each section. Like the brick kiln of this type, the sequence of operations is advanced by a chamber each day, and thus, as there are two sections, the equivalent to two chambers is being unloaded and two loaded daily. The limestone is stacked, with horizontal flues parallel to the length of the kiln formed at the base, and vertical flues formed under the feed-holes provided at the top. Coal slack is the fuel used, and this is fed to the line which is being subjected to the maximum temperature. The wickets to the drying and burning chambers are sealed with half-brick thick walls daubed over with grouted lime, and the face of the last stacked chamber in each section is covered with brown paper to exclude draught from the open wickets in front. Lightly burnt lime suitable for building purposes (mortars and plasters) is obtained at normal temperatures of 1 100° to 1 200° C. in the firing chambers, but proximity to the flues and longer heating periods produce a proportion of more solidly burnt lime suitable for the preparation of caustic soda. Whilst unloading the burnt lime, it is hand-picked, selected and graded, the lightly burnt being white in colour and the hard-fired or overburnt being dark coloured.

Slaking, Setting and Hardening of Lime.—Pure limestone or chalk is composed of carbonate of lime ($CaCO_3$). When this is heated in a kiln it yields calcium oxide (CaO) or *quicklime* and carbon dioxide (CO_2) which is driven off.

When the quicklime is *slaked* by the addition of water heat is evolved, and the lime expands and falls to powder. If just sufficient water is added to accomplish this action, the powder is dry and is called *hydrated lime* (see p. 21). This slaked or hydrated lime is calcium hydroxide ($Ca(OH)_2$), the action of slaking being expressed by the equation $CaO + H_2O = Ca(OH)_2$. If more water is added to the slaked lime it does not chemically combine with the lime but reduces it to a paste known as *lime putty.*

On lime putty being exposed to the atmosphere, it begins to set and gradually hardens to form carbonate of lime as the water evaporates and carbon dioxide is absorbed from the air. *This is known as " carbonation," and is an*

[1] At the Buxton Limeworks of Messrs Imperial Chemical Industries Ltd.

important property, as the hardness of certain lime mortars is dependent upon it. The chemical action which takes place on carbonation is represented by the equation $Ca(OH)_2 + CO_2 = CaCO_3 + H_2O$ (which is evaporated).

The slaking of hydraulic limes is referred to on page 21.

Classification.—The composition of various limestones differs considerably, and thus there are a number of different kinds of limes each having characteristic properties which influence the purposes for which they are used. This is one of several classifications[1] of lime : (1) Pure, Fat, White or Rich; (2) Lean, Poor, Grey Chalk or Stone; (3) Hydraulic or Blue Lias; and (4) Magnesian. The schedule below shows an approximate analysis of a typical specimen of each of these varieties.

1. *Pure, Fat, White or Rich Lime* contains less than 5 per cent. of impurities such as silica and alumina (in form of clay). In the analysis the specimen is shown consisting almost entirely of calcium oxide. It slakes rapidly, evolves much heat, and expands from two or three times its original bulk during the process, has a high degree of plasticity (hence the name " fat "), is slow setting and very slow in hardening. This stiffening up can only occur when the lime is in contact with the air (see preceding column). Whilst pure lime, which is white in colour, is extensively used for plastering, it is not so suitable for lime mortar on account of its slow-hardening characteristic and lack of strength (unless gauged with cement, see p. 27).

	Pure	Lean	Hydraulic	Magnesian
Calcium (CaO) . .	93·0	82·0	67·0	57·22
Magnesium oxide (MgO) .	0·4	0·6	1·0	38·38
Silica (SiO_2) . .	1·0	6·0	17·5	2·19
Alumina (Al_2O_3) . .	} 0·6	3·7	7·0	0·69
Iron oxide (Fe_2O_3) . .	}	1·7	2·5	0·68
Carbon dioxide, water, etc. .	5·0	6·0	5·0	0·84
	100·0	100·0	100·0	100·00

2. *Lean, Poor, Grey Chalk or Stone Lime* contains more than 5 per cent. of clayey impurities and is therefore less pure than fat lime. In the above analysis the impurities of silica, alumina and iron oxide amount to over 11 per cent. The characteristics are somewhat similar to those of fat lime, but on account of its impurities it slakes less rapidly (resulting in a diminution of heat and volume) and its iron content is responsible for its grey colour. Like fat lime, it sets and hardens slowly. It is used for both plaster and lime mortar.

3. *Hydraulic or Blue Lias Lime.*—This class of lime is capable of setting

[1] The latest classification appears in the British Standard Specifications for Building Limes, No. 890—1940, which divides quicklime into two classes, *i.e.*, Class A—Lime for plastering finishing coat, coarse stuff and building mortar, and Class B—Lime for coarse stuff and building mortar only. It gives particulars of several tests.

and hardening when not in contact with air and even if submerged in water, hence the name. Hydraulic lime is therefore unlike both pure and lean limes which, as already stated, will only stiffen when the water is evaporated from the putty and carbonation takes place as the CO_2 is absorbed from the air.

Limestones from which hydraulic limes are prepared contain varying proportions of silica and alumina (in the form of clay), in addition to the calcium oxide (see analysis). The clay and iron oxide play an important part in the setting and hardening of such limes. Quicklime is formed when the carbon dioxide is driven off the calcium carbonate as the limestone is burnt in the kiln. This quicklime, having a strong affinity for the clay, combines with it to form silicates and aluminates of lime.

Slaking.—If water is added to this burnt product after it has been finely ground the mass begins to set and harden as the water combines with the various products. As this action is not dependent upon the presence of carbon dioxide, the hardening will continue even when air is absent. The setting and hardening are therefore similar to the behaviour of Portland cement, the composition of which it closely resembles—compare the above analysis of hydraulic lime with that of Portland cement on p. 23.

These limes have been subdivided into (*a*) feebly hydraulic, (*b*) moderately hydraulic and (*c*) eminently hydraulic, according to the percentage of silica and alumina present.

(a) *Feebly Hydraulic Lime.*—This contains less than 15 per cent. of silica and alumina. The rate of slaking is slow (varying from five to sixty minutes) and the expansion on slaking is small. It produces a good mortar.

(b) *Moderately Hydraulic Lime.*—The silica and alumina content varies from 15 to 25 per cent. Slaking is very slow and the expansion is small. It makes an excellent mortar, is stronger than feebly hydraulic lime and is suitable for good-class brickwork and masonry.

(c) *Eminently or Very Hydraulic Lime.*—This contains from 25 to 30 per cent. of the important constituents of silica and alumina, and its chemical composition is very similar to that of ordinary Portland cement (see p. 23). It is also known as *blue Lias lime*, as it is found in the Lias formation which extends throughout part of Yorkshire and the Midlands. This lime is similar to, but stronger than, the moderately hydraulic variety. It must be very finely ground and must be screened before use to eliminate coarse unslaked particles. It closely resembles Portland cement (p. 22) and is used for similar purposes.

4. *Magnesian or Dolomitic Lime.*—The rocks from which such limes are produced are known as magnesian limestones or dolomites, as they contain up to 45 per cent. magnesium oxide.[1] The latter has similar characteristics to calcium oxide although it slakes much more slowly. This is an excellent lime and is generally used in the localities in which the magnesian limestones are found.

[1] The B.S. 890—1940 states that a lime which contains more than 5 per cent. of magnesium oxide shall be termed a magnesian lime.

Air Slaking.—The burnt lime should be slaked as soon as possi[ble] it arrives on the site, otherwise moisture and carbon dioxide from th[e atmos]phere will, in course of time, reduce the lime to a powder, *i.e.*, it wil[l become] air slaked. This is undesirable, for, carbonation having taken place, the[se particles] of carbonate of lime are incapable of setting, and thus adulterate any mortar with which they may be mixed. Hence the necessity of using only " freshly burnt " lime.

Hydrated Lime.—As explained on p. 20, hydrated lime is that produced when just sufficient water is added to the burnt limestone to satisfy the chemical action of slaking, and is in a dry powder form. The slaking process must be thorough, as any unslaked particles may cause considerable damage.

In addition to ordinary quicklime, certain lime manufacturers now supply lime in hydrated form. There is an increasing demand for this dry hydrated lime on account of the saving of time and labour resulting to the builder or plasterer. This lime is hydrated by a special plant at the lime-works and is supplied in bags, ready for use, in the form of a dry, fine powder. This process must be carefully controlled and the amount of water added must be just sufficient for the purpose, as an inadequate supply would result in some of the lime being unslaked, whilst an excess of water would produce plastic lime or putty.

At the Buxton works referred to on p. 20, hydrated lime, called " Limbux," is produced by the plant shown diagrammatically in Fig. 7. The burnt lime from the kiln is fed into the crusher A and reduced in size from 25 mm down, elevated to the hopper B and passed into the hydrator C. The latter consists of six steel tubes, each 760 mm diameter and 3·7 m long. A carefully regulated supply of water required to slake the lime enters the hydrator at D, the steam generated from the slaked lime

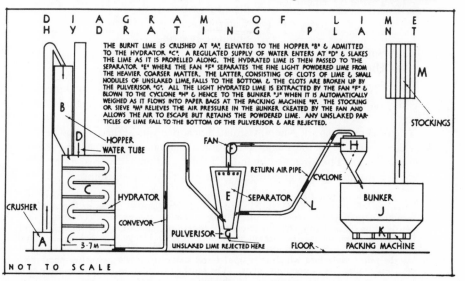

FIGURE 7

rising to heat the water. The lime is pushed forward by means of an auger and traverses the hydrator as indicated by the arrows. It is now in the form of a powder and proceeds to the separator E, where the fan F separates the fine light powdered hydrated lime from the heavier coarser matter. The latter, consisting of clots of hydrated lime and small nodules of unslaked lime, falls to the bottom and the clots are broken up by the pulverizer G. Any unslaked particles of lime, because of their density, fall to the bottom of the pulverizer and are rejected. The hydrated lime extracted by the fan is blown to the cyclone H and hence to the bunker J. The greater part of the circulating air is returned by the pipe L to the separator system. The increased air pressure in the bunker which is created by the fan is relieved by a tube which is terminated by a canvas sieve called the " stockings " M. This allows the air to escape, any of the fine powder drawn up with it being retained and returned to the bunker by periodically striking the canvas on the outside. Finally, the hydrated lime in the bunker, like Portland cement (see below), flows into paper bags and is automatically weighed. The usual size of bag contains 25 kg, but 100 and 200 kg bags can be obtained if required.

CEMENT

There are two groups of cement, *i.e.*, *natural and artificial*, but whilst the latter is one of the most important building materials, comparatively little natural cement is now produced. Natural cement is made from nodules consisting of lime (approximately 40 per cent.), clay (50 per cent.) and oxides of iron, etc. (10 per cent.); these lumps are burnt and crushed to a powder, which is a brown colour due to the iron content. Roman (produced near London) and Medina cements (Isle of Wight) are both quick-setting natural cements.

The artificial cement group includes :

(a) Portland Cement
- (i) Normal or ordinary.
- (ii) Rapid-hardening.
- (iii) White and coloured.
- (iv) Blast-furnace.
- (v) Waterproof.
- (vi) Sulphate-resisting.

(b) Super-sulphate Cement.

(c) High Alumina Cement.

(a) (i) **Normal or Ordinary Portland Cement.**—Chalk or limestone and clay are the raw materials from which this cement is manufactured (Chap. I, Vol. I).

The cement works are generally situated near deposits of these raw materials. A brief description of the manufacture and a diagram of a cement works are given in Fig. 8. The processes include : (1) Excavation and preparation of the materials; (2) mixing and grinding; (3) burning; and (4) grinding.

1. *Excavation and Preparation.*—The chalk is won from the limestone quarry by blasting. Gelignite charges are tamped in 150 mm diameter holes drilled at about 4·6 m intervals and at a distance of 4·6 m from the face (see sketch). On instantaneously firing these charges, huge masses of the limestone, amounting to several thousand kg. and varying in size from small fragments to large blocks, are dislodged. This loose stone is discharged into wagons from a mechanical navvy (p. 2) and hauled to the *jaw crusher* into which it is tipped and reduced by two powerful metal jaws to a maximum size of 200 mm cubes. The crushed stone passes on to a moving belt and is conveyed to the *cone crusher* which reduces it down to 20 mm maximum. This is delivered by a belt conveyer to the limestone silo.

The clay is excavated by mechanically dragging a *scraper-bucket* over the clay field; this is tipped into a *wash mill* (p. 1), and the washed clay, called *slip*, containing about 60 per cent. of water, is pumped through metal pipes to the *slip storage tank*.

2. *Mixing and Grinding.*—The chalk from the silo and the clay slip from the tank enter the *wet grinding mill* at A in the correct proportions (approximately 78 per cent. chalk and 22 per cent. clay). This is a cylindrical mill 11·3 m long by 2 to 2·6 m diameter, having a chromium steel lining and divided into three compartments by two slotted diaphragms. About 32 per cent. of the mill is occupied by steel balls graded in diameter from 100 to 75 mm in the first compartment, 64 to 38 mm in the middle compartment and 25 mm in the last compartment. The mill is caused to rotate at about 20 revs. per min., and as it rotates, the abrasive action of the balls as they strike against each other and against the metal casing grind the material as it comes between them. Fine grinding and thorough mixing reduce the materials to a creamy consistency, called *slurry*, the bulk of which, after leaving the mill, passes through a fine sieve (having a 0·09 mm mesh); that which fails to pass through the sieve is returned to the mill and re-ground.

After screening, the slurry is conveyed to the *open slurry tank*, which is 20 m in diameter and 4·5 m deep, where it is kept agitated by compressed air delivered through perforated pipes at the bottom of the tank. The slurry, now a uniform mixture, is then pumped to the upper or feed end of the kiln.

3. *Burning.*—The kiln is of the rotary type. It is a steel cylinder lined with firebrick, about 90 m long and 3 m diameter, slightly inclined and mounted on rollers; it revolves slowly at about 1 rev. per min. The fuel is dry pulverized coal. The raw coal is tipped from the railway trucks at C, elevated to the *raw coal silo*, passed to the *coal mill* where it is finely ground and also dried by hot air conveyed from the kiln by pipe D, elevated to the *pulverized coal hopper* and blown in at the lower or firing end of the kiln—see arrows. The temperature in the lower or burning zone is very intense (a white heat of approximately 1 538° C.) and gradually decreases to 232–260° C. at the top end, where the gases escape up the chimney stack. Thus the cold slurry, which is fed automatically and continuously, is first dried in the upper zone, and during its passage down the kiln is heated and finally partially fused into clinker. The chalk constituent, as it is heated, is converted into quicklime by the liberation of CO_2 and when subjected to the higher temperature the lime and clay chemically unite to form hard balls (3 to 19 mm in size) of Portland cement, called *clinker*, which is dark brown to black in colour.

This clinker, which is white hot, is cooled as it passes from the kiln at the lower end into drums or cylinders called *coolers*. There are twelve of these coolers, 1·2 m in diameter and at least 6 m long, parallel to and attached to the outside of the kiln. A draught of cold air is passed through the cylinders as the clinker gradually gravitates towards and emerges from the lower end on to a belt conveyor which delivers it to the *clinker storage bin* or shed.

4. *Grinding.*—Clinker is fed into the *clinker hopper* by means of an overhead travelling crane grab; the latter is also used to mix the coarse with the finer clinker. From the hopper the clinker passes to the *combination grinding mill, ball mill* or *dry mill*; this is of the same size and is similar to the wet mill, it being divided into three compartments which contain graded steel balls. These grind the clinker to a powder which is so fine that at least 90 per cent. of it must pass through a sieve of wire cloth having a mesh of 0·09 mm square size (see below).

A small quantity, from 1 to 3 per cent., of gypsum (calcium sulphate) is added at B from the *gypsum hopper* which adjoins the clinker hopper. This tends to lengthen the setting time of the cement to suit practical conditions.

The ground cement as it emerges from the dry mill is forced by compressed air up a pipe to silos or bins, each 6 m in diameter and about 21 m high, and having a capacity of 1·5 Mg.

Packing.—The cement from the silos is elevated to a hopper from which it flows to the *packing machine*. The cement was formerly packed into jute bags, but strong paper-valved bags of 50 kg capacity are now chiefly used. Each bag is placed by hand on the delivery nozzle of the machine, the cement is automatically weighed as it flows into it, and the filled and sealed bag is discharged and either stacked or placed direct into lorries or trucks. One machine can fill 1 200 bags per hour.

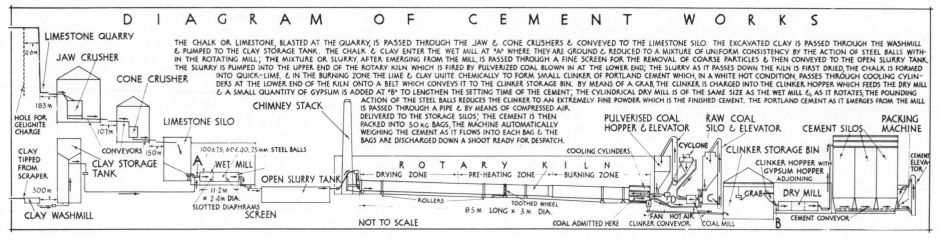

DIAGRAM OF CEMENT WORKS

THE CHALK OR LIMESTONE, BLASTED AT THE QUARRY, IS PASSED THROUGH THE JAW & CONE CRUSHERS & CONVEYED TO THE LIMESTONE SILO. THE EXCAVATED CLAY IS PASSED THROUGH THE WASHMILL & PUMPED TO THE CLAY STORAGE TANK. THE CHALK & CLAY ENTER THE WET MILL AT "A" WHERE THEY ARE GROUND & REDUCED TO A MIXTURE OF UNIFORM CONSISTENCY BY THE ACTION OF STEEL BALLS WITHIN THE ROTATING MILL; THE MIXTURE OR SLURRY, AFTER EMERGING FROM THE MILL, IS PASSED THROUGH A FINE SCREEN FOR THE REMOVAL OF COARSE PARTICLES & THEN CONVEYED TO THE OPEN SLURRY TANK. THE SLURRY IS PUMPED INTO THE UPPER END OF THE ROTARY KILN WHICH IS FIRED BY PULVERIZED COAL BLOWN IN AT THE LOWER END; THE SLURRY AS IT PASSES DOWN THE KILN IS FIRST DRIED, THE CHALK IS FORMED INTO QUICK-LIME, & IN THE BURNING ZONE THE LIME & CLAY UNITE CHEMICALLY TO FORM SMALL CLINKER OF PORTLAND CEMENT WHICH, IN A WHITE HOT CONDITION, PASSES THROUGH COOLING CYLINDERS AT THE LOWER END OF THE KILN ONTO A BELT WHICH CONVEYS IT TO THE CLINKER STORAGE BIN. BY MEANS OF A GRAB, THE CLINKER IS CHARGED INTO THE CLINKER HOPPER WHICH FEEDS THE DRY MILL & A SMALL QUANTITY OF GYPSUM IS ADDED AT "B" TO LENGTHEN THE SETTING TIME OF THE CEMENT; THE CYLINDRICAL DRY MILL IS OF THE SAME SIZE AS THE WET MILL &, AS IT ROTATES, THE POUNDING ACTION OF THE STEEL BALLS REDUCES THE CLINKER TO AN EXTREMELY FINE POWDER WHICH IS THE FINISHED CEMENT. THE PORTLAND CEMENT AS IT EMERGES FROM THE MILL IS PASSED THROUGH A PIPE & BY MEANS OF COMPRESSED AIR DELIVERED TO THE STORAGE SILOS; THE CEMENT IS THEN PACKED INTO 50 KG BAGS, THE MACHINE AUTOMATICALLY WEIGHING THE CEMENT AS IT FLOWS INTO EACH BAG & THE BAGS ARE DISCHARGED DOWN A SHOOT READY FOR DESPATCH.

FIGURE 8

Testing.—The manufacture is closely controlled at each stage, and samples of the clay slip and chalk before they enter the wet mill, slurry after leaving the mill, clinker after leaving the kiln, and cement at the packing machine are taken for laboratory examination.

The cement during and after manufacture is tested in accordance with the British Standard Specification for Ordinary Portland and Rapid-hardening Portland Cements, No. 12[1]. This specification includes the following tests with which Portland cement must comply : (*a*) Fineness, (*b*) chemical composition, (*c*) strength, (*d*) setting time and (*e*) soundness :—

(a) *Fineness.*—This is estimated by sieving for fifteen minutes a sample (about 0·11 kg) of the cement on a No. " 170 " (0·09 mm mesh) British Standard sieve, when the residue for ordinary Portland cement shall not exceed 10 per cent. As a general rule the finer the cement the more rapid the strength development of the concrete.

(b) *Chemical Composition.*—This clause in the specification limits the proportion of lime to the silica, alumina and iron oxide, and the ratio of the percentage of iron oxide to that of alumina. It also specifies the maximum percentage of insoluble residue (1 per cent.), magnesia (4 per cent.) and sulphur (2.75 per cent.), in addition to limiting the loss on ignition to 3 per cent.

The following may be considered as an approximate analysis of a typical Portland cement :—

	Per Cent.
Lime	64
Silica	23
Alumina	5
Iron oxide	3
Magnesia	2
Sulphuric anhydride . . .	2
Soda and potash	1
	100

[1] Published by the British Standards Institution, 28 Victoria Street, London, S.W.1.

The whole of the lime should combine with the silica and alumina. Any excess called *free lime*, may produce unsoundness (see p. 24). A deficiency of lime may produce a weak cement.

The presence of iron is responsible for the grey colour of cement (resembling that of Portland stone). If excessive, the iron oxide increases the difficulty of grinding the clinker.

Excessive quantities of magnesia and sulphur compounds cause unsoundness.

An excessive quantity of soda and potash may cause efflorescence in the cement, and these alkalis should therefore be kept to a minimum.

(c) *Strength.*—The specification requires that cement shall pass tests to determine its strength in tension or compression.

Tensile Strength Test.—The cement has to be mixed with sand to form a mortar composed of part 1 (by weight) cement and 3 parts of Leighton Buzzard sand (a very clean, white and well graded sand obtained from Bedfordshire) to which a specified amount of water is added. The mortar is formed in a brass mould of the shape shown at B, Fig. 9, the cross-sectional area at the " waist " of the briquette being 6·45 cm². The mould is carefully filled by consolidating the mortar with a standard steel spatula (knife) until it is flush with the top; the mould is reversed and the broad blade of the spatula is used to pat the mortar until water is brought to the surface, after which the surface is smoothed over and brought flush with the top of the mould by a trowel. The briquette is stored in a damp atmosphere and kept for twenty-four hours at a temperature of 14 to 17° C., when it is removed from the mould, submerged in clean water and left until required for testing.

It is required that twelve briquettes shall be prepared and stored in this manner, and that six of these shall be tested at three days after moulding, followed by the remaining six at seven days. The average minimum tensile breaking strength of ordinary Portland cement shall be 2·1 MN/m² at three days and 2·6 MN/m² at seven days after moulding.

One type of tensile testing machine is shown at A, Fig. 9. This has a pair of jaws of standard size and shape in which the briquette is placed. The lower jaw is fixed and the upper jaw is suspended at K to a system of levers consisting of lever R, pivoted on a knife-edge at J, and connected by a rod (having knife-edges at L and M) to lever Q, pivoted at N. A bucket is suspended at P to receive the load in the form of *shot* (lead pellets) fed from the container.

The testing is carried out in the following manner : A briquette is placed in the jaws, the spindle T is lifted to release the shot, which passes in a steady stream through a valve down the nozzle of the container into the bucket. This load is transmitted to the briquette through the system of levers and ultimately causes it to break across at the waist. Immediately this occurs the flow of shot is automatically stopped as the bucket falls on the pedestal below, depressing arm s, which in turn causes the spindle to drop and close the valve of the container. The bucket containing the shot is placed on some scales and weighed. A direct reading of the breaking load in kilograms is obtained from the scales, as they are calibrated in accordance with the ratio of the levers after the weight of the empty bucket has been allowed for. As this breaking load is applied on 6·45 cm² of the briquette, the breaking stress can be found.

A line diagram of the lever system of the apparatus is shown at c. The ratio of the lengths j'k' and j'l' in the lower lever is as 1 : 5 and that of m'n' and n'p' is as 1 : 10. Hence the magnifying ratio is 50, i.e., the stress on the briquette is 50 times as large as the load in the bucket. Thus, if the weight of the shot in the bucket when the briquette fails is 3 kg the load acting on ML equals $\frac{3 \times 10}{1} = 30$ kg multiplied by 5 equals 150 kg. This is the breaking load, and from it can be derived the breaking stress.

Compressive Strength Test.—If required by the purchaser the above tensile stress test may be substituted by a compressive strength test. The latter is applied to 70 or 75 mm cubes of a 1 : 3 mix, the mixing and compacting by vibration in a machine being specified. Three cubes are tested in a compression machine (see p. 32) at three days after moulding, and the average minimum compressive strength (calculated from the crushing load) for ordinary Portland cement shall be 10.7 N/mm². Three cubes are similarly tested at seven days, when the average minimum compressive strength shall be 17·2 N/mm² (see Table IV, p. 34).

(d) *Setting Time.*—When cement and water are mixed to form a paste, the mass remains plastic for a short while. The water combines chemically with the grains of cement to form hydrates. This is known as *hydration*. As this proceeds, the plasticity gradually disappears and the cement stiffens or *sets*. The cementing material between the particles of cement increases in amount, causing the mass to gain in strength and *hardness*, and this hardness increases for some considerable time after it has set.

The specification refers to " initial set " and " final set." Regarding the former, it is essential that the cement shall set slowly at first to allow time for the mixing and placing in position of the concrete, and to ensure thorough adhesion between adjacent batches of concrete. It is equally important that the concrete shall harden quickly after its initial set in order that it may be loaded as soon as possible and (in the case of reinforced concrete) permit the early removal of any formwork or shuttering (temporary timbering) which may be supporting it.

According to the specification, the initial setting time for normal setting cement shall be not less than thirty minutes and the final setting time not more than ten hours. If a quick-setting cement (see next column) is required, the initial setting time is reduced to not less than five minutes, and the final setting time to not more than thirty minutes. The Vicat apparatus, shown at D, Fig. 9, is used to determine the initial and final setting times of cement. A brass cylindrical mould, approximately 75 mm dia. and 38 mm deep, is placed upon a metal plate and filled to the top with neat cement to which sufficient water has been added to make it plastic. The filled mould is placed on the base as indicated by broken lines. The initial set is measured by means of a needle having a flat end, 1 mm square, which is screwed to the bottom of the rod in place of the final setting needle shown. The pin is withdrawn and the rod is lowered until it touches the smooth surface of the cement, when it is quickly released and allowed to penetrate the cement. This is repeated at intervals on different parts of the specimen until the needle fails to pierce it completely. The time which has elapsed between the addition of the water and this partial penetration of the needle is called the initial setting time and, as already stated, must not be less than thirty minutes for normal setting cement (or five minutes for quick-setting cement). The final setting time is determined in a similar manner, the initial setting needle being replaced by the final setting needle shown. The latter, of the same shape and section as the former needle, has a metal fitting attached at the end; the base of the fitting has a raised rim which is about 0·5 mm above the end of the central needle. The cement is considered to be finally set when, on a gentle application of the needle, the central flat point makes an impression on it, but the raised rim fails to do so. This final setting time must not exceed ten hours for normal-setting cement or thirty minutes for quick-setting cement.

(e) *Soundness.*—Unsound cement has a tendency towards excessive expansion. Sound cement is relatively free from this tendency and its volume remains constant. Most serious defects in cement products are caused by expansion which takes place during setting and may continue for some considerable time. Thus, reinforced concrete made of unsound cement may crack and disintegrate to such an extent as to permit the entrance of moisture and cause corrosion of the exposed steel. The soundness test which appears in the standard specification is therefore very important.

This soundness or expansion test is carried out in the Le Chatelier apparatus illustrated at F, Fig. 9. This is a brass split cylindrical mould having an indicator attached on each side of the split. The mould, resting on a glass plate and held together with the split edges touching, is completely filled with neat cement gauged with just sufficient water to make it plastic, and covered with another glass plate which is held down by a small weight. It is at once immersed in water (temperature 14·4 to 17·8° C.) and left for twenty-four hours. It is taken out, the distance w between the indicators is measured, the weighted mould is again immersed and then boiled for three hours. The mould is removed and, after cooling, the distance between the points is again measured. The difference between the two measurements indicates the expansion of the cement and shall not exceed 10 mm.

Good cements will show little (not more than 1 mm) if any expansion. The expansion of poor cements is often due to the presence of excess gypsum and other sulphates. The boiling water accelerates the reaction and resultant expansion.

A simple but effective test (not mentioned in the specification) is the *hot-pat test*. Water is added to neat cement and thoroughly mixed to a plastic condition. This is worked to the shape of a ball, placed on a piece of glass which is tapped on the bench until the cement flattens out to the shape of a disc about 75 mm in diameter, a little more than 6 mm thick at the centre and tapering to a knife-edge at the circumference. The surface is then smoothed over with a knife. After being covered over with a damp cloth and allowed to harden for twenty-four hours, the pat is boiled in water for four or five hours. If the cement is unsound, radial cracking (especially at the edges) and distortion will appear, due to expansion; the edges may curl up and surface flaking may appear. A pat of sound cement will remain unaltered after this treatment, although fine shrinkage cracks may appear.

The *cold-pat test* is similar to the above, except that the pat is not boiled but simply immersed in cold-water for twenty-four hours before examination.

(a) (ii) Rapid-hardening or High-early-strength Portland Cement.—

This is true Portland cement, and, as its name implies, its chief characteristic is the comparative rapidity with which it gains in strength in the early stages of hydration (see Table IV, p. 34).

B.S. 12, already referred to, applies to this cement. Whilst the residue of ordinary cement on a 170 sieve shall not exceed 10 per cent. (see p. 23), that of rapid-hardening cement shall not exceed 5 per cent. The ultimate tensile stress shall be not less than 2·07 N/mm² after one day and 3·1 N/mm² after three days. The compressive strength shall be not less than 11 N/mm² after one day and 24·1 N/mm² after three days. The initial setting time shall be not less than five minutes and the final setting time shall be not more than thirty minutes. These requirements should be compared with those stated in respect to ordinary Portland cement.

Rapid-hardening cement can be usefully employed in cold weather, as it is less liable than ordinary cement to damage from frost. It is preferred to ordinary cement in the construction of concrete roads, as it can take traffic within a few days, whereas concrete composed of ordinary cement should be left for twenty-eight days before roads are opened to heavy traffic. This advantage also applies to reinforced concrete floors, etc., made of rapid-hardening cement, as the lapse of time before the removal of the temporary timbering (formwork) and the application of loads is considerably reduced. The cost of rapid-hardening cement is slightly more than that of ordinary Portland cement. " Ferrocrete " and " Vitocrete " are some of the well-known brands of rapid-hardening cement.

(a) (iii) **White Portland Cement.**—The chemical composition and characteristics of white Portland cement are similar to those of ordinary Portland cement, except that the latter is of a grey colour. The colour of white cement is due to the raw materials used and the special precautions taken in its production. The materials are pure limestone and china (white) clay, the iron oxide content (which imparts the grey colour to ordinary Portland cement) being less than 1 per cent. The cement must not come into contact with iron or steel during its manufacture, the kiln is lined with special fireclay blocks, and oil is generally the fuel used. Aggregates used with white cement should be light coloured (see p. 28). White cement is more expensive than ordinary cement. It is in increasing demand for external rough-casting of walls, pointing of brickwork and masonry, and in the manufacture of reconstructed (artificial) stone and tiles. Well-known brands include " Atlas " and " Snowcrete."

Coloured Cement.—Cement, used for special purposes such as for plastering walls and in the manufacture of reconstructed stone and tiles, is now obtainable in a variety of colours. Pigments, such as black oxide of iron and manganese black (to produce a black colour), red oxide of iron (producing red), brown oxide of iron (producing brown), chromic oxide (producing green), etc., are thoroughly incorporated with the cement in a dry condition by machinery. Coloured cement can be obtained ready for use from the manufacturers, or the cement and pigments can be mixed on the job.

(a) (iv) **Portland Blast-furnace Cement.**—This is a mixture of ordinary Portland cement and blast-furnace slag. The latter is a product of the blast furnace in which iron ore is smelted as a preliminary in the manufacture of cast iron, steel, etc. Normally this slag is an impurity which is run into ladles and conveyed to the slag tip. When, however, it is used in the production of cement, the slag as it issues from the furnace is cooled by a stream of water which reduces it to a honeycombed, granulated condition. The slag is removed, dried and mixed with ordinary cement clinker and passed to a ball mill (see p. 22) for thorough incorporation and fine grinding. Not every slag is suitable for this purpose. The quality of this cement must comply with the British Standard Specification for Portland—Blastfurnace Cement, No. 146. The proportion of slag must not exceed 65 per cent., and that of Portland cement clinker must not be less than 35 per cent. (see p. 28).

(a) (v) **Waterproof Cement.**—This contains a waterproofing agent, and concrete made with it is less permeable to water than that made with normal P.C.

(a) (vi) **Sulphate-resisting Cement.**—Sulphate bearing clays attack normal P.C. and this cement offers some resistance to the action.

(b) **Super-sulphate Cement** is similar to (a) (vi) above, offering greater resistance to attack, used for concreting in contaminated ground.

(c) **High Aluminia or Aluminous Cement.**—(BS 915). This is made from a mixture of limestone and bauxite (aluminium ore) which is fired in a hot air blast in a furnace with coal. The heat liquefies the materials and the resulting cement is tapped off, eventually being ground extremely finely. The cement is much darker in colour than Portland cement. An approximate percentage analysis is: Lime 39, Silica 7, Alumina 39, Iron oxide 13, Magnesia, etc, 2.

Its chief characteristics are : Rapid-hardening, great strength, large amount of heat generated during the setting and hardening process, and its resistance to acids. Concrete composed of this cement develops a compressive strength of at least 34·4 N/mm^2 at the age of one day and 49 N/mm^2 at the age of seven days (see Table IV, p. 34). It is unaffected by frost on account of the heat which it generates. Because of these qualities, high alumna cement can be usefully employed when formwork is required to be removed with the minimum delay, for concreting ground floors on certain soils containing sulphates which may attack ordinary Portland cement concrete and for work requiring great strength, and when work must be done during low temperatures. The W/C ratio (see p. 31) should not exceed 0.4 and the strength of HAC cement concrete is affected adversely if the heat generated during hardening is not dissipated Thus, formwork encasing concrete should be removed as soon as practicable. Its use is not advocated for mass concrete exceeding 450 mm thick unless it can be deposited in thin layers, preferably 300 mm thick, and the dissipation of the evolved heat permitted. Another disadvantage of high alumina cement is its relatively high cost. It must not be mixed with or brought into contact with Portland cement, as a reduction in the strength of the former with result. One well-known brand is "Ciment Fondu"

During 1974 certain failures occurred in structural members made from HAC concrete due to the fact that "Conversion" occurs with this cement. The term conversion is used to describe physical changes arising during hydration which make the concrete porous. Hence HAC must not be used in buildings subject to excessive condensation or water penetration; the Building Regulations state it should not be used in structural work or foundations. The sole use now is as a heat resisting material.

MORTARS

Mortar is composed of an aggregate, such as sand, and a matrix or binding material of lime or cement or both (see p. 2, Vol. I).

Sand in mortar (1) reduces shrinkage and without it cracks would develop, (2) assists in the hardening of pure limes especially (p. 20) by allowing the penetration of air which provides CO_2 for the development of carbonization (p. 20) and (3) reduces its cost, as sand is much cheaper than lime or cement.

To give the best results sand should be well graded and must be clean.

Grading of Sand.—A suitably graded sand consists of particles varying in size from coarse to fine, with the smaller particles packing into the voids between the larger. A *coarse* sand is one the bulk of which is retained on a No. 52 British Standard Sieve (0·302 mm square mesh). If most of the particles of a sample pass through this sieve, the sand is classified as a *fine* one. Coarse sand produces what is known as a *harsh* mortar. Sand containing a large proportion of very fine particles, such as dust or silt, is not suitable, as an excessive amount of water is required to make the mortar workable, and this reduces its strength and increases shrinkage. It is therefore recommended that, for mortar, not more than 3 per cent. of sand should pass a No. 100 standard sieve (0.152 mm square mesh). To the experienced, the relative coarseness and fineness of a consignment of sand can be gauged approximately by its appearance and by rubbing some of it between the thumb and forefinger.

The strength of mortar (and concrete, see p. 28) is decreased if the particles of sand are of uniform size, owing to the presence of a large proportion of pore spaces. Tests have shown that the shape of the particles is not very important.

Cleanliness of Sand is most essential. Adhesion between the binding material and the sand is only possible if the particles of the latter are clean; the presence of dirt, especially if finely distributed to such an extent as to surround each small particle, interferes with the setting and reduces the strength of mortars and concretes. The chief impurities are clay, loam and organic compounds such as vegetable matter. The latter, not being inert, is liable to decay, and the organic acids produced may have an ill-effect on the mortar or concrete.

Clean sand when rubbed will not stain the fingers. A simple and effective test consists of half filling a glass vessel with the sand, water is added until it almost reaches the top, and after being agitated, the sand is allowed to settle. If the sand is clean, not more than a thin film of silt will be seen deposited on top of the sand, and the water above it will be clear; if, however, the sample is a dirty one, the bottom layer of the washed sand will be covered by a relatively thick dark layer of dirt, and small particles of suspended matter (generally organic and fine clay) may be seen floating in the water even if several hours have elapsed after agitation and examination.

Sand for general purposes may be considered satisfactory if a test similar to the above (but in a measuring cylinder) shows that it contains not more than 6 per cent. of silt. This is known as a *sedimentation* or *decanting test.*

A test for organic impurities consists of comparing the colour of the water above the sample of sand in a cylinder (to which a definite amount of 3 per cent. sodium hydroxide solution has been added) with that of a standard solution of tannic acid and sodium hydroxide. If, after standing for twenty-four hours following agitation, the colour of the former is darker than the standard colour, it indicates that the sand contains an excessive amount of organic matter which may be injurious and should be treated with suspicion.

If, on the score of economy, a local sand is to be used which is not sufficiently clean, much of the dirt can be eliminated by washing.

The following aggregates are used for mortars : (1) Pit or quarry sand, (2) river sand, (3) sea sand, (4) crushed stone and (5) ashes.

1. *Pit or Quarry Sand.*—The quality varies. Provided it is clean, it is a very good sand for mortar, concrete and plaster. Some pit sands are liable to contain organic matter in the form of coal which may interfere with the setting.

2. *River Sand.*—This is usually clean and is an excellent sand for all purposes. Some river sands may be deficient in *fines* (smaller particles) and thus produce harsh mortars.

3. *Sea Sand.*—Whilst this sand is commonly used locally for concrete, it is not suitable for mortar on account of its salt content which causes efflorescence (p. 13).

4. *Crushed Stone.*—This is now often used, especially for mortar required for ashlar work. The waste stone at the quarries is crushed to the size of sand particles. When this crushed stone is the same as that used for the ashlar work it assists in producing a mortar which closely conforms to the colour of the masonry and thus helps in making the joints inconspicuous.

5. *Ashes or Clinkers* from furnaces are crushed very finely and intimately ground with the lime in a mortar mill to produce a cheap and strong mortar, known as *black mortar.* The ashes should be free from unburnt coal and dust. Old broken bricks, which should be clean and especially free from plaster, are sometimes crushed and mixed with the lime in the mill.

Lime Mortar.—The slaked lime is mixed with the aggregate and water either by hand or in a mortar mill. Manual mixing should be done on a boarded platform to ensure that dirt will not be shovelled into the mix. The period of slaking, composition and strength of mortar depend upon the class of lime used.

The properties of the mortar should resemble those of the bricks. Thus, whilst a dense, strong impermeable mortar, such as cement mortar, should be used for bedding, jointing and pointing strong bricks of the engineering class, such mortar would be unsuitable for low-strength bricks of medium permeability if used in the construction of external walls. Existing brickwork has been known to develop defects in the bricks subsequent to re-pointing with rich, dense mortar. A possible explanation of the cause of this is that water absorbed by the bricks during wet weather can only be eliminated during dry periods by evaporation on the surface of the bricks and not through the joints, and any salts in the bricks may crystallize near the surface, causing disintegration of their faces.

Non-hydraulic Lime Mortars (from pure and lean limes, see p. 20) must be well slaked before use. This type can be stored in a heap for several days after mixing, provided the surface is smoothed over with a shovel to minimize carbonation by the exclusion of as much air as possible. As such mortars can only harden when exposed to the atmosphere (p. 20), a relatively large proportion of sand must be added to the lime to assist in the penetration of air. For this reason the proportion of sand may be as high as 4 parts by volume of sand to 1 part lime. These mortars are light-coloured. They are not likely to cause efflorescence.

These mortars are not suitable for work below ground level, especially if the ground is water-logged. Such mortars are improved if gauged with cement.

Hydraulic Lime Mortars (see p. 20) should be used within one hour after being mixed. This especially applies to eminently hydraulic mortar which sets quickly after the addition of the necessary amount of water. Any mortar which has stiffened and cannot be knocked up by means of a trowel to a sufficiently plastic condition should never be used. The proportions of lime to aggregate range from 1 part lime to from 2 to $3\frac{1}{2}$ parts sand, a common mixture being 1 : 3. These are excellent mortars for all purposes and are particularly suited for work below the ground level and in exposed positions.

Eminently hydraulic lime mortars rank next to cement mortars as regards strength. They may be a cause of efflorescence (p. 13) owing to the presence of salts.

Magnesian or Dolomitic Lime Mortars (see p. 21) have a slow-setting action and they should therefore be slaked for several hours before use. Their properties and uses are somewhat similar to those of hydraulic lime mortars.

Hydrated Lime (p. 21) should be reduced to a putty consistency by adding water and allowing it to stand (*soak*) for a day before being mixed with sand.

Black Mortars (see p. 26).—A usual proportion is 1 lime : 3 ashes or clinker (mixed in the mill). They are hard-setting and are suitable for internal walls and for brickwork and masonry where the colour is unimportant.

Cement Mortar (see Chap. I, Vol. I).—It is stronger than lime mortar and is therefore used in the construction of piers and load-bearing walls; it is also usefully employed for work below ground level and for external walls in exposed positions on account of its impermeability. Cement mortar is now extensively used during winter, as it is not so liable to damage by frost, owing to its relatively quick-setting property. It must be used immediately after mixing. Efflorescence may be caused, due to the presence in the cement of carbonates and sulphates of potash and soda (see p. 13). The usual composition is 1 cement : 3 sand; there is nothing to be gained by using a richer (and more costly) mix than this. A dense cement mortar should not be used for bedding and jointing low-strength bricks (p. 26).

Chemical additives are now available to improve the workability of mortar; these enable a coarser sand to be used and mixes leaner than 1 : 3 are practicable. They are added to the water in the proportion of about 3 per cent and allow the mortar to entrain air bubbles giving increased plasticity.

Cement-lime or Compo Mortars.—Compo is a mixture of lime, cement and sand. It is usual to mix the lime mortar as already explained, and then *gauge* (add to) this mixture with the necessary proportion of Portland cement immediately before the mortar is required for use. Non-hydraulic, feebly hydraulic and hydrated limes can be used for this class of mortar. The addition of the cement increases the hydraulicity of the mortar, besides increasing its strength, and the rate of hardening is therefore accelerated. This quality makes it a useful mortar to be employed in winter. Compo is more open textured than cement mortar and is therefore better suited for bedding and jointing bricks of moderate or low strength. The gauging also increases the workability of the mortar. The proportions vary from 1 cement : 2 to 3 lime : 6 to 9 sand. Eminently hydraulic and magnesian limes should not be gauged with cement.

> Compo is an excellent mortar for rubble, flint and similar walling where a large proportion of bedding material is required. When ordinary lime mortars are used for this class of work there is a tendency for excessive shrinkage to take place, and this may cause cracks through which water may penetrate. Compo for such work may consist of 1 part cement : 4 parts lime : 12 parts sand.
>
> FIRE-RESISTANT MORTAR.—Ordinary lime and cement mortars are unsuitable for setting firebricks or fireclay blocks used for lining furnaces, fireplaces, etc., as they shrink considerably when subjected to heat. There are several proprietary mortars specially produced for this class of work. A good fire-resisting mortar consists of a mixture of 1 part cement (preferably aluminous cement, see p. 25) to 2 parts finely crushed firebrick (p. 16).

Strength of Mortar.—Cement mortar produces the strongest brickwork, non-hydraulic lime mortar walling is approximately half the strength of that in cement mortar, and the strength of eminently hydraulic mortars is intermediate between that of cement and non-hydraulic lime mortars. The strength of compo mortars depends a good deal upon the cement content and may be very little less than cement mortar.

Colour of Mortar.—Whilst the colour of the mortar is immaterial if the brickwork is to be covered with plaster or roughcast, it is very important that the colour shall suitably conform with that of the bricks when these are to be used in the construction of faced work. The appearance of brickwork is often spoilt through inadequate attention being paid to the colour and texture of the jointing material, even when the bricks are expensive facings. The colour of mortar is influenced by both the lime or cement and the aggregate, and in order to obtain the desired result it is sometimes essential to try out different materials and proportions.

> The colour of lime mortar varies from white (when pure lime—p. 20—is used) to black (preceding column). Ordinary Portland cement mortar is grey in colour; white Portland cement with a light-coloured sand produces white mortar; different shades can be obtained by using coloured cements (p. 25). Sand varies in colour from white to dark brown or red. A yellow sand, mixed with grey lime, produces a satisfactory colour for certain sand-faced brickwork.
>
> Multi-coloured brickwork especially is apt to be disfigured by iron stains. As this staining disappears after the brickwork has weathered, it is advisable to defer the pointing of such brickwork.
>
> In masonry, and in order that the mortar shall harmonize with the stone, it is a common practice to use crushed stone (p. 26) in lieu of sand. Thus, for Portland stone ashlar work the proportions recommended are 2 parts Portland cement : 5 parts slaked lime : 7 to 12 parts crushed Portland stone.

Waterproofed Mortars.—There are now available a large number of proprietary substances, called *waterproofers*, which are mixed with mortars to render them impervious. They are marketed in the form of powders, pastes and liquids. Their object is to either fill the pores of the mortar or to line the pores with a film of water-repellent material. Most of these, such as

"Cementone," "Medusa," "Pudlo" and "Sika," are only suitable for cement mortars. As such mixtures must not be used after the initial set, it is necessary to apply the material without delay and in some cases within half an hour of the addition of water. Unused partially set mortar must be discarded.

> The amount of waterproof added varies and should be in accordance with the manufacturers' instructions. When in powder form, the mixture may consist of 1 part cement : 2 to 4 parts sand : 2 to 5 per cent. of the waterproofer; the required amount of the powder is added to and well incorporated with the cement before being spread over the sand; the whole is then mixed dry before the water is carefully added, after which it is mixed to an even consistency. When in the form of a paste, water is added very gradually to the waterproofer in the usual proportion of 1 part paste to 10 parts water whilst being well stirred to reduce the solution to a uniform consistency; the cement and sand are well mixed dry before the solution is added, and then mixed wet to a workable condition. If in liquid form, it is usual to add 1 litre of the waterproofer to every 15 litres of water; the cement and sand are mixed dry before this "gauging water" is added and finally mixed wet.
> Further reference to waterproofers is made on p. 36.
> Waterproofed cement is also used to make waterproof mortar.

CONCRETE

Concrete consists of a (1) matrix, (2) fine aggregate and (3) coarse aggregate thoroughly mixed with water. In general, a good concrete is required to be hard, strong, durable, dense, non-porous, fire resisting and economical, although for certain structures, such as internal partitions, strength and impermeability are not necessary requirements where a porous concrete may be desirable on account of its lightness and sound-insulating properties. The characteristics of concrete are influenced by the quality of the materials, grading of the aggregates, proportioning, amount of water used, and workmanship. Ideally, the variation in the size of the aggregates (known as *grading*) should be such that the fine aggregate will fit into the spaces between the coarse aggregate to leave a minimum percentage of voids to be filled by the matrix in cementing the whole mass together. Adequate grading is economical, as less cement is needed when the aggregates are well graded. A mixture which is too rich in cement may shrink excessively. It is most important to appreciate that the strength of mortar depends very largely upon the amount of water used in relation to the cement; *an excess of water results in a considerable reduction in strength* (see p. 30). Just sufficient water should be added to make the mix reasonably plastic and workable.

The expression "workable mixture" is applied to concrete of such consistency that it can be readily deposited in position in a uniform condition and rendered dense after a reasonable amount of punning (see p. 35).

Concrete when used by itself is known as *mass concrete* (used for foundations, certain floors, retaining walls, etc.); concrete reinforced with steel is called *reinforced concrete*.

1. **Matrix.**—The binding material used for most concretes is ordinary Portland cement (pp. 21 to 24). Rapid-hardening cement (p. 24) is suitable as a matrix for concrete structures which have to be speedily constructed. The fire-resisting and durable qualities of blast-furnace cement (p. 25) render this a satisfactory matrix for reinforced concrete and marine work. High alumina cement (p. 25), because of its high strength and rapid-hardening characteristics, is especially suited as a binding material for concrete used in structures which are to withstand high stresses and be speedily erected. Sulphate-resisting and super-sulphate (p. 25) cements are for use in concrete placed in sulphate bearing ground. Some clay subsoils and those containing industrial waste attack normal P.C.

2. **Fine Aggregate.**—According to B.S. 882—Concrete Aggregates from Natural Sources, a fine aggregate (conforming to the Code of Practice "The Structural Use of Concrete") is one which mainly passes a test sieve having a 4·8 mm square mesh. Sand (p. 25) is the chief material employed as a fine aggregate, and both quarry and river sands are extensively used for this purpose. Sea sand is also used locally as an aggregate, chiefly because of its low cost; if such sand is required for concrete which is to be exposed to view, it is advisable to eliminate as much as possible of the salt content by washing with *fresh* water, otherwise efflorescence may be objectionable. Cleanliness and suitable grading, already referred to, are essential requirements.

3. **Coarse Aggregate.**—This is classified as material which is mainly retained on a 4·8 mm meshed sieve. The maximum size varies; thus, for reinforced concrete work it is usually 19 mm, and for mass concrete, as for foundations, it is generally 38 mm and may be 64 mm. The materials must be clean (to ensure the thorough adhesion of the cement and the development of the setting properties of the concrete), strong (to resist stresses), durable (to withstand alternate weather conditions of wetness and dryness, frost and thaw, etc.), suitably graded (for economy and the development of the strength and workability of the concrete), free from combustible material (to ensure adequate fire-resistance) and inert in the presence of water (otherwise disruption of the concrete may result by expansion and contraction movement). In addition, aggregate for concrete floors and roads should be effective in resisting abrasion. Flaky and laminated material should be avoided.

The following materials are used for coarse aggregate : (*a*) Broken brick, (*b*) broken stone, (*c*) gravel, (*d*) slag, (*e*) pumice, (*f*) breeze and clinker, (*g*) foamed slag and (*h*) expanded slate. See also *sawdust concrete* and *fibrous wood cement* (Chap. I, Vol. III).

(*a*) *Broken Brick.*—Old bricks from demolished buildings, etc., are broken for use as aggregate. This is a good aggregate, provided the bricks are not porous and are thoroughly cleaned, *i.e.*, any lime and plaster must be removed. Soft and porous brick aggregate is particularly unsuited for reinforced concrete work, as such admits air and moisture to cause corrosion of the steel; broken well-burnt brick aggregate makes a valuable concrete because of its strong, durable and fire-resisting qualities. Adherent lime and plaster are very objectionable, as any calcium sulphate may cause expansion and disintegration of the concrete. Bricks having a high sulphur content are also unsuitable. Broken brick aggregate should be well watered before being mixed to prevent excessive absorption of the water used in mixing which may cause the concrete to crack.

(b) *Broken Stone* is an excellent aggregate provided the stone is free from any undesirable mineral constituents and is not soft, porous, friable or laminated. Granites, sandstones and close-grained limestones are all suitable. The stone is crushed and then screened.

There are several forms of crushers, such as the jaw, hammer, disc, gyratory and roll types, which break up large blocks of the rock into small pieces. There are also several types of screens, most of which have a vibrating action. In screening, the material is passed from the crusher by a belt conveyor to the primary screen, which has a large (76 mm) mesh. The screened material is then passed successively through a series of screens of various sized meshes, *i.e.*, 38, 19 and 4·8 mm. Thus, the 76-38 mm grade is retained on the 38 mm sieve and passed to the stock bin, that which passes through it is discharged on to the 19 mm sieve which separates the 38–19 mm grade (discharged to a second stock hopper) and allows the finer material to pass through on to the 4·8 mm sieve to be separated into 19–4·8 mm and finer grades, each of which is conveyed to a stock bin.

(c) *Gravel* is another very good aggregate and is extensively used. It is hard and durable, and is obtained from river beds, the seashore, and inland deposits which are quarried. The gravel is excavated by hand labour or mechanically. Clay is a common impurity and must therefore be removed by washing. Seashore gravel, if required for reinforced concrete, should also be washed in fresh water so as to eliminate as much as possible of the salts. This is also known as ballast (see below).

(d) *Blast-furnace Slag* (p. 25) is a very uncertain material as a coarse aggregate. Some slags readily disintegrate and are quite unsuitable, whilst others are inert and are commonly used locally in producing concrete of good quality. This is also referred to as " ballast " in districts where it is used (see also (g)).

Burnt Ballast is produced by burning clay in a kiln, and the slabs are then crushed and screened. It is a suitable material for coarse aggregate, provided it has been hard-burnt. Under-burnt ballast and that containing sulphur (from the fuel) should not be used.

(e) *Pumice* is a whitish or yellowish material of volcanic origin which is highly honeycombed. It was imported into this country, chiefly from Germany, and used as an aggregate for *lightweight concrete*. This concrete, although relatively weak, is, as its name implies, light and very suitable for partitions (Chap, I, Vol. III), covering flat roofs, encasing beams and pillars, and similar purposes where strength is not important. Pumice is crushed. Dust and shaly fragments should be removed. It does not contain sulphur and is inert.

(f) *Breeze and Clinker* are waste materials resulting from the burning of coal. Breeze is obtained from gasworks and coke ovens; clinker is the mineral matter or ash from furnaces. These materials produced from certain coals, especially when they contain small particles of the coal, are distinctly unsound and should be avoided. They have been responsible for a large number of concrete failures owing to the considerable expansion which takes place when

associated with cement. They may also have a large sulphur content, which will cause rapid and extensive corrosion of steel and the spalling off of the concrete. These are classified as " prohibited aggregates," are quite unsuitable for concreting, and they must not therefore be used for reinforced concrete work or for encasing beams, pillars, etc., in steel framed buildings. However, not all breeze and clinker are dangerous, and on account of cheapness and lightness, much is used for internal concrete block or slab partitions (Chap, I, Vol. III).

(g) *Foamed Slag*, which somewhat resembles pumice, is produced from blast-furnace slag by rapidly cooling the molten material with water. It is light in weight owing to its cellular structure and is crushed and graded as required. It is very suitable for the manufacture of partition slabs (Chap. I, Vol. III).

(h) *Expanded Slate* is another good lightweight aggregate which has not been extensively used, probably because its cost is higher than that of foamed slag. It is produced by heating waste slag to a high temperature until its thickness is considerably increased. This light honeycombed material is then crushed and graded.

Grading of Aggregates.—The importance of suitably grading the aggregates in order to obtain a concrete of good quality has been referred to on p. 28. It is therefore desirable that samples of the aggregate should be taken periodically and examined.

These samples should be representative, and therefore ten are taken from different parts of the consignment. These are well mixed together and a final test sample obtained. According to C.P. 114, the aggregates must comply with B.S. 882, both referred to on p. 28, and they must be tested as described in B.S. 812—Methods for Sampling and Testing of Mineral Aggregates (sands and fillers). The latter splits sands into four zones having different degrees of fineness, zones 1 to 3 are suitable for reinforced concrete work. Samples are taken of the aggregates and passed successively through a series of nine standard sieves, *i.e.*, 38·1, 19·1, 9·5, 4·8 mm, No. 7 (2.4 mm square mesh), No. 14 (1·2 mm mesh), No. 25 (0·6 mm mesh), No. 52 (0·3 mm mesh), and No. 100 (0·15 mm mesh). It will be observed that the size of opening of a sieve is double (or approximately so) that of the next smaller sieve. The aggregate retained on each sieve is then carefully weighed and the amount passed through each is expressed as a percentage.

The following figures shown in brackets are the limits of material passing through the sieves in respect to zone 1 fine aggregate : 4·8 mm sieve (90 to 100 per cent.), No. 7 sieve (60 to 95 per cent.), No. 14 sieve (30 to 70 per cent.), No. 25 sieve (15 to 34 per cent.), No. 52 sieve (5 to 20 per cent.) and No. 100 sieve (0 to 10 per cent.).

The following are the limits of material passing through sieves in respect to coarse aggregate of a specified size varying from a maximum of 38 mm to a minimum of 4·8 mm; 38 mm sieve (95 to 100 per cent.) 19·1 sieve (30 to 70 per cent.), 9·5 mm sieve (10 to 35 per cent.) and 4·8 mm sieve (0 to 5 per cent.); for 19 to 4·8 mm coarse aggregate, used in reinforced concrete work, the limits are : 19·1 mm sieve (95 to 100 per cent.), 9·5 mm sieve (25 to 55 per cent.) and 4·8 mm sieve (0 to 10 per cent.).

Not more than one-fifth and not less than one-twentieth of zone 1 sand of 4·8 mm maximum size should pass through a No. 52 sieve; for zone 3 sand the percentage passing the same sieve is 15 to 40. Unsuitable grading of the sand is a frequent cause of defects in concrete, and the strength and workability of the concrete depend a good deal upon the percentage of sand which passes through a No. 52 sieve. Thus, an excess of this fine material necessitates the addition of an *excessive amount of water* during mixing and a *decrease in the strength* of concrete results, whilst a deficiency of fine material causes unworkability and harshness. The above B.S. 882 requires that not more than 10 per cent. by weight of the sand (20 per cent. for crushed stone sands) shall pass through a No. 100 sieve. Fine dust must be excluded from the aggregate.

For coarse aggregate of 19 mm maximum size, not more than 55 per cent. and not less than one-quarter should pass through a 9·5 mm sieve.

The importance of correct grading cannot be over emphasized. The shape of the particles of aggregate influences the workability of the concrete. Thus, concrete with crushed aggregate having sharp edges will require more water than that made of rounded particles, and therefore the latter makes a stronger concrete for a given workability and is preferred to angular particles. The particles should be compact and not flat and elongated.

Proportioning Concrete.—The composition of concrete varies considerably, depending upon the specific requirements in respect to strength, durability, impermeability, workability and economy, in addition to the quality and characteristics of the materials. Thus, the proportions of materials for concrete required for a reinforced concrete beam will differ from those for a concrete non-load-bearing internal partition or for site concrete.

Great care should be taken to determine the correct proportions of the materials. Cement should always be specified by weight and it also good practice to express the proportions of the aggregates by weight. The Code of Practice (see below) require all materials to be weighed.

Sometimes the proportions of the aggregates are specified by volume; thus the Building Regulations stipulate the site concrete shall consist of not less than 50 kg of cement to every 0.11 m³ of fine aggregate and 0.16 m³ of coarse aggregate.

In practice, and during wet weather especially, it is difficult to obtain batches of concrete which are uniform when the fine aggregate is measured by volume. This is due to the increase in volume, known as *bulking*, of the sand which occurs when it is in a moist condition. Experiments show that 1 m³ of dry sand will approximately increase to 1·2 m³ if 3 per cent. of water is added to it, and therefore there is actually less aggregate in 1 m³ of moist sand than in the same volume of dry sand. If the water content increases to 4 per cent., the volume will be increased by approximately $\frac{1}{4}$; as the moisture increases beyond this percentage, the bulking gradually decreases, and when the sand becomes submerged the volume of the inundated sand is the same as that when dry. The finer sand, the greater the bulking. This bulking of moist sand should be allowed for; it is customary to assume that the volume has increased by 20 per cent., and therefore this amount of sand is added to the proportion of fine aggregate when mixing.

It is obvious that this is only an approximate correction. In wet weather, sand which has been deposited on a site has a variable water content. When high-grade concrete is required, the actual bulking may be obtained in the following manner: A small box is filled with the moist sand. This sand is dried, returned to the box, and

after being levelled off at the top the reduced depth of the sand is measured. The percentage of bulking equals

$$\frac{\text{Depth of box} - \text{depth of dry aggregate}}{\text{Depth of dry aggregate}} \times 100.$$

This method is not readily applied in practice and is only resorted to when specially called for.

The bulking of sand does not present any practical difficulties when the mixes are proportioned by weight. Coarse aggregates are not normally subjected to the phenomenon of bulking.

The Code of Practice for The Structural Use of Concrete provides for two methods of determining the mix proportions of concrete:—(*a*) *designed mixes* and (*b*) *standard mixes*.

(*a*) *Designed mixes.* In this method the designer specifies the concrete strength required and is free to select the proportions of the different materials to achieve this strength. The Code specifies a number of normal grades of concrete having different characteristic cube strengths. The following Table I gives three extracts from the Code; it will be noted that the grade number is the value in N/mm² of the 28 day cube strength.

TABLE I

Grade	Specified characteristic cube strength in N/mm² at	
	28 days	7 days
10	10	6·7
22·5	22·5	15·0
37·5	37·5	26·0

By adopting designed mixes economy of materials is obtained because the required strength and workability for the construction in hand can be obtained. This is done by, prior to the start of construction, making 6 cubes (see p. 32) from 4 separate batches of concrete (including one batch from full-scale production conditions). The actual materials to be used for the work are weighed and the slump (see p. 32) of each batch measured. Three cubes from each batch are tested (see p. 32) at 7 days and 3 at 28 days. If the desired strength is not attained the proportions are altered and the procedure repeated until attainment.

The concrete mix has to be designed to have a mean strength greater than the required characteristic strength by a margin of between 1·64 times and twice the standard deviation calculated on at least 40 separate batches but not less than 1/3rd of the specified strength for grades of 15 and below and 7·5 N/mm² for grades 22·5 and above.

The site procedure to ensure *quality control* of the mix includes the following. When the mix is first used on the site at least 40 cubes should be obtained (8 samples per day over a 5 day period). Thereafter samples should be obtained from about 4% of the batches made with at least one sample per day.

(b) *Standard mixes.* The Code gives a table of standard mixes wherein the weights (in kg) of cement and total aggregates are given for three sizes of aggregate and for medium and high workability. Table II below is an extract from the Code table for two grades of concrete using 19 mm maximum aggregate and medium slump (see p. 32) of between 25 and 50 mm. The grade number should give the 28-day cube strength in N/mm² of the mix.

TABLE II

Grade	Materials	Grade	Materials
10	cement 240 kg aggregate 1900 kg sand content 35-50%	15	cement 300 kg aggregate 1900 kg sand content 35-50%

If grade 15 concrete from this table is used with 35% sand content the proportions of fine and coarse aggregate to 1 part of cement can be found thus: 35% of the total aggregate weight of 1 900 kg=665 kg; leaving 1 235 kg of coarse aggregate. The mix proportion is thus 300 : 665 : 1 235 which is equivalent to 1 : 2·21 : 4·12. The latter is a very common mix for reinforced concrete work which, given good quality control, could have a strength of about 20 N/mm²; i.e., about 25% in excess of the grade number value.

The latter example shows that the use of standard mixes is not economical; the proportions of materials in them are chosen to reduce the possibility of poor concrete being produced. Standard mixes are intended for use on very small jobs where quality control by taking regular test cubes is not practicable.

It is convenient for the student to have some idea of concrete proportions for different classes of work. Thus, 1 : 3 : 6 is commonly used for strip foundations. 1 : 2 : 4 makes a general purpose reinforced concrete as does 1 : 1½ : 3. 1 : 1 : 2, having a high cement content, produces very strong impermeable concrete.

Water.—The water used for mixing concrete is required to produce a workable plastic mix, in addition to hydrating the cement. It must be clean and fresh. It is emphasized that the strength of concrete depends upon the quantity of water used in relation to the cement content, and *an excess of water, however slight,* reduces the strength of the concrete.

The following tests were carried out in the Building Laboratory of the Manchester University Institute of Science and Technology to demonstrate to students the marked effect that the water content has upon the compressive strength of concrete : Three different mixes of concrete were separately prepared. The materials in mix "A" were mixed dry in the proportion of 1 : 1 : 2. The cement used was normal Portland cement. The mix was divided and each half was separately mixed with water, one half having 30 per cent. more water added than the other. A 100 mm cube (see p. 32) was then made from each half of each batch and tested for compression strength at the end of twenty-eight days. Mixes "B" and "C" were dealt with in a similar manner, the excess water added to one-half of each mix being also 30 per cent. The following were the results :—

TABLE III

Mix	Proportions	Normal Mixes			Mixes with 30 per cent. Excess Water			Per Cent. Reduction in Strength
		$\frac{W}{C}$	Slump	Strength	$\frac{W}{C}$	Slump	Strength	
			mm	(N/mm²)		(mm)	(N/mm²)	
A	1 : 1 : 1	0·43	64	34·9	0·56	229	23·4	33
B	1 : 2 : 4	0·62	89	20·3	0·81	229	11·6	42½
C	1 : 3 : 6	0·85	50	10·7	1·10	179	5·91	44½

These figures illustrate the appreciable reduction in strength as a result of excess water content.

This relationship between the quantity of mixing water and amount of cement in a concrete mix is known as the *water-cement ratio*, expressed as $\frac{\text{“ W ”}}{\text{“ C ”}}\left(\frac{\text{Water}}{\text{Cement}}\right)$ either by volume, or by weight, or by the number of litres of water per 50 kg (weight of a bag) of cement. Thus, if expressed by volume, 1 m³ of water per 1 m³ of cement equals a ratio of $\frac{1}{1} = 1$; if by weight, this ratio becomes

$$\frac{1\ 000\ \text{kg (weight of 1 m}^3\text{ of water)}}{1\ 442\ \text{kg (weight of 1 m}^3\text{ of cement)}^1} = 0·69;$$

if 26·85 litres of water are used per 50 kg of cement, the ratio is

$$\frac{26.85\ \text{kg}}{50\ \text{kg}} = 0·54$$

Whilst in the laboratory the materials are usually taken by weight, it is more convenient for practical purposes to specify the number of litres per 50 kg bag of cement. The $\frac{W}{C}$ ratios and the corresponding strengths shown in Table III clearly indicate that the strength of the concrete is lowered as a result of the additional water.

It is not possible to state definitely the amount of water which should be used in a concrete mix, as this depends upon the desired workability, amount of water in the fine aggregate and that absorbed by the coarse aggregate. An approximate rule for finding the amount of water for concrete consisting of

[1] The weight of 1-cub. metre of cement depends upon its fineness; thus for normal Portland cement the weight is usually taken as 1 442 kg/m³; the finer ground rapid-hardening Portland cement may only weigh 1 282 kg/m³. The volume of 50 kg of normal P.C. is approx. 0·0347 m³.

dry and non-porous aggregate is to take 28 per cent. of the weight of the cement plus 4 per cent. of the weight of the aggregate. Thus, for a 1 : 2 : 4 mix requiring 50 kg cement, 0·0696 m³ sand (weighing 1 602 kg/m³) and 0·14 m³ gravel (weighing 1 570 kg/m³), the number of litres of water equals :

$$(\text{Cement}) \quad \frac{28}{100} \times 50 = 14 \text{ kg} \qquad\qquad = 14 \text{ litres}$$

$$(\text{Sand}) \quad \frac{4}{100} \times 0\cdot07 \times 1\,602 = 4\cdot48 \text{ kg} = 4\cdot48 \text{ ,,}$$

$$(\text{Gravel}) \quad \frac{4}{100} \times 0\cdot14 \times 1\,570 = 8\cdot8 \text{ kg} = 8\cdot8 \text{ ,,}$$

$$\overline{\qquad 27\cdot28 \text{ litres} \qquad}$$

Slump Test.—The best practical test for determining the desired workability of concrete and the required amount of water is that known as the slump test. This is now universally adopted both on the site during the progress of the work and in the laboratory. The apparatus simply consists of a metal mould, frustum of a cone in shape, with both ends open and provided with two handles; the dimensions are 305 mm high, 203 mm internal diameter at the bottom and 102 mm internal diameter at the top (see G, Fig. 9). A 610 mm long metal rod, 16 mm in diameter and bullet nosed, is also required.

In carrying out the test, the mould is placed on a flat surface which *must be non-absorbent*. It is filled with the freshly mixed concrete to a height of about 75 mm; this is puddled to expel the air by applying twenty-five strokes of the rod. The filling is completed in similar successive consolidated layers and the surface is struck off flush with the top by a trowel. The mould must be held firmly as it is being filled, and to prevent movement it may be provided with two flat footpieces, attached near the base, upon which the operator stands. Immediately it is full, the mould is carefully lifted *vertically* and placed on the mixing surface adjacent to the concrete specimen, which will have subsided or slumped. The amount of settlement, which varies according to the water content, is measured in mm by placing a rule across the top of the mould and measuring the height that its lower edge is above the top of the concrete. Thus, at H, Fig. 9, a 75 mm slump is indicated.

This is an excellent practical test, as it is simple and takes little time to carry out on the job. By its use it is possible to reasonably control and obtain a uniform consistency of the concrete. It is important to note that the slump will be affected if the cement and aggregates are changed, and therefore any such change of materials will necessitate preliminary trial tests to see if any alteration in the slump is necessary. A slump test is taken daily to check the consistency (or condition of wetness) of the concrete used for first-class work.

The slump values vary with different classes of work and the following may be taken as a general guide : For mass concrete and heavy reinforced concrete structures the slump varies from 25 to 100 mm. It may be necessary to increase the slump to 175 mm for columns, and for thin vertical and confined horizontal structures where adequate ramming of the concrete is not possible. For concrete roads the maximum slump should not exceed 25 mm in order that the necessary strength and wearing qualities may be obtained. Whilst a 175 mm slump is considered as a maximum for good quality mixes, it may be possible to increase this figure to 200 mm for concrete which does not require a high standard of strength. Concrete having a slump less than 50 mm must be well consolidated when placed in position to avoid honeycombing or pore spaces (see p. 35).

Compacting Factor Test.—This is another test applied to concrete, but it is only suitable for use in the laboratory. It is related to the workability of concrete, which is defined for this purpose as being the property which determines the amount of work required to compact or consolidate the concrete completely. The compacting factor may be defined as a measure of the density of a concrete achieved by a standard amount of work.

The apparatus used for this test consists of a frame which supports two truncated conical hoppers, one above the other, with a space between. A cylindrical mould, having a detachable base, is placed below these hoppers. Each of the latter has a hinged base which can be shot open.

The upper hopper is completely filled with the concrete immediately after mixing. The hinged door is released to allow the contents to fall into the lower hopper. The base of the latter is then opened and the concrete falls into the cylinder, completely filling it, the excess concrete being struck off level with the top. The compacting factor is then calculated in the following manner : The weight of the container when empty is subtracted from that of the container when full, and this net weight of concrete is divided by the weight of the concrete calculated from the known specific gravities of the cement, sand and coarse aggregate, in the correct proportions, required to fill the cylinder without pore spaces. Thus, if the net weight of the concrete is 3·56 kg and that of the contents of the cylinder (when no voids are left) is 3·79 kg, the compacting factor will be $\frac{3\cdot56}{3\cdot79} = 0\cdot94$. Experiments have shown that a compacting factor of 0·95 represents a concrete mix of high workability, that of 0·92 a medium workability, and 0·85 a low workability.

This is a useful test for comparing the workability of different mixes of concrete. Each specimen is brought to a standard condition (when deposited from the upper to the lower hopper) and is subjected to a standard amount of work when it falls into the cylinder.

Compression Test.—The quality of concrete is generally assessed by its crushing strength. This strength is determined by testing suitably prepared specimens of the concrete in a compression machine.

The form of standard test specimen favoured in this country is the 150 mm cube. This and the standard method of testing are specified in the B.S. 1881, Methods of Testing Concrete. The cement and fine aggregate, in correct proportions, are first mixed dry until a uniformly coloured mixture is obtained; the coarse aggregate is added and well mixed; the correct amount of water is then added and the composition mixed for at least two minutes. The concrete is tested for consistency by the slump test, described above, and after re-mixing it is placed in a steel mould of 150 mm by

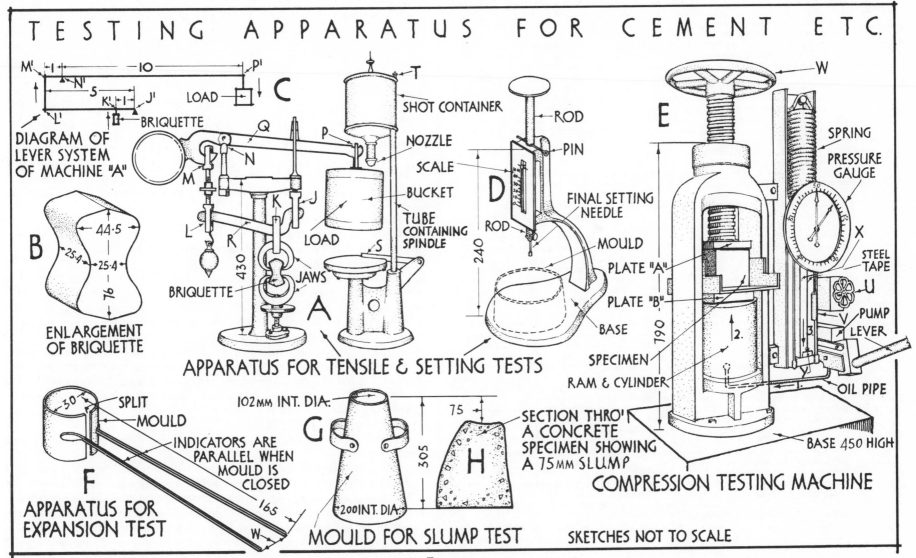

TESTING APPARATUS FOR CEMENT ETC.

DIAGRAM OF LEVER SYSTEM OF MACHINE "A"

LOAD

BRIQUETTE

C

B

44·5
25·4 25·4
76

ENLARGEMENT OF BRIQUETTE

Q
N
M
L
R
K
J
LOAD
JAWS
BRIQUETTE

A

SHOT CONTAINER
NOZZLE
SCALE
BUCKET
TUBE CONTAINING SPINDLE
LOAD
S
T

APPARATUS FOR TENSILE & SETTING TESTS

ROD
PIN
FINAL SETTING NEEDLE
MOULD
BASE
ROD
240

D

E
W
SPRING
PRESSURE GAUGE
PLATE "A"
PLATE "B"
BASE
SPECIMEN
RAM & CYLINDER
STEEL TAPE
X
U
V
PUMP LEVER
OIL PIPE
190
BASE 450 HIGH

COMPRESSION TESTING MACHINE

30
SPLIT
MOULD
INDICATORS ARE PARALLEL WHEN MOULD IS CLOSED
165
W

F

APPARATUS FOR EXPANSION TEST

102 MM INT. DIA.
75
305
200 INT. DIA.

G

SECTION THRO' A CONCRETE SPECIMEN SHOWING A 75 MM SLUMP

H

MOULD FOR SLUMP TEST

SKETCHES NOT TO SCALE

FIGURE 9

150 mm by 150 mm internal dimensions. The mould has a steel base plate attached and both this and the internal faces of the mould must be well oiled before filling to make the joint watertight, prevent sticking of the concrete and facilitate the removal of the cube without damage. The concrete is placed in the mould in three layers of approximately equal thickness, each layer being separately tamped 35 times if the slump is 38 mm or less (or 25 strokes for wetter mixes) with a 380 mm by 25 mm by 25 mm steel bar weighing 1·8 kg, after which the surface is carefully smoothed level with a trowel flush with the top of the mould. The mould is then stored in a damp cabinet for twenty-four hours, after which the concrete cube is removed from the mould, marked, and either immersed in water contained in a tank or buried in damp sand until the cube is ready for testing. This protection of the cube, called *curing*, is necessary to prevent evaporation of the water and to provide a favourable condition for setting and hardening of the concrete. The strength of the concrete is usually taken at either fourteen or twenty-eight days after it has been mixed; occasionally early date strengths are taken at three and seven days, and sometimes the strengths at three months and one year are required.

Test cubes prepared on the site during the progress of the work are kept damp for twenty-four hours and then removed from their moulds. After being marked to distinguish them, they are carefully packed in a wood box, encased in damp sand or sacking and dispatched to the laboratory where they are kept damp until required for testing.

One type of compression testing machine, manufactured by Messrs J. A. Amsler, and of 500 000 N capacity, is shown at E, Fig. 9. The concrete specimen is placed on the lower compression plate B attached to the ram or piston which operates within the press cylinder. The upper compression plate A is connected by means of a ball-and-socket joint to the large screw which is operated by the hand wheel W. The screw is adjusted to lower the plate A tightly on to the top of the specimen. Brackets at the right-hand side support the oil pump, subsidiary cylinder X with small piston, pressure gauge and spiral spring. Oil is conveyed by a pipe to the pump from a reservoir fixed to the back of the machine; the pump is connected to the press cylinder by an oil pipe, and a branch (not shown) from this pipe is connected to the subsidiary cylinder X.

After plate A has been tightened down and valve U closed, the pump is operated by raising and lowering the 915 mm long lever by hand. This forces the oil along the pipe (see arrow " I ") into the press cylinder to exert pressure on the underside of the ram. The latter and plate B gradually rise (see arrow " 2 ") to press the specimen against the stationary plate A. Meanwhile the oil forced along the branch pipe to cylinder X presses the piston downwards (see arrow " 3 ") and this extends the spiral spring. This extension of the spring is transmitted to the indicating hand or pointer on the gauge by a steel ribbon tape which is fixed at Y and passed round a pulley fixed to the spindle of the pointer and weighted at V. This causes the pointer to rotate round the dial, the scale on which is calibrated to give direct load readings. The pump is operated and the oil pressure increased, until the specimen is crushed. When this occurs the indicating hand gradually returns to zero, but a loose pointer, which the hand engages as it rotates during the test, remains to register the highest point reached when the specimen failed. The figure, expressed in kg, is divided by the area of the cross-section of the specimen to give the crushing strength of the concrete in kg per mm²; if this value is multiplied by 9·8 the stress in N/mm² is obtained. The specimen is removed by opening valve U and reversing the hand wheel W; this relieves the pressure on the press cylinder and the weight of the ram forces the oil from the cylinder to the reservoir.

Very little effort is required to hand-operate this machine and the time taken to carry out the test is approximately two minutes, depending upon the strength of the cube (about 15 N/mm² per min.).

For testing specimens requiring comparatively small pressures to crush them (such as timber), the spring on the 500 000 N machine is replaced by a lighter one and the dial is substituted by one reading to 200 000 N. This type of machine is also made having a capacity of 2 MN. This larger machine is necessary when 150 mm concrete cubes have to be tested, as a 500 000 N machine will only test 100 mm cubes at twenty-eight days.

The specimens referred to in Table III, p. 31 were tested in a 10 000 N machine. The following results of tests, which may be considered as typical, show how the strength of concrete, having a 50 mm slump, increases with age :—

TABLE IV

Type of Cement	Nominal Mix	Compressive Strength (N/mm²)				
		3 Days	7 Days	28 Days	3 Months	1 Year
Ordinary Portland .		9·65	17·2	26·8	33	45
Rapid-hardening P. .	1 : 2 : 4	17·2	24·1	34·4	38	48·2
High Alumina . .		48·2	49	55	No appreciable increase	

Mixing Concrete.—It is most important that the materials shall be thoroughly mixed in correct proportion. The mixing should be continued until the concrete is of a uniform colour and consistency. Concrete is either (1) hand-mixed or (2) machine-mixed.

1. *Hand-mixing.*—This method is sometimes adopted on small jobs. The mixing should never be carried out on the bare ground, as this results in the materials being contaminated by the earth which is scraped up. It should be done on a proper close-boarded platform or staging, 2·75 or 3 m square, preferably made of t. and g. floor boards fixed to five lengths of 100 mm by 50 mm battens. The joints of the boards must be close to prevent the escape of liquid grout. Sometimes the boards are protected by a covering of sheet iron or zinc plate, and a raised kerb round three of the sides is provided. The platform should be quite level to prevent the water from draining off, and it should be placed conveniently near to the place at which the concrete is to be deposited. A water point is brought near to the platform.

Careful measurement (by weighing) of the materials is essential for good quality concrete.

After proportioning the materials are mixed at least " twice dry and twice wet." Usually two men, one on each side of the heap, shovel the heap to one side, turning and sprinkling the materials in the process. This operation is repeated, the heap being thrown back to its original position. If necessary the materials are again turned over until the colour is uniform, free from streaks of brown and grey. Water is then added. Only the correct amount of water varying with the nature of the work and materials, and probably determined from a slump test (see p. 32), must be used. It may be measured by a bucket of known capacity. The water should not be thrown on to the heap from the bucket, as this washes the cement from the aggregate, but rather sprinkled on by means of a watering-can, having a rosehead, and which is filled from the measured pails. Usually a third man adds the water whilst the other two attend to the mixing and turn over the heap at least twice, as above described, until a uniform consistency is obtained.

An alternative method of mixing is to spread the measured sand in a layer of even thickness on the platform, the cement is distributed over this, both are mixed together until the colour is uniform, the coarse aggregate is thrown over the mixture which is turned over at least twice. Water is added and the whole again turned over two or three times.

2. *Machine-mixing.*—Concrete is now chiefly produced by mechanical mixing except where only small quantities are required. Machine-mixing is faster and cheaper than hand-mixing, and it generally produces a more thorough mix having additional strength.[1] There are two groups of mixers, *i.e.*, (*a*) batch mixers and (*b*) continuous mixers.

(*a*) *Batch Mixers*, which are portable, include the (i) tilting drum and (ii) closed drum types. Each is usually driven by either a petrol or oil engine or an electric motor.

(i) The *tilting drum mixer* (see line diagram J, Fig. 23) consists of a hopper and mixing drum. Correct quantities of cement and aggregates are loaded into the hopper, which is raised to discharge the materials into the drum. The coarse aggregate is first placed in the hopper, followed by the sand and the cement. The capacity of the drum varies considerably, one of 0·3/0·2 m^3 being useful for average work; the first number indicating the capacity (in cubic metres) of unmixed materials and the latter number that of the wet concrete produced. The correct amount of mixing water is discharged into the drum from an automatic tank fixed above it. Projecting metal baffle blades fixed to the inside of the drum assist in the distribution of the materials as they impinge against them whilst the drum is revolving. The period of mixing, which may be controlled automatically, should not be less than one minute and not more than two minutes after all of the materials have been added. The strength of the concrete is not materially increased if the latter period is prolonged; excessive mixing produces an undesirable stiffening up of the concrete. When mixing has been completed, the drum is rotated vertically to discharge the concrete.

(ii) The *closed drum mixer* has a hopper, a mixing drum which rotates on a horizontal axis, and a steel chute which is inserted into the drum after the mixing has been completed and down which the concrete is discharged.

(*b*) *Continuous Mixers.*—These are used on large engineering jobs. The aggregate, cement and water are mechanically measured and fed into the mixer from which the concrete is continuously discharged.

Central Mixing.—In connection with large contracts, a central batching and mixing plant is often installed on the site. This may consist of large elevated storage bins, below which are hoppers and mixing drums. The aggregate is conveyed to the storage bins and these feed the measuring hoppers below as required; the hoppers

[1] In the Code of Practice for The Structural Use of Concrete (see p. 28) it is stipulated that concrete should be mechanically mixed.

also receive the cement. The materials from the hoppers pass into the mixing water is automatically added, and, after being mixed, the concrete is deposited trucks and transported on rails to the required part of the site, where it is deposited.

Central batching plants are now being used to batch the materials and discharge them into mixing trucks which perform the actual mixing in course of transit from the plant to the job.

Placing Concrete.—Concrete should be placed in position as soon as possible and before setting has commenced. For short distances the concrete is usually shovelled from the mixing platform or discharged from the mixing drum into watertight steel wheelbarrows or handcarts and conveyed to the place of deposition. In order that the effect of the mixing will not be nullified, concrete must be carefully placed and not thrown from a height, otherwise its consistence becomes non-uniform by the separation of the heavier from the lighter particles. Concrete required for upper floors is hoisted by means of a *barrow-lift* (pulley block and tackle, attached to the scaffolding, for lifting the full barrows) or *concrete-hoist* (large hoppers containing the concrete are lifted to any desired height, the apparatus resembling the ordinary passenger-lift).

The placing of concrete on a large scale may also be effected either by tipping-trucks, towers or by pumping. Tipping-trucks, as already explained, run upon rails laid round the site and convey the concrete where required. A tower may reach a great height; a mechanical mixer is placed at the bottom, and this feeds concrete into large receptacles which are hoisted to the top of the tower where the concrete is passed down inclined shoots and deposited where required. Pumping concrete has been proved effective on large jobs where congested conditions prevent the placing of the mixture on the site; a pump forces the mixed concrete through a steel pipe 100 to 150 mm in diameter, to the place of deposition; concrete has been delivered in this manner to a height exceeding 30 m and for a horizontal distance of approximately 300 m.

Compacting Concrete.—Concrete after being placed in position should be well *rammed* or *punned* or *tamped* to consolidate it. This is done either by hand or mechanically. Two forms of rammers are shown at F and G, Fig. 23; these may be used for mass concrete. Metal pummels, similar to G, of various sizes are employed for consolidating the concrete round the steel bars in reinforced concrete structures. For mass concrete work the concrete is laid in layers not exceeding 300 mm thick, and each layer must be compacted before the next is spread. For reinforced work the concrete should be deposited in successive layers not exceeding 150 mm in thickness, and these must be rammed in turn. A 16 mm rod is useful for ramming (or " rodding ") concrete and expelling the air (see also p. 32).

For concrete work on a large scale, hand-compacting methods are being replaced by mechanical means. The concrete is consolidated by vibration, the *vibrators* being operated by compressed air or electricity. One form, called a *surface vibrator*, consists of a flat plate which is placed on the surface of the concrete, a vibrating appliance is attached, and this transmits rapid shocks or vibrations to the concrete which is consolidated as the plate is moved slowly over the surface. Another is the poker vibrator consisting of a needle, 760 mm long (or a fork with four prongs), which penetrates the concrete as the appliance,

...at the head, vibrates and consolidates. *External vibrators* ...rating reinforced concrete work. The vibrators are clamped ...temporary wood framing used to support the concrete until ...ese transmit shocks (some 9 000 per minute) through the ...concrete and consolidation results.

...ncrete is denser than that which is hand-compacted, and it is ...impervious and weather-resistant.

...oncrete.—The water must not be allowed to evaporate from the ...d the longer the concrete is kept moist, the more effective will be ...l combination of the cement with the water. The rapid drying out of the...er considerably reduces the strength of the concrete. The concrete should therefore be covered over immediately it has been consolidated. A layer of sand or sacking, upon which water is sprinkled each day for a week, is effective. Surface bituminous coatings are sometimes applied to prevent evaporation, the liquid being sprayed on the concrete.

Frost can do considerable damage to concrete before it has hardened, and once it has frozen it does not increase in strength. As a protection against frost, the concrete should be at once covered over with sacks, tarpaulins, straw, sawdust, etc. Canvas screens assist in protecting concrete from cold winds, and in severe weather the covering of windows affords a partial protection to internal concrete work in buildings in course of construction.

Waterproofed Concrete.—The production in a laboratory of concrete which is practically waterproof is a relatively simple matter when clean, well graded and best quality materials, properly proportioned, are thoroughly mixed with the correct amount of water under ideal conditions. In practice, however, where the conditions are less favourable, impervious concrete is not readily produced, and unless the various factors which tend to the production of good quality concrete are rigidly controlled, it will be interspersed with voids to such an extent as to render the product porous. Where the concrete is required to be impervious, it is now a common practice to use admixtures, known as waterproofers, which will have the effect of reducing the void space. Reference has been made to waterproofers on p. 27. The powder, paste and liquid forms are used for waterproofing concrete. The amount of waterproofer added to the concrete varies, but if in powdered form the usual proportion is 1·5 kg of the powder to 50 kg of cement. When hand-mixed, the concrete is prepared by adding the required amount of the waterproofer to the cement and thoroughly mixing them. If the concrete is machine-mixed, it is recommended that approximately half of the coarse aggregate, sand and cement are charged in this sequence into the hopper, all of the waterproofer is then spread over the cement, followed by the rest of the cement, sand and aggregate; these are placed into the drum, which is rotated for about one-quarter of a minute before the measured amount of water is added and the mixing is completed. The general proportion of paste waterproofer is 3% by weight of the cement, the paste being dissolved in the mixing water before the latter is added to the cement, sand and coarse aggregate.

When in liquid form, the waterproofer is usually in the proportion of 1 litre of the liquid to 15 litres of the mixing water (see pp. 27 and 56).

Certain of the waterproofers are just finely ground chalk, talc and iron filings which reduce the voids in the concrete. Others are chemically active, such as sulphate and sodium carbonate.

Waterproofed concrete can also be obtained by using waterproofed cement (p. 28), this is the most usual way of preparing large quantities.

BONDING

Students should revise the principles of bonding stated in Chap. I, Vol. I. The structural design of brick walls is given in Chap. IV, Vol. IV.

Squint Junctions.—Most junctions between walls are right-angled, as described in Chap. I, Vol. I, and squint or oblique junctions are not often called for.

Fig. 10 shows some typical examples of squint junctions. Those at A, B, C and D show English bond and the remainder are in double Flemish bond.

Details A and B show alternate courses of 215 mm and 327·5 mm squint walls connected at an angle of 45° to a 327·5 mm wall, and those at C and D indicate an angle of 60° between the walls. It should be noted in each case that (1) the heading course of the squint wall is bonded into the stretching course of the main wall, (2) the alternate stretching course of the squint wall butts against the heading course of the main wall and (3) the first brick at J in this stretching course is a three-quarter bevelled bat. For comparative purposes and convenience in setting-out, the angle between the walls in each detail has been made to coincide at J with the continuous transverse joint of the main wall. In practice, both the position and magnitude of this angle vary.

The double Flemish details at E to H show similar angles and thickness of walls. It will be observed that, for convenience, the 169 mm bevelled bat in each of the squint walls coincides with the through transverse joint of the main wall at J, and the first bonding brick in the alternate course of each squint wall is a header on face.

In this class of work the amount of cutting necessary to avoid continuous vertical joints should be kept to a minimum, the cut bricks should be as large as possible, and awkward shapes of bricks difficult to cut should be restricted.

Squint Quoins.—The description of the more usual right-angled or square quoins in Chap. I, Vol. I, should be referred to when considering squint quoins. The latter are of two forms, *i.e.*, (*a*) obtuse and (*b*) acute squint quoins.

(*a*) *Obtuse Squint Quoins.*—These are formed when two walls meet at an internal angle greater than 90°, such as at a bay window (see O, Fig. 11) and splay-corners of buildings adjoining streets. Typical examples are shown at A, B, C, D and E. Conforming to the general rule, the closer appears next to the quoin header, which latter is often less than 112·5 mm on face. It should be

SQUINT JUNCTIONS
ENGLISH BOND

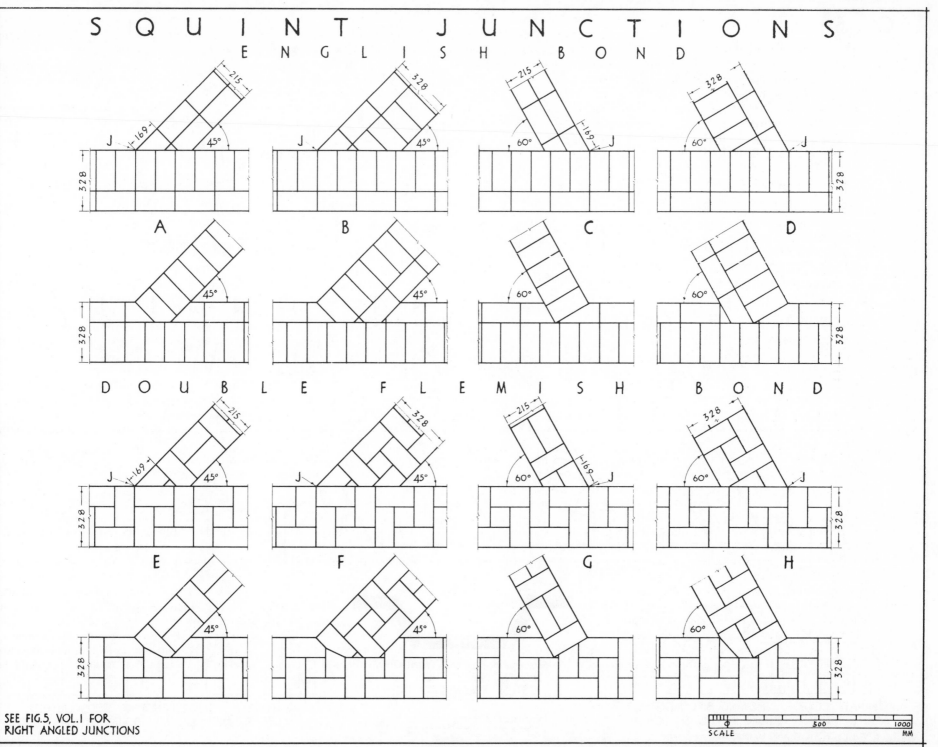

SEE FIG.5, VOL.1 FOR
RIGHT ANGLED JUNCTIONS

FIGURE 10

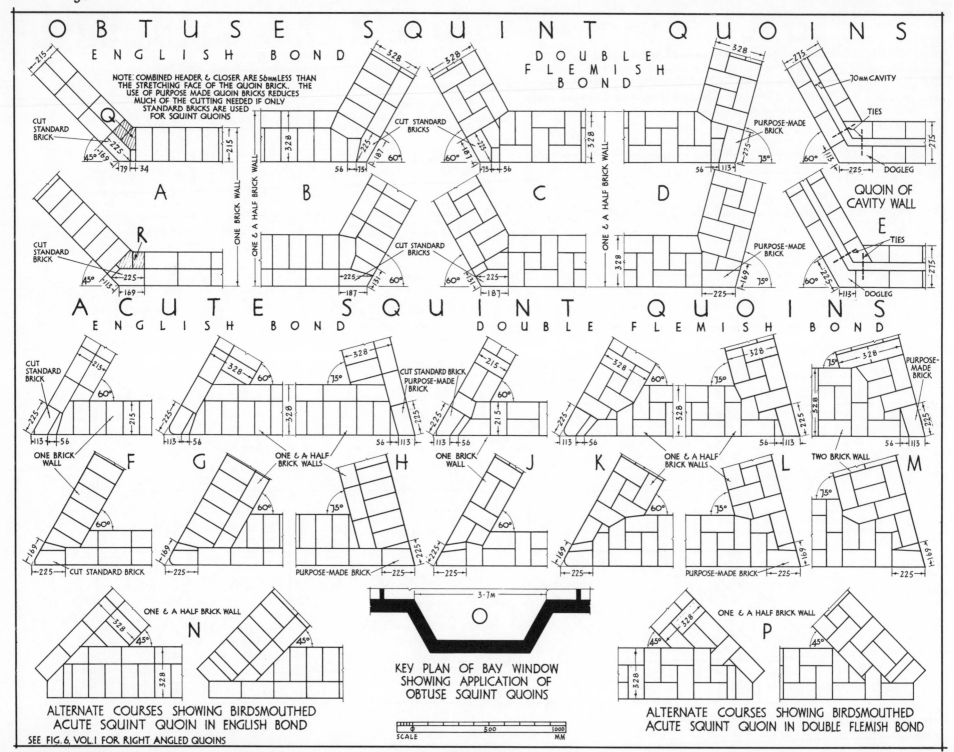

OBTUSE SQUINT QUOINS

ENGLISH BOND

DOUBLE FLEMISH BOND

NOTE: COMBINED HEADER & CLOSER ARE 56mm LESS THAN THE STRETCHING FACE OF THE QUOIN BRICK. THE USE OF PURPOSE MADE QUOIN BRICKS REDUCES MUCH OF THE CUTTING NEEDED IF ONLY STANDARD BRICKS ARE USED FOR SQUINT QUOINS

CUT STANDARD BRICK

CUT STANDARD BRICKS

PURPOSE-MADE BRICK

70mm CAVITY

TIES

DOGLEG

QUOIN OF CAVITY WALL

A   B   C   D   E

R   CUT STANDARD BRICK   CUT STANDARD BRICKS   PURPOSE-MADE BRICK   TIES   DOGLEG

ONE BRICK WALL   ONE & A HALF BRICK WALL   ONE & A HALF BRICK WALL

ACUTE SQUINT QUOINS

ENGLISH BOND   DOUBLE FLEMISH BOND

CUT STANDARD BRICK

CUT STANDARD BRICK PURPOSE-MADE BRICK

PURPOSE-MADE BRICK

ONE BRICK WALL   ONE & A HALF BRICK WALLS   ONE BRICK WALL   ONE & A HALF BRICK WALLS   TWO BRICK WALL

F   G   H   J   K   L   M

CUT STANDARD BRICK   PURPOSE-MADE BRICK   PURPOSE-MADE BRICK

ONE & A HALF BRICK WALL

N

ALTERNATE COURSES SHOWING BIRDSMOUTHED ACUTE SQUINT QUOIN IN ENGLISH BOND

SEE FIG. 6, VOL.1 FOR RIGHT ANGLED QUOINS

O

KEY PLAN OF BAY WINDOW SHOWING APPLICATION OF OBTUSE SQUINT QUOINS

3·7M

SCALE   0   500   1000   MM

ONE & A HALF BRICK WALL

P

ALTERNATE COURSES SHOWING BIRDSMOUTHED ACUTE SQUINT QUOIN IN DOUBLE FLEMISH BOND

FIGURE 11

noted that, in each case, the combined width of the header and closer is 56 mm less than the quoin stretcher. Thus, the alternate courses at A show the stretcher face to be 169 mm; therefore the return header, together with the closer, is 169−56=113 mm; as the header is 79 mm, the closer is 113−79=34 mm as shown. Joints which appear at the internal angles should be lapped as much as possible at successive courses. In this connection stability would be increased at the internal angle at A if purpose-made bricks Q and R (shown shaded) were used, as these would eliminate the 112·5 mm wide mitred joints at the angle.

For faced work it is now general to employ purpose-mades for the quoin bricks, and most of the larger manufacturers stock special bricks, such as A, B, C, D and J, Fig. 5, for this purpose. A much better appearance is thus obtained than when ordinary standard bricks are cut to shape. In the absence of purpose-made bricks, wire-cuts only should be shaped, as those with frogs produce ugly joints if the margins are removed.

(b) *Acute Squint Quoins* are rarely employed. They are necessary at corners of buildings abutting on streets which meet at an internal angle less than 90°. A few typical examples are detailed in Fig. 11, those at F, G, H and N showing alternate courses in English bond and those at J, K, L, M and P indicating alternate courses in double Flemish bond. In each case the rules of bonding which influence the face appearance have been complied with (see Chap. I, Vol. I).

Several expedients are sometimes adopted to dispense with the sharp arrises at very acute quoins, as such are readily damaged, difficult to cut (if standard bricks are used) and may cause injury to persons coming in contact with them. Thus, at F and J the corner is removed (or, preferably, purposely moulded to the shape shown) and bullnoses are shown at G and K. A simple and effective alternative is shown at N and P. where a bird's-mouthed appearance is obtained by the use

of standard bricks which require little cutting and which cut surfaces are not exposed.

The above are only a few examples of squint quoins. There are a number of alternatives. The aim should be to obtain the maximum lap with the minimum of cutting. Whilst the correct face appearance is not necessary if the walls are to be plastered, the principles of sound bonding should be observed and continuous straight joints avoided.

Piers.—Further examples of piers illustrated in Fig. 7, Vol. I, are shown at J, K, L and M, Fig. 12. The alternative plans of *detached squint piers* (J and K) are typical of those required in the construction of bay windows. The number of joints could be reduced, and greater strength therefore obtained, if purpose-mades were used instead of cut standard bricks.

An example of a *detached octagonal pier* is shown by plans of alternative courses at L, and an *attached octagonal pier* is detailed at M. Other polygonal forms, especially the hexagonal, are sometimes preferred. These may be constructed of standard bricks, cut to shape as required, but a better appearance is, of course, obtained if purpose-made bricks are used. Two further examples of detached piers are shown at R, Fig. 24 (see p. 64).

CAVITY OR HOLLOW WALLS

This type of construction is now very common and, for the reasons stated on pp. 42 and 43, is generally preferred to solid wall construction for many types of buildings, especially houses. Cavity walls are detailed in Figs. 13 and 14.

A cavity wall is usually an external wall, although it is sometimes adopted internally because of its good sound-resisting quality (see Chap. I, Vol. III). It consists of two separate walls[1], known as *leaves* or *skins*, having a cavity between, and connected together by metal ties. The Building Regulations require walls to be adequately insulated (see p. 43 where an external wall must have a maximum U-value of 0.45 W/m²K). A and P Fig. 13 shows such a wall having an external leaf of brick 102.5 mm thick, 50 mm cavity, a 115 mm thick inner leaf of aerated concrete block[2] with an internal lining of 12.5 mm plasterboard backed with 12.5 mm polystyrene fixed to the leaf with plaster dabs; giving a wall 292.5 mm thick. Such construction is satisfactory for a two-storey house. When a stronger wall is required blocks up to 200 mm thick are available.

The width of the cavity varies from 50 to 75 mm, the former being the minimum specified in the Building Regulations.

Ties.—These must be sufficiently strong for the purpose, be non-corrodible and so shaped that water from the outer leaf will not pass along them to the inner leaf. The metal ties are usually of mild steel, and these should be thoroughly galvanized or dipped in hot tar and sanded to protect them from rust. Either copper or stainless steel or similar durable and highly corrosive-resistant metal ties should be selected for important buildings and those near the sea.

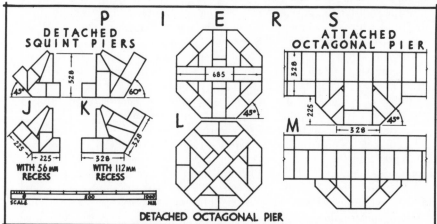

PIERS

DETACHED SQUINT PIERS

528

45° 60°

J K

225 328

WITH 56mm RECESS   WITH 112mm RECESS

SCALE

L

685

45°

ATTACHED OCTAGONAL PIER

528

225

M 328 45°

DETACHED OCTAGONAL PIER

FIGURE 12

[1] An alternative type of cavity wall is that built with V-bricks, see p. 17 and Fig. 5.
[2] Such as Thermalite Turbo block made from cement, lime, sand, pulverised fuel ash and aluminium powder. When these materials are mixed with hot water the aluminium powder reacts with the lime to form many tiny pockets of hydrogen. The latter subsequently diffuses to be replaced by air providing most of the insulation resulting in a strong, light weight well insulated block.

Three types of cavity ties which are made of any of these metals are shown at F, G and H, Fig. 13. The wire tie at F is commonly used, and, provided it is of sufficient thickness, is a useful type; the ends, which are twisted together and turned downwards, cause any water travelling along the tie from the outer leaf to drip into the cavity (see J) clear of the inner leaf; in addition, large accumulations of mortar droppings, which are a frequent cause of dampness (see adjoining column), do not readily lodge on the ties as the wire is comparatively thin. The wire should not be less than 3·2 mm thick; lighter ties, 2·7 mm are used for cheap work only. A similar pattern, of stainless steel with twisted ends, is shown at H, and is a good type. The flat bar tie shown at G, having forked ends and twisted in the middle, has been used for many years, and affords a stiff and durable connection.

According to the Building Regulations, these ties must be placed at distances apart not exceeding 900 mm horizontally and 450 mm vertically. The ties are staggered and the distribution is as shown at E. Ties must be placed at 300 mm vertical intervals at all angles and door and window jambs to increase stability (see Q and L, Fig. 13; E, Fig. 11; and D, Fig. 15).

Construction.— A cavity wall is often built with the outer leaf of facing bricks and an inner leaf of aerated concrete block. As the height of a block is 440 mm the ties will be placed vertically at every fourth joint of the brickwork. The brick leaf is commonly constructed in stretching bond. As this has a very unattractive appearance, the monotony is sometimes relieved by constructing the external leaf with a row of snap headers (half bricks) to three or five rows of stretchers (known as *English Garden Wall Bond*, see A, Fig. 18). Alternatively, the outer leaf may be built in Flemish bond or *Flemish Garden Wall Bond*, shown at B, Fig. 18, and A, Fig. 49, snap headers and not whole bricks being used as required. The cut surfaces of these snap headers should be flush with the internal face of the outer leaf.

Two methods of constructing the base of the wall are shown at A and P, Fig. 13. Brick footings are rarely employed. Method A, showing the cavity extending down to the concrete foundation, is common. This has one possible defect, namely, if the brickwork below the ground level is not soundly constructed, especially if the site is water-logged, water may pass through any open joints, collect in the cavity and escape through open joints in the inner leaf, to cause dampness below the floor by spreading over the site concrete. A sounder method, and one which is advocated, is that shown at J and P, where the bottom of the cavity is 150 to 300 mm below the damp proof course. Rain-water gaining access to the cavity through the outer leaf will stream down the inner face of this leaf. This should be prevented from accumulating at the base by providing narrow outlets or *weep-holes* in the course immediately below the damp proof course in the outer leaf, each third or fourth vertical joint between the stretchers being left open and not filled with mortar, otherwise the water may penetrate the brickwork above the damp proof course and cause dampness on the internal face of the wall. See note at J, which shows the detail at the foot of 367.5 mm cavity wall with inner leaf of 215 mm thick aerated concrete block and outer skin of brick. The lower portion of the cavity when continued to the concrete bed is sometimes filled with 1 : 2 : 4 concrete, the coarse aggregate being not more than 19 mm gauge. The top of this concrete should be at least 150 mm below the damp proof course and *not* as shown at F, Fig. 14, otherwise mortar droppings (see below) will accumulate through which water may be transmitted in the direction of the thick broken arrow to cause dampness and possibly dry-rot.

The position of the damp proof course is as for solid walls, *i.e.*, at least 150 mm above the ground level. This *must not* extend across the cavity for the reason stated below, and each leaf must therefore be provided with a separate damp proof course.

For cavity wall construction to be effective, it is essential that the inner wall shall be entirely disconnected (except for the cavity ties) from the outer leaf. Where this is not possible, as at door and window openings, special precautions have to be taken, as stated below. If the cavity is bridged by a porous material, water may penetrate and cause dampness on the inner face of the wall. Hence it is important that during construction mortar shall not be allowed to drop and lodge upon the ties (see E, Fig. 14). In order to maintain a clean cavity, a wood batten should be employed of a thickness slightly less than the width of the cavity and with a piece of cord attached to each end. This is supported upon the ties, raised as the work proceeds, and any intercepted mortar and brick chippings removed. Temporary openings should be left at the bottom of the cavity to afford access for the removal of droppings on completion of the wall. Similar gaps should be left at intervals up quoins and jambs through which a lath may be passed to dislodge any deposit on the ties. Another effective method is to flush the whole cavity with water, a hose pipe being used from the top of the wall for the purpose of dislodging any mortar and washing it to the base, from which it is removed through the temporary gaps. *Neglect of this precaution is a frequent cause of dampness in cavity walls.*

The reason why the cavity should extend below the damp proof course, and for the latter to be in separate widths, will now be appreciated. If the bottom of the cavity is level with the damp proof course, or if the latter is the full width of the wall, water may be conducted to the inner leaf through accumulated mortar droppings, and produce damp and unhealthy conditions.

Alternative details at the eaves are shown at A, B and P. That at A is sound as the solid portion of wall at the top distributes the weight of the roof over both leaves and the overhanging eaves prevents the transmission of moisture through this solid wall. This is a better detail than that at P, which shows the roof supported chiefly by the inner leaf. Detail B shows sound construction. Special precautions should be taken to prevent dampness at parapet walls. Defective construction is shown at A, Fig. 14, where water may be transmitted through the 215 mm solid parapet wall in the direction of the thick broken arrow to cause dampness and possible defect of the roof timbers. The cavity should

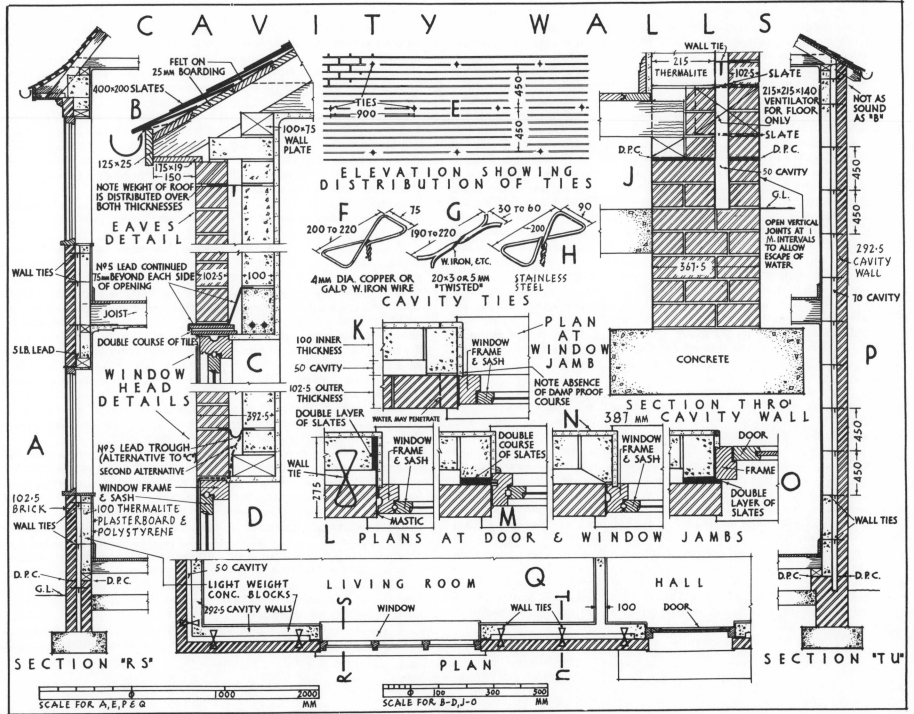

CAVITY WALLS

ELEVATION SHOWING DISTRIBUTION OF TIES

E — TIES 900 — 450, 450, 450

CAVITY TIES

F — 200 TO 220 — 75 — 4mm DIA. COPPER OR GALD. W.IRON WIRE

G — 190 TO 220 — W. IRON, ETC. — 20×3 or 5 MM "TWISTED"

H — 30 TO 60 — 90 — 200 — STAINLESS STEEL

EAVES DETAIL

B — FELT ON 25 MM BOARDING — 400×200 SLATES — 100×75 WALL PLATE — 125×25 — 175×19 — 150

NOTE WEIGHT OF ROOF IS DISTRIBUTED OVER BOTH THICKNESSES

WALL TIES

WINDOW HEAD DETAILS

Nº5 LEAD CONTINUED 75mm BEYOND EACH SIDE OF OPENING

102·5 — 100

JOIST

5 LB. LEAD

DOUBLE COURSE OF TILES

C

Nº5 LEAD TROUGH (ALTERNATIVE TO 'C')

SECOND ALTERNATIVE

WINDOW FRAME & SASH

100 THERMALITE PLASTERBOARD & POLYSTYRENE

392·5

D

A

102·5 BRICK

WALL TIES

D.P.C. — D.P.C.

G.L.

SECTION "RS"

50 CAVITY

LIGHT WEIGHT CONC. BLOCKS

292·5 CAVITY WALLS

LIVING ROOM

WINDOW

WALL TIES

Q

R — S — R — C

PLAN

100

HALL

DOOR

PLAN AT WINDOW JAMB

K — 100 INNER THICKNESS — 50 CAVITY — 102·5 OUTER THICKNESS — WINDOW FRAME & SASH — NOTE ABSENCE OF DAMP PROOF COURSE

DOUBLE LAYER OF SLATES

WATER MAY PENETRATE

PLANS AT DOOR & WINDOW JAMBS

L — 275 — WALL TIE — MASTIC

M — WINDOW FRAME & SASH — DOUBLE COURSE OF SLATES

N — WINDOW FRAME & SASH

O — DOOR — FRAME — DOUBLE LAYER OF SLATES

WALL TIE — 215 — THERMALITE — 102·5 — SLATE

215×215×140 VENTILATOR FOR FLOOR ONLY

SLATE

D.P.C. — D.P.C.

50 CAVITY

G.L.

J

OPEN VERTICAL JOINTS AT 1 M. INTERVALS TO ALLOW ESCAPE OF WATER

367·5

NOT AS SOUND AS "B"

292·5 CAVITY WALL

70 CAVITY

P

CONCRETE

SECTION THRO' 387 MM CAVITY WALL

450 — 450 — 450

WALL TIES

D.P.C. — D.P.C.

SECTION "TU"

SCALE FOR A, E, P & Q — 0 — 1000 — 2000 MM

SCALE FOR B-D, J-O — 0 — 100 — 300 — 500 MM

FIGURE 13

be extended to the coping. An example of defective construction associated with a flat roof is shown at D, Fig. 14. The cavity should have been continued to the coping, or, alternatively, either a lead or asphalt felt damp proof course should have been inserted above the cavity where indicated. It is always advisable to continue the asphalt roof covering (or lead flashing) for the full thickness of the wall to prevent the penetration of water through defective coping joints or porous stone or brickwork.

In the absence of adequate precautions dampness will readily occur round door and window openings. An example of unsound construction, commonly adopted, is shown at K, Fig. 13, where water may penetrate in the direction of the thick broken arrow through the solid jamb. A damp-resisting material should be provided as shown at M and O. The former detail shows a double layer of slates, bedded in cement, the outer layer projecting in a groove in the frame; this groove should be filled with oil mastic as the work proceeds. Effective construction is also shown at O, where lead, asphalt felt or a double layer of slates is applied at the slightly recessed jamb. A small reverse recessed jamb is shown at N, and the bevelled bricks forming the inner reveal only come into contact with the frame, which should be bedded in mastic; this detail is not recommended for adoption in exposed positions, although it is an improvement upon K. Detail L shows the cavity extending to the opening, and being closed by a double layer of slates in cement. This is quite satisfactory, although not so effective in withstanding heavy loads transmitted from lintels. An alternative and common method for preventing dampness at jambs consists of placing as the work proceeds a vertical layer of asphalt felt or lead in lieu of slates; this layer should be 215 mm wide, extending to the groove of the window frame at one edge and into the cavity at the other.

Dampness is very liable to be caused at the heads of openings if proper protection is not afforded. Thus, water passing through defective joints, etc., in the outer leaf will travel down its inner face until it comes into contact with a lintel, when it will spread along the top to the inside face of the inner leaf; the water will also drip at the soffit. The protection should take the form of a lead, copper or asphalt felt covering, stepped down from the inner leaf, as shown at C, Fig. 13, and continued over the tile course or window (or door) frame, as indicated at A and C, and by broken lines at D. This covering should extend for some 75 to 150 mm beyond each side of an opening or end of a lintel in order that the water may drip clear into the cavity. In addition, a few open vertical joints may be left in the brick head to allow any water to escape. The alternative lead trough, shown at D, is *not* recommended, as this does not prevent water from gaining access through defective joints in the head (or porous bricks) and causing dampness. Nor is it sufficient to use a narrow covering with the lower edge bedded in the joint level with the top or above a concrete lintel; contact between the lintel and the head or arch must be broken by the lead, which is continued as shown by broken lines at B, Fig. 14.

Dampness may also be caused at window sills, especially if these are of porous stone and are in direct contact with the inner leaf (see C, Fig. 14). An effective preventive is to break contact by means of a lead or asphalt felt covering as shown by broken lines, or by continuing the cavity (even if reduced in width) to the wood sill or window board. The ends of stone or terra-cotta sills should be notched with the back flush with the inner face of the outer leaf, otherwise rain may penetrate through mortar droppings which may lodge on the projecting ends.

If a lean-to or flat roof of a lower building adjoins a cavity wall the usual lead cover flashing should be continued for the full thickness of the outer leaf and be stepped up to the inner leaf. A few weep-holes should also be left in the course of the outer leaf above the flashing. Similarly, when a pitched roof abuts against a higher cavity wall, the stepped cover flashings at the intersection should be continued with upturned edge to 25 mm beyond the inner face of the outer leaf. Such provision is necessary to intercept rain-water streaming down the inner face of the outer leaf and causing dampness to the party wall below.

An additional cavity wall detail showing plans of successive courses at an obtuse squint quoin is given at E, Fig. 11. The external corner brick may be a purpose-made dogleg as shown, or the special squint C, Fig. 5. Alternate plans of an 275 mm circular wall are shown at D, Fig. 15 (see also p. 44). In both details wall ties are shown at the angles in each course to increase stability.

Floor Timbers.—Only sound, well-seasoned timber should be used for floor joists, wall plates, etc., otherwise dampness from the cavity may cause dry rot. It is also a wise precaution to have the wall plates and ends of built-in joists creosoted or treated with other preservatives (see Chap. I, Vol. III). The risk of dry rot to ground floor (or basement) timbers is considerably reduced if the joists are supported on wall plates bedded on sleeper walls.

Advantages of Cavity Wall Construction.—The chief merits of cavity walls are : (1) They prevent rain from penetrating to the internal face, (2) they have a high insulating value, and (3) they are economical.

1. *Prevention of Dampness.*—A cavity wall is more reliable than a solid wall of corresponding brick-thickness in excluding rain. Thus, an 292.5 mm cavity wall in an exposed position will prevent water from penetrating to the inner leaf, provided adequate precautions are taken in its construction and sound materials and workmanship are employed. But an external 215 mm solid wall (which is equivalent in thickness of brickwork to an 292.5 mm cavity wall) in an exposed position will *not* prevent rain from penetrating to the internal face unless the wall is rough-casted or similarly protected. As has been pointed out on p. 14, a solid wall is vulnerable to dampness by the penetration of rain through cracks in the mortar joints and to other causes, and it is recognized that external solid walls of buildings to be used for human habitation should be at least 328 mm thick, unless they are rough-casted.

2. *Insulation.*—As air is a good non-conductor of heat, it follows that the air in the cavity is effective in reducing the transmission of heat through the wall.

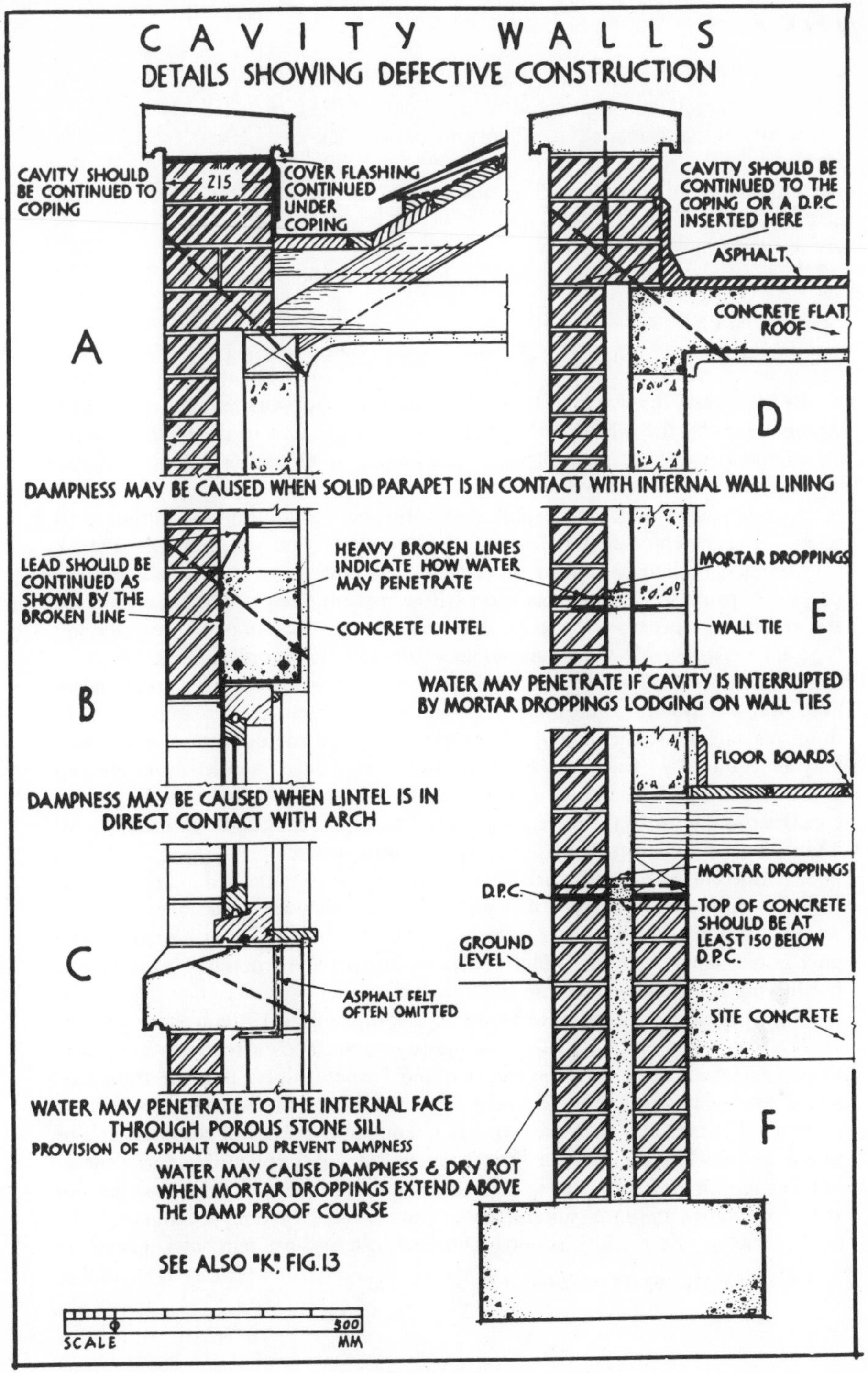

CAVITY WALLS
DETAILS SHOWING DEFECTIVE CONSTRUCTION

CAVITY SHOULD BE CONTINUED TO COPING

COVER FLASHING CONTINUED UNDER COPING

215

CAVITY SHOULD BE CONTINUED TO THE COPING OR A D.P.C INSERTED HERE

ASPHALT

A

CONCRETE FLAT ROOF

D

DAMPNESS MAY BE CAUSED WHEN SOLID PARAPET IS IN CONTACT WITH INTERNAL WALL LINING

LEAD SHOULD BE CONTINUED AS SHOWN BY THE BROKEN LINE

HEAVY BROKEN LINES INDICATE HOW WATER MAY PENETRATE

CONCRETE LINTEL

MORTAR DROPPINGS

WALL TIE

B

E

WATER MAY PENETRATE IF CAVITY IS INTERRUPTED BY MORTAR DROPPINGS LODGING ON WALL TIES

DAMPNESS MAY BE CAUSED WHEN LINTEL IS IN DIRECT CONTACT WITH ARCH

FLOOR BOARDS

MORTAR DROPPINGS

D.P.C.

TOP OF CONCRETE SHOULD BE AT LEAST 150 BELOW D.P.C.

GROUND LEVEL

C

ASPHALT FELT OFTEN OMITTED

SITE CONCRETE

F

WATER MAY PENETRATE TO THE INTERNAL FACE THROUGH POROUS STONE SILL
PROVISION OF ASPHALT WOULD PREVENT DAMPNESS
WATER MAY CAUSE DAMPNESS & DRY ROT WHEN MORTAR DROPPINGS EXTEND ABOVE THE DAMP PROOF COURSE

SEE ALSO "K". FIG. 13

SCALE
500
MM

FIGURE 14

Therefore the "heat losses" through an 292.5 mm cavity wall are about 50 per cent less than through a 215 mm solid wall, and a building of hollow wall construction is warmer in winter and cooler in summer than one built of solid outer walls. This affects fuel consumption, for less fuel is required to heat a building with cavity walls than that of solid wall construction. Thermal insulation is measured by the thermal transmittance coefficient (U-value, see Chap. XII, Vol. IV) and the Building Regulations require an exernal wall to have a U-value of not more than 0.45 W/m^2K., e.g. 102.5 mm outer leaf, 50 mm cavity, 115 mm aerated concrete block inner leaf (480 kg/m^3 density, with insulated plasterboard internal lining) (see p. 39).

An important matter affecting the heat insulating value of a cavity wall is the extent to which the cavity should be ventilated. Formerly, it was generally considered desirable to ventilate the cavity by means of air bricks fixed just above the ground level and also near the top. Whilst this circulation of air ensured a dry cavity and reduced the risk of defects arising in floor timbers, it also destroyed the insulating value of the wall. Therefore the only ventilation of the cavity which is now advocated is that provided by the weep-holes near the base of the cavity and at the head of door and window openings, as described on pp. 40 and 42. Of course the usual ventilation must be provided to ground floors of timber construction.

The sound insulating value of a 292.5 mm cavity wall is also higher than that of a 215 mm solid wall, and the former is therefore more effective in excluding external noises (see Chap. I, Vol. III).

3. *Economy.*—A 292.5 mm cavity wall costs less to construct than a 328 mm solid wall (which is the minimum thickness if dampness is to be avoided). Comparative figures show that the approximate cost of a 292.5 mm wall is at least 20 per cent. less than a 328 mm solid wall.

Summary of Special Precautions.—1. Wherever possible, contact between the two leaves should be avoided.

2. The cavity should be kept clear of droppings, and any on ties should be removed.

3. The main horizontal damp proof course must be in two separate widths, and the bottom of the cavity must be at least 150 mm below this.

4. Heads of openings must be properly protected by lead or similar damp proof material. Jambs must not be solid unless slate, etc., damp proof courses are provided. Projecting ends of stone or terra-cotta sills should be notched back from the inner leaf. Cover flashings at intersections of lower buildings adjoining cavity walls must extend to at least 25 mm beyond the inner face of the outer leaf.

5. Weep-holes should be formed immediately below the main horizontal damp proof course and above the damp proof courses over openings. No other ventilation to the cavity should be provided.

6. Built-in floor timbers should be sound and well-seasoned and their ends should be treated with a preservative (see Chap. I, Vol. III).

7. The cavity should be continued up a parapet wall to the coping.

8. Ties must be rust-proof, capable of preventing rain-transmission and easily cleaned of droppings.

At certain Bath stone mines (see p. 110) small pieces of waste but sound stone are sawn into blocks which are 140 mm high (or equal to two courses of brickwork) by 102·5 mm wide by 215 to 610 mm long. These are used as facings of cavity walls, the stone being in regular courses, a type of walling known locally as *range-work*.

Another type of cavity wall, suitable for public buildings, is shown at A, B and P, Fig. 16, Vol. III. This consists of an external leaf of ashlar, backed at alternate courses with brickwork, and an inner leaf of brickwork.

CIRCULAR WORK

Curved work is occasionally required as for segmental and semicircular bay windows, wells of staircases, apsed ends, and circular (on plan) factory, etc., chimney stacks. The plan of a portion of a room with a semicircular bay window is shown at A, Fig. 15, that on the left being above the sill level and that on the right below it. A sketch of this wall is shown at H, Fig. 29. The inner surface of the inner leaf has insulated plasterboard applied to it.

It will be seen at E and F, Fig. 15, that uncut standard bricks are quite unsuitable for circular work if normal bonding is to be maintained, as the stretcher faces of the bricks only conform approximately to the curve, and very wide joints on the convex surface are produced. The width of the joints can only be reduced by cutting each brick to a wedge-shape to form radial side joints. Not only is this an expensive procedure but the appearance is not satisfactory (especially if the curve is to a small radius), as the " curve " is made up of a succession of straight stretcher faces. In order to conform more closely to the curve, and when ordinary standard bricks only are available, heading bond (see Chap. I, Vol. I) may be adopted. But such a wall, where each course consists of headers, is unattractive and deficient in strength.

It is now the general practice, even in cheap speculative work, to use only purpose-made bricks for the exposed faces of circular walling. Such bricks are moulded to the required shape either by hand (see p. 4) or by the machine-pressure process (see p. 3).

Many of the larger manufacturers keep stocks of circular stretchers and headers, machine-pressed in dies shaped to curves of radii varying from 0·6 to 2·5 m as shown at L and M, Fig. 5. The contractor states the radius of the curve when ordering the bricks. If these do not conform to a stock radius, the plan of the wall is chalked out on the setting-out board and the position of the bricks marked after due allowance has been made for shrinkage in drying and burning. Two zinc templets are cut to the shape of a header and stretcher. Wood moulds (see p. 4) are prepared from these and handed to the moulder who proceeds to shape the bricks by hand.

Alternative plans of a portion of a 328 mm wall in English bond are shown

at C, and of an 275 mm cavity wall at D. Unless both faces of a curved wall are to be exposed, and as purpose-made circular bricks are relatively expensive (especially if hand-made), it is customary to back the curved facings with common bricks which are axed to give radial joints as shown at C. If the internal surface of a cavity wall is to be plastered, the inner leaf is usually built of common bricks see (D,) and unless the curvature is too sharp these commons are not cut to give radial joints.

The setting-out of circular work is described on pp. 71 and 73.

REINFORCED BRICKWORK

Reinforced Brickwork (see Fig. 16) is brickwork which has been strengthened by the introduction of steel or wrought iron in the form of either flat or rod bars, woven wire or expanded metal. This reinforcement is placed in the joints or in grooves or perforations in the bricks. Such brickwork is capable of resisting tensile and shear stresses, in addition to compression stress. It is essential that the bricks shall be sound and well burnt, the work well bonded in cement mortar or cement-lime mortar, and the reinforcement effectively protected against corrosion. Rusting of the reinforcement may cause serious damage because of the resultant expansion. Bricks of the engineering type are most suitable when heavy loads have to be supported. The mortar is usually composed of 1 part Portland cement to 3 parts sand; $\frac{1}{10}$ part of slaked lime may be added. Lime mortar should not be used, as this may have an injurious effect on the metal. It is generally considered that a brick wall may be reduced in thickness by 102·5 mm provided it is suitably reinforced and such reduced thickness is not less than 215 mm. Hence this type of construction increases the floor area of a building (or reduces the external size of a building) and decreases the dead load on foundations.

Reinforcement of brickwork also improves the longitudinal bond of thick walls. Whilst thick walls are strong transversely, they are weak longitudinally, as, with exception of the outer stretchers, they consist wholly of headers which only give a lap of 56 mm. The details in Fig. 16 show how the provision of reinforcing metal strips increase the longitudinal tie.

Fig. 16 shows examples of reinforced brick (a) walls, (b) pillars and (c) lintels.

(a) *Reinforced Brick Walls.*—The walls at B are shown reinforced at every third course with steel meshed strips called Exmet.[1] This is made from thin rolled steel plates which are cut and stretched (or expanded) by a machine to a diamond meshwork form (see A). It is known as " expanded metal." The junctions between the meshes remain uncut. It is supplied in 83 m coils or bundles of 5 m long flat strips in three standard widths, *i.e.*, 65 mm (suitable for 102·5 mm walls), 178 mm (suitable for 215 mm walls), 230 and 305 mm (used for thicker walls). Each width is obtainable in 1, 0·8 and 0·6 mm thicknesses. In

[1] Manufactured by The Expanded Metal Co. Ltd.

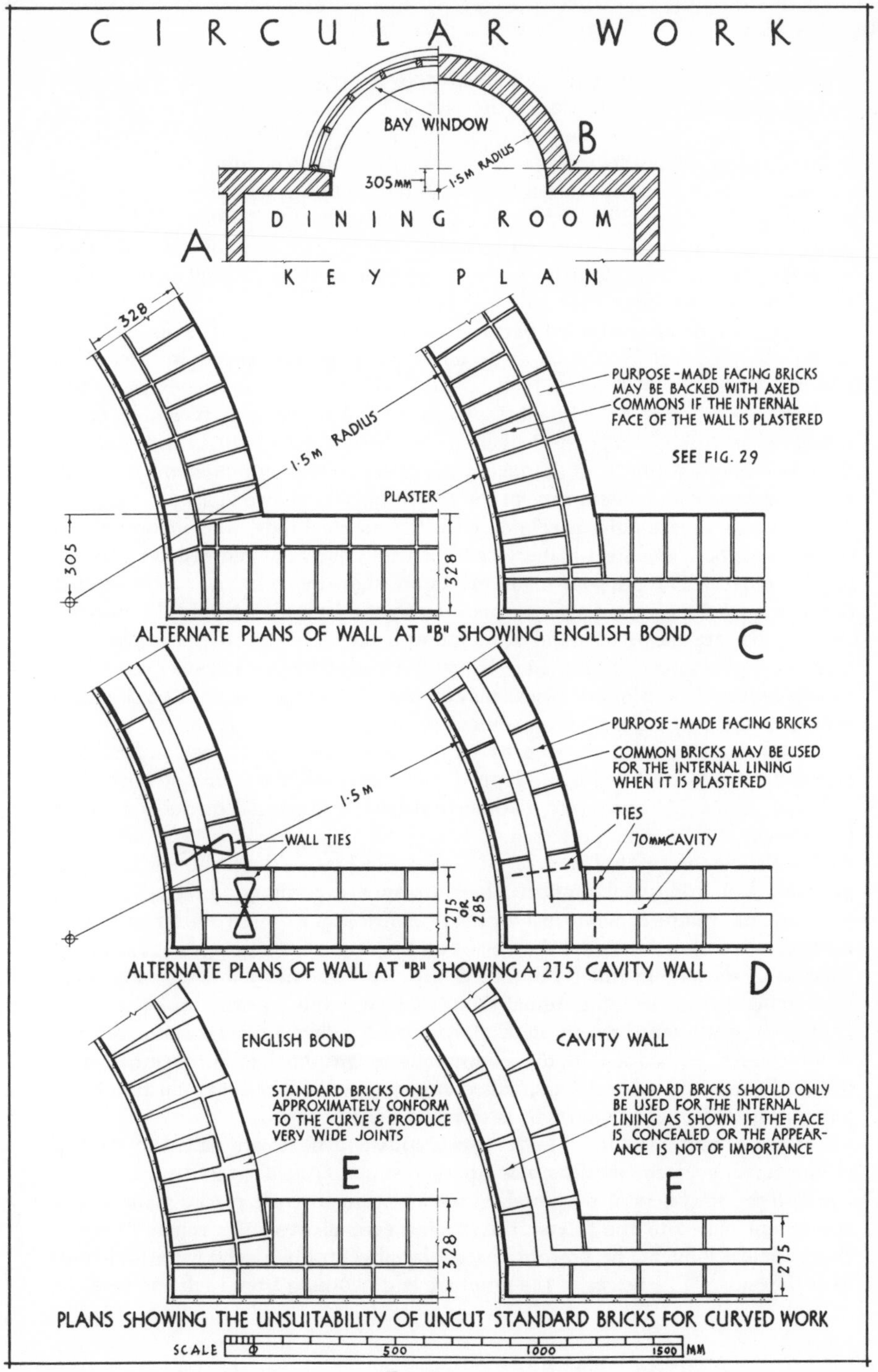

BAY WINDOW

305 MM   1.5 M RADIUS

A   B

DINING ROOM

KEY PLAN

328

1.5 M RADIUS

PURPOSE-MADE FACING BRICKS
MAY BE BACKED WITH AXED
COMMONS IF THE INTERNAL
FACE OF THE WALL IS PLASTERED

SEE FIG. 29

PLASTER

305   328

ALTERNATE PLANS OF WALL AT "B" SHOWING ENGLISH BOND   C

1.5 M

PURPOSE-MADE FACING BRICKS

COMMON BRICKS MAY BE USED
FOR THE INTERNAL LINING
WHEN IT IS PLASTERED

TIES

WALL TIES   70MM CAVITY

275 or 285

ALTERNATE PLANS OF WALL AT "B" SHOWING A 275 CAVITY WALL   D

ENGLISH BOND   CAVITY WALL

STANDARD BRICKS ONLY
APPROXIMATELY CONFORM
TO THE CURVE & PRODUCE
VERY WIDE JOINTS

STANDARD BRICKS SHOULD ONLY
BE USED FOR THE INTERNAL
LINING IF THE FACE
IS CONCEALED OR THE APPEAR-
ANCE IS NOT OF IMPORTANCE

E   F

328   275

PLANS SHOWING THE UNSUITABILITY OF UNCUT STANDARD BRICKS FOR CURVED WORK

SCALE   0   500   1000   1500 MM

FIGURE 15

addition, 100 mm width of material 0.8 and 0.6 thick is also produced. The size of the mesh (16 mm) is constant. To prevent corrosion the metal in the coil form is coated with oil and then dipped in asphaltum paint. Flat lengths are galvanized.[2]

The Exmet is uncoiled and pressed down into the mortar immediately the latter has been trowelled on the bed. It lies quite flat when uncoiled and the thickness of the bed joints is therefore not increased. Hand shears are used to cut the material into lengths as required.

The example at B shows the application of 65 mm (see A), 178 mm and 305 mm wide Exmet. Combinations of these widths are used for thicker walls, and when so employed, the material considerably improves the longitudinal tie which is especially weak in thick walls. The strips should be lapped 75 mm at the intersections, as shown, and at the joints. Sometimes only 65 mm wide strips are used for any thickness of wall, one strip to each half-brick thickness of the wall, and is thus similar to that shown at D. The amount of reinforcement used depends upon the nature of the loading, and whilst it may be necessary to reinforce every course, it is usual to provide reinforcement at every third or fourth course. Another arrangement consists of staggering the strips, thus in a 328 mm wall, one 65 mm strip is placed on one course at 25 mm from the external face, another strip is provided in the centre of the next course, and in the following course a 65 mm strip is placed 25 mm from the internal face; this is repeated for the full height.

Cavity walls (p. 39) may be reinforced by a 65 mm strip at every third course of each 102.5 mm lining. Partition walls, built with bricks laid-on-edge, may also be strengthened by the provision of 65 mm wide Exmet. The 65 mm wide strips especially are suitable for curved walls (p. 44), as this width can be readily bent as required. Expanded metal is also used to strengthen walls of chimney stacks and parapets built in exposed positions. Further applications include footings, walling over wide door and window openings, boundary and balcony walls and tall chimneys. Reinforcement of retaining walls, piers and arches is referred to on p. 46. It can also be usefully employed at toothings (see Chap. I, Vol. I) when the bond between new and existing walls at the indents is reinforced if the strips are left projecting beyond the old work and built-in as the new wall is constructed.

Another well-known form of meshed reinforcement, called Bricktor,[1] is shown at C. It is made of steel wire, black japanned as a protection, produced in 50 and 65 mm widths and sold in coils. The 50 mm width is suitable for brick-on-edge partitions and consists of four straight *tension wires* 1.4 mm thick interlaced with three 1.1 mm thick *binding wires*. The 65 mm strips have five tension wires and four continuous binding wires, each twisted to and

[1] One method of galvanizing, known as the *hot-dip process*, consists of cleansing the metal and removing any rust by placing it in dilute hydrochloric acid, washing it to remove the acid and then passing it through a bath containing liquid zinc.

[2] A product of Messrs Johnson's Reinforced Concrete Engineering Co. Ltd.

between a pair of tension wires as shown. One strip is provided at every half-brick thickness of the wall (see D). It is very easily handled, and is used for similar purposes and in like manner as described for Exmet.

> A type of reinforcement much used to strengthen brick walls in the past is shown at G and F. This consists of wrought iron (known as *hoop iron*, hence the name applied to the bond) or mild steel flat bars which vary in width from 22 to 32 mm and 0·25 to 1·6 mm in thickness. Protection against rust is provided by dipping the bars in hot tar; these are then at once sanded to increase adhesion of the mortar. One strip is provided per half-brick thickness of wall, and it is usual to reinforce every sixth course (see G). This detail shows the treatment at a right-angled quoin where the ends are double-hooked (see J) and beaten flat; alternatively, the middle and inner strips may be continued and single-hooked (see K) to the two outer strips. At an intersection (see H) the bars are interlaced and single-hooked. Any joints between long lengths are in the form of a welt (similar to D, Fig. 75, Vol. I). Although less effective, thin wire twisted round the bars may be used instead of the more expensive hook-and-welt joints. Hoop iron is now rarely employed, and whilst it is stronger than Exmet and Bricktor, it is more costly. It is also difficult to bed the bricks evenly unless the joints are unusually thick.

Retaining walls (those supporting earth, etc.) are often reinforced. If either of the meshed types are used, 65 mm strips may be embedded in the vertical joints to assist in resisting lateral pressure in addition to the bed joint reinforcement. Another form of reinforcement consists of vertical bars of circular section, and details of an actual retaining wall of such construction is shown at L, M and N. This 215 mm wall is built of engineering bricks in cement mortar (1 : 3) and reinforced with vertical mild steel bars near each face, in addition to steel meshed strips at every fourth course. The bricks opposite the vertical bars are purpose-made and grooved as shown at P. These grooves are slightly larger than the diameter of the bars to permit the latter to be grouted in with mortar to prevent corrosion. In constructing such a wall the bars are accurately placed in position, the ends being bent and anchored into the concrete foundation (see L). Erection of the bars is facilitated by the use of thin (3 mm thick) steel wire ties at every fourth course. These ties, which are built in as the work proceeds, are twisted round the bars, and those round opposite bars are tightened by twisting their ends. When the top course has been completed the grooves on face are well pointed so that the vertical rods are completely encased in cement mortar. Vertical damp proofing (see p. 52) completes the wall. If it is an area wall it may be finished with a stone or reinforced concrete coping and the ends of the vertical bars would be bedded in it to strengthen the work.

The walls are designed in accordance with the stresses to be resisted, and the size and spacing of the vertical reinforcement are therefore variable. Sometimes the bars are arranged near to both face lines of the wall, opposite to each other and in pairs at 215 mm centres with steel wire connections placed in the horizontal joints.

Perforated bricks may be used instead of grooved or slotted bricks, the centre of the perforations being about 19 mm from the external face. As these must be threaded over the vertical bars, they are not so convenient as the grooved bricks, although they are quite suitable for dwarf walls such as balcony, parapet and garden walls. The position of the vertical bars is concealed when perforated bricks are used in wall construction, and such are therefore preferred to grooved bricks when the appearance of the brickwork is of importance.

Small bars of circular section (usually 6 mm dia.) are sometimes used at the bed joints of walls in lieu of hoop iron or meshed reinforcement. Thin steel plates, 6 mm thick and 13 mm less in width than the thickness of the walls, may be embedded at every fourth course to provide heavy reinforcement. Such should be well tarred and sanded.

A patent type of reinforced partition is described in Chap. I, Vol. III.

(*b*) *Reinforced Brick Pillars.*—Detached piers are reinforced by providing a 65 mm wide strip of Bricktor or Exmet set back 25 mm from the external face at every second or third course or as required. Alternatively, 6 mm diameter rods may be embedded at the bed joints, each rod being bent to the shape of the pier, about 25 mm from the face, with each end overlapping about 150 mm at one corner. An excellent type of reinforced pillar is shown at S, T, U, V and W. This 215 mm square pillar is reinforced with four steel rods, well anchored into the concrete bed, and steel plates (see V) or wire ties (see W) embedded at every fourth course. The purpose-made bricks are shown at Q, T and U. Note that the bars are well protected against corrosion by the mortar. Details of a 440 mm square pillar are shown at X and Y, including a sketch of the special bricks at R; holed steel plates may be adopted in lieu of the wire ties when a heavier reinforcement is required. Perforated bricks may be used, but as these have to be threaded over the rods they are not so convenient as the grooved bricks.

Attached piers are reinforced by 65 mm wide strips of Exmet or Bricktor, placed 25 mm from the face and lapped over the continuous outer strips on the wall bed joints. Alternatively, two vertical bars with special bricks, similar to that shown at R, may be preferred.

(*c*) *Reinforced Brick Lintels or " Soldier Arches."*—These lintels must be provided with additional support when the span exceeds 900 mm. Omission of adequate reinforcement has been responsible for many failures. Two methods of reinforcement are shown at z and z′, Fig. 16 (see also Fig. 12, Vol. I). That at z shows the lintel reinforced with two 12 mm diameter mild steel bars embedded in the longitudinal joints and extending to 150 mm beyond the jambs. The alternative form at z′ shows two 6 mm diameter bars or tension reinforcement embedded in the continuous longitudinal joint, together with 6 mm diameter bent steel bars, called *stirrups*, bedded in every third vertical joint. The object of the stirrups is to resist shear stresses.

In constructing the lintel at z′, two small wood fillets are nailed to the top of the turning piece (used as a temporary support) at a clear distance apart equal to the thickness of the lintel. Pieces of thin wire are placed transversely across and nailed to the fillets at a spacing equivalent to the centre of every third vertical joint. The bottom bar is placed centrally on the wires and built in at the ends. The bricks of the lintel are laid (working from each end towards

REINFORCED BRICKWORK

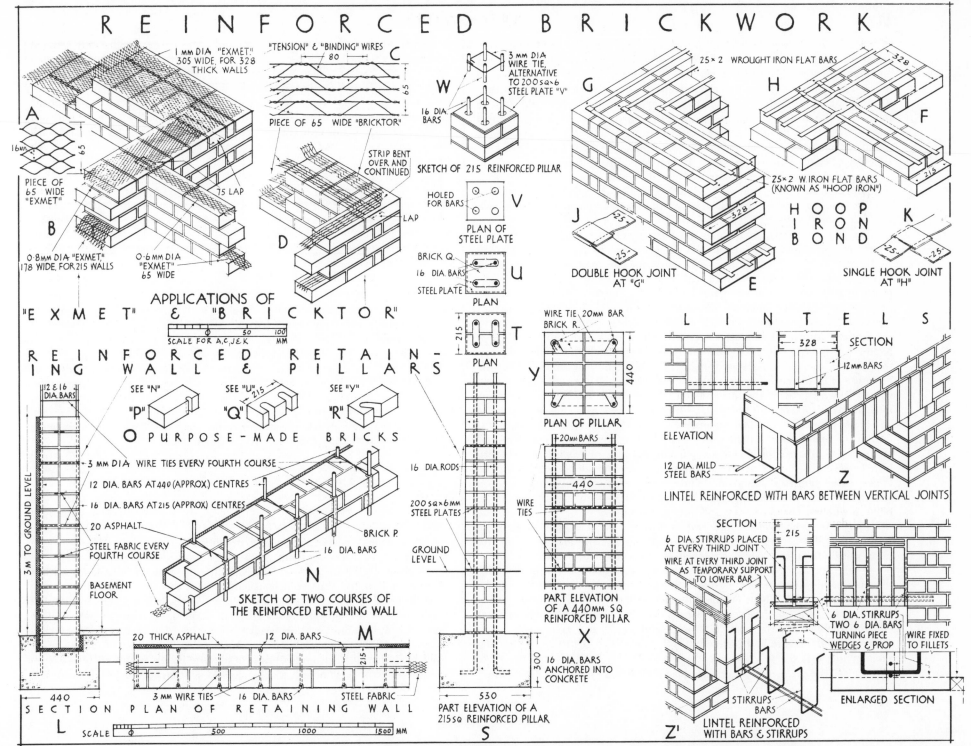

A – 1 mm DIA "EXMET" 305 WIDE FOR 328 THICK WALLS

16 mm — 65

PIECE OF 65 WIDE "EXMET"

B – 75 LAP

0.8 mm DIA "EXMET" 178 WIDE, FOR 215 WALLS

0.6 mm DIA "EXMET" 65 WIDE

C – "TENSION" & "BINDING" WIRES — 80 — 65

PIECE OF 65 WIDE "BRICKTOR"

D – STRIP BENT OVER AND CONTINUED — LAP

APPLICATIONS OF "EXMET" & "BRICKTOR"

SCALE FOR A,C,J&K — 0 50 100 MM

W – 3 mm DIA WIRE TIE, ALTERNATIVE TO 200 SQ × 6 STEEL PLATE "V" — 16 DIA. BARS

SKETCH OF 215 REINFORCED PILLAR

V – HOLED FOR BARS — PLAN OF STEEL PLATE

U – BRICK Q — 16 DIA. BARS — STEEL PLATE — PLAN

T – 215 — PLAN

G – 25 × 2 WROUGHT IRON FLAT BARS — 328

H – **F** – 25 × 2 W. IRON FLAT BARS (KNOWN AS "HOOP IRON") — 215

J – 25 — 25 — DOUBLE HOOK JOINT AT "G" — **E** — 328

H O O P   I R O N   B O N D

K – 25 — 25 — SINGLE HOOK JOINT AT "H"

REINFORCED RETAINING WALL & PILLARS

SEE "N" **"P"** — SEE "U" 215 **"Q"** — SEE "Y" **"R"**

O – PURPOSE-MADE BRICKS

N – 12 & 16 DIA. BARS — 3 mm DIA WIRE TIES EVERY FOURTH COURSE — 12 DIA. BARS AT 440 (APPROX) CENTRES — 16 DIA. BARS AT 215 (APPROX) CENTRES — 20 ASPHALT — STEEL FABRIC EVERY FOURTH COURSE — BRICK P. — 16 DIA. BARS — SKETCH OF TWO COURSES OF THE REINFORCED RETAINING WALL

3 M TO GROUND LEVEL — BASEMENT FLOOR

M – 20 THICK ASPHALT — 12 DIA. BARS — 215 — 3 mm WIRE TIES — 16 DIA. BARS — STEEL FABRIC

L – 440 — SECTION PLAN OF RETAINING WALL

SCALE — 0 500 1000 1500 MM

Y – WIRE TIE 20 mm BAR BRICK R. — 440 — PLAN OF PILLAR

X – 16 DIA. RODS — 200 SQ × 6 mm STEEL PLATES — GROUND LEVEL — +20 mm BARS — 440 — WIRE TIES — PART ELEVATION OF A 440 mm SQ REINFORCED PILLAR

S – 300 — 16 DIA. BARS ANCHORED INTO CONCRETE — 530 — PART ELEVATION OF A 215 SQ REINFORCED PILLAR

LINTELS

Z – 328 — SECTION — 12 mm BARS — ELEVATION — 12 DIA. MILD STEEL BARS — LINTEL REINFORCED WITH BARS BETWEEN VERTICAL JOINTS

Z' – SECTION — 215 — 6 DIA. STIRRUPS PLACED AT EVERY THIRD JOINT — WIRE AT EVERY THIRD JOINT AS TEMPORARY SUPPORT TO LOWER BAR — 6 DIA. STIRRUPS TWO 6 DIA. BARS TURNING PIECE WEDGES & PROP — WIRE FIXED TO FILLETS — STIRRUPS BARS — ENLARGED SECTION — LINTEL REINFORCED WITH BARS & STIRRUPS

FIGURE 16

the centre), and at the same time the stirrups, supported by the bottom bar, are bedded in position at every third joint, care being taken that the continuous longitudinal joint is filled with mortar for the lower 50 mm only. The top rod is inserted and pressed down to the stirrups or to a level slightly above them. The continuous vertical joint is then filled with grout from the top. Prior to the removal of the turning piece, the pieces of thin wire are cut flush with the two faces and the ends turned into the joints. Pointing completes the lintel. A 25 mm by 13 mm wood fillet may be used as a temporary support for the lower tension bar in lieu of the pieces of wire. This must be oiled before being built in to permit of its removal after the turning piece has been removed. The continuous joint is filled with mortar and the soffit pointed after removal of the fillet.

The size and number of bars vary with the span and loading. That shown at z′ is typical for a lintel having a maximum span of 2·5 m.

Flat and segmental arches may be strengthened by embedding meshed reinforcement in the bed joints of the walling which they support.

Reinforced brickwork has been adopted in the construction of fire-resisting floors. These slabs are reinforced with bars between the joints of the bricks placed on edge, both transversely and longitudinally, and these slabs are supported by steel beams at a maximum distance apart of 2·1 m. Reinforced slab construction is necessary for large brick canopies over doorways, etc.

Raking Bonds.—A characteristic defect in a thick wall built in English bond is a deficiency in the longitudinal bond due to the absence of stretchers in the heart of the wall. As stated on p. 45, this tie may be improved by the provision of metal reinforcement. An older method, and one which is now only occasionally adopted, is the introduction of courses of bricks set at a rake (or inclination) at intervals up the wall. These are known as raking bond courses and are of two forms, i.e., (a) diagonal bond, and (b) herring-bone bond.

(a) *Diagonal Bond* (see plan A, Fig. 17).—This is best suited for walls which are from 3 to 4-bricks thick, and is applied between the *stretching*[1] faces at every fifth or seventh course. Alternate raking courses should be inclined in the opposite direction to that shown. The method of setting-out is indicated on the figure. The triangular spaces formed near the stretching faces should be filled in with cut pieces of brick and not mortar only.

(b) *Herring-bone Bond.*—This form (so-called because of its slight resemblance to the spine of a herring) is shown at plan B, Fig. 17, and may be applied to walls which are at least 4-bricks thick at five to seven course vertical intervals. The bricks are laid at an angle of 45° in both directions from the centre. Like diagonal bond, alternate herring-bone courses are reversed. The setting-out is shown in the figure. Note (1) the construction lines F and G are drawn parallel to and equidistant from the centre line, with the 45° distance between (as 3-5) equal to 102·5 mm or the width of a brick, and (2) the long raking joint 1-2 is drawn from the centre and inclined at 45°, followed in sequence by the long raking joints 3-4, 5-6, 7-8, etc.

[1] Raking bond courses in brick footings should be between the normal *heading* faces.

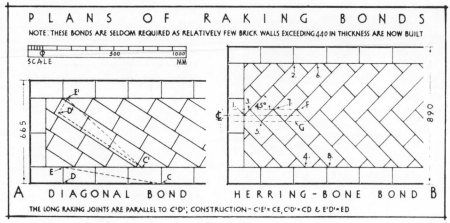

FIGURE 17

An alternative to raking bonds for increasing the longitudinal tie in thick walls is known as *longitudinal bond*. A course built in this bond consists entirely of stretchers, with exception of a row of queen closers adjacent to each outer row of stretchers. The inner rows of stretchers are arranged to break joint to give a 102.5 mm lap. This bond may be applied at every fifth course.

The above three bonds are seldom required for constructional purposes, as modern steel-framed and reinforced concrete construction has, to a large extent, eliminated thick walls. Both forms of raking bonds are, however, often used with good effect in decorated brickwork. Examples of such brickwork are shown in Fig. 24, the panel at M.1 indicating diagonal bond and that at M.2 showing the bricks arranged to a herring-bone pattern (see p. 62).

SPECIAL BONDS

Bonds which have not already been described include Garden, Cross, Dutch, Brick-on-edge and Facing Bonds.

Garden Wall Bond.—As its name implies, this bond is suitable for garden, division and similar walls which usually do not exceed 1-brick in thickness. Due to the slight variation in length of some bricks it is difficult to construct a 215 mm wall in English bond if a fair or uniform face is required on both sides (see Chap. I, Vol. I). As fewer headers are employed in garden wall bond than in either English or Flemish bonds, it is usually possible to select from the bricks available sufficient of the longer bricks of uniform length as headers for a garden bonded wall, the remaining bricks being used as stretchers and built flush with both faces of the headers. Fair faces on both sides of a garden bonded wall are thus ensured. Whilst garden wall bond is not as strong as English bond (the transverse tie being inferior), it is sufficient for most dwarf walls and for those not required to withstand large stresses. As mentioned on p. 40, garden wall bond is sometimes used instead of stretching bond for the construction of the outer leaves of cavity walls. It has a good appearance, and on this account is greatly to be preferred to stretching bond.

There are two forms of garden wall bond, *i.e.*, (*a*) English garden wall bond and (*b*) Flemish garden wall bond.

(*a*) *English Garden Wall Bond* (see A, Fig. 18).—This consists of one course of headers to three or five courses of stretchers. As in English bond, a queen closer is introduced next to the quoin header in the heading course. A header is placed at the quoin of each middle (or alternate) course of stretchers to give the necessary lap and face appearance of stretching bond (see also H, Fig. 3, Vol. I). The longitudinal vertical joint between each three (or five) successive stretching courses is continuous, and this causes the deficiency in transverse strength stated above. This bond, because of its economy, is very frequently adopted in the construction of 215 mm thick rough-casted external walls, especially for houses not exceeding two stories in height.

(*b*) *Flemish Garden Wall Bond* (see B, Fig. 18).—This is also known as *Sussex* and *Scotch* bond. It consists of three or five stretchers to one header in *each* course. A three-quarter bat is placed next to the quoin header in every alternate course, and a header is laid over the middle of each central stretcher.

In a modified arrangement at the quoin of a Sussex bonded wall, a queen closer is placed next to the quoin header of each alternate course, and this is followed by a series of three stretchers and a header. Each alternating course comprises a quoin stretcher with a stretcher adjoining, followed by a series consisting of a header and three stretchers. Excepting at the quoin the appearance is similar to the above, as each header is centrally over the middle stretcher.

Monk Bond is a variation of Flemish garden wall bond, *each* course consisting of a series comprising a header and two stretchers, the header falling centrally over the joint between a pair of stretchers.

English Cross Bond (see C, Fig. 18).—This is similar to English bond, in that it consists of alternate courses of headers and stretchers, with queen closers next to the quoin headers. Each *alternate stretching* course has, however, a header placed next to the quoin stretcher. This causes the stretchers to break joint in alternate courses.

Dutch Bond (see D, Fig. 18).—This is another modification of English bond. The bond consists of alternate courses of headers and stretchers, but *each stretching* course begins at the quoin with a three-quarter bat, and every *alternate stretching* course has a header placed next to the quoin three-quarter bat. This also has the effect of the stretchers breaking joint in alternate courses. The presence of the quoin three-quarter bats makes it unnecessary for queen closers to be placed next to the quoin headers as in English bond.

Brick-on-edge Bonds.—These differ from normal bond in that at least alternate courses are 102·5 mm high, the bricks being laid on edge and not on bed. They are economical as, compared with English bond, considerably fewer bricks and less mortar are required. Their strength is deficient, and the appearance is unsatisfactory on account of the large scale of the brick units and the light colour which is characteristic of the beds of most bricks. Only wire-cut bricks should be used. These bonds are sometimes employed for garden and similar walling, and occasionally for walls of cheap one-storied cottages. They can be employed effectively if their external faces are covered with vertical tiling (see Chap. III, Vol. III). The best known brick-on-edge bonds are (*a*) rat-trap bond and (*b*) Silverlock's bond.

(*a*) *Rat-trap Bond* (see F, Fig. 18).—All bricks are laid on edge, and, as shown, are arranged to give a face appearance of Flemish bond. Each alternate course L commences with a three-quarter bat, followed by a header, and each alternate course K commences with a header, succeeded by a stretcher. As indicated on the plans, there is a 85 mm cavity between each pair of stretchers, except at the jambs, which are solid (see also sketch). It is estimated that, compared with a 215 mm solid wall, a rat-trap bonded wall shows a saving of approximately 25 per cent. External walls of cottages built in this bond must be protected on their outer faces by rough-cast or vertical tiling, otherwise water may penetrate through the solid headers and mortar droppings.

Occasionally 215 mm rat-trap bonded walls are built solid, the cavity being filled by stretchers placed on edge.

(*b*) *Silverlock's Bond* (see E, Fig. 18).—This resembles English bond in that it consists of alternate courses of headers and stretchers, but, whereas the headers are laid on bed, the stretchers are placed on edge with a continuous cavity between. The jambs are solid, and a three-quarter bat at the beginning of each heading course gives the necessary bond. Whilst this is stronger than rat-trap bond, it is not so economical.

On the score of economy in materials and space, brick-on-edge stretching bond is frequently employed in the construction of 65 mm thick partition walls in lieu of 102·5 mm thick brick walls.

Facing Bond.—This is usually employed for solid walls exceeding 215 mm in thickness which are faced with thin bricks and backed by thicker and cheaper standard commons. The faced work is bonded to the backing in a series of blocks of a height which depends upon the difference in thickness between the two types of bricks. Thus, in the section through the 440 mm wall at G, Fig. 18, the height of four courses of 50 mm thick facings with their bed joints is shown to coincide with three courses of commons together with their joints, and the blocks of facings are alternately ½ and 1-brick thick. The facings may be built in either English, Flemish or any of the bonds A, B, C or D, Fig. 18 (with snap headers at the ½-brick thick blocks), and the backing is built in English bond. Somewhat similar construction may be applied to 1½ brick walls, with the backing to the alternating 215 mm thick facing blocks built in stretching bond.

A modified form of facing bond may be applied to 215 mm thick walls. Thus, the facings and commons would be built in ½-brick thick leaves in stretching bond with facing heading courses at suitable intervals. If the facing and backing bed joints coincide, as shown at G, such facing headers would appear at every fifth facing course.

Facing bond is not, of course, as strong as English bond, but the alternative would be to use thin bricks for the backing of the same thickness as the facings. And this would add considerably to the cost, especially if the facings were 50 mm or less.

ARCHES

A description of several forms of arches is given in Chap. I, Vol. I.

Semicircular Arch with Orders.—An opening in a thick wall is often finished with either splayed or stepped jambs and an arch comprising several rings of diminishing width or thickness. The arch is thus recessed or stepped by a series of rings known as *orders* (or " rows "). It is applied to both door and window openings and has a satisfactory appearance.

An example of this type of arch is shown at A, B and C, Fig. 19, which illustrates a main entrance to a house. Special attention is drawn to the section at C, which shows the bonding of the arch as each ring extends to the inner face. This is known as a *bonded* arch. It is much stronger than the alternative unbonded arch, often applied, when 102·5 by 102·5 mm by 65 mm voussoirs are used for each ring which is therefore only 102·5 mm wide on soffit. The impost is shown consisting of a double row of tiles which project 20 mm. An alternative is a thin stone course or a course of purpose-made bricks.

It is assumed that the door shown opens into an outer lobby, otherwise the thickness of the wall should be increased, with the inner ring at least 215 mm wide on soffit.

The two steps, of combined height equal to the brick-on-end plinth, are

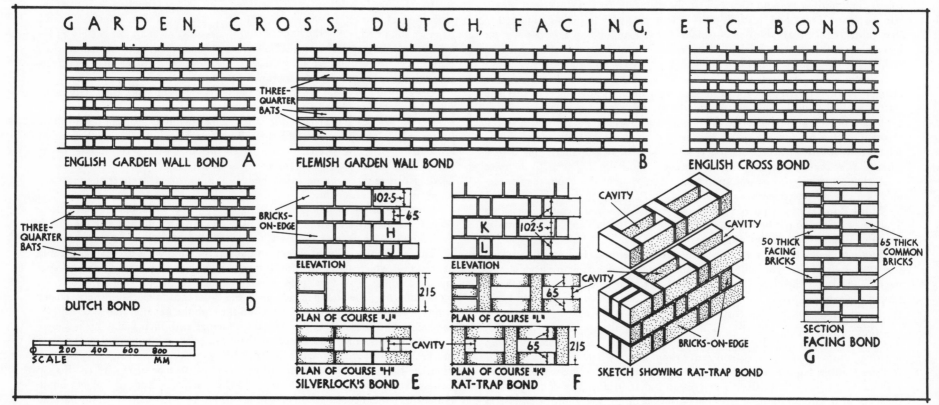

GARDEN, CROSS, DUTCH, FACING, ETC BONDS

ENGLISH GARDEN WALL BOND   A

THREE-QUARTER BATS

FLEMISH GARDEN WALL BOND   B

ENGLISH CROSS BOND   C

THREE-QUARTER BATS

DUTCH BOND   D

BRICKS-ON-EDGE   102·5   65   H   J   ELEVATION   215   PLAN OF COURSE "J"   CAVITY   PLAN OF COURSE "H"   SILVERLOCK'S BOND   E

K   102·5   L   ELEVATION   CAVITY   65   PLAN OF COURSE "L"   65   215   PLAN OF COURSE "K"   RAT-TRAP BOND   F

CAVITY   CAVITY   CAVITY   BRICKS-ON-EDGE   SKETCH SHOWING RAT-TRAP BOND

50 THICK FACING BRICKS   65 THICK COMMON BRICKS   SECTION   FACING BOND   G

SCALE   0   200   400   600   800   MM

FIGURE 18

formed with bricks-on-edge in cement. These bricks must be hard and durable, otherwise the arrises would be readily damaged. The bottom step is segmental with a 1·2 m radius, and consists of purpose-made bricks with a tile-on-edge infilling; the vertical joints are radial.

Another example of a semicircular arch with orders is shown at P.14, Fig. 24. This arch is three-ringed and the stepped recesses are continued down the jambs to the steps of the doorway. This is an alternative treatment to the splayed jambs shown at A, Fig. 19.

A semicircular arch with a toothed or *indented* extrados is shown at P.13, Fig. 24 (see also p. 62).

Stilted Semicircular Arch with Segmental Rere Arch (see U, V, W, X and Z, Fig. 19.)—A stilted (or elevated) arch is one which has its springing line above the impost. Thus, the amount of stilting of the semicircular arch at U is equal to two courses. In the absence of an impost the arch is continued below the springing line with several parallel voussoirs, any difference in texture and colour between the voussoirs and general walling producing the stilted effect. This arch is enriched by a slightly projecting crown course known as a *label* (see U and the section at Z). When the label consists of moulded bricks (or stone) it is called a *hood mould*. The voussoirs and label are of purpose-made bricks, and the arch is bonded on face.

When the jambs of an opening are rebated, the external arch need not necessarily be of the same shape as the internal arch. Thus the external arch at U is semicircular of 685 mm radius, and the inner arch is segmental of 1·81 m radius. As the internal jambs are splayed, as shown at W and X, the intersection between the soffit of the segmental arch and a splayed jamb will take the form of a curve as indicated at Z. This segmental arch is known as a *rere* (meaning " back " or " rear ") *arch*.

The development of the curved intersection is shown at X, V and Z. The plan at X and sectional elevation Z of the splayed jamb are each divided into four or any convenient number of equal parts. Vertical lines are projected from the quarter-points 1, 2 and 3 on the plan to the intrados of the segmental arch. Horizontal lines are drawn from the points 5, 1, 2, 3 and 4 on the intrados to intersect the corresponding vertical lines at Z. A line 5, 1, 2 3 and 4 drawn through these points of intersection gives the required curve, as shown at Z. Horizontal lines projected from the voussoir joints at the intrados of the segmental arch at V to Z give the level soffit joints in section YY.

Circular or Bull's-eye Arch (see H, Fig. 19).—This form of arch is chiefly adopted as an external decorative feature to receive either a fixed light or frame with a pivoted sash. Circular openings in internal walls are occasionally required through which metal smoke flues, ventilating tubes, etc., are passed. Purpose-made, rubber or axed bricks are used externally, and an internal arch is usually a rough ring.

Construction.—The lower half or *invert* of this arch is first built. The adjacent brickwork which will form the base for this lower half is built from course Z and

racked back up to course Y at the centre. A wood batten is laid across the oper weighed at the ends on course Y, and the trammel rod or *radius rod* (see C Vol. I) is screwed or nailed to it at the centre; allowance for the thickness bed joint at the extrados must be made in determining the length of the rod. Z is completed; stretchers 1, 2 and 3 are laid temporarily in position and m the required curve as the radius rod is traversed; these bricks are cut with and bolster (see 35, Fig. 19, Vol. I) and trimmed accurately to shape with a scut they are then laid permanently. Each course up to the middle line is completed in this manner, after which the purpose-made voussoirs forming the lower half of the arch are bedded in position, the radius rod being used to check the radial joints and curve. Finally, the upper half of the arch is constructed by the usual method, a wood centre on struts being used as a temporary support (see Chap. I, Vol. III).

Semi-elliptical Arch (see J, Fig. 19).—This shows half of an axed arch, bonded on face with a portion of a tiled key, and a half arch in three rough rings. Both purpose-mades and rubbers may be used for the former.

This form of arch has several demerits. It is not structurally sound, as defects such as shearing at the haunch joints may occur, especially if the rise is relatively small. Labour costs are high, as special care must be taken in its setting-out and erection if abnormally shaped curves at the intrados and extrados are to be avoided. It is sometimes preferred to the segmental arch where a comparatively large span is required and the height is restricted. The rise of the arch should be at least one-third the span.

As the student will be aware, an ellipse is produced when a cone is cut by a plane which does not intersect the base and is not parallel to it. A true elliptical curve cannot be constructed with compasses, as no part of it is circular. However, for reasons of economy and the need to reduce the number of voussoir templets to a minimum, it is usual to adopt a geometrical method for setting-out the intrados and extrados of a semi-elliptical arch. There are several methods, that set out from five centres shown at J being one of the best, as by it compound curves can be produced which closely conform to that of the true ellipse.

Setting-out.—Draw the major and minor axes; make cd = half span ab; construct circle with d as centre and db as radius, and mark off be and bf = radius db; draw lines dem, dfr, ken and hfo; g, e, k, f and h are the five required centres for both the intrados and extrados, and dm, kn, ko and dr are common normals. Construct tangential curves as, st, tu, uv and vw with g, e, k, f and h as centres respectively; construct the extrados in a similar manner; mark off the thickness of the voussoirs on the extrados (if the bricks are axed, purpose-made or rubbed) and draw the bed joints of the voussoirs. It is important to note that these joints are radial, as shown by the broken constructional lines; thus the voussoirs within the portion of the arch $mnts$ radiate from centre e, and those within portion $nout$ radiate from centre k. It will be seen that the bricklayer will only require three differently shaped templets to which axed or rubber voussoirs are shaped, i.e., one for the central voussoirs, one for those within the intermediate portions $mnts$ and $orvu$, and one templet for the voussoirs within the two end portions. Also for purpose-mades, three similarly shaped but larger (to allow for shrinkage) moulds will serve the moulder to shape the bricks.

Elliptical Arch (see K, Fig. 19).—This may be adopted as an alternative to the circular arch H. The method of setting out briefly indicated in the figure has been selected as an alternative to that described for the semi-elliptical arch J. It will be seen that only four centres *e*, *m*, *n* and *f* are required.

Setting-out.—After the major and minor axes have been drawn and their lengths decided upon, with centre *a* and radius *ab* describe arc *bc*; join *bh*, with centre *h* and radius *hc* describe arc *cd*; bisect *bd*, and the two centres *e* and *f* are at the intersection between this bisector and the two axes; the two remaining centres *m* and *n* are easily obtained by making *am* = *af* and *an* = *ae*. The voussoir joints of each of the four sections of the arch radiate towards its centre. Only two templets are required for the whole of the voussoirs.

Pointed Arches.—These are also known as Gothic arches, as the pointed arch is characteristic of this style of architecture. The intrados and extrados of each of the several forms of this type of arch are segmental curves which intersect at the pointed apex at which each half abuts to form a vertical joint on the centre line. It is therefore not usual to have a key.

There are five forms of pointed arch, *i.e.*, equilateral, drop, lancet, Tudor and Venetian.

The first three are illustrated at T, Fig. 19. The *equilateral arch* is shown at R, bonded on face; the radius of each curve of the intrados equals the span, the centres are at the *ends* of the springing line and the extrados is parallel to the intrados. A *drop arch*, as at Q, has its centres on the springing line and *within* it; in the example the span is 1·36 m and the radius is 1·14 m. A *lancet arch* has its centres on the springing line and *outside* the span; that shown by broken lines at S has a span of 0·69 m and the radius is 0·8 m. In each form the bed joints of the voussoirs radiate to their respective centres. The equilateral and drop arches are shown in section at O.

Tudor Arch (see N, Fig. 19).—This arch, commonly employed during the Tudor period, has four centres, all within the span; two of them are on the springing line and the other two are below it. The Tudor arch, like the semi-elliptical, is a weak form.

Setting-out.—There are several methods. In that shown, *ac* is set up and made equal to ⅝ (or ⅔) rise *em*; join *mc* and draw *mn* at right angles to it of indefinite length; mark off *mn* and *ar* = *ac*; join *nr*, bisect it and continue the bisector until it intersects *mn* continued at *s*; *s* and *r* are the required centres for the right half of the arch, and *sr* produced to *u* is a common normal. The remaining two centres *v* and *w* may be found by measuring from the centre line. The voussoir bed joints radiate from the respective centres. Two templets are required for the voussoirs.

Venetian Arch (see L, Fig. 19).—This pointed arch is deeper at the crown than at the springing line. The centres are on the latter. The voussoirs are radial from the centres of the *intrados* curves.

Florentine Arch (see M, Fig. 19).—This, like the Venetian arch, is deeper at the crown than at the springing. The intrados curve is semicircular, and the extrados has a pointed apex as it consists of two segmental curves, as shown.

Here also the voussoirs are normal to the *intrados* curve. Sometimes the extrados is semi-elliptical.

A semi-hexagonal arch and a *tiled segmental arch* are illustrated in Fig. 24 (see p. 63).

The centering for the above arches is described in Chap. I, Vol. III.

DAMP PROOFING OF BASEMENTS

The materials used for horizontal damp proof courses and their application are described in detail in Chap. I, Vol. I. Vertical damp proof courses will now be considered.

The materials chiefly used for vertical damp proof courses are (1) bituminous substances and (2) waterproofed cement and concrete.

1. Bitumen is a name applied to natural pitchy (see p. 54) substances consisting principally of hydrocarbons which vary in colour and hardness. It includes (*a*) natural asphalt, (*b*) artificial asphalt and (*c*) fibrous asphalt felt.

(*a*) *Natural* or *Native Asphalt* occurs in many parts of the world in either a pure (or moderately pure) condition or associated with a large proportion of mineral matter such as limestone, shale, etc., and known as *rock asphalt*. It is found in liquid form in springs, liquid or semi-liquid condition in lakes, and in impregnated rock formation. As there are no deposits in this country, asphalt has to be imported, the chief supplies being obtained from the British West Indies, France, Switzerland and Germany.

Natural asphalt is one of the most efficient materials employed for damp resisting purposes; it is black in colour, very durable, tough and elastic.

One of the largest deposits of asphalt exists on the Island of Trinidad, British West Indies. It is a lake, known as Trinidad Asphalt Lake, approximately circular, of 2 000 m in diameter and nearly 90 m deep. Whilst large quantities of asphalt have already been obtained from it, it is estimated that there still remain some 10 000 to 15 000 Mg. The consistency of the asphalt is such that it will permit men to work on the surface.

The chief supply from France comes from a large deposit in the Seyssel region and is commercially known by that name. Another source is that from a deposit mined in the south (St Jean de Maruéjols, Department of Gard). These are rock asphalt deposits, the limestone having a maximum asphalt impregnation of 12 per cent. It is both quarried and mined.

The largest deposits occuring in Switzerland are in the Val de Travers region, west of Lake Neuchatel, and well known as Val de Travers and Neuchatel asphalts. This is asphalt-impregnated limestone, the asphalt content varying from 8 to 12 per cent.

The principal deposit in Germany is situated at the village of Limmer (in the province of Hanover) and is marked as " Limmer Asphalt ". This is limestone which is impregnated with 8 to 20 per cent. of asphalt.

Winning and Refining.—The methods employed to obtain asphalt depend upon the nature of the deposits. Thus, Trinidad Lake asphalt is hand-picked

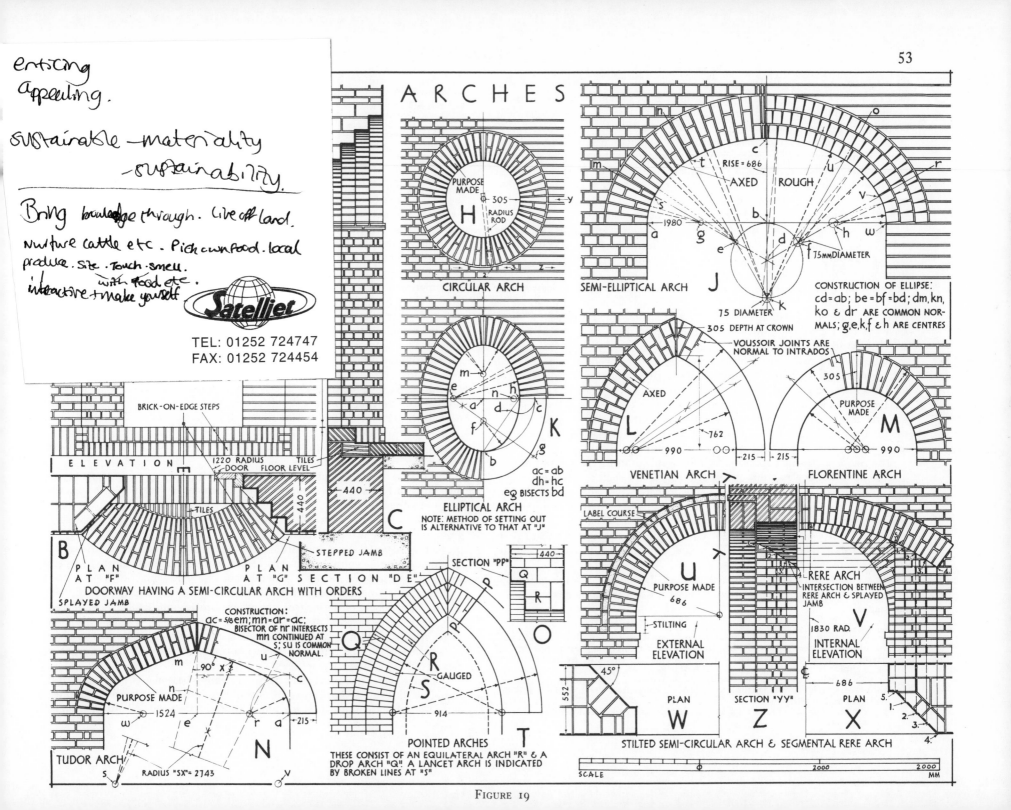

FIGURE 19

by men working on the surface, loaded into trucks which are hauled by cable over rails either to the refiners or to the shore (about 1·2 km distant) and loaded for direct shipment. Deposits of rock asphalt near the surface are open-quarried, blasting being resorted to. Deep deposits are mined.

Water is present in most natural asphalts. That from Lake Trinidad, for instance, has nearly 30 per cent. of moisture content. This must be removed. Dehydration is effected by heating the asphalt in open metal tanks, after which it is passed through a fine screen (to remove pieces of wood, etc.), and poured into barrels. Rock asphalts are crushed, ground and screened before being either heated in tanks or dried by exposure to the atmosphere.

Preparation of Natural Asphalt Mastic.—This is recognized as one of the most reliable materials for the damp proofing of walls, floors and flat roofs. As, for this purpose, most rock asphalts are deficient in bitumen, it is necessary to enrich them by the addition of Trinidad Lake asphalt. The rock asphalt or aggregate used in the preparation of the mastic should contain at least 90 per cent. of calcium carbonate and not less than 8 per cent. of bitumen. This rock is reduced by grinding to a powder so that the whole will pass a No. 8 sieve (mesh of 2 mm aperture) and at least 15 per cent. will pass a No. 200 sieve (mesh of 0·075 mm aperture). The required amount of Trinidad Lake asphalt is added and thoroughly incorporated by mechanical agitators with the powdered aggregate in a tank at a temperature of from 176° to 200° C. The total bitumen content should be at least 16 per cent. In order to stabilize the mastic and render it suitable for marketing, up to $12\frac{1}{2}$ per cent. by weight of fine grit such as sharp-grained sand is added during the mixing process. Finally, the mastic is discharged from the tank and cast into flat blocks weighing approximately 25 kg each. It is thus in a convenient form for handling.

(b) *Artificial Asphalt* is a cheap and inferior substitute for the natural product. The composition is a mixture of *tar* with aggregates such as sand, pulverized chalk and *pitch* (see below). It is liable to deteriorate and become brittle. Therefore, when used as a damp proof course, cracks may appear through which water may penetrate. The composition of artificial asphalt varies, a common mixture being 1 part tar (or tar and pitch), 1 part sand and $1\frac{1}{4}$ parts crushed chalk. These are boiled in a tank and thoroughly incorporated by stirring before being run into blocks.

Tar, a black, thick, oily, strong-smelling liquid, is obtained by the destructive distillation in a closed retort of bituminous coal, wood and certain other organic substances.

Coal tar is the largest group, and is recovered as a by-product in gas manufacture. The gases produced when the coal in the retorts (long vertical or inclined vessels of circular or D-section) is heated proceed through the hydraulic main (a large pipe), condensers (pipes in which the gases are cooled), tar extractor and scrubbers (where ammonia and impurities are removed) to the gasometer. During the process, tar is deposited in the hydraulic main, condensers, extractor and scrubbers, collected and mixed.

Valuable oils are obtained by subjecting the tar to fractional distillation. The process consists of heating the tar in a still (metal cylinder) and collecting the condensed vapours. Benzene, toluene, naphtha, carbolic acid, cresol, creosote, naphthalene and anthracene are some of these oils.

Pitch is the residue in the still after the oils have been evaporated. This black coloured material has a variable consistency, becoming brittle in winter and softening when subjected to heat in the summer, hence the reason why this is an unreliable material for damp proofing (see above).

(c) *Fibrous Asphalt Felt* (see Chap. I, Vol. I).—The continuous process is one of several used for manufacturing this material. The felt or hessian forming the base is passed in a continuous stretched sheet through a machine and successively (1) pre-heated as it travels over and under steam-heated cylinders, (2) impregnated with asphalt by being passed under and over a series of rollers in a tank containing hot liquid asphalt, (3) air-cooled as it traverses rollers, (4) passed through a second tank containing hot asphalt mastic and surface coatings of the liquid applied to each side of the sheet, (5) on emerging, sprayed by compressed air with grains of talc or similar material (to prevent the sheets from sticking together when coiled up) on the upper surface, (6) passed between a pair of rollers to embed the particles of talc and coiled by traversing air-cooled drums, (7) automatically cut into 22 m lengths, and (8) finally wound into coils by a winding machine.

Application of Vertical Damp Proof Courses.—As stated in Chap. I, Vol. I, the object of a horizontal damp proof course provided in a wall at least 150 mm above the ground level, is to intercept water absorbed from the soil and prevent it from rising up the wall. It is clear that this will not stop water from passing through a basement wall from the adjacent earth. Therefore it is necessary to introduce a vertical damp proof course which must extend from the above horizontal damp proof course down to a second horizontal course at or near the base of the wall.

Several alternative details showing the damp proofing of basements are illustrated in Fig. 20. A section through a basement is shown at A, in which a damp proof course in the thickness of the floor is continued vertically up each wall to the horizontal course placed at a minimum height of 150 mm above the ground level. The damp-resisting material thus forms a waterproof tank, preventing water from passing through the floor and walls adjacent to the earth, in addition to intercepting water absorbed from the ground which would otherwise pass up the walls above the ground level.

The damp proofing material in details B, C, D, E and G is natural asphalt mastic. The blocks of mastic (see above) are broken into small pieces, placed into a tank on the site, and gradually heated until the asphalt is sufficiently fluid to be applied. With exception of detail E, the vertical damp proof courses are situated within the thickness of the walls, and thus conform with what is considered to be the best practice.

Detail C shows one method of damp proofing a basement which has a joist and boarded floor. The $1\frac{1}{2}$ brick main wall has, in addition, a 102·5 mm thick outer leaf which is finished with a plinth course. This leaf is built in stretching bond, and its function is to protect and retain the vertical damp proof course.

The wall is built up to the level of the lower damp proof course of asphalt or other approved materials described in Chap. I, Vol. I. It is constructed in the following manner : The main 1½-brick wall is continued for three or four courses, and the joints on the outer face are raked out to a depth of about 20 mm to afford a key for the vertical asphalt. A similar number of courses of the outer leaf are built at a distance of 20 mm from the main wall. This cavity is maintained and mortar droppings prevented from falling into it, if a length of 300 mm by 20 mm board is placed next to the main wall as the leaf is constructed. This board is removed and the cavity is filled with molten asphalt from a pail; a length of floor board supported on the leaf by small splayed blocks and tilted towards the cavity facilitates this operation. A metal rod is used to consolidate the asphalt and prevent the formation of air voids. Care must be taken to ensure that the cavity is entirely free from mortar droppings before the asphalt is poured, otherwise water may be subsequently transmitted through such porous materials to the main wall. The wall and vertical damp proof course are formed in short " lifts " in this manner until the position of the upper horizontal damp proof course is reached. The latter course is then applied and the normal construction of the wall continued.

Attention is drawn to the means of ventilation provided to safeguard the floor timbers against dry rot. Vertical shafts or flues, of 215 mm by 102.5 mm cross section, are formed at approximately 1·8 m intervals in the centre of the main wall during construction; openings are left at the inner face below the basement floor, and the upper ends are completed with the usual perforated air bricks, as shown.

Detail D shows an alternative and efficient method of damp proofing. The bottom layer of concrete known as the *subfloor* is covered with a 20 mm thickness of asphalt laid in two separate coats (or a 30 mm thickness in three coats); this in turn is covered with a second layer of concrete, called the *loading floor* (as it counterbalances the upward pressure of subsoil water), and finished with wood block flooring (see Chap. I, Vol. III).

The asphalt covering the subfloor is continued as a vertical damp proof course, additional asphalt being applied at the intersection between the horizontal and vertical layers, and finished as a splayed angle fillet, to prevent possible creep of moisture at the intersection. The vertical layer is formed as follows. The outer 102·5 mm thickness of the wall is first constructed in stretching bond up to the level of the horizontal layer; the joints of the inner face are raked out and dust, etc., removed by means of a stiff broom; the first coat of the hot asphalt, approximately 10 mm thick, is then applied, it being spread or floated on by the aid of a *hand float* similar to that shown at D, Fig. 23. The latter is applied with sufficient pressure until a smooth surfaced homogeneous layer of asphalt is obtained, free from voids or blow holes. Any blow holes must be stabbed, filled in and smoothed over. The second coat must cover the joints of the first. The finished thickness of two-coat work is 20 mm. For special

work, and especially if water pressure has to be resisted, three separate coats are applied, the overall thickness being 23 mm or, preferably, 30 mm.

In order to provide a uniform backing for the asphalt, it is advisable to build the inner or main wall 20 mm from the face of the asphalt. Grouted cement is run into this cavity as each four courses of the brickwork is built. If this is not done, spaces will be left between the asphalt and the outer face of the main wall, and any water from the soil forced through the outer leaf may seriously damage the unsupported patches of asphalt and gain entrance into the building. The cement grouted backing to the asphalt is shown in detail B.

The upper horizontal damp proof course may only cover the wall from the vertical layer to the outer face, or, preferably, extend for the full thickness of the wall as indicated by broken lines at D.

Sometimes the provision of subsoil drainage is made to remove the risk of damage to the vertical damp proof course. Thus, as shown at D, small diameter drain pipes (see Chapter Two) are laid butt-jointed in the trench and covered with about 600 mm of gravel before the trench is filled in with soil. This subsoil drain is continued round the building, laid with adequate fall, and continued to a hedge ditch or other suitable outlet. Hence the level of the subsoil water is lowered to that of the drain, eliminating pressure on the vertical damp proof course, as the water passes through the open joints of the drain and is removed.

Another form of internal vertical damp proof course is shown at G. The wall is constructed in two block-bonded thicknesses with a continuous double layer of asphalt between, the height of the blocks being five courses each.

The detail at E shows the vertical asphalt applied on the external face of the walls. The joints must be well raked out to afford an adequate key for the asphalt, otherwise there is a risk of the covering becoming detached from the wall. There should be a minimum width of 760 mm working space between the wall and the timbering of the trench to enable this to be done. In order that the asphalt will not be exposed to view and the hot rays of the sun, it is turned in 102·5 mm just below the ground level and continued vertically to the upper horizontal course. This method is not so efficient as either of those shown at C, D and G, especially if the damp proof course is subjected to subsoil water pressure. The construction of the floor, in which Bull Dog clips are employed, is described in Chap. I, Vol. III.

Detail F shows the application of sheets of fibrous asphalt felt. This bituminous sheeting is generally in 915 mm widths and is laid vertically with 75 mm wide lapped joints. In the given example it is shown applied to the internal face of the main 1½-brick wall. This face is first rendered with cement mortar (1 : 3) of 10 mm thickness to provide an even surface for the sheeting.

It is usual for three men to work together when applying the felt. The roll is supported by two men holding the projecting ends of a wood roller which is passed through it. Commencing at the upper horizontal damp proof course previously laid, and working downwards, the underside of the roll as it is gradually uncoiled is heated by a blow lamp manipulated by the third man. Meanwhile, one of the other men holding an end of the rod with one hand, presses a hand float over the sheet as it uncoils and attaches it to the rendered face of the wall. This is continued, the roll being slowly uncoiled as it is heated and attached, until the base is reached. The upper edge must be thoroughly heated and *sealed* to the horizontal damp proof course, and the lower edge should be heated and lapped 75 mm over the floor damp proof course previously laid. Each successive vertical layer of sheeting must be thoroughly sealed by heat and pressure at the lapped joints.

The inner 102·5 mm wall is built after the concrete loading floor has been formed, a 10 or 13 mm cavity being left between the leaf and the asphalt and filled with grouted cement as described on p. 55 in connection with detail B. It is usual for this inner leaf to be continued up to the basement ceiling.

Bituminous sheeting may also be applied next to a 102·5 mm leaf as at D or externally as at E.

Damp Proofing of Floors.—The concrete floors shown at D, E, F and G are shown with a damp proof course over the concrete subfloor. Such provision is necessary if the site is damp (see waterproofed concrete floors below). The course may be either of asphalt mastic or fibrous asphalt felt.

> The surface of the concrete must be absolutely dry before the asphalt is applied, otherwise adhesion will be adversely affected. It should be level and well brushed down. In order to promote adhesion, hot liquid asphalt, known as a *primer*, is brushed over the surface before the first coat of asphalt mastic is applied; alternatively, the concrete may be covered with bituminous paper or *building paper* (one type consists of two layers of hemp impregnated with bitumen and covered with brown or kraft paper). This first coat of mastic, 10 mm thick, is spread and floated over in bays not exceeding 1·4 m; the joint between a bay and that last formed is properly sealed by spreading the hot asphalt some 75 mm over the edge of that already laid to soften it, and after the superfluous asphalt has been removed, the joint is well floated or ironed until both edges are properly bonded and levelled. The second coat is applied direct on to the first, care being taken that the joints do not coincide with those below. If a third coat is required, this must also break joint with the second.
>
> If fibrous asphalt felt is to be used, as shown at F, the concrete subfloor is primed and the bituminous sheeting is laid with 75 mm lapped joints, as described in the preceeding column for vertical sheeting, the sheets being heated as they are uncoiled and floated on to the floor. As any sharp projections on the surface of the subfloor may tear the sheeting, it is advisable to cover the concrete with a 13 mm thick layer of cement mortar to prevent damage when the concrete of the loaded floor is deposited. This also ensures a good backing for the damp proof course, which is very essential if water pressure has to be resisted.
>
> In order to prevent damage being caused to the horizontal damp proof course by the upward pressure of subsoil water, it is often necessary to reinforce the concrete by a continuous layer of expanded metal or other steel reinforcement placed about 25 mm below the damp proof course. Similar reinforcement, placed approximately 25 mm from the top, is also usually provided in the concrete loading floor. Such reinforcement resists the tension stresses created.[1] In all such construction the loading floors should be tied or built-in to the walls, as shown at D, E, F and G.

Treatment of Damp Existing Basement Walls.—The absence of vertical damp proof courses is a frequent cause of dampness in walls of existing basements.

One method of curing such dampness is to apply a bituminous sheeting vertical damp proof course to the internal face of the wall, similar to that shown at F and described on p. 55, and to construct a 102·5 mm brick (or concrete) wall from the floor to the ceiling.

Alternatively, asphalt mastic may be applied to the internal faces of the walls after any plaster has been removed and the joints well raked out. Two coats of

[1] See Vol. IV.

asphalt may be rendered as described in connection with detail D and a 102·5 mm brick lining constructed, or this inner lining may be built with 20 mm cavity between, into which the liquid mastic is poured (see description on p. 55 in respect to detail C). If a wall exceeds 2·7 m in height, it is desirable to bond the new 102·5 mm brick lining to it; this is effected by forming 125 mm by 125 mm by 100 mm high pockets (one per square metre) in the existing wall, lining these with asphalt mastic, and building in headers from the new wall during its construction.

If the wall can be treated externally, the vertical asphalt damp proof course may be applied on the outer face, as shown at E.

When the floor, in addition to the walls, of an existing basement is damp, it is advisable to take up the floor, replace it with at least 150 mm thickness of concrete (1 : 2 : 4) and cover it with a 20 mm double layer of *coloured asphalt* before the walls are treated. This can be obtained in various colours, and provides a noiseless, damp-resisting and hygienic finish. Occasionally the layer of asphalt may be placed direct upon the existing concrete floor; this is rarely satisfactory, as the concrete is usually defective.

Waterproofed cement (see below) is also applied to walls and floors of damp existing basements in lieu of bituminous materials.

2. Waterproofed Cement Renderings and Concrete.—Waterproofers, as described on p. 27, are used for cement renderings and concrete (see p. 36) for damp proofing basements. The composition of the mixes varies according to the waterproofer, water pressure (if any) to be resisted, and the particular requirements of the building. In all cases the directions of the proprietors of the waterproofers should be complied with, and only best materials and workmanship employed.

The construction may be somewhat similar to that shown at E, except that the floor consists of one layer only of waterproofed reinforced concrete covered with a rendering of waterproofed cement mixture; the rendering is continued vertically on the outer face of the wall to the upper horizontal damp proof course as shown.

> The composition of the concrete recommended by one firm whose product is a well-known waterproofer in powder form is 1 part Portland cement, 2 parts sand, 3 parts coarse aggregate (graded from 19 mm down to 6 mm) and 3 kg of waterproofer to 100 kg of cement. The reinforcement is placed at 25 mm from the upper surface, the thickness of the floor and amount of reinforcement depending upon the span and water pressure to be resisted. The concrete is at once covered with a 20 mm mixture composed of 1 part Portland cement, 2 parts sand and 5 kg of waterproofer to 100 kg of cement. The vertical rendering is of similar composition, but is 25 mm thick in three coats.

To cure dampness in an existing basement, it is recommended that a 150 mm layer of waterproofed reinforced concrete, composed as above, be formed on the old concrete floor; this is rendered with a 20 mm layer of waterproofed cement mortar, as above, and continued as a 25 mm thick vertical layer on the inner face of the walls.

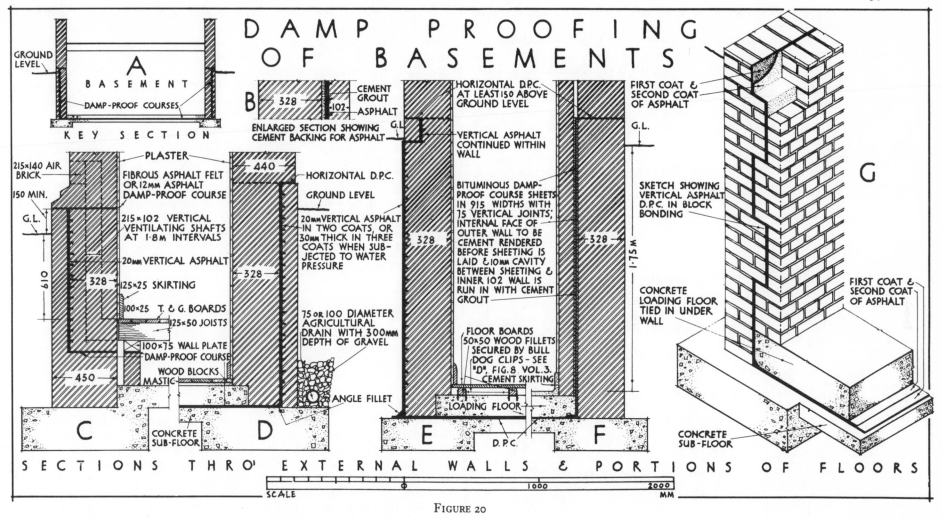

DAMP PROOFING OF BASEMENTS

A
GROUND LEVEL
BASEMENT
DAMP-PROOF COURSES
KEY SECTION

B
328
102
CEMENT GROUT
ASPHALT
ENLARGED SECTION SHOWING CEMENT BACKING FOR ASPHALT

C
215×140 AIR BRICK
150 MIN.
G.L.
PLASTER
FIBROUS ASPHALT FELT OR 12MM ASPHALT DAMP-PROOF COURSE
215×102 VERTICAL VENTILATING SHAFTS AT 1·8M INTERVALS
20MM VERTICAL ASPHALT
125×25 SKIRTING
100×25 T. & G. BOARDS
125×50 JOISTS
100×75 WALL PLATE
DAMP-PROOF COURSE
WOOD BLOCKS
MASTIC
610
328
450
CONCRETE SUB-FLOOR

D
440
HORIZONTAL D.P.C.
GROUND LEVEL
20MM VERTICAL ASPHALT IN TWO COATS, OR 30MM THICK IN THREE COATS WHEN SUBJECTED TO WATER PRESSURE
328
75 OR 100 DIAMETER AGRICULTURAL DRAIN WITH 300MM DEPTH OF GRAVEL
ANGLE FILLET

E / F
HORIZONTAL D.P.C. AT LEAST 150 ABOVE GROUND LEVEL
VERTICAL ASPHALT CONTINUED WITHIN WALL
BITUMINOUS DAMP-PROOF COURSE SHEETS IN 915 WIDTHS WITH 75 VERTICAL JOINTS; INTERNAL FACE OF OUTER WALL TO BE CEMENT RENDERED BEFORE SHEETING IS LAID & 10MM CAVITY BETWEEN SHEETING & INNER 102 WALL IS RUN IN WITH CEMENT GROUT
G.L.
328
FLOOR BOARDS 50×50 WOOD FILLETS SECURED BY BULL DOG CLIPS—SEE "D", FIG.8 VOL.3.
CEMENT SKIRTING
LOADING FLOOR
D.P.C.
1·75 M
328

G
FIRST COAT & SECOND COAT OF ASPHALT
SKETCH SHOWING VERTICAL ASPHALT D.P.C. IN BLOCK BONDING
CONCRETE LOADING FLOOR TIED IN UNDER WALL
FIRST COAT & SECOND COAT OF ASPHALT
CONCRETE SUB-FLOOR

SECTIONS THRO' EXTERNAL WALLS & PORTIONS OF FLOORS

SCALE 0 1000 2000 MM

FIGURE 20

The following is the sequence of operations : (1) Chases are formed in the walls to receive the edges of the waterproofed concrete floor; (2) any plaster, limewash or paint is removed from the walls, the joints are raked out or the brickwork (or stonework) is hacked over by using a hammer and punch to give a key for the rendering, the walls are brushed down with a stiff broom to remove dust and afterwards copiously watered to prevent excessive absorption of moisture from the rendering; (3) the surface of the existing floor is well hacked, brushed and washed; (4) a 5 per cent. grout of waterproofed cement is brushed over the cleaned surface to effect a bond between it and the waterproofed concrete layer which is at once laid before the grout sets; (5) this is rendered without delay; (6) each prepared internal face of the wall is grouted, and after the fillet has been carefully formed at the bottom corner (this is important, as the intersection is vulnerable) and before the grout has set, the first coat of the wall rendering is applied, followed by the subsequent coats.

Defects in this form of damp proofing may occur through cracks which may develop in the rendering coats through which water may penetrate.

In modern construction, basements are frequently constructed of solid reinforced concrete walls, the concrete being waterproofed.

A double course of slates, bedded in cement (as described in Chap. I, Vol. I), may be used as a cheap, but less effective, alternative vertical damp proof course to those described above.

Finally, the practice adopted in cheap work of rendering the *inside* faces of basement walls with two coats of cement mortar to a finished thickness of 20 mm is highly undesirable, as dampness will ultimately appear through this thin un-waterproofed layer. The covering of damp walls with wood *cleading* or panelling should also be discouraged, as this only hides the defects, and, whilst the unhealthy conditions still remain, the wood is likely to be attacked by dry rot.

The provision made for damp proofing walls built on sloping sites is described on p. 59.

Dry or Open Areas.—Fig. 21 shows a section through a typical open area. Such provision is necessary to afford natural lighting and direct access to a basement.

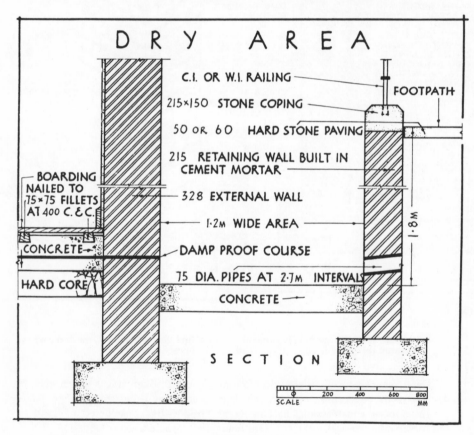

FIGURE 21

The ground is supported by a *retaining wall* some distance from the outer wall of the building. The area must be paved and drained, gullies (see p. 78) being placed as required and connected by drains to the public sewer. The retaining wall must be built in cement mortar, and is usually surmounted by a metal railing or balustrade, as this obstructs little light; either small *weep-holes* must be formed, or pipes, as shown, provided near the base of the wall to allow the escape of subsoil water, otherwise the pressure may overturn it, especially if the water becomes frozen. The floor of the basement is an alternative to those shown in Fig. 20; the floor is waterproofed with a 20 mm asphalt d.p.c.

A *closed dry area* may consist of a 102·5 mm independent wall, extending from a few millimetres below the basement floor to the ground level, 51 to 102·5 mm from the main wall and finished at the ground level with a brick-on-edge coping which closes the cavity; the latter may be ventilated by vertical shafts formed in the main wall, similar to that shown at c, Fig. 20. This is an undesirable form of construction, as water may gain access through the thin retaining wall and cause dampness as it accumulates. To overcome this defect the closed cavity is sometimes increased in width, the bottom is concreted and a gully provided which is connected to the sewer by a drain. This gully will, however, become unsealed (see Chapter Two) in dry weather owing to the evaporation of the water in the trap, and thus gases from the sewer will escape into the inaccessible cavity. Such provision cannot be too strongly condemned.

STEPPED FOUNDATIONS FOR SLOPING SITES

Foundations must be horizontal irrespective of the character of the site. If a site has little or no fall, the foundations of walls of the same thickness are generally level throughout. On a sloping site, however, it would be un-economical to construct all foundations at the same level as that of the lowest, and it is therefore the practice on such a site to arrange the foundations at different levels according to the slope. Such are known as stepped foundations. The steps should be in relatively short lengths and preferably of uniform height not exceeding 900 mm, the smaller the better. Hence when the slope is con-siderable, it is desirable to form the foundation of a wall of appreciable length in a series of small steps; if the steps are high owing to their inadequate number, there is a risk of unequal settlement occurring due to the large variation in the loads transmitted to the foundation on each side of a benching (see below) and the difference in shrinkage of the mortar joints between the larger number below each benching and those above; this may cause cracks to appear in the wall immediately over the changes of depth. The lengths of the steps need not be uniform, and they may vary considerably if the fall is very irregular.

Two typical arrangements of stepped foundations are shown at A and B, Fig. 22.

The site at A has a fairly regular slope, with a total difference in level in the length of the wall of 1·2 m. The two steps are of uniform height. The sketch detail c shows the concrete continued vertically from the lower to the upper concrete beds. This is known as a *benching* and should be of a width at

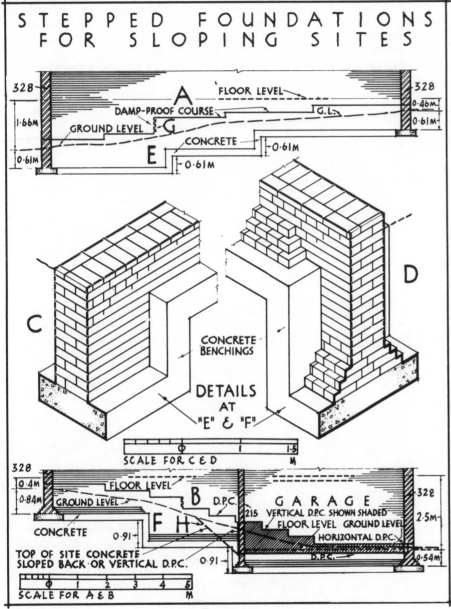

STEPPED FOUNDATIONS FOR SLOPING SITES

Details at "E" & "F"

SCALE FOR C D

CONCRETE BENCHINGS

FLOOR LEVEL
DAMP-PROOF COURSE
GROUND LEVEL
CONCRETE

GARAGE

VERTICAL D.P.C. SHOWN SHADED
FLOOR LEVEL   GROUND LEVEL
HORIZONTAL D.P.C.
D.P.C.

TOP OF SITE CONCRETE
SLOPED BACK OR VERTICAL D.P.C.

SCALE FOR A & B

FIGURE 22

least equal to the thickness of the concrete bed. In this example the floor level is the same throughout.

The sectional elevation at B shows the ground to have an irregular fall, the total difference in level being 2·1 m. Advantage has been taken of the fall to obtain garage accommodation as shown; a building should be designed to obtain accommodation in this manner in order to reduce the cost and avoid " dead walling " at the lower level. The foundation consists of brick footings on concrete as an alternative to that at A. The detail at D shows the footings (and wall) of the lower section abutting against the concrete benching, and those above it returned, the lowest course of footings being 150 mm from the edge of the benching.

Site Concrete.—This has not been shown in order to avoid complication. No attempt would be made to arrange this in a series of level steps; the top 150 mm of virgin soil would be removed and the 150 mm of site concrete would be formed to a slope more or less conforming to that of the ground. The floor of the garage at B would be of concrete. The site concrete under the floor on the left of the division wall could be laid to fall as described above, in which case the division wall would require a vertical damp proof course; alternatively the latter can be dispensed with if the earth is excavated to a depth of 230 mm below the horizontal damp proof course in the wall, sloped back and covered with 150 mm of site concrete as shown at H.

Damp Proofing.—The horizontal damp proof courses are stepped as shown, care being taken that none come within 150 mm of the ground; the vertical joint should be as short as possible in order not to weaken the walls, otherwise the steps should be as shown at G where asphalt mastic is applied and the adjacent walling toothed. A vertical damp proof course, indicated by a thick line, would be required on the back face of the garage division wall unless the earth is removed and the site concrete sloped as explained above. The vertical damp proof course is required to be continued round the side walls of the garage as the floor is below the ground level; this may be applied to the internal faces, as shown by the shaded area, but if this is objected to on the score of appearance, it may be formed within the thickness of the wall in the usual manner.

CONCRETE FLOOR CONSTRUCTION

A concrete floor may consist of a single layer, known as *one-course work*, or two layers called *two-course work*. The former is commonly adopted for floors of garages, cellars, coal houses, etc., and those which are to be covered with other materials such as boarding and asphalt; site concrete is in one layer only. Two-course work is generally employed in good practice, and consists of a base layer on which an insulating material such as 15 mm thick polystyrene is laid, covered by a finishing surface or wearing coat which should not be less than 50 mm thick. A common mix for the base is grade 15 concrete (see p. 31), just sufficient water should be used to give a 50 mm slump. A hard

wearing surface, known as a *granolithic* finish, is obtained from a mixture of 1 part cement, 1 part sand and 2 to 3 parts clean granite or whinstone chippings (crushed granite) capable of passing through a 6·4 mm square mesh sieve and excluding dust; approximately 60 per cent. of the chippings should be retained on a 3·2 mm mesh sieve; the surface concrete should give a 25 mm slump (see p. 32). The concrete is either machine or hand mixed, as described on p. 34. An excess of water, cement and trowelling (see below) should be avoided, as this brings the cement to the surface and produces what is known as a dusty floor. The surface should be applied to the base before the latter has hardened. The ground should be firm, any soft patches being replaced with concrete or hard stone. Sometimes a 150 to 300 mm layer of broken bricks or stone is first laid to receive the base layer; this sub-base is called *hard core* or *penning* (see Fig. 21).

Methods of forming a Concrete Floor.—Large floors are formed in a series of bays or sections, a convenient size being 3 m square, concreted alternately. One of several methods of forming a two-coursed floor is as follows : As shown at A, Fig. 23, 38 mm thick *edge-boards* or battens are nailed to wood stakes (or secured by staples to 20 mm diameter metal rods) driven in along the boundaries of the bays at about 1·2 m centres, the top edges of the battens being brought to the required floor level by the use of a long straight edge and spirit level. The base concrete is deposited in a bay, spread, and shovelled up to a height slightly more than the finished level. A wood *strike-board, tamper,* or *striking-off board* is then used to consolidate and bring the concrete to a uniformly level surface; as shown at B, this strike-board is notched at each end, the depth of the notch being equal to the thickness of the surface coat of the floor. It is manipulated by a man at each end who, working together, tamp down the concrete by lifting and releasing it as they proceed slowly backwards and forwards, any excess concrete being struck off as the tamper is brought forward when traversing the battens, and any low patches being filled in before the surface is given a final light tamping.

The wearing coat should be laid within an hour of mixing the base concrete. The ends of the strike-board used for forming the finishing coat are not notched

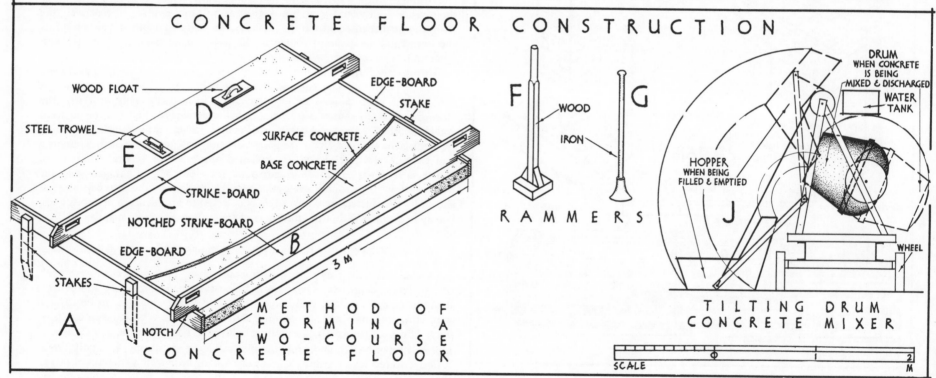

FIGURE 23

(see C). The granolithic mixture (see p. 60) is deposited and then levelled as the strike-board is caused to traverse the edge-boards with a to-and-fro and zigzag motion. When sufficiently hard, the surface is tamped and floated with the wood *float* D, any irregularities being made good. Final trowelling is by means of the *steel trowel* E, which is worked in a circular motion. Excessive trowelling brings to the surface a liquid scum, called *laitance*. Such should be avoided, as this destroys the initial set and produces a friable, non-wearing surface having a glossy finish which has a tendency to dust and craze.

> Not all surfaces are finished in this manner. Thus, for common work, the concrete is often *spade-finished*, *i.e.*, the surface is beaten down and smoothed over with the back of the spade. Another finish, often adopted for paths and roads, is produced by jumping the strike-board up and down as it traverses the edge-boards, to form a serious of small corrugations. A hard-wearing surface of attractive appearance may be produced by mechanically operated grinding discs which are applied to the floor after it has become sufficiently hard. This exposes and polishes the coarse aggregate.
> *Terrazzo* is another finish used in first-class work. One method is to cover the concrete base with a 25 mm thick wearing coat composed of 1 part cement and 2 parts sand; crushed marble of 6 mm gauge (free from dust) is sprinkled and rolled into this coat whilst it is still soft; when sufficiently hard (three or four days after laying) it is ground down to a smooth surface by stone discs mechanically operated. Another terrazzo finish consists of a 25 mm coat of 1 part cement and 2½ parts crushed marble of 13 mm gauge or less, which is machine ground after it has been allowed to partially harden.
> An alternative method of forming a two-course floor is as follows : The floor is divided into bays, as above described, by temporarily bedding wood battens, called *screed rules*, on narrow strips of concrete; these are firmly tapped in position until their top edges are brought to the required level by means of a straight edge and spirit level; each alternate bay is dealt with in turn; the base concrete is deposited and levelled off to the top of the screeds by a straight edge which is drawn over them in a zigzag manner; the concrete is compacted or *punned* with a *wood rammer* (see F) or *iron rammer* or *punner* (see G); the top layer of concrete is then spread over the base, brought to a level surface flush with the screeds by means of the straight edge, floated (D) and trowelled (E) as already described; the screeds are removed, and the holes filled in with concrete and levelled off.

The floor should be covered with damp sacks or 25 mm thickness of sand, kept moist by occasionally spraying water on it from a hose to prevent the concrete from drying out too rapidly. Alternatively the floor may be covered with a sheet of polythene. It should be kept damp for at least ten days (see p. 36).

DECORATED BRICKWORK

The decorative value of brickwork is influenced by the size, shape, colour and texture of the bricks and mortar joints, in addition to the face arrangment of the bricks and form of the feature.

Bricks.—The thickness of the bricks affects the appearance of faced brickwork considerably. Whilst a wall built of thick bricks looks strong, and these are therefore suitable for engineering work, it is generally agreed that the appearance of most walls is enhanced if 50 mm bricks are employed. Bricks which are uniform in shape, with straight, sharp arrises, give a mechanical appearance to a wall, which is avoided by the use of the somewhat irregularly edged and surfaced hand-made variety.

A wide range of colours and textures of bricks is now available (see pp. 12 and 13). Some walls are purposely built of bricks which are uniform in colour; such bricks must be carefully selected if a dull, monotonous appearance is to be avoided. Within recent years there has been an increased demand for multi-coloured bricks; these have a very pleasing appearance, provided the selected shades suitably blend and violent contrasts are avoided. Regarding texture, bricks having a smooth surface can be readily cleaned and are therefore often employed for external walling in towns where they quickly become discoloured in the dust-laden atmosphere; otherwise sand-faced or richly textured bricks are generally preferred because of the excellent effect they produce.

Jointing and Pointing.—Particular attention should be given to the colour of the mortar, and the shape and texture of the joints used for facing work. Various forms of jointing and pointing are described in Chap. I, Vol. I. The appearance of a wall constructed of sound materials and workmanship may be completely ruined by the adoption of unsuitable joints. Thus, for example, joints least suitable for sand-faced bricks of rich texture and warm colouring are those of black or dark blue mortar (see p. 27) which are struck-jointed, on account of the colour and the *smooth* mechanical appearance.

The texture of the joints should conform with that of the bricks. Joints smoothed over with the trowel should not be associated with rough textured bricks, for which flush and recessed joints (see Vol. I) give the best results. If neither of the latter can be adopted because of expense, a satisfactory finish to rustic brickwork is obtained if the joints are just left as the mortar is cut off with the trowel, no attempt being made to smooth the surface; the fairly rough texture of such joints gives a more satisfactory finish to this class of work than that produced by smooth struck joints.

The colour of mortar is referred to on p. 27, to which attention is drawn. Marked contrasts between the colour of the jointing material and the bricks should be avoided, hence white joints should not be used with bright red facings. Generally, black mortar should be avoided for faced work. The design of a façade can be influenced by mortar joints; thus, horizontality can be effectively stressed if the vertical joints are made inconspicuous by flush-pointing them with mortar of the same colour as that of the bricks (which should be uniform), and a lighter coloured mortar is used for the flush-pointed bed joints.

That the shape of the joint affects the appearance of brick walling may be appreciated by comparing work which has been flush jointed and that with recessed joints. Whilst both are attractive, there is a big contrast between the flat appearance of the former and the deep shadows formed by the latter, in which each brick unit in the mass is clearly defined. An effective modification, in which both of these joints may be employed in conjunction, consists of flush vertical joints and recessed bed joints.

The thickness of the joints is also important. With few exceptions, such as

...ckwork, thin joints should be avoided. Most first-class work has ...ed joints, and sometimes this thickness is increased to 13 mm.

... of plain brick walling is relieved by using bricks either of con-... or texture or face appearance, or a combination of all three, at ...ions, such as at parapets, quoins, string courses, door and window ... The judicious use of stone and tiles at these positions assists ...ng interesting contrasts. A few examples of these are illustrated in Fig. 24.

Parapets (see A, B, C, D, E and F).—That at A shows a simple finish to the quoin of a brick-on-edge parapet. The double course of tiles at B is surmounted by brick-on-end and brick-on-edge courses, both of which may be set slightly back from the face and at the quoin. The parapet course at C consists of stretchers alternating and coursing with bricks laid on end bed-faced; this is bedded on a slightly projecting stretching course and is finished with one or more projecting courses of tiles. Bricks-on-end (which may be slightly set back from the face), surmounted by two courses of thick tiles, comprise the parapet at D, and an interesting finish at the quoin is provided by the tiles as shown. A simple but effective detail is shown at E, where the top four heading courses are set back (or *indented*) 13 to 25 mm from the face and at the quoin, and these alternate with stretching courses of suitable contrasting colour flush with the wall face; a 50 mm thick stone coping serves as a finish. That at F simply consists of a brick-on-edge course surmounted by a similar stone coping.

Additional designs suitable for parapets, modified as required, include the string courses at N.7, 8 and 9, diagonal pattern at M.1 (or a course of bricks laid diagonally), herring-bone pattern at M.2 (two inclined courses laid horizontally), pattern M.3 (see below), pattern M.5 (arranged horizontally), bricks-on-end as shown at P.10, and one or more courses of basketweave shown at P.14.

The top courses of bricks, tiles or stone of a parapet should be well bedded and jointed in cement mortar in order to exclude water and increase stability. The provision of a horizontal damp proof course, below the parapet and extending the full thickness of the wall, is an additional requirement.

Built-up cornices, involving the use of moulded bricks, rarely find a place in modern design.

Quoins (see G, H, J, K and L).—Additional interest may be provided by simply using at the quoins bricks of contrasting colour to that of the rest of the walling, and producing a toothed effect, as at G and L; the quoin bricks may be darker than the adjacent walling (*i.e.*, " purple " quoins against a mass of " buff brindles ") or lighter, such as " cherry red " quoins contrasting with " dark strawberry " coloured adjoining brickwork. The appearance of additional strength is obtained by using rusticated or indented quoins, as shown at H, J and K. The elevation and sketch at H show projecting blocks of two-course depth alternating with three-course projecting blocks, the blocks being of uniform length. The treatment at J is somewhat similar, but the shorter alternate blocks give a toothed effect. Projecting blocks at greater intervals are shown at K.

In general, indented courses should not have a greater set-back than 25 mm if a coarse appearance is to be avoided.

This form of treatment is also employed at door and window openings.

String Courses.—A few suggestions are shown at N.6, 7, 8 and 9, and at J. Most of the parapets described above may also be adopted for string courses or friezes. Moulded brick courses are not now greatly favoured.

Panels.—Large masses of plain walling may be relieved by the provision of decorative panels. A few designs are shown at M.1, 2, 3, 4 and 5. That at M.1 shows square panels of bricks laid diagonally with header divisions; the infilling bricks may be of contrasting colour. The panel at M.2 consists of a herring-bone infilling, short brick-on-end head and sill, and header verticals. Panel M.3 comprises three " piers " of purpose-made bricks with bevelled faces which project (see plan), alternating with bricks arranged on end, and finished with two courses of tiles top and bottom, the latter projecting as shown on plan. The simple rectangular panel at M.4 projects (see plan) and is of contrasting colour. A somewhat complicated design, suitable for a large panel, is shown at M.5; such provides an interesting feature, especially if surrounded by a large mass of brickwork; the panel may be given a slight projection. Another form of panel, much favoured, consists of an infilling of bricks arranged in basketweave pattern (see P.14).

Arches.—Apart from their design, arches may emphasize such salient features as doors and windows by the employment of bricks of contrasting colours and textures, and the introduction of differing materials forming the keys and imposts. Thus, for example, a pleasing effect to a façade constructed of dark coloured bricks may be obtained if rubbers or similar coloured voussoirs are used for the arches, and points of interest provided if tiles or stone are used for key blocks.

Several arches having tiled keys are shown in Vol. I and in Fig. 19 of this volume; additional examples are illustrated in Fig. 24. That shown at P.10 shows a lintel or soldier arch with several projecting voussoirs. P.11 shows a segmental arch constructed entirely of tiles.

> The mortar joints at the tiled soffit (and sometimes on the face) are usually recessed (see P.11). This effect is obtained by spreading a 20 mm layer of sand on the wood centre; each tile is forced down until it touches the lagging, and mortar is spread on the bed of the tile above the sand. Pointing is applied on removal of the centre. This ensures clean exposed edges of the tiles, which are otherwise liable to become stained with the mortar and rendered inconspicuous.

The semi-hexagonal arch at P.12 embodies tiles at the corners. The semicircular arch P.13 consists of a tiled key block and purpose-made long voussoirs alternating with shorter ones; this toothed arrangement is continued down the jambs; owing to the difficulty in accurately cutting to the required shape the bricks adjacent to the extrados, this form of arch is usually associated with rough-casted walls, and rough cutting is therefore only necessary. A semicircular arch, with stepped rings, over a door opening is shown at P.14; the core or tympanum is filled with bricks arranged in basketweave pattern; an equally effective treatment is to arrange the bricks forming the core in herring-

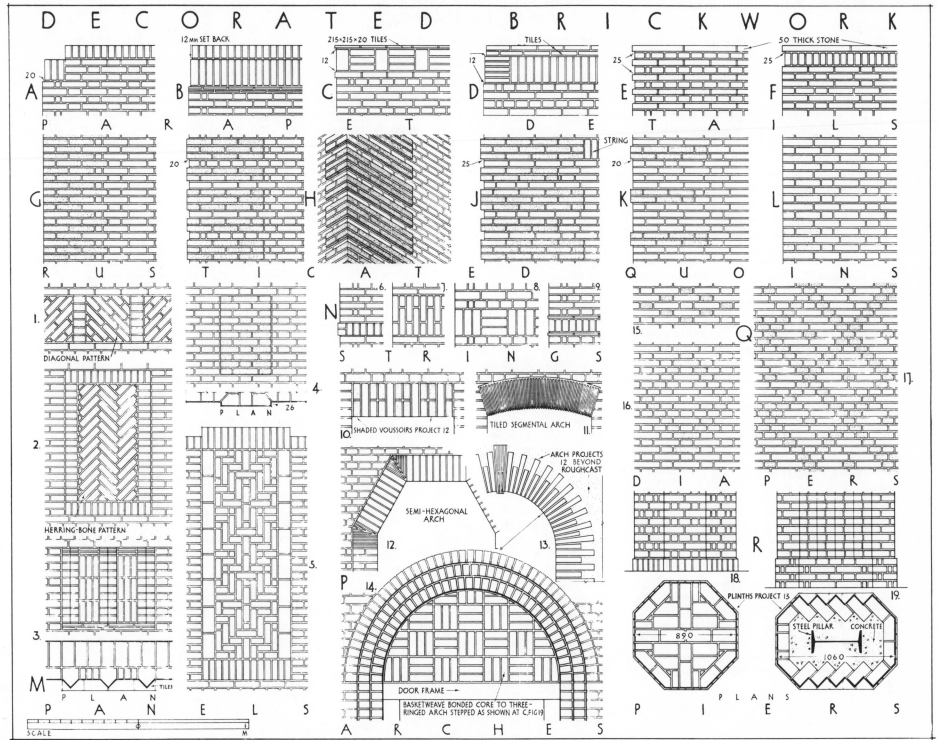

DECORATED BRICKWORK

PARAPET DETAILS

A — 20

B — 12MM SET BACK

C — 215×215×20 TILES — 12

D — TILES — 12

E — 25

F — 50 THICK STONE — 25

RUSTICATED QUOINS

G

H — 20

J — STRING — 25

K — 20

L

PANELS

1. DIAGONAL PATTERN

2. HERRING-BONE PATTERN

3. — PLAN — TILES — M

4. — PLAN — 26

5.

STRINGS

N — 6. 7. 8. 9. — S

10. SHADED VOUSSOIRS PROJECT 12

11. TILED SEGMENTAL ARCH

ARCHES

12. SEMI-HEXAGONAL ARCH

13. ARCH PROJECTS 12 BEYOND ROUGHCAST

14. P — DOOR FRAME — BASKETWEAVE BONDED CORE TO THREE-RINGED ARCH STEPPED AS SHOWN AT C, FIG 19

DIAPERS

Q — 15. 16. 17.

R

18. — 890

19. PLINTHS PROJECT 13 — STEEL PILLAR — CONCRETE — 1060

PIERS PLANS

SCALE — M

FIGURE 24

bone formation. This core is supported on a stout oak frame, and one or more courses of tiles (with 13 mm projection) are often introduced between the top of the frame and the brickwork.

Diaper Work.—Variegated coloured or diaper work in which dark coloured bricks, arranged in pattern form, are associated with lighter coloured brickwork (or light coloured brick patterns contrasting with general walling of dark bricks) is less prevalent in modern construction than formerly. The present tendency, when multi-coloured bricks are employed, is to lay the " darks " in haphazard fashion, no attempt being made to arrange them to any mechanical pattern.

A few examples of diapers or chequer work are shown at Q.15, 16 and 17. In each case the general wall bond is adjusted to suit the particular design of the diapers.

Piers.—These have been referred to on p. 39. The detached octagonal pier shown in plan and part elevation at R.18, with a simple brick-on-edge plinth having a 13 mm projection, has a pleasing appearance. Indented courses, set back about 20 mm and at six to eight course intervals, are sometimes provided in this form of structure. An alternative design (occasionally employed in modern churches) is shown in plan and part elevation at R.19. Steel pillars (which support the steel roof trusses and any steel beams) are encased in concrete and finished with brickwork. The plinth is four courses high above the floor and has a 13 mm projection. The bricks forming the two longer faces of the pillar shaft are arranged diagonally (those in alternate courses being laid in the opposite direction) to give a serrated effect. As shown, these bricks are not purpose-made; special bricks, shaped somewhat like those indicated at M.3, are sometimes used. The concrete is placed in position as the brickwork proceeds. Although this brickwork does not support any load, other than its own weight, it is advisable to tie the shorter faces into the concrete by placing 25 mm by 6 mm by 150 mm long copper strips in the bed joints at sixth course intervals.

FIREPLACES, FLUES, CHIMNEY BREASTS AND STACKS

As a means of heating a living-room of a house the open fire is still the most popular in this country, despite the fact that it is very largely responsible for the pollution of the atmosphere by the smoke and other products of combustion emitted from it. Air pollution is now reduced in this country by the insistence contained in the Building Regulations that only smokeless fuels should be used in heating appliances. Such fuels are anthracite, coke (including patent solid smokeless fuels), oil and gas.

Fireplace, etc., construction must comply with the Building Regulations which give differing requirements according to the type of heating appliance, and differentiate between high and low output appliances.

A high-rating appliance is defined either as one with a heat output exceeding 45 kW (most domestic appliances do not exceed this value), or as large incinerators—they are beyond the scope of this volume.

Low-rating appliances are split into two types : Class I—solid fuel or oil-burning types with an output rating not exceeding 45 kW and medium-sized incinerators; and Class II— gas-burning types having a rating not exceeding 45 kW and small incinerators.

The requirements of the Building Regulations have been briefly incorporated in the following description, and most of them are illustrated in Fig. 25. This shows the plan B, vertical section C and elevation A of a two-storied chimney breast (which accommodates two fireplaces and flues), together with enlarged details.

Each heating appliance must be provided with a *flue* or duct for the removal of smoke. If the chimney in which the fireplace opening and flue are formed projects (and it generally does) it is known as a *chimney breast* until it penetrates the roof, when it is called a *chimney stack*.

Foundations.—The foundations of a chimney must be similar to those of the adjacent wall, *i.e.*, they must comply with either of those shown at A, B, C or D, Fig. 10, Vol. I (see A, C and Z, Fig. 25). The chimney must be well bonded to the adjacent wall (see plan at Z) and be provided with a proper damp proof course (see A and section Z).

Chimney Stacks.—A chimney breast which is to penetrate the ridge of a roof is gradually reduced in width above the ceiling until that of the chimney stack is obtained, which should occur just below the penetration (see A, Fig. 25). For a stack at the ridge or nearer than 600 mm from it the minimum height is 600 mm above its highest penetration of the roof (1 m high if it is further than 600 mm from the ridge). For reasons of stability, it is advisable that the height of a stack is to be not more than six times its least width (unless otherwise secured) measured from the highest point of intersection (see T). The minimum thickness of the walls of a stack is 100 mm. If the stack only accommodates one flue, the appearance is considerably improved if this thickness is increased to 215 mm. The 102.5 mm thick *withes* (or divisions) should be well bonded into the external walls. Plans showing typical bonding are shown at J and X. Chimney stacks should be built in waterproofed cement mortar from 300 mm below the lowest point of intersection of the roof. A metal or slate damp proof course can also be inserted. Rain is thus prevented from soaking down the walls.

It is usual to terminate a flue with a fireclay pot, although this is not always necessary and its omission is sometimes preferred. Chimney pots are of various shapes and sizes, a simple type being cylindrical, of 200 mm (or 215 mm) internal diameter 13 to 20 mm thick, and with a flange at the base; its height varies, 300 mm being common; it is often tapered to about 190 mm (internal) at the top to give a restricted outlet which is considered to have the effect of increasing the velocity of the ascending current. The pot should be supported on the brickwork (see W) and securely built in cement mortar between two or three

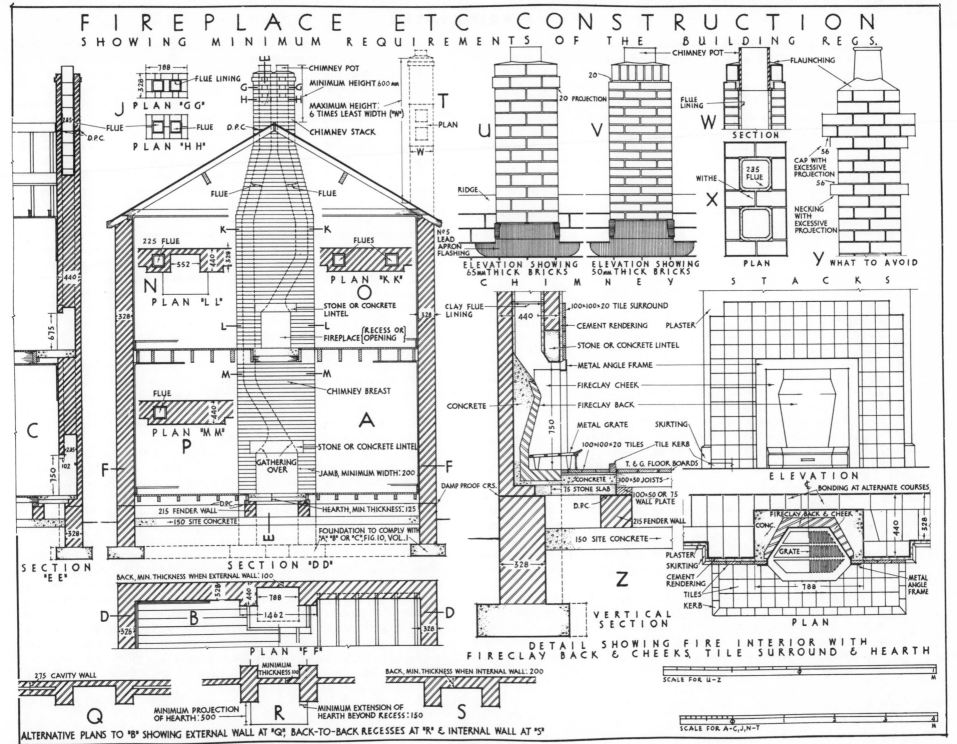

Figure 25

courses of brickwork (or a stone cap or several courses of tiles); the top of the stack is *flaunched*, *i.e.*, covered with cement mortar, which is weathered to throw off the water.

> Many buildings are marred by unsightly chimney stacks which penetrate the roofs at random. As a rule, stacks should be of simple design. A frequent mistake is to complete stacks with *cappings* of oversailing courses with excessive projections. The coarse finish which these give is shown at Y, where the capping and necking courses are given a 56 mm projection. Ugly chimney pots are common. Tall chimney pots are unnecessary, unless the flues are short or have been improperly constructed, or high trees and buildings are in such close proximity as to produce down-draughts. An unobtrusive but effective finish may be obtained if the chimney pots (or short lengths of drain pipes) are caused to project not more than 25 mm above the flaunching; this is usually sufficient to prevent eddies of wind which may be created if the top surfaces of the stacks were flat.
>
> Two simple designs are shown at U and V. The former stack is constructed of standard 65 mm bricks with an oversailing course having a small projection. The stack at V is built of 50 mm bricks, and is finished with a brick-on-edge course set back 20 mm; part section and the plan are shown at W and X. The appearance of a chimney stack is much improved if thin bricks are employed. The leadwork conforms with the details shown in Fig. 75, Vol. I.

Fireplace Recesses for Class I Appliances.—Heating appliances of the open fire type have to be built into a recess; free-standing enclosed heating appliances (e.g. room heaters, ranges, etc.—see Vol. IV) are often placed in a recess but this is not essential.

The *jambs* (attached piers at the sides of a fireplace opening or recess) must not be less than 200 mm wide. Their projection varies according to the type of range to be accommodated, thus a greater projection is required for a kitchen range than for a small fireplace recess. The size of a fireplace recess also varies, thus a modern kitchen range (with oven) of medium size needs a space of 1 m wide by 1·2 m high, whilst the smallest room fireplace recess need only be 440 mm wide and 610 mm high. The width of a chimney breast may be varied according to the size and importance of a room, thus, for a long drawing-room, the breast may be at least 1·8 m wide in order that it may be of suitable proportions.

The *head* of a fireplace recess is normally finished with a reinforced concrete lintel. Very occasionally a stone lintel or brick arch may be used, the latter usually being segmental in two rough rings. Where a breast projects more than 102·5 mm and the jambs are less than 330 mm wide, a brick arch must be built on a wrought iron or steel bar, 215 mm longer than the opening at each end; the object of this *cambered chimney bar* is to tie in the narrow abutments.

The *back* of a fireplace recess in an *external* wall (see B and Q) or between two recesses built *back-to-back* (see R) in a wall, *other than a party wall*, shall be at least 100 mm thick. A party wall is a division wall between two buildings occupied by differing tenants or belonging to different owners. The back of every other recess (thus including a single opening in an *internal* wall as at S, and back-to-back recess in a party wall) shall be not less than 200 mm thick.

The backs shall be continued for the full height of the recess at the thickness stated. The above thicknesses around a fireplace recess are exclusive of the fireback and sides.

Hearths for Class I Appliances must be of non-combustible materials and securely supported. The *back hearth* (that within the fireplace recess) is bedded on the walling of the breast (see C) or as shown at Z. The *hearth* must have a minimum thickness of 125 mm (see A), a minimum extension beyond the opening at each end of 150 mm (see R), and a minimum projection from the breast of 500 mm, as shown at R. The support and trimming of front hearths are illustrated in Figs. 32, 33 and 34, Vol. I; the section at Z shows an alternative treatment of a ground floor hearth. The Building Regulations state that no combustible material shall be built under a hearth within 250 mm from its upper surface unless such material is separated from the underside of the hearth by an air space of at least 50 mm. (An exception to this requirement permits the use of timber fillets supporting the edges of the hearth where it adjoins a floor.) In addition to the requirement that the hearth should project 500 mm beyond the breast the distance from the front of an appliance to the edge of the hearth shall be not less than 300 mm (in the case of an open fire or room heater which can be used as such) and 225 mm in other cases. The distance at the back and sides shall be not less than 150 mm. If the hearth extends to a wall the latter distance may be reduced for free-standing appliances providing the wall thicknesses given above are observed.

Chimneys for Class I Appliances.—The smoke from heating appliances is carried away via the chimney which is defined as being any part of the structure of a building forming any part of a flue other than a flue pipe. Most chimneys in domestic work are of brick incorporating a flue lining (see below), some consist of a separate flue pipe. A brick flue is normally 215 mm by 215 mm and this should be uniform.

The brickwork above the fireplace opening is corbelled or *gathered over* in order to reduce the opening to the size of the flue and avoid a large space which may produce eddies and reduce the upward current (draught) in the flue (see A, Fig. 25). This reduced opening is known as a *throat*. The two flues at A, Fig. 25, are indicated by broken lines (see also C). That from the lower fire-place must be bent in order to negotiate the upper fireplace. The gathering over should be arranged to bring the narrowest part of the throat centrally over the fire. It is generally agreed that, whereas a flue should be as straight as possible for most of its height, it should have at least one bend in order to reduce down-draught and the admission of rain; hence the reason for not continuing the upper flue in a straight line to the chimney pot; if this flue was straight through-out, it would undoubtedly produce a smoky chimney because of its short length. Any bends must be gradual and flues should not be less than 45° to the horizontal. The brickwork enclosing flues shall be at least 100 mm thickness (see J, w and x); the minimum thickness of the back of a flue in a wall separating buildings which is not back to back with another flue shall

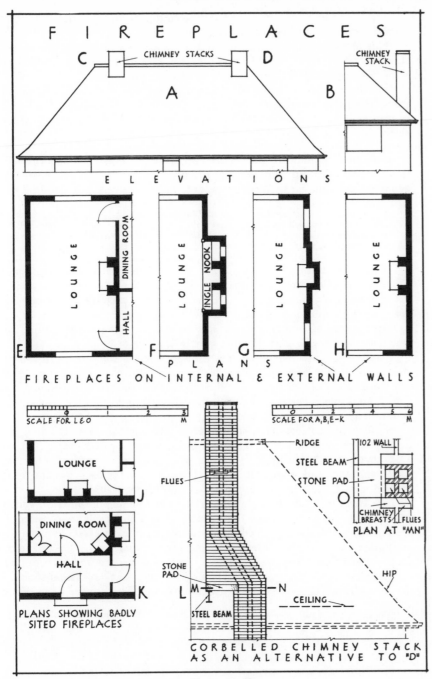

FIGURE 26

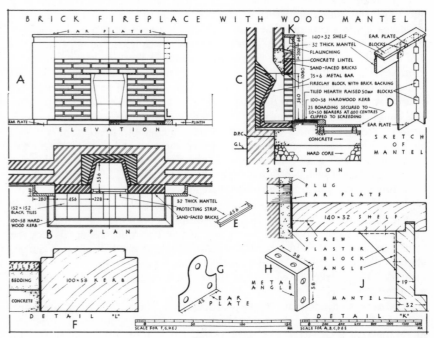

FIGURE 27

be not less than 200 mm thick (or if a cavity wall, having each leaf at least 100 mm thick) up to the roof level.

In the U.K. the Building Regulations specify that for Class I appliances the flue must be lined with any of the following : rebated or socketed flue linings of clay (*a*) complying with B.S. 1181 (Fig. 28) or of (*b*) vitrified clay pipes complying with B.S. 65 (see p. 76); or (*c*) high alumina cement and kilnburnt aggregate pipes. The most commonly used of these is (*a*). As an alternative to the above linings chimneys may be constructed with concrete flue blocks made of kiln-burnt aggregate and high alumina cement. Both linings and blocks must be pointed with 1 : 4 cement mortar and the linings must be built with the socket uppermost, care being taken to keep the bore of the flue free from mortar. Linings are built into the flues as the chimney is constructed and backed with mortar. Flue linings complying with B.S. 1181 are detailed in Fig. 28. The bottom length of liner in a flue should rest on corbels projecting from the chimney flue; linings should not be cut because it is important to preserve the socket or rebate intact.

Before the insistence of flue linings the inside of brick flues was rendered (known as *parged*) to a thickness of at least 13 mm with a mixture of 1 cement : 3

lime : 10 sand. This proved very satisfactory for open fires but with enclosed heating appliances where the products of combustion are less diluted with air there was a danger of tarry compounds leaching through the flue and discolouring internal walls. The Scottish Building Regulations permit the use of parged flues for open fires but the Regulations applying to England and Wales do not.

Flue pipes for Class I appliances.—A flue pipe is sometimes adopted in lieu of a chimney and can be conveniently used when fixed on the outside of a wall to serve, for example, a central heating boiler which is being added to an existing house that has not got a conveniently situated chimney. It must not pass through an internal wall, floor or roof space. It is also used in the form of a short connecting flue between a room heater or range and a chimney flue.

A flue pipe must be of cast iron to B.S. 41 Cast Iron Flue Pipes, or 3 mm thick mild steel, or stainless steel 1 mm thick, or vitreous enamelled low carbon steel 0.9 mm thick for pipes upto 113 mm diameter (1.2 mm if larger).

Where a flue pipe discharges into the side of a chimney flue (*e.g.* from a free-standing appliance) any combustible material in the chimney or attached wall must be separated from it by non-combustible material at least 200 mm thick if the combustible material is beside or below the pipe (300 mm if above). A similar provision applies if the flue pipe discharges into the bottom of a chimney flue. If a flue pipe passes through a roof or external wall otherwise than for discharging into a chimney flue it must be either (*a*) placed at a distance of not less than three times its external diameter from any combustible material in the roof or wall; or (*b*) (*i*) (in the case of a pipe passing through a roof) separated from any combustible part of the roof by a minimum of 200 mm thick solid non-combustible material; or (*b*) (*ii*) in the case of a pipe passing through an external wall be protected as described above for a flue pipe passing into the side of a chimney flue; or (*c*) enclosed in a metal or asbestos-cement sleeve which projects 150 mm beyond any combustible material in the roof or wall—a minimum of 25 mm space is required between the pipe and the sleeve which is to be packed with a 25 mm minimum thickness of non-combustible thermal insulating material such as asbestos rope. Alternatively the Building Regulations allow protection by a specially constructed sleeve.

Supply of Combustion Air to all Appliances.—These are specified by the Building Regulations thus. For solid fuel *open* fires a permanent air entry of 50% of the appliance throat area. For other solid fuel appliances the minimum area of such air entry is at least 550 mm² per kW of rated output above 5kW. For oil burning appliances the minimum air entry must be 550 mm²/kW of appliance rated output above 5 kW. Comparable rules exist for gas fired appliances.

Chimneys for Class II Appliances.—As these are for gas-burning appliances which produce a greater amount of water vapour in the products of combustion than is the case with an open fire the flue linings have to be any of the materials given on p. 67. Alternativey the flue may be constructed with dense concrete blocks made with high-alumina cement; these are detailed in Vol. IV, they provide a flue size of 305 by 64 mm.

The flue must be surrounded and separated from any other flue in the chimney by solid material at least 25 mm thick.

Flue pipes for Class II appliances can be as for Class I appliances plus sheet metal to B.S. 715 Metal Flues for Gas Burning Appliances and Asbestos-cement to B.S. 567 Asbestos-cement Flue Pipes.

The flue pipe must be at least 50 mm from any combustible material and if it passes through a combustible roof, floor, ceiling or wall it must be in a sleeve of non-combustible material leaving an air space of 25 mm between it and the sleeve.

Additional Building Regulation requirements for Class I appliances are as follows : No combustible material (*e.g.* a floor joist) is to be placed nearer than 200 mm from a flue or fireplace recess (150 mm in the case of a wood plug).

> Fires have been caused by plugs (used for fixing skirtings, picture rails, grounds for panelling, etc.) which have been driven through joints and actually penetrated flues. It is therefore important that joiners should know of the position of flues when fixing wood members round chimney breasts.

Where the thickness of solid non-combustible material surrounding a chimney flue is less than 200 mm, no combustible material, other than a floor board, skirting, dado rail, picture rail, mantle shelf or architrave shall be placed nearer than 38 mm to the outer surface of the chimney.

Metal fastenings such as nails, screws, etc., in contact with combustible materials, shall not be placed within 50 mm of a flue or fireplace recess.

Class I appliances which are not fixed in a recess conforming to the provisions given on p. 66 must not be fixed nearer a wall than 150 mm unless the wall for a height of 300 mm above the top of the appliance is of 200 mm thick non-combustible material (if the wall is less than 50 mm from the appliance) or 75 mm thick (in any other case).

If the flame of a Class II appliance is less than 225 mm above the floor, then the appliance must be placed on a hearth of non-combustible material at least 12.5 mm thick. This hearth must extend (*a*) at least 225 mm in front of the flame in the appliance and (*b*) not less than 150 mm beyond the back and sides of the appliance or, if there is a wall within 150 mm, up the wall.

Fire Interiors[1] and Fireplaces.—Details of a simple fire interior, suitable for the ground floor recess at A, are shown at z, Fig. 25. This consists of a fireclay block with base, inclined back and splayed sides or *cheeks*, a metal (cast iron) grate, metal (stainless steel, etc.) angle frame, and a surround of 100 mm square glazed tiles. The fireclay block is bedded on mortar and backed solidly with lean concrete or brickwork. The upper surface of this backing should be sloped as shown to prevent soot from accumulating; if left square, like F, Fig. 28

---

[1] These are more fully described in Vol. IV, together with other forms of heating.

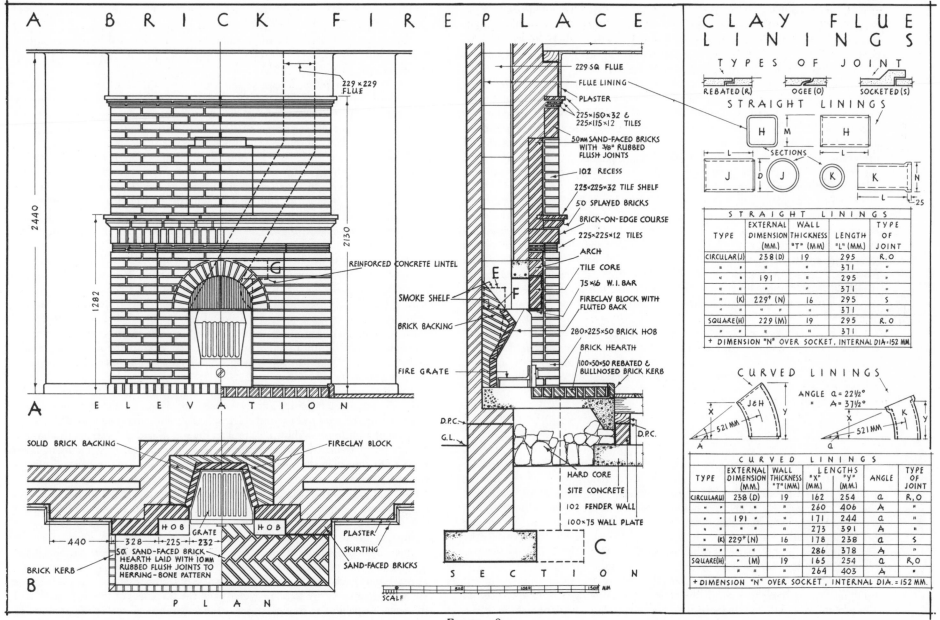

A BRICK FIREPLACE

ELEVATION

- 2440
- 2130
- 1282
- 229 × 229 FLUE
- G
- REINFORCED CONCRETE LINTEL

A

PLAN

- SOLID BRICK BACKING
- FIRECLAY BLOCK
- HOB — GRATE — HOB
- 440
- 328 — 225 — 232
- 50. SAND-FACED BRICK HEARTH LAID WITH 10MM RUBBED FLUSH JOINTS TO HERRING-BONE PATTERN
- BRICK KERB
- PLASTER
- SKIRTING
- SAND-FACED BRICKS

B

SECTION

- 229 SQ FLUE
- FLUE LINING
- PLASTER
- 225×150×32 & 225×115×12 TILES
- 50MM SAND-FACED BRICKS WITH 3/8" RUBBED FLUSH JOINTS
- 102 RECESS
- 225×225×32 TILE SHELF
- 50 SPLAYED BRICKS
- BRICK-ON-EDGE COURSE
- 225×225×12 TILES
- ARCH
- TILE CORE
- 75×6 W.I. BAR
- FIRECLAY BLOCK WITH FLUTED BACK
- 280×225×50 BRICK HOB
- BRICK HEARTH
- 100×50×50 REBATED & BULLNOSED BRICK KERB
- SMOKE SHELF
- BRICK BACKING
- FIRE GRATE
- E   F
- D.P.C.
- G.L.
- D.P.C.
- HARD CORE
- SITE CONCRETE
- 102 FENDER WALL
- 100×75 WALL PLATE

C

SCALE 500 1000 1500 MM

CLAY FLUE LININGS

TYPES OF JOINT

REBATED (R)   OGEE (O)   SOCKETED (S)

STRAIGHT LININGS

H   M   H
L   L
SECTIONS
J   D   J   K   K
L   25
N

STRAIGHT LININGS

TYPE	EXTERNAL DIMENSION (MM.)	WALL THICKNESS "T" (MM)	LENGTH "L" (MM.)	TYPE OF JOINT
CIRCULAR (J)	238 (D)	19	295	R.O
" "	"	"	371	"
" "	191	"	295	"
" "	"	"	371	"
" (K)	229⁺ (N)	16	295	S
" "	"	"	371	"
SQUARE (H)	229 (M)	19	295	R.O
" "	"	"	371	"

⁺ DIMENSION "N" OVER SOCKET, INTERNAL DIA.=152 MM.

CURVED LININGS

J&H   X   Y   ANGLE a = 22½°   " A = 37½°
521 MM   A
K   X   Y   521 MM   a

CURVED LININGS

TYPE	EXTERNAL DIMENSION (MM.)	WALL THICKNESS "T"(MM.)	LENGTHS "X" (MM.)	"Y" (MM.)	ANGLE	TYPE OF JOINT
CIRCULAR (J)	238 (D)	19	162	254	a	R.O
" "	"	"	260	406	A	"
" "	191	"	171	244	a	"
" "	"	"	273	391	A	"
" (K)	229⁺ (N)	16	178	238	a	S
" "	"	"	286	378	A	"
SQUARE (H)	" (M)	19	165	254	a	R.O
" "	"	"	264	403	A	"

⁺ DIMENSION "N" OVER SOCKET, INTERNAL DIA. = 152 MM.

FIGURE 28

as is sometimes advocated, the large accumulation of soot will be blown into the room in the event of down-draughts. The tiles are bedded on the cement rendering. The tiles and simple kerb forming the front hearth are bedded in cement mortar. The back of the block is inclined forward and its sides splayed in order to throw the maximum heat into the room.

Fig. 26 shows alternative positions of the fire, that at E being recommended because heat transmitted at the back of the fire is not wasted as is the case with those on an external wall at F, G and H. A fireplace should not be placed opposite a door as this creates draughty conditions; also, there should be sufficient room at the sides for chairs, this weakness is shown at J and K. Stacks should preferably rise through the ridge as previously explained and in a hipped roof the treatment at C is more pleasing than that at D. If necessary, the stack can be corbelled over as shown at L and O.

The fireplace in Fig. 27 has a simple brick surround built against the wall. A timber mantel is pre-fabricated from 32 mm thick timber, the top and sides being tenoned together as shown at A and D; glued blocks and tongues and grooves are used to fix the parts to each other, these are shown at D and J, and in addition, metal angles as at H fix the mantel to the shelf. Ear plates (G) fasten the mantel to the wall and floor as given at A and D. A timber curb at F is placed round the tiled hearth, the space between the tiles and the fireclay is closed with a chromium plated metal protecting strip drawn at E.

The brick fireplace at Fig. 28 is more elaborate. The hearth is of brick and the fire opening is arched over with a tiled core resting on a wrought iron bar as noted at C. Two positions E and F of the smoke shelf are shown; although this feature is advocated by some, as explained above, it is less satisfactory than the sloping finish.

SETTING OUT

A brief description of the construction of walls is given in Chap. I, Vol. I.

Prior to the commencement of building operations the site must be surveyed and any differences in level of the surface obtained by means of an instrument called a *dumpy level*. The trenches to receive the foundations must be first *set out* or *pegged out* before their excavation is begun. If the site is sloping, and before the trenches are set out, it may be necessary to level the surface by excavating the higher parts and removing the soil to the lower portions as required. *Boning rods*, as described on p. 83, are used for levelling.

The first line to be set out is generally that of the main frontage of the building. As a linen tape stretches and is unreliable, a steel tape is used to measure off its length and fix its relative position. A wood peg or stake is driven in at each end, the centre of the pegs indicating the position of the quoins. The lines of all other walls are measured off from this front wall line.

The plans of most buildings must be approved by the local authority before building operations are commenced. A plan submitted for approval will include the *block plan* of the building on which is shown the site, drainage, relative position to adjacent streets, etc. If the site adjoins existing buildings or a highway, it is very important that the *frontage line* shall be accurately set out in order that it shall not encroach beyond the *building line*, the position of which is obtainable on application to the local authority.

If a building is rectangular, right angles are set off from the main line by using the " 3 : 4 : 5 " method, *i.e.*, a distance of 12 m is measured along the line from one end and a *pin* (or *arrow*, made of stout wire, about 230 mm long, ring-shaped at one end and pointed at the other) is inserted; a tape is held at each end of this length, the 9 m division on one of the tapes is held at the 15 m division on the other, both tapes are stretched taut and a pin is inserted at the intersection. The 9 m line thus set off is at right angles to the main line, as, in a right-angled triangle, the sum of the squares on the two sides containing the angle equals the square on the hypotenuse, *i.e.*, $9^2 + 12^2 = 15^2$. The large wood square shown at R, Fig. 29, is also used for setting out and checking right angles.

It is necessary to fix the height of one of the floors of the building, usually the ground floor level, to which all other heights are related. If possible, this should be a permanent level, such as the top of a plinth or step of a conveniently situated existing building; otherwise a peg is driven in a position on the site, preferably opposite a door opening where it is not likely to be disturbed, until its top coincides with the required level as determined by a dumpy level or other means. The height that the top of this peg is above the ground should be noted and booked in case the peg is surreptitiously or accidentally lowered and a subsequent check is required.

Profiles are used to ensure the accurate setting out and construction of the walls. These are temporary guides, consisting of boards nailed to wood pegs which are driven into the ground. Details of profiles are shown in Fig. 29. A key plan of a building is shown by broken lines at A, and the various profiles are indicated at the corners and opposite to division walls. Enlargements of these profiles are shown in the plan G and the sketches B and C. A corner profile is made of three pegs, well driven in, to which two boards are nailed. One profile is placed at each corner (see A and G), with the boards parallel to and at 610 to 900 mm from the outer trench lines. The top of the corner peg at least of each profile is often the level of the ground floor. A steel tape should be used when setting out these profiles, and the measurements checked. A useful check is obtained by taking diagonal measurements between opposite corners, and if the building is rectangular, these should, of course, be equal. Permanent dimensions are marked on each board indicating the width of the concrete bed, brick footings (assuming that these are to be provided) and the thickness of the wall (see B and G). Saw-cuts, about 13 mm deep, are made down these marks in the upper edge of each board to receive the ends of the bricklayer's line. Each profile used for division walls consists of two pegs and a board, and the latter is similarly marked and cut (see C and G). The centre lines of the walls are sometimes marked.

The position and correct alignment of the trenches, footings and walls are obtained by plumbing down from lines which are stretched in turn between opposite profiles. Thus, assuming that the trenches have been lined out and excavated, and the concrete[1] has been placed in position, the bottom course of footings would be aligned in the following manner : One end of a line (see M and P at B and C) is passed down the saw-cut at the top of the appropriate mark and wrapped round the board, and after the line has been stretched taut the opposite end is fixed in a similar manner. The plumb-rule, sometimes stayed as shown (the stay being nailed to the rule), is held by one hand against the line near one end of the trench and, when vertical, a mark is made by the point of the trowel in a little mortar trowelled on the concrete bed. A brick is laid temporarily on this mortar with the outer face in line with the mark; the plumbing of this face is checked. Another brick is laid in a similar manner at the other end. A bricklayer's line, with pins, is fixed between and level with the top of these bricks. The bottom course of footings is then built, commencing at the corners, the position of each of which is found by plumbing down at the intersection of the two lines (see L at B). Similarly, the wall is set off correctly by plumbing down from lines N and Q shown at B and C.

Sometimes two profiles, like E shown at G, are used for the two walls forming a quoin instead of a corner profile. Profiles for division walls are often dispensed with, the right-angled intersections being then checked by the use of the large square R. Corner profiles for setting out squint quoins (see Fig. 11) have their boards parallel to the sides of the walls, and a division wall which forms a squint junction (see Fig. 10) is set out by placing the two profiles, one at each end, at right angles to its length.

Whilst profiles assist in the accurate setting out and construction of walls, their use by no means is general. In the absence of profiles the lines of the trenches are pegged out, two pegs being driven in at each end of a trench at a distance between their outer faces equal to its width; the line is stretched in alignment with these outer faces; these pegs, like the profiles are placed some 610 mm outside the lines of trenches. After the trenches have been excavated to the required depth and the concrete beds formed, the alignment of each wall is maintained by placing the quoin bricks in correct position, as described above, and stretching a line between.

Circular Work.—This may be set out by using either (*a*) a *trammel* or (*b*) a *templet*.

[1] *Levelling Concrete Bed.*—A peg is driven in the bottom and at each corner of the trenches until the top of each is at the required depth below the floor level: this depth is obtained by means of a 1 metre rule and the use of a spirit level and short straight edge applied on the corner peg of the nearest profile. If this depth is in accordance with the gauge of the brickwork decided upon, the floor level will course with the bed joint of the brickwork. Intermediate pegs are then driven in the bottom of the trenches at convenient intervals until their tops are at the same level as the corner pegs. This is assured if three boning rods (see p. 83) of the same height (about 1·2 m) are used, one on each of a pair of corner pegs and the third on the intermediate pegs in turn, and " sighting through " from one end. The concrete is carefully deposited and brought approximately to the level of the peg tops. A horizontal surface is obtained by using a striking-off board (see p. 60) on each pair of adjacent pegs in turn. These wood pegs must be removed before the concrete has set, and the holes filled with concrete. If allowed to remain the pegs may rot and be responsible for the onset of dry rot in floor, etc., timbers (see Chap. I, Vol. III).

(a) *Trammel Method.*—The application of a trammel for the bay window indicated at A is shown at H, Fig. 29. The bonding of this wall is shown in Fig. 15. A trammel is a 13 mm thick board, not more than 150 mm wide, and holed at one end. A 20 mm diameter metal bar is set up vertically in a slab of concrete at the centre of the circle; the length of the bar must be sufficient to reach to the top course of the proposed wall, and must be vertical, as tested by a plumb-rule. Alternatively, the rod may be tightly fitted into a wood peg or post which has been driven into the ground at the centre. The trammel is threaded over and passed down the bar, and the width of the concrete (and footings) and the thickness of the wall are accurately marked on its upper face. The setting out and construction of the semicircular (or segmental) wall are aided by the trammel as it is caused to rotate, and by plumbing. As the brickwork proceeds above the ground level, the trammel, which must be horizontal, is supported at its holed end by a piece of cord which is fastened under it to the bar, the cord being raised as each course is completed.

(b) *Templet Method.*—This is often preferred to the trammel on account of its convenience and the accurate check which it affords. A templet consists of two wide thin pieces of board, overlapped and nailed to each other, as shown at J. The outer edge is sawn and carefully planed to the required curve. A wood tie connects and projects beyond the two ends, and the outer edge of this tie must coincide with the external face of the main wall. Three wood struts or stays are fixed as shown; these make the templet rigid and convenient for handling. The templet is placed as required on top of each course during and after its construction, any bricks not conforming to the curve being tapped in or out until their outer faces correspond to the curve. Plumbing provides a further check on the work. It is most important that the outer edge of the tie is in true alignment with the main wall face each time the templet is used.

General.—In conclusion, it is most important that the following requirements be observed if best results are to be obtained when setting out facing work :—

1. *The normal face appearance of the selected bond must be maintained over and under openings.* Hence the average length of the bricks should be carefully noted and, as stated in Chap. I, Vol. I, the width of each opening should be a multiple of 1 brick for English bond, and for Flemish bond the width should be a multiple of $1\frac{1}{2}$ bricks after 440 mm wide; the combined thickness of the vertical or cross joints must, of course, be allowed for.

If these dimensions are departed from when the above bonds are adopted, broken bond is inevitable. An example of broken English bond above an opening is shown at N, Fig. 19; note the stretching course immediately over the crown. Unsatisfactory features of broken bond are the non-maintenance of the perpends and unbalanced treatment at the jambs of openings (such as a stretcher at one side and a header or bat in the same course at the other).

2. *The length of walling between openings and the width of external attached piers should be in accord with the average length of the facing bricks.* Thus, for

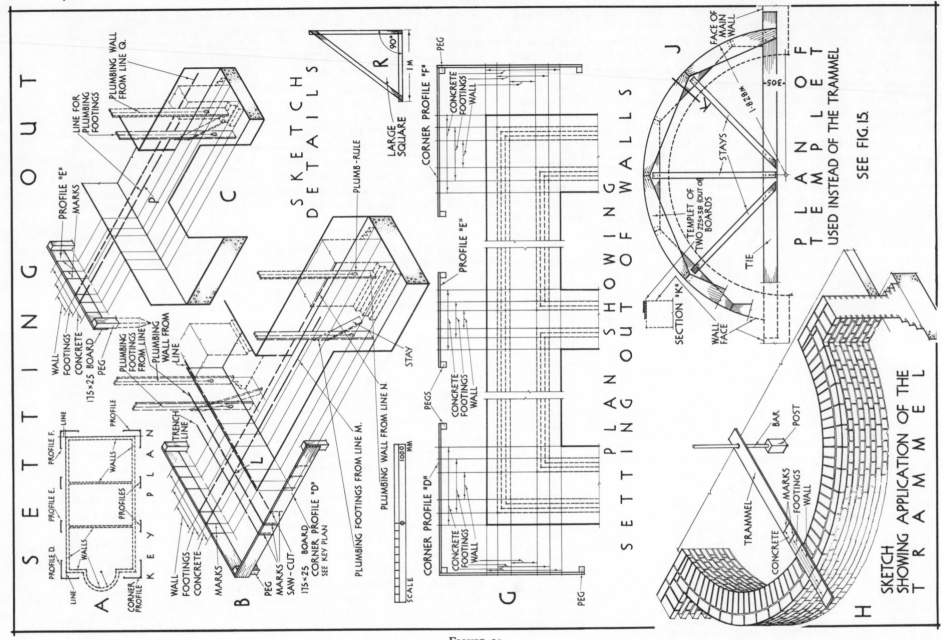

FIGURE 29

example, broken bond will be avoided if these lengths and widths are multiples of whole bricks (plus the total thickness of the vertical joints) and the bond is either stretcher, English or English garden wall.

It is usual to mark the above position of door and window openings, etc., on the course of common brickwork (generally 65 mm below the ground level) and when constructing the faced work to make certain that the appropriate perpends are vertically under the reveals concerned.

3. *Split courses above arches and lintels* (see Chap. I, Vol. I) *and below sills must be avoided.* Therefore the average thickness of the bricks and the bed joints must be taken into account when deciding upon the height of most openings and the construction must conform to the gauge rod (see Chap. I, Vol. I) on which the courses are indicated. It is good practice to arrange that a stretcher is the first (reveal) brick in each of the courses immediately above the sill and below the arch. To attain this, it is necessary that the number of courses between the ground level and the sill course shall be carefully ascertained and the bonding arranged accordingly.

Accurately set out brickwork is no more expensive than that which is constructed in a haphazard fashion, and whilst the above preliminaries to actual construction will involve some thought and the expenditure of a little time, the results obtained are well worth while.

CHAPTER TWO

DRAINAGE

Syllabus.—Surface water and subsoil drainage, sewage disposal, Septic tank. Characteristics and brief description of the manufacture of drain pipes, including bends, junctions, channels and tapers pipes, gullies and interceptors. Setting out and construction of drains. Drainage system for small buildings; inspection, interception and ventilation; soil stacks.

Surface Water Drainage.—Provision has to be made for the drainage and disposal of rainwater which falls on to roads, including paved areas, and open spaces. In the former case, this is arranged by having street gullies (see below) placed along the kerbside which discharge into the sewerage system. In country districts the disposal may be by means of *soakaways* in permeable ground—these are holes filled with broken stone from which the water percolates naturally; alternatively, the water may be conducted to ditches and watercourses.

Gullies are made sufficiently deep so that silt and grit can collect in the bottom and not be washed into the sewers. For the same reason, surface water drains should be connected to the sewers through a sediment chamber—a brick enclosure about 900 mm by 900 mm by 760 mm deep, with inlet and outlet near to the top, the chamber collects the grit and sediment which can be removed periodically as is the case with street gullies.

Subsoil Drainage.—Fields and other open spaces should be provided with subsoil drains placed about 1 m deep. The agricultural pipes used for this purpose are 60, 75 and 100 mm diam., they are without sockets (see below) and are laid butt jointed to allow the water to enter; it is preferable to cover the pipes with 25 mm size broken stone 150 mm thick before the trench is back filled. The main pipes will follow the natural depressions in the ground, and can discharge to ditches, watercourses, soakaways, or sewers and drains. In the latter event, a sediment chamber is required as above and an interceptor (see below) can be used at the junction with the drain. The main pipes (75 or 100 mm dia., according to conditions) are fed by branches 75 mm dia., laid herring-bone pattern at an average distance apart of 4·5 m, or closer if site conditions are bad. Subsoil drains are used for several purposes such as round basements (Fig. 20), to prevent flooding, or to improve the soil conditions for agricultural purposes.

Sewage Disposal.—In addition to rain water, the waste and refuse required to be disposed of from houses and other occupied buildings include (1) liquid wastes from sinks, lavatory basins and baths, (2) excrement and (3) ashes and household refuse. B.S. 8301 Code of Practice for Building Drainage is relevant.

Where there is an inadequate water supply, such as in certain rural districts, the rain water is usually collected in galvanized iron tanks and used for houshold purposes, and fixed receptacles known as *privy middens*, *earth closets* or *ash closets* are provided for excrement, ashes and other refuse. Another objectionable but less insanitary form of accommodation existing in certain districts, including a number of large townships, consists of *pail closets* or *tub closets* in which movable receptacles for faecal matter are provided, ashes being received in small dust bins. This is known as the *dry* or *conservancy system* of sanitation.

The best system, now in general use, is known as the *water-carriage system*. This provides for the admission to and removal by pipes of the liquid wastes from sinks, baths, etc., and excreta. These combined wastes and excreta are called *sewage*.

A complete sewerage or drainage system consists of a network of pipes conveying sewage, the smaller pipes being connected to larger ones and these ultimately combining to form what is called a *main outfall sewer*.

The method of disposal of sewage depends a good deal upon the location of the district. Thus, that from a coast town is simply disposed of by continuing the outfall sewer some distance on the sea bed and allowing the sewage to discharge into the sea during the ebb-tides. Otherwise the outfall sewer is continued to the *sewage disposal works*, where the sewage is treated and rendered innocuous. One form of treatment, known as the *activated sludge system*, consists of passing the sewage through a screen and a settling tank prior to admitting it to a large rectangular tank where it is agitated by compressed air admitted at the floor level. In another method the sewage after being screened and settled is sprayed over a *percolating filter* consisting of a 1·8 m deep bed of gravel or similar material. Another method, now being gradually superseded by the activated sludge system, consists of the admission of sewage to one or more *contact beds* of gravel of broken bricks, etc., where it is allowed to remain for several hours. If only a comparatively small system, the sewage, after preliminary screening and settling to eliminate as much as possible of the solid matter (called *sludge*), may be distributed over land. After being treated by one of these methods, the purified liquid or *effluent* is discharged into the nearest watercourse. In each of these systems the sewage is rendered harmless by the action of bacteria and oxygen.

In the absence of a conveniently situated public sewer (see Fig. 30), and where no nuisance is likely to occur, the sewage from a country house may be conveyed to a *septic tank* or " cesspool " and then allowed to percolate through the soil (provided it is gravel or is otherwise suitable) or passed over a small filter bed of clinker, etc.

In some districts the rain water is kept separate from the sewage, one set of pipes taking the former and another the sewage; this is known as the *separate system*. Most local authorities, however, adopt the *combined* or *single-sewer system*, in which one set of pipes takes both sewage and rain water.

The channels or pipes which convey sewage are called *drains* or *sewers*. The essential difference between a drain and a sewer is concerned with ownership. A sewer belongs to a local authority, who is therefore responsible for its maintenance; a drain is the property and responsibility of an individual. Briefly, according to the Public Health Act, 1875, a drain is a channel by which sewage is conveyed from a single house or premises within the same boundary; if it serves more than one house, the channel is a sewer. Much litigation has resulted in determining whether pipes were drains or sewers, and whilst the above is a broad distinction, it may not apply in districts where local authorities have obtained special powers under private acts or have adopted provisions under the Public Health (Amendment) Acts.

Septic Tanks.—These are used to treat sewage from isolated country houses when a piped sewage system is not available; they are also used occasionally for small communities of about 100 persons. The Building Regulations require a septic tank to be of suitable depth and adequate size, having in no case a capacity less than 2 700 litres (this is a suitable size for the average house); it must be covered or fenced in and if covered, adequately ventilated and having means of access for inspection, cleansing and emptying.

A septic tank is a chamber wherein sewage is collected and solids broken down by bacteria into liquid and sludge. The effluent from it should either be filtered or dispersed by soakaway drains (subsoil irrigation) if the ground is suitable. A septic tank should only receive foul water; rainwater being passed separately to soakaways. Grease should be excluded from it as this tends to clog the drains disposing of the effluent and impairs decomposition of the sewage; hence the kitchen sink should discharge through a grease trap (see p. 82) which must be cleaned regularly. The over-generous use of detergents and disinfectants also affects adversely the treatment of the sewage.

A septic tank partially liquefies and breaks up, by gasification, the solids so that about 70 per cent. of these collect on the bottom as sludge. *Anaerobic* (without air) bacteria develop and particles rise to the surface to form a scum which, because it assists the action, should be left undisturbed until the tank is emptied. The bulk of the sludge is pumped out by the local authority or private contractor at about six-monthly intervals, leaving a small amount to restart the bacterial action in the newly-admitted sewage. Hence, in addition to the requirements given above, the tank must be (*a*) conveniently placed for access, (*b*) not nearer than, and down wind 15 m from, habitable buildings, and (*c*) where it will not contaminate water supplies; also if the effluent from it is discharged to a stream or watercourse, then (*d*) the approval of the local River Board must be sought.

A septic tank will not function well if it has a capacity less than 1 818 litres and in order to take full advantage of the reduction of the solids it should allow for 48-hrs. storage of liquid. As the Building Regulations demand a minimum capacity of 2 700 litres (*i.e.* or 1 350 litres per day) this is equivalent to 225 litres per person per day in a household of 6 persons; this is adequate and allows

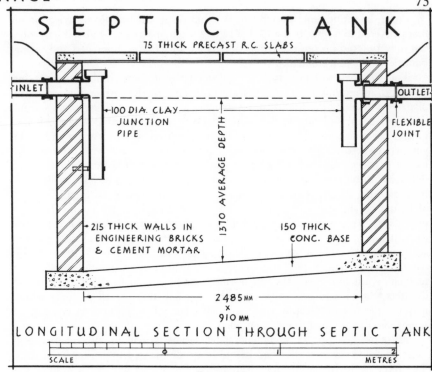

FIGURE 30

a margin of safety bearing in mind that the average use of water per person is nearer 182 litres per day. Hence as 1 litre = 1 000 cm³ then a 2 700 litre tank requires a volume of 2 700 × 1 000 cm³ = 2·7 m³. Allowing for an average depth of liquid in the tank of 1·37 m its area must be 2·7 ÷ 1·37 = 2 m² (approx.). So as to allow an even flow from the inlet to the outlet the length of the tank should be about three times its width. Therefore if the width is taken as 910 mm its length could be about 2 485 mm, which gives a surface area of liquid of almost 2·3 m².

The above dimensions are observed in Fig. 30, which shows the longitudinal section of a typical rectangular septic tank for a house. It is constructed with 215 mm thick walls of engineering brick on a 150 mm thick concrete base. The top is formed of five 75 mm thick reinforced concrete panels set loosely on the walls to allow for ventilation and removal for cleansing and emptying at about 6-monthly intervals thus the tank should be within 30 m from vehicular access. The inlet to the tank is made with a T-junction clay drain pipe set in the wall, the outlet is similarly formed; these provisions prevent the sewage from passing straight through and the former directs it to the bottom of the tank and preserves intact the crust which forms on the surface of the liquid.

From the septic tank the effluent is either dispersed by subsoil irrigation or first delivered to a filter bed and thence to a ditch or stream. Subsoil irrigation can only be used on porous ground; it is cheaper than a filter bed and, being odourless, less objectionable.

The trenches and pipework for subsoil irrigation are similar to those for subsoil drainage but the objectives are different; in the former the idea is to disperse and aerate the liquid so the trenches are shallower. They are 450 mm wide and deep, and dug to follow the natural ground slope at a gradient not greater than 1 : 200. The irrigation length required is between 3·7 and 18 m per person according to the porosity of the ground. A 150 mm thick bed of ballast (25 to 50 mm size stone) is spread over the trench bottom and 100 mm dia. agricultural pipes with open joints (about 3 mm) laid on it. To prevent silt from entering the pipes strips of felt are laid over the joints. A further 50 mm of ballast is laid over the pipes and the trench filled over with soil. If space permits the irrigation area can be duplicated, this allows one area to rest whilst the other is in use; it can be accomplished by having a small chamber at the septic tank outlet which has two outlet pipes capable of being used alternately by having a simple gate valve fitted to them. A further improvement of the septic tank effluent is to increase the size of this second chamber to about 2 m³. This, in effect, then becomes a settlement chamber and traps small particles which may emerge from the septic tank; the particles fall to the bottom and can be removed when the main tank is emptied.

Filter bed.—Septic tank effluent which is not treated by subsoil irrigation must be delivered to a filter bed before being discharged to a ditch or stream. The filter comprises a chamber containing filter media and is built adjoining the septic tank; its object is to aerate (hence the action is *aerobic*) and purify the effluent, good ventilation is therefore essential. It is for this reason that it should be placed as far away from property as possible, otherwise it becomes a smelly nuisance. Two filters, allowing alternate use, are preferred as this prevents anaerobic growth which would clog the media. Each should have a capacity of 1 m³ of media per 415 litres of effluent. Hence for the above 1 350 litres a day scheme the volume is about 3·3 m³; a suitable depth is 1·2 m, so the requisite plan area would be about 2·75 m square. The floor of the bed is made with concrete and on this are laid agricultural drain pipes; these are covered with 0·15 m bed of stone (75 to 100 mm size) topped with a bed 1·05 m deep of 25 to 50 mm clinker. Various means of delivering the effluent on to the filter bed are available; in one system the effluent discharges over a tilting hopper having a cross-section of W shape. Each half of the W is a trough which when full tilts over to spill the contents on top of the filter bed; as one half is emptying the other is being filled.

DRAIN PIPES AND TRAPS

An important consideration in the design of drainage systems is the type of joint used to connect the pipes. It has been found that in certain cases the traditional cement and sand joint used to join clay pipes (see p. 78) is too rigid to permit movement resulting from settlement in ground liable to subsidence or in ground consisting of shrinkable clay which expands and contracts according to its water content. The Building Regulations recognise this fact and stipulate that the joints must remain watertight in all working conditions, including differential movement between the pipe and the ground or any structure through or under which the pipe passes. The Building Regulations require that the joint for rigid pipes (asbestos, clay, concrete and iron) must be of the flexible type like G and H, Fig. 33. The cement-mortar joint has proved satisfactory in most cases since its introduction at the start of the 20th century; prior to that clay was used, this has flexibility but cannot resist the ingress of tree roots into the pipes. The Building Regulations do not permit the use of the cement mortar joint; because it has been used for many years, usually satisfactorily, it is described briefly in this book.

Drain pipes are made of clay or shale, cast iron, asbestos-cement, concrete, pitch fibre and plastic.

Clay Drain Pipes and Traps.—Much drainage work is done with clay pipes. They are sometimes referred to as *stoneware, fireclay, earthenware* or simply *ware* pipes and are to B.S. 65 Specification for Vitrified Clay Pipes, Fittings and Joints. Vitrification is a process where the clay is burnt to a high temperature to render the pipe impervious. The B.S. defines three types of pipe. *Normal* which are suitable for all drains and sewers other than where extra chemical resistance is required. *Surface Water* for the transport of surface water only. *Perforated* for land drains. The B.S. also defines *Extra Chemically Resistant* pipes.

Clay drain pipes are sometimes referred to as *stoneware, fireclay, earthenware* or simply *ware* pipes. The clay from which the stoneware pipes are made is found in this country in the south and midlands, and fireclays in the north. Both produce drain pipes and traps of first quality.

Clay pipes in the form of straights, bends, junctions and tapers are made and they may be provided with a socket end for the polyester joint (see p. 79), or they may be without a socket for a special sleeve joint (see p. 79). Clay traps and channels are also available.

A sound clay pipe should be well vitrified throughout, straight in the barrel (twisted or warped pipes cannot be properly jointed), truly cylindrical, smooth, and free from cracks and blisters. It should ring sound when struck with a hammer. B.S. 65 specifies the maximum and minimum bore diameters. Thus for a nominal 100 mm bore *normal* pipe the maximum bore is 105 mm and the minimum is 96 mm. For the *surface water* type these two dimensions are 107 mm and 95 mm respectively. The B.S. also specifies the permissible deviation from straightness, crushing strength, bending moment resistance and impermeability.

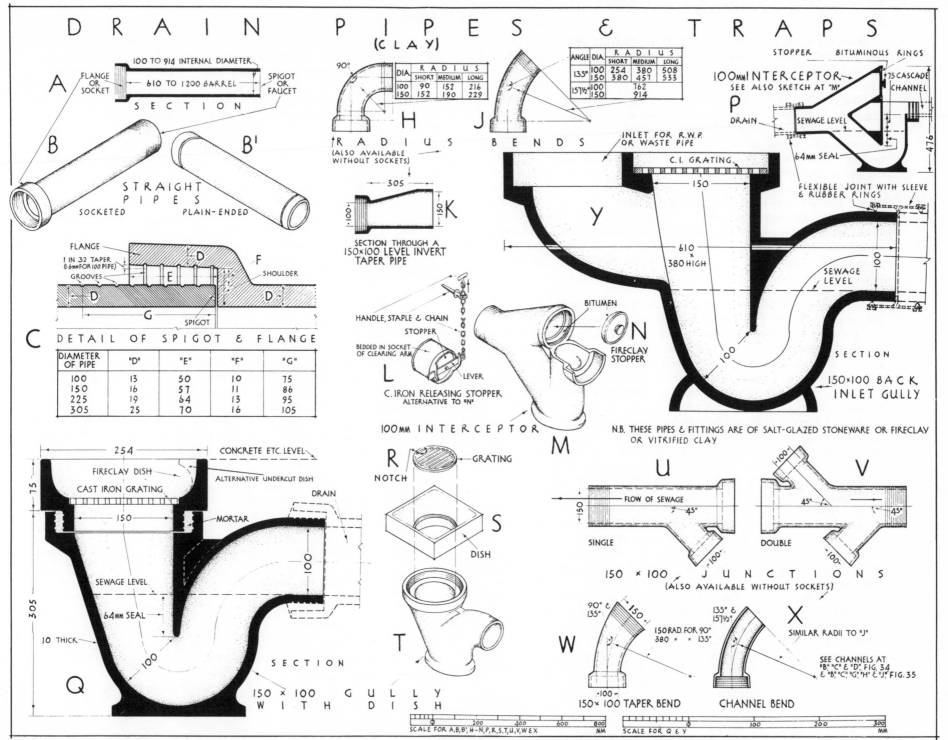

Figure 31

Ware pipes including straights, bends, junctions, tapers and channels are shown in Fig. 31 and also in Fig. 33 which shows the various means of jointing; similar cast iron fittings are shown in Fig. 32, and described on p. 80. *Clay pipes and traps* are described as follows :—

Straight Clay Pipes (see A, B and C, Fig. 31).—In the socketed pipes the cylindrical barrel has a *flange* or *socket* at one end, and the opposite end is called the *spigot* or *faucet*. The interior of the flanges and the exterior of the spigots are grooved to a minimum depth of 1·6 mm to afford a key for the jointing material. The *internal* diameter varies from 75 to 900 mm. The Building Regulations stipulate that the diameter of drains conveying soil water must not be less than 100 mm; this size is sufficient for most house drainage systems of average size, and very rarely are pipes exceeding 150 mm diameter required for this purpose. The minimum size of a drain carrying surface water only is 75 mm. The larger pipes are used for public sewers and 50 and 75 mm pipes are utilized for subsoil or agricultural drainage. The length of the barrel, *exclusive* of the flange, varies from 0.3 to 2 m; the 1.2, 1.5 and 2 m lengths are commonly used. The *minimum* thickness of pipes, size of flanges, etc., are shown in the table at C, Fig. 31.

Radius Bends (see H and J, Fig. 31).—These are required at horizontal and vertical changes of direction of straight lengths of drains. The standard radii of 100 and 150 mm pipes are shown. They are described in accordance with the number of bends required to make a complete circle, thus that at H is known as a quick or *quarter bend*, the 135° example at J is called an *eighth circle bend*, and the slow bend having a contained angle of 157½ ° (see J) is called a *sixteenth circle bend*. A bend required to change the direction of a drain on plan should be slow or " easy," and two eighth circle bends are preferable to a single quarter bend. The latter should never be used for this purpose unless the drain conveys rain water only. A single quarter bend should not be used at the foot of a soil stack extending through two storeys in height (see p. 93) but it can usefully be adopted for a ground floor W.C. where the vertical drain is short in length.

Similar radius bends are made in the socketless type of pipe.

Clay Junctions (see U and V, Fig. 31).—Such are necessary at connections between drains. That at U is called a *single junction* and is specified according to the internal diameters of the connecting pipes, *i.e.*, 100 mm by 100 mm, 150 mm by 100 mm, 150 mm by 150 mm, etc. The branch or *arm* of a junction should be obliquely inclined in the direction of the flow of the sewage. Right-angled or square junctions must never be used; a branch pipe which is unavoidably at right angles to a main drain should be connected by means of an oblique junction and a slow bend. A *double junction* is shown at V; they are not advocated, an inspection chamber (see p. 88) being preferred; the arms should be the maximum distance from each other, and a better arrangement is to use two adjacent single junctions.

Similar junctions are made in the socketless type of pipe.

Clay Taper Pipes (see K, Fig. 31).—These are necessary when the size of a drain has to be increased on account of one or more additional branches which may be connected to it lower down its length. The socketed one shown is of the *level invert* or *straight invert* type, the invert being the lower internal surface. Another type has the socket concentric with the spigot, and thus there is a slight fall in the invert from the socket to the spigot. Tapers are specified according to the size of the adjacent pipes, *i.e.*, 150 mm by 100 mm, 225 mm by 150 mm, etc. Very occasionally, as for alteration work, a taper pipe is required having the socket at the larger end. A standard 150 mm by 100 mm *taper bend* is shown at W.

Similar socketless taper pipes are also made.

Clay Channel Pipes, required at inspection and disconnecting chambers, are described on p. 88 and illustrated in Figs. 34 and 35. A standard channel bend is shown at X, Fig. 31.

Clay Traps.—The purpose of a trap is described on pp. 82-83 and 90; there are two main kinds: *gully traps* or *gullies* and *intercepting traps*. Clay gullies are shown at Q, R, S, T and Y, Fig. 31 and their application is illustrated in Figs. 34, 35 and 36. A clay intercepting trap (or *disconnecting trap* or *interceptor* is shown at M and P, Fig. 31, its application is shown in Fig. 34, and described on pp. 89 and 90; such traps are now seldom used—see p. 89. The seal increases from 64 mm for a 100 mm interceptor to 76 mm for 150 and 225 mm traps.

Joints for Clay Pipes.—It has been mentioned on p. 76 that joints must be watertight; in addition none of the jointing material must remain in the pipe, and the invert (the inside of the bottom of the pipe) must be in true alignment throughout. The following joints are used for clay pipes : (1) *Polyester and rubber ring joint*, (2) *Sleeved joint*. Prior to the introduction of these two joints the cement-mortar joint was universal (p. 76), for this reason a brief description is given of it.

Cement-mortar Joint for Clay Pipes (see G', Fig. 33.).—The recommended mortar composition is 1 cement : 3 sand, sometimes 2% waterproofer (see p. 27) is included. Neat cement has been employed but this can cause cracking of the pipe sockets. In addition, a piece of *yarn* is used at the bottom of the joint.

The joint is formed in the following manner : The spigot of a pipe is placed within the socket of the last laid pipe and closely butted against the shoulder. A piece of yarn, after being dipped into a pail of cement grout to preserve it (unless it has been previously tarred) is wrapped two or three times round the spigot and well caulked against the shoulder by means of a blunt chisel, cement mortar is packed in by hand to completely fill the annular space, and this is neatly finished by a fillet splayed by a trowel at an angle of about 60°. The object of the yarn is twofold, as it prevents the entrance of the mortar to the inside of the drain and assists in centering the pipes to maintain a properly aligned invert.

Some jointers prefer to omit the preliminary packing of the joints with yarn. Accordingly, unless the mortar is of a stiff consistency, much of it will pass within the drain and a "dropped invert" will result as the pipes, because of their weight, will subside and squeeze out some of the material. Such a faulty joint is shown at H'. If the projecting mortar is not removed, as explained on p. 85, paper and solids may accumulate to cause an obstruction in the drain; lodgement may also be caused by the dropping of the spigot.

The unsightly appearance produced by an excess of mortar and the absence of a fillet is also shown.

1. *Polyester and Rubber Ring Joint for Clay Pipes* (G†, Fig. 33).—In order to give dimensional accuracy for the ring joint both the socket and the spigot of the pipe have special mouldings made of polyester (a type of plastic) cast on to them during the manufacture of the pipe. In making the joint the inside of the socket is coated with a special lubricant, the adjacent pipe length then has a rubber joint ring (to B. S. 2494) slipped over the spigot and to engage in the groove of the polyester moulding. The spigot is then pushed home into the mating socket, this compresses the ring to make a watertight joint.

2. *Sleeved Joint for Clay Pipes* (H‡, Fig. 33).—Joints of this kind are likely to be increasingly adopted for joining plain ended (*i.e.* socketless) pipes and the acceptance in modern drain laying practice of such joints will lead to the declining demand for the more expensive socketed pipe. The one shown has a sleeve or coupling made of polypropylene (a type of plastic) which has an internal groove at each end containing a specially shaped rubber ring. Also round the inside of the sleeve there are a number of small locating lugs on the centre line which serve to position the pipes when these are pushed into place; the lugs ensure that the sleeve is placed centrally round the pipe ends. Also the pipes themselves have a very small groove round the outside about 50 mm from the ends; the position of this groove corresponds to the distance from the edge of the sleeve to the face of the locating lugs. It is thus possible to inspect the joint after it has been made and check that the sleeve is in the correct place.

In making the joint the first pipe length can be stood on end. Its upper end is then covered on the outside for a length of about 50 mm with a special lubricant and the coupling pressed on to it. The pipe is then placed in the trench and held against a stake driven into the ground; the next pipe has its lubricated end pushed into the other end of the sleeve to complete the joint.

Manufacture of Clay Drain Pipes and Traps.—The processes vary according to the class of clay and the plant available, but, as in brick manufacture, they are divided into the preparation of the clay, moulding, drying and burning.

The clay is finely ground and screened as described on pp. 2 and 3. Grog (or powdered burnt clay—see p. 3—or crushed burnt and damaged pipes) is added to the clay to reduce the shrinkage, some clays requiring 25 per cent. of this material.

Straight Pipes are made by an extrusion process which may be either vertical or horizontal. In the vertical method the clay is fed into a machine, the pipe is extruded downwards and cut to length by a wire; if a socketed pipe is being made the socket is automatically formed. The ends of the pipe are trimmed and, in the case of socketed pipes grooves are formed in the socket and at the spigot end.

After moulding, the pipes are transported and placed vertically on the drying floor and gradually dried in a temperature of 27° C. for one or two days.

They are then taken to the kiln; this, in the older installations, is of the circular down-draught type (see p. 6), whilst the more modern method is to use the tunnel kiln (see p. 10). The pipes are carefully stacked vertically upon their sockets, one above the other, to a height of from 2·4 to 3·7 mm

Circular Down-draught Kiln.—The heat is gradually applied until a maximum temperature of about 1 100° C. is reached; this is known as the vitrification stage. Burning may occupy from three or four days, and cooling, which must be carefully controlled, takes the same time.

Tunnel Kiln (see p. 10).—This is used for the ceramic glazed pipes where the glaze is applied immediately after extrusion. The pipes move slowly along the kiln for a length of time dependent upon the pipe diameter; in the case of a 100 mm pipe this would be about 30 hrs. The kiln heat is gradually increased to a maximum of 1 070° C.

Junctions are made from straight pipes moulded as described above. Thus, a small socketed piece required for an arm of a junction is cut from a freshly moulded pipe, its end is shaped by hand (or by a special machine), the cut edge is covered with liquid clay and fitted on to a recently moulded pipe. On the following day the required hole in the latter pipe is cut at the joining of the arm, trimmed with a knife and smoothed over with the fingers.

Bends are formed either by a machine, to which various dies can be fitted, or by hand. If the latter, a straight pipe as it emerges from the machine, is bent to the approximate radius, and then fitted over a core of the correct shape and trued up by hand.

Channels.—Two half-round channels are obtained from a whole green pipe. The latter is placed in a plaster-of-Paris mould which is half-round in section and the length of a pipe, and it is divided longitudinally by a piece of wire drawn along the top edges of the mould. The cut edges are then trimmed.

A three-quarter channel bend, such as is shown at G, H and J, Fig. 35, consists of a half-round channel bend (obtained by dividing a green radius bend) together with a length cut by hand to the required shape. These are stuck together with liquid clay and the joint neatly trimmed off.

Traps are moulded by hand in moulds made of plaster of Paris. Two moulds are required per trap. Each mould is shaped with its internal surface the reverse of the exterior of the trap to be moulded. Thus, for a gully such as that at T, Fig. 31, the moulds would be shaped to the exterior shown in section Q. A clot of prepared clay is flattened to the required thickness, and this is taken by the moulder who work it into the mould to the desired shape. When the two pieces have been moulded in this manner, the two moulds are brought together and clamped by bands of hoop iron. When the clay has sufficiently set, the moulds are removed and the junction is neatly trimmed and smoothed off. Interceptors are hand-moulded in a similar manner.

Junctions, bends, channels, traps, etc., are dried, burnt and placed in the kiln as described above.

Whilst most channels are vitrified, they are sometimes required to be *white glazed* or *enamelled*. Enamel consists of powdered flint, china clay, powdered zinc,

---

† By Naylor Bros. (Denby Dale) Ltd.
‡ By the Hepworth Iron Co. Ltd., Sheffield.

etc., well mixed together and water added to form a slurry. Glaze is a somewhat similar mixture with the addition of whiting, felspar and soda. The channels must be thoroughly dry before the enamel is applied. In best work three or four coats of enamel are first brushed on the internal surface and edges of each channel, and this is followed by two coats of glaze. This film is fused when the channels are heated in the kiln and forms a hard, durable, impervious and white coloured surface.

Cast Iron Drain Pipes and Traps (see Fig. 32[1]).—These are made to conform to B.S. 497, they are coated with a tar based composition for protection and are mainly used inside buildings or underneath them. They are an alternative to drains of weaker materials which must be encased in concrete if they pass beneath a building.

The straight pipes are made in standard 2·74 m lengths (excluding the socket depth) and other lengths and in the diameters shown at A; for 100 mm pipes, the socket depth is 75 mm and the wall thickness is not less than 9·5 mm.

Radius bends are made resembling the ware range and are of two main types—short or long radius. An example of the latter is shown at B, both types are made in the different angles given; there are also similarly angled branches or junctions. The special long branch at C can be used in internal ducts to serve a range of W.C.'s as indicated at D. This detail shows the branches connected to vertical pipes of varying length with a large diameter socket to receive the W.C. outlet. Both pipes and bends can be made with removable access plates for inspection or rodding purposes.

A cast iron inspection chamber which can be used inside a building is shown at G, this is one of many standard types which can be had with from one to six branch inlets at 135° on either or both sides, others can be obtained with 90 or 112⅓° bend inlet branches. The removable cover is fixed with galvanised steel, bronze or gunmetal bolts and nuts and has a greased felt washer.

The cast iron gully at E is one of several available with differing angled outlets as shown, they can be made with access doors noted by the broken line. The example given is jointed to a *bellmouth back inlet* gully top having a grating. The one at F is used to trap the large volume of grease from hotels and similar premises; both inlet and outlet are below the level of the water, and there should be enough of this to cool the grease which is removed at intervals by taking off the cover and lifting the perforated tray. The outlet is fitted with a cap to permit of cleaning and there is a bellmouth back inlet top similar to that at E. Should this type of gully be used internally beneath a sink, then the outlet is supplied with a vent pipe connection adjacent to the cap in lieu of the grating near the inlet.

Another type of gully is that designed to prevent flooding of the building by sewage backing up the drains. This may occur if there is a blockage in the system or in coastal areas where the drains from low buildings discharge to the sea and may suffer periodic tidal inundation. Such an anti-flooding gully (or interceptor) is provided with a copper ball float which allows outward flow but closes against a rubber seating if the water level rises due to back flow.

[1] By Messrs, Burn Bros. Ltd.

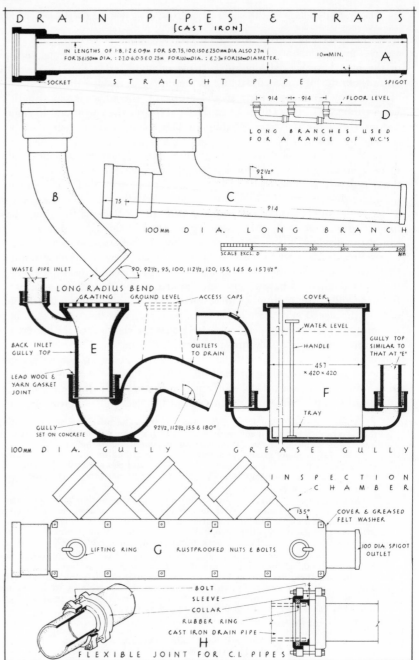

FIGURE 32

Joints for Cast Iron Pipes.—The traditional non-flexible joint for cast iron pipes was either made with lead (molten lead or lead wool) as described in Chap. VI, Vol. I and shown at z, Fig. 77, in the same volume; or by a stiff mix of neat cement and water. For the reasons given on p. 76 a flexible type of joint is now required and one of these is shown at H, Fig. 32.

This joint must be used with socketless pipes or with the socketed pipes as described above in which case the socket must be cut off and so must the bead at the spigot end. It comprises a coupling formed with a sleeve, two collars and two rubber rings of square section. In making the joint a collar and a rubber ring are pushed on to the end of each pipe, the pipes are then placed inside the sleeve and on tightening the nuts on the two bolts the rubber rings are compressed between the collars and the sleeve to make a watertight joint.

> *Manufacture of Cast Iron Pipes.*—Pipes of all sizes are produced by two methods : centrifugal casting (or spinning) and sand moulding.
>
> Spun pipes are made in either metal or sand-lined flasks which are rotated at high speed. Metal is introduced either along the wall of the rotating cavity or from one end. The centrifugal force exerted by the spinning mould spreads the molten metal evenly, giving a uniform wall thickness.
>
> Sand moulded pipes are made by hand moulding or, more usually, by mechanical methods; both techniques are similar requiring a sand mould into which a sand core is placed to give the internal shape of the pipe. In the mechanical manufacture a pattern of the pipe being made is placed within a moulding box and clay-bonded sand is thrown around it by a sand slinger (a machine which throws the sand at high speed to give a ramming effect). When the box is full it is stripped from the pattern to leave an accurate reproduction of the outside shape of the required pipe indented in the sand. The inside shape of the pipe is produced by making a sand core which is located in the mould cavity. The casting of the pipe is then done by pouring molten metal into the mould cavity at a number of points simultaneously.
>
> After casting the pipes cool briefly in the mould and are then removed from the box. Dry sand adhering to the casting is brushed off; the castings are then ground smooth and inspected before being treated with a coat of paint or coating solution.

Asbestos-Cement Drain Pipes are made to conform to B.S. 3656; they are plain ended (without a socket) and are available in the standard length of 4 m, but half and quarter lengths of 2 m and 1 m are also provided. Asbestos-cement bends and junctions are stocked in sizes similar to those for clay pipes.

Joints for Asbestos-cement Pipes are of the flexible kind employing an asbestos-cement sleeve or collar and two rubber rings for each pipe end. One example[1] is shown at J, Fig. 33.

The rings are placed on the pipe by using a taper plug one end of which is placed in the pipe; the other end of the plug, being of a smaller diameter than the pipe, allows the rings to be placed easily over it. The rings are rolled along the plug on to the pipe; each pipe end is mounted with two rings in this way. The sleeve is then pushed on to the end of one of the pipes over the two rings which become compressed. The next pipe length with its two rings is then put into position and the sleeve is slid back until it is central over the joint.

[1] By Turners Asbestos Cement Co. Ltd.

Manufacture of Asbestos-cement Pipes.—In Chap. III, Vol. III there is a description of the manufacture of asbestos-cement; this states how, at one stage, a thin film of the material is obtained. This continuous film, of width slightly greater than the pipe length, is fed on to a rotating mandrel; the successive layers of asbestos-cement are consolidated by hydraulic pressure and the process is continued until the requisite thickness, which forms the pipe wall, is achieved. The resulting pipe is then withdrawn from the mandrel leaving a smooth and well polished bore. After a seven day maturing period in a tank of water the pipe is trimmed to length and its ends turned to accurate limits to ensure correct fitting at the joints.

Concrete Drain Pipes are made to conform to B.S. 5911 in lengths from 914 mm to 3·66 m and diameters from 100 to 600 mm. They are socketed and the detail at J', Fig. 33 shows the flexible joint made with a rubber ring. Concrete bends and junctions similar to the clay range are also made.

> *Manufacture of Concrete Drain Pipes.*—One way of making the smaller (100 to 225 dia.) pipes is to cast them vertically. The outside of the pipe is formed by a fixed mould inside which is a rotating mandrel which shapes the inside of the pipe; the concrete is charged into the space between the two. The mandrel has two lugs fitted to it which spread the concrete and transfer part of the weight of the mandrel to the wall of concrete to consolidate it. The bottom part of the mandrel smoothes the inside of the pipe wall as it rotates and so the pipe is successively built up. The outer mould with enclosed pipe is then taken away for steam curing as described below.
>
> The larger sized concrete pipes (225 mm dia. and upwards) are produced by a combination of centrifugal spinning and vibration which gives a high degree of consolidation, impermeability and strength. A typical manufacturing bed has seven horizontal axles each with a wheel at each end; one of the outer axles is motor driven. Resting over and in between the axles are six steel pipe moulds, the enlarged ends of these sit over the wheels so that once the drive is switched on all the wheels and moulds rotate. The moulds which are sprayed with mould oil before the concrete is placed in them, are shaped to form the pipe socket at one end. The carefully batched cement, sand and gravel mix is fed into the rotating moulds and after spinning, centrifuging and vibration (produced by the wheels) the wet concrete is compressed against the mould. Any internal unevenness in the pipe is removed by the application of a long-handled trowel which is curved to approximate to the inside curve of the pipe barrel. The resulting degree of compaction enables the mould for a 225 mm pipe, for example, to be removed from the machine after about nine minutes (35 mins. for a 760 mm pipe). The mould with enclosed pipe is then taken to a steam curing chamber where the temperature is between 37·8 and 51·6° C. and humidity about 98 per cent. After a curing period of 2½-hrs. for a 225 mm pipe (6 hrs. for a 760 mm pipe) the moulds are stripped (they are in two halves) and the pipes transferred to the stock yard where they cure for 28 days after which they are ready for use.

Pitch Fibre Drain Pipes (see B' and B", Fig. 33).—These are made to conform to B.S. 2760 in 2·44 m lengths for the 50, 75, 100, 150, 200 and 230 mm dia. sizes and also in 3·05 m lengths for the 100 mm dia. Bends, junctions, tapers and gullies are available and channels can be formed by cutting a pipe in two with a saw. Being more flexible and resilient than the above kinds of pipe they are frequently specified where ground movement is expected such as in coal mining areas. They may not be suitable for factory effluents and the manufacturers should be consulted before they are installed for non-domestic services. The ends of the pipe have a 2° taper and the dry joint is made by hammering *home* a pitch fibre coupling, using a wooden dolly to protect it (in the enlargement at B" a slight gap is shown for clarity). The pipe can be cut with a saw and the ends tapered on site with a hand-lathe. An alternative type of joint employs rubber rings and a sleeve. Joints between the pipe and a clay one are made with a rubber ring, a special adaptor being required for connecting to the spigot end of earthenware.

> *Manufacture of Pitch Fibre Pipes.*—Cellulose fibre in the form of waste paper (newspaper cannot be used because of the print) is mixed with water into a slurry and fed to a container where it is picked up by revolving colander rollers on the outer perimeter and deposited on to a pipe mandrel. The rollers have a mesh surface through which water drains, leaving a thin mat of fibre which builds up on the mandrel to the requisite thickness; pressure is applied by rollers to the mandrel to form the white coloured pipe. The pipes are then passed through a drying oven and dipped in a tank containing hot pitch. By means of vacuum and applied pressure the pipes become impregnated with pitch before being cooled, cut to length and having their ends machined.

Plastic Drain Pipes.—Suitable only for domestic drainage, these are made of p.v.c. (polyvinyl chloride) in 1·2, 3·01 and 6·1 m lengths. The pipes are plain ended and the joint is made by a sleeve and rubber rings similar to the sleeved joint for clay pipes (p. 79). Being made of a flexible material they are ideal for the sort of situations given under pitch fibre pipes above. Plastic drains must be laid on and surrounded by compacted granular bedding (9 to 5 mm gravel).

Traps include *gully traps, grease traps, intercepting traps* and the larger *petrol and grease chambers.* The object of a gully is to prevent drain air escaping from a drain and polluting the atmosphere near ground level. A grease trap, and a petrol and grease chamber are used to prevent these substances from entering the drain. An intercepting trap can be used to prevent sewer gases from entering the drainage system; they are now rarely used (see p. 89).

Gully Traps or *Gullies* (see Q, R, S, T and Y, Fig. 31 and A, Fig. 36) are mentioned on p. 78. A gully is used to take the discharge from a waste pipe from a lavatory basin, bath or sink which is situated *at or about ground level.* (The Building Regulations allow such waste pipes to be outside the building; but waste pipes from sanitary appliances at higher levels (*e.g.*, first floor and above) must be placed *internally* (except for buildings not more than 3 storeys high-see p. 86). A gully is also used[1] to receive the flow from a rainwater pipe and at the sides of paths, roads and in yards and other paved areas (see the car wash at A, Fig. 35).

A gully trap takes the form of a bent pipe (see Q, Fig. 31) with the inner fold projecting into the retained liquid and 64 mm below the outlet to form the *seal.* The internal surface is curved throughout, varying from 150 mm at the inlet and 100 mm at the outlet. It is of the *self-cleansing* type, as it permits of the free passage of waste liquids, and the absence of angles and corners prevents any accumulation of small pieces of organic, etc., matter. The flat base enables the gully to be bedded correctly, and as shown at D, Fig. 36, it is set on 150 mm of concrete.

The clay gully shown at Q, R, S and T, Fig. 31, is suitable for taking the

[1] Gullies are not *essential* when a separate sewage system is used (see p. 74).

flow from a rainwater pipe. The gully inlet has a flange to receive the cylindrical rim of the square dish (see S), the joint between the two being of cement and sand mortar; the dish is slightly rebated for the cast iron *grid* or *grating* (see R). If the undercut type of dish is used as indicated by broken line at Q there is less danger of water splashing on to the surrounding ground. The type of gully shown at Q with circular top and separate dish is much preferred to the *square grid gully* which has a square rebated top to receive the grating direct. As the latter has no separate dish, it is often impossible to fix it square with the wall of a building unless a bend (on plan) is provided at the beginning of the branch drain. The gully at Q can also be used for a waste pipe discharge if the type of grating which is notched out to receive the end of the waste pipe is used as indicated by the broken line at R. (Note that it is a B.R. requirement that an *external* waste pipe can be used in the circumstances mentioned in the adjacent column provided that the pipe discharges *above* the water level in the gully but *below* the grating.)

Another type of clay gully is shown at Y, Fig. 31; this is the back inlet gully used for ground floor waste pipe discharges (note that it complies with the last mentioned B.R. requirement) and to receive the end of a R.W.P. When used for the latter purpose it is preferred to the gully at Q in the dish of which leaves may accumulate to block the grating and cause flooding in a rain storm. A similar cast iron back inlet gully is shown at E, Fig. 32. As traps may become unsealed by evaporation during hot weather, it is advisable that water be poured down them occasionally during such prolonged periods.

All gullies should be fixed outside the building, but see permitted exception on p. 80; in order to comply with this requirement in connection with a basement, it may be necessary to construct a small area (at least 760 mm wide for access) adjacent to an external wall, in the concrete floor of which the gully is fixed.

Applications of gullies are illustrated in Figs. 34-36.

Intercepting Traps or Disconnecting Traps of Interceptors.—One of several types of this ware trap is shown at M and P, Fig. 31, and a similar trap is shown at B, Fig. 34. The seal increases from 64 mm for a 100 mm interceptor to 75 mm for 150 mm and 225 mm traps. The trap is fixed in an intercepting chamber (see Fig. 34), and its object is to intercept the sewer gases from the drainage system. Its adoption is becoming less frequent, and its merits and demerits are discussed on p. 89.

Grease Traps.—One type of cast iron grease trap is shown at F, Fig. 32. Its purpose is to prevent fat and grease collecting inside drain pipes from large kitchens, schools, canteens, etc., and it is described on p. 80. Smaller and similar models are made in clay and as mentioned on p. 75, one of these should be used in septic tank installations.

Petrol and Grease Chambers.—These are both constructed in a similar way to a septic tank; their purpose is to collect grease and petrol and prevent these from being discharged into a drainage system. They are used at garages and in places having large kitchens, such as schools and canteens. A typical grease and petrol chamber is 610 mm deep and 610 mm square formed with 215 mm brick walls on a flat concrete base; the top has loose 50 mm thick timber planks which permit ventilation and can be removed to enable the grease and petrol to be taken off the surface of the liquid. The inlet to the chamber is just a straight pipe 50 mm above outlet level; the outlet has a T-pipe junction like the septic tank in Fig. 30.

SETTING OUT AND EXCAVATION OF DRAIN TRENCHES

Gradient of Drains.—A drain must be laid to an adequate inclination or gradient. This is expressed as a ratio between the total fall (or difference in level between the upper and lower ends of the drain) and the horizontal length of the drain. Thus, if the fall is 2 m and the horizontal length is 60 m, the gradient is 1 in 30. A 100 mm drain should have a *minimum* fall of 1 in 60 and a 150 mm drain a *minimum* fall of 1 in 120, these would be adequate for up to 20 and 100 houses respectively.

Before deciding upon the gradient to which a drain is to be laid, it is necessary to obtain the depth of the public sewer (or existing drain or septic tank) and the level of the ground. The depth of the sewer below the ground level at the proposed point of connection may be obtained by inspection on the site, such as at a convenient manhole or chamber (see p. 88), or from the surveyor to the local authority; the level of the ground along the proposed line of the drain is determined by using a dumpy level and levelling staff or the straight edge and spirit level. The longitudinal section, such as is shown at E, Fig. 34, can then be plotted. Besides having an adequate fall, the drain should be laid to a uniform gradient up to the boundary of the site, or from chamber to chamber (see p. 88), after which the fall may be increased up to the connection. Thus, at E the drain has a uniform inclination of 1 in 32 up to the intercepting chamber M, from which point the gradient is increased. In this example it would be uneconomical to maintain a uniform gradient from the gully to the sewer because of the addtional excavation which would be entailed.

Unless the drain is a short one the setting out of the trench is performed in the following manner : A wood peg is driven in on the proposed centre line of the drain at each point where it changes direction. The sides are pegged out, pegs being inserted at half of the width from each centre peg; a cord is stretched taut and tied to one pair of side pegs, the side is marked with a pick or spade, and the opposite side is similarly marked.

The correct level of the bottom of the trench is obtained and a uniform fall maintained by the use of two *sight rails* and a *boning rod*. A sight rail is a wood board, having straight edges, and about 38 mm thick. It is fixed to a pair of 100 mm by 50 or 75 mm wood posts, having pointed ends, which are securely driven into the ground at one end and clear of the proposed trench; each post is sometimes packed with earth, gravel, etc., within a 150 or 225 mm drain pipe

placed vertically with its flange resting on the ground. The sight rail is nailed to the two posts at any convenient height and with its upper edge horizontal as tested by a spirit level. The second sight rail is fixed at the correct level in a similar manner at the opposite end of the trench; the level of the top edge of this rail must be such that an imaginary line, called the *line of sight*, drawn from it to that of the other is parallel to the proposed gradient of the drain; a dumpy level and levelling staff should be used to fix the height of this second sight rail to ensure that the difference in level between the two rails is that decided upon. An application of sight rails is illustrated at A, C and D, Fig. 33, where the inclination of the line of sight is 1 in 60 and is 2·3 m above the bottom of the proposed trench. The required gradient of the trench bottom is maintained by use of the boning rod. This rod resembles an elongated tee-square having a wood blade with cross head attached (see A, B, C and D). The height of the rod must equal the vertical distance between the line of sight and the predetermined level of the trench bottom, *i.e.*, 2·3 m in this example.

The excavation is proceeded with until the level of the bottom of the trench is reached as determined by " sighting through." Thus, the foreman standing immediately behind one of the sight rails looks towards the far sight rail so that he can just see the top edges of both rails, and the required depth is indicated when the top of the boning rod, resting upon the bottom of the excavation and held vertically by an assistant, coincides with the line of sight. This is repeated, the rod being held at intervals along the trench. The boning rod W at D, Fig. 33, shows that the required level of the trench at that point has been reached and that additional excavation is necessary further up if, when sighting through as the rod is held in turn at positions U and V, its head appears above the line of sight as indicated. Excavation of the last few centimetres may be deferred until just prior to the laying of the drain, when the earth is trimmed off and the bottom rammed solid. Alternatively, when the trench is machine excavated, this more expensive hand trimming which would be necessary, is avoided by over excavating with the machine by about 100 mm which is made good with bedding (see below).

Timbering, as required, is provided as a temporary support to the sides of the trench (see Fig. 40, Vol. I, and Fig. 21, Vol. III).

Joints.—These must be airtight and watertight; none of the jointing material must remain within the bore of the pipes, and the invert must be in true alignment throughout. The joints for clay pipes are described on pp. 78-79; those for cast iron, asbestos-cement and concrete pipes on p. 81; and for pitch fibre and plastic drain pipes on pp. 81 and 82 respectively. For the reasons given on pp. 76 and 79 the sleeved type of joint which permits flexibility is much preferred.

CONSTRUCTION OF DRAINS

As the structural load-carrying capacity of a pipe depends on its crushing strength and the way it is supported it is important that the pipes be properly

SETTING OUT & CONSTRUCTION OF DRAINS

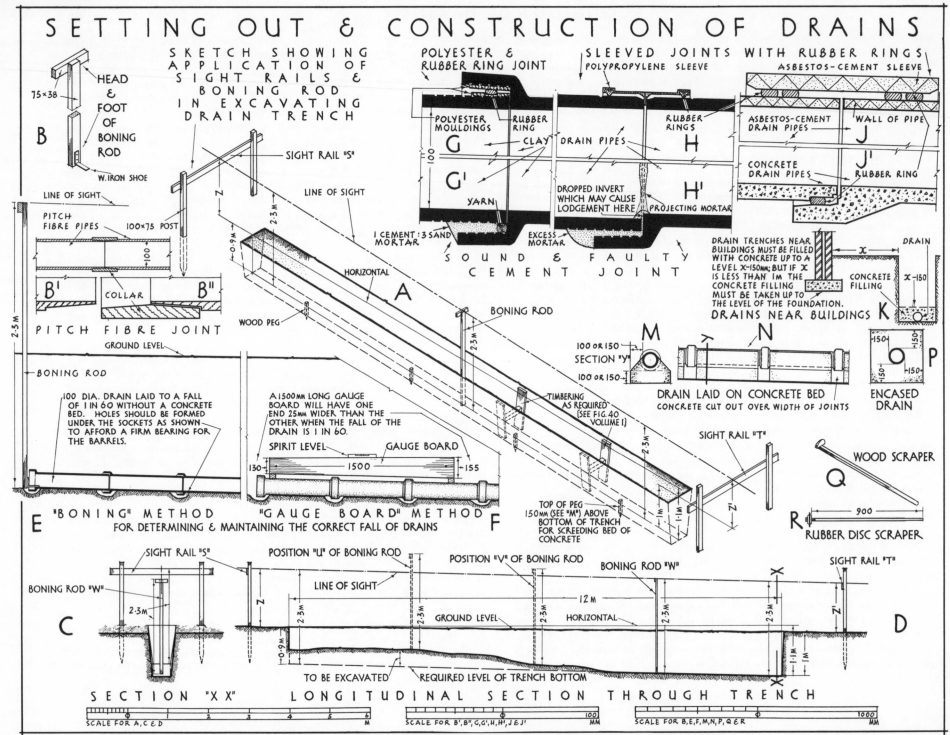

SKETCH SHOWING APPLICATION OF SIGHT RAILS & BONING ROD IN EXCAVATING DRAIN TRENCH

HEAD & FOOT OF BONING ROD

75×38

B

W.IRON SHOE

SIGHT RAIL "S"

LINE OF SIGHT

LINE OF SIGHT

100×75 POST

PITCH FIBRE PIPES

100

B' COLLAR **B"**

PITCH FIBRE JOINT

GROUND LEVEL

BONING ROD

100 DIA. DRAIN LAID TO A FALL OF 1 IN 60 WITHOUT A CONCRETE BED. HOLES SHOULD BE FORMED UNDER THE SOCKETS AS SHOWN TO AFFORD A FIRM BEARING FOR THE BARRELS.

E "BONING" METHOD

HORIZONTAL

A

WOOD PEG

BONING ROD

TIMBERING AS REQUIRED (SEE FIG. 40 VOLUME I)

A 1500mm LONG GAUGE BOARD WILL HAVE ONE END 25mm WIDER THAN THE OTHER WHEN THE FALL OF THE DRAIN IS 1 IN 60.

SPIRIT LEVEL   GAUGE BOARD

130   1500   155

"GAUGE BOARD" METHOD **F**
FOR DETERMINING & MAINTAINING THE CORRECT FALL OF DRAINS

TOP OF PEG 150mm (SEE "M") ABOVE BOTTOM OF TRENCH FOR SCREEDING BED OF CONCRETE

SIGHT RAIL "T"

POLYESTER & RUBBER RING JOINT

SLEEVED JOINTS WITH RUBBER RINGS

POLYPROPYLENE SLEEVE

ASBESTOS-CEMENT SLEEVE

POLYESTER MOULDINGS   RUBBER RING

G   CLAY   DRAIN PIPES   **H**

G'   YARN

RUBBER RINGS

ASBESTOS-CEMENT DRAIN PIPES   WALL OF PIPE   **J**

CONCRETE DRAIN PIPES   RUBBER RING   **J'**

DROPPED INVERT WHICH MAY CAUSE LODGEMENT HERE   PROJECTING MORTAR

1 CEMENT : 3 SAND MORTAR   EXCESS MORTAR

H'

SOUND & FAULTY CEMENT JOINT

DRAIN TRENCHES NEAR BUILDINGS MUST BE FILLED WITH CONCRETE UP TO A LEVEL X-150mm; BUT IF X IS LESS THAN 1M THE CONCRETE FILLING MUST BE TAKEN UP TO THE LEVEL OF THE FOUNDATION.

DRAINS NEAR BUILDINGS **K**

x   DRAIN

CONCRETE FILLING   x-150

100 OR 150

SECTION "Y"   **M**

100 OR 150

y   **N**

DRAIN LAID ON CONCRETE BED
CONCRETE CUT OUT OVER WIDTH OF JOINTS

150   150

O   **P**

150   150

ENCASED DRAIN

WOOD SCRAPER

Q

900

R

RUBBER DISC SCRAPER

SIGHT RAIL "S"

BONING ROD "W"

2.3M

SECTION "XX" **C**

POSITION "U" OF BONING ROD

POSITION "V" OF BONING ROD

BONING ROD "W"

SIGHT RAIL "T"

LINE OF SIGHT

Z

2.3M   2.3M   2.3M   2.3M   2.3M   Z'

12M

GROUND LEVEL

0.9M   HORIZONTAL   1.1M 1M

TO BE EXCAVATED   REQUIRED LEVEL OF TRENCH BOTTOM

X   X

D

LONGITUDINAL SECTION THROUGH TRENCH

SCALE FOR A,C & D
0 1 2 3 4 5 6 M

SCALE FOR B',B",G,G',H,H',J&J'
0 100 MM

SCALE FOR B,E,F,M,N,P,Q,E R
0 1000 MM

FIGURE 33

bedded on to a firm foundation otherwise settlement may occur and cause cracked or broken pipes and an irregular invert. Rigid pipes can be laid direct onto hand trimmed ground, flexible pipes must be laid on a 100 mm thick bed of granualar material. Although as mentioned above, if trenches are machine cut, it is cheaper to over excavate slightly and make good with granular bedding. In the case of the larger sized sewer pipes, a granular bed or concrete bed must be adopted. A granular bedding comprises 1 part coarse sand to 2 parts 13 or 10 mm stone; this gives a good seating to the barrel of the pipe. A bedding, used to strengthen the larger sewer pipes and also beneath smaller drain pipes in weak ground to strengthen the pipeline, is concrete (see M, Fig. 33). When it is placed and partially set it should be cut out over the width of the pipe joints so as to maintain flexibility in the pipeline (see N, Fig. 33). Drains beneath buildings, if not of cast iron, should be completely encased (see p. 86). Whatever bedding is used, in the case of socketed or sleeved pipe joints, it should be scraped away at the joints to ensure that the pipe barrel is properly supported. 100 mm rigid pipes must have a minimum cover of 0.4 m in gardens; for flexible pipes this cover must be 0.6 m. Pipes under roads need greater cover.

Drains Adjacent to Walls of Buildings.—The Building Regulations stipulate that, except where the nature of the ground makes it unnecessary, if a bottom of a drain trench is below an adjacent wall foundation is must be filled with concrete to a level not lower than the bottom of the wall foundation by more than the distance from the foundation to the near side of the trench less 150 mm—see K, Fig. 33. Where, however, a drain trench is within 1 metre of a wall foundation the trench must be filled with concrete to the level of the underside of the foundation (see K). Expansion joints over the width of the drain joint must be left at 5 m intervals in such concrete filling. Also where a drain passes through or under a building precautions must be taken to prevent damage to drains by differential settlement; damage is avoided by using cast iron pipes or surrounding the pipes of weaker materials in concrete, using a flexible joint where they pass through walls and leaving a gap round the pipe at this point which can be filled with a compressible material (puddled clay or mastic).

Laying of Drains.—Both the (1) *boning* and (2) *gauge-board* methods are adopted in the laying of drains.

The following is how these methods are applied to a drain which is laid directly on the ground. After the trench has been excavated and the bottom formed to the required gradient as described on p. 83, the construction of a drain is proceeded with, commencing at the lower end. In the case of socketed pipes the sockets should be facing upwards against the flow, also with such pipes it will be necessary to form holes in the trench bottom under the sockets to ensure that the barrels have a firm bearing (see E and F, Fig. 33). These hand-holes also enable the joints to be made and are formed as each pipe is laid, sufficient earth being removed by the pipe layer to enable him to get his hand

under the sockets to form the joints. Smaller handholes are required in the case of sleeved joints. When the socketed or sleeved pipes are laid on a granular bedding part of this is scraped away at each joint.

1. *Boning* is the more accurate method. The boning rod used is similar to that referred to on p. 83, except that it is provided with a projecting wood or metal shoe as shown at B, Fig. 33. It is held on the invert of each pipe in succession, as indicated at E, any adjustment of the pipes being made until the head coincides with the line of sight. Thus, the position of each pipe is fixed independently and therefore any errors are not accumulative. The formation of sinkings under the sockets as mentioned above is often omitted, and instead a brick is placed under each barrel near the socket; this is an undesirable practice as such partially supported pipes may be fractured by the weight of the earth above or by traffic. The pipes are then jointed. When cement mortar joints, were used, any mortar which may have entered the drain was removed before it has set. This was done immediately each joint was made by using a wood scraper Q or scraper R (consisting of a disc of rubber bolted between two wood discs) or a *badger* (having two discs similar to R with a steel spiral spring between) or a bag containing shavings.

2. *Gauge-board or Straight-edge Method.*—This is illustrated at F, Fig. 33. The board is tapered as required. Thus, if the drain is to be laid to a fall of 1 in 60, a 1 500 mm long board will be $\frac{1}{60} \times 1\ 500 = 25$ mm deeper at one end than the other; a thin block is nailed on the splayed edge at each end so that the board will clear the sockets. The gauge-board is used as each joint is formed, the level of the pipe being adjusted until the bubble of the spirit level is in the centre of its run when the level is placed on the board as shown. This method should only be used for short lengths and branches of drains. It is not so accurate as the boning method, for, unlike the latter, any errors are accumulative. Also, as the thickness and bore of pipes may vary slightly, it follows that the invert may not be parallel to the required gradient. Special care must therefore be taken when using this method to a drain having only a slight fall.

The gauge-board is often used without blocks, and is then laid upon the sockets; when so applied, errors may occur by irregularly shaped and eccentric sockets. A straight edge, having a projecting screw at one end which is adjusted as required, is sometimes used instead of the gauge-board. A lath, having a small fillet attached at one end of a thickness equal to the required difference in level, is a further substitute.

The concrete foundation for a drain referred to above is formed in the following manner : The bottom of the trench is laid to fall as previously explained, additional depth being allowed for the concrete. Wood pegs are driven in along the trench bottom at about 3 m intervals with their tops 100 to 150 mm (according to the thickness of the concrete) above the ground. The concrete forming the rectangular bed is placed in position and screeded off (see p. 61) level with the tops of the pegs. The top of the concrete is thus given a fall parallel to the line of sight. The pipes are then laid by either the boning or gauge-board methods with their flanges resting upon the concrete. The concrete benching is formed after the joints of the drain have set, the concrete being well packed under the pipes and neatly flaunched midway up the drain pipes or to the crown (see M and N, Fig. 33). Some prefer to provide additional room for making the joints by laying the barrel of each pipe on a brick laid flat upon the concrete bed near to the socket, followed by packing and benching. A better method is to embed bricks flat at 50 mm depth and 610 mm centres (or socket intervals) in the concrete foundation during formation; these are removed before the concrete has set, and the holes thus formed for the sockets are filled in with fine concrete after the joints have set and during benching. Gaps must be left in the concrete at each joint as explained on p. 85.

Testing Drain Pipes.—No drain shall be covered up before it has been tested and approved by the local authority.

The test most generally applied to new drains is the *hydraulic* or *water test*, the Building Regulations demand that such a water test be carried out. Briefly, after the joints have set, the lower end is plugged, the drain is filled with water and allowed to remain for 2 hours and topped up. A 1.5 m head of water is provided above the invert at the head of the drain. The leakage over 30 minutes must not cause the water level to drop more than 6.4 mm per metre run of drain. Any cracked or otherwise defective pipes are replaced by sound ones, and any defective joints are made good.

Another test, now falling into disfavour because of the cost entailed, is the *smoke test*. Smoke from burning oily cotton waste is pumped by a machine into the lower end of the drain, the upper end is plugged, and pumping is maintained until a certain pressure is reached. Any defects are exposed by escaping smoke.

Ball Test.—A drain may be airtight and watertight and pass either of the above two tests and yet be of defective construction owing to the presence of jointing material within the drain and an improperly aligned invert. It is for this reason that many authorities now apply the ball test to newly constructed drains in addition to the hydraulic (or smoke) test. This test merely consists of passing a solid rubber ball down each length of drain. The diameter of the ball is 6.5 mm less than that of the drain. The ball is put into the drain at the top end, and if it emerges at the lower end it is a sufficient indication that the drain is true in bore and free from obstructions. If the ball does not traverse the full length of the drain, the cause of the stoppage is ascertained and any defects remedied. This is an important test.

Refilling Trench.—After a drain has been approved, the trench should be carefully refilled in 150 mm thick layers. The finer earth is placed with care next to the drain so as not to damage the pipes and joints. This is spread and lightly consolidated, after which the remainder of the refilling is completed, each layer being well rammed.

DRAINAGE SCHEMES

The drainage plan of a building (with certain exceptions) must be submitted to and approved by a local authority before building operations are commenced.

The following is usually required to be indicated on such a plan : (1) The position of rain water pipes, gullies, and the various sanitary fittings such as lavatory basins, baths, sinks and water closets; (2) arrangement of the various drains, the sizes of which must be specified; (3) inspection chambers, and, if necessary, the intercepting chamber (see p. 89); (4) means of ventilation; and (5) the position of the public sewer (or other outlet) to which the main drain is shown connected.

A typical plan showing the drainage scheme for a small house is shown at A, Fig. 34, and a part system is shown at A, Fig. 35. These are referred to on p. 91.

Principles of Drainage.— These are given below, all except item 4 form part of the Building Regulations.

1. Drains must be airtight and watertight under all working conditions including any differential movement between the pipe and the ground or any structure through or under which it passes, constructed of sound materials and workmanship, with an even invert and a clear bore; all traps must remain self-cleansing with an adequate seal.

2. They must be provided with a sound foundation, laid with an adequate and uniform gradient and in straight lines between points and where the direction changes.

3. Adequate means of inspection and cleaning must be provided, inspection chambers being constructed at change of direction points and in convenient positions to receive the maximum number of branch drains.

4. A drain *may* be required to be disconnected from a sewer (or cesspool) by the provision of an intercepting chamber (see p. 89).

5. Adequate ventilation must be provided.

6. Branch drains should be as short as possible and laid in straight lines to the nearest inspection chamber.

7. Bends must be slow and junctions oblique.

8. Rain water pipes must discharge into gullies (unless stormwater drains are separate from foul drains—see p. 74). Where R.W.P.'s are placed internally they may discharge into properly constructed soil stacks (see p. 91).

9. Ground floor sinks, lavatory basins and bath waste pipes may discharge into gullies *outside* (see p. 82); or be connected to a soil stack (see p. 91) These appliances at higher levels in buildings up to 3 storeys high may discharge into an *external* soil stack but the stack must be *inside* for buildings of more than 3 storeys.

10. Ground floor water closets are usually connected direct to drains. W.C.'s at ground level (or higher) in buildings of more than 3 storeys must discharge into an *internal* soil stack; for buildings of 3 storeys and less the stack may be *outside*.

11. Unless unavoidable, no drain shall pass under a building. If laid under a building precautions to avoid damage to it must be taken. This means either using a cast iron pipe or one of the other pipe materials surrounded in 150 mm thick concrete (P, Fig. 33).

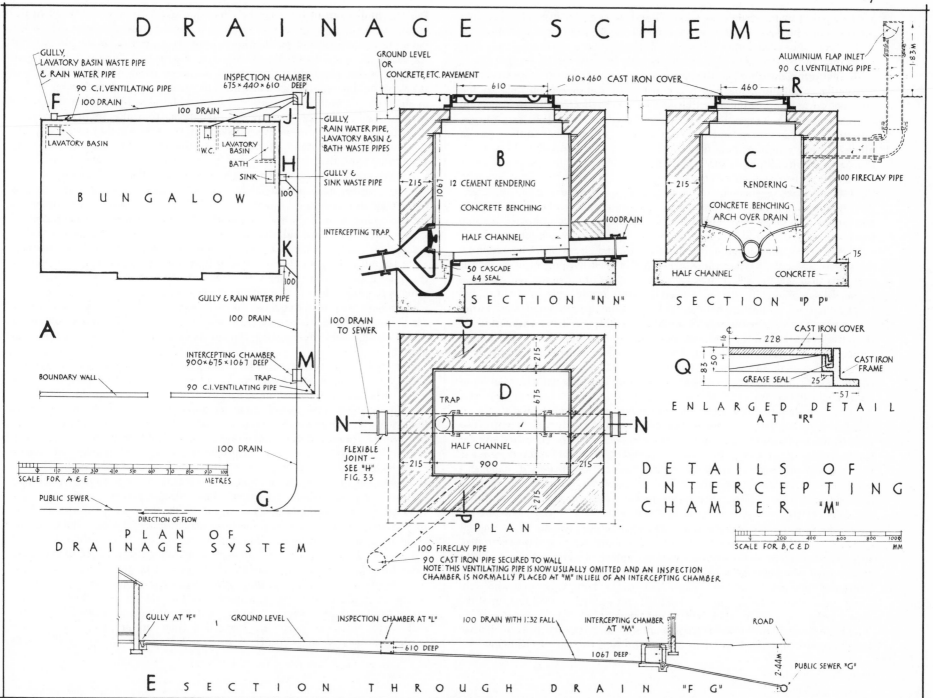

D R A I N A G E   S C H E M E

GULLY,
LAVATORY BASIN WASTE PIPE
& RAIN WATER PIPE
90 C.I. VENTILATING PIPE
100 DRAIN

F

LAVATORY BASIN

B U N G A L O W

INSPECTION CHAMBER
675 × 440 × 610 DEEP
100 DRAIN
J L
W.C.
LAVATORY BASIN
BATH
SINK
H
100

GULLY,
RAIN WATER PIPE,
LAVATORY BASIN &
BATH WASTE PIPES

GULLY &
SINK WASTE PIPE

K
100

A

BOUNDARY WALL

GULLY & RAIN WATER PIPE

100 DRAIN

INTERCEPTING CHAMBER
900 × 675 × 1067 DEEP
M
TRAP
90 C.I. VENTILATING PIPE

100 DRAIN

SCALE FOR A & E
METRES

PUBLIC SEWER
G
DIRECTION OF FLOW

P L A N   O F
D R A I N A G E   S Y S T E M

GROUND LEVEL
OR
CONCRETE, ETC. PAVEMENT
610
610 × 460 CAST IRON COVER

B
215
190
12 CEMENT RENDERING
CONCRETE BENCHING
HALF CHANNEL
100 DRAIN

INTERCEPTING TRAP
50 CASCADE
64 SEAL

S E C T I O N   " N N "

ALUMINIUM FLAP INLET
90 C.I. VENTILATING PIPE
1·83 M

460
R
C
215
RENDERING
CONCRETE BENCHING
ARCH OVER DRAIN
100 FIRECLAY PIPE
HALF CHANNEL   CONCRETE
75

S E C T I O N   " P P "

100 DRAIN
TO SEWER
P
215
675
215
TRAP
D
HALF CHANNEL
N N
215   900   215
215
FLEXIBLE
JOINT —
SEE "H"
FIG. 33
P

P L A N

100 FIRECLAY PIPE
90 CAST IRON PIPE SECURED TO WALL
NOTE: THIS VENTILATING PIPE IS NOW USUALLY OMITTED AND AN INSPECTION
CHAMBER IS NORMALLY PLACED AT "M" IN LIEU OF AN INTERCEPTING CHAMBER

¢
16
228   CAST IRON COVER
Q
83
50   CAST IRON
GREASE SEAL   FRAME
25
57

E N L A R G E D   D E T A I L
A T   " R "

D E T A I L S   O F
I N T E R C E P T I N G
C H A M B E R   " M "

SCALE FOR B, C & D
200   400   600   800   1000
MM

GULLY AT "F"   GROUND LEVEL   INSPECTION CHAMBER AT "L"   100 DRAIN WITH 1:32 FALL   INTERCEPTING CHAMBER
AT "M"
ROAD
610 DEEP
1067 DEEP
2·44 M
PUBLIC SEWER "G"

E   S E C T I O N   T H R O U G H   D R A I N   " F   G "

FIGURE 34

12. The plumbing system carrying soil and waste water inside the building must be designed so that the traps to the different sanitary appliances remain sealed with water (see p. 91).

Several of these principles have been already referred to.

Inspection Chambers.—All drains should be conveniently accessible, and, in accordance with principle No. 3, adequate means of inspection and cleaning must be provided. The Building Regulations require that there be an inspection chamber and : (1) changes in direction and gradient; (2) within 12·5 m of a junction between drains and between a drain and a sewer, unless one is placed at that junction; in addition (3) no part of a drain shall be further than 45 m from an inspection chamber.

A typical inspection chamber is shown in Fig. 35. The floor is of concrete, the walls of brick or concrete and a cast iron cover provides means of access. The minimum internal dimensions are 460 mm square when the depth is 460 mm or less, 685 mm by 460 mm when the depth is 900 mm, and 910 mm (preferably 1 135 mm) by 685 mm when the depth exceeds 900 mm, the latter size being necessary to enable a man to pass down and do any operation required.

The concrete floor is 150 mm thick and this need not project more than is necessary to enable the walls to be constructed, *i.e.*, 75 to 150 mm. The thickness of the walls need only be 102·5 mm when the depth is under 760 mm, but should be 215 mm thick for deeper chambers. The 215 mm English bonded brickwork can be of engineering bricks or hard sound common bricks in cement mortar; in the latter event the inside of the walls must be rendered (see below); the bond is shown at C, Fig. 35. An alternative form of wall construction is shown at H, the walls being in two separate half-brick leaves in stretching bond with a continuous 13 mm thick layer of waterproofed mortar between which serves as a watertight lining.

The drains are run in straight lines to the *internal* faces of the walls, and the channels to which they are connected are jointed and bedded in cement. The ends of the pipes through the walls may be either arched or concreted over as shown at C, Fig. 34 and C, Fig. 35, respectively; if roughly bricked round (a common practice) leaks may occur. The Building Regulations demand that where a drain passes through the wall of an inspection chamber (or wall of a building) precautions must be taken to prevent damage to the drain by differential movement; one way of achieving this is to use a flexible joint for the first drain joint outside the chamber. The channels are usually of vitrified or white-glazed ware, they should not be formed in the concrete. Two alternative forms of branch connections at chambers are shown at B and G, Fig. 35. These show three branches delivering at the main drain. The construction at B consists of one double and one single half-round channel junction; the right hand and lower left-hand branches are gradually curved in the direction of the flow by the provision of slow half-round channel bends (see also sketch C). The alternative plan G shows the application of three-quarter branch channel bends which provide gradual leads and prevent sewage overflowing and fouling the bottom of the chamber; they are particularly effective when the curvature is sharp; as shown, the inverts of these bends are above that of the half-round main channel, as their lower ends are supported on the top edges of the latter (see also sketch H). A selection of standard three-quarter branch channel bends, alternative to those at G and H, is shown at J. The spaces between the channels are filled in with concrete and this is sloped or *benched* up as shown at B and C, Fig. 34 and C, Fig. 35. The object of the benching is to prevent fouling of the base from discharges from the branch channels. Sometimes the benching is given a slope of 45°; this is rather excessive, as a workman can only stand upon it with difficulty. The form of benching recommended is that shown at C, Fig. 35, although that indicated at C, Fig. 34 is adequate when the chamber only accommodates the main channel.

The chamber must be watertight to prevent leakage of sewage in the event of the main drain below it becoming choked. For this reason, if common bricks are used, the inside of the walls is sometimes rendered with a cement mixture composed of 1 part Portland cement and 3 parts sand; a 2 per cent. waterproofer is sometimes added to the mix. The thickness of this rendering should be from 13 to 10 mm and it should be continued from the top and over the benching to the inner edges of the channels as shown. Chambers over 900 mm deep are sometimes rendered up to that height, above which the joints are neatly pointed with cement mortar. Rendering is not required when better class bricks, e.g. blue engineering bricks, are used for the internal lining. In ground containing sulphate salts, sulphate-resisting cement must be used for the concrete and mortar.

Access to the chamber is provided by a *galvanized cast iron cover with frame*. These are of many different patterns and of various strengths and sizes. They must be large enough to allow a man to pass through, common sizes being 610 mm by 460 mm (see B and C, Fig. 34, and C, Fig. 35) and 690 mm square in the clear. The cover for this purpose must be airtight, and therefore the joint between the frame and cover has either a single, double or triple seal. A single seal joint is shown at Q, Fig. 34, the groove in the frame being filled with grease into which the lower rim of the cover projects; a band of solid rubber, known as a *rubber ring*, may be used instead of the grease to form a seating for the rim. Both of these materials may be used, thus a double seal cover may have the outer groove filled with grease or tallow, and the inner groove fitted with a rubber ring or tarred cord. If required, the cover may be locked, four gun-metal screws being used for this purpose. The top of the brickwork is corbelled over as shown, and the frame is bedded in cement mortar on it, the face of the cover being brought level with the surface of the ground or pavement. Unless the adjacent surface is paved, a 150 mm wide concrete curb, rendered smooth in neat cement, should be provided as a margin to the frame (see C, Fig. 35); this covers the flange of the frame and keeps it in position; a rebated hard stone curb serves the same purpose. Inspection chambers are sometimes needed inside buildings when, in order to prevent leakage of sewage in the event of the drain becoming blocked at a lower level, the cover must be bolted down.

Chambers which exceed 1.5 m in depth should be provided with *step-* or *foot-irons*. These may be of galvanized cast iron, horse-shoe shaped, as shown at c and D, Fig. 35, and fixed at every fourth course, or they may simply consist of 25 mm by 10 mm flat wrought iron bars (dipped in hot bitumen to preserve them) fixed at vertical intervals across one of the corners. They should be well bedded in to make them secure and prevent leakage.

A *drop inspection chamber* is used to connect a shallow drain to a deeper one, it is constructed as above and the shallow drain is joined to a vertical *drop pipe* (surrounded in concrete) placed outside the wall. The pipe has a slow bend at the bottom which enters the chamber and connects to a channel junction at invert level. The drop pipe is continued up to ground level where it is fitted with a cast iron cover, a short length of pipe extends laterally from the junction of the drop pipe and the shallow drain into the inside of the chamber where it is provided with a removable cap; these provisions allow for rodding of both the drain and the drop pipe. A drop inspection chamber is thus a means of reducing excavation depths for drains where these must connect to a deeper drain or sewer.

Rodding.—As implied, inspection chambers are provided as convenient means of inspecting, testing and cleansing drains. In the event of a drain becoming choked, the cause of the stoppage is removed by the application of *cleaning rods* (also known as *clearing rods* or *drain rods*). A rod consists of a bundle of malacca canes or Sarawak bamboo canes (or 6·5 mm diameter bronze rods) in 610 to 914 mm lengths; these lengths are screwed together by means of locking joints. Several varieties of tools are available for screwing to the first length, such as screws, plungers, rollers, brushes and scrapers for the withdrawal of obstructions and the removal of grease, etc. which tends to accumulate on the internal surface of the drains.

In small deep chambers especially, the insertion of a drain rod is facilitated if a ware *drain chute* is provided. An application of these is shown at H, Fig. 35, type E being fixed at the exit and type F at the entrance of the main drain.

Intercepting or Disconnecting Chambers.—Principle No. 4 refers to drain disconnection. An intercepting chamber is similar in all respects to an inspection chamber except that an intercepting trap or interceptor is fixed to the drain at the lower end of the chamber for the purpose of disconnecting the sewer gases from the drainage system. Of course, it also provides means for inspection and rodding. The position of such a chamber should be on the line of the main drain and as near as possible to the boundary. Plan and sections of an intercepting chamber are shown at B, C and D, Fig. 34. The trap has been referred to on p. 78, one type being shown at L, M, N and P, Fig. 31, and a somewhat similar form is shown at B and D, Fig. 34. The seal in each case is 64 mm and the water level is 50 to 75 mm below the channel invert. This drop is called the *cascade* and its object is to increase the velocity of the sewage during its passage through the trap. This cascade cannot always be obtained owing to the available fall from the head of the drain to the sewer being inadequate, and therefore under such conditions a trap having the outlet level with the inlet is used. The latter form of interceptor is a frequent cause of stoppage in a drain, especially if the drain has less than the required minimum fall, owing to the resulting inadequate scour through the trap leading to an accumulation of solids. The trap is provided with a *clearing arm* (also called a *raking arm* or *cleaning arm*) through which a drain rod can be passed to clear any obstruction between the trap and sewer. A *stopper* or *cap* is fitted to the arm. There are several types of stoppers, including (1) a simple ware disc which is cemented to the socket; (2) a ware disc having a bituminous rim, which, when smeared with grease or a non-setting composition, is fitted to a similar bituminous ring on the socket of the arm (see M, N and P, Fig. 31); (3) a cap which is screwed to the socket to form a bituminous joint; and (4) that shown at L and known as a *releasing stopper*.

The latter is the best form. The body of the fitting is cemented into the socket of the arm; the stopper is tightly forced in position by means of a lever which engages in slotted projecting lugs; a chain is attached to one end of the lever and passes through a staple fixed near the top of the chamber. It is an airtight stopper; it cannot be forced out by pressure of gases in the sewer, and in the event of the trap becoming choked and the chamber filled with sewage, the latter is caused to escape down the raking arm by jerking the chain and releasing the stopper; otherwise, unless the obstruction can be removed by prodding the trap, the sewage can only be removed by baling or pumping.

None of the above stoppers (1), (2) and (3) can be removed like the releasing stopper to empty a chamber filled with sewage. In addition, when stopper (1) is cemented in, it is difficult to remove without causing damage; if left uncemented (as is general) the joint is not airtight and the cap is readily forced out, by excessive pressure of sewer gases, into the trap to cause stoppage of the drain. Stopper (2) is an improvement upon (1) as it is easily removed when required and the joint is air-tight; it has, however, a similar defect in that it can be forced out by back pressure from the sewer.

The trap has a flat base, and it must be set level.

Formerly, most local authorities insisted upon the disconnection of house drains from sewers by the provision of intercepting traps. *In many districts now, however, the use of such traps is optional, and an increasing number of authorities advocate their abolition* for the chief reasons that (1) the trap is liable to become choked, preventing the escape of the sewage and causing it to overflow at the gullies; (2) the air in soundly constructed sewers is not more harmful than drain air, and disconnection therefore serves no useful purpose; and (3) increased ventilation of the whole sewerage and drainage system results when interceptors are omitted. The generally accepted view now is that interceptors are unnecessary if the sewers are properly constructed and adequately ventilated, but such traps are essential if the sewers are neither self-cleansing nor suitably ventilated. An intercepting trap should be used at the junction between a drain carrying roof water only and a foul drain if trapped gullies are not used at the rainwater pipes.

Both inspection and intercepting chambers are commonly referred to as

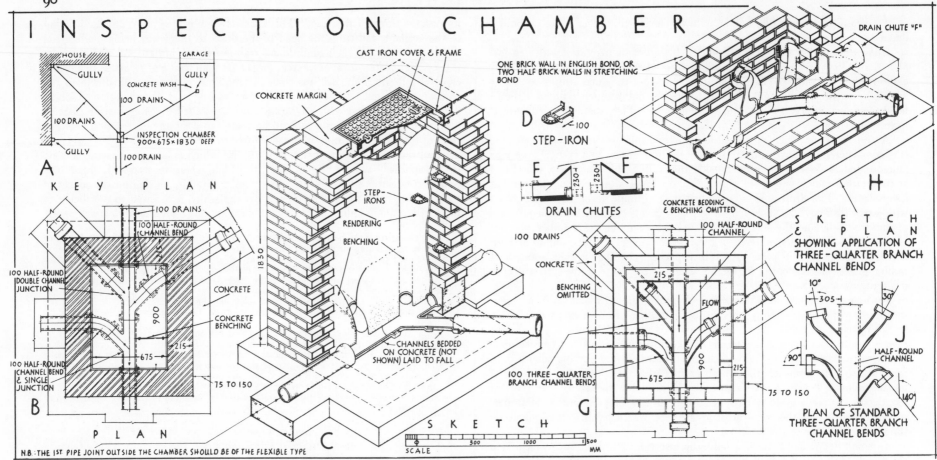

FIGURE 35

manholes, but this term should not be used in connection with house drainage owing to its ambiguity.

Ventilation.—Drains must be efficiently ventilated (see principle No. 5), at least *one* ventilating pipe should be provided to a drainage system as far as possible from the connection to the sewer. The chief aim in drain ventilation is to reduce the pressure of the foul air within the drains by providing for its discharge into the open where it will not cause a nuisance or endanger health; otherwise the accumulation of the gases may be such as to unseal traps and thereby permit of the escape of noxious air into buildings or at the ground level.

One means of ventilation, generally accepted up to within recent years (see below), was to provide an inlet at the lower end of the drain and an outlet at its upper end or head. The inlet is usually a short length of ware pipe taken from near the top of the intercepting chamber and continued by a vertical cast iron pipe, 1·5 or 1·8 m high, fixed to the boundary wall or fence; this is finished with a head having a louvred opening, behind which is a hinged aluminium or mica valve or flap (see C and D, Fig. 34). The outlet is a cast iron pipe provided at the head of the drain. Such an outlet ventilating pipe is shown at F, Fig. 34; this would be fixed to the wall of the building and continued at least 610 mm above the eaves and distant from dormer, etc., windows. Its foot would be connected to the 100 mm by 100 mm junction in the main drain by means of a 100 mm diameter bend. Thus, air entering the drain through the valve at the lower end traverses the drain before escaping at the head. *In practice, however, the* INLET *pipe is often found to be an unsatisfactory feature owing to the valve becoming either stuck or damaged or detached, and thus acting as an outlet. It is for this reason that the provision of ventilating inlets is no longer advocated, and existing inlets are often abolished, especially if they are adjacent to buildings or public footpaths.*

The Building Regulations insist that the open end of a ventilating pipe shall be protected against obstruction, such as a bird's nest, by the provision of a spherical galvanized iron (or copper) wire cage (see Fig. 36). A soil stack must always terminate as a vent pipe (see B, Fig. 36).

Drainage Systems shown in Figs. 34 and 35.—A drainage plan of a small one-storied house is shown at A, Fig. 34. It complies with the principles given on pp. 86 and 88. The gully at F receives a rain water pipe and the lavatory basin waste pipe, and the 100 mm drain from it is laid with a uniform gradient of 1 in 32 to the inspection chamber L. The water closet is connected direct to the drain which is also taken to the chamber. A rain water pipe and the lavatory basin and bath waste pipes discharge into gully J connected to a 100 mm drain. As these drains are laid in straight lines to the inspection chamber they can be easily rodded if necessary. The main drain is continued at the same gradient to the intercepting chamber M,[1] collects the short branch drains from the gullies at H and K, and proceeds with an increased gradient to the public sewer to which it is connected in the direction of the flow. A ventilating outlet is connected to the head of the system at F; *if required*, a ventilating inlet is provided at M (see p. 90). A section through the main drain is shown at E. In order to provide additional protection to the upper portion of the drain (which will be necessary if there is likely to be any traffic over it) it may either be encased in concrete (see P, Fig. 33 and p. 86) for two or three pipe lengths, or the drain at the connection to gully F may be given additional fall. Details of the intercepting chamber are shown at B, C and D and have been explained on p. 89. The construction of the inspection chamber L is somewhat similar to, but smaller than, that illustrated in Fig. 35 and described on p. 88.

A key plan of portion of another drainage system is shown at A, Fig. 35. This has been introduced to show the application of a deep inspection chamber, detailed on this drawing, and which has been already described.

INTERNAL SOIL AND WASTE PIPEWORK [2]

On p. 86 it has been stated that the Building Regulations:—(1) permit *waste* pipes from appliances at or about ground level to show on the *outside* of a building of any storey height; (2) permit *soil* and *waste* pipes to show on the outside for buildings of *not more* than 3 storeys; (3) for buildings of *more* than 3 storeys *soil* and *waste* pipes [except *waste* pipes given in (1)] must be *inside*. A main sanitation pipe transporting soil and waste water is called a *soil stack* (Fig. 36) and regardless of the number of storeys it is good practice to have this always inside; there are two reasons for this—it avoids the risk of the smaller waste pipes becoming frozen and the unsightly appearance of pipework on the elevation of the building. Ventilation pipes may show on the outside of a building but as the top of a soil stack forms the vent pipe and *internal* soil stacks are recommended only the upper portion of the vent above the roof is visible (Fig. 36). from the outside.

An essential feature in the installation of soil and waste pipework is the trap. This has a water seal like that of the gully and is provided for the same reason, *i.e.*, to prevent the escape of drain air into a building. Systems must be designed so that the water seal is not destroyed. Certain effects, caused by suction or increased pressure described below, can arise to impair the seals in waste pipes connected direct to a soil stack. Trap seals to waste pipes discharging into gullies are not affected because the pressure is atmospheric above and below the trap; in such cases it is usual to employ a trap with a 38 mm seal. The trap can be an S-trap as at C, Fig. 36, or a P-trap as at D. Such are, therefore, used for ground floor appliances and the waste pipes discharge into a gully below the grating (see p. 82 and C, Fig. 36), or into a back inlet gully (see p. 82).

W.C.s have a seal which is 50 mm deep and in the case of those at ground floor level they are merely connected direct to the drain, normally the S-trap W.C. is used (E, Fig. 36); if the P-trap kind were used part of the soil pipe would be outside the wall. A W.C. at the upper floors in a building must discharge into an internal soil stack for buildings more than 3 storeys high.

Preservation of Trap Seals.—The effects mentioned above which may occur to impair trap seals are three[1] : *self-siphonage, induced siphonage* and *back pressure*, they are summarised below and described in more detail in Vol. IV.

Self-siphonage.—This can happen in small bore pipes from sinks and washbasins. If the outfall end of a waste pipe is full of water and only partially full between there and the trap, suction may develop in the pipe length and draw water from the trap. This would reduce the depth of seal; it is prevented by having a 76 mm deep seal P-trap (not an S-trap) and limiting the slope and length of the waste pipe as described in the rules (see p. 93).

Induced Siphonage.—When a soil stack is temporarily and partially filled by a short column of water passing a waste pipe junction, the waste pipe trap suffers induced siphonage; this draws water from the seal. The discharge from a W.C. can be responsible for filling the stack but the effect is reduced by having a swept junction between the stack pipe and the W.C. pipe (*i.e.*, a curved angle (Y) as shown at B, Fig. 36).

Back Pressure.—This is an increase of pressure in pipes. It may happen at

---

[1] This has been shown as an intercepting chamber to satisfy the requirements of those local authorities who still advocate the use of the intercepting trap. As pointed out, however, on p. 89, many local authorities deprecate the use of interceptors, and therefore in those districts coming under their jurisdiction the trap may be omitted at the chamber at M which would then serve as an inspection chamber only.

[2] This is considered in greater detail in Vol. IV.

[1] There is another, caused by evaporation of water seals particularly in warm weather in unoccupied buildings.

SANITARY FITTINGS

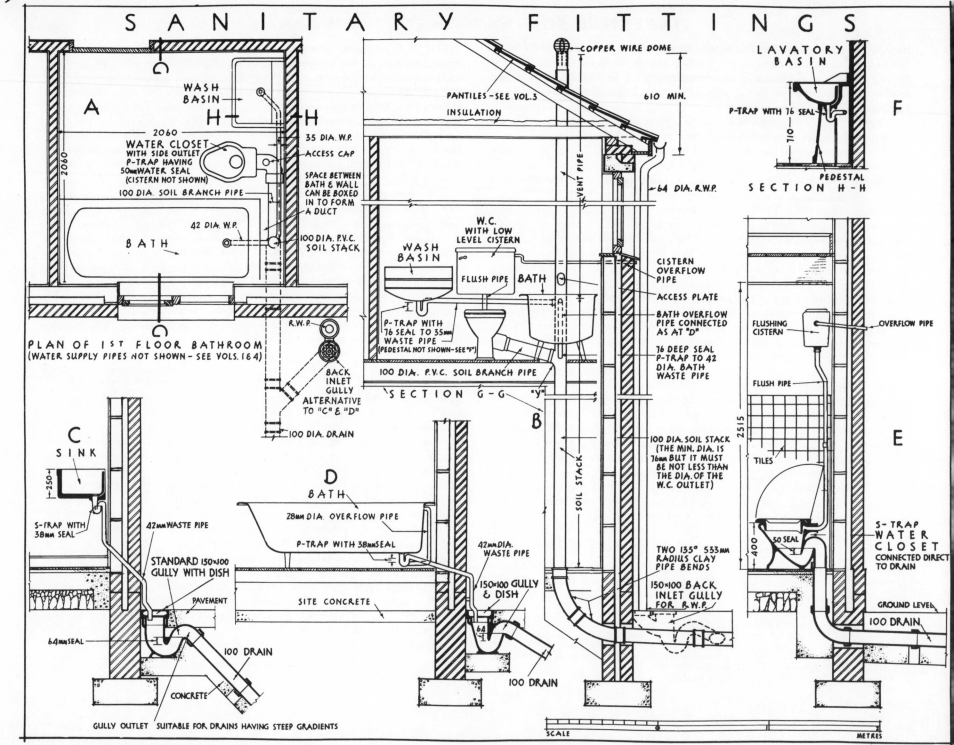

PLAN OF 1ST FLOOR BATHROOM (WATER SUPPLY PIPES NOT SHOWN - SEE VOLS. 1 & 4)

A

WASH BASIN

2060

WATER CLOSET WITH SIDE OUTLET P-TRAP HAVING 50mm WATER SEAL (CISTERN NOT SHOWN)

100 DIA. SOIL BRANCH PIPE

42 DIA. W.P.

BATH

2060

35 DIA. W.P.

ACCESS CAP

SPACE BETWEEN BATH & WALL CAN BE BOXED IN TO FORM A DUCT

100 DIA. P.V.C. SOIL STACK

R.W.P.

BACK INLET GULLY ALTERNATIVE TO "C" & "D"

100 DIA. DRAIN

SECTION G-G

PANTILES - SEE VOL. 3

INSULATION

COPPER WIRE DOME

610 MIN.

VENT PIPE

64 DIA. R.W.P.

WASH BASIN

W.C. WITH LOW LEVEL CISTERN

FLUSH PIPE

BATH

P-TRAP WITH 76 SEAL TO 35mm WASTE PIPE (PEDESTAL NOT SHOWN - SEE "F")

100 DIA. P.V.C. SOIL BRANCH PIPE

CISTERN OVERFLOW PIPE

ACCESS PLATE

BATH OVERFLOW PIPE CONNECTED AS AT "D"

76 DEEP SEAL P-TRAP TO 42 DIA. BATH WASTE PIPE

"Y"

B

SOIL STACK

100 DIA. SOIL STACK (THE MIN. DIA. IS 76mm BUT IT MUST BE NOT LESS THAN THE DIA. OF THE W.C. OUTLET)

TWO 135° 533mm RADIUS CLAY PIPE BENDS

150×100 BACK INLET GULLY FOR R.W.P.

C

SINK

250

S-TRAP WITH 38mm SEAL

42mm WASTE PIPE

STANDARD 150×100 GULLY WITH DISH

64mm SEAL

PAVEMENT

100 DRAIN

CONCRETE

GULLY OUTLET SUITABLE FOR DRAINS HAVING STEEP GRADIENTS

D

BATH

28mm DIA. OVERFLOW PIPE

P-TRAP WITH 38mm SEAL

SITE CONCRETE

42mm DIA. WASTE PIPE

150×100 GULLY & DISH

64

100 DRAIN

F

LAVATORY BASIN

P-TRAP WITH 76 SEAL

710

PEDESTAL

SECTION H-H

E

FLUSHING CISTERN

OVERFLOW PIPE

FLUSH PIPE

TILES

2515

50 SEAL

400

S-TRAP WATER CLOSET CONNECTED DIRECT TO DRAIN

GROUND LEVEL

100 DRAIN

SCALE

METRES

FIGURE 36

the foot of a soil stack near the bend connection to the drain. If the bend is sharp and the stack is full of liquid at a higher level any pipes connected to the stack between these levels will suffer increased pressure. It is for this reason that it is preferable to deliver ground floor waste pipes to a gully outside and not connect them to the stack. This effect is reduced by having a slow bend at the base of the soil stack (see B, Fig. 36).

Rules for Maximum Slope of Sink and Washbasin Waste Pipes.— The minimum slope is 21 mm per m and the pipe should not be longer than 1·7 m measured from the trap weir to the junction of the soil pipe. The maximum slope for waste pipes 1 700, 1 1140, 890, 710 mm long is 21, 41, 62 and 83 mm per m respectively.

Typical Soil and Waste Pipework for a House¹ (Fig. 36).—The detail at C shows a ground floor sink with 38 mm deep S-trap joined to a waste pipe which delivers below the grating of a gully. A similar arrangement applies for a ground floor bath (see D) or lavatory basin. At E there is the normal detail of a ground floor W.C. with 50 mm seal S-trap connected direct to the drain.

The remaining details are of first floor appliances connected to a soil stack; the plan of the bathroom which contains bath, washbasin, and W.C. is given at A. The soil stack is placed at the end of the bath where it can, if desired, be boxed in to form a duct. The bath has a 76 mm deep seal P-trap connecting to the 38 mm dia. bath waste pipe which delivers to the soil stack. A similar arrangement applies for the washbasin but it has a 32 mm dia. waste pipe (the minimum size demanded by the Building Regulations).

¹ See Vol. IV for pipework in larger buildings.

The W.C., with a side outlet P-trap, has the usual 50 mm water seal; it has a 100 mm dia. soil branch pipe connected to the stack. Note that the foot of the stack (see p. 78) has a slow bend formed from two 135° angle bends of clay drain pipes. The top of the stack is protected against obstruction with a garvanised iron (or copper) wire cage. The top of the stack (which is actually a ventilation pipe for its length above the top waste pipe connection) finishes 610 mm above eaves level to ensure that foul air cannot enter the house. The bath waste pipe connection to the stack should be either above or 205 mm below the junction of the W.C. branch with the stack to avoid siphonage effects on the waste pipe by discharges from the W.C. and prevent such discharges from backing up into the bath waste.

It is good practice to have an access cap in the stack near to the waste pipe connections to simplify cleansing in the event of a blockage. For the same reason the use of a W.C. with an access cap (or connection for a small dia. vent pipe—see Vol. IV) at the back of the water seal is advocated; this enables the soil branch pipe to be rodded—if a blockage does occur it is usually in this branch pipe.

The materials for the above pipework are described in Vol. IV; briefly, cast iron, galvanised steel, copper and pitch fibre, but, more often nowadays, plastic are used for the soil stack; with the same materials for the soil branch pipe and copper or plastic for the waste pipes and traps.

Tests for Soil, Waste and Ventilation Pipes—Such pipes must be capable, according to the Building Regulations, of withstanding a smoke or air test (see p. 86) for at least three minutes at a pressure equivalent to 38 mm of water, whilst maintaining a minimum water seal of 25 mm.

CHAPTER THREE

MASONRY

Syllabus.—Formation and classification of stones; characteristics, tests. Quarrying, mining and machine dressing. Stone dressings to door and window openings. Cornices. Stone steps and stairs.

BS 5390 Code of Practice for Stone Masonry is relevant.

Formation and Classification of Stones.—As stated in Chap. I, Vol. I, rocks are divided into three principal classes, *i.e.*, (1) igneous, (2) sedimentary and (3) metamorphic. These are considered in greater detail in this chapter.

Geology, which is the science concerned with the composition, structure and history of the materials of the earth, is briefly referred to here as an introduction to a study of the rocks used for building purposes.

The basic rocks of the earth's crust were formed from material molten by intense heat at the interior of the earth. Some of this material, such as granite (see next column), was consolidated at a great depth below the surface, whilst molten paste erupted from volcanoes solidified on the earth's surface to form rocks, such as, for example, those contained in the mountains of the Lake District, North Wales and the Scottish Highlands. Other rocks were formed from fragments of minerals disintegrated from the originally formed rocks by natural agencies, such as the expansive action of frost and the expansion and extraction due to alternate heat and cold, and removed by streams to form successive layers of sand, gravel, etc.; the pressure on the lower layers squeezed out the water and interlocked the grains, and, in addition, water charged with substances such as carbonate of lime and silica acted as cementing agents and hardened the mass of such sedimentary rocks during percolation; example of rocks formed in this manner are sandstones and limestones (see pp. 97–103). Marbles (see p. 105) and slates (see Chap. V, Vol. I) are examples of another class of rock formed from basic or sedimentary rocks which have been metamorphosed (altered) in structure as a result of lateral (side) pressure or heat or both. Yet another class of rocks is formed from the remains of marine organisms, and certain limestones (see p. 103), consisting of shells, corals, etc., are examples of these.

A classification of the known rocks of the earth's crust is given in Table VI on p. 96.

1. Igneous Rocks.—These have been formed of material which has been molten by the intense heat within the interior of the earth and become solidified. They are divided into (*a*) *plutonic* rocks, (*b*) *hypabyssal* rocks and (*c*) *volcanic* rocks.

(*a*) *Plutonic Rocks* are igneous rocks which have been consolidated at a considerable depth below the earth's surface; the erosion (wearing away) of the upper and softer strata has caused such rocks to appear at the earth's surface. Consolidation was gradual owing to the extremely slow rate of cooling, and such rocks are therefore completely crystalline and have a coarse-grained texture.

These rocks consist of silica in combination with bases such as iron, lime, magnesia, potash and soda, and they are classed as *acid*, *intermediate* or *basic*, according to the percentage of silica content. Thus, acid rocks have over 66 per cent. of silica, intermediate rocks have from 52 to 66 per cent. of silica, and the silica content of the basic group is less than 52 per cent.

The (i) *granites* are included in the acid group of plutonic rocks, the (ii) *syenites* and (iii) *diorites* are of the intermediate group, and the (iv) *gabbro* family forms the basic group. These are described below.

Constituent Minerals of Igneous Rocks.—These include quartz, felspar, mica, hornblende, augite, diallage, magnetite and pyrites.

Quartz is pure silica. The grains are hard and *extremely durable*; they are commonly colourless, although those of granite especially may vary in colour from pink, yellow, purple, red and brown to black.

Felspar is the group of minerals which is usually the most abundant. The grains are silicates of alumina combined with one or more of the bases—lime, potash and soda. Potash felspar is known as *orthoclase*; soda felspar or *albite* and soda-lime felspar or *oligoclase* are called *plagioclase* felspars. The colour of the plagioclases is usually white or light grey, and that of orthoclase crystals may be yellowish-pink, red or green.

Mica.—These crystals are silicates of alumina with potash or magnesia. The potash micas are silver white and have a bright lustre; one of the most important of these is known as *muscovite*. The magnesiam micas are dark brown or black, and the principal of these is called *biotite*. Mica appears as short, glittering scales or flakes parallel to the natural bed; these flakes are therefore an indication of the position of the natural bed. The white mica is very durable, but the biotite variety is softer and liable to decomposition.

Hornblende is of the *amphibole* group and is a silicate of magnesia, lime, aluminium and iron. The colour is green, brown or black.

Augite is a modification of hornblende, it being similar in comparison and colour but differing somewhat in the shape of the crystals.

Diallage is a variety of augite, green in colour the crystals are usually laminated.

Magnetite, or magnetic ore, has a bluish-black metallic lustre; it influences the colour of stones.

Pyrites is another iron ore. It occurs as small yellow specks. Crystals of the " white iron pyrites " variety, called *marcasite*, readily decompose, as the pale yellow changes to white efflorescence and the sulphuric acid formed in the process sets up decay in the stone.

(*a*) (i) *Granite.*—There are several kinds of this crystalline granular rock and these vary in colour and texture. The chief constituents are felspar, quartz and mica, the former being predominant; horneblende and augite are sometimes represented in addition to or in place of mica. If the mica present is the white variety, the rock is called a *muscovite granite*; a *biotite granite* contains the dark mica only; when both micas are present, it is known as a *muscovite-biotite granite*. A *hornblende-biotite granite* has a hornblende and dark mica content, and if hornblende without mica is present it is a *hornblende granite*.

The colour of granite is influenced chiefly by that of the felspar. The texture is also estimated by the size of the felspar crystals; thus, it is considered that granites containing felspar grains which exceed 10 mm in length are coarse-grained, those having felspars between 5 mm and 10 mm are medium-grained granites, and fine-grained granites have felspars less than 5 mm long.

Granites are extremely hard, durable and strong. Those with plagioclase felspars and dark micas are relatively less durable than granites having orthoclase felspars and light micas. As described on p. 114, granites are capable of taking a high polish and are therefore easily kept clean when employed in polluted atmospheres. Owing to their great hardness, granites are difficult to work and are thus expensive. This accounts for their restricted use for building purposes. Their very high strength and durable qualities render granites the best natural

stones for resisting high stresses and severe exposure; in addition, the rich mottled or speckled coloured appearance of certain granites make them most suitable for decorative use, as for wall and floor coverings, pillars, etc. Granites have been used on many important buildings (for plinths, external walls of lower storeys, and dressings to principal entrances, etc.), for memorials, and for engineering works (including docks, sea walls, embankments, lighthouses and bridges). In districts near the quarries, granites have been used exclusively for the construction of external walls of buildings; thus, the external walls of many of the buildings in Aberdeen are constructed of this material. Granite, because of its hard-wearing quality, is used for kerbs of streets, and for the same reason it has been extensively employed for road setts, although this form of road paving is not now favoured on account of the noise from traffic which results when streets are laid with setts. It is also used for coarse aggregates for concrete.

The principal centres in England where granites used for building purposes are quarried are Cornwall and Cumbria (Shap). Scottish granites are worked chiefly in Grampian Region (the most important centres being Aberdeen and Peterhead) and Dumfries and Galloway. The principal granite districts in

TABLE V

GRANITES

REF. No. (see Fig. 37)	NAME OF GRANITE	SITUATION OF QUARRY	NAME AND ADDRESS OF OWNER	CRUSHING STRENGTH MN/m²	WEIGHT kg/m³	CHARACTERISTICS
2	CORRENNIE .	Alford, Grampian Region	John Fyfe Ltd., Blaikie's Quay, Aberdeen, Scotland	0·183	2 600	A muscovite-biotite. Salmon red; medium grained.
8	CREETOWN .	Fell Hill and Silver Hill Quarries, Creetown, Dumfries and Galloway	Stewart & Co. Ltd., 25 Fraser Road, Aberdeen	0·148	2 700	A biotite. White (when hammered) and bluish-white (when polished); fine grained.
64	DE LANK SILVER GREY	De Lank, St Breward, Bodmin, Cornwall	Cornish De Lank Granite Quarries Ltd., De Lank, Bodmin, Cornwall	0·126	2 640	A muscovite-biotite. Light greenish-grey; medium grained.
3	KEMNAY . .	Near Aberdeen, Scotland	John Fyfe Ltd., Blaikie's Quay, Aberdeen, Scotland	0·213	2 640	A muscovite-biotite. Light silver-grey speckled with black mica; medium grained.
4	LOWER PERSLEY	Near Aberdeen, Scotland	George Hall, 17 Back Hilton Road, Aberdeen	0·138	2 660	A muscovite-biotite. Light bluish-grey; fine grained.
1	PETERHEAD, RED	Stirling Hill, Boddam, Peterhead, Grampian Region	Heslop Wilson & Co. Ltd., Peterhead Granite Works, Boddam, Grampian Region	0·138	2 800	A biotite. Brilliant red; coarse grained.
6	RUBISLAW .	Aberdeen, Scotland	Rubislaw Granite Co. Ltd. Queen's Road, Aberdeen	0·118	2 500	A muscovite-biotite. Bluish-grey; fine ground.
5	SCLATTIE .	Bucksburn, near Aberdeen	A. & F. Manuelle Ltd., 59 Marischal Street, Aberdeen	0·091	2 560	A muscovite-biotite. Light bluish-grey; medium grained.
16	SHAP . .	Shap, Cumbria	The Shap Granite Co. Ltd., Shap, Cumbria	0·161	2 640	A biotite. Greyish-pink (" Light Shap ") and reddish-brown " Dark Shap "); medium grained.
62 63	TOR BRAKE and TOR DOWN	St Breward, Bodmin, Cornwall	Wm. Nankivell & Sons Ltd., St Breward, Bodmin, Cornwall	0·161	2 610	A muscovite-biotite. Silvery-grey; medium grained.

TABLE VI

CLASSIFICATION OF STRATA

This classification of the known rocks of the earth's crust shows the complete geological history divided into three great *eras*, the Eozoic (meaning "dawn of life"), Palæozoic ("ancient life)" and Neozoic ("new life"). The eras are divided into *periods* and the latter are divided into *epochs*. The mass of rock of an era is known as a *group*, the rocks of each period a *system*, and those of an epoch are referred to as a *series*. The strata are shown in correct sequence, the oldest (those in the Eozoic group) being at the bottom of the table.

Group or Era	System or Period	Series or Epoch	Building Stones, Slates, Marbles, Granites, Limes, etc., Found
NEOZOIC — Cainozoic	Post-pliocene	Recent Strata / Glacial Beds / Forest Bed	... / ...
	Pliocene	Norwich Crag / Red Crag / Caralline Crag	Gravels.
	Miocene		...
	Oligocene	Hamstead Beds / Bembridge Beds / Osborne Beds / Headon Beds	Clays and sands.
	Eocene	Bagshot Beds / Barton Clay / Bracklesham Beds / London Clay / Woolwich Beds / Thanet Sands	Clays, sands and gravels.
NEOZOIC — Mesozoic	Cretaceous	Upper Cretaceous / Middle Cretaceous / Lower Cretaceous / Upper Oölites	... Kentish Rag Stone. Portland Limestone. Limestone yielding Lime
	Jurassic	Middle Oölites / Lower Oölites	Limestones, including Ancaster and Clipsham
		Lias	Limestones, including Blue Lias Stone yielding lime (see p. 20).
	Triassic	Rhætic / Keuper / Bunter	... Sandstones, including Hollington. Sandstones, including Corsehill, St. Bees and Shawk.

Group or Era	System or Period	Series or Epoch	Building Stones, Slates, Marbles, Granites, Limes, etc., Found
PALÆOZOIC — New Palæozoic	Permian	Upper Permian / Middle Permian	Sandstones, including Lazonby. Magnesian Limestones, including Anston, Linby and Park, Nook.
		Lower Permian	Magnesian Sandstones, including Red and White Mansfield.
	Carboniferous	Coal Measures	Sandstones, including Springwell, and Woodkirk.
		Millstone Grit	Sandstones, including Dunn House and Stanton in Peak. ...
	Devonian	Yoredale Beds / Carboniferous Limestone / Upper Devonian / Old Red Sandstone	English Marbles, including Hopton-Wood. Limestone yielding lime. Slates, including Cornish (Delabole). Sandstones, used locally in Gloucestershire, Northumberland, etc. (see p. 94).
		Middle Devonian	Certain limestones and English Marble ...
PALÆOZOIC — Older Palæozoic	Silurian	Lower Devonian / Ludlow Beds / Wenlock Beds	... Welsh Slates, including Corwen and Llangollen.
	Ordovician	Llandovery Beds / Bala Beds / Llandeilo Beds	... Welsh Slates, including Festiniog and Precelly. Lake District Slates, including Buttermere, Honister, Elterwater, Kentmere and Tilberthwaite; also Burlington Quarry. ...
	Cambrian	Arenig Beds / Olenus Beds / Paradoxides Beds / Olenellus Beds	... Welsh Slates, including Bangor, Dinorwic and Penrhyn.
EOZOIC	Pre-Cambrian	...	Mainly igneous (including Granites, see Table III). Scottish Slates from Argyll, Dumbarton and Perth.

Ireland are in counties Down, Dublin, Wexford and Wicklow. Norwegian (grey) and Swedish (grey, red and black) granites are also imported into the United Kingdom, much of it being dressed in the Aberdeen district. The distribution of granites in Great Britain is shown in Fig. 37[1] and listed in Table V.

As indicating the composition of granite, that of the De Lank Silver Grey Granite (see Table V) consists of quartz 46 per cent., orthoclase felspar 30 per cent., plagioclase felspar 6 per cent., muscovite (white mica) 11 per cent. and biotite (black mica) 7 per cent.

> (a) (ii) *Syenite.*—None of the true syenite quarried in this country is used for building purposes. It occurs in Leicestershire, Gwynedd, the Highlands of Scotland and the Channel Islands, where it is quarried and used for road material. A well-known syenite, called "Pearl Granite," is imported from Norway and used for plinths to shop fronts, etc.; it has a mottled appearance, with dark green markings and light-coloured patches. Syenite is hard, durable, strong and more easily worked than granite. Quartz is usually absent, felspar is the prevalent mineral, hornblende is present, and the mica content is usually less than in granite.
>
> (a) (iii) *Diorite.*—This occurs in Leicestershire and Gwynedd. It is difficult to work, and this, in addition to its dull green or black colour, renders it unsuitable for building purposes. It is sometimes known as *greenstone*, and is used as road metal. *Whinstone* is the name applied in Scotland to this stone, although in certain localities this name is given to any stone which is difficult to work or to stone used in road construction. Felspar, hornblende, augite and dark mica are present, and quartz is usually absent.
>
> (a) (iv) *Gabbro* is quarried in Cornwall, certain parts of Wales, and in the Scottish Highlands. It is rarely used for building purposes on account of its bad weathering qualities and its dull appearance. Felspar, hornblende, augite or diallage are the chief minerals of gabbro.
>
> (b) *Hypabyssal Rocks.*—These were masses of molten material which penetrated the overlying strata, and erosion of the latter has exposed these rocks at the surface. Cooling of the masses was more rapid than with the plutonic rocks, and their texture is therefore finer. Hypabyssal rocks, like plutonic rocks, are classed as acid, intermediate and basic. The rocks of the acid group are called *quartz porphyries*, those of the intermediate group are *porphyries* and *porphyrites*, and *dolerites* and *diabases* are of the basic group. The quartz porphyries and porphyrites occur in Cornwall and Devon (when they are known as *elvans*), North and South Wales and in Scotland; some of them readily take a polish and have been used for ornamental purposes and general walling; they are now used chiefly for breaking up into aggregates for concrete and road purposes. The porphyrites are quarried in Leicester, Somerset, Gwynedd, etc.; they are very tough and are commonly used for road metal. The dolerites and diabases have a wide distribution throughout Great Britain and are employed extensively for roads (the stone being sometimes crushed, screened, dried and coated with bitumen to form tarmacadam) and rough walling; this stone is known in the north as "whinstone."
>
> (c) *Volcanic Rocks* have been formed from lava poured out at the surface from volcanoes. Rapid cooling and hardening caused the material to be fine grained and of glassy character. Their group classification are *rhyolites* (acid), *trachytes* and *andesites* (intermediate) and *basalt* (basic). They are quarried in England, Scotland, Wales and Ireland, and are employed for road construction.

2. Sedimentary or Aqueous Rocks.—This division comprises those stones which are chiefly employed for building purposes. Most of these rocks are

[1] Only some of the important quarries producing granite for building purposes are indicated here. A number of well-known quarries have been closed down because of the absence of demand, and a large number of igneous rock quarries produce stone which is used solely as road metal and for concrete aggregates.

formed of fragments of igneous rocks which have been deposited by water in layers or strata. As successive layers were formed, these sediments became hardened and consolidated by great pressure and were cemented together by sandy or clayey paste or by a chemical substance (such as carbonate of lime) conveyed by the percolating water. Other rocks of this division are formed from the remains of marine organisms (shellfish, etc.) and chemically by precipitation. The principal sedimentary rocks are (a) sandstones and (b) limestones.

(a) *Sandstones.*—These consist of grains of quartz (sand or silica, see p. 94) held together by a cement or matrix. In addition to quartz, sandstones may contain such minerals as mica, felspar, hornblende and oxides of iron (see p. 94). The texture of the stone is influenced by the size and distribution of the grains; thus, a stone may vary from fine to coarse-grained, and be either compact or the grains may be more sparsely distributed in the cementing material. As the quartz grains are practically indestructible, the durability of sandstones and grits (see p. 98) depends chiefly upon the cementing material. With the exception of freestones (see p. 98), sandstones are highly stratified, the *bedding* or natural bed being clearly visible as a general rule. The beds vary in thickness from a few cm to many metres.

The principal cements, the composition of which varies considerably, are *siliceous*, *calcareous*, *ferruginous* and *argillaceous*; two or more of these substances may be present in the cement. Sandstones are classified according to the nature of the binding material, thus (i) *siliceous sandstones*, (ii) *calcareous sandstones*, (iii) *ferruginous sandstones* and (iv) *argillaceous sandstones*. They may also be classified as (v) *micaceous sandstones* and (vi) *felspathic sandstones*, if either mica or felspar respectively is present in fair quantity. In addition, sandstones are classified according to the character of the grains and degree of the stratification, *e.g.*, (vii) *gritstones*, (viii) *flagstones*, (ix) *tilestones*, (x) *liver stones*, (xi) *freestones* and (xii) *York stone*.

(a) (i) *Siliceous Sandstones.*—The grains of these stones are held together by siliceous cement (silica deposited from solution in water). Such sandstones are exceedingly durable, as the silica has good cementing properties and is not attacked by acids in the atmosphere. They are very hard and are usually difficult to work. Examples of siliceous sandstones are the gritstones (see p. 98 and Table VII).

(a) (ii) *Calcareous Sandstones.*—The grains are bound together by calcareous cement, which is composed of *calcite* (crystals of carbonate of lime) or a combination of carbonate of lime and carbonate of magnesia and known as *dolomite* (when they are called *dolomitic sandstones*). Whilst both calcite and dolomite have good binding qualities, they are not durable if exposed to polluted atmospheres owing to the acids attacking the matrix and loosening the grains of sand which gradually become removed by the weather. These stones are easily worked. White Mansfield is an example of a dolomitic sandstone (see p. 101).

(a) (iii) *Ferruginous Sandstones.*—The cementing material is largely ferruginous, *i.e.*, oxides of iron deposited from solution. This influences the colour (such as brown, red, brownish-yellow, etc.) of the stone. These are good weathering stones, although they may be affected by frost action in very exposed situations. Hollington and Woodkirk Brown are of this class (see Table VII).

(a) (iv) *Argillaceous Sandstones* are of inferior quality and unsuitable as building stones owing to the argillaceous (clayey) cement becoming soft when wetted by rain.

(a) (v) *Micaceous Sandstones* are those in which white mica (muscovite, see p. 90) is prominent. The mica is clearly visible as glittering flakes lying with their longest faces parallel to the bedding planes. The presence of mica thus assists in indicating the direction of the natural bed of a stone. An example is Red Corsehill (see Table VII).

(a) (vi) *Felspathic Sandstones* contain felspar in subsidiary amounts. Stones of this class are quarried in different parts of the country, including Hereford & Worcester and Salop, and are used locally.

(a) (vii) *Gritstones* or *Grits*.—These are strong, hard and durable stones. The sand grains are often coarse and angular, giving a rough texture, and the cement is siliceous. An example is Dunn House, (see Table VII).

(a) (viii) *Flagstones* are strongly laminated and are therefore readily split along the bedding planes. They are used as paving or flagging stones, treads of steps, etc. Many quarries in Yorkshire produce sharp, annular-grained, hard-wearing and clearly laminated stone suitable for these purposes.

(a) (ix) *Tilestones*.—These are thinner-bedded stones than flagstones and are used for covering roofs, *e.g.*, traditional in the Cotswold District (thin bedded limestone) and in Yorkshire (thin bedded sandstone). See Vol. III.

(a) (x) *Liver or Knell Stones*.—These are known as " thick-bedded," and, as implied, large blocks of the stone can be obtained. Many sandstones and limestones are in this class.

(a) (xi) *Freestones* are those which are fine-grained. They have no well-defined bedding planes and can be easily dressed. Examples are Red Corsehill and Locharbriggs (see Table VII).

(a) (xii) *York Stone*.—This is a term applied to sandstones from Yorkshire, and more particularly to those from that county which are specially hard, strong and durable, and specified as being suitable for steps, sills, lintels, copings, landings, etc.

Whilst the present demand for every description of stone for building purposes is less than formerly, those of the sandstone class form one of the most valuable walling materials. The weathering properties of stones are discussed on p. 106, and reference is made to the severe test imposed on stone by sulphuric acid from smoke polluted atmospheres. It has been pointed out that the durability of sandstones depends very largely upon the cementing material (see p. 97) as the quartz is practically indestructible. Siliceous sandstones (p. 97) are therefore generally considered to be the most durable of the sedimentary rocks, as the binding material of silica is highly resistant to acid attack. The excellent state of preservation of many ancient buildings built of this stone is evidence of this. Unfortunately, city buildings constructed of sandstone often assume a drab appearance owing to the dark discoloration which results. Many sandstones are exceptionally hard, and for this reason are selected for steps, sills, etc. Some are difficult to work, but others of the freestone (see preceding column) class are good chiselling stones and are very suitable for moulded work. Sandstone is an excellent and frequently used material for road construction and concrete aggregates.

Sandstones are very widely distributed throughout the British Isles. The distribution of some of the more important quarries producing building stone is shown in Fig. 37. This does not include the large number of small quarries which are worked, often intermittently, to supply sandstone for building purposes locally.

A selection of some of the principal quarries producing sandstones used for building purposes is listed in Table VII. The chemical composition of a few building sandstones is shown in Table IX. An enlarged sketch showing approximately the structure of a sandstone such as is seen under the microscope[1] is shown at A, Fig. 38. See footnote to p. 102.

Whilst granites and certain slates are obtained from the Pre-Cambrian and Cambrian systems respectively (see Table VI), much of the stone is either inaccessible, or too difficult to work or is of unsatisfactory appearance. The Ordovician system does not provide building sandstones beyond beds of flagstones which are quarried for local use. Flagstones and grits are quarried from the Silurian system and used locally. Good building sandstones are quarried from the Old Red Sandstone series of the Devonian system and used locally in counties Gloucestershire, Hereford & Worcester, Salop, Gwent, Northumberland and Grampian Region; sandstones from the other series of this system are unimportant. Several good quality building sandstones have in the past been quarries in the North of England and in Scotland from the Carboniferous Limestone and Yoredale Beds series of the Carboniferous system and used on important buildings, but they are now chiefly used locally.

The most prolific sources of best sandstone employed for building purposes are obtained from the (i) Millstone Grit and (ii) Coal Measures series of the Carboniferous system (see Tables VI and VII).

(i) *Millstone Grit*.—Whilst this series of strata, consisting of regular beds of gritstone, has a wide distribution throughout the country, it has been most extensively developed in Derbyshire, Lancashire and Yorkshire, where much excellent building stone is quarried.

(ii) *Coal Measures*.—This formation is widely distributed. The chief quarries are situated in Durham, Glamorgan, Strathclyde and Lothian Region. The stone is quarried in other counties and used locally. In general, this stone is hard, durable and of a good colour.

Sandstones for building purposes from the Permian system are quarried in Cumbria (Lazonby); local stone is also used from this system in the south-west of this country. The Bunter and Keuper series of the Triassic system yield good building sandstones in Cheshire, Cumbria, Lancashire, Salop, Staffordshire, Warwickshire, Hereford & Worcester, and Dumfries & Galloway.

Building sandstones are rare in the Jurassic system. There is none of much importance in the Cretaceous strata, and stone in the Cainozoic group is too soft for building purposes.

---

[1] A thin piece of the stone, approximately 16 mm square with smoothed faces, is mounted (secured by an adhesive), on a piece of glass known as a *slide*. The specimen is then reduced to the required thickness, which may be not more than 0·025 mm; this is done by rubbing it on a piece of glass on which water and an abrasive (carborundum) is applied. An examination of the slide under the microscope will show the structure of the stone.

TABLE VII
SANDSTONES

Ref. No. (see Fig. 37)	Name of Stone	Situation of Quarry	Name and Address of Owner	Geological Identification		Crushing Strength (MN/m)	Weight (kg/m³)	Characteristics	Porosity (per cent.) (see p. 107)	Saturation Coefficient (see p. 107)	Result of Frost Test (see p. 110)	Crystalli- sation Test (see pp. 109) % age Weight Loss
				Series	System							
20	CORSEHILL, RED	Annan, Dumfries & Galloway	Dunhouse Quarry Ltd, Bishop Auckland, Durham	Bunter	Triassic	0·0684	2 080	coarse grained Pink pastel; durable; close grained; good working	22	0·60	Weathered a little at arrises	93
21	DUNHOUSE	Darlington, Durham	Dunhouse Quarry Ltd, Bishop Auckland, Durham	,,	,,	0·0503	2 160	Light brown; very durable; medium grained; very free working	15	0·66	..	86
22	HOLLINGTON	Hollington and Great Gate, Stoke-on-Trent	J. Oldham & Co, Hollington, Stoke on Trent	Keuper	Triassic	0·028 (W. and S.) 0·031 (Red) 0·035 (Mottled)	2 130 2 160 2 210	White and salmon : very dur- able; fine texture; free work- ing. Red and motttled : very durable; harder than above; free working	19	0·75	..	90
23	KERRIDGE	Macclesfield, Derbyshire	Macclesfield Stone Quarries Ltd, Stoke on Trent	Millstone Grit	Carbonif- erous	0·0623	2 450	Buff; very hard and durable; fine to medium texture; good working; obtainable in large blocks	5	0·90	Undamaged	2
24	LAZONBY	Penrith, Cumbria	Realstone Ltd, Chesterfield	Upper Permian	Permian	..	2 340	" Red " (light terra-cotta) and " White " (light yellowish- pink); very hard and dur- able; coarse grained; diffi- cult to work	9.3	0.47	Undamaged	22
25	LOCHARBRIGGS	Dumfries, Scotland	Baird & Stevenson Ltd, Locharbriggs, Dumfries	Bunter	Triassic	0·044	2 000	Pale salmon pink; durable; medium texture; free work- ing; obtainable in large blocks	25	0·70	Weathered a little at arrises	22
26	SHAWK	Thursby, near Carlisle	John Laing Construction, Carlisle	Bunter	Triassic	..	2 210	Red, white and flecked; very durable; fine texture; free working; very suitable for carving	18	0·68	..	45
27	SPRINGWELL	Gateshead, Co. Durham	Natural Stone Quarries Ltd., Gateshead	Coal Measures	Carbonif- erous	..	2 560	Yellow; very durable; medium grained; fairly easy to work	..	..	..	..
28	ST. BEES, RED	St. Bees, Cumbria	Natural Stone Quarries Ltd, Gateshead	Bunter	Triassic	0·042	2 280	Bright red; very durable; fine grained; good working	..	..	..	38
29	STANCLIFFE	Darley Dale Derbyshire	Realstone Ltd., Chesterfield	Millstone Grit	Carbonif- erous	0·0695	2 320	Honey to very light drab; very hard and durable; uniform texture, close-grained; good working	13	0·65	..	95
30	STANTON Moor	Stanton in Peak, Matlock	Stancliffe Stone Co. Ltd., Tideswell, Derbyshire	,,	,,	0·055	2 240	Brown; very durable; fine texture	16	0·68	..	..
31	WOODKIRK BROWN	Morley, Near Leeds	Pawson Bros. Ltd, Morley	,,	,,	0·0552	2 280	Brown; durable; fine grained; good working	14	0·65	..	86

TABLE VIII—LIMESTONES

REF. No. (see Fig. 37)	NAME OF STONE and Durability class (see pp 109)	SITUATION OF QUARRY	NAME AND ADDRESS OF OWNERS	GEOLOGICAL IDENTIFICATION SERIES	SYSTEM	CRUSHING STRENGTH (MN/m²)	WEIGHT (kg/m³)	CHARACTERISTICS	POROSITY (per cent.) (see p. 107)	SATURATION COEFFICIENT (see p. 107)	CRYSTALLISATION TEST (see pp. 109) % AGE WEIGHT LOSS
32	ANCASTER BROWN WEATHER BED D to F	Ancaster, Lincolnshire	The Gregory Quarries Ltd., Mansfield, Notts	Lower Oölites	Jurassic	0·0163	2 500	Brown with grey and buff mottling; not durable in polluted atmospheres; coarse grained; free working; takes high polish	..	..	19
33	CLIPSHAM A to D	Clipsham, Leics	P.G. Medwell & Son, Clipsham	Lower Oölites	Jurassic	0·0314	2 240	Pale cream; durable in non-polluted atmospheres; medium grained; free working	16	0.80	16
34	HOPTON-WOOD A to B	Wirksworth, Derbyshire	Tarmac Roadstone, Matlock, Derbyshire	Carboniferous Limestone	Carboniferous	..	2 400	(See p. 104)	7.6	0.61	..
35	HORNTON A to C	Edge Hill, Oxfordshire	Hornton Quarries Ltd., North Bar, Banbury, Oxfordshire	Lower Oölites	Jurassic	..	2 120	Brown, blue and mixture of both; close grained; easily worked; takes a good polish	21	0.7	..
36	PORTLAND[2] A to D	Isle of Portland, Dorset	Kingston Minerals., Ltd., Portland	Upper Oölites	Jurassic	0·0308	2 210	Whitbed most suitable for general building purposes; light brown or white; durable; medium grained; good working	18	0.67	12
37	WELDON C	Weldon Northants	Weldon Stone Enterprises, Castle Ashby	Lower Oölites	Jurassic	..	1 920	Pinkish-brown; not durable in polluted atmospheres; coarse grained; easily worked	29	0.75	13
MAGNESIAN LIMESTONES											
38	PARK NOOK B	Park Nook, Skelbrooke, Near Doncaster	Neil Butcher, Skelbrooke	Middle Permian	Permian	0·37	2 180	Cream; durable in non-polluted atmospheres; fine grained and compact; easily worked; suitable for carved work	23	0.80	30
MAGNESIAN SANDSTONE											
39	MANSFIELD, WHITE B	Mansfield, Nottinghamshire	The Gregory Quarries Ltd., Mansfield, Notts	Lower Permian	Permian	0·495	2 240	Creamy-yellow; not durable in polluted atmospheres; fine even grained	15.3	0.63	59

[1] Portland stone is also quarried by The South-Western Stone Co. Ltd. (Thessaly Road, Battersea, London, S.W.8) in the Isle of Portland.
[2] Red Mansfield stone (warm red colour due to greater iron oxide content) is also quarried.

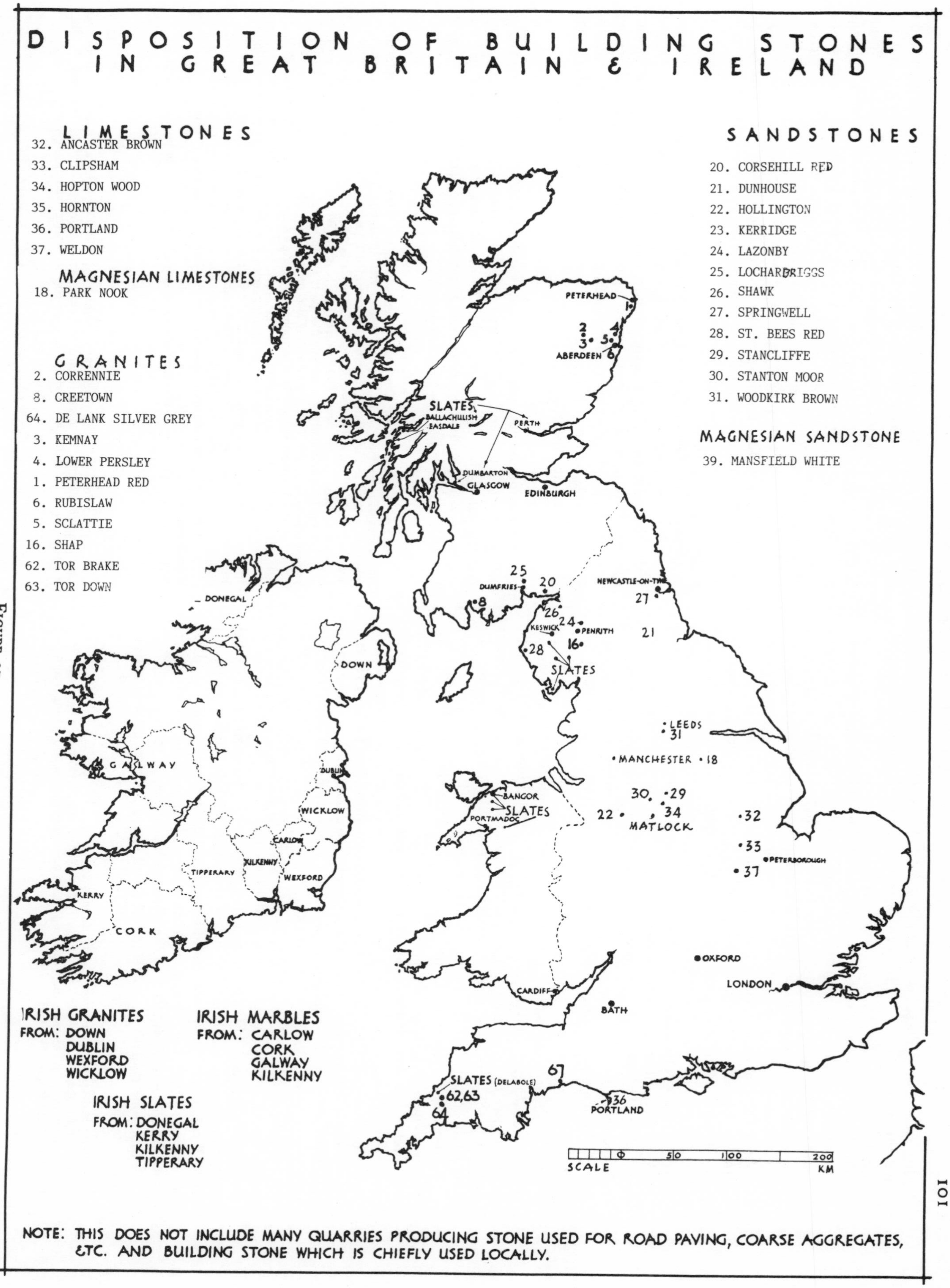
DISPOSITION OF BUILDING STONES IN GREAT BRITAIN & IRELAND
LIMESTONES
32. ANCASTER BROWN
33. CLIPSHAM
34. HOPTON WOOD
35. HORNTON
36. PORTLAND
37. WELDON
MAGNESIAN LIMESTONES
18. PARK NOOK
GRANITES
2. CORRENNIE
8. CREETOWN
64. DE LANK SILVER GREY
3. KEMNAY
4. LOWER PERSLEY
1. PETERHEAD RED
6. RUBISLAW
5. SCLATTIE
16. SHAP
62. TOR BRAKE
63. TOR DOWN
SANDSTONES
20. CORSEHILL RED
21. DUNHOUSE
22. HOLLINGTON
23. KERRIDGE
24. LAZONBY
25. LOCHARBRIGGS
26. SHAWK
27. SPRINGWELL
28. ST. BEES RED
29. STANCLIFFE
30. STANTON MOOR
31. WOODKIRK BROWN
MAGNESIAN SANDSTONE
39. MANSFIELD WHITE
PETERHEAD
ABERDEEN
SLATES
BALLACHULISH
EASDALE
PERTH
DUMBARTON
GLASGOW
EDINBURGH
DUMFRIES
NEWCASTLE-ON-TYNE
KESWICK
PENRITH
SLATES
LEEDS
MANCHESTER
MATLOCK
BANGOR
SLATES
PORTMADOC
PETERBOROUGH
OXFORD
LONDON
CARDIFF
BATH
SLATES (DELABOLE)
PORTLAND
DONEGAL
DOWN
GALWAY
DUBLIN
WICKLOW
CARLOW
KILKENNY
TIPPERARY
WEXFORD
KERRY
CORK
SCALE 0 50 100 200 KM
IRISH GRANITES
FROM: DOWN
DUBLIN
WEXFORD
WICKLOW
IRISH MARBLES
FROM: CARLOW
CORK
GALWAY
KILKENNY
IRISH SLATES
FROM: DONEGAL
KERRY
KILKENNY
TIPPERARY
NOTE: THIS DOES NOT INCLUDE MANY QUARRIES PRODUCING STONE USED FOR ROAD PAVING, COARSE AGGREGATES, ETC. AND BUILDING STONE WHICH IS CHIEFLY USED LOCALLY.

FIGURE 37

(b) *Limestones.*—These are called *calcareous* (" limey ") *rocks*, as they consist mainly of carbonate of lime. They are formed either by (i) organic or (ii) chemical agencies.

(b) (i) Those of organic origin are formed of the fossil remains of mulluscs (minute animal organisms, such as snails, furnished with shells which consist of calcium carbonate), corals, etc., that have been deposited in lakes or in sea basins, and the accumulations subsequently hardened into rocks by pressure and cementing material. These are known as *shelly limestones*, well-known examples being Ancaster, Clipsham and Weldon (see Table VIII and D, Fig. 38).

(b) (ii) Limestones of the chemically formed group consist of grains, each having a central core or nucleus (probably a sand grain or a fragment of a shell) round which concentric layers of calcium carbonate have been deposited from water. These grains, having the appearance of eggs or roe of a fish, are called *oölites*, and the stone is sometimes referred to as " egg stone "[1] or " roe stone " (see B and C, Fig. 38). The grains vary in size, stones having large grains being called *pistolite*. Fragments of shells may be present. Portland stone, Clipsham and Hornton are well-known examples of oölitic limestones (e.g. Portland, Fig 38[2]).

The grains are cemented together by a matrix consisting of carbonate of lime, called *calcite*, or a mixture of carbonate of lime, silica, alumina and magnesia. In some cases the grains are only cemented together at their points of contact (see B, Fig. 38), in other types (see C and D, Fig. 38) the cementing material completely occupies the spaces between the grains.

Carbonate of magnesia is present in most limestones (see Table X). Stones containing a relatively high proportion of this carbonate are called *magnesian limestones*. If the magnesium carbonate and calcium carbonate are present in approximately equal proportions, the rocks are called *dolomites* or *dolomitic limestones*; Park Nook is an example of dolomites (see Tables VIII and X). A magnesian stone containing a large proportion of silica is classed as a *calcareous* or *dolomitic* or *magnesian sandstone*; White Mansfield stone is of this type (see p. 97 and Tables VIII and IX).

Limestones are used extensively for building purposes. Their weathering properties are referred to on p. 105. Many are excellent for internal work on account of their agreeable colour and free working qualities, and for external walling in districts free from atmospheric pollution. Whilst certain limestones are well established as suitable building stones and have been widely used for this purpose, others are quite unsuited for external walls of buildings in districts where acid gases are produced by the burning of coal (see p. 105).

A limestone generally considered to be well suited for external ashlar work subjected to acid attack is Portland stone. It has been employed during the past three hundred years for many important buildings in London and the provinces, and whilst the external faces are liable to become affected, the erosion is usually so slight (sheltered surfaces being possibly an exception, see p. 107) and uniform as not to be detrimental. Another reason for its popularity is the attractive appearance of light and shade produced on the weathered surfaces of this stone. As mentioned in Chap. I, Vol. I, there are three[1] beds in a Portland stone quarry which yield stone used for constructional work, *e.g.*, the roach bed, whitbed and basebed, the whitbed being most suitable for general purposes. The structure of whitbed stone is illustrated at B, Fig. 38.

Many limestones are fine grained and easily worked. Some like Weldon are so soft immediately after being quarried that they can be readily sawn and chiselled, and their fine grain and even texture render them particularly suited for delicate carving. It is because of these characteristics, together with their agreeable appearance, that they are selected for internal ecclesiastical work such as pulpits and altar screens. Kentish Rag, a hard siliceous limestone (see Chap. I, Vol. I) is not easy to work.

The distribution of certain important limestone quarries and mines is shown in Fig. 37. These limestones are listed in Table VIII. The chemical composition of some of them is given in Table X. Some idea of the structure of limestones may be obtained by reference to the enlarged sketches at B, C and D, Fig. 38.

The Pre-Cambrian, Cambrian and Ordovician systems do not contribute any building limestones of importance. The Silurian system yields building limestones in Shropshire where it is used locally. Good limestone is obtained from the Middle Devonian series; some are finely veined and are of a rich colour. The Carboniferous Limestone series furnishes highly decorative limestone in Derbyshire (*e.g.*, Hopton-Wood); this takes a high polish and is classed commercially as a marble (see p. 104); stone from this series is used locally in Somerset and South Wales; local use is also made in Yorkshire. Magnesian limestone occurs in the Permian system in Nottingham and Yorkshire. The Triassic system does not yield any building limestones.

The Jurassic system, especially the Oölites series, furnishes many important building limestones. A few are from the Lias series, including those quarried and employed locally in Oxfordshire, Hereford & Worcester, Warwickshire and Wales. Ancaster and Clipsham stones are from the Lower Oölites, and Portland stone is from the Upper Oölites series.

Kentish Rag, used for rubble masonry in the South of England, is from the Lower Cretaceous series and the white Beer stone is from the Middle Cretaceous series. As mentioned on p. 98, none of the rocks in the Cainozoic group is sufficiently hard for building purposes.

---

[1] Oölite is derived from *oon* = egg and *lithos* = stone.

[2] It will be observed that, in order to provide a useful comparison, A, B, C and D, Fig. 38, have been sketched on the same scale, a portion of each prepared slide being magnified and projected to permit of this.

[1] In some Portland stone quarries, a bed of stone below the whitbed has been discovered which yields a highly decorative hard and compact limestone, known as "Perrycot." This is sawn into 25 mm thick slabs and is used for decorative wall linings, etc.

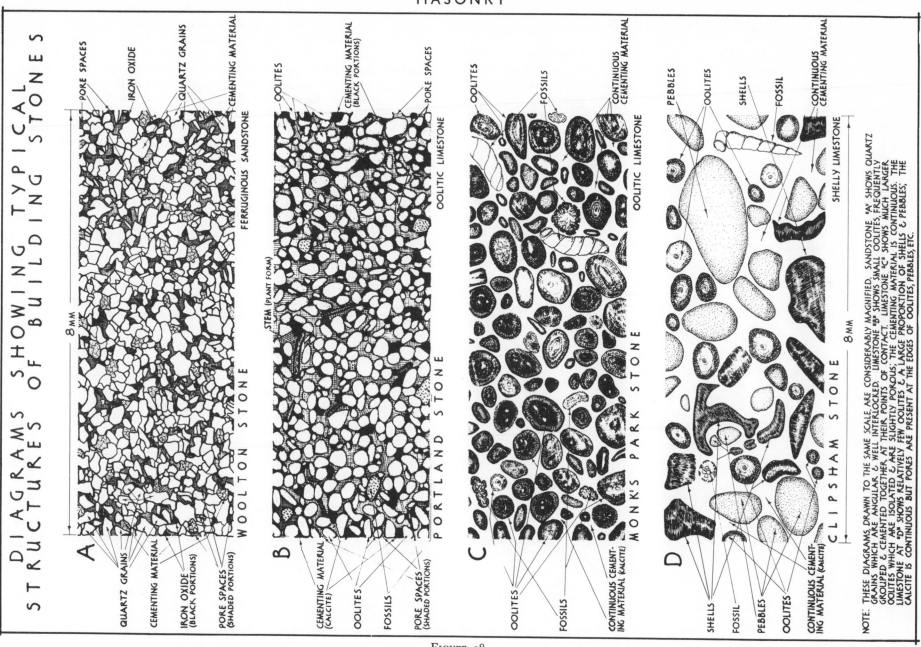

DIAGRAMS SHOWING TYPICAL
STRUCTURES OF BUILDING STONES

A — WOOLTON STONE — FERRUGINOUS SANDSTONE

8MM

PORE SPACES
IRON OXIDE
QUARTZ GRAINS
CEMENTING MATERIAL

QUARTZ GRAINS
CEMENTING MATERIAL
IRON OXIDE (BLACK PORTIONS)
PORE SPACES (SHADED PORTIONS)

B — PORTLAND STONE — OOLITIC LIMESTONE

OOLITES
CEMENTING MATERIAL (BLACK PORTIONS)
PORE SPACES

STEM (PLANT FORM)

CEMENTING MATERIAL (CALCITE)
OOLITES
FOSSILS
PORE SPACES (SHADED PORTIONS)

C — MONK'S PARK STONE — OOLITIC LIMESTONE

OOLITES
FOSSILS
CONTINUOUS CEMENTING MATERIAL

OOLITES
FOSSILS
CONTINUOUS CEMENTING MATERIAL (CALCITE)

D — CLIPSHAM STONE — SHELLY LIMESTONE

PEBBLES
OOLITES
SHELLS
FOSSIL
CONTINUOUS CEMENTING MATERIAL

8MM

SHELLS
FOSSIL
PEBBLES
OOLITES
CONTINUOUS CEMENTING MATERIAL (CALCITE)

NOTE: THESE DIAGRAMS, DRAWN TO THE SAME SCALE, ARE CONSIDERABLY MAGNIFIED. SANDSTONE "A" SHOWS QUARTZ GRAINS WHICH ARE ANGULAR & WELL INTERLOCKED. LIMESTONE "B" SHOWS SMALL OOLITES, FREQUENTLY GROUPED & CEMENTED TOGETHER, AT THEIR POINTS OF CONTACT. LIMESTONE "C" SHOWS MUCH LARGER OOLITES WHICH ARE ISOLATED & ARE SLIGHTLY POROUS; THE CEMENTING MATERIAL IS CONTINUOUS. THE LIMESTONE AT "D" SHOWS RELATIVELY FEW OOLITES & A LARGE PROPORTION OF SHELLS & PEBBLES; THE CALCITE IS CONTINUOUS BUT PORES ARE PRESENT AT THE EDGES OF OOLITES, PEBBLES, ETC.

FIGURE 38

TABLE IX
CHEMICAL COMPOSITION OF SANDSTONES

Reference No. (see Fig. 37)	Name of Stone	Silica	Alumina	Oxides of Iron	Carbonate of Lime	Carbonate of Magnesia	Titanium Oxide, Potash, etc.	Soda, etc.	Water and Loss
20	Corsehill, Red .	95·33	0·59	1·28	1·49	1·31	...	...	...
21	Dunhouse .	97·30	0·85		0·30	0·25	...	...	1·30
22	Hollington .	86·64	8·78	1·02	0·72	0·44	...	0·40	2·00
25	Locharbriggs .	97·88	0·38	0·80	0·25	0·10	...	...	0·59
39	Mansfield, White .	51·62	1·58		26·58	18·16	...	...	2·06
28	St. Bees Red .	85·20	2·00	7·00	0·10	0·30	...	3·30	2·10
31	Woodkirk Brown .	83·00	8·02	3·43	0·12	0·07	0·55	0·65	4·16

TABLE X
CHEMICAL COMPOSITION OF LIMESTONES

Reference No. (see Fig. 37)	Name of Stone	Carbonate of Lime	Carbonate of Magnesia	Alumina and Oxide of Iron	Silica	Water and Loss	Remarks
32	Ancaster Brown .	93·59	2·90	0·80	...	2·71	
33	Clipsham Old Quarry	97·56	0·54	0·83	0·84	0·23	
34	Hopton-Wood .	98·40	0·32	0·31	0·77	0·20	Referred to as a marble.
18	Park Nook . .	56·10	42·20	0·50	...	1·20	A magnesian limestone.
36	Portland . .	95·16	1·20	0·50	1·20	1·94	
37	Weldon . . .	93·43	3·55	1·09	0·80	1·13	

3. Metamorphic Rocks.—These are either igneous or sedimentary rocks which have been altered or metamorphosed by heat (from the earth's interior) or pressure (caused by the weight of superimposed layers of material or to the movement of the earth's crust) or a combination of both. As a result of this metamorphism, the original structure of the rocks has been destroyed, the arrangement of the particles (or stratification) being changed. The chief metamorphic rocks used for building purposes are (a) marbles, (b) slates and (c) quartzite.

(a) *Marbles.*—True marbles are metamorphosed limestones consisting of aggregates of granular crystals of calcium carbonate (calcite). The composition varies, but some marbles comprise approximately 98 per cent. of calcium carbonate with traces of magnesium carbonate, silica and oxide of iron. Many hard, compact limestones, capable of taking a good polish, are referred to in the trade as marbles, although the metamorphosis has been only partial; examples of these so-called marbles are obtained from Derbyshire and Devonshire (see below). Marbles are obtained in a great variety of colours, some of them being richly marked or veined (due to the presence of iron oxides) and others are richly fossilized; many are finely grained and can be elaborately carved. Because of their delicacy of colouring and capacity of taking a high polish (p. 113), marbles are chiefly used for decorative purposes; they are thus employed as wall linings (the slabs being usually 20 mm thick—see Chap. VIII, Vol. IV), pavement or floor coverings (of 20 to 25 mm thick slabs), staircase treads, risers and balustrades, internal columns, shop fronts, fireplaces, etc.; they are also in demand for ecclesiastical work, such as altars, screens, fronts and statues.

The best known so-called marbles quarried in this country (and known as "English marbles") are Ancaster Brown Weather Bed (Lincolnshire), and Hopton-Wood (Derbyshire), although neither is a true marble.

Ancaster Brown Weather Bed is of the Lower Oölites series (Jurassic system). It is brown with grey and buff mottling. It is coarse grained, free working and takes a high polish.

Hopton-Wood Marble.—This Derbyshire marble is marketed under five classifications, *i.e.*, (1) Light Hopton-Wood (cream-coloured ground spotted with small light brown crystals; suitable for both internal and external—if in clean atmosphere—purposes); (2) *Dark Hopton-Wood*[1] (similar to (1) but more densely marked with slightly darker patches); (3) *Black Bird's-eye* (black with slight brown cast having light coloured fossil spot markings, hence the name; only suitable for internal work); (4) *Grey Bird's-eye* (similar to (3) but of grey-brown colour); and (5) *Derbyshire Fossil* (deep grey colour, richly fossilized, some of the fossils being 50 mm long; only suitable for internal work).

[1] Both Light and Dark Hopton-Wood stone were used after the First World War by the Imperial War Graves Commission for 120 000 headstones.

Ashburton Marble—This Devonshire marble has a most attractive appearance, it being dark grey in colour, verging on black, with bright red and white crystalline veins, together with fossils.

Irish Marbles in demand in this country include : *Black* (quarried in Kilkenny and Carlow); *Connemara Irish Green* (quarried in Galway, green ground with grey and black patches and veins); *Victoria Red* (from Cork, mottled light red with thin dark veins).

Many foreign marbles are imported and used for decorative purposes in this country, and the following are some of these :—

BELGIAN : *Belgian Black* (deep black); *Belgian Fossil* or *Petit Granite* (very dark grey with lighter grey spots—fossils—and veins); *Blue Belge* (black or deep blue-black ground with white, light or bluish-grey streaks); *Rouge* (various, light reddish-brown ground with white, grey or dark brown irregular veins); *St Anne* (dark grey with white cloudy patches and irregular veins).

FRENCH : *Brocatelle Jaune* (yellow with brown and white veins); *Brocatelle Violette* (purplish-grey with brown and yellow patches); *Comblanchien* (light brown with fossils); *Jaune Lamartine* (rich yellow with fine brown, grey and red veins); *Lunel* (light fawn with few markings); *Napoleon* (light fawn with brown and red veins); *Rose* (red with black veins).

GRECIAN : *Cippolino* (pinkish-white with dark green wavy bands); *Skyros* (creamy-white or delicate yellow ground with gold and purple veins); *Tinos* (dark green ground with lighter green streaks and narrow irregular black and white veins); *Verde Antico* (light and dark green mixture with occasional whitish patches).

ITALIAN : *Breccia* (grey, purple and yellow mixture with white veins); *Dove* (lavender or dark grey, slightly veined); *Fleur de Peche* (rich purple with white mottling); *Levanto Rosso* (dark red, purple and green mixture); *Pavonazzetto* (ivory ground with irregular orange and rusty veins); *Pavonazzo* (similar to Pavonazzetto with purple veins; scarce); *San Stefano* (dark buff with stippled darker flecks); *Second Statuary* (white with grey or greyish-green veinings); *Statuary* (pure white and expensive; so called as it is principally used for statues); *Sicilian* (white with bluish cast); *Sienna* (all shades of yellow with purple and black veins); *Travertine*[1] (straw, amber and golden ground with irregular darker graining; bands of small pores characteristic).

NORWEGIAN : *Brêche Rosé* (pale rose-pink ground with white mottling); *Norge Clair* (white).

SWEDISH : *Swedish Green* (pale green ground with darker green ribboning and white mottling).

Alabaster, used for ornaments, electric light bowels, etc., is sulphate of lime. It is white when in its pure form. The true alabaster comes from Algeria and has been deposited as stalactites and stalagmites.[2] So-called alabaster is found in Derbyshire, Somerset and other parts of this country.

Onyx Marbles from Algeria, Brazil and Mexico are of calcium carbonate produced as stalactites and stalagmites. They are richly figured and are of many colours, varying from white to yellow, the characteristic veining being due to the presence of metallic oxides.

Marbles are obtained from the Devonian and Carboniferous systems.

(b) *Slates.*—A true slate is a metamorphic sedimentary clay rock. Originally the clay was deposited as a fine silt; this was compressed by vertical pressure

---

[1] *Travertine or Calcareous Tufa* consists of hardened masses of carbonate of lime deposited by springs; the compact variety is known as " travertine " and the light and spongy type is called " tufa."

[2] These are produced by the dropping of water containing carbonate of lime through fissures in the roofs of caves. Icicle-like stalactites (masses hanging from the roof) and stalagmites (deposits gradually built up on the floor) of calcium sulphate (or calcium carbonate) are thus formed.

into shale, which, when subsequently subjected to enormous lateral pressure accompanied by intense heat, was converted into slate. The forces producing this side pressure contorted the original horizontal *bedding planes*, and, in addition, rearranged the particles into inclined *cleavage planes*. An example of this formation is shown in Fig. 69, Vol. I, and, as there described, a block of slate is readily converted into relatively thin roofing slates by splitting it along the parallel planes of cleavage. The preparation, characteristics, etc., of slates are described in Vol. I.

Welsh slates are obtained from the Cambrian, Ordovician and Silurian systems. The Bangor, Dinorwic (or Velinheli) and Penrhyn slates are worked from the Cambrian (Olenellus Beds) rocks; the Festiniog (or Portmadoc) and Precelly slates are mined or quarried from the Ordovician (Llandeilo Beds) rocks; slates from Corwen and Llangollen are obtained from the Wenlock Beds (Silurian system) and are softer than most of those mentioned above (see Table VI).

Lake District green slates (Buttermere, Honister, Elterwater, Kentmere and Tilberthwaite) and those from the Burlington quarries are of the Ordovician age (Llandeilo Beds).

Cornish (Delabole) slates are obtained from the Upper Devonian series.

Scottish slates from Argyll (Ballachulish and Easdale), Dumbarton and Perth are from the Pre-Cambrian system.

Irish slates from Tipperary, Donegal, Kerry and Kilkenny are of the Ordovician age.

(c) *Quartzite* is a very compact, hard and durable metamorphic rock. Like slates, it is ready split into thin slabs, but it is very difficult to saw to panel sizes. When converted, the slabs have a very pleasing textured surface and attractive colour, ranging from grey, olive to golden. Whilst for centuries this has been used as a building material in Italy, where it is quarried, it has only recently been employed in this country on buildings as a floor and external and internal wall covering, the 10 to 20 mm thick slabs being bedded in mortar.

DEFECTS IN STONE

Certain defects in stone are mentioned in Chap. I, Vol. I, and include clay-holes, mottle, sand-holes and vents.

Decay of stone may be due to (1) incorrect bedding, (2) atmospheric impurities, (3) careless selection, (4) association of dissimilar stones, (5) efflorescence, (6) frost action and (7) corrodible metal fastenings. Regarding decay caused by :

1. *Incorrect Bedding.*—Serious weathering defects occur if stone is incorrectly bedded (see Chap. I, Vol. I), and especially if face-bedding (*e.g.*, with the natural bed vertical and parallel to the face of the wall) is resorted to. Blocks of stone must be built with the natural bed perpendicular to the pressure (see also under 6 on p. 106).

2. *Atmospheric Impurities.*—A polluted atmosphere is the principal cause of decay of certain stones. Those containing calcium carbonate, such as limestones (ordinary and magnesian) and calcareous sandstones, are especially liable to attack.

The chief sources of atmospheric pollution are domestic coal fires and industrial furnaces. Such pollution occurs principally in the vicinity of large towns and manufacturing centres. The products of combustion of coal mainly responsible for decay of stone are acid gases, such as sulphur dioxide and trioxide, and soot; sulphurous acid and sulphuric acid are formed when the dioxide and trioxide respectively come into contact with water, such as rain. Although the acid gases are most concentrated in cities and industrial areas, they are readily carried by air currents and do damage for a considerable distance from the source of pollution.

When these sulphur acids descend with the rain, snow or fog upon the calcium carbonate of ordinary limestones, calcium sulphate is formed and carbon dioxide is liberated. The rain washes away the sulphate, causing *erosion* (wearing away) of the surface of the stone. The action of these acids on magnesian limestones has a similar weathering effect, the small quantities of magnesium sulphate and calcium sulphate produced are dissolved by the water present and tend to form a surface skin when the water dries out. Such erosion occurs chiefly on those external walls of buildings which are exposed to the prevailing wind (which in this country is from the south-west) and the washing action of the rain. The defect is not serious when the erosion is very gradual and uniform, and is considered by some to be an advantage on account of the different texture of wall surfaces which results. This natural washing by rain is responsible for the attractive dark and light appearance of Portland stone and similar limestone buildings.

Serious decay occurs when the sulphur acids cause the formation of a hard layer or skin on the outer surface of limestone, which subsequently blisters and flakes off, the latter condition being known as *exfoliation*. Such layers consist chiefly of salts (calcium sulphite and calcium sulphate). When the skin scales off, a fresh surface is exposed and a new hard layer is formed. Constant repetition of this process results in a weakening of the wall, and the appearance is, of course very ugly. The decay only occurs on the surfaces of external walls which are sheltered from the washing action of rain; exposed surfaces are not affected, as the rain removes the salts and thus prevents the formation of the surface skin. Some limestones are less liable to this form of decay than others.

Soot is a product of combustion of coal and is largely responsible for the discoloration of stone. It may also cause decay. That from domestic fires especially consists of a large proportion of tarry matter and this causes the soot to adhere to stone surfaces. Sandstones are very liable to become discoloured, and in course of time most sandstone buildings in industrial towns become black and assume a drab appearance as the pores of the surface of the stone become filled with soot deposit. Limestone buildings are not so disfigured, except those sheltered walls which are not rain-washed and on which the soot is allowed to accumulate.

Decay of stonework can be effectively retarded if soot and dirt are removed at sufficiently frequent intervals by washing or cleaning by means of jets of steam or abrasive.

Stonework is washed with water from a hose pipe (such as a fire hose) connected to the water main; a pumping machine is used if the pressure of the water is inadequate. Ladders, scaffolding or suspended cradles are required, as the stone must be scrubbed by hand with bristle brushes. An effective method for limestone buildings is to apply water in the form of a fine spray through nozzles to the stonework for one or two hours, and after a short interval the surface is lightly brushed with comparatively soft scrubbing brushes.

Steam cleaning is very effective when applied to walls which are much discoloured. The steam, generated by a boiler, is passed up a flexible tube from which it emerges on the stone. A wire brush fitted on the nozzle of the tube is used to scrub the black surfaces.

The value of these processes in maintaining a clean appearance of buildings and arresting decay is being appreciated by an increasing number of property owners, and some buildings in towns where the atmosphere is highly polluted are washed yearly; other buildings only require such treatment every five or six years.

The practice which is sometimes adopted of using special cleaning preparations, such as caustic soda and other alkalis, is condemned, as such chemicals damage the stonework.

3. *Careless Selection.*—Stone obtained from soft beds in a quarry or mine will weather more quickly than that from the harder beds. A wall becomes unsightly if it consists of stones which do not weather uniformly. Careful selection should ensure that only the hardest and most durable stone is used.

4. *Association of Dissimilar Stones.*—Decay of sandstones may result if both limestones and sandstones are used together in a wall. Thus, for example, a limestone string course or limestone dressing to door and window openings in a wall mainly constructed of sandstone may be the cause of decay of the adjacent sandstone; plinths of sandstone have been known to decay because of the limestone above them.

The following is the reason for the decay: When salts, such as calcium sulphate, are formed (see preceding column), they may be washed from the limestone on to the surface of the sandstone. These salts may be absorbed and crystallize; as an increase in volume occurs when these crystals are formed, the resulting pressure just behind the surface disintegrates the stone; such decay may become extensive.

Similarly, when ordinary limestone is associated with magnesian limestone, decay of the former may occur due to the absorption of magnesium sulphate (see preceding column) from the magnesian limestone.

5. *Efflorescence* (see p. 13).—Decay may arise from unsuitable jointing material. The salts in cement and lime mortars may be absorbed by the stone; crystalization of the salts may occur and either set up decay of the stone (due to the resulting pressure) or cause efflorescence on the surface. Such defects are especially likely to occur if the jointing material is a rich impermeable cement mortar, for, in wet weather, water will be absorbed by the stone and not the mortar; as this water dries out from the stone surface only (and not from the joints), the salts are either brought to the outer face of the stone to cause efflorescence or they crystallize in the pores immediately behind it.

Brown or yellow staining of limestone walling may result from alkalis in the mortar. Discoloration of the limestone facing of compound walls may be caused from brickwork backing which is bedded and jointed with black mortar. It is desirable, therefore, that either suitable lime mortar (see Chap. I, Vol. I) or asphalt be used to back the ashlar blocks, the latter being preferred, as the waterproof material effectively prevents the salts from the backing mortar penetrating the stone.

6. *Frost Action.*—This is described on p. 15 and is also referred to on p. 110. Porous and laminated stone is especially liable to decay caused during the winter by the absorption of water, which expands in the pore spaces and bedding planes when it becomes frozen, and thus disintegration of the stone occurs. Copings, unprotected cornices and string courses, walls of unsuitable materials and inferior workmanship below the ground level, and retaining walls are most vulnerable to damage by frost action. Blocks of face-bedded stone are particularly liable, as any water penetrating the stone and becoming frozen will cause patches of the skin to spall off.

7. *Corrodible Metal Fastenings.*—Reference is made in Chap. I, Vol. I, to the damage caused to stonework which is secured with corrodible metal, such as wrought iron. The expansion which occurs when embedded wrought iron corrodes is sufficient to split huge blocks of stone, such as cornices, copings and upper spire stones.[1] Metal which does not rust, such as bronze, stainless steel and copper, should be used for these fastenings.

Preservation.—The best method of preserving stone is by washing or steam cleaning (see p. 106). Most so-called " preservatives " have proved to be unsatisfactory.

TESTS APPLIED TO STONES

It is recognized that the most reliable indication of the durability of a stone required to withstand certain atmospheric conditions is obtained by a careful inspection of that used in the construction of buildings which have been subjected to similar exposure for a lengthy period. Such is not, however, a conclusive guide, as the quality of stone obtained from different parts of a quarry may vary considerably, and it does not therefore follow that the characteristics of recently won stone are similar to that obtained from older workings in the same quarry and which was used for the inspected buildings. Further, the quality of stone from a new quarry cannot be judged in this manner. Laboratory tests are therefore valuable for supplying information which could only be otherwise obtained by trial and error methods.

The following are tests which may be carried out for estimating the durability of stone : (1) Rate of water absorption or permeability, (2) percentage porosity, (3) saturation coefficient, (4) resistance to frost and (5) crystallisation test. They provide information which can be compared with stones whose durable qualities and other properties are known, and whilst such comparative tests are not decisive,

[1] The apex of a stone spire consists of blocks of stone which are usually connected together by a central vertical metal rod. It is fairly common experience to find that these blocks have developed cracks, and investigations have shown that the defects were caused by the corrosion of the rods. The work of restoration is costly, as scaffolding has to be erected, and the whole of the defective stonework must be removed and replaced with new blocks which are " threaded " over a non-corrodible vertical rod.

they do give data which may be of value when selecting a stone for a specific purpose. Students should refer to the footnote on p. 14 for, brief definitions of absorption, permeability and porosity.

1. *Rate of Water Absorption or Permeability Test.*—This is described on p. 14, the brass cover being fitted to the stone specimen whose four vertical faces are rendered impermeable by the application of wax. As already explained, the test conditions are not likely to be exceeded, even in the most exposed positions, by those met with in practice.

2. *Percentage Porosity Test.*—In order to understand the significance of the expression " percentage porosity," the student should revise the definitions of *bulk density* and *solid density* which he would have considered in his study of Building Science and for which convenience are repeated here.

Density (in kg/m³) $= \dfrac{\text{weight (in kg)}}{\text{volume (in m}^3)}$; therefore the *bulk* or *total density* (in kg/m³) $= \dfrac{\text{weight (in kg)}}{\text{bulk volume (in m}^3)}$. If the specimen to be examined is of irregular shape, the bulk volume is obtained by using an apparatus such as the *overflow tank* shown at A, Fig. 39. The specimen is carefully lowered into the tank which has been previously filled with water to the " weir " level indicated; the water displaced passes from the outlet into a vessel of convenient size and transferred to a glass measuring cylinder; this gives the volume of the water, which is equal to that of the specimen.

The solid or powdered density (in kg/m³) $= \dfrac{\text{weight (in kg)}}{\text{solid volume (in m}^3)}$. Actually, the solid density of most stones, in addition to bricks and concretes, is approximately the same, namely, 2 660 kg/m³. The adoption of this figure therefore simplifies the routine, as it obviates the necessity of powdering the specimen and obtaining its volume.

The *percentage porosity* is found after the bulk and solid densities have been determined, thus :

$$\text{Percentage porosity} = \frac{\text{volume of voids}}{\text{bulk volume}} \times 100$$

$$= \frac{\text{bulk volume} - \text{solid volume}}{\text{bulk volume}} \times 100$$

$$= \left(1 - \frac{\text{solid volume} \times \text{weight}}{\text{bulk volume} \times \text{weight}}\right) 100$$

$$= \left(1 - \frac{\text{solid volume}}{\text{weight}} \times \frac{\text{weight}}{\text{bulk volume}}\right) 100$$

$$= \left(1 - \frac{\text{bulk density}}{\text{solid density}}\right) 100$$

$$= \left(1 - \frac{\text{bulk density}}{2\ 660}\right) 100.$$

Thus, taking the Corsehill Red stone which heads the list in Table VII, the bulk density being 2080 kg/m³ the percentage porosity $= \left(1 - \dfrac{2\ 080}{2\ 660}\right) 100 = 22$ approx., the figure given in the table.

3. *Saturation Coefficient Test.*—Damage caused by frost is referred to above Very porous stones will absorb more water than others less porous and are therefore more vulnerable to damage due to frost action. If the voids are completely filled with water and this water freezes, the resulting pressure will tend to disrupt the cell walls by internal pressure. If, however, the interconnected pores (see p. 14)

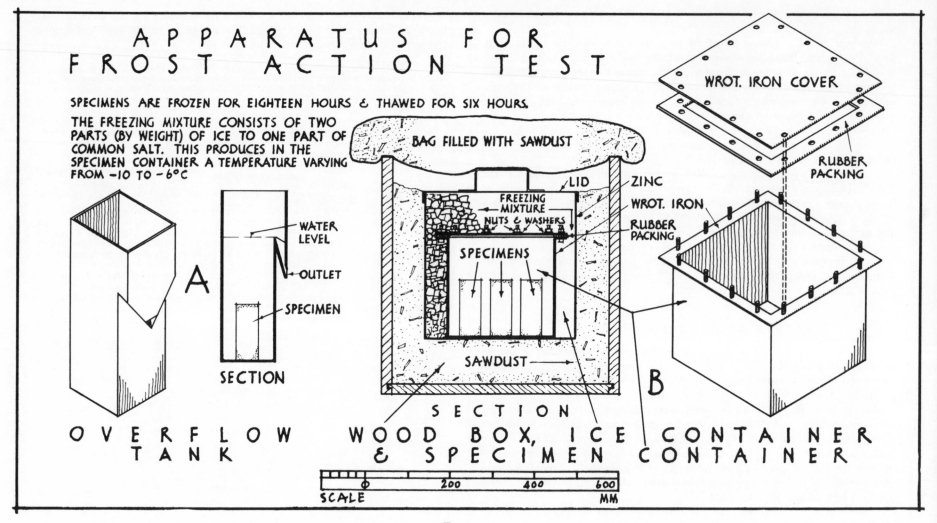

APPARATUS FOR FROST ACTION TEST

SPECIMENS ARE FROZEN FOR EIGHTEEN HOURS & THAWED FOR SIX HOURS.

THE FREEZING MIXTURE CONSISTS OF TWO PARTS (BY WEIGHT) OF ICE TO ONE PART OF COMMON SALT. THIS PRODUCES IN THE SPECIMEN CONTAINER A TEMPERATURE VARYING FROM −10 TO −6°C

WATER LEVEL

OUTLET

SPECIMEN

A

SECTION

OVERFLOW TANK

BAG FILLED WITH SAWDUST

LID

ZINC

FREEZING MIXTURE

WROT. IRON

NUTS & WASHERS

RUBBER PACKING

SPECIMENS

SAWDUST

SECTION

WOOD BOX, ICE & SPECIMEN CONTAINER

WROT. IRON COVER

RUBBER PACKING

B

CONTAINER

SCALE   0   200   400   600   MM

FIGURE 39

are only partly filled with water, there may be sufficient space within them to allow for this expansion, and damage to the stone structure will not occur. Hence the ratio of water absorbed to the volume of void space may be taken as a measure of the capacity of the stone to resist frost action; this ratio is known as the *saturation coefficient*. It is usually expressed as follows :—

$$\text{Saturation coefficient} = \frac{\text{water absorbed after twenty-four hours' soaking}}{\text{total water absorption after five hours' boiling}}.$$

This test is carried out as follows : The stone specimen is dried in an oven, allowed to cool, weighed, soaked in cold water for twenty-four hours, removed and wiped with a cloth, and re-weighed. The difference between these two weights is that which is placed in the numerator (p. 107). The specimen is then returned to the water and boiled for five hours; it is then allowed to cool under water, removed, wiped and weighed; the difference between this latter weight and the dry weight is the figure which appears in the denominator.

The saturation coefficients supplied in Tables VII and VIII were obtained in this manner. Thus, taking the Portland stone listed in Table VIII, the dry, soaking and boiling weights were 1·028, 1·084 and 1·111 kg respectively, giving a saturation coefficient

$$= \frac{\text{(water absorbed after twenty-four hours' soaking)}}{\text{(total water absorbed after five hours' boiling)}}$$

$$= \frac{\text{weight after soaking (1·084 kg)} - \text{dry weight (1·028 kg)}}{\text{weight after boiling (1·111 kg)} - \text{dry weight (1·028 kg)}}$$

$$= \frac{56}{83} = 0·67 \text{ (see Table VIII).}$$

This coefficient has a practical value as it is considered to be a helpful guide to the capacity of the stone to withstand frost action. As a general rule, it is regarded that a stone having a saturation coefficient of 0·80 and under should not be liable to damage from frost action. As, however, there are exceptions to this, it is desirable to submit a stone of unknown frost resistance to a freezing test (see below).

4. *Frost Resistance Test.*—The apparatus used[1] for this purpose is illustrated at B, Fig. 39. It consists of a wood box (560 mm by 560 mm by 530 mm deep of 25 mm thick timber), a zinc ice container (356 mm by 356 mm by 330 mm deep) with lid, a wrought iron specimen container (267 mm by 254 mm by 230 mm deep) with cover, and a bag filled with sawdust (or similar insulating material) as a cover to the wood box.

The test is performed in the following manner : Sawdust (or granulated cork) to a depth of about 100 mm is placed at the bottom of the wood box; the ice container is placed on top of this sawdust and this or similar insulating material is packed at the sides as shown in the section; the stone specimens are placed in the specimen container, the metal cover is tightly screwed down to ensure that the rubber packed joint is watertight, and this container is placed within the ice container. The freezing mixture is then placed in the ice container, the lid is fitted on it and, finally, the sawdust bag is placed over the outer box (see section). The freezing mixture consists of 2 parts (by weight) of ice to 1 part (by weight) of common salt. This produces a temperature in the specimen container varying from −9° to −7° C. approx. The specimens are subjected to this temperature for eighteen hours, after which they are removed and gradually thawed in water for six hours; after examination, they are replaced, again frozen for eighteen hours, removed, thawed for six hours and examined. This cycle is repeated until the samples have undergone ten freezings.

The specimens listed in Table VII were tested in this manner. It will be seen that some were unaffected and others showed damage at the arrises. Stone of poor quality is seriously damaged when subjected to this test, some splitting and showing similar signs of disruption after only the first or second freezing.

The weather conditions experienced in this country are not sufficiently severe to cause frost damage to stonework in general walling, unless the stones are face-bedded and the stone is of inferior quality, but coping, etc., stones are liable to disintegration if subjected to prolonged periods of rain followed by frost (see p. 107).

Other tests include a chemical test (such as subjecting the specimens in a closed tank to hydrochloric acid fumes) and that for determining the compressive strength; a machine used for the latter is shown at E, Fig. 9, and described on p. 32.

"5.*Crystallisation Test.* This, most important test, deals with the main cause of stone decay caused by the crystallisation of soluble salts within the pores of the stone. It measures the ability of a stone to withstand the pressure caused by the repeated crystallisation and hydration of the salts which derive from atmospheric pollution (see pp.105 and 106) and rising damp. The test amplifies the pollution effects by causing soluble salts to crystallise in the pores.

The test method subjects samples of stone to 15 cycles of immersion in a saturated aqueous sodium sulphate decahydrate solution of specific gravity 1.68. The samples are then dried in a humid oven, they are weighed before and after immersion and the weight loss found. The greater this loss the less durable is the stone. Tables VII and VIII gives the percentage loss.

There are 6 durability classes from A to F for limestones, examples are given in Table VIII. The percentage crystallisation C, 5-15%; D, 15-35%; E more than 35%; F, the sample shatters early in the test.

The extent of decay in a building depends on four factors: the amount of pollution at the building site; the severity of frost in the locality, the position of the stone on the building and whether it is inland or at an exposed coastal area. The parts of a building (and the surround to it) can be numbered from 1 to 4 thus: Part 1—paving stones and steps suffer the greatest decay. Part 2—copings, chimneys, cornices, open parapets and plinths suffer less than 1. Part 3—solid parapets, strings, cills and mullions suffer less than 2. Part 4—plain walling which suffers least of all.

Thus Class A stones can be used for all parts. Class B for all parts except 1, although in the case of a cornice it could be of Class C if covered in lead (see Chapter 6, Vol. 1). Class C for Part 3 features in low pollution areas and also for plain walling in such areas. Class D for general walling at an inland site, it is not suitable for exposed sites. Class E could be used at inland sites which are not liable to frost. Obviously in important buildings which have to last only Class A stones are used.

QUARRYING AND MINING

A description of quarrying appears in Chap. I, Vol. I. Open quarrying is not resorted to when building stone is at a considerable depth below the surface, as the removal of the overburden would be too costly. Beer stone and most of the limestones (including Congrit, Corsham Down, Monk's Park and St.

[1] At the Department of Building, Manchester University Institute of Science and Technology.

Aldhelm Box Ground) obtained in the Bath district are mined. A typical stone mine consists of an adit or tunnelled opening made in the side of a hill at the level of the best stone.   The adit is continued as the stone is removed and follows the bed.   Branch tunnels are formed from this main gallery.   In the Box Ground mine the underground workings pass from one side of the hill to the other, a distance of 5 kilometres, and the galleries in some places are nearly 30 m below the surface.   The height of the tunnels is at least equal to the thickness of the good stone beds, which may be up to 3 m, and the width may exceed this.

The roof and floor of a tunnel consist of hard coarse stone.   The first operation in winning the limestone is to pick out the top 230 mm of the stone just below the roof; this is called the *picking bed*, and the tool used is a long-handled pick.   When the picking has proceeded some 1·5 or 1·8 m, a long hand saw is employed (which is operated at the handle by both hands) to divide the rock by vertical cuts extending from the top to the next bed and at about 1·5 m horizontal intervals; this operation is comparatively easy as the stone is very soft.   A block, having three free sides, is removed either with large crow bars or by a crane, the rope from the latter being attached to a lewis bolt inserted in the face of the block. The blocks, which may weigh from 6 000 to 8 000 kg, are squared up with saws, and then lifted by crane on to bogies which run on lines along the tunnel to the surface depot.   The roof is supported at intervals by strong cross-beams supported by props at the sides; falls of the roof are also averted by the insertion of oak wedges in any vertical cracks or vents.

When Bath stone has just been removed it contains much quarry sap; it is soft, and if used immediately it would weather badly.   It is therefore allowed to *season* for a period before being fixed.   The time allowed for the blocks of stone to remain in the stacking ground depends very largely upon the demand, but normally the stone is seasoned for several months before being dressed,

If necessary, the stone can be dressed soon after mining if obtained between the late spring to the end of September, but that mined during the winter months is stored underground till the following spring before it is worked.   Damage from frost is thus prevented.

MACHINE DRESSING

A brief description of certain machines used for dressing stone is given in Chap. I, Vol. I.   Some of these are illustrated here in Fig. 40.

Frame Saw (see A and B).—This machine, which is used for sawing large blocks into several smaller slabs, has a swing frame which holds the desired number of steel saw blades.   The frame is suspended by four rods, and operates with a backward and forward motion by means of a connecting rod, secured to the frame and the crankshaft of the flywheel which is driven by electric or other power.   The blades are either corrugated (see C) or wavy or plain in section, the former being commonly used for sandstone, limestone, slate and granite, and the plain type for marble; they are 75, 100, 125 or 150 mm wide by 3·2 mm thick (for marble), 5 mm thick (for sandstone and limestone) and 6 mm thick (for granite).   This machine is made in various sizes, the maximum size of stone that can be dealt with varying from 2·4 to 4·2 m long 1·2 to 2·4 m wide and 1·2 to 1·8 m thick.

The block of stone to be converted is placed on a bogie or trolley, packed firmly and level, and wheeled in position under the swing frame. The required number of blades is fixed in the frame at the necessary distance apart. The maximum number of blades which may be fitted to the frame depends upon the hardness of the stone and the power of the machine; generally the number does not exceed twelve, and this may be reduced to four or five blades if the stone is very hard; for marble slabbing when the thickness of the slabs may be only 13 mm, the number of blades (which are secured by special fittings) may reach thirty. The machine is set into operation causing the saw frame to descend the long worm screws in the four legs at a predetermined speed and regulated by the ratchet arrangement controlled by the levers shown at A. The rate of the downward feed is regulated according to the hardness of the stone, the number of blades used, etc.; as a guide, the cutting speeds of one 3·7 m long machine, having twelve blades, are 12, 30 and 76 cm per hour for hard sandstone, Portland stone and Bath stone respectively; a similar machine, with four blades, will saw granite at the rate of from 2·5 to 4 cm per hour; for cutting thin slabs of marble, the speed is reduced to about 4 cm per hour in order to secure the desired accuracy.

An abrasive material, such as chilled shot (steel pellets), sharp sand or carborundum, in addition to water, must be used to facilitate the sawing operation. The water is supplied from a tank situated above the machine and is automatically distributed over the stone through small taps fixed in two transverse pipes which either swing backwards and forwards with the frame or are kept stationary. The abrasive, placed as required over the cuts or kerfs in the stone by the sawyer (man in charge of the machine), is carried by the water down the cuts to the lower edges of the blades, and thus deepens the cuts during the reciprocating action of the blades; in addition, the water cools the blades and thus prevents undue wear of the steel. Steel shot is generally used for corrugated blades, except for limestone, when sand should be used, as shot rusts and would cause discoloration.

The cross-section at A shows a block of stone partially sawn into seven slabs.

On completion of the " slabbing," the frame is stopped and raised, the bogie is run clear of the frame and the stone is removed.

The frame saw is the most useful machine for cutting hard stone.

Another machine, known as the *rip saw*, is somewhat similar to the above with the exception that its width is greater than its length and the wide bogie runs on a track at right angles to that shown at B; the swing frame has thus a transverse reciprocating motion. The rip saw is usefully employed for cross-cutting blocks and especially those which are too wide for the ordinary frame saw.

Diamond Saw (see D).—This machine is used for rapidly and accurately cutting relatively small blocks of stone, such as slabs from the frame saw. It has a circular steel saw blade which is caused to rotate by an electric motor at a high speed to cut the stone which travels towards it on a moving table. The size of saw blade varies from 0·6 to 2 m. Saw blades must be carefully tensioned (Chap. I, Vol. III). Welded to the rim of the blade are U-shaped steel sockets or clips into each of which a half carat diamond is securely fixed; an enlargement of a portion of a blade is shown at E; the diamonds are staggered, as indicated, in order that the width of the cut is fully covered; four sockets per 25 mm diameter of blade are provided, thus a 1·5 m blade is fitted with 240 sockets provided with the same number of diamonds. The maximum speed of the blade varies with its diameter; that of a 1·5 m diameter blade is 575 revs. per min. whilst a 1·8 m diameter blade has a maximum velocity of 480 revs. per min. This speed is regulated according to the character of the stone, it being much less for a hard sandstone than for a soft limestone; in order to avoid damage to the arrises of the stone, the speed of the blade is lowest when the blade is just entering and leaving the block. The deepest cut that a saw blade will make is less than half the diameter of the blade, thus, for example, the maximum depth of cut of an 2·1 m blade is approximately 0·9 m and the thickness of stone would be restricted to this.

A water feed, necessary to cool the blade, is provided as shown at D. The pipe can be raised or lowered as required to deliver water on top of the stone. A guard is fixed to the upper half to prevent splashing.

The stone is placed upon, but not necessarily fixed to, a cast iron table which moves on rollers. After the blade has been brought to the required position by traversing the frame, the table is advanced quickly to bring the stone up to the blade and proceeds at the desired speed until the cut has been formed, after which the table is quickly returned. The machine has four changes of feed for cutting, in addition to the quick advance and return, and these changes are readily effected by the sawyer operating a lever.

The cutting speed depends upon the horse-power, hardness of the stone and depth of cut. A 22·5 kw machine will saw a 0·9 m thick block of Portland stone at the rate of 1 390 cm² per min. of sawn area. This rate is much higher than that of the frame saw, but whilst the latter can deal with all types of stone, including granite, a diamond saw is only suitable for relatively soft stones, such as limestones, as hard stones would quickly damage the blade and wear out the sockets.

The machine can also be provided with two tables which can be either used together or one can be loaded whilst the stone on the other is being cut.

This machine may also be provided with two circular saw blades, when it is called a *twin blade* or *duplex machine*. It has either one or two tables, the latter moving on separate tracks parallel to each other. The blades, with a lateral movement, are independent and may be traversed in the same or opposite direction as required. These blades can be raised or lowered (known as a *rising and falling motion*) and are thus invaluable for forming cuts less than the thickness of the stone (an operation called *checking*) as required for grooves in window sills, etc., for *channelling* (removal of portions of the backs of stones such as are required to be fixed to steel beams and pillars of steel-framed buildings, etc.), *recessing* (*e.g.*, jamb stones) for sinking mouldings of cornices, etc. The maximum vertical movement is 0·9 m. The area of sawn surface of Portland stone when the cut is 0·9 m deep and both blades are operating is approximately 5160 cm² per min. This machine has largely replaced the single blade type.

Cross-cut or Beam Saw.—This consists of a long *transverse* cast iron beam, supported by a pillar at each end, along which a circular saw blade is caused to travel; it is obtainable in two sizes, allowing a maximum traverse of blade of 2·4 and 3·7 m. The largest size of blade is 1·5 m and this gives a maximum depth of cut of approximately 0·6 m. A wide table, mounted on wheels or moving on inverted vee-slides (as shown at J), is usually provided, although side-by-side twin tables are also available.

The table, with the stone in position, is brought under the blade, adjusted and locked; the blade is then made to traverse and cut the stone. Both *fixed height* and *rise and fall movement* types are available, the former being useful for plain sawing and jointing (such as squaring ends of blocks of stone, edges of marble slabs, etc.) and the latter, which permits of a maximum vertical movement of the blade of 380 mm, is invaluable for checking, channelling and recessing.

The blade may be of either the diamond or carborundum (see below) type. A typical cutting speed by a diamond saw is 1 410 cm² per min. for Portland stone; this speed is reduced to from one-third to one-half if the blade is of the carborundum type.

Gravity Saw (see F).—This type is so called as the table supporting the stone is pulled forward partly by the force of gravity. A counter-weight, adjusted according to the weight of the stone, is suspended by a wire rope which passes over pulley " 1 " (the block of which is secured to a roof, etc., beam), under the lower pulley " 2 " and is attached to the forward end of the moving table. Thus, a smooth pull, with a distinct economy in power, is obtained throughout the cut. The backward movement of the table is accomplished by operating the handwheel " 1 "

The cast iron table has transverse and longitudal slots to receive clamps for the accurate setting and expeditious fastening down of the stone; it has a deep longitudinal slot to allow the blade to pass below the under surface of the stone. One type, of maximum size 3 m by 1 m, is known as a *cross traverse table*, as it can be given a transverse movement by operating the handle of screw " 2 ". The maximum cross movement is 0·76 m. A number of parallel cuts can thus be formed with one placing of the stone. The other type, called a *plain table*, cannot be moved transversely.

This machine may be provided with either a diamond blade or a *carborundum blade*. The latter is a steel blade with a 50 to 75 mm wide rim of carborundum (an abrasive material, being a crystalline compound of carbon and silicon); the carborundum, mixed with shellac, is heated and pressed round the periphery of the steel blade, which is dovetailed to provide a key. Carborundum blades give better finished

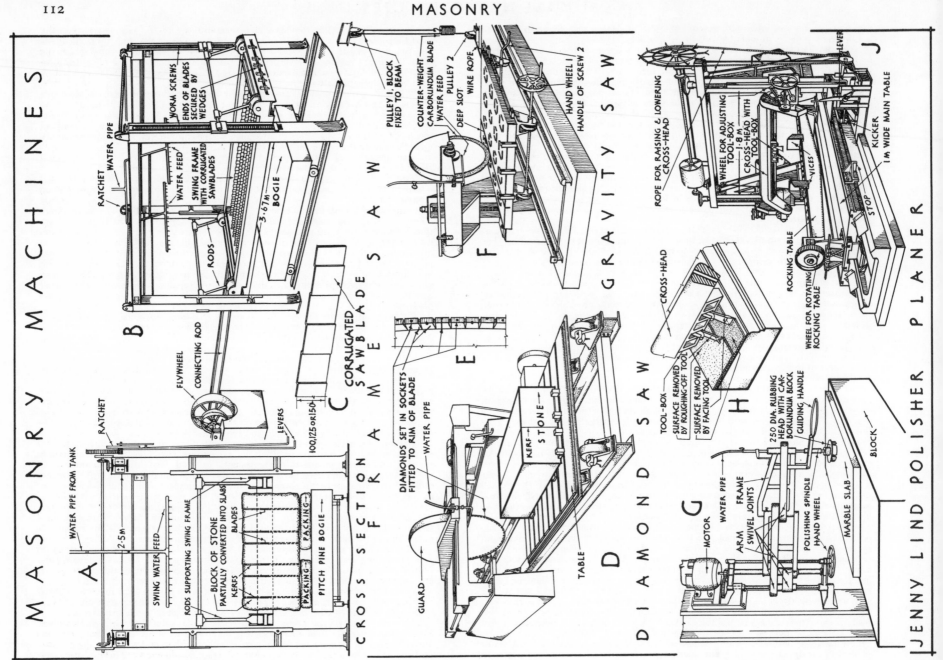

MASONRY MACHINES

A CROSS SECTION FRAME SAW

WATER PIPE FROM TANK

2·5 M

SWING WATER FEED

RATCHET

RODS SUPPORTING SWING FRAME

SWING WATER FEED

BLOCK OF STONE PARTIALLY CONVERTED INTO SLABS

BLADES

KERFS

PACKING

PACKING

PITCH PINE BOGIE

100, 125 or 150

LEVERS

FLYWHEEL

CONNECTING ROD

B

RATCHET

WATER PIPE

WORM SCREWS

ENDS OF BLADES SECURED BY WEDGES

WATER FEED

SWING FRAME WITH CORRUGATED SAWBLADES

RODS

3·67 M

BOGIE

C CORRUGATED SAWBLADE

D DIAMOND SAW

DIAMONDS SET IN SOCKETS FITTED TO RIM OF BLADE

WATER PIPE

KERF

STONE

GUARD

TABLE

E

F GRAVITY SAW

PULLEY 1, BLOCK FIXED TO BEAM

COUNTER-WEIGHT

CARBORUNDUM BLADE

WATER FEED

PULLEY 2

DEEP SLOT

WIRE ROPE

HAND WHEEL 1

HANDLE OF SCREW 2

G

MOTOR

WATER PIPE

ARM

FRAME

SWIVEL JOINTS

POLISHING SPINDLE

HAND WHEEL

250 DIA. RUBBING HEAD WITH CARBORUNDUM BLOCK

GUIDING HANDLE

MARBLE SLAB

BLOCK

H

TOOL-BOX

SURFACE REMOVED BY ROUGHING-OFF TOOL

SURFACE REMOVED BY FACING TOOL

CROSS-HEAD

J JENNY LIND POLISHER PLANER

LEVER

ROPE FOR RAISING & LOWERING CROSS-HEAD

WHEEL FOR ADJUSTING TOOL-BOX

1·8 M

CROSS-HEAD WITH TOOL-BOX

VICES

STOP

KICKER

1 M WIDE MAIN TABLE

WHEEL FOR ROTATING ROCKING TABLE

ROCKING TABLE

FIGURE 40

surfaces and finer cuts than those formed by diamond blades, and they can be used for both hard and soft stones. Their cutting speeds are, however, not more than half those of diamond blades; thus, typical speeds are 200 mm per min. for 150 mm slabs of Portland stone and 100 mm per min. for 300 mm slabs, and these rates are approximately doubled if diamond blades are used.

Gravity saws are made of three types, namely, (1) *fixed height*, suitable for plain sawing and jointing, (2) *rise and fall* for checking, channelling and sinking, and (3) *universal*, which cuts the stone at any angle from vertical to horizontal, as it has a swivelling head which can be adjusted to a vertical or inclined plane as required. The latter can be provided with a carborundum wheel (400 mm diameter and from 25 to 50 mm thick) in lieu of the circular blade, which rotates in a vertical spindle and grinds and moulds the edges of the stone or marble.

Planing and Moulding Machines.—As implied, these are used for machining the exposed face or faces to the desired finish and for moulding blocks of stone. One of the simplest, known as the *canting arm* or *reversible planer*, is shown at J. For surfacing, the stone (of a maximum length of 2·7 m) is fixed upon the *rocking table* between the two vices, with the face to be dressed uppermost. Wide blocks of stone fixed on the rocking table (which may be only 165 mm wide) are accommodated by supporting the overhanging portions by wood resting upon wedges on the main table. One or more tools are fixed by wedges in the *tool box* and the latter is moved along the *cross-head* to the required position by manipulating the handwheel shown; the cross-head is lowered by power or by the operator pulling down on the rope until the edge of the tool is just below the surface of the stone. As the main table which supports the loaded rocking table moves forward on inverted vee-slides, the surface of the stone is cut as indicated at H; the cross-head (or *canting arm* or *reversible head*) swings over on the return travel of the stone which automatically occurs when the *stop*, adjusted as required at the side of the main table, comes in contact with the *kicker* which moves the driving belt from one pulley to the other. It thus cuts in both directions, and for this reason is recognized to be the best machine for surfacing.

The cross-head is lowered as required after each cut. The rate of surfacing stone is dependent upon several conditions, but an approximate average speed is 0·9 m² per min.

Whilst essentially used for surfacing, this machine can also be used for moulded work. Thus, for cornices and similar members, a *plate box* into which is fitted a plate or tool having an edge smithed to the reverse of the required mould is fixed in the tool box. The rocking table is rotated and fixed at the desired angle so as to bring the surface of the stone to be moulded into a convenient position relative to the tool which cuts the stone during the forward movement of the table. Before a stone is placed on the machine for moulding, one end is " cut in " to the required section by hand by the mason.

The rocking table can be removed so that large blocks can be machined by fixing them directly on to the main table.

For circular work, such as column " turning," two metal brackets are fixed to the main table. The block of stone is supported by two horizontal metal " centres " which are attached to the brackets and are let into the ends of the stone. The cutting process is as described above, the main table moving forward towards the tool box fixed in the middle of the cross-head and the stone rotated after each cut by means of gearing fixed on one side of the brackets. Flutes are formed, after the turning has been completed, by specially shaped tools fixed in the tool box. A column shaft up to 2·4 m long and 1·4 m diameter can be worked on this machine.

Circular column shafts, caps and bases, balusters, etc., are also turned in a *lathe*. Like the wood-working lathe described in Chap. I, Vol. III, the stone is fixed to two centres, and as it rotates it is cut by a tool fitted in a holder which traverses the length of the stone. Flutes are formed by the planing machine or by hand.

Other machines cut the stone in the forward direction only, and are known as *rigid head planing machines*. They have a quick return. They are especially invaluable for forming intricate moulded work. No hand finishing is necessary, as the machined-cut surfaces are excellent.

One of these rigid head planing machines, called an *open-side planer*, has two tool boxes, one within the cross-head (or cross-arm) and the other at the side of the single pillar. The upper tool box traverses the cross-arm and the tools can be made to move vertically; the side tool box has a rise and fall motion and the horizontally fitted tools can be moved horizontally. The top tools cut the upper surface of the stone whilst the side tools mould the vertical surface at the same operation. A big saving of time thereby results. This machine is particularly effective for deep cornices. Unlike the canting-arm planer (see J), it has only one pillar and it can therefore deal with wide (up to 2·1 m) blocks; it is employed for forming return mouldings on stones such as quoin cornices and string courses, square pillar and pilaster bases and caps, etc.

Another rigid head planing machine is the *four-head planer*. As implied, this has four tool boxes, *i.e.*, two in the cross-head and one at the side of each of the two pillars. Like those in the open-side planer, these tool boxes are independently operated and the machine is therefore capable of moulding and surfacing the top and side faces of two blocks of stone at the same time.

For marble, granite and similar brittle stone, carborundum wheels of the required shape may be fitted into the tool boxes in lieu of steel tools. The abrasive action of these wheels, assisted by water delivered on the stone, forms the desired section as they rotate at a high speed.

Polishing Machines.—These include the (*a*) Rubbing Bed, (*b*) Jenny Lind Polisher and (*c*) Disc Polisher.

(*a*) *Rubbing Bed.*—This consists of a circular metal table, 1·8 to 4·2 m diameter and 50 to 64 mm thick, which revolves on a vertical spindle at a speed varying from 20 (the largest size) to 45 revs. per min. It has a circular trough round the rim to carry away the liquid slurry produced during the rubbing operation.

This machine is now used chiefly in marble and granite works, and whilst it was formerly employed for surfacing limestone and sandstone blocks, it is now rarely used for this purpose, as the circular saw—especially the carborundum saw—and planers give a surface which is satisfactory for most purposes at a cheaper cost.

The block or slab of marble, etc., is placed on the table, and sharp sand or steel shot, together with water, is applied as the table rotates. The friction created by the action of the abrasive between the table top and the stone produces a smooth surface. Large blocks are kept in position by a wood beam fixed across and slightly above the table. Small blocks are controlled by hand.

(*b*) *Jenny Lind Polisher.*—One of several types, known as the *rise and fall* model, is shown at G. It is used for smoothing and polishing flat surfaces of marble and granite blocks or slabs. The machine, which is fixed to a pillar or wall, consists of a metal frame carrying an arm and a vertical rotating *polishing spindle* to which is connected a *rubbing head* or a *polishing disc*; the diameter of the head is 250 mm and that of the disc is 300 mm; the discs of larger machines are up to 750 mm diameter. As shown, the frame with arm is in two sections and the swivel joints allow the head or disc to be easily guided in any direction; each section of the arm is 0·9 m long and a 2·7 m by 1·2 m slab can be covered by the head at one fixing. The frame has a 0·6 m vertical adjustment by means of the hand wheel and screw and, in addition, the polishing spindle can be vertically adjusted through 175 or 200 mm. The rubbing head revolves at a speed of 250 revs. per min.; some machines have two speeds, one for smoothing and a quicker one for polishing.

A smooth surface is imparted to the marble or stone by carborundum blocks, which are of four grades, *i.e.*, coarse, medium, fine and finishing. These are fixed in turn in this order to the rubbing head; the abrasive action of these blocks as they rotate, together with the water which is delivered through the hollow polishing spindle, gives the smooth surface. This is followed by the final polishing process, the fine carborundum block being replaced by the *polishing disc*, which is a metal plate faced with felt; oxide of tin, known as *putty powder*, is applied, in addition to water; the rotary action gradually imparts a high polish to the stone.

A marble slab, after being sawn, is smoothed and polished (or " glossed ") in the following manner : The slab is set on the stone bench, the coarse carborundum block is fitted to the rubbing head and the spindle is adjusted to the required height. The motor is started, the water is turned on and the operator, holding the guiding handle, gradually directs the rotating block over the whole surface. The pressure of the carborundum block is increased or diminished by the operator lowering or raising the handle. When the surface has been rubbed down to an even surface, the coarse carborundum block is replaced by the medium block and the process is repeated.

After the fine and finishing blocks have been applied in a similar manner, the surface should be very smooth. Any grit on the marble must now be removed, the polishing disc is fixed, putty powder is sprinkled over the slab, and the surface is traversed as described until a high polish is obtained.

A splash-board, not shown in the sketch, is used to protect the operator from the slurry; it is fitted to the bench between the slab and the operator and with its upper edge about 150 mm above the top of the slab.

Slabs longer than 2·7 m must be re-set on the bench to allow the untreated surface to be dealt with. This is obviated if, instead of the fixed bench, a bogie—which runs on a track—is available.

A *fixed-height* model of this machine, cheaper than the one described, has no rise and fall main adjustment, but the polishing spindle has a 175 mm vertical movement.

(c) *Disc Polisher.*—This has a long vertical rotary spindle attached at its upper end by a universal joint to the motor above and with a 380 mm diameter disc at its lower end. The spindle is telescopic to allow for the adjustment of the disc at the required height, and the universal joint permits an area of approximately 2·1 m diameter of marble or granite to be polished.

Moulded surfaces of marble cannot be smoothed and polished by these machines and are dealt with by hand. Such work is smoothed or "grounded" by using different grades of carborundum powder; a piece of *snake stone* (Water of Ayr stone) is then applied to complete the smoothing process, after which the surface is polished by applying putty powder on a felt " jack " or pad.

Granite surfaces, especially when they have been axed (see below), are sometimes smoothed by the application of steel shot and emery powder instead of the carborundum blocks. During the first or *shotting* process, the rough surface is rendered perfectly flat by the abrasive action of the shot and water and the rotary cast steel plate of the Jenny Lind Polisher head. The second process is called *emerying*, as emery is used in lieu of shot; this completes the grinding operation. All traces of the emery are removed, and the glossing or polishing operation is performed with the felted disc and putty powder. Sometimes oil is rubbed into the granite to give a rich gloss.

Instead of hand grinding and polishing moulded granite surfaces, these operations may be performed by a *pendulum* or *slider*. A metal casting of the reverse shape of the required granite section is made and attached to one end of a long rod which is connected at the opposite end to a vertical member which is caused to swing sideways like a pendulum. After the casting has been correctly placed on the moulded granite, it is caused to swing to and fro as the pendulum swings; shot, emery, putty powder and water are applied in turn during the process.

Pneumatic Dressing and Carving Plant.—This comprises an air compressor, air receiver, cast iron main air pipe, flexible branch air pipes or hoses, pneumatic hammers and chisels. The latter tools include the punch or puncheon, plain, broad or flat, tooth (having serrated edges) and bush chisels; the bush chisel consists of several steel blades, having sharpened edges, bolted together, and is used for dressing the roughest blocks. The tools are fitted into the pneumatic hammers and the latter are attached to the flexible air hoses; a cock is fitted near the end of each hose by which the compressed air can be turned on or off by the operator. When the air is admitted to the hammer, the piston within the latter strikes in rapid succession the head of the shank of the tool; the effect of this percussion action is therefore similar to that obtained by the mason when he strikes a chisel with a mallet. Hence the dressing operation is comparatively simple, as the operator is only required to turn on the air, place the tool on the surface of the stone and guide it in the required direction. Those tools are very rapid in action and are capable of doing work ranging from the heaviest dressing to elaborate carving. They are especially effective for dressing intractable stone, such as granite and certain marble. The size of the plant varies, the largest being capable of operating fifteen hammers and employing the same number of masons.

Pneumatic hammers and machinery, such as the frame and carborundum saws, have largely superseded hand-dressing of granite.

Where the latter is still employed, the operations are somewhat similar to those described in Chap. I, Vol. I. The scappling hammer or pick is used for hammer-faced and picked work; fine picked work is produced by a fine-pointed pick or a hammer having a serrated edge; punched work is obtained by a punch or puncheon which unlike that shown at N, Fig. 19, Vol. I, is in the form of a hammer resembling a blunt pick. Single axed work is done with an axe or hexagonal headed hammer after the surface has been picked; this produces parallel lines on the surface which are barely visible in fine axed work. The finest surface given to a block of granite before being smoothed and polished is produced by a hammer called a *patent axe* after the face has been dressed with the ordinary axe; the head of the patent axe consists of sharp steel blades, one end of the head has a larger number and finer blades than the other and is used after the end with the thicker blades has been employed.

Helicoidal Wire Sawing Plant.—This is used for quarrying stone and for reducing large blocks to a size suitable for the frame saw. It consists of a long wire (of 5 to 6·5 mm diameter) which travels over and under several pulleys at a rate of approximately 60 m per min. as it produces a vertical cut in the stone. The system has not been commonly adopted in this country.

STONE DRESSINGS TO OPENINGS

Examples of dressing to openings additional to those illustrated in Vol. I are shown in Figs. 41–46 inclusive.

Six elevations of entrances are shown in Fig. 41. The same treatment may also be applied to window openings. Those at A, B, C, D and E show semicircular arches, and that at F is segmental. All of the arches have stepped extradoses.

The voussoirs forming the semicircular arch at A have ears or crossettes. The keystone extends to a string course. A satisfactory proportion of opening is obtained if the 60° diagonal intersects the top of the transome, as shown (see also C). The ashlar consists of alternate thin and thicker courses, that on the left having rusticated joints (such as the channelled joint at A, Fig. 45) and that on the right being flushed-jointed.

In all of the examples, broken diagonal lines indicate the size and shape of each voussoir, etc. Ambiguity is thus removed and the bonding is made clear. A working drawing should also have the amount of bed of each stone specified by ringed figures (see Fig. 24, Vol. I).

The treatment at B gives a bold appearance which is particularly effective for large openings. Plain courses alternate with those consisting of blocks having a large projection. The latter, detailed at S, shows a rock-faced middle portion of each block which is emphasized by the contrasting smooth or plain finished mouldings. With certain exceptions, the joints are channelled; the exceptions include the plain vertical joints necessary to limit the size of some of the voussoirs. The courses above the springing are wider than those below, and a moulded course at the impost, such as is shown on the left, may be preferred to separate the two. The broken construction lines show that the channelled joints and cyma mouldings of the voussoirs are parallel, and thus the rusticated portions are tapered.

The opening at C shows a recessed jamb (see plan K). The arch is similarly recessed and consists of two rings—note the value of the broken diagonal lines as indicating this. The voussoirs of the outer ring are moulded as shown at M. The bold appearance is here shown of the steps detailed in section at M, Fig. 49.

STONE DRESSINGS TO DOOR OPENINGS

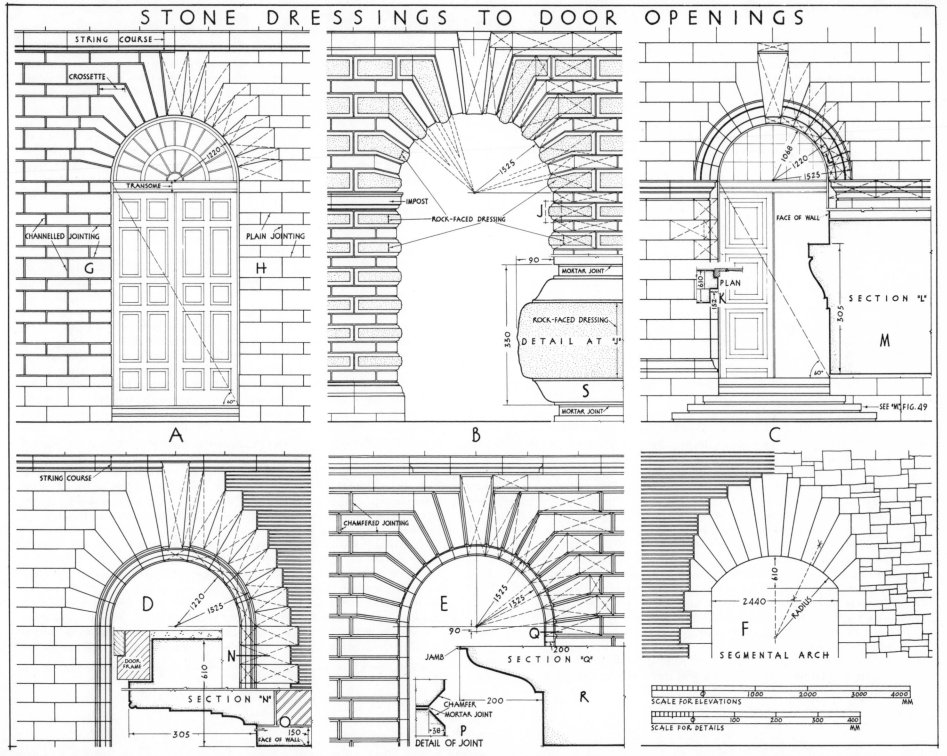

STRING COURSE

CROSSETTE

1220

TRANSOME

CHANNELLED JOINTING

PLAIN JOINTING

G

H

60°

A

1525

IMPOST

ROCK-FACED DRESSING

J

90

MORTAR JOINT

350

ROCK-FACED DRESSING

DETAIL AT "J"

S

MORTAR JOINT

B

1068
1220
1525

FACE OF WALL

610
152

PLAN

K

SECTION "L"

305

60°

M

SEE "M" FIG. 49

C

STRING COURSE

1220
1525

D

DOOR FRAME

N

610

SECTION "N"

305

150

FACE OF WALL

D

CHAMFERED JOINTING

1525
1325

E

90

Q

200

SECTION "Q"

JAMB

CHAMFER
MORTAR JOINT

200

38

P

R

DETAIL OF JOINT

E

610

2440

RADIUS

F

SEGMENTAL ARCH

SCALE FOR ELEVATIONS
0   1000   2000   3000   4000   MM

SCALE FOR DETAILS
0   100   200   300   400   MM

F

FIGURE 41

Another example of a two-ringed arch is shown at D. This differs from C in that the inner ring is moulded (see O) and the bed joints of its voussoirs coincide with alternate bed joints of the outer ring voussoirs. The voussoirs course with the ashlar shown on the left. For brick walls the voussoirs should course with the brickwork as shown on the right.

The arch at E differs from the two preceding examples, as it is only a single-ringed arch, each voussoir being moulded as shown at R. The general jointing is chamfered (see P) and the vertical joints of the voussoirs may be also chamfered as an alternative to the plain joints shown.

The application of a stepped extradosed arch to a segmental headed opening is shown at F; the voussoirs are shown coursing with brickwork on the left and, as an alternative, with squared rubble walling on the right. The bed joint of the lower voussoir or springer is below the springing line; this is necessary in order that the springer may be of satisfactory proportions.

Each of the openings shown in Fig. 41 may accommodate a pair of folding doors and a transome light, such as are faintly indicated at A and C.

Examples of six square-headed door openings are illustrated in Fig. 42. Enlarged details of this stonework are shown in Fig. 43.

The height of a classic door opening is at least twice its width, but this proportion is not habitually followed. The example at B and C, Fig. 42, is in accordance with tradition, whilst E and H show the height to be 1·31 m greater than the width, a proportion which conforms to that of most of the standard internal doors listed in Chap. IV, Vol. I.

The doorway shown in elevation at A, Fig. 42, suitable for a house, is provided with an entablature. The latter consists of a moulded architrave, frieze and cornice. The student is recommended to study a classic entablature, such as that shown at A and B, Fig. 47, in order to become conversant with the proportions of the traditional type. Whilst these general proportions are often departed from in current practice, such divergence should be strictly limited. Two alternative details of this entablature are shown at A and B, Fig. 43. That at A conforms most closely to the elevation; because of the cushion-shaped appearance of the frieze, which is said to be *pulvinated*, the centre of the arc forming the pulvination is obtained as shown at L, Fig. 45. A flat frieze is shown at B, Fig. 43; whilst this is of the same height as that at A, it is usual to make a pulvinated frieze three-quarters of the height of the architrave and a plain frieze equal to the architrave. In accordance with tradition, the width of an architrave is about one-sixth the width of the opening, and the cornice is from one and a quarter to one and a third the height of the architrave. Thus, the classical proportions of this doorway would be as follows: Architrave, $\frac{1}{6} \times 1\cdot 07\text{m} = 180$ mm wide; frieze, $\frac{3}{4} \times 180$ mm $= 135$ mm high (if pulvinated) and 180 mm (if plain); and cornice, $\frac{5}{4}$ to $\frac{4}{3} \times 180$ mm or about 230 mm (see also G, Fig. 44, and L and M, Fig. 45).

The elevation at A shows ashlar walling on the left and brickwork as an alternative on the right. The moulded jambs may be coursed as shown on the left, or the number of bed joints in the architrave may be reduced as indicated on the right; a bond stone in the architrave, shown by broken lines at S, may be used, or a good bond may be obtained if alternate jamb stones are shaped as shown by full lines at D, Fig. 48. In order to minimize awkward cutting of the brickwork at the cornice, the latter may be finished square as shown by broken lines at T.

A pedimented doorway[1] is shown in elevation at C and in section at B, Fig. 42. A pediment is a triangular feature which crowns a doorway, window, gable, etc.; its lower boundary being the horizontal corona and bedmould, and its sloping boundaries being the complete cornice; the triangular space between these horizontal and raking members is occupied by one or several stones and is called the *tympanum* or core. A modification of this triangular pediment is the segmental pediment, the cornice being curved to the shape of a segment.

The pediment is often made excessively high. This is avoided, and a satisfactory proportion obtained if the geometrical construction shown at C is adhered to. Thus, with one end " *a* " of the fillet of the corona as centre and its whole length " *ab* " as radius, an arc is drawn to intersect the centre line at " *c* "; with " *c* " as centre and " *cb* " as radius an arc is struck intersecting the centre line at " *d* "; the latter should be the point of intersection of either the bottom of the raking corona as shown or the bottom of the raking bedmould.

It will be observed that the raking cornice consists of the crown mould comprising a cyma recta with fillet, the corona and bedmould. This is shown more clearly in the enlarged detail at C, Fig. 43, where P equals Q. The jointing of the stonework should be carefully studied. The lower end stone or *springer* comprises portions of the cornice, the horizontal corona and bedmould; it courses with the adjacent ashlar, forming top and bottom horizontal bed joints, a vertical joint at the end of the cornice, and the fourth boundary consists of a vertical joint at the horizontal corona and bedmould which is continued as a normal joint at the raking cornice; this latter joint coincides with the intersection between the bottom of the raking bedmould and the fillet of the horizontal corona. The apex stone is also coursed in with the ashlar, the cornice being stopped against the wall face and the upper bed coinciding with the horizontal bed joint of the ashlar. A departure from the latter bed joint is usually made if the stone pediment occurs in a brick wall; here the projecting sloping surface of each stone of the cornice is continued to the back and the brickwork is cut to intersect this raking surface.

A detailed section through the architrave is shown at S, Fig. 43, and a portion of the elevation is shown at R. The stonework at the principal entrance of an important building may be enriched by carving. Many existing examples show very elaborate enrichment, but owing to the high cost of such work, the present tendency is to economize in this direction. Where such decoration is applied, it is usual to limit it to the bedmould, one or two members of the architrave and occasionally to the crown mould. An example of ornamentation is indicated at R. Care should be taken to provide adequate material in the member for the

[1] This type is usually deferred to the third year of a course, and the pediment is therefore elaborated in Vol. IV.

carver to produce the required ornament. Thus, the bead U at S, Fig. 43, formed by the moulding machine (J, Fig. 40), is suitable for the carving of the *bead and reel* ornament shown at R; similarly, the ovolo bedmould is suited to receive the *egg and dart* ornament indicated in Fig. 46. An alternative ot this architrave is detailed at T, Fig. 43. Whilst some of the close grained sandstones can be finely carved, the limestone class is generally most suited for this purpose.

The architrave of the entrance D, Fig. 42, is detailed at D, Fig. 43. Note that it outer members are returned on the plinth block, which latter must, of course, have an adequate projection to receive it. The head of this architrave (like that at E, G and H, Fig. 42) is formed of three stones with secret joggle joints (see D, Fig. 25, Vol. I). An additional feature may be provided either at U or V in the form of brackets or *consoles* similar to, but much shorter than, that detailed in Fig. 46 and placed below an increased projecting cornice.

The entrance at E, Fig. 42, has a wide architrave which is detailed at E, Fig. 43. The broad outer flat band is continued to form the upper member of the plinth. The shadow produced at the deep sinking emphasizes the rather bold curved member.

The detail of the architrave at F and G, Fig. 42, is shown at F, Fig. 43. The prominent moulded member is effective, but see the note below regarding protection of projecting masonry. It will be observed that the stonework courses with the brickwork.

> Principal doors of buildings of importance are frequently of bronze. The door, with pediment and entablature, shown at F and G is an example. Briefly, the bronze of the entablature and pilaster is of 6·5 mm thick cast bronze, and, for best work, the external face of the door is formed with 6·5 mm thick bronze cast in the form of panels, and an 3 mm thick sheet bronze backing; the door is 50 mm thick, with a space between the facing and backing.

An example of a very wide architrave is shown at H, Fig. 42, and detailed at G, Fig. 43.

> The necessary lead covering of cornices has been purposely omitted in order to make the stone details as clear as possible. It cannot be too strongly emphasized that all projecting stone members should be protected as shown in Fig. 76, Vol. I. This is especially necessary in smoke-laden districts (see p. 106). Thus, for example, in addition to the cornice shown at B and C, Fig. 42, the upper surface of the horizontal corona should be given a very slight weathering and be covered with lead. The value of the drip and throating should also be appreciated (see Fig. 47 and p. 124). The modern tendency of omitting projecting courses, such as cornices, string courses and sills—with their drips and throatings—has resulted in many recent buildings becoming horribly disfigured within a very short time after erection. Such disfigurement is very pronounced at door and window openings which have been finished simply with wide, plain but slightly projecting bands of fillets. Referring again to some of the entrances illustrated in Fig. 42 and detailed in Fig. 43, it is seen that certain of the details should be slightly modified unless protection by string courses, porticoes, etc., is afforded. Thus, for example, a small throat could with advantage be formed at E (see broken lines at X) and F (Y to be widened to allow for the small throat), Fig. 43.

Additional doorways are shown in Fig. 48, and, as already pointed out, these door dressings can also be applied to windows.

Six examples of the stone treatment at windows are illustrated in Fig. 44 and detailed in Fig. 45.

The opening at A, Fig. 44, accommodates a pair of metal casements (see Fig. 62, Vol. I) and a hopper light. The elongated channelled bed joints, detailed at A, Fig. 45, are an effective contrast to the adjacent plain jointing.

The double-hung sashed window shown at C and D, Fig. 44, has a stone segmental head backed with a two-ringed rough brick arch, and the architrave consists of alternate moulded and projecting plain blocks. This is detailed at C, Fig. 45.

The opening at G, Fig. 44, shows an entablature. Traditional proportions are indicated. Two alternative details are shown at L and M, Fig. 45.

The metal casement in a wood frame (see Fig. 62, Vol. I) shown at J and L, Fig. 44, is detailed at D, Fig. 45. The latter figure also shows two alternative details of the window sill at J and K.

The openings at M and O, Fig. 44, are detailed at E and G, Fig. 45.

An elevation and vertical section of a double-hung sashed window are shown at J and K, Fig. 46. The stone dressings include an entablature with consoles or brackets. The latter are often elaborately enriched with carving and usually take the form of a *scroll* (resembling a partially unrolled scroll of parchment) or *volute*. Detail A shows the side view of a console and one of several methods of contrasting a scroll is there shown and explained at H. The elevation is shown at B and the architrave is detailed at N. An application of consoles to an entrance is illustrated at H, Fig. 48.

CORNICES

Several cornices are illustrated in Fig. 47 as alternatives to those shown in Vol. I.

The plan and elevation of a classic (Corinthian) entablature are shown at A and B, Fig. 47. Many important buildings have been completed with entablatures of proportions which conform very closely to those indicated in this traditional example.[1] Students should study these proportions very closely and be guided by them when designing stonework for upper features of buildings and dressings at door and window openings.

The cornice may be provided with a gutter as shown by broken lines at A, or be similar to that at N, or it may be weathered in the more usual manner as shown at L. The outlet from the gutter, such as a lead branch pipe, would be connected to a rain-water pipe fixed in an inconspicuous position; in order to avoid mutilation of the stonework, the outlet sometimes takes the form of a swan-neck bend connected to an internal rain-water pipe. Enrichment, in the form of a carved bedmould, cymatium (occasionally), modillions (in the form of horizontal scrolls) and sunk panels (often rose-shaped and therefore known as *roses*), may be provided.

The sections at F, G, H and J show cornices having a small projection. They

[1] The proportions of a classic entablature are based upon the diameter of a column just above its base. Details of an order, comprising columns, entablature, etc., are given in Vol. IV.

STONE DRESSINGS TO DOOR OPENINGS

NOTE: ENLARGED DETAILS OF THE STONE MOULDINGS ARE SHOWN IN FIG. 43

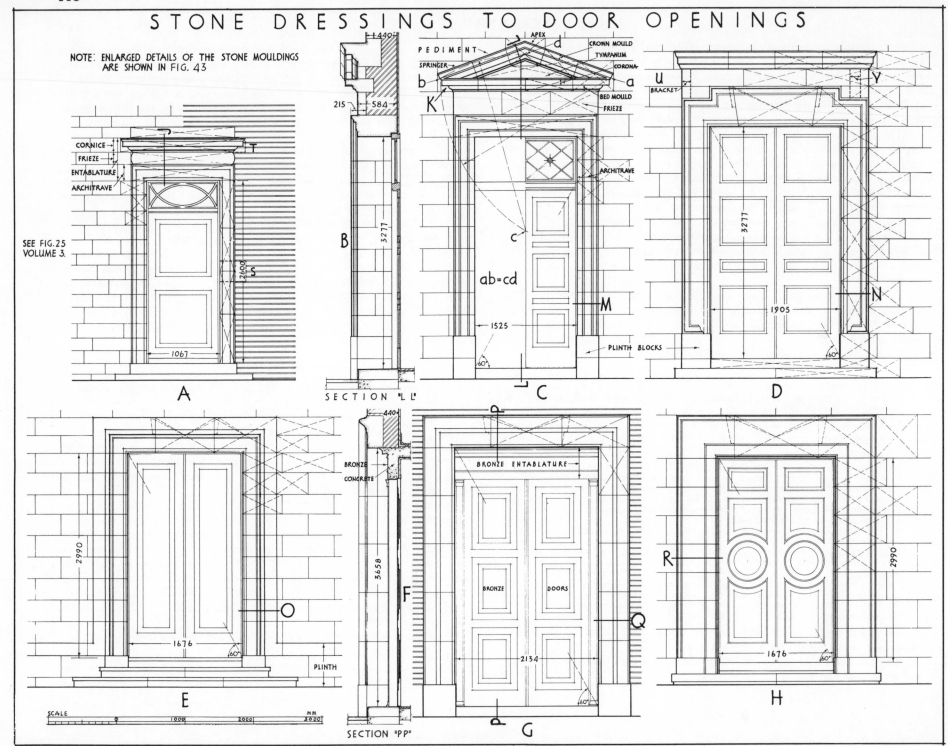

SEE FIG. 25 VOLUME 3.

CORNICE
FRIEZE
ENTABLATURE
ARCHITRAVE

2600
1067
S

A

±440
215 | 584
3277

SECTION "LL"

B

PEDIMENT | APEX | d | CROWN MOULD
SPRINGER | | TYMPANUM
b | | CORONA
K | | a
| | BED MOULD
| | FRIEZE
ARCHITRAVE
c
ab=cd
M
1525
60°
PLINTH BLOCKS

C

U | BRACKET | Y
3277
1905
N
60°

D

2990
1676
60°
O
PLINTH

SCALE | 1000 | 2000 | MM 3000

E

440
BRONZE
CONCRETE
3658
F

SECTION "PP"

F

BRONZE ENTABLATURE
BRONZE | DOORS
2134
60°
Q

G

R
2990
1676
60°

H

FIGURE 42

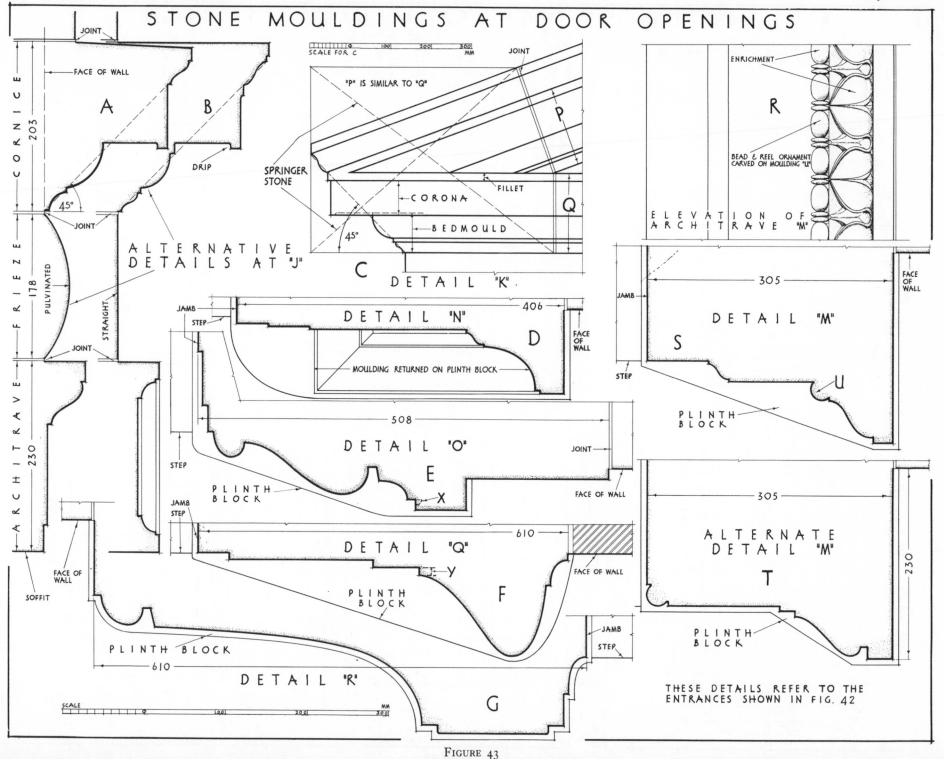

STONE MOULDINGS AT DOOR OPENINGS

ALTERNATIVE DETAILS AT "J"

CORNICE 203
FRIEZE 178
PULVINATED
ARCHITRAVE 230

JOINT
FACE OF WALL
A B
DRIP
45°
JOINT
STRAIGHT
JOINT
FACE OF WALL
SOFFIT

SCALE FOR C
0 100 200 300 MM
JOINT
"P" IS SIMILAR TO "Q"
SPRINGER STONE
P
FILLET
Q
CORONA
BEDMOULD
45°
DETAIL "K".
C

ENRICHMENT
R
BEAD & REEL ORNAMENT CARVED ON MOULDING "L"
ELEVATION OF ARCHITRAVE "M"

JAMB
305
FACE OF WALL
DETAIL "M"
S
STEP
U
PLINTH BLOCK

DETAIL "N"
JAMB
STEP
406
D
FACE OF WALL
MOULDING RETURNED ON PLINTH BLOCK

508
DETAIL "O"
STEP
E
PLINTH BLOCK
JOINT
X
FACE OF WALL

JAMB
STEP
610
DETAIL "Q"
Y
F
PLINTH BLOCK
FACE OF WALL
JAMB
STEP

ALTERNATE DETAIL "M"
T
230
PLINTH BLOCK

PLINTH BLOCK
610
DETAIL "R"
G

THESE DETAILS REFER TO THE ENTRANCES SHOWN IN FIG. 42

SCALE
0 100 200 300 MM

FIGURE 43

STONE DRESSINGS TO WINDOW OPENINGS

NOTE: ENLARGED DETAILS OF THE STONE MOULDINGS ARE SHOWN IN FIG. 45

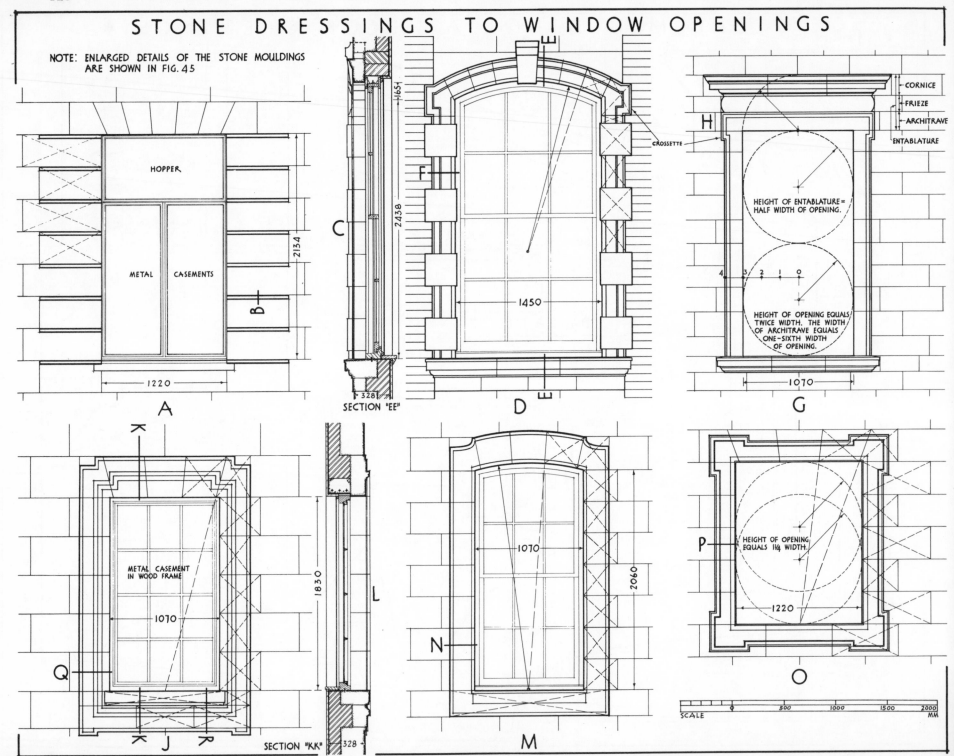

HOPPER

METAL CASEMENTS

1220

A

SECTION "EE"

1651

2438

328

C

1450

D

CORNICE

FRIEZE

ARCHITRAVE

ENTABLATURE

CROSSETTE

H

HEIGHT OF ENTABLATURE = HALF WIDTH OF OPENING.

4 3 2 1 0

HEIGHT OF OPENING EQUALS TWICE WIDTH. THE WIDTH OF ARCHITRAVE EQUALS ONE-SIXTH WIDTH OF OPENING.

1070

G

METAL CASEMENT IN WOOD FRAME

1070

1830

328

SECTION "KK"

K

Q

K J R

L

1070

2060

N

M

HEIGHT OF OPENING EQUALS 1¼ WIDTH.

1220

P

O

SCALE

0 500 1000 1500 2000

MM

FIGURE 44

DETAILS OF MASONRY AT WINDOW OPENINGS

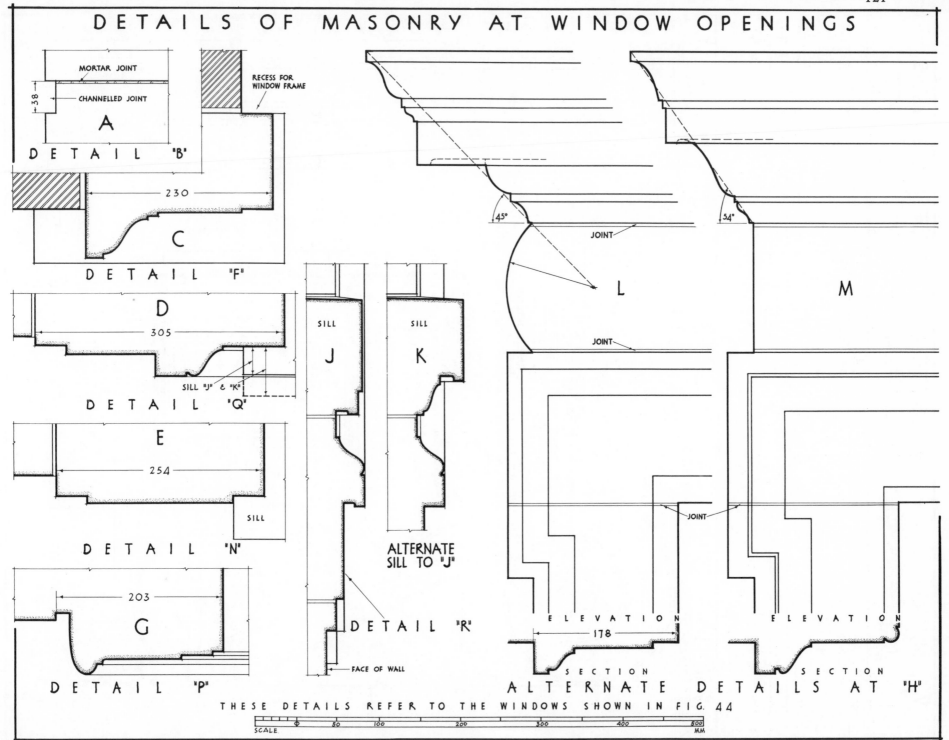

MORTAR JOINT

RECESS FOR WINDOW FRAME

38

CHANNELLED JOINT

A

D E T A I L "B"

230

C

D E T A I L "F"

D

305

SILL "J" & "K"

D E T A I L "Q"

E

254

SILL

D E T A I L "N"

203

G

D E T A I L "P"

SILL

J

SILL

K

ALTERNATE
SILL TO "J"

DETAIL "R"

FACE OF WALL

45°

54°

JOINT

L

M

JOINT

JOINT

E L E V A T I O N

E L E V A T I O N

178

S E C T I O N

S E C T I O N

A L T E R N A T E   D E T A I L S   A T "H"

THESE DETAILS REFER TO THE WINDOWS SHOWN IN FIG. 44

SCALE   0   50   100   200   300   400   500
MM

FIGURE 45

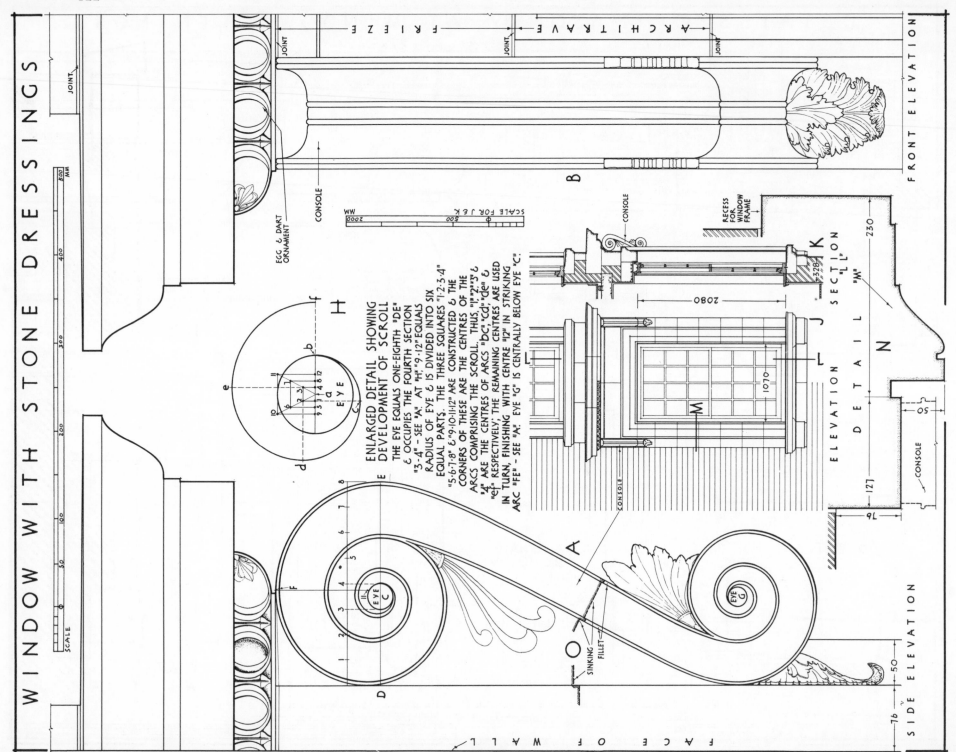

WINDOW WITH STONE DRESSINGS

ENLARGED DETAIL SHOWING
DEVELOPMENT OF SCROLL

THE EYE EQUALS ONE-EIGHTH "DE"
& OCCUPIES THE FOURTH SECTION
"3-4" – SEE "A" AT "H". "9-12" EQUALS
RADIUS OF EYE & IS DIVIDED INTO SIX
EQUAL PARTS. THE THREE SQUARES "1-2-3-4"
"5-6-7-8" & "9-10-11-12" ARE CONSTRUCTED & THE
CORNERS OF THESE ARE THE CENTRES OF THE
ARCS COMPRISING THE SCROLL. THUS, "1"-"2"-"3" &
"4" ARE THE CENTRES OF ARCS "BC"-"CD"-"DE" &
"EF" RESPECTIVELY; THE REMAINING CENTRES ARE USED
IN TURN, FINISHING WITH CENTRE "12" IN STRIKING
ARC "FE" – SEE "A". EYE "G" IS CENTRALLY BELOW EYE "C".

FRONT ELEVATION

SIDE ELEVATION

FIGURE 46

C O R N I C E S

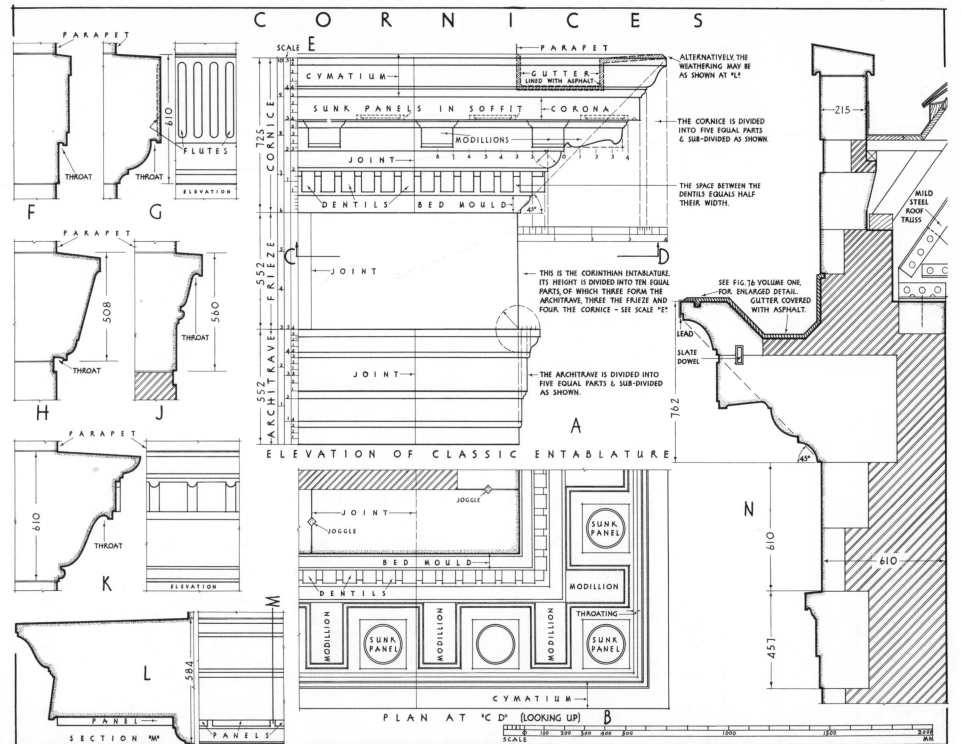

PARAPET

FLUTES

ELEVATION

THROAT

THROAT

610

F

G

PARAPET

THROAT

508

560

THROAT

THROAT

H

J

PARAPET

610

THROAT

K

ELEVATION

PANEL

584

SECTION "M"

M

PANELS

L

SCALE

E

CYMATIUM

PARAPET

GUTTER LINED WITH ASPHALT

ALTERNATIVELY, THE WEATHERING MAY BE AS SHOWN AT "L".

SUNK PANELS IN SOFFIT

CORONA

CORNICE

725

MODILLIONS

THE CORNICE IS DIVIDED INTO FIVE EQUAL PARTS & SUB-DIVIDED AS SHOWN.

JOINT

8 7 6 5 4 3 2 1 0 1 2 3 4

DENTILS

BED MOULD

45°

THE SPACE BETWEEN THE DENTILS EQUALS HALF THEIR WIDTH.

1 2 3 4

C

D

FRIEZE

552

JOINT

THIS IS THE CORINTHIAN ENTABLATURE. ITS HEIGHT IS DIVIDED INTO TEN EQUAL PARTS, OF WHICH THREE FORM THE ARCHITRAVE, THREE THE FRIEZE AND FOUR THE CORNICE – SEE SCALE "E".

SEE FIG. 76 VOLUME ONE, FOR ENLARGED DETAIL. GUTTER COVERED WITH ASPHALT.

ARCHITRAVE

552

JOINT

JOINT

THE ARCHITRAVE IS DIVIDED INTO FIVE EQUAL PARTS & SUB-DIVIDED AS SHOWN.

A

ELEVATION OF CLASSIC ENTABLATURE

LEAD

SLATE DOWEL

762

N

45°

MILD STEEL ROOF TRUSS

215

610

610

457

JOINT

JOGGLE

JOGGLE

BED MOULD

SUNK PANEL

SUNK PANEL

MODILLION

DENTILS

MODILLION

MODILLION

MODILLION

SUNK PANEL

SUNK PANEL

THROATING

CYMATIUM

PLAN AT "C D" (LOOKING UP)

B

SCALE

0 100 200 300 400 500 1000 1500 2000

MM

FIGURE 47

could also be used as string courses. The section and elevation at G show a fluted band. A somewhat similar motif is used at the cornice K. Cornice L has a relatively large projection; the soffit of this type may be relieved by raised panels or *mutules*.

The section at N shows a cornice complete with parapet, etc. An economy in stone results when a cornice is of this compound type, as a relatively small block is required as a crowning member.

Note that all the cornices are throated to prevent staining of the masonry below.

STONE STEPS AND STAIRS

The design and construction of wood stairs are introduced in Chap. IV, Vol. I (Fig. 65), and fully described in Chap. II, Vol. III. As the terms, essential requirements, proportions of steps, etc., are dealt with in these volumes, and as they apply equally well to stone steps and stairs, it is unnecessary to repeat such information here, and students are therefore recommended to defer consideration of the following until they have studied the principles of wood stair construction.

The stone selected for steps and landings must be hard, strong and durable, and it should not readily wear to a smooth and slippery surface. Certain of the sandstones best satisfy these requirements, and " York " stone (see p. 98) is usually specified.

Steps are either (1) rectangular, (2) built-up, or (3) spandril in cross-section.

1. *Rectangular Steps.*—These are illustrated at H, J, K, L, M, N and O, Fig. 48, Fig. 42 and in Vol. I. They are the strongest type. A flight of such solid steps may be constructed with the front lower edge of one step supported on the top back edge of that below (see L and N, Fig. 48), but the rebated or checked joint (similar to that at G, Fig. 48) is the best. These steps may be provided with moulded nosings (see G and H, Fig. 48, Fig. 41, and Fig. 42).

2. *Built-up Steps* (see E and P, Fig. 48).—The tread and riser of each step are formed of relatively thin sawn slabs, and the construction is therefore economical. They are not so strong as solid rectangular steps, and whilst occasionally used without any bedding or backing (see P), they are more often applied as a facing to concrete steps (see E). The minimum thickness of treads which are only supported at the ends is 50 mm and this should be increased by at least 13 mm for every extra 300 mm of unsupported length beyond 915 mm. Slabs which are less than 50 mm thick can be easily fractured, even when being handled before and during fixing, and thin treads constructed as shown at E can readily snap by a weight suddenly applied unless solidly bedded throughout.

Steps formed of stone treads only, known as *skeleton stone steps*, are sometimes employed for short, narrow flights, which are not subjected to heavy traffic and where the absence of risers is not objected to.

3. *Spandril Steps* (see A, B, C, D and E, Fig. 49).—Excepting the ends which are built into the wall, these steps are approximately triangular in cross-section,

and are therefore lighter than the solid rectangular type. Such steps add greatly to the appearance of a stair and the maximum headroom is obtained by their use. The soffit may be flush (see A and B), broken (see C) or moulded (see D). A splayed rebated joint is formed between each step, the splay of the rebate being normal to the pitch of the stair. To avoid weak construction and damage to the step at its back edge (where it is thinnest), it is usual to have a 50 mm splay (see A) for stairs not exceeding 1·2 m width, and this is increased by 13 mm for every additional 300 mm in width.

Thresholds.—In addition to those illustrated in Vol. I, there are several thresholds shown in Figs. 41, 42 and 48. An example of one in which built-up steps are employed is shown at A, B, C, D and E, Fig. 48. The treads and risers are solidly bedded and well jointed in cement mortar (1 cement to 3 sand). The treads of all external steps should be given a slight fall to throw off the weather; the fall shown at E is 3 mm. The top edge of the nosing should be slightly rounded off (it is sometimes chamfered), otherwise it maybe easily damaged. The nosings may be moulded; several examples of moulded nosings are shown at G, Fig. 48; A, B, C, D, K, L and M, Fig. 49; Figs. 41 and 42. Solid rectangular steps may also be used as an alternative. Alternative facings to the wall are shown, that on the left being of ashlar with a brick backing, and on the right a brick cavity wall is shown, having a Flemish garden wall facing (see B, Fig. 18).

The application of solid rectangular steps forming an unimportant entrance is shown at L, M, N and O, Fig. 48. The steps are built solidly into a wall at one end and supported at the other by a dwarf wall (see L and M). The front lower edge of one step is bedded in cement mortar on the top back edge of the step below (see N). Whilst this form of a joint is good enough for a flight of this description, it is not employed in first-class work as open joints appear if the mortar bedding becomes defective. Note that the going (254 mm), plus twice the rise (178 mm) as shown at N, equals 610 mm (see Chap. IV, Vol. I).

The detail at P shows the construction of built-up steps which could be adopted as an alternative to the above. The treads and risers are connected together by means of three pairs of copper (or slate or other non-corrodible material) cramps or dowels bedded in cement mortar.

The simple balustrade consists of 25 mm square wrought iron balusters to which a handrail of similar material is screwed (see K, Fig. 49), holes being drilled through the handrail and the ends of the balusters (which would also be tapped) to receive the screws; one end of the rail is also built into the wall to ensure greater rigidity. The balusters are secured to the steps and landing in a manner shown at K and M, Fig. 49; dovetailed mortices are formed to receive the ends (preferable ragged to give a key) of the balusters; molten lead is then run in, well caulked (consolidated when cool with a blunt chisel) and covered flush with cement mortar to exclude water from the lead and thus prevent discoloration of the stone. Grouted cement is a cheaper alternative to lead. As an alternative to the metal balustrade, the wall may be continued to a convenient height and finished with a coping.

STONE STEPS

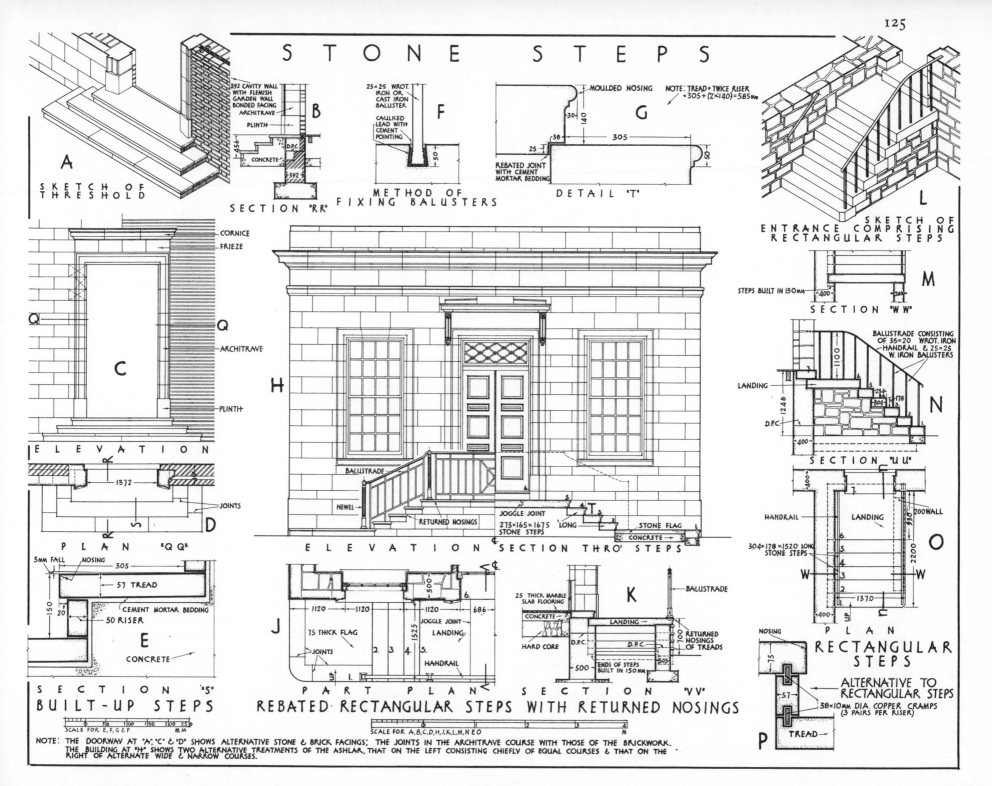

A — SKETCH OF THRESHOLD

B — SECTION "RR"
- 392 CAVITY WALL WITH FLEMISH GARDEN WALL BONDED FACING
- ARCHITRAVE
- PLINTH
- D.P.C.
- CONCRETE
- 456
- 392

F — METHOD OF FIXING BALUSTERS
- 25×25 WROT. IRON OR CAST IRON BALUSTER
- CAULKED LEAD WITH CEMENT POINTING
- 50

G — DETAIL "T"
- MOULDED NOSING
- NOTE: TREAD + TWICE RISER = 305 + (2×140) = 585 MM
- 30
- 140
- 38
- 25
- 305
- 50
- REBATED JOINT WITH CEMENT MORTAR BEDDING

L — SKETCH OF ENTRANCE COMPRISING RECTANGULAR STEPS

C — ELEVATION
- CORNICE
- FRIEZE
- ARCHITRAVE
- PLINTH
- Q Q

D — PLAN "Q Q"
- 1372
- JOINTS

E — SECTION "S" — BUILT-UP STEPS
- 3 MM FALL
- NOSING
- 305
- 57 TREAD
- 50 RISER
- 150
- 20
- CEMENT MORTAR BEDDING
- CONCRETE

SCALE FOR E, F, G & P
50 100 150 200 250
MM

H — ELEVATION SECTION THRO' STEPS
- BALUSTRADE
- NEWEL
- RETURNED NOSINGS
- JOGGLE JOINT
- 273×165×1675 STONE STEPS
- 'LONG'
- STONE FLAG
- CONCRETE
- T

J — PART PLAN — REBATED RECTANGULAR STEPS WITH RETURNED NOSINGS
- 500
- 1120 1120 1120 686
- 1525
- 75 THICK FLAG
- JOGGLE JOINT
- LANDING
- 2 3 4 5
- JOINTS
- HANDRAIL
- UP

K — SECTION "VV"
- 25 THICK MARBLE SLAB FLOORING
- BALUSTRADE
- CONCRETE
- LANDING
- RETURNED NOSINGS OF TREADS
- HARD CORE
- D.P.C.
- D.P.C.
- 700
- 305
- ENDS OF STEPS BUILT IN 150 MM
- 500

M — SECTION "WW"
- STEPS BUILT IN 150 MM
- 400 200

N — SECTION "UU"
- BALUSTRADE CONSISTING OF 35×20 WROT. IRON HANDRAIL & 25×25 W. IRON BALUSTERS
- 1100
- LANDING
- 254
- 178
- 304
- D.P.C.
- 124.6
- 400

O — PLAN — RECTANGULAR STEPS
- 400
- HANDRAIL
- LANDING
- 200 WALL
- 304×178×1520 LONG STONE STEPS
- 93.0
- 2200
- 6
- 5
- 4
- 3
- 2
- W W
- UP
- 1370
- 400

P — ALTERNATIVE TO RECTANGULAR STEPS
- NOSING
- 75
- 57
- TREAD
- 38×10 MM DIA. COPPER CRAMPS (3 PAIRS PER RISER)

SCALE FOR A, B, C, D, H, J, K, L, M, N & O
1 2 3 4
M

NOTE: THE DOORWAY AT "A", "C" & "D" SHOWS ALTERNATIVE STONE & BRICK FACINGS; THE JOINTS IN THE ARCHITRAVE COURSE WITH THOSE OF THE BRICKWORK. THE BUILDING AT "H" SHOWS TWO ALTERNATIVE TREATMENTS OF THE ASHLAR, THAT ON THE LEFT CONSISTING CHIEFLY OF EQUAL COURSES & THAT ON THE RIGHT OF ALTERNATE WIDE & NARROW COURSES.

FIGURE 48

Another application of rectangular steps is given at H, J and K, Fig. 48. The elevation is that of the façade of a small public building, such as offices or a bank. Whilst this is not a common arrangement of steps for an entrance, it is given here as an alternative to the more usual form shown at C, and it has an advantage in that the balustrade is useful, especially to the infirm and older members of the public who may visit the building. A detail of the steps is given at G; these are of good proportions, with the bottom of the front edges square rebated and the tread nosings moulded; these nosings are returned on the outer ends of the step (see H and K). The steps and landing are built 150 mm into the main wall and are supported on a wall at the outer ends. The landing consists of three stone slabs (see H and J) connected together by *joggle joints* (see the section at H and also the detail at F, Fig. 49). Each bottom step consists of an edging of stone blocks cut to the section shown at G, with a 50 to 75 mm thick flag solidly bedded on a concrete bed (see section at H). The metal balustrade is secured to the steps as described on p. 124. Alternative designs of the latter are shown in Fig. 49.

Stairs.—Stone was commonly preferred to timber in the construction of principal staircases of municipal and commercial, etc., buildings. This material has been largely superseded and such stairs are now chiefly of reinforced concrete construction (see p. 129). Where stone is still specified for this purpose, it is generally in districts where suitable local sandstone is employed.

A stone open well stair is detailed in Fig. 49. The plan H shows twenty steps, including landings, arranged round a 710 mm wide well. As shown in the sections G and J, these steps are of the spandril type already described. They are also known as *cantilever* or *hanging steps*, as each is fixed at one end only, the other being free and finished with a returned moulded nosing as detailed at A. The sketch at E shows the built-in end of a spandril step; the spandril soffit is stopped at the face of the wall (or plaster) and a square seating is formed at the end which is built into the wall (which latter is preferably constructed in cement mortar), the wall hold varying from 102·5 to 215 mm. The ends of these steps are bedded in cement and solidly fixed all round—especially at their top surfaces—with sound pieces of slate, etc. set in cement; the steps are also jointed in mortar.

Each of the alternative spandril steps shown at B has its returned nosing continued to line with the face of the riser of the second step above it. Of good appearance, they are stronger than those at A because of their increased thickness. The steps at C form a broken soffit, the appearance of which is less satisfactory than the above. The moulded soffit formed by the steps at D is attractive. Alternative nosings are shown at C, K, L and M, the bold appearance of the latter being especially effective (see C, Fig. 41 and H, Fig. 42). Note that the proportions of these steps agree with the rules stated in Chap. IV, Vol. I.

The half space landing consists of four slabs, joggle jointed, which are solidly built into the walls. The thickness of this landing may be either 165 mm or 210 mm (see R); whilst the latter gives a satisfactory finish on the underside where it joins step 19, it results in a large increase in weight of each slab. The joggles are stopped at the free ends at least, and thus only butt joints are exposed as shown at F. Each of the quarter space landings may consist of two slabs, joggle jointed, to facilitate handling and fixing.

The steps may be built-in as the walls are being constructed, or fixing may be deferred until the walls have been built and the building is nearer completion. The latter is the usual course adopted and risk of damage to the steps is thereby minimized; the pockets which receive the ends of the steps are formed and temporarily filled in with bricks laid in sand as the walling proceeds, which bricks are thereby easily removed when required. A storey-rod is used to ensure that the steps are built in at the correct heights (the bottom one being fixed first) and the free ends of the steps are securely strutted down to the floor; these vertical wood struts must not be removed until the work has set. If built-in as the general work proceeds, the steps must be adequately protected with rough wood casings; these must be well secured and should be frequently examined, as a dislodged casing may result in a damaged nosing.

The weight of wall tailing down the fixed ends of the steps must be adequate to ensure stability of a cantilevered stair. The strength of the stair shown in Fig. 49 would be considerably increased if, as shown at S, a mild steel beam was provided to support the half space landing at its outer edge and a steel channel or beam was introduced at the soffit of each flight and near to the free ends of the steps. The detail S shows the connection between the landing beam (which would have a 215 mm bearing on the walls) and the top flight channel. Such steelwork is necessary for wide stairs, especially if subjected to heavy traffic. Incidentally, it assists in preventing a total collapse of the stair in the case of fire. If desired, such steelwork may be encased in concrete and either plastered or finished with thin stone slabs bedded to the concrete, as shown at B, Fig. 50.

Balustrade.—Two alternative designs of wrought iron balustrades are shown at G and J, Fig. 49, and alternative details of these are shown at K, L and M. The fixing of the balusters at K has been described on p. 124; as indicated, the dovetail mortice which receives the baluster must be set back from the end face of the step (unless the nosing is of the type shown at M). This reduces the effective width of the stair, and to avoid this the balustrade may be of the design shown at G and J where balusters of small section, connected at their lower ends to a 38 mm by 7 mm bar, alternate at intervals with 25 mm square *bracket balusters*. The latter are so called because they are connected to the *ends* of the steps in a similar manner to that described, the balusters being curved to clear the nosings (see also detail L); the cover plate shown may be used to provide a good finish and it may be either bedded on cement or fixed by small screws secured to plugs driven into holes drilled into the stone. This detail also shows the method of fixing a wood handrail to a metal balustrade; the upper ends of the balusters are screwed to a 32 by 7 mm wrought iron bar and the handrail is secured to this with screws, the latter being fixed from below at intervals between the balusters. An alternative wood handrail, fixed in a similar manner, is shown at M. The balustrade may be of bronze as an alternative to wrought iron (see also B, Fig. 50).

The Building Regulations make certain rules about the height of balustrades

STONE OPEN WELL STAIRCASE

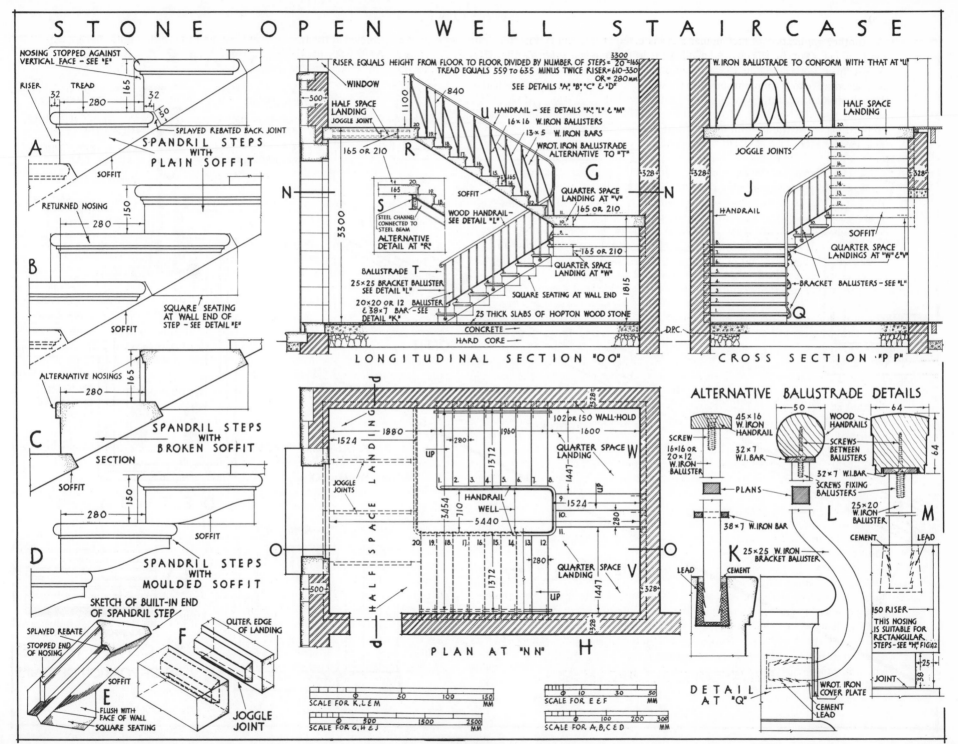

FIGURE 49

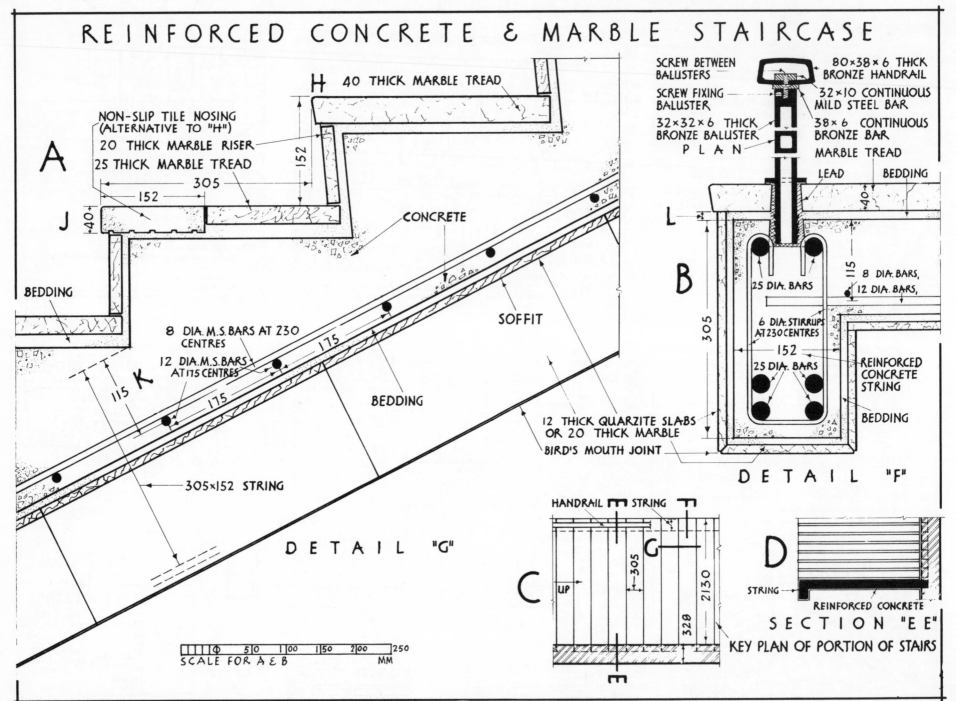

128

REINFORCED CONCRETE & MARBLE STAIRCASE

H 40 THICK MARBLE TREAD

NON-SLIP TILE NOSING
(ALTERNATIVE TO "H")
20 THICK MARBLE RISER
25 THICK MARBLE TREAD

A

152

305

152

J

40

CONCRETE

BEDDING

8 DIA. M.S. BARS AT 230 CENTRES
12 DIA. M.S. BARS AT 175 CENTRES

175

SOFFIT

BEDDING

115 K

175

305×152 STRING

12 THICK QUARZITE SLABS OR 20 THICK MARBLE

BIRD'S MOUTH JOINT

DETAIL "G"

SCREW BETWEEN BALUSTERS
SCREW FIXING BALUSTER
32×32×6 THICK BRONZE BALUSTER
PLAN

80×38×6 THICK BRONZE HANDRAIL
32×10 CONTINUOUS MILD STEEL BAR
38×6 CONTINUOUS BRONZE BAR
MARBLE TREAD
LEAD BEDDING

40

L

B

305

25 DIA. BARS

6 DIA. STIRRUPS AT 230 CENTRES

152

25 DIA. BARS

115

8 DIA. BARS,
12 DIA. BARS,

REINFORCED CONCRETE STRING

BEDDING

DETAIL "F"

HANDRAIL   STRING
G
305
UP
328
2130

C
E

DETAIL "G"

STRING

D

REINFORCED CONCRETE

SECTION "EE"
KEY PLAN OF PORTION OF STAIRS

SCALE FOR A & B
50 100 150 200 250
MM

FIGURE 50

and handrails to " private stairways " (those in a building used by one family) and " common stairways " (those in buildings used by more than one family). Briefly, the rules are as follows. Both types of stairway are to be guarded on each side by a wall or balustrade placed between 840 mm and 1 m above the pitch line (the line joining the step nosings); those stairways less than 1 m wide require a handrail on one side and those 1 m or more wide require a handrail on both sides. The side of a landing must be guarded by a wall or balustrade 900 mm high for a private stair and 1 m for a common stair.

The brick walls of this staircase may be either plastered of faced with ashlar of similar stone to that of the steps. If left exposed, the brickwork would be finished with flush mortar joints. As shown, the floor covering can be of stone slabs bedded on concrete.

If there is not sufficient width available for an open well stair, it would be designed as a dog-leg type (see Chap. II, Vol. III).

Reinforced Concrete Stairs.—It has been already stated that important stairs, especially those required for public buildings, are now constructed of reinforced concrete and that this has largely replaced masonry for this purpose. The reasons for this are : A reinforced concrete stair, suitably finished, (1) has a more attractive appearance, (2) it may be more fire-resistant, (3) its width is less restricted, as it can be designed to take heavy traffic over a large transverse span without resorting to any intermediate support (such as walls which encroach upon the hall), (4) the treads can be rendered non-slip (stone treads wear smooth and may become dangerous), and (5) it can be more easily kept clean.

Although reinforced concrete design is deferred until the advanced years of a course (see Chap. II, Vol. IV), a stair of contemporary construction is briefly referred to here in order that a comparison may be made between stairs of traditional design and those in which newer materials are employed.

A key part plan and cross-section of a portion of a flight of a *typical* open well reinforced concrete stair are shown at C and D, Fig. 50. The section shows the structure to be built into the wall at one end and supported by a string at the other. The details show that the concrete (which resists the compression stresses) is reinforced with 12 mm diameter mild steel transverse bars (which resist the tension stresses) at 175 mm centres; 8 mm diameter longitudinal bars are placed immediately over and wired to these transverse bars at 230 mm centres; the thickness of the concrete at K is 115 mm; the upper surface of the concrete is shaped to suit the risers—two alternative forms being shown at A. The concrete string is reinforced with four 25 mm diameter steel longitudinal (tension) bars and two similar (compression) bars near the top surface; 6 mm diameter steel stirrups are wired to these bars at 230 mm centres and at right angles to the pitch of the stair. *Note the above sizes vary according to the width of the stair and the load to be supported*, and are determined by calculation.

Because of its unattractive appearance a stair constructed entirely of reinforced concrete would not be suitable for a public building in which it was to be an important feature. Hence the structure is covered or veneered with marble, tiles, terrazzo or other suitable material.

Detail A shows alternative forms of risers, one being vertical and the other inclined. These risers are formed of 20 mm. thick slabs of marble bedded to the concrete. The tread at H is formed of a 40 mm thick slab of marble, solidly bedded. As polished marble, especially when wet, has a slippery surface, non-slip tile nosings, which are artificial products, are often incorporated with the treads; that shown at J is grooved to give a key for the bedding. Care must be taken to use a mortar for bedding which will not stain the marble.

The string and soffit are also shown covered with marble or quartzite (a natural very hard stone, imported from Italy, and obtainable in several attractive colours—see p. 106) slabs. The walls may also be covered with 20 mm. thick marble, etc., slabs.

As these covering materials are costly, the soffit may be finished with Keene's or similar cement.

The string shown is of the " open " type; " close " strings (see Chap. II, Vol. III) may be employed.

Expensive veneers are only applied when the appearance is of importance. Reinforced concrete stairs, such as are required for warehouses, etc., are often left uncovered, the treads only being provided with non-slip nosings.

The stair shown in Fig. 50 is cast *in situ*, *i.e.*, it is constructed on the site. It is therefore necessary to provide a temporary wood support, called *formwork* or *shuttering*, for this purpose. Briefly, this consists of butt-jointed boards or sheets for the soffit, fixed at the correct level and pitch to bearers supported by struts. This would be continued to form a suitable frame or box for the string, and this would be strutted; riser boards, etc., would also be fixed. The concrete is placed in position after the reinforcement has been fixed, and the formwork is not removed until the concrete has adequately set. Formwork for reinforced concrete is detailed in Chap. II, Vol. IV.

Concrete steps for narrow stairs are often pre-cast, *i.e.*, are separately formed in wood moulds of the required shape. These, when sufficiently set, are removed and fixed as described for stone steps.

Details of the bronze balusters and handrails are shown at B. These are alternative to those illustrated in Fig. 49 and are fixed as previously described.

NOTE.—The section through the string at B has been taken at a normal from the intersection between the concrete tread and riser (bottom). The baluster has been shown in section to illustrate more clearly the construction; as this would be in the centre of the tread, the distance L would be approximately 100 mm, and therefore the bottom of the baluster is well clear of the top main reinforcement.

CHAPTER FOUR

MILD STEEL ROOF TRUSSES

Syllabus.—Mild steel roof trusses up to 12 m[1] span, with alternative details.

Mild steel[2] is much stronger than timber, it is more fire-resisting and its sections can be readily assembled to form comparatively simple connections. It is principally for these reasons that mild steel is now employed extensively for roof trusses of small and medium spans and for its supersedence of wood as a material for trusses of large span.[3] Whilst wood is still preferred to steel for trusses of open (unceiled) roofs of certain buildings, well-designed steel trusses for large spanned open roofs of buildings of the industrial, etc., type have a light and satisfactory appearance, chiefly because of the small size of the member, and the simple joints. Mild steel roof trusses must be painted at intervals to prevent corrosion.

A steel roof truss, like the built up roof truss (see Chap. III, Vol. I), is a triangulated structure. The principal rafters (abbreviated to " rafters ") are prevented from spreading by connecting their lower ends by a tie (*main tie*), and struts and subsidary ties are provided at intermediate points to afford adequate bracing. Struts should be kept as short as possible. The centre line principle is adopted throughout (see p. 131), and thus the point of attachment of each purlin coincides with the intersection of the axes of the truss members. Secondary stresses, such as bending moments in the rafters, are thereby avoided.

All of the members of a modern metal roof truss are of mild steel, and most, if not all, of them are angles (see D and E, Fig. 80, Vol. I). Angles effectively resist both compression and tension stresses; they can be conveniently attached and they are produced economically. Thus, whereas formerly T-bars were used for rafters, either a single angle or two angles placed back to back are now employed. Struts consist of either single or double angles, and either one or two angles placed back to back are used for a main tie. Until comparatively recently, it was a common practice to use single or double flat bars for a main tie, as they were suitable for resisting tension stresses. However, owing to wind pressure and the abnormal strain imposed during the transporting and erection of trusses, members may be subjected to changes of stresses, and flats will not resist compression. *Flat main ties therefore tend to become buckled.* If a ceiling is to be provided, ceiling joints can be readily fixed to a main tie of double angles and this is an additional reason why they should be used instead of flats, which latter are useless for this purpose unless metallic lathing is employed in the ceiling plaster. Flat bars are still used, but less frequently than formerly, for subsidary tie members (see Fig. 54); angles are preferred.

The members of a truss are connected together normally by means of bolts[1] and thin plates, called *gussets;* sometimes the members are welded[1] to the gussets; formerly rivets[1] were also used.

The *pitch* of rivets is the distance between their centres. Accordng to the British Standard Specification for " The Use of Structural Steel in Building," (*a*) the minimum pitch shall be not less than $2\frac{1}{2}$ times the diameter of the bolts *(b)* the maximum pitch must not exceed 32 t* or 300 mm and *(c)* the minimum distance from the centre of any bolt to the end of a member or edge of a gusset shall be 28 mm and 32 mm for 16 mm and 20 mm diameter respectively. The size of the bolts depends upon that of the members to be connected, thus 16 mm diameter bolts are commonly employed for angles and flats up to 60 mm wide and 20 mm diameter bolts for larger members. When making a joint, a member, even if subjected to a small stress, should be connected to a gusset by at least two bolts,

The thickness of gussets theoretically depends upon the bearing value of the bolts employed, The minimum thickness is 6 mm and these have been used for the small truss detailed in Fig. 51; 8 mm gussets are used for roofs of larger span up to at least 12 m and the thickness rarely exceeds 10 mm even for very large trusses. The size and shape vary according to the pitch of the bolts,

---

[1] In many syllabuses the span is limited to 9 m.

[2] The manufacture and characteristics of mild steel and other metals are described in Vol. IV.

[3] An exception is the bow-string or similar laminated wood type of truss which is still occasionally adopted for large spans.

[1] Welding, as an alternative to bolting, is described in Vol. IV. Gusscts are sometimes dispensed with and the members, all angles, are welded together. Thus, referring to the detail at F, Fig. 52, the strut could be connected directly on to the rafter by means of *fillet welds.* An electric current or gas (an oxy-acetylene flame) is employed to melt a steel rod or wire (called an *electrode*) and the adjacent edges of the members in such a manner that the molten metal from thc electrode is deposited along the points of contact and fused into them.

* t = thickness of the thinner outer plate.

size and inclination of the connecting members and the appearance desired. Several examples of gussets are given in Figs. 51–53 and will be referred to later. If a member consists of double angles, gussets are always placed between them.

Small trusses are fabricated (welded or bolted together) at the works and transported to the site. Owing to the difficulty of conveying larger trusses, these are fabricated in parts at the works and assembled together on the job (see the reference to Fig. 53 on p. 136). Sometimes trusses are made "piece small," i.e., the various members, cut to length and holed for the bolts are conveyed to the site and the trusses are there assembled.

Trusses are erected by a crane (or sheer legs) and connected by holding-down bolts to the building (see below). The distance between trusses up to 12 m span varies from 3 to 4·5 m. Wider spacing results in heavy purlins and uneconomical sizes of members. The pitch of steel roof trusses, like those of timber construction, depends upon the nature of the covering material and the architectural effect desired.

Details of roof trusses up to 12 m span are given in Figs. 51–53. These are typical only, and several alternative details are provided for reference. It is appreciated that the sizes of the members are influenced by the weight of the covering material,[1] the distance between the trusses and purlins, the provision or otherwise of a plastered ceiling, and the degree of exposure of the building to wind pressure. Briefly, the sizes of the members, number and sizes of the bolts etc., are dependent upon the forces in the members. The trusses illustrated in Figs. 51, 52 and 53 have been designed to supports ceilings, and in each example the covering material is slates.

Truss suitable for a 6 m Span (see Fig. 51).—This is a slated roof, having a pitch of 30°. The effective span (distance between the centres of bearings) is 6 m and the maximum distance between the trusses is 3·7 m. It is assumed that the building is of the single storied workshop type and the external walls are only required to be 215 mm thick (see S). Increased bearings for the trusses are provided by internal piers, as shown. If required to prevent the transmission of moisture, the walls would have to be rough-casted (or similarly treated) externally, or be built in cavity construction as shown at C, Fig. 52.

Sound concrete pads of sufficient thickness and area must be provided to give a reliable and level bearing for the ends of the truss and to receive the steel fixing bolts. The pads course with the brickwork. The bolts are called ragged lewis bolts or rag bolts.[2] A sketch of one of these holding-down bolts is shown at B; its thickness is equal to the diameter of the upper threaded shank and the lower portion is tapered in its width; its edges are jagged as shown to

afford a key for the fixing material, which is usually molten lead run in to secure the bolt when placed in the hole in the padstone. The lead should be well caulked, otherwise water may enter and set up corrosion which may split the padstone. These bolts, which are provided with nuts, are obtainable in overall lengths of 100, 150, 230 and 380 mm and of 16, 20, 22, 25 and 32 mm diameter. That shown at B is suitable for the truss illustrated in Fig. 53, but as indicated at C, Fig. 51, smaller bolts will serve for this small truss. Two are required at each end and these are fixed in readiness to receive the truss.

All of the members consist of single angles. These and the gussets are only 6 mm thick, the minimum thickness stipulated in the aforementioned B.S.S. 449. The preferred maximum unsupported length of the 100 mm by 50 mm wood spars is 2·34 m (see Chap. III, Vol. I), and so only one purlin is required at each side.

The centre line principle has been observed in setting out, and, to prevent confusion, these lines have been shown to be those of the bolts.

Although the centre lines of members are taken when drawing force diagrams, it should be pointed out that the details of a structural engineer's working drawing, on which the position of each bolt hole at every connection is indicated, show the intersecting lines of members to be what are termed gauge lines, scratch lines or scratters. These are the setting out lines which are "scratched" on the backs of members at the fabricating shop and along which the centres of the holes for the bolts are spaced. The following bracketed figures give the position (measured down the back from the intersection between the two legs of the gauge lines for angles having 50 mm (28 mm—see H, Fig. 52), 6 mm (35 mm)—see C, Fig. 51), 80 mm (45 mm—see C), 90 mm (50 mm), 100 mm (58 mm), etc., legs. The setting out of the details in Fig. 50 shows the intersecting lines to be those of the scratter lines.

It will be observed that at A, Fig. 51, in order to obtain symmetry, the rafters and inclined tension angles (known as diagonal ties) are fixed to the gusset plates on one side, and that the main tension angle, called the main tie, and the struts are fixed on the other. This results in a better balanced truss than if all the members were fixed on the same side.

Details of the foot or shoe of the truss are shown at C, D and E. A short angle cleat is fixed at each side of the gusset and these rest upon a bearing plate or base plate or sole plate. Both the cleats and the bearing plate are holed at a distance apart equal to that of the lewis bolts, i.e., 96 mm (see E). The plates are placed in position and the truss is hoisted and lowered until the holes in the cleats are engaged by the shanks of the lewis bolts. The cleat holes are larger than the diameter of the bolts (see D) to facilitate fixing and allow a slight margin for any error in the setting out. This obviates an erection difficulty which would be otherwise caused if such an allowance was not made and a slight inaccuracy occurred in either the setting out of the lewis bolts or the position of the holes in the cleats. The nuts are finally tightened with a spanner. The section at E shows the rafter at one side of the gusset and the main tie at the other.

The details at the apex are shown at F and G. The ends of the rafters are mitred and those of the diagonal ties are square cut. The wood ridge is secured by two 12 mm diameter bolts to two bent plates or flats which have been either

---

[1] The weight of asbestos-cement corrugated sheets is approximately 167·5 N/m² and that of clay tiles may be as much as 695 N/m². Thus, if the trusses are 3·7 m apart and the purlins are at 2·4 m centres, the difference in weight of these covering materials (ignoring that of the spars necessary for the tiles and not required for the sheets) over the area concerned is approximately 5 kN.

[2] A "rag bolt", unlike a lewis bolt, is not tapered, and resembles an ordinary bolt shank, part of which is jagged and part threaded.

STEEL ROOF TRUSS

SUITABLE FOR A 6 METRE SPAN

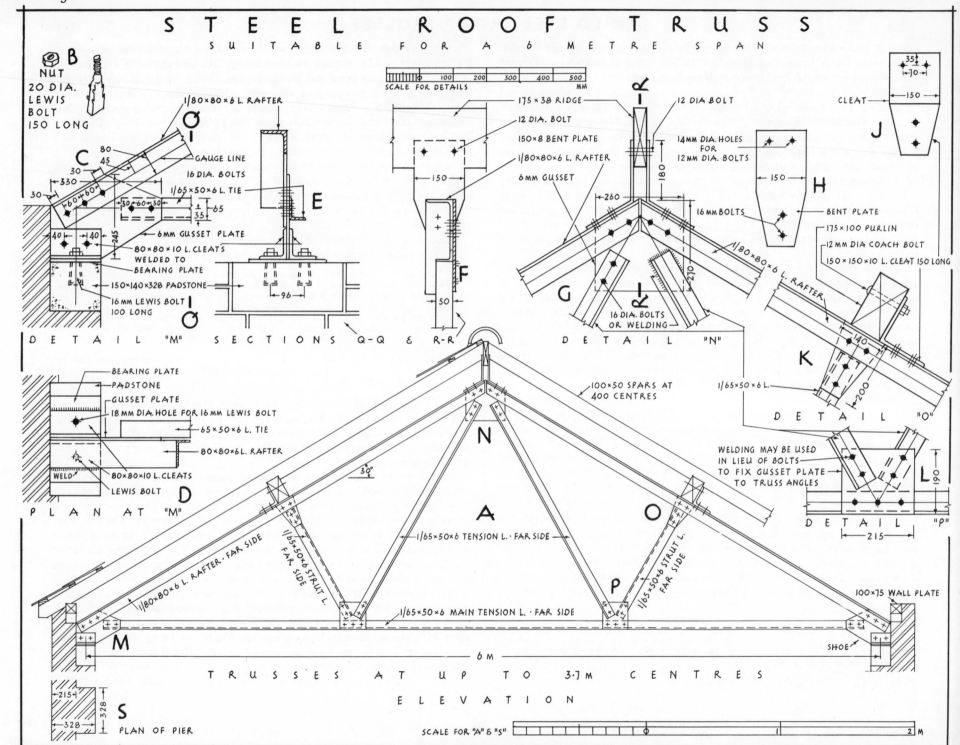

B NUT 20 DIA. LEWIS BOLT 150 LONG

100 200 300 400 500
SCALE FOR DETAILS
MM

1/80×80×6 L. RAFTER

Q

C
80
45
30
330
30
+60+60+
245
40 40

GAUGE LINE
16 DIA. BOLTS
1/65×50×6 L. TIE
30 60 30
35 65
6MM GUSSET PLATE
80×80×10 L. CLEATS WELDED TO BEARING PLATE
150×140×328 PADSTONE
16 MM LEWIS BOLT 100 LONG

Q

E

96

DETAIL "M" **SECTIONS Q-Q & R-R**

175×38 RIDGE
12 DIA. BOLT
150×8 BENT PLATE
1/80×80×6 L. RAFTER
6MM GUSSET
150

R
12 DIA BOLT
14MM DIA. HOLES FOR 12 MM DIA. BOLTS
180
260
210
16MM BOLTS
1/80×80×6 L. RAFTER
16 DIA. BOLTS OR WELDING
R

G
50
F

DETAIL "N"

J
35
70
150
CLEAT

H
150
BENT PLATE
175×100 PURLIN
12 MM DIA COACH BOLT
150×150×10 L. CLEAT 150 LONG

K
140
200
1/65×50×6 L.

DETAIL "O"

BEARING PLATE
PADSTONE
GUSSET PLATE
18 MM DIA. HOLE FOR 16 MM LEWIS BOLT
65×50×6 L. TIE
80×80×6 L. RAFTER
WELD
80×80×10 L. CLEATS
LEWIS BOLT
D

PLAN AT "M"

WELDING MAY BE USED IN LIEU OF BOLTS TO FIX GUSSET PLATE TO TRUSS ANGLES

L
190

DETAIL "P"
215

100×50 SPARS AT 400 CENTRES

30°

N

A

O

1/80×80×6 L. RAFTER - FAR SIDE
1/65×50×6 STRUT L. FAR SIDE
1/65×50×6 TENSION L · FAR SIDE
1/65×50×6 STRUT L. FAR SIDE
1/65×50×6 MAIN TENSION L · FAR SIDE

P

100×75 WALL PLATE

M
SHOE

6 M

TRUSSES AT UP TO 3·7 M CENTRES

ELEVATION

S
215
328
328

PLAN OF PIER

SCALE FOR "A" & "S"
2 M

FIGURE 51

bolted or welded to the rafters, the former being preferred. A detail of one of these plates before bending is shown at H. *Care must be taken in setting out that the bolts connecting these plates to the rafters do not foul the bolts fixing the latter to the gusset.*

The purlins are of wood, and each is bolted to a cleat bolted or welded to the rafter (see K). A detail of the cleat is shown at J. Joints between purlins must occur at the trusses, and for such connections the cleats are 305 mm long to enable two bolts being fixed at the end of each purlin (see Q, Fig. 53). The bolts now commonly used for fixing these wood members are called *carriage bolts or coach bolts.* As shown at K, a carriage bolt has a flat cup head and a square *neck* (portion of the shank next to the head). Washers are not required.[1] Square nuts are used. Alternative purlins are shown at N, S, T and U, Fig. 53.

The detail at L shows the connection between the main and diagonal ties and the strut.

All the bolts are 16 mm diameter. The pitch of the bolts is figured on the drawings. The "32–58 mm" pitch shown is common for this size of bolt. It will also be noted that the sizes of the gussets are figured. A structural engineer's working drawing shows all of these dimensions. Many of them have been omitted in the following drawings in order to prevent a mass of figures from obscuring the details.

Truss suitable for a 9 m Span (see Fig. 52).—An outline of the truss is shown at A, the rafters being equally divided by two purlins on each side, and the main tie also equally divided.

Like the previous example, each member is a single angle, and to obtain a suitable balance some members are fixed at the near side of the gussets and others at the far side.

Details of the shoe are given at C, D and E. The main tie extends for the full width of the base plate and secured to it by a welding. A short cleat is provided at the opposite side of the gusset and welded to the base plate. As shown at D, two 20 mm diameter holes are formed in the plate to receive the lewis bolts. Unlike that shown at C, Fig. 51, the gusset does not project below the main tie, and this arrangement is therefore more suitable if a plastered ceiling without cornices is to be provided.

The details at F and G are those at the heads of the struts.

The connections at the apex are shown at H, and those between the gusset, main tie, struts and diagonal tie are shown at K. The section at J shows a strut on each side of the gusset. The size of these struts and the diagonal tie is that of the smallest angles used in roof construction, *i.e.*, 50 mm by 50 mm by 6 mm.

[1] A hole, of diameter equal to that of the bolt, is bored in the wood purlin. The bolt is inserted and the square-necked portion driven home. The latter prevents rotation of the bolt when the nut is being tightened.

The purlins in this example are of steel (see F and G). These are sometimes preferred to the timber purlins shown in Fig. 51. It will be noted that the purlins are fixed to the rafters by means of bolts. It should also be observed that the centre line principle has been complied with and that the nut comes centrally between the pair of bolts below. Wood plates, called *fillers*, must be bolted at 760 to 915 mm intervals to the purlins as shown to provide fixings for the spars. They are in short lengths. An alternative arrangement is shown at B, where the purlins are reversed and the fillers are placed against their backs. Whilst this is as sound as the type shown at F and G, the fillers are not so readily fixed. The wood plates, not being in continuous lengths, can be laid on the purlins if fixed as shown at F until required to be bolted, but such a temporary support is not available if the purlins are arranged as shown at B. The latter detail is adopted if soffit boarding is required and which is nailed direct to the fillers. The form of end joint between steel purlins is described on p. 136.

The detail at the ridge shows an alternative but more costly arrangement to that detailed at G, Fig. 51; this is usually adopted for the direct fixing of asbestos-cement sheets (see Chap. III, Vol. III). The steel members are continuous and the spars are nailed to the fillers.

The usual type of tapered gutter is detailed at C and the external cavity walls are 378 mm thick.

Truss Suitable for a 12 m Span (see Fig. 53).—The outline elevation at A shows the setting out. Each rafter is divided into four equal parts. The struts are normal to the rafters and the foot of each main diagonal tie scratter line meets the intersection between those of the 80 mm by 80 by 8 mm main strut and main tie. When arriving at the sizes of the members it was assumed that the roof covering was slates, that a plastered ceiling had to be supported and that the distance between trusses was 3·7 m.

This is known as a *Fink, French* or *Belgian* truss and is of good design, each half consisting of a symmetrical triangulated frame. The king tie is only necessary if a ceiling is required and serves as an additional support for the main tie.

As stated on p. 131, the gauge or scratter lines and the the centre lines have been drawn when setting out these details. This is in conformity with the usual practice adopted by structural engineers when preparing working details showing the position of the bolts, etc. The spacing of the bolts is fully dimensioned.

The rafters, main tie and diagonal ties, consist of double angles placed back to back and between which the 10 mm gussets are fixed.

The shoe is detailed at N, O and P. The padstone is 215 mm thick (or equal to three courses of brickwork), as it has to accomodate two 20 mm lewis bolts which are 150 mm long (see B, Fig. 51). Two cleats are bolted or welded to the gusset and these are welded to the bearing plate in which slotted holes for the fixing bolts are provided. The section at P shows the double rafter and main tie bolted to the gusset.

STEEL ROOF TRUSS

SUITABLE FOR A 9 METRE SPAN

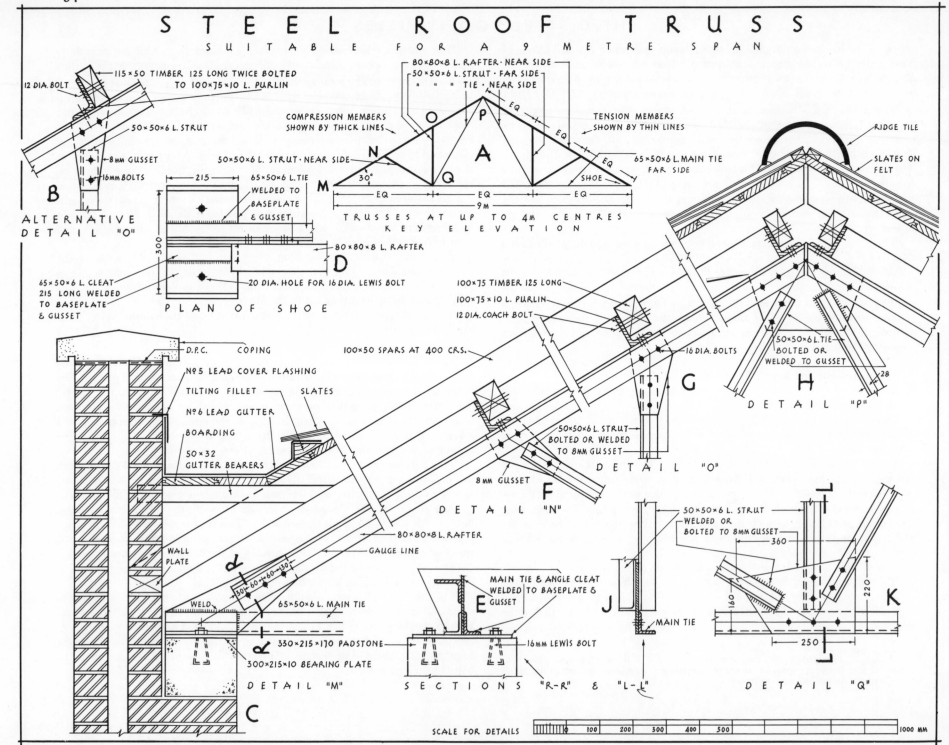

115×50 TIMBER 125 LONG TWICE BOLTED TO 100×75×10 L. PURLIN

12 DIA. BOLT

50×50×6 L. STRUT

8mm GUSSET

16mm BOLTS

B

ALTERNATIVE DETAIL "O"

65×50×6 L. CLEAT 215 LONG WELDED TO BASEPLATE & GUSSET

215

300

65×50×6 L. TIE WELDED TO BASEPLATE & GUSSET

80×80×8 L. RAFTER

D

20 DIA. HOLE FOR 16 DIA. LEWIS BOLT

PLAN OF SHOE

80×80×8 L. RAFTER · NEAR SIDE
50×50×6 L. STRUT · FAR SIDE
" " " TIE · NEAR SIDE

COMPRESSION MEMBERS SHOWN BY THICK LINES

TENSION MEMBERS SHOWN BY THIN LINES

O   P

N   A

M   Q   SHOE

65×50×6 L. MAIN TIE FAR SIDE

50×50×6 L. STRUT · NEAR SIDE

30°

EQ   EQ   EQ
9m

TRUSSES AT UP TO 4M CENTRES
KEY ELEVATION

RIDGE TILE

SLATES ON FELT

100×75 TIMBER 125 LONG
100×75×10 L. PURLIN
12 DIA. COACH BOLT

16 DIA. BOLTS

50×50×6 L. TIE BOLTED OR WELDED TO GUSSET

28

H

DETAIL "P"

D.P.C.   COPING

Nº5 LEAD COVER FLASHING

TILTING FILLET   SLATES

Nº6 LEAD GUTTER

BOARDING

50×32 GUTTER BEARERS

100×50 SPARS AT 400 CRS.

8mm GUSSET

G

50×50×6 L. STRUT BOLTED OR WELDED TO 8mm GUSSET

DETAIL "O"

F

DETAIL "N"

80×80×8 L. RAFTER

GAUGE LINE

30× 60× 60× 130

WALL PLATE

WELD   65×50×6 L. MAIN TIE

330×215×170 PADSTONE

300×215×10 BEARING PLATE

DETAIL "M"   **C**

MAIN TIE & ANGLE CLEAT WELDED TO BASEPLATE & GUSSET

E

16mm LEWIS BOLT

SECTIONS "R-R" & "L-L"

MAIN TIE   **J**

50×50×6 L. STRUT WELDED OR BOLTED TO 8mm GUSSET

360

160   220

250

K

DETAIL "Q"

SCALE FOR DETAILS

0   100   200   300   400   500   1000 MM

FIGURE 52

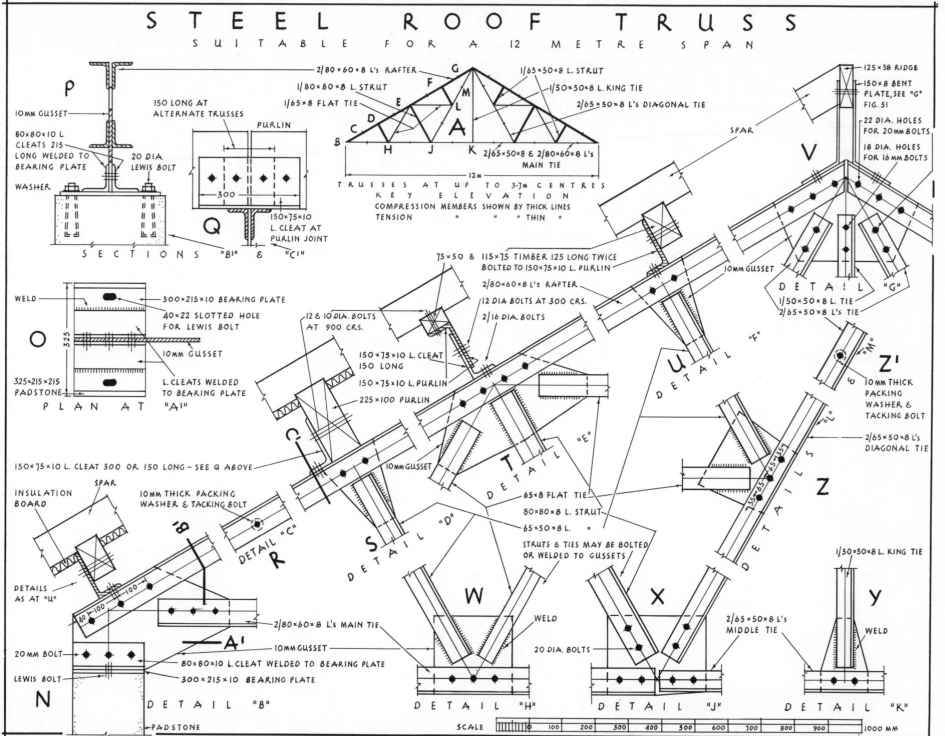

FIGURE 53

Trusses of this size cannot be conveniently transported as complete structures from the works to the building site. Each truss is therefore fabricated in two halves at the works and conveyed in parts to the building. Thus the left half detailed in Fig. 53 would be bolted together with the gusset plate at the apex connected as shown and holed in order that the right half may be readily bolted to it on site. The gusset at the bottom of the diagonal tie will be fixed and holed similarly, and the detached *middle* main tie will have a holed gusset plate bolted at its centre to receive the lower end of the king tie. On arrival on the site each truss is quickly assembled by (*a*) connecting the upper ends of the rafter and diagonal tie of the right half to the apex gusset, (*b*) bolting the middle main tie to the gusset at x and to the corresponding plate on the right half truss, and (*c*) connectiog the king rod to the apex and middle main tie gussets. When the joints are being made, the nuts are not finally spannered until all the bolts have been inserted. It will be observed that the diameter of the holes is 2 mm larger than that of the bolts shanks.

As the stress in the main tie decreases towards the centre, the middle portion consists of smaller angles, as shown at x.

The king tie is sometimes omitted if the roof is to be open, *i.e.*, no ceiling is required.

The detail at z is somewhat similar to that at w, and, with exception of those of the purlins, a description of it and the remaining details is unnecessary.

Four different types of purlins are shown at N, S, T and U. That connecting the feet of the trusses (N) is similar to that detailed at F and G, Fig. 52, described on p. 133. Members such as this may be provided at the shoes of each of the trusses shown in Figs. 51 and 52 if preferred to fixing the feet of the spars to wall plates.

An alternative to the above is shown at U. Here the purlin is reversed and the short plates are bolted at the back. For the reason stated on p. 133, this is not so convenient for fixing the fillers.

The large wood purlin shown at S is fixed in a similar manner to that illustrated at K, Fig. 51, but the cleat leg fixed to the rafter is shorter, as the required two bolts are provided when one is fixed to each of the angles of the rafter. The purlins should be sufficiently long to span across two bays (7·4 m) to allow their ends to come over alternate trusses. The cleats will be 300 mm long at the purlin ends (see Q) and 150 mm long at the intermediate trusses. These purlin joints should be staggered to ensure that all the joints do not come over the same pairs of trusses. The type of end joint used for steel purlins, like those in Figs. 52 and N and U, Fig. 53, usually consists of a 80 mm by 80 mm by 10 mm angle cleat, twice bolted to the back of the rafter, to which each purlin end is twice bolted.

The steel purlin at T is bolted to an angle cleat bolted or welded to the two angles of the rafter. A 75 mm by 50 mm wood plate is carriage-bolted or coach-screwed (see Chap. IV, Vol. I) to it at 915 mm intervals to provide a fixing for the spars. This type of purlin, without the wood plate, is commonly employed for fixing asbestos-cement or corrugated iron sheets (see Chap. III, Vol. III).

HOMEWORK PROGRAMME

The following schedule follows closely that provided in Vol. I; a suggested guide to reading has been added. For the reasons there stated, it is not possible to compile a programme of homework which will suit every class of student, especially for such a comprehensive subject as Building Construction. A lecturer will, of course, select subject-matter for homework which will be of most value to his students, having regard to their capacity and specific needs. The following subjects have therefore been selected to meet what are considered to be average requirements.

Although the proposed guide for reading covers the whole book, it will be appreciated that much of the description, especially that related to materials, is for reference purposes, and students will therefore concentrate upon those sections which have special reference to their own particular syllabuses.

As stated in Vol. I, it is assumed that the drawing sheets will be A2 size and that the maximum number of sheets which may be produced varies from twenty-four to twenty-eight, according to the length of session.

The homework programme for the second year of the course is continued in Vol. III, and deals with carpentry, joinery and roof coverings.

Sheet Number				Subject of Drawing	Reading (Pages)
Number of Lectures per Session					
24	25	26	27		
1	1	1	1	CAVITY WALLS.—Draw one-fifth full size details B, D (including proper damp proof course), A (lower portion) and J, Fig. 13.	1-12, 36-44.
2	2	2	2	REINFORCED BRICKWORK.—Sketch details showing the application to walls B, pillars and lintels, Fig. 16.	12-19, 44-51.
3	3	3	3	ARCHES.—Draw, to 1 : 10 scale, A, B, C and J (half), Fig. 19, and P. 14. (half), Fig. 24.	19-27, 51-52.
4	4	4	4	DAMP PROOFING.—(a) Draw, to 1 : 10 scale, details C and E, Fig. 20. STEPPED FOUNDATIONS.—(b) Draw, to a scale of 1 : 50, elevation of a 328 mm wall, 12 m long, with stepped foundations, assuming the ground to have an irregular fall of 1·8 m (see Fig. 22).	28-36, 52-58. 59-60
5	5	5	5	FIREPLACE, ETC.—(a) Draw, to 1 : 20 scale, A, B, C, N, O and P, Fig. 25; (b) draw 1 : 10 scale details V, W and X, Fig. 25.	60-64, 64-73.
6	6	6	6	DRAINAGE.—Sketch: (a) A, J, Q, U and V, Fig. 31; (b) C, D, F, G′ and H, Fig. 33.	74-86.
7	7	7	7	DRAINAGE.—(a) Draw, to a scale of 1 : 100, block plan of a detached house and show the drainage scheme to meet the requirements of the Building Regulations. There are three rain water pipes and the sanitary fittings include a sink, two lavatory basins, bath and two water closets. The sewer, boundaries, etc., must be shown. Refer to Fig. 34. (b) Draw 1 : 10 scale plan and cross-section of an inspection chamber. Refer to Figs. 34 and 35.	83-93.
8	8	8	8	MASONRY.—Draw : (a) 1 : 10 scale plan, vertical section and elevation of entrance A, Fig. 42, assuming a 318 mm cavity wall with 140 mm stone outer leaf; (b) half full-size detail at A or B, Fig. 43.	94-106, 114-122
			9	MASONRY.—Draw : (a) 1 : 20 scale elevation C, section B and plan of entrance, Fig. 42; (b) full-size detail of head of architrave at S or T, Fig. 43.	106.
9	9	9	10	MASONRY.—Draw : (a) 1 : 10 scale elevation J, section L and elevation M of windows, Fig. 44; (b) full-size details at D and E, Fig. 45.	106-116, 122-129
10	10	10	11	STEEL TRUSS.—Draw : (a) 1 : 10 scale elevation A, Fig. 51; (b) one-fifth size details at C, G, K and L, Fig. 51.	130-133.
11	11	11	12	STEEL TRUSS.—Draw: (a) to a scale of 1 : 50, elevation A, Fig. 52; (b) one-fifth full size details at C, F, H and K, Fig. 52.	132-136.
12	12	12	13	STEEL TRUSS.—Draw : (a) to a scale of 1 : 100 elevation A, Fig. 53; (b) one-fifth full size details at N, R, S, T, U, V, W, X, Y and Z, Fig. 53.	136.

INDEX